W9-CEY-421

# RAGTIME

An Encyclopedia, Discography, and Sheetography

# RAGTIME

# DAVID A. JASEN

Routledge
Taylor & Francis Group
New York   London

Routledge
Taylor & Francis Group
270 Madison Avenue
New York, NY 10016

Routledge
Taylor & Francis Group
2 Park Square
Milton Park, Abingdon
Oxon OX14 4RN

© 2007 by Taylor & Francis Group, LLC
Routledge is an imprint of Taylor & Francis Group, an Informa business

Printed in the United States of America on acid-free paper
10 9 8 7 6 5 4 3 2 1

International Standard Book Number-10: 0-415-97862-9 (Hardcover)
International Standard Book Number-13: 978-0-415-97862-0 (Hardcover)

---

**Library of Congress Cataloging-in-Publication Data**

---

Jasen, David A.
    Ragtime : an encyclopedia, discography, and sheetography / David A. Jasen.
        p. cm.
    ISBN 0-415-97862-9
    1. Ragtime music--Encyclopedias. 2. Ragtime music--Discography. I. Title.

ML3530.J373 2007
781.64'5--dc22                                                                                           2006031343

---

**Visit the Taylor & Francis Web site at**
**http://www.taylorandfrancis.com**

**and the Routledge Web site at**
**http://www.routledge-ny.com**

# Dedication

To my favorite (and only) grandson,

Alex Jasen

With the hope that this book will encourage a lifelong interest in this subject.

# Contents

# Thematic Contents

## The Joplin Tradition or Classic Ragtime

## Novelty Ragtime (1918–1928)

## Stride Ragtime (1918–1929)

## Jelly Roll Morton Ragtime

## Ragtime Revival

# Acknowledgments

This work is the culmination of over fifty-five years of study, research, collecting, and performing. I have been most fortunate to have several friends with whom I have collaborated in the past and who share my love of this subject. From the time we first met, on his home ground of St. Louis, Missouri, at the Goldenrod Showboat, Trebor Jay Tichenor and I have shared a life of performing; collecting sheet music, flat-disc recordings, piano rolls, catalogs, trade publications, periodicals, original ragtime artifacts (Would you believe the door to the Rosebud bar?); and talking about and writing about the living history of ragtime. Much of these thoughts are to be found in this volume.

Another great friend and collaborator is Gene Jones, who has spent these past twenty-five years egging me on, researching, collecting, reading and listening, thinking creatively about the various histories of ragtime, and providing rare insights as we tackled several projects together. His invaluable help is also to be found here.

Other friends who have shared their interest include Richard Allen, Walter C. Allen, George A. Blacker, Rudi Blesh, August Caminiti, Caleb Crowell, Bob Darch, John R. T. Davies, Neville Dickie, Bo Esselius, Vince Giordano, Sol Goodman, Oliver Graham, Thornton Hagert, Roger Hankins, Carl Kenziora, Jr., James Kidd, Ross Laird, Keith Miller, Mike Montgomery, Max Morath, Dennis Pash, Nick Perls, Charlie Rasch, David Reffkin, Brian Rust, Richard Spottswood, Carl Seltzer, Vincent Terbois, Edward S. Walker, John Wallace, Les Zeiger, and Dick Zimmerman.

Major dealers who throughout the years have taken special pains to provide materials include Beverly Hamer, Joel Markowitz, Sandy Marrone, Wayland Bunnell, Paul Riseman, and Mike Schwimmer. They, too, are good friends.

Special thanks to my friend and editor, Richard Carlin, who continues to support my endeavors.

# Ragtime: An Overview

For a little more than 100 years since ragtime was created and burst on the scene in the United States, it has become the basis for dramatic change in the popular music landscape and has infused its sparkling rhythms onto every aspect of our musical culture. During this time, we have seen ragtime undergo several transformations: from its beginning in 1896, when the word was first printed to indicate a special ingredient in musical accompaniment, or later applied to a type of song or dance or an entire musical composition or style of playing, to when it wasn't even called *ragtime* or *rag* — as in its last phase during the 1920s when the special Novelty rags had such titles as "Kitten on the Keys," "Knice and Knifty," "Doll Dance," and the Stride rags were called "Carolina Shout" and "Handful of Keys" — to the first full-scale revival in the 1940s and 1950s. Though the revival started in San Francisco in the early forties by Lu Watters's Yerba Buena Jazz Band and its pianist, Wally Rose, featuring rags nightly, it was in 1950 that Capitol Records, a major record company with worldwide distribution, turned Lou Busch, one of its artist-and-repertoire men, into the recording artist Joe "Fingers" Carr. He was a brilliant composer of rags; an arranger and pianist who recorded more rags than anyone during the decade of the fifties.

Gone were the coon songs, the simple pop songs, syncopated or not, with the word *rag* or *ragtime* in its title. Gone were the syncopated dances (except for the same three or four cakewalks) and other tunes not in the 2/4 rhythm, which were all called ragtime. Gone was the honky-tonk style of playing pop songs called ragtime, which were incorporated into the general popular music repertoire during the mid-teens for a decade, mostly found on piano rolls and in dance and jazz bands. What remained to be recorded in this first revival period, performed in festivals and concerts, studied, researched, and written about, were the body of piano rags composed and published across this country from 1897 to roughly 1927. This, then, was what was called now and forevermore, ragtime — a musical composition for the piano comprising three or four sections containing sixteen measures each, which combines a syncopated melody accompanied by an even, steady duple rhythm.

When the second revival took place in the seventies, with its use of Scott Joplin's rags in the movie *The Sting* in 1974, classical piano players "discovered" the rags of Joplin and tried to superimpose a classical sound to ragtime. At the same time, original turn-of-the-twentieth-century orchestrations were found and classically trained instrumentalists replaced the Dixieland bands (who had replaced the military bands during the ragtime years) and called themselves Ragtime Orchestras. For these past thirty or so years now, ragtime has evolved into being performed by trained musicians with a great mix of sensibilities to give ragtime a wide variety of performance sounds. Contemporary ragtime composers, along with adding fifty years' worth of harmonies and taking inspiration from a host of extra-ragtime sources, have even extended the sixteen measure melodies to reflect today's view of ragtime.

1897–1927: Ragtime's original heyday; thirty years of growth and development.
1928–1940: Ragtime's decline end absorption into mainstream popular music; twelve years of oblivion.

1941–1971: Ragtime's first revival as nostalgic good-time music; thirty years of research and redefinition.

1972–present: Ragtime's second revival as a classical and contemporary music; thirty years of technical skill and experimentation, broadening its scope.

Selections from the discography and rollography have been chosen for your listening pleasure in the individual listings of the major rags.

# Categories of Ragtime

Through the years, the sounds of ragtime varied considerably, as did its publications in printed form. When studying the scores, it becomes obvious that several distinct groupings can be distinguished, especially among major composers who spent considerable time developing their works. For the convenience of studying the larger picture of the development of ragtime composition, ragtime has been divided into several categories of rags, each with its own history, overall sound, major compositional influences, and outstanding performers. For the most part, these groups have definite time periods and geographic locations:

Early ragtime (1897–1905). The Folk rag came from the Midwest and South, which took local and regional floating strains and unusual rhythms in unorthodox patterns.

The Joplin tradition or Classic ragtime. This used the formula devised by Scott Joplin to combine the Instrumental folk music of the Midwest with the formal European tradition of the classical music of the nineteenth century.

Popular ragtime (1906–1912). Reducing the ragtime approach where simple syncopated melodies were turned out by professional pop composers in Tin Pan Alley during ragtime's heyday.

Advanced ragtime (1913–1917). This brought about a renewed creativity in expanding the harmonies to give a richer sound for the composer–performer.

Novelty ragtime (1918–1928). This brought forth highly complex rhythms and harmonies derived in part from the French Impressionists and piano roll arranging techniques.

Stride ragtime (1918–1929). This came mainly from the black composers who settled in New York City and performed in vaudeville, saloons, and bawdy houses.

Jelly Roll Morton's ragtime. This reflected his unique and varied approaches to ragtime as a performance art, as captured in print and especially on record.

# A

## Advanced Ragtime, 1913–1917

After ragtime's popularity peaked around 1912, there was not the sudden dismissal that occurs with musical fads of today. Ragtime in 1913 still had a powerful draw, not only in the United States but in England and Europe as well. Tin Pan Alley was continuing to grind out large quantities of songs with the magic word *rag* in their titles. But other things were also happening to ragtime.

Composers were starting to experiment with the Popular rag, not in form but in content—creating new musical ideas within the same structure. Now that the pressure to create popular hits was removed, other composer–performers were attracted to ragtime as a composed music. Unusual harmonies were initially used by Georgia-born Malvin Franklin when he came to New York City and published "Hot Chocolate Rag." As New York-born Harry Jentes entered the field with "California Sunshine," and later "Bantam Step," people noticed a decided difference in the rags. There were colorations and new dissonances to be used later in jazz: Blues elements and the blues form integrated with traditional ragtime writing to tantalize the by now jaded listener. But it was not all confined to New York City: Sydney K. Russell in Berkeley was turning out imaginative rags like "Too Much Raspberry"; Irwin P. Leclere in New Orleans with the inventive "Triangle Jazz Blues"; and Fred Heltman in Cleveland with "Fred Heltman's Rag." And the cradle of ragtime, St. Louis, was maintaining its creativity with the widest variety of musical ideas incorporated into the ragtime form as demonstrated by Artie Matthews and his five diverse "Pastime Rags," Rob Hampton's "Cataract Rag" and "Agitation Rag," Lucien P. Gibson's "Jinx Rag" and "Cactus Rag," and, finally, Charles Thompson's unassuming but highly exciting ragtime compositions, "The Lily Rag" and "Delmar Rag."

The black ragtime pianist–composers from the East Coast started being heard from. Luckey Roberts from Philadelphia was the first of this crowd to be published and to record. Unfortunately, his earliest recordings, which were made for Columbia, were not issued at the time and have since disappeared, presumably destroyed. At the time they were recorded in 1916 only Mike Bernard and Englishman-turned-Canadian Harry Thomas had made ragtime piano discs of major consequence, but they were soon to be joined by the touring vaudeville favorite, Roy Spangler, who can be heard on "Piano Ragtime of the Teens, Twenties and Thirties," (Herwin 402), performing songwriter–publisher Abe Olman's "Red Onion Rag." The "Pride of Baltimore," Eubie Blake, followed Luckey in publishing rags, but his numbers fell between the pop song and the rag tradition. Finally, New Jersey-born James P. Johnson composed several rags that, like Luckey's and Eubie's, had a pronounced lyrical quality seldom found in the rags of the time. It is not surprising, then, that a few years later all three would make significant contributions to the world of popular music by writing beautiful ballads, memorable dances, and sparkling, foot-tapping music. Their creativity easily matched their counterparts in St. Louis, but their originality took on a completely different character.

One of the oldest show business devices is to take a classical composition and syncopate it. The ragging of the classics suddenly blossomed forth in this era with great skill and cleverness. Julius Lenzberg led the pack with "Operatic Rag" and "Hungarian Rag," whereas Edward Claypoole from Baltimore published the widely copied and wildly successful "Ragging the Scale." Paul Pratt contributed "Springtime Rag," which was given twenties dance band treatment in an unusual recording by Vic Meyers and his orchestra. George L. Cobb created the masterpiece "Russian Rag," from Sergei Rachmaninoff's Prelude, op. 3, no. 2, which was so successful that a few years later he was forced to write another one called "The New Russian Rag."

Throughout these imaginative years, Folk rags were still being written and published in small towns, and the Joplin school was well represented by James Scott and Joseph Lamb. The Advanced rag writers were no longer writing for the at-home amateur pianist, as were the Popular rag composers, but were writing for themselves and for other professional performers. Consequently, the Advanced rag was not only harmonically advanced but was also more difficult to play than the preceding Popular rag.

A revolution in producing player piano rolls took place around 1913. This was the advent of hand-played rolls. Before then all rolls were created by technicians who read music scores and punched out the notes they wanted on a continuous sheet of paper placed on a table with the piano keyboard marked. In many cases the rolls exactly reproduced the sheet music score. One firm, however, hired a brilliant arranger to enrich the plain, unadorned sound. When pumping alone in a living room or parlor, a full, rich series of sounds would make the pumping seem worthwhile. U.S. Music Rolls employed Mary "Mae" Brown, the most gifted arranger of mechanically cut popular rolls.

Two outstanding player–artists in these years created certain rags that are found only on rolls. These rags were never published or recorded on disc, and many were never even copyrighted. The men were Imperial Industries manager Charley Straight and QRS's eventual owner, Max Kortlander.

# "African Pas'" (Maurice Kirwin)

## December 29, 1902, John Stark & Son, St. Louis

*Pas'* means *step* in the sense of African dance. This is the rag Stark advertised for aspiring ragtime pianists as "easy and brilliant—good to catch the ragtime swing." Section A, marked *pianissimo,* gets the rag rolling gently and interestingly uses the lowered sixth chord (E flat, in the key of G).

# "African Ripples" (Thomas Waller)

## April 20, 1931, Joe Davis, Inc., New York

A section is the same as the A section of "Gladyse."

# *African Suite* ("Mississippi Shivers," "High Hattin'," "Kinda Careless") (Zez Confrey)

## July 16, 1924, Jack Mills, Inc., New York

The suite consists of three Novelty rags, only the first of which has been recorded. It is also the most versatile, as it incorporates the blues with an early Romantic period flavor and a popular ballad into the Novelty rag framework.

# "Agitation Rag" (Robert Hampton)

## January 10, 1915, Stark Music Co., St. Louis

The D section has a treble figure that became a favorite later in Stride ragtime.

# "Alaskan Rag" (Joseph Lamb)

## *They All Played Ragtime*, 3d ed., 1966, Oak Publications, New York

An extension of his great complex rags of the teens and a beautiful addition to the Classic rag repertoire. It is certainly Lamb's most intricate and detailed conception. His final breakthrough in Classic rag composition, he begins the A section with rests in both hands.

# "Amazon Rag" (Teddy Hahn)

## February 11, 1904, John Arnold & Co., Cincinnati

The most advanced of the rags published by this firm, noted for their adventurous rags. Section A is the most pianistic with a descending broken chord C minor pattern much like later Novelty rags. B is an unexpected interlude in G minor, C has a startling harmonic change, and D is a dramatic through-composed section in the manner of Lamb's *"Dynamite Rag."*

# "American Beauty Rag" (Joseph Lamb)

## December 27, 1913, Stark Music Co., St. Louis

One of the greatest rags of all and a splendid example of the best of the Classic rags, it simply must be heard to be appreciated. It reveals the depth of Lamb's conceptions, his bold originality, and his use of unusual harmonies. The melodic lines alternate between long, sweeping phrases and short, skipping melodies. While section B compliments the A section, the tour de force comes with the short introduction into the C section and throughout C leading to section D with its powerful development into the finale. These sections are more rhythmic than melodic. Austere yet elegant in its sweeping beauty, it is an astonishing yet fitting rag in the development following the "Excelsior Rag."

# "Angel Food" (Al F. Marzian)

## December 16, 1911, Forster Music Publisher, Chicago

A string bass player from Louisville, who published several rags of others, this is his only rag and is an absolute joy. The interlude in minor recalls the *Dance of the Seven Veils* and provides a wonderful contrast to the rest of the piece.

# "Applejack, Some Rag" (Charles L. Johnson)

## April 7, 1909, Vandersloot Music Publishing Co., Williamsport, PA

An inspired A section leads to a most lyrical B section, a high point in his rags.

# "Arctic Sunset" (Joseph Lamb)

## *Ragtime Treasures,* Mills Music, Inc., New York, 1964

A section begins with a Novelty rag influence and proceeds to an ambitiously syncopated B section crossing the bar lines. C, however, brings an almost Joplinesque change of mood with a brief serenade marked to be played slow. The final section again designates a tempo change, marked *allegretto.* Such a format is rare with Lamb.

# Donald Ashwander

## (b. July 17, 1929, Birmingham, Alabama; d. October 26, 1994, New York City)

A most unusual man, whose southern heritage is very much a part of his musical life, Ashwander worked for NBC-TV, was a seaman, and composed ballet music and music for advertisements. For twenty-five years he was the musical director, performer, composer, and actor with The Paper Bag Players, a most creative children's theater, with costumes and scenery made from paper bags. His contemporary rags, mostly written between 1965 and 1970, extended the scope of ragtime. His performing style was unique, and his particular bounciness attracted other contemporary players. He was a thoughtful, sensitive musician with great technique and charm.

Donald Ashwander.

## Ragtime Compositions

"Astor Place Rag Waltz," 1977, *The Ragtime Current,* Edward B. Marks Music, New York

"Business in Town," 1966, *They All Played Ragtime,* 3d ed., Oak Publications, New York

"Cascade Plunge," not copyrighted or published

"Empty Porches," not copyrighted or published

"Friday Night," 1966, *They All Played Ragtime,* 3d ed., Oak Publications, New York

"Harlem River Houseboat Rag," not copyrighted or published

"Late Hours Rag," not copyrighted or published

"Mobile Carnival Rag Tango," not copyrighted or published

"Moon Walk," not copyrighted or published

"Peacock Colors," not copyrighted or published

"The Ragtime Pierrot," not copyrighted or published

"Sea Oats," not copyrighted or published

"Upstairs Rag," not copyrighted or published

"Voices, Voices," not copyrighted or published

"Waterloo Rag," not copyrighted or published

"Winter Fields," not copyrighted or published

# May Frances Aufderheide

## (b. May 21, 1888, Indianapolis, Indiana; d. September 1, 1972, Pasadena, California)

A popular pianist whose first rag was a hit. The large sale of "Dusty Rag" impressed her father, John H. Aufderheide, enough to start his own music publishing company. Located in the Lemcke Building, the firm was managed by Paul Pratt who, along with May's friends Julia Niebergall and Gladys Yelvington, also contributed three rags to the catalog. May married Thomas M. Kaufman, who worked for her father in his Commonwealth Loan Company and permanently left the music business. They had one son.

## Ragtime Compositions

"Dusty Rag," February 6, 1908,
Duane Crabb Co., Indianapolis
"Richmond Rag," December 12, 1908,
   J. H. Aufderheide, Indianapolis
"Buzzer Rag," September 4, 1909,
   J. H. Aufderheide, Indianapolis
"The Thriller," September 4, 1909,
   J. H. Aufderheide, Indianapolis

"A Totally Different Rag," July 16, 1910,
   J. H. Aufderheide, Indianapolis
"Blue Ribbon Rag," October 3, 1910,
   J. H. Aufderheide, Indianapolis
"Novelty Rag," April 11, 1911,
   J. H. Aufderheide, Indianapolis

# B

## "Back to Life" (Charles Hunter)

### November 18, 1905, Charles K. Harris, New York

One of the most curious rags ever published. Though the form appears typical enough for a Folk rag, the use of keys is not. The rag begins on a G minor chord, which is the II chord, the supertonic, of the A section's tonic, F. The B section moves abruptly to D flat, after which A is repeated. C is also in the key of F. D moves up a fourth to B flat. Finally, A returns to end the rag. Without section B, the tune is fairly orthodox, but as it is it has the overall effect of a medley, with the A strain barely holding it together.

## "The Baltimore Blues" (Henry Lodge)

### June 20, 1917, Jerome H. Remick & Co., New York

A weird tonal plan for a blues concept. It begins in the key of D major, modulates to C and then onto F, and finishes with a repeat of the first section. A touch of true blues feeling occurs at the start of the C section, where a very pianistic bass run in triplets ends on a minor seventh.

## Banjo Ragtime

The banjo, like ragtime, is an American product. Joe Sweeney, of Appomattox, Virginia, is credited with designing its four long gut strings and one short one with a rim and wooden resonator for backing. Banjoists would pick the strings with their fingers using three basic motions with their right hand while fingering the frets on the neck with their left hand.

The history of recorded ragtime banjo music started with the first commercially made flat discs. All these recordings were made acoustically. The recording studios were crude affairs with six or seven horns lined up in racks. The disc made from the one in the center usually had the best sound to it. As there were no duplicating facilities, every disc was an original recording.

The pioneer recording banjoists were Cullen and Collins from Washington, D.C., Ruby Brooks of the vaudeville team of Brooks and Denton, Olly Oakley in London, and the Banjo King, Vess L. Ossman.

Although ragtime was composed primarily for the piano, the earliest recordings featured military concert bands and five-string banjoists. The banjo soloists were usually backed by the military bands or, perhaps, by a piano. Recording virtuosi were made famous by their records, went into vaudeville, and toured around the country, some touring in England and Europe.

The two greatest five-string banjoists during ragtime's first two decades were Ossman (1868–1923) and Fred Van Eps (1878–1960). Both were pioneers, first recording on cylinders and then on flat discs. Though they each made many recordings of diverse musical genres, it is on their ragtime recordings that they fully demonstrate their remarkable techniques and musicianship. They did their own arranging, showing off their incredible skills.

Approaching the 1920s, the five-stringed banjo gave way to the four-string tenor and plectrum banjos, both of which were used mainly as rhythm backing in the jazz and dance orchestras. The absolute ruler of the four-string tenor banjo was Harry Reser (1896–1965), who was the first to show that the tenor was capable of being a solo instrument. He was not only the acknowledged leader among solo banjoists, but he also composed rags for the banjo that compared favorably to the Novelty piano rags being composed at the same time. What started out to herald the new instrumental popular music remained to champion it and to create additional pieces in the repertoire.

# "Bantam Step" (Harry Jentes)

## February 21, 1916, Shapiro, Bernstein & Co., New York

One of the most singular Advanced rags. Section A's unusual harmonies achieve a haunting quality, unlike most late rags. His piano-roll performance is important because it illustrates how he altered some of the harmonies of the score in performance and is especially enjoyable because of his great broken bass octave figures that are at variance from the printed score.

# "Barber Shop Rag" (Brun Campbell)

## Not copyrighted or published

The C strain is an asymmetrical fifteen and one-half measures. The most striking, however, is the eight-measure B section, which is identical to the first half of "Muskrat Ramble." Perhaps this was a floating folk strain, as it is very pianistic.

# Roy Fredrick Bargy

**(b. July 31, 1894, Newaygo, Michigan;
d. January 16, 1974, Vista, California)**

Bargy grew up in Toledo, Ohio, where at the age of five he started piano lessons. He wanted to be a concert pianist but realized at seventeen that unless he studied in Europe there would be no opportunity for such a career in this country. He hung around the district in Toledo listening to such black pianists as Johnny Walters and Luckey Roberts, started making good money playing piano and organ for silent movies, and formed his own dance orchestra. Through a friend who did artwork for Imperial Player Rolls, he auditioned for Charley Straight in 1919 and in September of that year worked at Imperial full time for more than a year. His main job at Imperial was to edit the popular song rolls. Occasionally he was asked to arrange and play some himself as well as to compose and record one Novelty rag a month. He collaborated on two with Charley Straight, who introduced him to booking agent Edgar Benson. Benson formed a band to record for the Victor Talking Machine Company and hired Bargy as pianist, arranger, and director. "Ma" (Victor 18819) and "Say It While Dancing" (Victor 18938) feature him at the piano and serve to illustrate his fine abilities as arranger. He joined Isham Jones and his orchestra in the same capacity and toured the country with them for two years. During this time, the band recorded for Brunswick, and "The Original Charleston" offers a superb piano solo by Bargy (Brunswick 2970, also available on *The Dancing Twenties*, Folkways RBF-27). Bargy began a twelve-year stint with Paul Whiteman, who had the greatest dance orchestra of all, in February 1928 as solo pianist, arranger, and assistant conductor. He went into radio as conductor–arranger for the Lanny Ross Show and in 1943 became musical director for Jimmy Durante, an association that lasted twenty years, until both of them retired.

A distinctive Bargy device was the extensive use of the *break*—a musical interruption of the melody—incorporating it as part of his melodic line. Famous ragtime artist–composer–pianist Jelly Roll Morton specifically pointed out the advantages of using breaks as a performance device. Bargy uses it as a compositional device, integrating it as part of the melodic conception. For freshness, he always used new and rhythmically different breaks throughout his rags, never boring the listener by using the same breaks over and over.

## Ragtime Compositions

"Rufenreddy" (with Charley Straight), November 14, 1921, Sam Fox, Cleveland

"Slipova," November 14, 1921, Sam Fox, Cleveland

"Knice and Knifty" (with Charley Straight), February 7, 1922, Sam Fox, Cleveland

"Sunshine Capers," February 7, 1922, Sam Fox, Cleveland

"Behave Yourself," June 27, 1922, Sam Fox, Cleveland

"Jim Jams," June 27, 1922, Sam Fox, Cleveland

"Justin-Tyme," June 27, 1922, Sam Fox, Cleveland

"Pianoflage," June 27, 1922, Sam Fox, Cleveland

"Sweet and Tender," April 17, 1923, Will Rossiter, Chicago

"A Blue Streak," 1921, Forster Music, Chicago

"Ditto," not copyrighted or published

"Omeomy," not copyrighted or published

# "Bee Hive" (Joseph Lamb)

## March 27, 1959, unpublished

Of all the unavailable Lamb rags, this is most like his hard-to-play classics. The trio is one of his most monumental creations, with frequent chord changes occurring in rapid succession in a heavy texture of diminished chords that seems to be Lambs's answer to the trio of his favorite Joplin rag, "Gladiolus."

# "Bees and Honey Rag" (Les Copeland)

## Not copyrighted or published

This is one of several that stay in one key, recalling the Turpin approach. However, the three-over-four device in the A section is an accretion of Popular rag writing that betrays its later date. His last four rags were done exclusively as piano-roll performances and were never written down.

# Theron Catlen Bennett

## (b. July 9, 1879, Pierce City, Missouri; d. April 6, 1937, Los Angeles)

Local pianist who went to work for the Victor Kremer Co., Bennett later became a music publisher, purchasing W. C. Handy's first success, "Memphis Blues." Afterward, he owned a chain of music stores in New York City, Chicago, Omaha, St. Louis, Memphis, and Denver. Finally, he settled in Denver, where he operated the famous Dutch Mill Cafe, rendezvous for musicians and artists. His big hit was "Around Her Neck She Wore a Yellow Ribbon."

## Ragtime Compositions

"Pickaninny Capers," March 16, 1903, Cornelius J. Shea, Springfield, MO

"Satisfied," January 2, 1904, Victor Kremer Co., Chicago

"St. Louis Tickle" (as Barney & Seymore), August 20, 1904, Victor Kremer Co., Chicago

"Sweet Pickles" (as George E. Florence), October 23, 1907, Victor Kremer Co., Chicago

"Pork and Beans," January 26, 1909, Victor Kremer Co., Chicago

"Pudnin' Tame," March 25, 1909, Jerome H. Remick & Co., New York

"Sycamore Saplin," April 9, 1910, Jerome H. Remick & Co., New York

"Chills and Fever," August 27, 1912, Sam Fox, Cleveland

"Some Blues, for You All," January 8, 1916, Joe Morris Music, New York

# Mike Bernard

**(b. March 17, 1881, New York;
d. June 27, 1936, New York)**

The most famous of the music hall or variety pianists was Mike Bernard (the pseudonym of Mike Barnett), who accompanied the greatest artists in vaudeville while he was resident pianist at Tony Pastor's Music Hall, the most famous variety hall in the United States. Playing or otherwise performing at Tony Pastor's was what performing at the Palace Theatre in New York City was to a later generation of show business folk: the highest accolade a performer could have. Only headliners played at Pastor's, and Mike Bernard, often a show by himself, manned the keyboard. The greatest display of his pianism is amply demonstrated on the recording "Blaze Away" (Columbia A-2577) which illustrates his whirlwind approach to ragtime and reaffirms his title of "Rag Time King of the World," a title and diamond-studded medal so stated when he won the National Ragtime Piano Contest at Tammany Hall on January 23, 1900, sponsored by the *Police Gazette*. His performance of an earlier rag, "Tantalizing Tingles" (Columbia A-1386), supports the theory that for ragtime to mean anything to its audience, the performer must incorporate his own individualized style within the rendition. Bernard was a crowd pleaser for many years.

# "Bert Williams" (Jelly Roll Morton)

**June 29, 1948, unpublished**

This was originally titled "Pacific Rag," but when the great comedian expressed appreciation, it was changed to honor him.

# "Billiken Rag" (E. J. Stark)

## February 21, 1913, Stark Music Co., St. Louis

Named after the St. Louis University basketball team, which had been named after a coach who bore a marked resemblance to the traditional good luck doll *Billiken,* used by Stark on the cover. Section A features an unusual chromatic descent that lasts for three measures.

# "Bird-Brain Rag" (Joseph Lamb)

## *Ragtime Treasures,* 1964, Mills Music, Inc., New York

Expansive later style with thinner texture to allow for ranging melodic line. In sections C and D, tenths are in the bass instead of the conventional octaves.

# "Black and White Rag" (George Botsford)

## Not copyrighted, published 1908, Jerome H. Remick & Co., New York

This was an early ragtime hit—the third million-selling rag in sheet music—and the biggest success of Botsford's seventeen rags. Vaudeville virtuoso pianist Albert Benzler, also an expert percussionist and marimba soloist, probably made the first piano recording of a rag when U.S. Everlasting issued his version on their cylinder (#380) in early 1910. Benzler performs this rag at a fairly fast clip, and his virtuosity is apparent. He appears not to deviate from the printed score and is content to deliver the happy sounds as they were written. This rare cylinder first appeared on LP in the historical reissue series on the Herwin label (Herwin 405).

Because of its immediate popularity, it is incredible that this rag was not copyrighted initially. Not until November 13, 1924, did Botsford have it copyrighted in a revised arrangement. Its most appealing feature was the three-over-four device in the A section. The C section comes from Max Hoffman's rag of 1904, "Yankee Land." Later that same year, Cy Seymour (pseudonym of William C. Polla) used it for his trio in "The Black Laugh."

# "A Black Bawl" (Harry C. Thompson)

## June 16, 1905, W. C. Polla Co., Chicago

Sections C and D bear a strong resemblance to parts of McFadden's medley, "Rags to Burn" (see also Brun Campbell).

# "A Black Smoke" (Charles L. Johnson)

## Not copyrighted, published 1902, Carl Hoffman, Kansas City, MO

An imaginative Folk Rag essay all in one key, but one that achieves surprising variety. The introduction and vamp are extended ideas leaving no doubt that the home key is G. Section A has syncopation crossing the bar line, a rarity in early rags, and has a rather complex stop-time ending. B, by contrast, uses a different syncopation and shorter phrasing. C is a buck dance executed with careful dynamics in the call-and-response pattern. D has the cleverest harmonies, bringing in the relative minor.

# "Black Wasp Rag" (H. A. Fischler)

## February 21, 1911, Vandersloot Music Publishing Co., Williamsport, PA

One of a half-dozen or so rags published by Vandersloot, which specialized in easy-to-play rags, mostly scored in single-note melody lines and phrased with rather busy, relentless syncopations that vary greatly in inventiveness.

# James Hubert (Eubie) Blake

## (b. February 7, 1887, Baltimore; d. February 12, 1983, Brooklyn)

From early lessons on the organ (at age six) and piano (at age seven) to the sporting houses where he learned the latest rags as an adolescent, Blake began to compose rags ("Charleston Rag," 1899), ballads, and waltzes with equal facility and invention. He studied with Margaret Marshall and later with Llewellyn Wilson and became a star attraction in cafes, first in Baltimore and then in Atlantic City. He began his professional career on July 4, 1901, as a dancer and accompanist in a medicine show. Blake met singer and lyricist Noble Sissie on May 15, 1915, at the River View Park in Baltimore. This was the start of a lasting partnership until Sissie died December 17, 1975. They immediately became a songwriting team, the Dixie Duo, and headliners in vaudeville. On May 23, 1921, the team's first Broadway musical, *Shuffle Along,* was produced at the 63rd Street Theatre. The success of this show gave other black songwriters a chance to write for Broadway. Throughout the twenties and early thirties Blake wrote for many such shows, both in New York and in London. During World War II he toured with the U.S.O. With the ragtime revival, starting in 1951, Blake came out of retirement to record and to perform at ragtime and jazz festivals around the world. He frequently appeared on radio and television, composed a number of new rags, and formed a record company in 1971, Eubie Blake Music, which produced both albums and sheet-music folios. Robert Kimball and William Bolcom compiled an excellent pictorial book on Blake's life, *Reminiscing with Sissie and Blake* (Viking Press, 1973). Standard popular songs include "I'm Just Wild about Harry," "Memories of You," and "You're Lucky to Me."

Eubie Blake and Noble Sissie.

Eubie Blake at 90.

David Alan Jasen and Eubie Blake.

## Ragtime Compositions

"The Chevy Chase," October 28, 1914, Jos. W. Stern & Co., New York

"Fizz Water," October 28, 1914, Jos. W. Stern & Co., New York

"Bugle Call Rag" (with Carey Morgan), January 27, 1916, Jos. W. Stern & Co., New York

"Charleston Rag" (a.k.a. "Sounds of Africa"), August 8, 1917, unpublished until *Sincerely, Eubie Blake,* Eubie Blake Music (1975), New York

"Baltimore Todalo," October 29, 1962, *Sincerely, Eubie Blake,* Eubie Blake Music (1975), New York

"Brittwood Rag," September 11, 1962, *Sincerely, Eubie Blake,* Eubie Blake Music (1975), New York

"Dicty's on Seventh Avenue," July 24, 1962, *Giants of Ragtime,* Edward B. Marks Music (1971), New York

"Kitchen Tom," October 20, 1962, *Sincerely, Eubie Blake,* Eubie Blake Music (1975), New York

"Melodic Rag," January 3, 1972, not published

"Novelty Rag," January 3, 1972, not published

"Poor Jimmy Green," October 13, 1969, *Sincerely, Eubie Blake,* Eubie Blake Music (1975), New York

"Poor Katie Red (Eubie's Slow Drag)," August 18, 1960, *Sincerely, Eubie Blake,* Eubie Blake Music (1975), New York

"Rhapsody in Ragtime," March 6, 1973, *Sincerely, Eubie Blake,* Eubie Blake Music (1975), New York

"Tricky Fingers," October 14, 1959, *Giants of Ragtime,* Edward B. Marks Music (1971), New York

"Troublesome Ivories" (a.k.a. "Ragtime Rag"), May 14, 1971, *Giants of Ragtime,* Edward B. Marks Music (1971), New York

# "Blame It on the Blues" (Charles L. Cooke)

## March 3, 1914, Jerome H. Remick & Co., New York

One of the most inspired and original of these later rags, without the composer's resorting to odd harmonies or dissonances. Cooke became famous during the twenties when he recorded as Doc Cook & His Dreamland Orchestra. He was one of the few black musicians who obtained a doctor of music degree. He graduated from the Chicago Musical College.

# Rudi Blesh

## (b. January 21, 1899, Guthrie, Oklahoma; d. August 25, 1985, Gilmanton, New Hampshire)

Rudi Blesh, coauthor with Harriet Janis, wrote the first history of ragtime, *They All Played Ragtime* (Alfred A. Knopf, 1950). The idea came from Janis, who persuaded Blesh to help her research and write it. He was reluctant, as he had just finished researching, writing, and publishing a controversial book on the history of jazz called *Shining Trumpets* (Knopf, 1946). He was finally committed to this ragtime project after they went to the Library of Congress and the copyright office where they were given a tip to visit Harlem journalist Bucklin Moon. Moon helped them locate New York musicians and told them to look up black pioneer publisher and songwriter Shep Edmonds at his home in Columbus, Ohio. Edmonds gave them names and addresses of other ragtime composers and performers and the best advice for finding others by going to any city and asking the local undertakers for their addresses. Their research was conducted throughout 1949 and within the year of its publication, more than half of those Blesh and Janis interviewed were dead. The book set the stage for giving prominence to Scott Joplin and told ragtime's story with Joplin center stage along with his followers James Scott, Arthur Marshall, and Joseph Lamb. The book provided further impetus to the ragtime revival by telling ragtime's important musical history and by inspiring many new fans to collect and play the music. It also encouraged a few ragtimers to continue researching ragtime's interesting past. Blesh continued to inspire young ragtimers by speaking at ragtime festivals and major concerts, writing record liner notes, teaching courses at New York City universities as an adjunct professor, and giving his support to other ragtime scholars and enthusiasts.

## "Blooie-Blooie" (Edythe Baker)

### Not copyrighted or published

She was one of the most creative piano-roll artists. This work features a striking key change from G to D flat at the trio.

## Rube Bloom

### (b. April 24, 1902, New York; d. March 30, 1976, New York)

Bloom went to public school in Brooklyn, New York, which he left at age seventeen to become an accompanist for vaudeville stars. He was entirely self-taught, composed directly at the piano, then memorized it and got someone else to write it down for publication. An extraordinarily fine pianist, he was in great demand for recording work, as a soloist, accompanist (especially for Jane Gray on Harmony), and in dance and jazz bands. Over the years he recorded with Bix Beiderbecke, Miff Mole, Frankie Trumbauer, the Dorsey Brothers, Red Nichols, Ethel Waters, and Noble Sissle. His own group was called Rube Bloom and His Bayou Boys. In 1928 he won first prize of $5,000 in the Victor Talking Machine Company's contest for his composition "Song of the Bayou." His songwriting career included such hits as "Give Me the Simple Life," "Penthouse Serenade," "Big Man from the South," "Truckin!," "Stay on the Right Side, Sister," and "Fools Rush In." Although he never studied counterpoint, harmony, or composition, he wrote several piano method books and was a much sought-after arranger of hit songs for various publishers.

## Ragtime Compositions

"That Futuristic Rag," April 9, 1923, Jack Mills, Inc., New York

"Spring Fever," June 21, 1926, Triangle Music, New York

"Soliloquy," June 21, 1926, Triangle Music, New York

"Silhouette," May 9, 1927, Triangle Music, New York

"Jumping Jack" (with Bernie Seaman & Marvin Smolev), July 3, 1928, ABC Standard, New York

"Aunt Jemima's Birthday," May 15, 1931, Robbins Music, New York

"One Finger Joe," May 15, 1931, Robbins Music, New York

"Southern Charms," May 15, 1931, Robbins Music, New York

# "Blue Clover Man" (Max Kortlander)

This Novelty rag was copyrighted on June 18, 1920, and only exists on a hand-played piano roll performed by the composer (QRS 100879). This piano-roll performance is the most sophisticated ever produced. Kortlander's use of exotic harmonies and totally different rhythms within the same ragtime composition was unique for its time.

# "Blue Goose Rag" (as Raymond Birch)

## January 3, 1916, Forster Music Publisher, Chicago

Unusual C section not written in syncopation.

# "Blue Grass Rag" (Joseph Lamb)

## *Ragtime Treasures,* Mills Music, Inc., New York, 1964

One of Lamb's very best. It remained unfinished until during the 1950s when he finally wrote its trio. The bass is varied in section B and the rousing D section is capped by a Novelty rag break.

# "Blue Rag" (Brun Campbell)

## Not copyrighted or published

The blue quality is the melodic flavor. Structurally, it has three sections of sixteen, eight, and thirty-two measures, respectively.

# "A Blue Streak" (Roy Bargy)

## 1921, Forster Music Publisher, Chicago

One of Bargy's masterpieces of 1921, the published sheet music was taken from Bargy's roll (Imperial 513600). The A section is an amazing blend of the blues with the Novelty rag and features an ascending walking bass consisting of a bottom tonic note walking with the dominant and tonic together leading to an exciting tremolo in the right hand.

# "Bohemia" (Joseph Lamb)

## February 17, 1919, Stark Music Co., St. Louis

Most advanced use of tonality by Lamb, with the key in section A not sure until the twelfth measure. A most unusual beginning, starting in the minor mode and ending up in the major. The grace and charm of the B section is achieved by the subtle use of passing tones and syncopation crossing the bar lines, which enhances the delicate quality. This section also has an alternate "ad lib" bass in octaves at its start. The high spirits of the C section give way to an interesting but unusual device for a Classic rag: the twelve-measure interlude leading to a repeat of the C section, which is a throwback to an old cakewalk pattern, much as Joplin did in "Eugenia." The repeat marks indicate that the interlude is to be included in the last repeat. A thoroughly delightful rag.

# William Elden Bolcom

## (b. May 26, 1938, Seattle)

Bolcom studied composition and piano beginning at age five. He entered the University of Washington at age eleven and continued the study of classical music until he received a doctor of musical arts degree from Stanford University. With Arnold Weinstein in 1963 he wrote an award-winning opera for actors called *Dynamite Tonite*. He became interested in ragtime in 1967 and started composing it. Recordings followed in 1971. He married singer Joan Morris, with whom he gives concerts and makes records.

## Ragtime Compositions

"Brass Knuckles" (with William Albright), not copyrighted or published

"California Porcupine—Grand Rag Fantasy," May 24, 1971, not published

"Garden of Eden: Rag Suite," May 24, 1971, not published

"Glad Rag," May 24, 1971, not published

"Graceful Ghost," May 24, 1971, Edward B. Marks Music, New York

"Seabiscuits Rag," May 24, 1971, Edward B. Marks Music, New York

# "Bolo Rag" (Albert Gumble)

## November 11, 1908, Jerome H. Remick & Co., New York

A fine rag climaxed by a sweeping descent of sixteenth notes in the trio. Instructions read to be played "slowly but surely."

# "Bombshell Rag" (Thomas R. Confare and Morris Silver)

## Not copyrighted, published 1909, Charles I. Davis Music Pub., Cleveland

An important recent discovery indicating that Confare, who arranged the famous "Cannon Ball," might have had a heavier hand in the rag than the so-called composer, Jos. Northup. This is in the same style but is a more complex work.

# "Bon Ton" (Luckey Roberts)

## May 7, 1915, G. Ricordi & Co., New York

An inverted version of "Junk Man Rag."

# "Bone Head Blues" (Leo Gordon)

## Not copyrighted, published 1917, Walter Jacobs, Boston

Some of the silent movie music issued by Jacobs includes excellent original rags with frequently daring and involved harmonies. This one begins section A with a startling dissonance of augmented chords cleverly worked out over a standard dominant seventh in the bass.

# George Botsford

**(b. February 24, 1874, Sioux Falls, South Dakota;
d. February 11, 1949, New York)**

Although born in South Dakota and raised in Iowa, Botsford spent his professional life as a composer–conductor in New York City. His second rag was a smash hit and established him as a professional. His "Grizzly Bear Rag" was also a tremendous hit and became an even greater seller when Irving Berlin wrote words for it. "Sailing down the Chesapeake Bay" was another enormous success, and with its proceeds he started his own publishing firm, experimenting with miniature opera to be sung by only three or four people. The idea did not catch on, so he went to work for Remick Music Corporation as arranger and chief of their harmony and quartet department. He arranged music for amateur minstrel shows and became director of the New York Police Department's Glee Club.

Though overall the Botsford rags are a fine group, he was more dependent on the three-over-four formula than other writers for major companies. Half of his rags have the following pattern: A BB A CC B. In general, he preferred not to repeat A before stating the B section and moved directly to the trio after the second A.

## Ragtime Compositions

"Klondike Rag," January 23, 1908, William R. Haskins Co., New York

"Black and White Rag," not copyrighted, published 1908, Jerome H. Remick & Co., New York

"Old Crow Rag," April 13, 1909, Jerome H. Remick & Co., New York

"Pianophiends Rag," May 11, 1909, William R. Haskins Co., New York

"Texas Steer," October 15, 1909, Jerome H. Remick & Co., New York

"Wiggle Rag," October 15, 1909, Jerome H. Remick & Co., New York

"Grizzly Bear Rag," April 18, 1910, Ted Snyder Co., New York

"Lovey-Dovey Rag," May 19, 1910, Ted Snyder Co., New York

"Chatterbox Rag," October 4, 1910, Jerome H. Remick & Co., Detroit

"Royal Flush," March 27, 1911, Jerome H. Remick & Co., Detroit

"Hyacinth," December 11, 1911, Jerome H. Remick & Co., New York

"Honeysuckle Rag," December 19, 1911, Jerome H. Remick & Co., New York

"Universal Rag," February 14, 1913, George Botsford, New York

"Rag, Baby Mine," March 28, 1913, Jerome H. Remick & Co., New York

"The Buck-Eye Rag," June 11, 1913, George Botsford, New York

"The Incandescent Rag," October 21, 1913, Jerome H. Remick & Co., New York

"Boomerang Rag," June 21, 1916, Jerome H. Remick & Co., New York

# "The Bounding Buck" (Henry Lodge)

## March 1, 1918, M. Witmark & Sons, New York

One of his most lyrical, yet certainly his most advanced rag. The A section is masterful: After establishing the tonality of E flat, he introduces a sequence that suggests the key of E natural. The eighth measure ends on a $B_7$, which has the feeling of the lowered sixth chord because it is followed by a return to the first four measures, which reestablishes E flat. The B strain is one of the composer's most beautiful, enhanced by his clever use of minors. C extends the mood of B and is the most melodic of the three.

# "Bowery Buck" (Tom Turpin)

## March 6, 1899, Robt. De Yong & Co., St. Louis

A typical folk rag, especially in form and use of tonality, sometimes described as linear or additive. Such a rag simply states a section, repeats it, and moves onto the next. It also stays in the same key throughout. Here the repeats of B and C are written out, with added treble notes in the B repeat, filling out the texture. This became a standard scoring device much later in the popular rags. As with "Harlem Rag," the A section is a busy one with a syncopated single-note line with an emphasis on a flatted ninth. Section B breaks away in strutting fashion, but the highlight is C. According to St. Louis ragtime pianist Charles Thompson, Turpin adapted it from a street-organ melody heard often in Chestnut Valley. Sparked by a triplet rip in the bass, it is an unusual concept that avoids the oompah bass and causes a brief but very notable suspension in which the beat must be inferred—quite a sophisticated device for such an early rag. De Yong sold this piece the same year to Will Rossiter, who at first used the original plates but later made a new set to conform to the familiar Rossiter style. The music is identical in all editions, with the addition of an "ff" in the final Rossiter one. All editions were "Dedicated to my friend, E. J. Morgan," but the interesting "N. B., 'The Most Original Rag-Time Two Step Ever Written'" was not on the original De Yong issue.

# Euday Louis Bowman

## (b. November 9, 1887, Fort Worth; d. May 26, 1949, New York)

Composer of the most famous and biggest-selling rag in sheet music and recordings, Bowman has a life that is surprisingly shrouded in obscurity. From the turn of this century through the depression he was an itinerant pianist, typical of his time, wandering throughout the Midwest and South. After Pee Wee Hunt made his sensationally best-selling recording of "12th Street Rag"—with over three million copies sold—Bowman decided to cash in on that popularity by recording it on his own label, using the piano on which he originally wrote it. He came to New York City to promote the sale of his record and died there three days later. A product of the districts, his ragtime compositions reflect this atmosphere. The numbered streets, 6th through 12th, cut across Calhoun Street in Fort Worth, which was the heart of the district, whereas Petticoat Lane was in the red light district in Kansas City, where his major publisher was located. Of his other compositions, mostly blues numbers, "Kansas City Blues," "Colorado Blues," "Fort Worth Blues," and "Tipperary Blues" are the most idiomatic midwestern blues ever scored—real blues tunes with ragtime flavor in the traditional soulful style.

## Ragtime Compositions

"Twelfth Street Rag," January 30, 1914, August 24, 1914, January 2, 1915, Euday L. Bowman, Fort Worth
"Sixth Street Rag," November 11, 1914, unpublished
"Tenth Street Rag," November 11, 1914, unpublished
"Petticoat Lane," June 1, 1915, unpublished, August 14, 1915, Copyright transferred to J. W. Jenkins' Sons, Kansas City, MO, who then published it

"Shamrock Rag," January 21, 1916, Euday L. Bowman, Fort Worth
"Eleventh Street Rag," November 16, 1917, unpublished, July 15, 1918, Ward & Bowman, Gary, IN
"Chromatic Chords," February 12, 1926, unpublished

# "Brain-Storm Rag" (Bud Manchester)

## June 3, 1907, Stark Music Co., New York

Manchester was an alias used by E. J. Stark. Section D is only eight measures long.

# "A Breeze from Alabama" (Scott Joplin)

## December 29, 1902, John Stark & Son, St. Louis

Advertised by Stark as "a story in transitions," this is an ambitious experiment in tonality, far ahead of any other rag writer of the day. After two sections in the key of C, the composer begins the C section abruptly in the key of A flat; this is a favorite harmonic change in folk ragtime, but more thoroughly explored here. Within this C section, Joplin modulates to E natural, and back again to A flat, telescoping the effect of the previous C–A flat change. Then he moves to F and finally ends in the key of C.

# "Bric-a-Brac Rag" (Maurice Porcelain)

## Not copyrighted, published 1906, Vinton Music Co., Boston

Rambling, ebullient rag that appears to consist of a series of improvisations. The interlude has a written break on board, or in front of the keys. The cover illustrates a broken willowware plate, once the most popular chinaware in America.

# "The Buffalo Rag" (Tom Turpin)

## November 2, 1904, Will Rossiter, Chicago

This is a Turpin rag with no indicated arranger, and its idiosyncrasies may give the best clues as to how he sounded as a performer. It is all in one key in a linear format, closing with the introduction as coda. Of all his rags, this one seems to be the most folk rooted in flavor: there are banjoistic ideas as the ascending figure in B and in the quick 32nd-note bass descents in D. The entire composition has a capricious air: The treble texture is punctuated with quick chords and abrupt phrasing, contrasted with longer, lyrical single-note melody lines. The Turpin flair for contrast, surprise, and creativity was never better displayed, as C evolves beautifully from B. The title may reflect Turpin's hunting days and his western adventures but most probably refers to the Benevolent Order of Buffaloes, a St. Louis lodge in which he was very active.

# Louis Ferdinand Busch

## (b. July 18, 1910, Louisville; d. September 18, 1979, Camarillo, California)

The family name was Bush, but he added the *c* because he thought it looked good. He took private piano lessons, starting at the age of nine, and left high school and home at sixteen to tour with Clyde McCoy and

Joe "Fingers" Carr.

other local bands. With no formal training, he became an arranger as well as pianist for Henry Busse, Leo Reisman, Horace Heidt, Vincent Lopez, George Olsen, and Hal Kemp. He married vocalist Janet Blair and settled in Los Angeles. In December 1941 he was Lena Horne's accompanist. He joined the army in 1942 and served for the duration of the war. He went to work for Capitol Transcription Service in 1946 and became musical director for Peter Lind Hayes and Mary Healy. From May 1949, he was an artist and repertoire executive for Capitol Records. He and his second wife, singer Margaret Whiting, have one daughter. Busch created the ragtime pseudonym Joe "Fingers" Carr in April 1950 and became the best-known ragtime pianist worldwide through his more than thirty-six singles and fourteen albums. He created an atmosphere for ragtime that highlighted the ebullient, rollicking aspects of this happy music. His carefully thought-out arrangements and inspired performances encouraged many of the leading ragtimers of today. In 1958 he went to Warner Bros. Records as producer–artist, where he made five albums as Joe "Fingers" Carr. In 1960 he went to Dot Records where he performed on three albums. He became Allan Sherman's musical director, arranger, composer, and conductor. Among his compositions are "Roller Coaster," used as the closing theme in television's long-running panel show, "What's My Line"; "Ivory Rag," which became the first segment in the ragtime medley, "The Crazy Otto"; and Allan Sherman's big hit, "Hello Mudduh, Hello Fadduh." As Lou Busch, he made a lovely mood album called "Lazy Rhapsody" (Capitol T-1072), in which he was arranger, conductor, and featured pianist. Not only did he create memorable arrangements of 1920s hits and a body of clever rags, but he recorded more published rags than anyone else, and of them many were recorded for the first time. He was a major rediscoverer of ragtime at a time when no one else was looking.

## Ragtime Compositions

"Baked Alaska," November 23, 1959, not published

"Barky Roll Stomp," December 12, 1955, unpublished

"Boogie Woogie Rag," September 2, 1952, unpublished

"Carr's Hop," March 5, 1952, Chatsworth Music, New York

"Doo Wacky Rag," May 31, 1956, unpublished

"Fingers Medley," not copyrighted or published

"Finicky Fingers," March 5, 1952, Chatsworth Music, New York

"Fourth Man Rag" (by Dick Hamilton & Jill Leland), not copyrighted or published

"Hook and Ladder Rag," May 31, 1956, unpublished

"Hot Potatoes," February 27, 1958, unpublished

"Ironfingers Rag" (with Alvino Rey), June 20, 1960, unpublished

"Looney Louie," February 27, 1958, unpublished

"Piano Picker Rag," October 24, 1966, unpublished

"Piccadilly Rag," May 31, 1956, unpublished

"Raggedy-Ann Rag," March 5, 1952, Chatsworth Music, New York

"Rapscallion Rag," March 5, 1952, Chatsworth Music, New York

"Rattlesnake Rag" (with Eddie Hanson), December 29, 1952, Chatsworth Music, New York

"Tin Pan Rag," March 5, 1952, Chatsworth Music, New York

"Two Dollar Rag," not copyrighted or published

"Waltz in Ragtime," March 5, 1952, Chatsworth Music, New York

# C

## Cakewalk

This dance sensation, along with the jaunty music written for it, first appeared in music halls and theaters in the mid 1890s. Its popularity was based on tuneful, lightly syncopated music written for high-strutting, prancing dance steps. It was composer–publisher Kerry (Frederick Allen) Mills who started the rage for this

Kerry Mills.

dance music with his first publication, "Rastus on Parade" (1895). The tune had the distinction of establishing what soon became a harmonic cliché of cakewalks by beginning in a minor key and moving to the relative major, a construction that later writers followed with a subdominant trio section. Another Mills cakewalk, however, "At a Georgia Camp Meeting" (1897), became the standard against which all other cakewalks were measured. Although a highly singable and danceable number, it was rejected by all major publishers of the day. Their costly mistake firmly set up the house of F. A. Mills for the next twenty years. His 1899 hit "Whistling Rufus" successfully competed with E. T. McGrath's "A Breeze from Blackville," Bernard Franklin's "Blackville Society," Arthur Pryor's "A Coon Band Contest," Jean Schwartz's "Dusky Dudes," George Rosey's "A Rag-Time Skedaddle," and Abe Holzmann's "Smokey Mokes"—all winners in the glorious year of the cakewalk. The following year, J. Bodewalt Lampe published "Creole Belles" in his hometown of Buffalo, New York. Not until Whitney-Warner purchased it the following year did it became a million seller. Although Mills went on to compose several lovely Tin Pan Alley songs, such as "Meet Me in St. Louis, Louis" and "Red Wing," which became standards, he occasionally harked back to his cakewalk roots, with "Kerry Mills Ragtime Dance" (1909) and "Kerry Mills' Cake Walk" (1915).

In their Tin Pan Alley form, cakewalks were 2/4 instrumentals, with occasional vocal trios, founded on a simple march framework and using simple syncopation in a single rhythm pattern. Compositionally, they were unpianistic pieces involving single note, easily remembered melody lines that one could sketch out on a piano with one finger without disturbing their harmony. Though cakewalks were often arranged for piano (as were marches), their sheet music covers typically displayed other instruments, usually trombones and banjos, and they were often performed by marching or circus bands, as well as by string bands consisting of violin, banjo, and string bass. The earliest cakewalk hits were popularized by the premier concert band of John Philip Sousa, who was responsible for the cakewalk's European popularity. Sousa detested the cakewalk but clearly perceived its commercial possibilities. He had his solo trombonist, Arthur Pryor, make the arrangements and conduct the Sousa band when it recorded cakewalks.

# "California Sunshine" (Harry Jentes)

## November 29, 1913, Theron C. Bennett Co., New York

Only last section is in ragtime.

# "Calliope Rag" (James Scott)

## *They All Played Ragtime,* 3d ed., 1966, Oak Publications, New York, arranged and edited by Donald Ashwander

An enchanting work discovered by Robert Darch, who obtained the manuscript from one of Scott's sisters, with the information that Scott played it on the steam calliope at Lakeside Park, located between Carthage and Joplin, Missouri. Probably written prior to 1910.

# Sanford Brunson Campbell

### (b. March 26, 1884, Oberlin, Kansas;
### d. November 23, 1952, Venice, California)

Born with a natural interest in music, Campbell was given piano lessons at ten, ran away from home to Okla-homa City when he was fifteen to attend a celebration, and earned pocket money playing at the Armstrong-Byrd Music Company where Joplin's friend and colleague Otis Saunders asked Campbell to play from the manuscript of the "Maple Leaf Rag." Shortly thereafter he went to Sedalia where he then met Joplin, who taught him his four earliest rags. As he wrote,

> Joplin was playing a version of "Maple Leaf Rag" as early as 1889, that is, at least the years before it was actually pub-lished. Joplin himself told me. As you know, I was Scott Joplin's only white pupil in 1898 Sedalia, and I learned to play "Maple Leaf" from the original hand-notated pen-and-ink manuscript. Today (1950), I can still play the trio part which Joplin used in the 1880's before his pal Otis Saunders helped him arrange it as it appears in the present day piano copy. When Saunders lent a hand, he re-wrote the last half of the trio. However, when I made my record I used Scott's original trio, not the later one, in order to do a really authentic job. I became a kid ragtime pianist, and met almost all of the early Negro pianists and composers of ragtime in the 1890's, such great musicians as Tom Turpin, Scott Joplin, Otis Saunders, Scott Hayden, James Scott, Arthur Marshall, Louis Chauvin, Tony Williams, Tony Jackson, Melford Alexander, Jelly Roll Morton, Ida Hastings (a Negress), and "Ink" Howard. I am very proud of the fact that I could call these Negro musicians my friends.

He traveled over the Midwest and South, playing in honky tonks, barrelhouses, pool halls, roadhouses, confectionery stores, theaters, hotels, steamboats, nautch houses, restaurants, and saloons. He retired from active playing in 1908 when he married and became a barber. His writings about ragtime and recordings date from the mid 1940s and early 1950s.

Unlike most composers, especially the classic rag pioneers, Campbell does not use secondary-chord relationships such as relative minor or minor of the dominant but instead sticks close to the basic I-IV-V harmony, with heavy use of the basic circle of fifths. In folk ragtime, the minor tonality is touched on lightly, usually as a regular II chord or brief use of the relative minor. It is rarely prolonged, as in some Joplin rags, except where it is a carryover from the A section cakewalk tradition of beginning in a minor key—descriptive of an exotic setting of dancers preparing for the competition. Campbell's avoidance of minors and especially his recurring use of the circle of fifths is reminiscent of Charles Hunter's rags, however, Hunter did make skillful use of minor keys, briefly, for a change of color, and early country string band music. Campbell's playing is in the typical Folk rag style of the earliest ragtime performers, placing strains of diverse or similar feelings in a random fashion. In several of his works a blues–rag mixture of slurs, flatted thirds, and sevenths can be heard in a twelve-measure form. There is a great deal of improvisation in his playing: part of the transformation of syncopating folk tunes, marches, popular songs, and classical material. It is most dramatically demonstrated on his two different recordings of "Essay in Ragtime." The patchwork of using floating folk music within an original conception is evident in his playing. Some of the idiosyncrasies of the earliest scoring of folk rags appear in these performances, such as adding extra beats to a measure ("Barber Shop Rag") and placing harmonic changes in unexpected places ("Campbell Cakewalk").

## Ragtime Compositions (not copyrighted or published)

| | |
|---|---|
| "Barber Shop Rag" | "Ginger Snap Rag" |
| "Blue Rag" | "Grandpa Stomps" |
| "Campbell Cakewalk" | "Rendezvous Rag" |
| "Chestnut Street in the 90s" | "Tent Show Rag" |
| "Essay in Ragtime" | |

# "Campbell Cakewalk" (Brun Campbell)

## Not copyrighted or published

This is his most eccentric, unorthodox solo. Only the B and C sections contain sixteen measures. A has twenty-eight (in a form of twenty plus eight), whereas D is almost formless—fourteen and one-half measures with chords and harmonies changing at unexpected places. Folk ragtime in the rough.

# "Can Ragtime Be Surpressed?"

## By Axel W. Christensen

(Reprinted from the May, 1918 issue of Melody Magazine. Christensen was the foremost ragtime instructor of the day, having a nationwide chain of ragtime schools.)

"Almost three years ago some college students in one of our smaller cities, perhaps for the want of something else to do, organized a 'Society for the suppresion of Ragtime Music in America'.

"They have not been seen or heard of since.

"No doubt they were sincere in their convictions, as there are some people who do not like ragtime, but I feel that they were just a little bit selfish in trying to take it away from people who do like it. Fortunately, however, the people who like ragtime are in such great majority that the Society for the Suppression of Ragtime found it harder than they expected to sweep the country with their movement.

"Nearly every true red-blooded American citizen likes real snappy ragtime, and he asks for it and gets it wherever he is, whether it is at the restaurant, at the theatre, at the dance or at home—and if he cannot play it himself he will have Mike Bernard, John Philip Sousa and others play it for him through the phonograph.

"Believe me, the Society for the Suppression of Ragtime in America had some job on its hands, and it's no wonder they were doomed to disappointment.

"Having spent several years on the vaudeville stage, during which time I have had the opportunity of studying audiences in every part of the country, I have always noticed that no matter how dormant or listless people might seem at the opening of the performance, they instantly come to life when the orchestra played a good ragtime number, and the performer on the stage who used ragtime in his or her act was sure of the heartiest appreciation. And when an audience applauded a ragtime act, it was not the desultory applause that marks the spots in the average vaudeville act where the audience is kindly supposed to applaud; it was spontaneous, electrical, unanimous—applause that filled the house from the orchestra pit to the uttermost hidden regions in the gallery.

"I have seen grand opera quartets that possessed wonderful merit—artists who had spent years in hard, painstaking training—fall flat and leave the stage at the end of their act with barely enough applause to take them to the entrance (in fact, I have seen them run to get to the entrance before the applause died out). On the other hand, I have seen a slip of a girl go out on the stage and deliver a half dozen snappy songs and simply 'stop the show' the continued applause making it practically impossible for the next act to go on. When it came to art, she was not to be compared with the grand opera quartet—she had never spent any time in musical training—but when she sang her syncopated songs she struck the responsive chord that is to be found in the soul of every American man or woman, and so she was successful.

"Some time ago the London Times discussed ragtime at great length in its columns. The London Times is of the opinion that ragtime is the typical American music, the true music of the hustler, and that it is filled with the spirit and bustle of American life.

"Some ragtime is easy to play, and there is some that is quite hard to master. We have our 'classic' ragtime that would baffle many a music teacher who has never played anything but the orthodox music—and if the truth were known, many of the persons who are crying 'Down with Ragtime' could not play ragtime as it ought to be played if their lives depended on it. I am willing to admit that ragtime in the hands of some musicians (who would play a song like 'Some Sunday Morning' with the same ponderous dignity that they would render 'Asleep In The Deep') should be suppressed.

"Sasanoff, the eminent Russian orchestra leader, became so enthusiastic on hearing an American orchestra play some real ragtime that he decided he would have it scored to be reproduced by his own orchestra in Russia. In his opinion, ragtime is to America what the folk songs are to Norway, Sweden, Italy or other foreign lands.

"Many writers have endeavored to trace ragtime down to its origin, but there are almost as many opinions as to where ragtime had its source as there are writers on the subject. Ever since there has been such a thing as ragtime, there have been people who would tell you that ragtime was on the decline, and that it would soon be a thing of the past. Twelve or thirteen years ago a well-known music publisher told me in all seriousness to devote my efforts to something besides ragtime, because the knell of ragtime had been sounded; it had run itself to death and the publishers would soon stop printing it altogether. He sagely told me that if I had only gone into business a few years previous I might have made something out of it, but there was no longer any hope. That was twelve years ago, and ragtime is now stronger than ever. The ragtime of today, however, is not the same as that written twenty years ago. Such rags as the 'Mississippi Rag,' 'The Georgia Camp Meeting,' etc., depended mostly upon plain syncopation, while today it is not a matter of mere syncopation, because in addition to the syncopated rhythm there is the peculiar and pleasing breaking up and grouping of the chords.

"Many millions of dollars are spent annually in America for popular sheet music, and in the greater portion of it you will find the ragtime rhythm somewhere. I would recommend that the 'Society for the Suppression of Ragtime in America' devote its efforts to helping suppress the war in Europe, as something that might be accomplished with greater ease."

# "Canadian Capers"
# (Henry Cohen, Gus Chandler, and Bert White)

## March 26, 1915, Roger Graham, Chicago

An interesting rag, it is part of a much larger work by San Franciscan pianist Sid Le Protti. Cohen happened to hear Le Protti doing his specialty in a saloon, requested him to play it over many times during the next few weeks, and tipped him a couple of dollars each time it was requested. Cohen wrote out that portion of the piece he wanted and got Chandler and White to write the lyrics. It has become one of the ragtime favorites of this period.

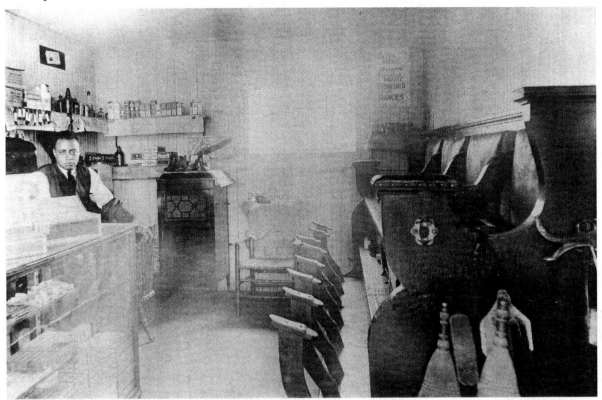

# "Cannon Ball" (Jos. C. Northup)

## April 17, 1905, Victor Kremer Co., Chicago

One of the most popular of the early rags written by a still unknown—not to be confused with Theo. Northrup—and arranged by Thomas R. Confare, who collaborated on a follow-up titled "Bombshell Rag." Section A is a floating folk theme, as it appears in Chas E. Mullen's "Levee Rag" (1902) and in A. H. Tournade's "Easy Money" (1904). B is blazingly pianistic and starts with a dramatic circle of fifths and climaxes in a fast, downward run of treble triads.

# "Caprice Rag" (James P. Johnson)

## Not copyrighted or published

Johnson preferred a busy single-note melody line in many of his rags, especially his first two, "Caprice" and "Daintiness." This one is spiced with quick triplets with the traditional octave-chord ragtime bass.

# "Car-Barlick-Acid Rag-Time" (Clarence C. Wiley)

## August 9, 1901, C. C. Wiley, Oskaloosa, IA

Though copyrighted in 1901, the earliest known copies bear a 1903 copyright date published by the composer. Sold to Giles Bros. in 1904 and then to Jerome H. Remick & Co. in 1907, the cover states, "Something new in Rag-time…an excellent piano piece for rag-time lovers." Indeed, for once the blurb is right; it is one of the most rollicking Folk rags ever written.

# "Carolina FoxTrot" (Will H. Vodery)

## July 7, 1914, Jos. W. Stern & Co., New York

Vodery was an accomplished composer and arranger who knew Scott Joplin in New York City. This tune is one of the first published in the Stride style and has the same feeling as found in the earliest of Luckey Roberts's rags. The A section is remarkably similar to the corresponding section of James P. Johnson's "Carolina Shout."

# "Carolina Shout" (James P. Johnson)

## October 16, 1925, Clarence Williams Music Publishing Co., New York

To the East Coast ticklers, this was their "Maple Leaf Rag," the tune used in all cutting contests. The QRS roll, in fact, was learned note for note by both Fats Waller and Duke Ellington. It was originally written around 1914 for cotillion dancing, was made into a roll in 1918, and was recorded on disc in 1921. The A section begins with a descending progression based on a floating folk strain that was adapted and modified by rag composers and jazz musicians alike, most particularly in the respective A strains of "Wild Cherries," "Perfect Rag," "Buddy's Habits," and "Little Rock Getaway." The remainder of the rag is built on call-and-response patterns shifting back and forth from treble to bass registers with dramatic syncopations. Like "Maple Leaf Rag," it is a folk essence finely honed into a definitive masterpiece of its kind. A comparison between the QRS roll and the earlier, stilted Artempo reveals how the characteristic stride sound bloomed only after 1920.

# "The Cascades" (Scott Joplin)

## August 22, 1904, John Stark & Son, St. Louis

Inspired by the spectacular water display that became the symbol of the 1904 St. Louis World's Fair, this masterpiece of syncopation displays ragtime's grace and majesty. Section C is a high point in ragtime literature, with a thick, complex texture of fast-moving octaves in both hands, which when properly executed reveals a new, wider command of the piano's resources by the composer. D section is a full and grand movement with a more profound ending rather than the flamboyant ones used earlier.

# "Castle House Rag" (James Reese Europe)

## March 9, 1914, Jos. W. Stern & Co., New York

Named after the famous dance team of the teens and their most famous teaching place. Section A is interesting in that it begins in C minor but ends up in C major. Section C is an inventive stop-time melody.

# "The Cat's Pajamas" (Harry Jentes)

## January 10, 1923, Jack Mills, Inc., New York

The QRS piano roll is one of the most exciting Novelty rag performances of the era.

# "Cataract Rag" (Robert Hampton)

## July 27, 1914, Stark Music Co., St. Louis

The masterpiece of the virtuosic late-St. Louis style in ragtime. It has an intricate structure characterized by quick sixteenth-note movements in octaves and dramatic ascending and descending arpeggios in thirty-second-note triplets, descriptive of a waterfall. Charley Thompson, Hampton's contemporary, recalled that the composer's performance was even more complex than the score, containing more "fill-ins."

# "Champagne Rag" (Joseph Lamb)

## September 15, 1910, Stark Music Co., St. Louis

An eloquent rag in a light vein, revealing ragtime's link with the march and cakewalk forms. The A section has a lovely melody with a march-like quality. In the B section that quality is more insistent, with a descending chromatic flow of the melody. C section has the stately but sprightly quality of the cakewalk. When repeated, it has an added burst of optimism that is more richly scored, with the melody in octaves. A march interlude with dramatic stop-time effects follows. With old-world charm, it glides into the repeat of the A section, but this time in the subdominant, as in the structure of the cakewalk.

# "Charleston Rag" (Eubie Blake)

## August 8, 1917, unpublished until *Sincerely, Eubie Blake*, Eubie Blake Music, 1975

One of the uniquely original rags and one of the most important in the entire repertoire. No part of it was ever used by anyone, including Eubie, who has reused others of his work much as Mozart did. This major work is brilliantly inspired. An interesting feature is that all of the lettered sections are thirty-two measures long instead of the traditional sixteen. The walking bass in combination with the ambitious syncopation in the A section was truly innovative in 1899 when he composed it.

# "Chatterbox Rag" (George Botsford)

## October 4, 1910, Jerome H. Remick & Co., Detroit

An imaginative rag with a trio combining features from sections A and B effectively.

Chatterbox Rag.

# Louis Chauvin

## (b. March 13, 1881, St. Louis; d. March 26, 1908, Chicago)

A shadowy figure from ragtime's obscure past, this towering genius, heralded as the King of Ragtime Players and easily the finest pianist in the early years of this century in and around St. Louis, was also of tremendous importance to the musical development of Scott Joplin. The haunting, bittersweet quality much admired in Joplin's later work was due to the influence of this musically inventive performer who could not read music and did not care to have his compositions preserved in writing. Charles Thompson recalled Chauvin as "strictly an ear player" and ranked him the best of St. Louis pianists. He also remembered that Chauvin played an entire musical show score from memory after hearing it only once. During the 1904 St. Louis World's Fair, when the best pianists from around the country came there to earn fame and fortune, Chauvin won the most important ragtime contest from among the finest in the land. After flirting with vaudeville and enjoying the wandering life in show business as part of vocal quartets and duos (singing and playing piano), he settled down to the life of a professor in the district of St. Louis. At the end of his life, in Chicago's district, he died of multiple sclerosis.

In the recently discovered *Palladium*, a black Republican newspaper published in St. Louis from 1893 to 1907, the following article appeared in the February 27, 1904, issue concerning a pre-World's Fair ragtime piano contest sponsored by the Rose Bud Club on February 22, 1904.

> On Tuesday last the Rose Bud club gave its third annual ball and piano contest at the New Douglass hall, corner Beaumont and Lawton avenue (formerly Chestnut Street), and it was one of the largest, finest and best conducted affairs of the kind ever held in St. Louis. The hall was packed and jammed, many well-dressed, good-looking and orderly people, from all classes of society. A great many of the best people in town were present, among them being The *Palladium* man, to enjoy the festivities and witness the great piano contest.

Louis Chauvin.

# THE DOUGLASS THEATORIUM.
### Beaumont and Lawton Avenues.
## REFINED VAUDEVILLE.
### Week Beginning Monday, July 30th.
## MISS VELLA CRAWFORD
### The Renowned Prima Donna.
### RICHARD D. BARRETT
Premier Baritone, late of Black Patti Troubadors

## MEYERS and WALKER
### Comedy Sketch Artists.
## LEWIS CHAUVIN
### The Black Paderewski.
## J. ED. HUNN
### Comedian.
## EDDIE SUTTON
### Lyric Tenor.
### Dancing Each Evening After Performance.
## MUSIC
### By W. D. Flowers' Orchestra.
Doors Open 7:30.          Curtain at 8:30.

Admission, 15c, 25c and 35c.
Box office open every day at 10:30 a. m.
Secure Seats now and avoid the rush.

Louis Chauvin playbill.

# First GRAND BALL
### GIVEN BY THE
## LADY PIANO PLAYERS CLUB,
MASONIC TEMPLE,  18 South Tenth St.,  MONDAY EVENING, OCT. 30, 1905.
### GENERAL ADMISSION, 25 CENTS.

OFFICERS—Bettie Taylor, president; Goodie Taylor, vice-president; Mattie Brown, treasurer; Ethel Wilson, secretary; Philip Hawkins, manager; L. E. Terrell, musical director; Sam Patterson, master of ceremonies; Louis Chauvan, king of rag time players.

Women's ragtime contest.

Mr. Tom Turpin presented an elegant gold medal to the successful contestant, Mr. Louis Chauvin. Messrs. Joe Jordan and Charles Warfield were a tie for second place, Mr. Mann Reynolds, Mr. Conroy Casey and Mr. Ed Williams were all close up in the contest, and were well received by the crowd. Music was furnished by the matchless World's Fair band. Mr. Tom Turpin was general manager, ably assisted by Messrs. Tom Watkins, John H. Clark, George Isabell, Lonnie Johnson, Charles Warfield, Sam Patterson, Willie North, Alonzo Brooks, Howard Anderson, Dick Curry, Louis Chauvin, Richard Kent, George Kinsey, Mr. Helms, E. J. Bruner, and several others. The bar was presided over by Messrs. Charles Turpin, Charles Weinstock, Ed Isabell, Walter Nevels, Dave Young, Henry Taylor and "Fatima." Messrs. Ike Commodore and "Nubba" Watson sold tickets. The union waiters promised to do better next time. The club desires to thank their many friends for their very gracious support, and promise on the occasion of their next annual ball to see to it that every piano player of note in the United States enters, and will give an elegant diamond medal to the winner, and hold the contest at the Exposition coliseum, where there will be plenty of room, and all can hear and see to the very best advantage.

Mr. Samuel Patterson came from Chicago just to attend the Turpin ball. Clarence Goins danced with every girl that would look pleasant at him. He went out of his cravat, but still held on to his half-smoked cigar.

## Ragtime Compositions

"Heliotrope Bouquet" (with Scott Joplin), December 23, 1907, Stark Music Co., New York

# "Chestnut Street in the 90s" (Brun Campbell)

### Not copyrighted or published

The title is a reference to the Chestnut Valley sporting district in St. Louis, which centered around Union Station on Market and Chestnut Streets. Generally, Market Street had the saloons and Chestnut Street the houses. In the late '90s, Campbell was following Joplin and Saunders around, from Sedalia to St. Louis. This solo, in his Folk rag style, is his best and draws substantially from an 1899 Kansas City-published Folk rag medley, "Rags to Burn," by an acquaintance, Frank X. McFadden (Listen to Wally Rose's performance on "Whippin the Keys," Blackbird C-12010). It is a composite of Campbell's favorite phrases and a rare example of early midwestern ragtime performance at its best. It is in one key (B flat) until the F section (a circle of fifths), which leads to the exquisite final section in D flat. Campbell once described the E blues section as copying "Chauvin's barrelhouse style." In an interview, Charles Thompson confirmed that Chauvin also played the blues.

# "The Chevy Chase" (Eubie Blake)

### October 28, 1914, Jos. W. Stern & Co., New York

The B section breaks away from A with great syncopation. The high point in this rag is the trio.

# "Chicago Breakdown" (Jelly Roll Morton)

### January 12, 1926, Melrose Bros. Music Co., Chicago

This is also known as "Stratford Hunch," the only difference being an introduction to "Hunch."

# "Chicago Tickle" (also known as "The Tierney Rag") (Harry Tierney)

### August 8, 1913, unpublished

C section is very fine but like Botsford's "Hyacinth Rag."

# "Chicken Chowder" (Irene Giblin)

## April 12, 1905, Jerome H. Remick & Co., Detroit

Her first popular hit rag and a favorite with string groups because of the chromatic runs.

# "Chills and Fever" (Theron Bennett)

## August 27, 1912, Sam Fox Publishing Co., Cleveland

His most conventional rag, with a bucolic-sounding device used in the Tin Pan Alley rags called Barnyard rags. B uses clichés, almost identical with Percy Wenrich's last section of "Peaches and Cream." The thirty-two-measure trio features a dynamic (mf-pp) call-and-response pattern.

# Axel Christensen

## (b. March 23, 1881, Chicago; d. August 17, 1955, Los Angeles)

Axel Waldemar Fritchoff Christensen had taken piano lessons as a child, but it was not until he heard the new syncopated songs in 1896 that he considered a musical career. In 1903, he decided to open a music

Axel Christensen record label.

school devoted to teaching ragtime. He offered his lessons at fifty cents for each lesson and advertised them in the Chicago *Daily News* with the headline "Ragtime Taught in Ten Lessons." Within the year, he had over 100 students and self-published a folio called *Christensen's Instruction Book No.1 for Rag-Time Piano Playing*, which he sold for one dollar a copy. In 1912, he issued an instruction book for the vaudeville pianist. He himself created a vaudeville act in 1913 and billed himself as the Czar of Ragtime, booking his act in the cities that had a branch of his school. He composed and published his own rags, which were so-so affairs, not too difficult for the intermediate students. He was one of ragtime's great proselytizers, and in December 1914, he started publishing a monthly magazine, the *Ragtime Review*, which extolled and reprinted many of John Stark's rags. Like Stark, he used the phrase *real Ragtime* to distinguish piano rags from syncopated songs and dance music. His magazine lasted until the January 1918 issue. He continued writing about ragtime in Walter Jacobs's *Melody* magazine throughout the 1920s. He created his own record label in 1923 featuring his own rags and a monologue from his vaudeville act. He continued his school with over twenty-five branches throughout the country including a correspondence course for the more rural student and kept up with the changing styles of popular music by issuing folios during the mid thirties on *Modern Swing Music* and *Swing Breaks and Bass Figures*. Christensen retired during the early fifties and moved to Los Angeles, where he died in 1955.

# "Chromatic Rag" (Will Held)

## March 10, 1916, Stark Music Co., St. Louis

The chromaticism is both harmonic and melodic. Section A features long chromatic runs. By contrast, the fine trio is extremely lyrical.

# "Cleopatra Rag" (Joseph Lamb)

## June 16, 1915, Stark Music Co., St. Louis

A light, high-stepping prance-like A section indicates an extensive use of dotted notes to form a single-note melody line—a device rarely found in a Classic rag, as this group preferred a legato melody line. An excellent example of the variety of Lamb's syncopations.

# "Climax Rag" (James Scott)

## March 5, 1914, Stark Music Co., St. Louis

A section begins with the echo that usually comes at the end section. It has been suggested that this piece was inspired by the silent movie accompaniments. The C section is extraordinarily clever in the descending approach of the left hand, which swells from being part of the right hand to a full traditional left hand. The effect is orchestral and provides a welcome break from the usual approach.

# "Clover Club" (Felix Arndt)

## May 9, 1918, Sam Fox Publishing Co., Cleveland

A fine rag with Novelty-style breaks by an early piano-roll artist and composer of "Nola," the most popular of the nonrag Novelties.

# "Coaxing the Piano" (Zez Confrey)

## March 6, 1922, Jack Mills Inc., New York

Yet another variation of "Kitten." Rhythmically more complex than "Witch," it is also more melodic in its way. B section is unusual in that the melody is in the left hand. Altogether a first-rate rag filled with inventive figures.

# George L. Cobb

## (b. August 31, 1886, Mexico, New York; d. December 25, 1942, Brookline, Massachusetts)

Cobb attended the School of Harmony and Composition at Syracuse University in 1905. He won a contest for the best composition in Buffalo. He was a distinguished arranger and composer for the Boston publisher

Walter Jacobs. His rags covered three phases: Popular, Advanced, and Novelty. During the teens, he wrote several very popular songs, including "Are You from Dixie," "All Aboard for Dixie Land," "Listen to that Dixie Band," and "Alabama Jubilee."

## Ragtime Compositions

"Rubber Plant Rag," June 14, 1909, Walter Jacobs, Boston

"Aggravation Rag," March 1, 1910, Walter Jacobs, Boston

"Canned Corn Rag," March 1, 1910, Bell Music Co., Buffalo

"That Hindu Rag," October 15, 1910, Walter Jacobs, Boston

"Bunny Hug Rag," August 4, 1913, Chas. E. Roat Music, Battle Creek, MI

"The Midnight Trot," April 5, 1916, Will Rossiter, Chicago

"Nautical Nonsense," not copyrighted, published 1917, Walter Jacobs, Boston

"Cracked Ice," not copyrighted, published 1918, Walter Jacobs, Boston

"Irish Confetti," not copyrighted, published 1918, Walter Jacobs, Boston

"Russian Rag," April 27, 1918, Will Rossiter, Chicago

"Feedin' the Kitty," not copyrighted, published 1919, Walter Jacobs, Boston

"Say When," not copyrighted, published 1919, Walter Jacobs, Boston

"Stop It," not copyrighted, published 1919, Walter Jacobs, Boston

"Water Wagon Blues," not copyrighted, published 1919, Walter Jacobs, Boston

"'Dust Em Off," not copyrighted, published 1920, Walter Jacobs, Boston

"Hop Scotch," not copyrighted, published 1921, Walter Jacobs, Boston

"Piano Salad," January 18, 1923, Walter Jacobs, Boston

"The New Russian Rag," May 16, 1923, Will Rossiter, Chicago

"Chromatic Capers," June 12, 1925, Walter Jacobs, Boston

"Procrastination Rag," June 29, 1927, Walter Jacobs, Boston

"Piano Sauce," August 13, 1927, Hub Music Co., Boston

"Cubistic Rag," October 14, 1927, Walter Jacobs, Boston

"Snuggle Pup," March 4, 1929, Walter Jacobs, Boston

# "Cole Smoak" (Clarence H. St. John)

## December 28, 1906, John Stark & Son, St. Louis

Noted in a surviving ledger of John Stark, "St. John is the king of present-day ragtime invention…[he] seems to be crowding Joplin off the perch." These comments are somewhat hyperbolic, but this is a first-rate rag.

# "Colonial Glide" (Paul Pratt)

## January 13, 1910, J. H. Aufderheide, Indianapolis

The title reflects the popular dance craze of the teens with its plethora of glide tunes. The joke here is a very brief suggestion of the minuet in the introduction, which yields to a rag of imagination and skill. The changes come up one measure at a time and are rapid harmonic rhythm for a rag written in 1910. Section A begins on a diminished chord and arrives at the home key thus: A flat°/A flat/F$_7$/B flat minor/B flat$_7$/E flat$_7$/A flat. But the real tour de force occurs in section C: Fm/C/A flat$_7$/D$_7$/D flat$_7$/Fm/C$_7$/Fm (it repeats for the last eight measures).

# Edward Elzear (Zez) Confrey

## (b. April 3, 1895, Peru, Illinois;
## d. November 22, 1971, Lakewood, New Jersey)

Confrey was the youngest of five children born to Thomas J. and Margaret Brown Confrey. When he was four, his eldest brother, Jim (who played seven instruments), was taking piano lessons. After one of the lessons, Confrey toddled over to the piano and picked out the same piece Jim was being taught. Lessons for precocious Confrey began soon after. While attending LaSalle-Peru High School, he played in and conducted his own orchestra. As a senior, he played piano on Chicago river steamboats. After graduation, he went to study at the famous Chicago Musical College with Jesse Dunn and Frank Denhart. There he was exposed

Zez Confrey.

Kitten on the Keys.

Kitten on the Keys record label.

to the French Impressionists, whose work had a profound influence on him, later reflected in his compositions. In 1915 he obtained a job demonstrating music for the Chicago branch of the Harry Von Tilzer Music
Publishing Company. His first pieces were songs (e.g., "On the Banks of Dear Old Illinois"), one-steps (e.g.,
"Over the Top"), and a revolutionary rag, "My Pet," which combined the Impressionist harmonies with the
rhythmic complexities of the roll arrangements in a ragtime format. With "My Pet," he achieved that which
established Scott Joplin nineteen years earlier. At the start of World War I, he enlisted in the navy and was
featured in a skit with a touring show, *Leave It to the Sailors.* Part of the routine featured Confrey and a
violinist from Waukegan who eventually became known as Jack Benny. When the show broke up, Confrey
auditioned for the QRS piano-roll company. Since both he and the company were in Chicago, he was hired
as pianist and arranger. Earlier, he had a taste of rollmaking when he cut his first roll for the rival Imperial
Player Roll Company (*Over the Top,* Imperial 511340). During his stay with QRS, he played and arranged
123 rolls. His arrangements were consistently tasteful and filled with inspiration. His success in making rolls
and composing hit tunes led him into recording—piano solos for Brunswick, Edison, and Emerson and
playing with an orchestra for Victor—and appearing in vaudeville. During 1922 he composed three popular
songs that further stimulated demand for his services: "Stumbling," "Tricks," and "Dumbell." The following
year Mills published his phenomenally successful book, *Modern Novelty Piano Solos,* a folio still in print as
late as the 1960s. On February 12, 1924, Confrey participated as soloist in the historic concert at Aeolian
Hall. It was billed as "Paul Whiteman and his Palais Royal Orchestra will offer an Experiment in Modern
Music, assisted by Zez Confrey and George Gershwin." Later that year, he was to make rolls exclusively for
Ampico. As popular music was turning more and more to jazz bands—at first small combos and then large
orchestras—he turned to composition as his chief source of enjoyment and financial security. His compo-
sitions ranged from his complex Novelty rags to concert studies, miniature operas, popular songs, mood

pieces, and simple children's works for beginners. He retired from active composing after the Second World War. He was a victim of Parkinson's disease.

## Ragtime Compositions

"My Pet," March 11, 1921, Jack Mills, Inc., New York

"Kitten on the Keys," March 11, 1921, Jack Mills, Inc., New York

"You Tell 'Em Ivories," July 19, 1921, Jack Mills, Inc., New York

"Poor Buttermilk," July 22, 1921, Jack Mills, Inc., New York

"Greenwich Witch," August 4, 1921, Jack Mills, Inc., New York

"Stumbling Paraphrase," July 1, 1922, Leo Feist, Inc., New York

"Coaxing the Piano," March 6, 1922, Jack Mills, Inc., New York

"Nickel in the Slot," April 6, 1923, Leo Feist, Inc., New York

"Dizzy Fingers," November 17, 1923, Jack Mills, Inc., New York

"African Suite" ("Mississippi Shivers," "High Hattin'," "Kinda Careless"), July 16, 1924, Jack Mills, Inc., New York

"Humorestless," March 12, 1925, Jack Mills, Inc., New York

"Jay Walk," February 12, 1927, Jack Mills, Inc., New York

"Jack in the Box," December 30, 1927, Jack Mills, Inc., New York

"Smart Alec," December 27, 1933, Mills Music, New York

"Giddy Ditty," October 24, 1935, Exclusive Publications, New York

# "Contentment Rag" (Joseph Lamb)

## January 10, 1915, Stark Music Co., St. Louis

Written as a present for the Starks's wedding anniversary in 1909, it was not published then because of Mrs. Stark's illness, which lead to her death the following year. Illustrating a more subdued side of Lamb, it makes a perfect counterpart to "Ethiopia Rag." The B section quotes two measures of the B section of "Maple Leaf Rag" but quickly returns to the body of the development. In an unusual design, the C section is used as an introduction to the D section (as the A section of "Maple Leaf Rag" introduces the B). This is a most delightful section which is striking in its strength and grandeur.

# Leslie C. Copeland

## (b. June 4, 1887, Wichita; d. March 3, 1942, San Francisco)

An anomaly among eccentrics, Copeland started out in minstrelsy, playing with the famous minstrel troop of Lew Dockstader and appearing before the King of England and other European royalty. He then graduated into vaudeville, making piano rolls in the early teens. He composed in the archaic style of the original itinerants of fifteen years earlier but was published by Remick, the largest commercial publisher of popular music.

He is usually categorized as a Tin Pan Alley writer because of the time in which he wrote and because of his publisher. However, his style is decidedly of the earliest in ragtime's history. He was, moreover, a contemporary

Leslie C. Copeland.

of Brun Campbell, who recalled that both he and Copeland were auditioning for the Dockstader job and Campbell lost out only when he demanded more money. Copeland uses only three sections and usually ends with a repeat of an earlier section. Harking back to the Turpin era, "Race Track Blues," "Invitation Rag," and "Bees and Honey" stay in the same key for all three sections. "Dockstader Rag" and "French Pastry Rag" have thirty-two-measure sections, recalling the march influence, a la Hunter. "Race Track Blues" and "Rocky Mountain Fox" contain strong blues–rag mixtures, a hallmark of the midwestern players. The use of floating folk strains which occurs in the B section of "French Pastry" and in "Dockstader Rag," features what is probably the most popular recurring folk strain in ragtime. The markings on the sheet music of "Invitation Rag" are identical with Ben Harney's "Good Old Wagon": a dotted pattern alternating with a straight, even one. Many notes are also marked staccato. His piano-roll performances indicate a loose, rhythmic feeling, and perhaps the dotted notes represent an attempt to notate it. He also uses a four-note crash chord that Jelly Roll Morton remembered in his Library of Congress recordings as being used by "piano sharks with a four-fingered bass."

## Ragtime Compositions

"Cabbage Leaf Rag," November 2, 1909, Marsh & Needles, Wichita

"Invitation Rag," December 20, 1911, Jerome H. Remick & Co., New York

"The Dockstader Rag," November 29, 1912, Jerome H. Remick & Co., New York

"38th Street Rag" (a.k.a. "Les Copeland's Rag"), January 17, 1913, Waterson, Berlin & Snyder, New York

"42nd Street Rag" (with Jack Smith), December 2, 1913, Waterson, Berlin & Snyder, New York

"French Pastry Rag," September 1, 1914, Jerome H. Remick & Co., New York

"Bees and Honey Rag," not copyrighted or published

"Race Track Blues," not copyrighted or published

"Rocky Mountain Fox," not copyrighted or published

"Twist and Twirl," not copyrighted or published

# "Coronation Rag" (Winifred Atwell)

## April 22, 1953, Jefferson Music Co., New York

This was composed, recorded, and published by Trinidad-born and educated Winifred Atwell (1914–1983). She had a superb classical piano training and came to London, England, for a concert career in 1947. By a series of accidents, she was called on to play boogie-woogie as a last-minute replacement, achieved great acclaim, forsook her concert career, and spent the rest of her professional life playing popular music mostly in England. This rag celebrated Queen Elizabeth II's coronation ([E] Decca F-10110).

# "Cotton Bolls" (Charles Hunter)

## June 7, 1901, Frank G. Fite, Nashville

One of his prettiest and more unorthodox rags. All sections are in the key of D flat except section B, which is in A flat. The high point is C, which alternates a raggy pattern in the treble with syncopated bass breaks.

# "A Cotton Patch" (Chas. A. Tyler)

## July 31, 1902, J. W. Jenkins' Sons, Kansas City, MO

A melodious Folk rag with an unusual structural feature characteristic of several Folk rags: The D section closes with the last half of the previous section (see also Theron Bennett's "Sweet Pickles"). B is a fine stop-time buck and wing, contrasting with the flowing melodies of A and C.

## "Cotton Time" (Charles Neil Daniels)

### September 26, 1910, Jerome H. Remick & Co., Detroit

An infectious folk-inspired rag by one of the most influential men in ragtime publishing who, curiously, wrote few rags. It was also issued as a vocal piece the same year.

## "Cottontail Rag" (Joseph Lamb)

### *Ragtime Treasures,* 1964, Mills Music, Inc., New York

A marvelous rag in the Classic rag tradition, even the D section being a variation of the same section in his "Top Liner Rag." Elegant, sparkling with rich harmonies and beautiful flowing melodies.

## "Country Club" (Scott Joplin)

### October 30, 1909, Seminary Music Co., New York

Seemingly like earlier works, this is an advanced working out of syncopated marches contrasted with long-flowing ballad-like melodies. Much of the treble voicing is in thirds (especially the B section). Section D contains an early example of a written break. The break is a musical interruption that separates musical ideas within a phrase and that jazz bands featured as a performance trick rather than as a compositional device. The major ragtime composer to use the break as an integral part of the composition was, of course, Jelly Roll Morton.

## "Crab Apples" (Percy Wenrich)

### January 27, 1908, Brehm Bros., Erie, PA

One of his more inspired rags and with his characteristic folk touch. Section B has imaginative harmonic changes.

## "Cradle Rock" (Abe Frankl and Phil Kornheiser)

### August 11, 1916, Leo Feist, New York

Section A is a genuine down-home blues over a repeated bass pattern marked "Cradle."

# "Crazy Bone Rag" (Charles L. Johnson)

## March 29, 1913, Forster Music Publisher, Chicago

A section is the reverse of the A section to "Dill Pickles."

# "The Crazy Otto"

## Medley

This was the name of a medley of tunes put together by a German studio musician named Fritz Schulz-Reichel who called himself Crazy Otto. It was a German production issued there by the Polydor label (22009) in March 1955. The opening tune was Lou Busch's "Ivory Rag," and the closing number was Irving Berlin's "Simple Melody." It clearly hit the European public as a nostalgic look back at the good old days, as it featured an out-of-tune honky-tonk piano and boisterous singers getting drunk at a party chiming in from time to time. After Decca Records imported the Polydor recording into this country, Randy Wood, head of Dot Records, heard it and wanted his ragtime champ Johnny Maddox to do what is known as a cover recording of it. As the medley consisted of five compositions, each of them controlled by a different publisher, they could not get together to allow publication of what was recorded on this medley. As time was growing short and Maddox could not get a printed score, Dot gave the assignment to Perry Como's accompanist, studio musician Billy Rowland. Having perfect pitch, Rowland copied the German version and adapted it slightly, making a better recording of it. This version (Dot 15325) sold over one million copies in the United States.

# "Cum-Bac" (Charles L. Johnson)

## December 22, 1911, Jerome H. Remick & Co., Detroit

One of his best. A section features unusual bass. A bouncy, happy rag. Fun to play. Introduced to records in 1966 by Charlie Rasch (Ragtime Society RSR 4).

# D

## Bob Darch

### (b. March 31, 1920, Detroit;
### d. October 20, 2002, Springfield, Missouri)

Robert Russell Darch truly lived a ragtime life. From the time he was thirteen taking piano lessons from Tom Turpin's nephew, Gene, till just before he died, Ragtime Bob entertained mostly in saloons first starting in the Red Dog Saloon in Juneau, Alaska, and then going to Las Vegas, Carson City, Nevada; Joplin, Missouri; Fort Wayne, Indiana; Carthage, Missouri; even Tombstone, Arizona and all over the country, playing a fine saloon in Washington, D.C., and later, the White House. It made no difference where Darch entertained, playing the rags he heard in his travels, reading them from the original sheet music he collected, telling his stories, and singing outrageous funny songs as well as the pop songs from the ragtime era. He made every-one—from the school children to the Chamber of Commerce—in places like Sedalia, Missouri, aware of the ragtime heritage of their community. He then staged concerts, getting former residents like Arthur Marshall back to talk about the ragtime years and to play some of his great rags. On August 21, 1959, he opened Club '76 in Toronto, Canada, bringing with him Eubie Blake out of retirement and, for his only profes-sional piano engagement, Joseph Lamb, performing his own rags. He was instrumental in bringing together Toronto fans and starting the Ragtime Society in 1962 that lasted for twenty-five years and included an annual get-together, a record label, a bimonthly publication *The Ragtimer,* which reported on all the ragtime news, including recent record reviews, concert and festival reviews, and articles of great historic interest. In that same year, Darch brought Charlie Thompson and Joe Jordan together with a reactivated Eubie Blake to make a series of recordings, singly and together, on several LPs, one for sale to the public titled *A Reunion in Ragtime.* He continued his rounds of playing clubs, lounges, and saloons, exciting his audiences for ragtime. At the end of May 1976, Darch put together a ragtime festival for Carthage, Missouri, introducing its audi-ence to their hometown ragtimers James Scott and Clarence Woods. During his researches into ragtime's history, Darch managed to locate and have published heretofore unknown rags by Scott Hayden, Eubie Blake, Joseph Lamb, and James Scott. In his later years, from the 1980s on, Darch traveled and performed all over the world in such places as Norway, Sweden, Germany, Holland, Ireland, and Italy. He even found time to inaugurate a turn-of-the century saloon in the Edgewood Resort at Alexandria Bay in upper New York State with a twice-yearly ragtime and Dixieland jazz festival. As his friend Gene Jones wrote in a dedication

Bob Darch and Arthur Marshall.

to him in *That American Rag* (Routledge, 2000), "If a town or a city has any ragtime connection at all, people know what it is, after Bob has been there. Because of him, the music of many long-forgotten local composers, players and publishers has been kept alive."

## Ragtime Compositions

"Flicker Red Rag," December 30, 1953, Red-Dog Saloon, Juneau
"Opera House Rag," August 19, 1960, The Ragtime Music, Virginia City, NV

# "Darkey Todalo, A Raggedy Rag" (Joe Jordan)

## November 15, 1910, Harry Von Tilzer Music Publishing Co., New York

Though *Todalo* signifies a dance tune, this is more of an involved piano rag. Section A has a descending melodic figure out of the folkways (see "Wild Cherries Rag"). The overall structure then becomes unusual as section B takes on the character of an interlude leading to the folk-like call-and-response of section C. The trio is then delayed by a return to section A. In this sense, the trio acts like a melodic section at the end and is not the usual third section of a rag. This final section has the St. Louis Rosebud Bar flavor, which Jordan's music recalled.

# "Delmar Rag" (Charles Thompson)

## Not copyrighted or published

This is named after a St. Louis street formerly called Morgan Street. The A section is similar to Joe Jordan's "J. J. J. Rag" in its A section. Both Jordan and Thompson credited the idea to Conroy Casey, a St. Louis pianist whom Joplin also admired. This rag also shows the influence of Robert Hampton.

# "Deuces Wild" (Max Kortlander)

## November 17, 1923, Jack Mills, Inc., New York

Kortlander's most innovative rag; an asymmetrical effect is achieved by repeating the motive of the introduction as the first two measures of section A. At first it sounds like an extended introduction, but as the motive reappears again and again, at the middle of the A strain and at repeats of A, the idea lends the performance a seamless effect.

# "Dew Drop Alley Stomp" (Sugar Underwood)

## Unpublished

Never published, this Folk rag was recorded by its itinerant black composer in Savannah (Victor 21538). Underwood was an amazingly sophisticated pianist who improvises his essentially two-section rag in cohesive steps. Notice how he builds his six variations of the second section toward a climax.

# "Dill Pickles Rag" (Charles L. Johnson)

## Not originally copyrighted, published 1906, Carl Hoffman, Kansas City, MO, September 16, 1907, Jerome H. Remick & Co., Detroit

Syncopation is marked in the music to point up the three-over-four idea. Left hand in the B section suggests a trombone used in the military bands. C is the most lyrical section. It sold over a million copies of sheet music.

Dill Pickles Rag.

## "Dixie Dimples" (James Scott)

### Not copyrighted, published 1918,
### Will L. Livernash Music Co., Kansas City, MO

Unlike the other Scott rags, this one is written in dotted rhythm—in the style of foxtrots of the late teens. The A section cleverly uses the final section of "Climax Rag." In the B section, which is linked and can be considered a development of A, can be heard what would become in 1950 part of "The Old Piano Roll Blues." This rag is a most charming addition to the Scott catalogue.

## "Dixie Kisses" (Phil Ohman)

### Not copyrighted or published

An astounding 1919 piano-roll performance (QRS 100884) featuring a pyrotechnical break executed in double time and in contrary motion.

# "Dixie Queen,
# A Southern Ragtime" (Robert Hoffman)

## Not copyrighted, published 1906, Victor Kremer Co., Chicago

As in "I'm Alabama Bound," Hoffman used a floating folk strain here recalled years later by Jelly Roll Morton in his recording of "Mama's Got a Baby, Tee-Nah-Nah." It was also used as a song by J. Russel Robinson, who had then recently visited New Orleans ("Te Na Na").

# "The Dockstader Rag" (Les Copeland)

## November 29, 1912, Jerome H. Remick & Co., New York

Section B emerges with an odd harmonic progression: B flat/Gm/F/Dm/E flat/B flat. The final B flat resolution is spiced with a characteristic treble slur best described as funky. It is one of the most successful stylistic features of the Copeland rags: a direct carryover from performance practices. Section C is apparently a floating folk strain, as it bears a close relationship with Jelly Roll Morton's "Naked Dance," both melodically and harmonically. Even the minor of the subdominant is used here at the end, consistent with the Morton performance.

# "Doctor Brown" (Fred Irvin)

## October 27, 1914, Jerome H. Remick & Co., New York

Whimsical, unforgettable early foxtrot. The A section is ingenious as it has the feeling of two melodies being played at once in the right hand. Section B has the characteristic atmosphere of the Stride style.

# "Dog on the Piano" (Ted Shapiro)

## September 5, 1924, Jack Mills, Inc., New York

This is a great Novelty rag. Famed vaudeville accompanist Ted Shapiro (1899–1980) made a career of accompanying Nora Bayes, Eva Tanguay, and, from 1921 until her death in 1966, Sophie Tucker. The best dance band recording was made by the Isham Jones Orchestra (Brunswick 2646) in April 1924. Their pianist–arranger was Roy Bargy who had just left the Benson Orchestra. The fine trumpet playing is that of Louis Panico, who was a mainstay of the organization. Jones, an outstanding composer of popular songs, performed on the tenor saxophone.

# "The Doll Dance" (Nacio Herb Brown)

## July 6, 1927, Sherman, Clay & Co., San Francisco

One of the most famous Novelty rags written and one of the last rags to sell a million copies of sheet music, it was also the basis of countless imitations (as was Scott Joplin's "Maple Leaf Rag"). The finest piano solo was provided by Jimmy Andrews (Banner 6116) and the finest orchestral arrangement by the Sam Lanin Orchestra (Perfect 14800). This talented studio band from New York included Red Nichols on cornet, Tommy Dorsey on trombone, Jimmy Dorsey and Andy Sanella on clarinet and alto sax, Harry Reser on banjo, and the truly amazing artistry of Arthur Schutt at the piano.

# "Don't Jazz Me-Rag"
# ("I'm Music") (James Scott)

## September 18, 1921, Stark Music Co., St. Louis

Undoubtedly a John Stark title (he was known to have disliked jazz). Ironically, the rag uses many devices that would become common in twenties jazz band performances.

# "Double Fudge" (Joe Jordan)

## December 20, 1902, Jos. F. Hunleth Music Co., St. Louis

A fascinating concept that sounds as though it were written in the Rosebud Bar with Tom Turpin looking over the composer's shoulder. It opens with an odd minor strain that weaves a genteel romantic aura rather more involved than a simple cakewalk minor strain. B moves to the relative major smoothly by opening on the regular II chord and features a call-and-response pattern. C has the strongest Turpin flavor, only suggested in B and returns to the quick triplets used in A.

# "Down Home Rag" (Wilbur C. S. Sweatman)

## September 18, 1911, Will Rossiter, Chicago

A most apropos title for perhaps the most basic bucolic rag essay of all time. The composer had a vaudeville act that featured his playing three clarinets at the same time.

# "Dusty Rag" (May Aufderheide)

## February 6, 1908, Duane Crabb Publishing Co., Indianapolis

An unadorned rag in a folk style, but with the emphasis on nonchord tones and melodic chromaticism that bring about a softer lyricism than older Folk rags. This was the first hit rag of the Indianapolis–Ohio Valley ragtime group, which surfaced at this time.

# E

## Early Ragtime, 1897–1905

The term *Folk rag* has been applied carelessly in the past—most frequently to designate a later country music style that loosely adapted some of the principles of ragtime—but there appears to be an actual subtradition within the ragtime idiom that should be considered more of the basic folk art. This comprises written rags as well as a body of recordings of performances that is a much more variegated expression than the precise literature of Classic rags. The term indicates the folksy, idiosyncratic character of all the rags that contain a variety of folk qualities. The term is more literal or traditional when applied to the informal recorded ragtime of Brun Campbell, which was never written down—the equivalent of a pure oral folk tradition—but also applies to a finished published rag of Charles Hunter, which reflects a feeling of basic folk roots. Thus, the Folk rag refers not to one specific type of rag but rather a body of performances and compositions that have folk elements of various sorts enumerated in the discussion of each individual rag.

The works of Tom Turpin and Hunter conceptually precede the Classic rag, though most are contemporary with the rags of Scott Joplin. In their informal, unpredictable format and simple, direct use of folk materials, they can be viewed as a link to Classic ragtime composition. However, the Turpin and Hunter rags are also the beginning of a Folk rag tradition that continues throughout the literature of ragtime. Turpin and Hunter are the progenitors, but a Folk rag in an early style might have been published or played at any point in the ragtime era.

All ragtime deals with folk elements, but in varying ways. The early written rags are more direct expressions of the richly varied, frequently unorthodox ragtime playing styles that abounded in the Mississippi Valley as ragtime blossomed. Joplin took these folk elements and formalized them into a new art form: the Classic rag. Later, Tin Pan Alley writers such as Charles L. Johnson and George Botsford formulated the most tantalizing of these elements, and the ragtime cliché was born. Still later, the best writers of Advanced ragtime hybridized the form by adapting newer folk elements. Finally, with the expansion of new harmonies and complex rhythmic patterns of Novelty ragtime, the folk tradition became more stylized and more of an abstraction. But the best ragtime of even this last age—that of Zez Confrey and Roy Bargy—is firmly rooted in the folk tradition, and most of the writers were midwesterners who began by mastering the older idioms.

Folk rag characteristics determine what is or what is not a Folk rag, and it is harder to isolate them than the criteria for a Classic, Tin Pan Alley, or Novelty rag. In general, a Folk rag has an informal, untutored approach. It is frequently a less polished but more spontaneous concept than a Classic or Popular rag, featuring a direct use of folk materials. Some Folk rags are original creations, but others have floating folk strains—not simply folk songs but favorite instrumental music passages that pop up in many rags. It is not known where they originated or who first used them.

Most Folk rag compositions, particularly those published after the early period (1897–1905), are the products of small-town midwestern composers, many of whom published their own works. Though some of these reveal the influence of some big rag hits, notably Joplin's "Maple Leaf Rag," most are indigenous to their locale, expressions of rural America. In Kansas City, the prolific Charles L. Johnson influenced the other Folk rag composers in his area with such original devices as those found in "Scandalous Thompson" and "A Black Smoke." The extraordinary ragtime in Nashville, for instance, could well be called a *school* of Folk rag composition. There is a consistent style here and an ebullient mix both of black folk sources and white Tennessee hill music, a distinctly *southern-fried* concoction. The leading composer was blind pianist Charles Hunter. Although there are a few rural black rags, notably in Texas, the small-town Folk rags are mostly by white composers, considering most of the black writers sought larger urban audiences.

As Folk rags became more popular, they were bought up by larger publishers, signaling the end of an era for the small publisher. In this way, Tin Pan Alley began to control the music of America. A good example of an early Folk rag building fame is the printing history of Oskaloosa, Iowa, pharmacist Clarence Wiley's "Car-Barlick-Acid," which Wiley copyrighted in 1901. Wiley then published the work himself in his hometown in 1903. It sold so well that a year later, the Giles Brothers—of the river towns of Quincy, Illinois, and Hannibal, Missouri—purchased the rights from the composer–publisher. Three years later Jerome H. Remick & Co., Tin Pan Alley's largest publisher, now in New York City, bought it and sold it throughout the country.

Another example is the fine Folk rag by aspiring doctor Calvin L. Woolsey of Braymer, a town near Joplin, Missouri. He helped work his way through medical school by writing and publishing his own rags. His most ambitious use of syncopation, not found in the Classic rags, appears in "Medic Rag," which Remick also purchased and set on its popular way.

The man responsible for both these purchases, and indeed all of Remick's vast output of rags, was composer–publisher Charles N. Daniels, who first appeared on the publishing scene when he bought Joplin's "Original Rags" in 1898 and arranged it for the Carl Hoffman Music Company of Kansas City, Missouri.

The important centers of Folk ragtime publications came from Nashville (Frank G. Fite and H. A. French), Memphis (O. K. Houck Piano Company), Kansas City, Missouri (Carl Hoffman Music Co. and J. W. Jenkins' Sons Music Co.), St. Louis (John Stark and Son, Jos. F. Hunleth Music Co., Buck and Lowney, and Placht and Son), Chicago (Will Rossiter, Victor Kremer, and Thompson Music Co.), Cincinnati (Philip Kussel, John Arnold, Joseph Krolage & Co.), and New Orleans (Puderer, Gruenewald, and Hackenjos).

A great part of the Folk ragtime heritage is preserved on certain gramophone recordings and piano rolls. Most of these were made from ragtime's start in 1897. Many of the recordings were made after the Folk rag period, but the approach to the music is the unifying element.

Folk ragtime on recordings provides a chance to explore rags, not as composed music but as music performed by the largely untutored itinerants who wandered from village to town, from saloon to whorehouse.

None of the Folk rags recorded—many on the spur of the moment—were ever published. The performances are as varied and diverse as the written and published compositions. The recordings are as definitive as the rag sheets—even more so, because the performer is giving a full interpretation, not a watered-down simplification for the amateur piano players.

Recordings are also important when famous performers reminisce about their musical beginnings. Jelly Roll Morton, for instance, remembered hearing an early rag in St. Louis on his Library of Congress sessions (Classic Jazz Masters CJM-9) and played one strain of "Randall's Rag." Willie "The Lion" Smith, raised in upper New York State, shared his recollection of "Don't You Hit That Lady Dressed in Green" (Dial 305-10" LP). The interesting thing about these two stories, in addition to being unusually colorful and informative, is that the strains of both rags are similar. Eubie Blake recalled on the LP *The Eighty-Six Years of Eubie Blake* (Columbia C2S 847) hearing "Poor Katie Red" and "Jimmy Green" as played by the early ragtime pianists in his hometown of Baltimore.

The contrast between Alonzo Yancey playing "Everybody's Rag" and Blind Leroy Garnett doing "Louisiana Glide" (both versions of the same rag and appearing on *Black and White Piano Ragtime,* Biograph BLP 12047) is very great, which illustrates vividly the enormous diversity of performed ragtime.

The sophistication of Sugar Underwood playing his own "Dew Drop Alley Stomp" (Victor 21538) sharply contrasts with Will Ezell's rhythmic barrelhouse playing of his "Mixed Up Rag" (Paramount 12688) and the archaic yet lilting sounds of Arnold Wiley performing "Arnold Wiley's Rag" (*Piano Ragtime of the Teens, Twenties & Thirties,* Herwin 402). Campbell, discovered to have been Joplin's only white pupil, made only five formal recordings but also made informal tapes (issued on Euphonic 1201 and 1202), which illustrate his folk roots and how he developed his musical ideas.

Few Folk rag performances of the early midwestern days were recorded, since recording companies were headquartered in New York. After the First World War, Chicago became a major recording city. But few ragtime pioneers were around then to record, and the companies did not want their old-fashioned sounds. Thus, Campbell's recordings are the closest we have to that era. He was not a great composer or a flashy vaudeville pianist, but he was the typical itinerant player who roamed the countryside having a good time, listening to all available music, adding ideas remembered from times past, and earning enough to sustain this good-natured life. He was an active player in both cheap dives and fancy saloons from 1898 through 1908, when he retired from music to become a barber, a decision forced on him by his wife when they married. He was musically inactive and lived in Venice, California, until the West Coast Revival of Lu Watters's Yerba Buena Jazz Band focused on ragtime in the early 1940s and Campbell was discovered and persuaded to record. These discs show him playing the same way he did in the original era as a Folk ragtime performer. Not all of what Campbell played was simply from his memory, however; he had a trunk full of old sheet music. One in particular, "Rags to Burn" by Frank McFadden, whom he knew and remembered, formed the basis for at least two of his best compositions: "Chestnut Street in the 90s" and "Ginger Snap Rag." In Folk style, he put strains together in random fashion, with a stomping, rhythmic playing style. As with Hunter's compositions, Campbell's ragtime is liberally mixed with traditional Southern hill music.

A further use of floating folk strains is evident in at least two more of his tunes: "Tent Show Rag," which uses the verse to "Memphis Blues," and "Barber Shop Rag," which is based on the first section of "Muskrat Ramble."

Will Ezell was one of several midwestern pianists who featured folk blues and, occasionally, rags. This group includes Charles "Cow Cow" Davenport, Fred Longshaw, and Rob Cooper; all can be heard on *Piano Ragtime of the Teens, Twenties & Thirties* (Herwin 402). Throughout the twenties and later, piano solos in the Folk rag tradition were recorded sporadically. Performances tended to include not only the floating folk strains but also favorite sections of published rags; typical was Davenport's treatment of Carey Morgan's 1915 "Trilby Rag," in both his own "Atlanta Rag" and "Texas Shout." Ezell's three ragtime solos, for example, are both patchworks: "Mixed Up Rag" is based on the Original Dixieland Jazz Band's piece, "Sensation Rag" (which is not a rag); "West Coast Rag" (Paramount 12549), is based on Jay Roberts' 1910 "Entertainer's Rag" and probably other West Coast strains; and "Bucket of Blood" (Paramount 12773), a popular name for saloon dives, is reminiscent of the B section in Tad Fischer's "Encore Rag."

Thus, the principle of early Folk ragtime composition continues: patching tunes together in a medley format. Other examples are "Mr. Crump's Rag" by Jesse Crump (Biograph BLP-12047), "Mr. Freddie's Rag" by J. H. Shayne (Decca 7663 and Circle 1011), "Hobo Rag" by Alonzo Yancey (Session 10-003), and Herve Duerson's "Easy Drag" and "Avenue Strut" (Origin OJL-15).

The improvisatory ragtime school, in particular the Storyville pianists, led by Tony Jackson, were recalled by Morton in his Library of Congress sessions (Classic Jazz Masters CJM-2-9), all of whom performed rags, blues, and pop songs. In *Storyville, New Orleans* by Al Rose (University of Alabama Press, 1974), an ex-prostitute fondly recalled the blues playing of Buddy Carter. Morton played a sample of how Carter played ragtime. Other legendary figures during the earliest years of this century were conjured up by Morton, including Alfred Wilson, Sammy Davis, and Kid Ross.

The basic principles of Folk ragtime, and much of the folk material on sheet music, rolls, and recordings, are still viable, as evidenced in the recent Folk-flavored rags of Tom Shea and Trebor Jay Tichenor. Because ragtime is piano music, written for and performed on an instrument of fixed diatonic tonality, the primary ragtime impulse was toward a set form with a sense of established, formal musical disciplines. Some of the earliest and finest Folk rag scores—those of Turpin, Hunter, and Northrup—have a finished quality. Many problems of early scoring were solved by the professional arrangers hired by the Tin Pan Alley publishers, namely D. S. DeLisle, Charles N. Daniels, Theodore Northrup, Max Hoffman, Ben Jerome, and Robert S. Roberts.

In this sense, then, the earliest Folk rags are something of a compromise, though a glance at some of the less polished scores—Walter Starck's December 15, 1897, "Darktown Capers" and Fred Neddermeyer's October 7, 1898, "In Colored Circles"—shows that the schooled arrangers added a much-needed sense of order to a world of improvisatory, unpredictable, patchwork conceptions. Lacking the vital manuscripts and documentary recordings of the pioneers, it is impossible for us to assess, for example, DeLisle's work on Turpin's rags. As most later rags written by the schooled musicians, such as Joplin, follow much the same basic patterns and principles of these fine early Folk rags, it can be assumed that these early arrangers had a constructive effect on the published music. Some of the irregular idiosyncrasies can be heard in those folk performances recorded on 78s and piano rolls, where undoubtedly a few playing characteristics were lost (probably in the way of bass patterns), but the rag was destined to become more formalized, a disciplined form of broader and more varied expression.

## "The Easy Winners" (Scott Joplin)

### October 10, 1901, self, St. Louis

Continuing in his advanced and mature use of instrumental folk materials, this piece vividly illustrates Joplin's development as the leading ragtime composer. In the Stark Ledger, there is a comment that if one could play this rag as well as Joplin, one could borrow five dollars from anyone present. After Shattinger Music Co. of St. Louis bought the piece—issuing a simplified edition that apparently was not successful—Stark finally published it from Joplin's original plates, with the blurb that it was "Joplin's favorite." The A section is a beautiful adaptation of an improvisatory Folk ragtime pattern that lies well in the right hand in the key of A flat and is best done in Morton's "Naked Dance." It is the first instance of an idea that eventually became one of the most popular ragtime clichés (also see comment on "Paragon Rag"). The B section is outstanding in its thorough realization of a syncopated chromatic melody line. An interesting device used to unify the composition is in using the same ending for both C and D sections. The strong echo-like effect in the D section was a favorite device later exploited with great success by his leading disciples, James Scott and Joseph Lamb.

## "Eccentric" (J. Russel Robinson)

### October 17, 1923, Jack Mills, Inc., New York

Because this rag has an orchestral feeling, it is a favorite with jazz bands. Noteworthy is the dotted-note writing in the melody of the D strain, which is done to effect a swinging feeling, as used on many late ragtime and dance tunes. Robinson's idea to swing, and to indicate it in the music, is unusual and compares favorably to Morton's musical ideas.

# Willie Eckstein

## (b. December 6, 1888, Pointe St. Charles, Canada; d. September 23, 1963, Montreal)

Eckstein was a child prodigy, touring the world giving classical recitals at the age of seven. By the time he was ten, he could sight-read anything placed in front of him. When he was twelve, he won a music scholarship to McGill University. In his early teens, he toured in American and Canadian vaudeville as a child wonder, earning $15,000 a year. In 1912 he found his permanent niche, when he became an interpreter, or pianist for Montreal's Strand Theatre, a position he held for the next twenty years. Axel Christensen, on seeing and hearing Eckstein perform at the silent movie house, asked why he was frittering away his talents accompanying silent films and learned that Eckstein was making more than twice what Christensen was making in vaudeville while staying at home. Eckstein began recording in Montreal around 1923 and was the first to record Joplin's "Maple Leaf Rag" as a piano solo. The fact that he arranged it as Novelty rag made the recording even more impressive. Eckstein became the foremost interpreter of Novelty rags, recording several of Zez Confrey's most inspired rags, as well as Novelties by Roy Bargy, Larry Brier, and Ted Shapiro. What made Eckstein's versions so memorable is that he added many embellishments to the compositions at high speed. Remarkable displays of the highest virtuosity, almost overwhelming the listener, made Eckstein's performances memorable. For the last thirty years of his life, Eckstein entertained at two Montreal nightclubs, dazzling customers and fellow musicians alike. Surely, the most impressive ragtime pianist of the twentieth century.

# "Efficiency Rag" (James Scott)

## January 10, 1917, Stark Music Co., St. Louis

A great rag reflecting the joyousness and sunny spirits inherent in the ragtime tradition. Contains all of Scott's hallmarks and could be used to sum up the best of Scott.

# "Eleventh Street Rag" (Euday Bowman)

## November 16, 1917, unpublished, July 15, 1918, Bowman & Ward, Gary, IN

It is a loose collection of very funky ragtime phrases. The introduction is modified from the one used in "12th Street Rag." Each section has the same ending. The rag builds intensity through the use of slurs ending in a rip-roaring style rarely preserved on paper. A musical kissing cousin to "12th Street Rag."

# "Elite Syncopations" (Scott Joplin)

## December 29, 1902, John Stark & Son, St. Louis

An excellent example combining Joplin's use of folk strains with a lyrical melodic line. The A and D sections use folk materials where sections B and C are effectively contrasted with flowing melodies. The juxtaposing of differing musical ideas was a favorite compositional device first used by Joplin. The A section beautifully incorporates one of the earliest ragtime clichés, usually overdone for the effect of hands chasing each other. The D section features an especially strong finish.

# "The Entertainer" (Scott Joplin)

## December 29, 1902, John Stark & Son, St. Louis

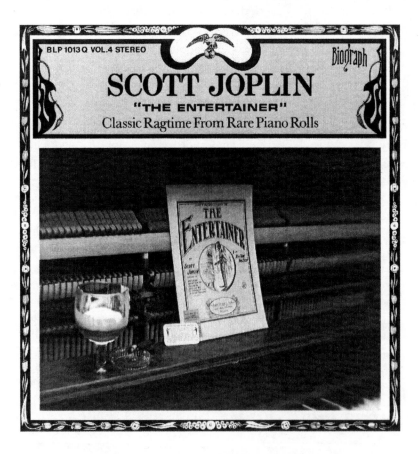

This was the number-one song on the top ten popular song charts during 1974—a phenomenal occurrence seventy-two years after it was published. Section A features an advanced use of a pianistic call-and-response pattern with dynamic markings indicated by the composer. In section B, the third and fourth measures act as a fill-in between the first two and the fifth and sixth, similar to arrangements of pieces for string orchestra. In the rare two-mandolin-and-guitar arrangement issued by Stark, the string concept is clearly realized, especially in the trio. It was even dedicated to "James Brown and His Mandolin Club." Just six months after it appeared on sheet music counters, Monroe H. Rosenfeld, a prominent Tin Pan Alley lyricist-composer, wrote about Joplin in the *St. Louis Globe-Democrat* of June 7, 1903: "Probably the best and most euphonious of his latter day compositions is 'The Entertainer.' It is a jingling work of a very original character, embracing various strains of a retentive character which set the foot in spontaneous action and leave an indelible imprint on the tympanum."

## "The Entertainer's Rag" (Jay Roberts)

### September 30, 1910, Pacific Coast Music Co., Oakland

One of the most popular rags of its day, written by a virtuoso vaudeville pianist. Actually, it is a collection of rather hackneyed, though dazzling, ragtime licks. It was used by pianists to win contests, as the counterpoint of "Yankee Doodle" and "Dixie" assured the contestant a hand from both sides of the Mason–Dixon Line.

## "Erratic" (J. Russel Robinson)

### October 17, 1923, Jack Mills, Inc., New York

Section A features unusual harmonies in a downward chromatic run, which suggests the title. B has a touch rarely encountered: The bass in the fifth and sixth measures join the syncopated treble pattern, abandoning briefly the traditional ragtime bass.

## "Essay in Ragtime" (Brun Campbell)

### Not copyrighted or published

Both solos start with slightly different introductions (West Coast 114 and Euphonic ESR 1201). The essay idea is the middle part of the performance, the B section followed by two variations. C is a twelve-bar blues. The Euphonic solo is Campbell's most rollicking, with a strong, self-assured rhythmic drive.

## "Ethiopia Rag" (Joseph Lamb)

### Not copyrighted, published 1909, Stark Music Co., New York

A startling change of style from "Sensation Rag." The trio is one of the most imaginative found in ragtime featuring varied bass patterns with single notes as well as octaves. The riff pattern here (measures 5, 6, and 7) is unique.

# "Eugenia" (Scott Joplin)

## February 26, 1906, Will Rossiter, Chicago

An incredibly lovely work showing a growing maturity in dealing with beautiful melodic lines in each section. For the first time, Joplin extends a musical bridge between sections to the entire length of a section. However, this interlude-C interlude-C is among the oldest cakewalk patterns. The fast bass octaves in sixteenths midway in the A and C sections, as well as in the first ending of A, are similar to the embellishments in the hand-played rolls Joplin made. This stylistic feature occurs in some of the earliest of Joplin's rags, including the trios for "Swipesy and Sunflower Slow Drag" (see also Arthur Marshall's remarks). In an unprecedented blurb, Rossiter advertised this rag as "rather difficult." The title was undoubtedly suggested by Eugenia Street, behind the Rosebud in the St. Louis District.

# "Euphonic Sounds" (Scott Joplin)

## October 30, 1909, Seminary Music Co., New York

More of a musical exercise, it is one of Joplin's most ambitious creations. The entire conception illustrates his heaviest leanings toward European romanticism. The A and B sections have eliminated the standard left hand of ragtime (octave-chord, octave-chord). Interestingly, the ending of section A is similar to the comparable ending of A in "Pine Apple Rag." The B section is one of his most high-reaching ragtime selections. The use of the minor tonality combined with diminished chords and the usual major tonality gives this rag a wide variety of expression, creating several moods.

# "Evergreen Rag" (James Scott)

## Not copyrighted, published 1915, Stark Music Co., St. Louis

A charming departure from Scott's excursions into the heavier textured rags. Lightly syncopated, it is dance music. The B section evokes pleasant memories of such pieces as Scott Joplin's "Elite Syncopations" and "Weeping Willow."

# "Evolution Rag" (Thomas S. Allen)

## December 16, 1912, Walter Jacobs, Boston

The best in a fairly impressive series of rags by Allen, a prolific writer of instrumentals, who had a flair for syncopated melodic lines in long phrases.

# "Excelsior Rag" (Joseph Lamb)

## Not copyrighted, published 1909, Stark Music Co., New York

This reveals Lamb's genius for intricate rhythmic forms and full, rich harmonies. A beautifully complex structure of syncopation, built on sequences (measures 6, 7, and 8), it in reality pays homage to Joplin, as the A, B, and C sections are inspired improvisations on the respective sections of "Maple Leaf Rag." It is also the only Classic rag published in the keys of D flat and G flat. When John Stark saw it, he asked Lamb to transpose it to the keys of C and F. After he heard it, he agreed with Lamb that it sounded better in the more difficult keys.

# F

## "The Fascinator" (James Scott)

### September 23, 1903, Dumars Music Co., Carthage, MO

Scott's cleverness is clearly illustrated in this rag. His long, elegantly flowing melody is amply demonstrated in the B section, heralding beautiful melodies to come. The C section takes a Joplinesque turn: In tune with the heavy influence of the 1901–02 Joplin rags, he modulates at the trio from A flat to C, copying the same idea in Joplin's "Breeze from Alabama." The D section has ideas incorporated from the "Peacherine Rag" trio by Joplin.

## "The Favorite" (Scott Joplin)

### June 23, 1904, A. W. Perry & Sons' Music Co., Sedalia, MO

Although published in 1904, it was written in 1900. In fact, the B section with its minor tonality (G minor) going to its relative major (B flat) is similar to the writing of the "Ragtime Dance," probably written at the same time. D section harks back to the A section, very march-like.

## "Felicity Rag" (Scott Hayden with Scott Joplin)

### July 27, 1911, John Stark & Son, St. Louis

This was probably written during the early years in St. Louis when Hayden and Joplin lived together and, with "Kismet Rag," were the Joplin rags to which John Stark referred (see "Sugar Cane"). The melodic lines are fresh and very busy, with a contrasting trio, probably Joplin's contribution.

## "Fig Leaf Rag" (Scott Joplin)

### February 24, 1908, Stark Music Co., St. Louis

A masterpiece, Joplin's genius is evident everywhere, from the expansive conception, through the exploring C section, to the jubilant D section. Its subtitle, "A High Class Rag," is certainly apt. The unexpected harmonies in the majestic D section may be described as chromatic writing, but it sounds more as if the whole idea was dictated by the extraordinary harmonic concept. In general, Joplin was more of a pentatonic writer and used less chromaticism than his disciple Joe Lamb.

## "The Finger Breaker" (Jelly Roll Morton)

### November 23, 1942, unpublished

A stomp taken at breakneck speed in the spirit of the Harlem cutting contest pieces, but in Morton style. It is derived in part from "Frog-I-More Rag." He transforms the basic syncopated pattern of ascending chromatic harmonies into a more complex Novelty rag style exchange between the bass and treble. The climax of the performance comes with quick register jumps up and down the keyboard, a favorite device of Classic rag composer James Scott, here employed more dramatically with a riff-like feeling.

## "Firefly Rag" (Joseph Lamb)

### *Ragtime Treasures,* 1964, Mills Music, Inc., New York

Contains his most unusual harmonic touch: A break midway into the A section is spiced with chromatic augmented chords, revealing Lamb's knowledge of the later twenties writing style.

## "Fizz Water" (Eubie Blake)

### October 28, 1914, Jos. W. Stern & Co., New York

Both this and "Chevy Chase," early tunes of Blake's, are in the mold of the popular one-step and foxtrot dance tunes of the teens.

# "Floating Along" (Henry Fredericks)

## August 8, 1914, McKinley Music Co., Chicago

A strain is the same as its counterpart in William Tyers's "Maori."

# "Florida Rag" (George L. Lowry)

## September 25, 1905, Jos. W. Stern & Co., New York

Highlight is the trio with barbershop-style harmonics: F-E$_7$-F.

# "Fourth Man Rag" (as written by Dick Hamilton and Jill Leland)

This rag was composed especially for a recording (Capitol 1091) by Lou Busch who under the pseudonym Joe "Fingers" Carr created an unbeatable atmosphere and single-handedly established a ragtime revival throughout the '50s worldwide. Here, on this 1950 recording, he combined with the fantastically successful Dixieland band of Pee Wee Hunt's, for this first-time dual appearance. Busch's great arranging skills manage to keep both the Carr and Hunt sounds distinctive yet blendable for a real musical collaboration. They would collaborate further on two LPs (Capitol T-783 and Capitol T-935).

# "Frances" (Jelly Roll Morton)

## January 10, 1931, unpublished

Also known as "Fat Frances."

# "Freakish" (Jelly Roll Morton)

## September 28, 1929, unpublished

A masterful blend of Morton's style with a series of ninth chords characteristic of Novelty writing.

## "Freckles" (Larry Buck)

### November 25, 1905, W. C. Polla Co., Chicago

Ambitious Folk rag woven skillfully together by repeating motives and using the same ending in sections A, B, and D.

## "Fred Heltman's Rag" (Fred Heltman)

### February 16, 1918, self, Cleveland

A fine pianistic rag by Cleveland's leading ragtime composer–performer (1887–1960), who was also one of the all-too-few rag composers who cut rolls of their own compositions (Heltman for QRS Autograph series).

# "French Pastry Rag" (Les Copeland)

## September 1, 1914, Jerome H. Remick & Co., New York

A melodic rag with an extended C section of thirty-six measures. Section B was recently discovered to be a floating folk strain. Claude "Chauff" Williams, once an itinerant ragtime pianist, included it as part of his "Williams' Rag." He announced it to a festival audience as "one of the rags we all played."

# "Fried Chicken Rag" (Ella Hudson Day)

## February 27, 1912, Thos. Goggan & Bros., Galveston

This publisher had branches in five Texas cities. This has an interesting A section, which uses an ambitious and seldom encountered syncopation (but see "Lion Tamer Rag").

# "Frog-I-More Rag" (Jelly Roll Morton)

## May 15, 1918, unpublished

Research by Mike Montgomery tends to support the view that Morton appropriated the opening section from a pianist–contortionist named Froggie Moore. In the early twenties, Morton turned the trio into the popular song "Sweetheart of Mine."

# "Frog Legs Rag" (James Scott)

## December 10, 1906, John Stark & Son, New York

His first real masterpiece, it contains many of what were to become typical Scott devices. The crisp freshness of the A section gives way to a sophisticated use in the B section of the "Maple Leaf Rag" B section. The lyrical C is an interesting development in feeling of the A section, with similar harmonics. The D section introduces us to one of Scott's favorite devices, the echo, or call-and-response phrasing in which an idea, usually of one measure, is stated and then repeated an octave higher. This theme develops the feel of B, once again, with the use of similar chords. The modulation at the trio is unusual in that it goes to the dominant (A flat) instead of the subdominant, which would have put sections C and D in the key of G flat. Perhaps Stark objected to a score with six flats—he did later with Joseph Lamb's "Excelsior," but then gave in.

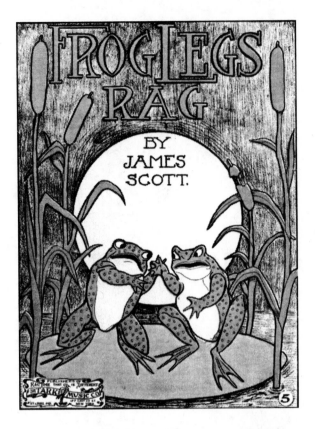

## "Funeral Rag" (Max Kortlander)

### Not copyrighted or published

A spirit antithetical to ragtime is nevertheless transformed into a fairly successful rag. It is based on Chopin's "Funeral March."

## "Funny Bones" (Calvin Woolsey)

### July 17, 1909, Jerome H. Remick & Co., New York

Section D contains full treble octaves and chords after a C section full of busy sixteenth notes. The phrasing is one measure repeated, reminiscent of James Scott, who usually went an octave higher for the repeated measure.

## "Funny Folks" (W. C. Powell [Polla])

### February 25, 1904, W. C. Polla Co., Chicago

The title is a reference to foreign visitors at the 1904 St. Louis World's Fair.

# G

## "Georgia Grind" (Ford T. Dabney)

### March 12, 1915, Jos. W. Stern & Co., New York

The *grind* was usually a slow blues, but as done here is a beautiful rag equally effective taken at a fast or slow tempo. The Victor recording is a street-piano or hurdy-gurdy roll recording that captures a mood of bygone urban life (see comment for Tom Turpin's "Bowery Buck").

## "Giddy Ditty" (Zez Confrey)

### October 24, 1935, Exclusive Publications, Inc., New York

Confrey's last Novelty rag, very melodic, yet not without pitfalls. More swingy, jazzy, but with those syncopated triplets and unusual harmonies.

## "Ginger Snap Rag" (Brun Campbell)

### Not copyrighted or published

Another patchwork solo (Euphonic ESR 1202), beginning with the introduction of "Peaceful Henry" and proceeding to a familiar "Salty Dog" circle of fifths, whereas sections B and C once again draw on "Rags to Burn."

# "Glad Rag" (Ribe Danmark [pseud. for J. B. Lampe])

## May 18, 1910, Jerome H. Remick & Co., Detroit

One of only two known rags by an early and very prominent arranger of Tin Pan Alley, Danmark was also a leading cakewalk composer at the turn of the twentieth century. The pseudonym is a slight change from his birthplace, Ribe, Denmark.

# "Gladiolus Rag" (Scott Joplin)

## September 24, 1907, Jos. W. Stern & Co., New York

This closely follows the sound of the "Maple Leaf Rag," especially in the A and B sections. A comparison of the two reveals the change in Scott Joplin's writing style. It has a grand air about it. Section C produces the most unusual harmonies, which enlarge the scope of this fine work. As in "Search Light Rag," this D section harks back to the ebullient ending.

# "Good and Plenty Rag" (Joseph Lamb)

## *Ragtime Treasures,* 1964, Mills Music, Inc., New York

An exciting and thrilling work. Mixing the Joplin and Folk rag styles with his own originality, this unusual rag creates a happy-go-lucky atmosphere. One in his experimental group of rags from the 1907–1914 period.

# "Grace and Beauty" (James Scott)

## November 12, 1909, Stark Music Co., St. Louis

Undoubtedly Scott's most brilliant ragtime work. In the finest Classic rag tradition, this scintillating composition flows smoothly from one section to the next, progressively developing fresh ideas. Section C starts with the echo device, which is imaginatively used again in the D section.

# "Grandpa Stomps" (Brun Campbell)

## Not copyrighted or published

In the style of several Folk rags, the last half of section B quotes the last half of section A (also see Theron Bennett's "Sweet Pickles"). C section modulates to the subdominant and forms a trio in the regular rag style of construction.

# "Grandpa's Spells" (Jelly Roll Morton)

## August 20, 1923, Melrose Bros. Music Co., Chicago

A Morton classic and probably his favorite cutting contest piece. In the Peppers recording he arranged sparkling breaks for sections A and B. In the piano score, the trio opens with instructions to "Crash-Strike bass open-handed." The "spell" here alternates with a flowing lyrical line, providing marvelous contrast.

# "Greased Lightning" (Joseph Lamb)

## March 27, 1959, unpublished

Section A recalls "Excelsior Rag." B and C are folksy, but D is an astounding finale—a bold through composed theme with ascending and descending runs capped by a blaze of Novelty devices.

# "Great Scott Rag" (James Scott)

## August 18, 1909, Allen Music Co., Columbia, MO

A lovely rag filled with Scott's reworkings of favorite ragtime devices. The first two measures of A are identical with the opener of Chas. L. Johnson's "Scandalous Thompson" (1899). Though the two Kansas City composers never met, it is highly probable that Scott was familiar with this fine early work. The B section contains another variation of Scott Joplin's B section to "Maple Leaf Rag," with the Scott echo effect interwoven. The C section has the interesting device of alternating the syncopation between the left and right hands, the bass in syncopated octaves similarly done in "Kansas City Rag."

# "Greenwich Witch" (Zez Confrey)

## August 4, 1921, Jack Mills, Inc., New York

A charming inversion of "Kitten," it has its own distinctiveness. Section B cements its relationship to the more famous piece but uses the groupings in a rhythmic accent rather than melodically. C section is another flagwaver but highlights the melody rather than the rhythm.

# "Gulbransen Rag" (Herb Willet)

## Not copyrighted or published

C section is like Aufderheide's A section of "Dusty Rag." This rag is a piano roll only original (U. S. Music 66036).

# H

## "Ham And!" (Arthur Marshall)

### February 24, 1908, Stark Music Co., New York

It is here that the Marshall style is best exemplified. A fascinating intermediary style between the less formalized Folk ragtime and the subtle restraint of the Joplin style. As the only active performer of the Classic rag pioneers, he incorporated many folksy, explicit performing devices into his own rags, much as Artie Matthews did later with his various "Pastime" rags. Once again, this rag highlights an intense series of slurs (found in section C), a sound usually associated with the midwestern and southern folk blues players. The entire rag has the feeling of spontaneity.

## "Handful of Keys" (Thomas Waller)

### December 29, 1930, Southern Music Publishing Co., New York

Waller's tour de force as a cutting contest, rent party piece, matched only by James P. Johnson's "Carolina Shout" and Luckey Roberts's "Nothin'."

## "Harlem Rag" (Tom Turpin)

### December 17, 1897, Robt. De Yong & Co., St. Louis

This is a pioneering Folk rag masterpiece, one of the earliest rags deliberately written for the piano. The A section is a busy melodic line—a Turpin hallmark. He always included one such strain for contrast. The rest of the rag is constructed of three sections and their variations. Beyond the older tradition of syncopating an unsyncopated melody, here the B, C, and D sections are written with simple syncopation followed by more involved syncopated variations of them ($B_1$, $C_1$, and $D_1$). In addition, it further illustrates the older tradition of performing themes with variations by writing them out, thereby providing insights as to how the pioneer ragtime pianists thought. The Father of St. Louis ragtime here demonstrates in his own personal style how original rag strains were developed. At the same time, this is a rare documentation of the improvisatory performer-oriented side of ragtime, the same impulse that spawned jazz. There are two different De Yong editions, both arranged by D. S. DeLisle, bearing the identical copyright but with completely different C sections. In 1899, Jos. W. Stern & Co. purchased the rights and published an arrangement by their chief arranger, William H. Tyers, which eliminated the first section and is generally simplified. The Wally Rose version (Good Time Jazz 51) follows the first printed edition. The original C section is the first published example of what became the Folk ragtime staple—ragging a basic circle of fifths. The D section has a march-like character, and its folk-song flavor indicates an adaptation.

# Scott Hayden

## (b. March 31, 1882, Sedalia, Missouri; d. September 16, 1915, Chicago)

Raised in the very place where Scott Joplin formally created his concept of ragtime, Hayden was a schoolmate of Arthur Marshall's and attended and graduated from Lincoln High School. Under Joplin's tutelage, their

collaborations are among the finest rags ever written. Hayden had a light, airy, delicate style with single notes and flowing melodic lines indicating his personal pianistic approach, much admired by Joplin. He married Nora Wright and lived with the Joplins in St. Louis in 1901. Nora died after the birth of their daughter. Hayden moved to Chicago, where he married Jeanette Wilkins, who continued to live in Chicago after his death. The last twelve years of his life were spent as an elevator operator in the Cook County Hospital, where he died of pulmonary tuberculosis.

## Ragtime Compositions

"Pear Blossoms," November 1, 1960, published in
*They All Played Ragtime,* 1966, Oak Publications,
3rd ed., 1966
"Sunflower Slow Drag" (with Scott Joplin),
March 18, 1901, John Stark & Son, St. Louis
"Something Doing" (with Scott Joplin),
February 24, 1903, Val A. Reis Music, St. Louis

"Felicity Rag" (with Scott Joplin), July 27,
1911, John Stark & Son, St. Louis
"Kismet Rag" (with Scott Joplin), February 21,
1913, John Stark & Son, St. Louis

# "Heavy on the Catsup" (Lewis F. Muir)

## December 26, 1913, F. A. Mills, New York

Muir (1883–1915) was a self-taught pianist who played exclusively in the key of F sharp. He played on the pike at the 1904 St. Louis World's Fair and later became one of the great Tin Pan Alley songwriters.

# "Heliotrope Bouquet" (Louis Chauvin with Scott Joplin)

## December 23, 1907, Stark Music Co., New York

The first two sections (A and B) of this rag are by Chauvin and the last two (C and D) are by Joplin. The first half of this exquisite masterwork (advertised by Stark as "the audible poetry of motion") has stylistic idiosyncrasies not found in other rags by Joplin, features he took great care to notate, providing the sole example of Chauvin's ragtime style. The structure of A is a most effective variation on the usual pattern: Here the last four measures are detached from the idea of the first twelve, forming a release to the end of the section. The rhythmic riff-like lilting B section was taken in the twenties for the chorus of a jazz classic, "Heebie Jeebies." It has eccentric thirty-second-note triplets and a break of descending diminished triads. The ending here is also unusual and features the Scotch snap rhythmic pattern, encountered infrequently in the Classic rags. The C and D sections are more predictable. Rudi Blesh recalls that Sam Patterson played the entire piece as a tango.

# "Hilarity Rag" (James Scott)

## September 15, 1910, Stark Music Co., St. Louis

A highlight in the development of the Classic rag. Sections A and D are in the Folk rag style and enclose two richly harmonic and heavily syncopated sections. The C section is an ingenious extension of the B section. The D section is Joplinesque in its strong finish but distinctively original in concept.

# History of Ragtime Recordings

Emile Berliner was the inventor of the flat disc, seven inches in diameter and made of hard rubber, which he produced experimentally in 1895. He was the first to produce flat discs commercially—as opposed to cylinders, a Thomas Edison invention—and invented the process to reproduce them in quantity from stampers, making lateral acoustical discs. The Berliner Gramophone Company incorporated on October 8, 1895. Berliner also opened the first professional recording studio in 1897. The composition of these commercial discs from this point forward consisted of shellac, lampblack, byritis, and cotton flock as a binder.

There were two processes for making flat discs: acoustic and electric—the first produced entirely by the power and energy of sound alone and the latter dependent on electric currents through a microphone powered by an amplifier. There were also two methods of cutting a record groove. The most commonly used method was the lateral cut with the needle moving in a horizontal plane. The other, developed by Edison, was the vertical, or hill-and-dale, method with the needle moving in a vertical plane.

The history of the record industry has been told in great detail in *From Tin Foil to Stereo* (Howard W. Sams, 1959) by Oliver Read and Walter Welch. What has not been stressed is the history of ragtime recordings. Throughout this discography one finds recurring names, such as Vess L. Ossman, Fred Van Eps, Olly Oakley, Harry Reser, Mike Bernard, Joe "Fingers" Carr, Wally Rose, Ralph Sutton, Arthur Pryor's Band, Prince's Orchestra, the Victor Military Band, Zonophone Concert Band, and the New Mayfair Dance Orchestra.

The most important American companies recording ragtime in the 78 revolutions per minute (rpm) era were Victor, which was directly descended from Berliner and incorporated as the Victor Talking Machine Company on October 3, 1901; Columbia, originally known as the Columbia Graphophone Company, which started manufacturing flat discs during the latter part of 1901; Okeh, through the General Phonograph Corporation from May, 1918; Zonophone, as the Universal Talking Machine Company from October 1899; Brunswick, as Brunswick–Balke–Collender Company from June 1919; Emerson, known as Emerson Phonograph Company from February 1921; Edison, who produced vertically cut flat discs from October, 1913; Capitol, formed as a company to produce records from July 1942; Circle, which made its first ragtime recordings May 1946; and Good Time Jazz, which made its first recordings from May 1949.

Like the variations of ragtime styles, each company set its own speed—the uniform 78 rpm speed was not achieved for over a quarter of a century. Speeds varied from a low of 72 rpm to a high of 86 rpm. The size of a disc also varied from five to fourteen inches in diameter with the ten- and twelve-inch formats becoming the most popular.

Though ragtime was music composed mainly for the piano, ragtime on records featured such diverse solo instruments as saxophone (Rudy Wiedoeft, Six Brown Brothers), accordion (Guido and Pietro Deiro), piccolo (George Schweinfest), guitar (Nick Lucas, Chet Atkins), trombone (Arthur Pryor, Leo Zimmerman, Harry Raderman), and xylophone (Chris Chapman, El Cota, George Hamilton Green, Ed King, Harry Robbins, and

Rudy Starita). However, the majority of the earliest recordings featured the banjo, brass band, and piano—but not altogether.

The banjo was especially suited to the acoustic process of recording, for its pinging strings provided adequate power to cut a deep groove in the master disc. The earliest ragtime recording was done by the king of the banjo virtuosi, Sylvester Louis Ossman, in 1897 for Berliner. He continued to make recordings until 1917.

Fred Van Eps, who began recording ragtime on the five-string banjo for flat discs around 1910, not only replaced Ossman as the premiere recording banjoist but also by rerecording those compositions made famous by Ossman years before. The trio was a popular combination—Ossman having been featured in the Ossman-Dudley Trio while Van Eps starred in the Van Eps Trio. His longtime pianist was Frank Edgar Banta, son of Frank P. Banta who accompanied Vess Ossman in his early recordings. Van Eps had invented a particular technique for his style, abandoned later in his career for another unique style that he perfected and that can be heard on his last recordings in 1952.

The twenties produced four-string banjo virtuosi playing Novelty rags, by far the most complex of the ragtime styles. The most outstanding was Harry Reser, who composed and recorded his Novelty rags with matchless brilliance. Among others were Len Fillis, Pete Mandell, Michael Danzi, Joe Brannelly, Lou Calabrese, Roy Smeck, Emile Grimshaw, Michele Ortuso, Eddie Peabody, and Mario De Pietro.

Bands were a natural for these early recordings. Not only did brass bands enjoy a great popularity throughout the country during the 1880s and 1890s, but the instruments also recorded well. Almost immediately after a piano rag was published by a major house, there appeared a band arrangement. Though such an arrangement might lose a charming subtlety of the music, it highlighted the melody and rhythm in a straightforward manner. Touring throughout Europe at the turn of the twentieth century, John Philip Sousa and other great bandleaders played the joyous cakewalks and rags during their concerts, which decisively helped in the spreading of this infectious music throughout the world.

The earliest ragtime recording made by a band was also done in 1897 by the Berliner house band, the Metropolitan Orchestra. Recordings with the Sousa Band quickly followed under the leadership of the band's trombone virtuoso, Arthur Pryor. Although Sousa consented to lend his name, he would not personally conduct only part of his band for discs. Only a small part of his band could record because the small studio was crammed with recording equipment.

The influence of marches was a strong one in ragtime, and it can be seen that this, too, is a natural occurrence. With the brass bands playing marches, composers like Abe Holzmann, William Krell, and J. Bodewalt Lampe, who also functioned as band leaders, would create rags for their bands to perform with a march feeling. The major composer of rags for band was Arthur Pryor, whose inventiveness and musicianship is fully documented in the discography.

Every recording company had its military band, the most famous being the Victor Military Band led by the virtuoso trumpeter, Walter B. Rogers. In addition to their house band, Victor also recorded the Patrick Conway and Arthur Pryor bands. At Columbia, Charles A. Prince held sway, directing his band under various pseudonyms. The Zonophone Company, through its Concert Band and Hager's Orchestra, made a sizeable contribution to the recorded ragtime repertoire, much of which was recorded only by them.

In the recording infancy of the flat disc, piano ragtime is rare. The first known syncopated piano solo was the one made for the Victor Talking Machine Company of "Creole Belles" by its studio pianist, Charles H. H. Booth, on November 1, 1901. But it was not until the 1912 recordings by Mike Bernard for Columbia that piano ragtime began to appear with more frequency. One reason often given for the extremely few early ragtime piano recordings was that the piano was unable to make loud enough sound vibrations to cut a deep enough groove into the wax compound used for making the master disc. This was sheer nonsense and is clearly disproved by the fact that most singers prior to 1912 were accompanied by pianists, and these accompaniments are distinctly heard. It is amusing to see prominent classical pianists shown in advertisements of their records seated at a grand piano, for studio recordings only used upright pianos, which gave a more faithful reproduction of sound than the grand. Probably the real reason that ragtime pianists were not widely recorded on discs was that it did not pay very well. Also the early ragtimers were mainly in the Midwest and the recording companies in the East. The player piano was the great novelty during the early years of the century. Pianists could make up to fifty dollars a roll, and a good ragtime pianist could make five or six rolls in a day. Vaudeville gave employment to many a ragtime pianist, and because he would tour a large circuit, he would not want his material to become well known to his audiences. Consequently, pianists did not start making discs on a regular basis until the beginning of the twenties. By that time Missouri or St. Louis ragtime and Tin Pan Alley ragtime were on their way out, and the new Novelty rags were taking over as exemplified on records by Zez Confrey, Roy Bargy, Willie Eckstein, Billy Mayerl, Victor Arden and Phil Ohman, Frank Banta, Constance Mering and Muriel Pollock, Frank Herbin, Raie Da Costa, Jean Paques, Sid Reinherz, Edna Fischer, Sidney Williams, Vee Lawnhurst, Vera Guilaroff, Fred Elizalde, Harry Jentes, and Rube Bloom.

As the phonograph record established itself as a moneymaker, higher fees were paid to the artists for recording them. The Harlem Stride men, who also made piano rolls, added recordings to their considerable laurels. And so it is that we have exciting performances by James P. Johnson, Fats Waller, and Eubie Blake. By mid 1925, the new electrical recording process was being used; it enlarged the sound spectrum to the listener, making it easier for the listener to hear more of the nuances.

By the time the first ragtime revival on records in the forties had become worldwide in the fifties, recording techniques had become more sophisticated. The brass band gave way to the Dixieland band. The bands of Pete Daily, Pee Wee Hunt, Lu Watters, the Firehouse Five Plus Two, the Southern Jazz Group, Graeme Bell, and Doc Evans made significant contributions to ragtime with their arrangements. In England, such groups as the Ballihooligans, Bugle Call Raggers, Harry Gold, Sid Phillips, and Harry Roy bands kept ragtime alive during the thirties, and they continued it in the forties and fifties. The banjo was relegated to a scattered few (most notably Bob Roberts, The Banjo Kings—Dick Roberts and Luther "Red" Roundtree—and Nappy Lamare), and the piano finally came into its own and dominated the scene with such exponents as Wally Rose, Paul Lingle, Winifred Atwell, Johnny Maddox, Del Wood, Marvin Ash, Ray Turner, Bill Krenz, Poppa John Gordy, Sid Nierman, Knocky Parker, Billy Rowland, and Ralph Sutton.

Although the Lu Watters's Yerba Buena Jazz Band in 1941 could be said to have started the ragtime revival on disc recordings, largely due to its pianist Wally Rose, the worldwide prominence of ragtime as a successful accomplishment belongs to one man who, as an astoundingly thorough musician, made the world ragtime conscious. This man was Lou Busch, who recorded as Joe "Fingers" Carr. Busch dealt in every medium—solo piano, arranger, composer, producer, director of singing groups, bands in various unique combinations—recording a huge amount of ragtime, all of it exciting to listen to, sparkling with originality, and with a freshness of sound unusual in any field. Ragtime could have no better champion.

Toward the end of the first revival and strongly active during the second ragtime revival were pianists Ragtime Bob Darch, Max Morath, Dick Hyman, John Arpin, Dave Jasen, Trebor Tichenor, Neville Dickie, Terry Waldo, and Dick Zimmerman. Instrumental groups began making ragtime recordings during this period as the St. Louis Ragtimers, Chrysanthemum Ragtime Band, and the Dawn of the Century Ragtime Orchestra.

To handle the swelling demand for ragtime, independent record companies were formed, gaining distribution outlets in the new chain stores that were taking over the mom-and-pop stores of the 78 rpm era. Sam Goody began selling long-playing albums at a discount, followed by Strawberries, Cocoanuts, and Tower Records. Folkways' RBF label began its famous reissue series in 1973, whereas Herwin started its ragtime reissues in 1971 with "They All Played the Maple Leaf Rag," a unique concept at the time featuring one tune performed over a seventy-year period by fifteen artists. By selling over 8,000 copies, it encouraged other companies to come out with their compilations of 78 rpm reissues on LP. Stomp Off came into existence in 1980 issuing brand new LP recordings of rags by the newer ragtime performers—solo pianists as well as orchestras. They continue to record and issue ragtime, now on CDs.

The recording that has sold the most copies of a ragtime composition was the 1948 disc of Pee Wee Hunt and his Orchestra doing "12th Street Rag." It sold over three million copies, more than all of the other versions on 78s combined. The Hunt arrangement has been so widely imitated that practically all versions recorded since 1948 have copied the Hunt interpretation, standardizing it comparably to the obligatory traditional clarinet solo in "High Society" and to the "Oh, play that thing!" vocal in "Dippermouth Blues."

# "Honey Moon Rag" (James Scott)

## August 15, 1916, Stark Music Co., St. Louis

The Steve Williams piano roll (Artempo 9935) is one of the finest Classic rag performances on roll. The A section of "Honey Moon" is a variation to the A section of "Maple Leaf Rag."

# "Honey Rag" (Egbert Van Alstyne)

## July 7, 1909, Jerome H. Remick & Co., New York

Extraordinary harmonic color is achieved in section A with the use of the major seventh and sixth. He attended the Chicago Musical College.

# "Honeysuckle Rag" (George Botsford)

## December 19, 1911, Jerome H. Remick & Co., New York

One of the composer's best. A section is in minor using the three-over-four syncopation. B breaks away beautifully on the dominant of the relative major and has longer phrases of syncopation using another pattern, the delayed entrance of the melody in the right hand. The trio is another fascinating excursion using several ragtime devices in a fresh manner.

# "Hoosier Rag" (Julia Lee Niebergall)

## November 1, 1907, Jerome H. Remick & Co., New York

An apt title for an Indiana rag, and one of the best. A characteristic lyricism is achieved here and in other rags of this Ohio Valley group by emphasis on major sevenths, sixths, and ninths.

# "Hop Scotch" (George L. Cobb)

## Not copyrighted, published 1921, Walter Jacobs, Boston

An ingenious and moving composition. Section A begins as an updated movement through a circle of fifths with a chromatic melody line, stressing flatted ninths and fifths with ninth and thirteenth chords. The phrasing and bass movement in B suggests the title. The C section is an inspiration with a wistful blues flavor.

# "Horseshoe Rag" (Julia Lee Niebergall)

## April 1, 1911, J. H. Aufderheide & Co., Indianapolis

Section A is perhaps her finest melody. It alternates four even eighth notes in the treble with the pattern and has a Classic rag style ending à la Joplin. C has parts of the bass in chromatic sixths, a characteristic of midwestern rags that Jelly Roll Morton picked up.

Julia Lee Niebergall.

# "Hot Chocolate Rag" (Malvin Franklin and Arthur Lange)

## April 6, 1909, Jos. W. Stern & Co., New York

Melodic phrasing in the A section teases one's perception of the actual tonic key.

## "Hot Cinders" (Joseph Lamb)

### *Ragtime Treasures,* 1964, Mills Music, Inc., New York

This was one from his Novelty rag days when Mills, publishers of Zez Confrey's super Novelties, asked for the same from Lamb. He obliged with this clever, un-Classic rag.

## "Hot Hands" (Charley Straight)

### February 16, 1916, Jerome H. Remick & Co., New York

A comparison of the score with the piano-roll performance (QRS 100223) reveals how many rag scores are compromises for the commercial market. The melody in the published version is voiced mainly in harmonic thirds, fifths, and sixths. The bass is the usual octave-chord structure. The roll, on the other hand, has the melody voiced in octaves with their harmony notes for a richer texture. The bass features tenths and alternates with the midwestern Folk rag device of octaves with a moving added note that gives the performance a slightly funky sound.

## "Hot House Rag" (Paul Pratt)

### July 27, 1914, Stark Music Co., St. Louis

A truly brilliantly inspired conception by the crack pit-band pianist of Indianapolis. The first two measures of section A anticipate the Novelty rag with its descending octaves broken into a three-eight figure, executed with both hands.

## "Humorestless" (Zez Confrey)

### March 12, 1925, Jack Mills, Inc., New York

Ragging the classics but in the Novelty idiom. This time Dvorak's famous "Humoresque" gets the Novelty treatment. Section D, in fact, puts "Humoresque" in counterpoint with "Swanee River."

## "Hungarian Rag" (Julius Lenzberg)

### June 26, 1913, Jerome H. Remick & Co., New York

A superb example of ragging the classics. This one owes its inspiration to Franz Liszt (1811–1886).

JULIUS LENZBERG,
*Composer and Musical Director.*

# Charles Hunter

## (b. May 16, 1876, Columbia, Tennessee;
## d. January 23, 1906, St. Louis)

Hunter attended the School for the Blind in Nashville, where he was taught the trade of piano tuning. He worked for the Jesse French Piano Company in Nashville, where he taught himself to play the piano and had his rags published. He was transferred to the St. Louis branch of the French company, which he soon left for the easy life of the District. He contracted tuberculosis and died before reaching thirty. He was buried by the Knights of Pythias.

Though Tom Turpin and Hunter both wrote in a Folk rag style and are the most important early rag composers, there are basic differences in approach. There is more of an orthodox march–cakewalk feeling in the Hunter rags that is almost completely absent from the eccentric, twisting and turning pianistics of Turpin. Form for Hunter was a more complex matter. Whereas Turpin approached the standard Classic rag format (inspired by the "Maple Leaf Rag") only once (in "St. Louis Rag"), Hunter uses a familiar Folk rag emphasis on pentatonic melodies. These he mixes with an ambitious use of nonchord tones, a feature that reveals a decided influence of white folk music, presumably that which the composer heard in the Tennessee hills where he grew up. Though black rags generally make use of nonchord tones, they do so in a much more

limited fashion and are usually overwhelmingly pentatonic, whereas the flair for nonchord tones pervades all Caucasian rags to a great extent. In contrast, the Hunter rags are less restless and more bucolic than Turpin's. Hunter preferred the more deeply flatted keys of A flat and D flat in his writing. This is a characteristic of much Mississippi Valley Folk rag writing, and many writers in this genre preferred to work in these keys.

## Ragtime Compositions

"Tickled To Death," May 11, 1901, Nashville (first appeared in 1899), Frank G. Fite

"'Possum and Taters, A Ragtime Feast," April 20, 1900, Henry A. French, Nashville

"A Tennessee Tantalizer," November 19, 1900, Henry A. French, Nashville

"Cotton Bolls," June 7, 1901, Frank G. Fite, Nashville

"Queen of Love—Two-Step," June 21, 1901, Henry A. French, Nashville

"Just Ask Me," April 5, 1902, Frank G. Fite, Nashville

"Why We Smile," September 28, 1903, Frank G. Fite, Nashville

"Back to Life," November 18, 1905, Charles K. Harris, New York

# "Hyacinth" (George Botsford)

## December 11, 1911, Jerome H. Remick & Co., New York

A graceful rag with long flowing melodic lines at the end of the extended sixteen-measured introduction and again in section B. The trio is one of the finest in all Popular ragtime.

# Richard Roven Hyman

## (b. March 8, 1927, New York)

Hyman was thoroughly trained in the classics by his famed uncle Anton Rovinsky. Later he studied with Teddy Wilson. He spent a year in the navy and then two years at Columbia University. He made his professional debut in 1948 and has played with such diverse musicians as Tony Scott, Red Norvo, Victor Lombardo, Benny Goodman, and Mundell Lowe. During the mid fifties he recorded ragtime under a variety of pseudonyms (Knuckles O'Toole, Willie "The Rock" Knox, Slugger Ryan) and composed several rags under other aliases (J. Gaines, Jack Schwartz, Arthur Charleston). In the seventies, he recorded examples of practically every type of rag. His biggest ragtime project has been the five-disc set of Scott Joplin rags, including a wonderful series of improvisations for RCA.

## Ragtime Compositions

"New Orleans Rag," not copyrighted or published
"The Old Professor," April 18, 1955, Hollis Music, New York
"Ragtime Razz Matazz" (as J. Gaines), September 2, 1958, Record Song, New York

"Ragtime Revelation" (as J. Gaines), September 2, 1958, Record Song, New York
"Ragtime Fantasy for Piano & Orchestra," March 15, 1976, Eastlake Music, New York

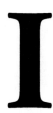

# I

## "I'm Alabama Bound" (Robert Hoffman)

### September 28, 1909, Robert Ebberman, New Orleans

Section A was one of the best-known folk songs of the Southern Mississippi Valley, recalled in later years by Jelly Roll Morton. It is also part of Blind Boone's "Southern Rag Medley #2," published the same year.

## "The Incandescent Rag" (George Botsford)

### October 21, 1913, Jerome H. Remick & Co., New York

An excellent rag featuring the three-over-four device in section A spiced with anticipatory syncopation and an intricate B section climaxed by a great ascending break (measures 7 and 8). This is an ambitious syncopated figure, apparently first used in "Mandy's Broadway Stroll," later more dramatically by Joseph Lamb in his B section of "Ethiopia," and finally most advanced in Mark Janza's "Lion Tamer."

## "Invitation Rag" (Les Copeland)

### December 20, 1911, Jerome H. Remick & Co., New York

Section A is a development from the B section of "Cabbage Leaf Rag." B begins with incipient Novelty rag phrasing using a 3/8 figure. C reflects Copeland's best approach to the down-home feelings by using treble slurs.

# J

## "J. J. J. Rag" (Joe Jordan)

### April 17, 1905, Pekin Publishing Co., Chicago

A section preserves a rag idea floating around St. Louis, which Charlie Thompson used in "Delmar Rag." The trio is a typical bit of Jordan's eccentric Folk ragtime, characterized here by unusually wide jumps in the melodic line.

## "Jack in the Box" (Zez Confrey)

### December 30, 1927, Jack Mills, Inc., New York

Confrey's imitation musically of the children's Jack-in-the-box toy. Lightly syncopated, it achieved popularity with the home piano players.

## "Jamaica Jinjer, a Hot Rag" (Egbert Van Alstyne)

### March 19, 1912, Jerome H. Remick & Co., New York

The composer's version on piano roll (QRS 100036) is interesting because he slows down for the final repeat of C. Vintage recordings of ragtime reveal that this device, as well as its reverse, was a common practice in performance.

# David Alan Jasen

## (b. December 16, 1937, New York)

Jasen began picking out tunes on the piano at age two. Dr. Kurt List recorded his early efforts. At six, he auditioned for Isabella Vangerrova to take theory and classical piano lessons. He studied with Helen Shafranek for eleven years. During this time he discovered ragtime and purchased recordings because sheet music was not available. Having relative pitch enabled him to learn rags from recordings. He started composing his own rags. With the appearance of the Joe "Fingers" Carr recordings, he imitated Carr and learned how to arrange a rag for performance. He earned a bachelor of arts degree in communication arts from American University. He met humorist P. G. Wodehouse and became his official biographer and bibliographer. Jasen has the most extensive archive of Wodehousiana in the world. From 1959 to 1966 he was supervisor of network news videotape for the Columbia Broadcasting System. He obtained a master of science degree in library science from Long Island University, is a professor in the School of the Arts at C. W. Post Center, and founder of the Department of Media Arts. He married Susan Pomerantz in 1963, and they have one son, Raymond Douglas. He is author of the pioneer ragtime discography *Recorded Ragtime* (Archon, 1973) and has the largest collection of ragtime on records and research materials on ragtime. Jasen is a producer of ragtime collections on LP and CD, a writer of articles on ragtime, and is cited by others in scholarly journals, doctoral dissertations, master's theses, liner notes, and specialist books and articles. He is editor of "100 Greatest Ragtime Hits" (The Big 3) and has appeared in leading ragtime and jazz festivals in the United States, England, and Europe. His lecture–concerts are in great demand, especially on college campuses. He formerly hosted a weekly half-hour radio program, "Ragtime and Riverboat Jazz," and produced, hosted, and performed at the ragtime concert, "Rags to Riches," at C. W. Post on October 30, 1976. *New York Times* jazz critic John S. Wilson said of him, "Ragtime is still vital today wherever Dave Jasen happens to be."

Dave, Busch, and Tichenor.

## Ragtime Compositions

"Dave's Rag," June 28, 1979,
  *Ragtime: 100 Authentic Rags,* Big 3, New York
"Everybody's Rag" (with Alonzo Yancey), not
  copyrighted or published
"Festival Rag," June 28, 1979,
  *Ragtime: 100 Authentic Rags,* Big 3, New York
"London Rag," June 28, 1979,
  *Ragtime: 100 Authentic Rags,* Big 3, New York
"Macadamian Scuffle," not copyrighted or published
"Make Believe Rag," June 28, 1979,
  *Ragtime: 100 Authentic Rags,* Big 3, New York
"Mike's Washboard Rag," June 2, 2002, Katherine
  Reynolds, Minneapolis
"Nobody's Rag," June 28, 1979,
  *Ragtime: 100 Authentic Rags,* Big 3, New York

"Piano Roll Jazz Rag," July 25, 1955, unpublished
"The Player Piano Rag," not copyrighted or
  published, composed August 1954
"Qwindo's Rag," June 28, 1979,
  *Ragtime: 100 Authentic Rags,* Big 3, New York
"Raymond's Rag," June 28, 1979,
  *Ragtime: 100 Authentic Rags,* Big 3, New York
"Shoe String Rag," June 28, 1979,
  *Ragtime: 100 Authentic Rags,* Big 3, New York
"Somebody's Rag," not copyrighted or published
"Susan's Rag," June 28, 1979,
  *Ragtime: 100 Authentic Rags,* Big 3, New York
"That American Ragtime Dance," June 28, 1979,
  *Ragtime: 100 Authentic Rags,* Big 3, New York
"Two Reel Rag," July 25, 1955, unpublished

# "Jay Walk" (Zez Confrey)

## February 12, 1927, Jack Mills, Inc., New York

A rollicking Novelty rag showing further refinements in the art of composition mainly with the various ways to use triplets in syncopation.

# Harry Jentes

## (b. August 28, 1887, New York; d. January 19, 1958, New York)

Jentes was a pianist in vaudeville who made a few piano rolls and gramophone records. He composed such early teen favorites as "Put Me to Sleep with an Old Fashioned Melody," "I Don't Want to Get Well," and "All by Myself."

## Ragtime Compositions

"Rhapsody Rag," January 17, 1911, Maurice Shapiro,
  New York
"California Sunshine," November 29, 1913, Theron
  C. Bennett Co., New York
"Soup and Fish Rag" (with Pete Wendling), December
  11, 1913, George W. Meyer Music, New York
"Bantam Step," February 21, 1916, Shapiro, Bernstein
  & Co., New York

"The Cat's Pajamas," January 10, 1923, Jack Mills,
  Inc., New York
"Tricky Trix," June 13, 1923, Jack Mills, Inc.,
  New York
"Rag-O-Rhythm," May 17, 1924, Harry Jentes
  Co., New York
"Twinkles," June 1, 1925, Robbins-Engel,
  New York

Harry Jentes.

# "Jersey Rag" (Joseph Lamb)

## March 17, 1959, unpublished

One of the Folk-style rags written during the same time as "Sensation Rag." A pure joy, the C section contains a startling key change from G flat to G natural, affected cleverly by way of a $D_7$ chord at the beginning of the section. D section extends the motive of the "Maple Leaf Rag" B section for a whirlwind finish.

# "Jim Jams" (Roy Bargy)

## June 27, 1922, Sam Fox Publishing Co., Cleveland

It is one of the great Novelty rag masterpieces. An unusual feature occurs in the left hand of the B section, which starts chord-octave, chord-octave instead of the usual octave-chord, octave-chord, thus adding the effect of more syncopation to an already thoroughly syncopated rag. Compare Bargy's 1924 recording (Victor 19320) with his 1920 piano roll (Imperial 513140).

# "Jingles" (James P. Johnson)

## July 1, 1926, Clarence Williams Music Publishing Co., New York

A great Novelty rag by the Father of Stride. Johnson was one of the very few black composers who wrote in the Novelty rag idiom and shows a complete mastery of this complex form. His 1930 recording (Brunswick 4762) demonstrates his extraordinary performing capabilities with this recorded example. The third section nicely integrates elements of Stride in the overall Novelty frame.

# "Jinx Rag" (Lucian Porter Gibson)

## December 7, 1911, Lucian P. Gibson, St. Louis

Named after a famous cartoon, this was originally published by the composer. However, it was later published by Stark in a much more complex version, arranged by Artie Matthews. A comparison between the two is fascinating and demonstrates how Matthews's skill turned a mediocre rag into an interesting one. The B section is stolen from Joe Jordan's "That Teasin' Rag."

# "Joe Lamb's Old Rag" (Joseph Lamb)

## Written in 1908, originally titled "Dynamite Rag," copyrighted in 1962, not yet published.

One of the best of the unpublished experimental rags and certainly one of the most adventurous. It is in a romping Folk rag style throughout. The through-composed D section is a major achievement.

# Charles Leslie Johnson

## (b. December 3, 1876, Kansas City, Kansas; d. December 28, 1950, Kansas City, Missouri)

By the time he was six, Johnson was pounding away on his neighbor's piano, composing and creating music. The neighbor, Mrs. Cree, gave him his first piano lessons. When he was nine, his parents bought him his own piano. He continued to play the popular music of the day while taking classical lessons. After three years, he suddenly quit when his teacher, Mr. Kreiser, complained about his playing ragtime. At sixteen he studied harmony and theory. He had a fine ear and taught himself to play several stringed instruments. He became proficient on the violin, banjo, guitar, and mandolin. Mandolin and guitar clubs were fashionable, and Johnson joined several. His earliest published tunes were written for the various groups with which he played.

Charles Leslie Johnson.

He became well known in the Twin Cities by organizing several string orchestras that played in theaters, hotels, restaurants, and dance halls. During the day, he demonstrated songs and pianos for the large J. W. Jenkins & Sons Music Company, which published his first rag in May 1899. He married Sylvia Hoskins in 1901, and they had a daughter, Frances. Shortly after, he entered a partnership in the Central Music Publishing Company, which published his Indian song hit, "Iola." Interestingly, both this one and Charles N. Daniels's earlier "Hiawatha" were named after towns in Kansas and not Native Americans. The lyrics to both songs were added after they had become successful as instrumental numbers; *"Iola"* did not become a big hit until Charles N. Daniels bought it for Whitney–Warner and exploited it nationally. Coincidentally, Johnson was working for Daniels's old firm, Carl Hoffman Music Company, at the time of the purchase. It was at that same time that Johnson was working over a new rag late one Saturday afternoon when the bookkeeper came in and asked him what the name of it was. The man was carrying a carton of dill pickles for his dinner, and Charlie looked at them and said, "I'll call it 'Dill Pickles Rag.'" Of his more than thirty rags, it remained his favorite. When he first joined Hoffman's, he arranged Harry Kelly's only hit, "Peaceful Henry," named after the Hoffman janitor. Fun-loving, practical joker though he was—and his music reflects his good humor and zest for living—he composed steadily in all areas of popular music throughout his life and made a good living as an arranger for publication of the works of others. After Remick bought "Dill Pickles" in 1907—having been published by Hoffman the year before—Johnson started his own publishing house, which was finally sold to Harold Rossiter in 1911 with the stipulation that Johnson not enter the business again for one year. This did not stop him from being published by other firms (notably by Remick, Vandersloot, Sam Fox, Forster, and Will Rossiter). His biggest moneymaker was "Sweet and Low," for which he earned $30,000. He was so prolific as a composer that he had to use pseudonyms. In addition to writing

rags under his own name, he also wrote as Raymond Birch, Fannie B. Woods, and Ethel Earnist. His ragtime output is impressive and abounds in midwestern folk roots. He married a second time during the twenties, to Mrs. Eva Johnson, who survived him. Johnson's ragtime compositions really fall into two categories: Folk ragtime and Popular ragtime. Johnson's early work reveals a creative folk talent and a skill at composition that heightens the style. Though his rags became more predictable after "Dill Pickles," he maintained a respectable level of folk inspiration in his work. He, in turn, became the inspiration for several other rag composers in Kansas City. Unlike other successful Tin Pan Alley writers, Johnson elected to stay in his hometown. Most of the Kansas City Folk rags were published by Hoffman and Jenkins, as well as by Johnson's own company. The Kansas City rags are mostly simple folksy tunes, lyrical melodies voiced in thin textures of single notes and triads more often than octaves. Almost all are three-sectioned rags in the keys of C, F, G, and B flat. They have an affinity with the older marches and cakewalks in their simplicity and directness, but are more clearly the product of the ragtime era than transition pieces. Other composers of this genre are Ed Kuhn, E. Harry Kelly, Irene Cozad, Maude Gilmore, and Mamie Williams.

## Ragtime Compositions

"Scandalous Thompson," May 27, 1899, J. W. Jenkins' Sons, Kansas City, MO

"A Black Smoke," 1902, Carl Hoffman, Kansas City, MO

"Dill Pickles Rag," 1906, Carl Hoffman, Kansas City, MO, September 16, 1907, Jerome H. Remick & Co., Detroit

"Sneeky Peet," January 10, 1907, J. W. Jenkins' Sons, Kansas City, MO

"Southern Beauties," October 12, 1907, Jerome H. Remick & Co., Detroit

"All the Money" (as Raymond Birch), March 13, 1908, Charles L. Johnson & Co., Kansas City, MO

"Powder Rag" (as Raymond Birch), August 20, 1908, Charles L. Johnson & Co., Kansas City, MO

"Beedle-Um-Bo" (as Raymond Birch), December 17, 1908, Charles L. Johnson & Co., Kansas City, MO

"Silver King Rag," April 5, 1909, Thompson Music Co., Chicago

"Apple Jack," April 7, 1909, Vandersloot Music, Williamsport, PA

"Pansy Blossoms," June 28, 1909, American Music, Chicago

"Pigeon Wing Rag," July 26, 1909, Will Rossiter, Chicago

"Porcupine Rag," September 15, 1909, M. Witmark & Sons, New York

"Kissing Bug," 1909, Keith Music, Louisville, KY

"Lady Slippers" (as Raymond Birch), May 26, 1910, Charles L. Johnson & Co., Kansas City, MO

"Golden Spider," November 3, 1910, Vandersloot Music, Williamsport, PA

"Cloud Kisser" (as Raymond Birch), January 3, 1911, Johnson Pub., Kansas City, MO

"Melody Rag" (as Raymond Birch), January 3, 1911, Johnson Pub., Kansas City, MO

"Tar Babies," January 3, 1911, Johnson Pub., Kansas City, MO

"The Barber Pole Rag," April 3, 1911, Hal G. Nichols Co., Denver

"Peanuts, a Nutty Rag" (as Ethel Earnist), July 20, 1911, Johnson Pub., Kansas City, MO

"Cum-Bac," December 22, 1911, Jerome H. Remick & Co., Detroit

"Hen Cackle Rag," January 31, 1912, J. W. Jenkins' Sons, Kansas City, MO

"Swanee Rag," March 18, 1912, Sam Fox Pub., Cleveland

"Crazy Bone Rag," March 29, 1913, Forster Music, Chicago

"Pink Poodle," May 6, 1914, Forster Music, Chicago

"Peek-a-Boo Rag," September 28, 1914, Forster Music, Chicago

"Alabama Slide," July 21, 1915, Forster Music, Chicago

"Blue Goose Rag" (as Raymond Birch), January 3, 1916, Forster Music, Chicago

"Teasing the Cat," August 19, 1916, Forster Music, Chicago

"Snookums," February 9, 1918, Forster Music, Chicago

# James Price Johnson

## (b. February 1, 1894, New Brunswick, New Jersey; d. November 17, 1955, Jamaica, New York)

Johnson grew up in Jersey City, where his mother gave him rudimentary instruction on the piano. Born with perfect pitch, he sampled all types of piano music, taking classical lessons from Bruto Gianinni for four years. In 1908, the family moved to New York City, where he heard the latest styles of playing from performers in cabarets and sporting houses from the South and West. His first professional job was in 1912 at Coney Island. He then played the popular Atlantic City resort in summers and various New York dance halls in the San Juan Hill section and clubs in Harlem during the winters. In 1919 he played in Toledo, Chicago, and other midwestern cities. Like all top pianists, he had to play in every key. As he told Tom Davin in *The Jazz Review* (1959), "I would hear tunes and to make sure, go home and 'woodshed' them in every key, put them in major and minor and all the ninth chords." In 1917 he began making piano rolls. They sold so well that he produced them for the next ten years. He was called the Father of Stride Piano and composed the most famous Stride rag, "Carolina Shout," which was used as a cutting contest piece. He recorded it twice, first in 1921 (Okeh 4495) and again in 1944 (Decca 24885).

He began making records in 1921 and stopped in 1947. He became musical director for musical revues, touring the country and making a trip to England early in 1923. Later that year he collaborated on the Broadway musical, *Runnin' Wild,* from which came his popular song hit, "Old Fashioned Love." Also from that show was a tune destined to be forever associated with the roaring twenties—the "Charleston." He never recorded his most famous tune, but Isham Jones and his orchestra, featuring Roy Bargy at the piano (Brunswick 2970), and the Tennessee Tooters, featuring Rube Bloom at the piano (Vocalion 15086), made up for it. That rhythm was insinuated into every fast fox-trot from 1925 to 1927.

During the twenties he became the favorite accompanist of blues singers, most notably Ethel Waters and Bessie Smith. Other great tunes of his were the outstanding syncopated waltz, "Eccentricity," the unforgettable ballad, "If I Could Be with You," and his most popular blues, "Snowy Morning Blues." During the thirties he devoted his time to composing large works: symphonies, ballet music, operas, and rhapsodies.

James Price Johnson.

During the forties he recorded, played in bands, took part in the Eddie Condon New York Town Hall concerts, appeared on the Rudi Blesh "This Is Jazz" radio show over the Mutual network, and gave a concert of his classical works with the Brooklyn Symphony Orchestra. His most memorable club date was at the Pied Piper, where he entertained his devoted fans nightly. A second stroke in 1951 made him an invalid for the last four years of his life.

## Ragtime Compositions

"Caprice Rag," not copyrighted or published

"Carolina Balmoral," not copyrighted or published

"Carolina Shout," October 16, 1925, Clarence Williams Music, New York

"Daintiness Rag," not copyrighted or published

"Gut Stomp" (with Willie the Lion Smith), not copyrighted or published

"Harlem Strut," not copyrighted or published

"Innovation," not copyrighted or published

"Jersey Sweet," not copyrighted or published

"Jingles," July 1, 1926, Clarence Williams Music, New York

"Keep Movin'," not copyrighted or published

"Keep Off the Grass," July 1, 1926, Clarence Williams Music, New York

"Mule Walk," not copyrighted or published

"Scoutin' Around," September 18, 1925, Perry Bradford Music, New York

"Steeplechase Rag" (a.k.a. "Over the Bars"), not copyrighted, piano roll in 1917.

"Over the Bars," February 15, 1939, Clarence Williams Music, New York

"Stop It," August 21, 1917, F. B. Haviland Co., New York

"Toddlin'," September 18, 1925, Perry Bradford Music, New York

"Twilight Rag," not copyrighted or published

"You've Got to Be Modernistic," November 3, 1933, Clarence Williams Music, New York

# Scott Joplin

## (b. November 24, 1868, Bowie County, Texas; d. April 1, 1917, New York)

Joplin came from a musical family where his ex-slave father Giles played the violin for plantation parties in North Carolina. His mother, Florence Givens of Kentucky, was freeborn and sang and played the banjo. One of six children (the others were Monroe, Robert, William, Myrtle, and Ossie), Joplin showed musical ability, so his mother, who was by then raising the family alone, let him take music lessons. For financial reasons these were sketchy, but they helped to provide enough background for him to make his way as a roving pianist throughout the Mississippi Valley. In 1885 he was working at "Honest John" Turpin's Silver Dollar Saloon in St. Louis. In 1893 he went, along with thousands of other itinerant musicians, to Chicago for the World's Fair. He then went for the first time to Sedalia, Missouri, where he became the second cornetist in their Queen City Concert Band. Then he organized the Texas Medley Quartette, which sang its way to upstate New York and back to Sedalia, where Joplin played at the Williams Brothers's saloon, whose social club was named the Maple Leaf Club. At this time he attended the George R. Smith College and studied theory, harmony, and composition. While studying, he was befriended by Marie Walker, who owned a music store in Hannibal, and she helped him write his songs down on paper. During his studies, in 1897, he started writing rags; it is more than likely that Walker also helped with these. Though he composed his greatest and most influential piece, "Maple Leaf Rag," in 1897, it was not until 1899, however, that John Stark and Son of Sedalia published it. It became the first rag to be popular nationally, eventually selling a million copies of sheet music and establishing ragtime as a genre. "Maple Leaf Rag" was the most imitated rag of all time and

set the musical structure of rags from that time forward. It is no wonder, then, that Stark proclaimed in his advertising that Joplin was "King of Ragtime writers." Joplin's use of several sixteen-measure musical themes of complex syncopation with an even, steady duple rhythm was a most revolutionary musical idea at the turn of the twentieth century. Popular music would never be the same again. The essential gaiety of the beat fit the national mood; the toe-tapping qualities of this new music filled the air with excitement. This syncopated piano music eclipsed the nonpianistic cakewalk's popularity soon after the slightly syncopated coon song made its debut. The piano rag was more sophisticated musically and technically harder to play than any popular music had been up to this time. Still, the infectious lilt of its syncopated melodies charmed and delighted listeners, and sheet music sales soared. Joplin moved from Sedalia to St. Louis, following his publisher, John Stark, there in 1900. After Stark's successful publication of the "Maple Leaf Rag," Joplin married Belle Hayden, a young widow who was Scott Hayden's sister-in-law. The young couple moved to St. Louis when Stark established his printing company there. Thanks to a royalty arrangement on "Maple Leaf," Joplin gave up playing for the more enjoyable pursuits of teaching and composing ragtime. Joplin's next works were in a different vein, combining the traditions of Afro-American folk tunes with nineteenth-century European romanticism. His imaginative use of black midwestern folk materials led Alfred Ernst of the St. Louis Choral Symphony Society to call Joplin, in a 1901 article in the *St. Louis Post-Dispatch*, "an extraordinary genius as a composer of ragtime music." That same year saw the publication of "Peacherine Rag" and "The Easy Winners." His "Elite Syncopations" and "The Entertainer" of 1902 proved equally exciting, this last rag being revived in 1973 as background and theme music for the award-winning motion picture "The Sting." A recording of the rag that year sold over a million copies and topped the charts as the number-one record for several weeks, seventy-one years after its initial publication (MCA 40174).

PYTHIAN TEMPLE.

3137 Pine St.

JAMES W. GRANT PRESENTS

Blue's Concert Band

Every Sunday Afternoon at 3:30.

WM. BLUE, Band Master.

Specials, Sunday, Nov. 18.
Messrs. D. E. Gordon and Scott
Joplin; Misses George A. Scott and
E. E. Sevier.

Scott Joplin Story.

For the 1904 St. Louis World's Fair, Joplin composed "The Cascades," which became well known. After the death of their two-month-old girl, the Joplins became estranged, and Belle died in 1906. Emotionally shattered, he wandered around Chicago, visited family in Texarkana and then came to New York City in 1907, where he set up an office at 128 West Twenty-Ninth Street in which to compose and arrange ragtime. He made his first New York sale to Joseph W. Stern and Company, which published his "Search Light Rag" and "Gladiolus Rag" that year. His masterpiece in the exceptional year of 1908 was "Fig Leaf Rag," and it was fitting that his mentor, Stark, issued it. His "Maple Leaf" variation, "Sugar Cane," was published by the new Seminary Music Company of New York in 1908, as was his brilliant "Pine Apple Rag," later that year. This last tune was such a successful seller that two years later words were added to make a charming "rag song." Joplin was the first to create a syncopated tango instrumental, and his "Solace" of 1909 remains hauntingly beautiful.

He met Lottie Stokes, whom he married in 1909. She provided him with the comfort, love, and understanding he needed to further inspire his musical ideas. It was at this time that he expended most of his energy working on *Treemonisha,* the folk opera that occupied his thoughts for the rest of his life. Joplin's life is a lesson on how a black artist could rise above the district life. He opposed the life chosen by Louis Chauvin and Charles Hunter on basic principle and rejected the attendant performer dimensions of a ragtime life. It is bitterly ironic that in the end, the district life caught up with him: He died of complications arising from syphilis.

Joplin was the most influential ragtime composer of all time, mainly because he wrote the first popular ragtime hit, "Maple Leaf Rag." Except for the small-town Folk rag composers, all other writers emulated the formula of this great rag. As for influencing others, only a few were aware of being so influenced. That two of them turned out to be among the finest ragtime composers is indeed a tribute to Joplin. He collected the black midwestern Folk rag ideas as raw material for the creation of original strains. Thus, his rags are the

Scott Joplin ad.

most heavily pentatonic, with liberal use of blue notes and other outstanding features that characterize black folk music. In this creative synthesis, the syncopated folk art was wedded with formal principles of European composition; the traditional march became the dominant form, and the result was a new art form, the Classic rag—a unique conception that paradoxically both forged the way for early serious ragtime composition and at the same time developed along insular lines, away from most other ragtime playing and composing. He infused early Folk ragtime with a moving, bittersweet quality and made the rag a more sophisticated and complex expression.

His work can be divided into three periods. The first is the early Sedalia/St. Louis phase (from "Original Rags" to "The Favorite"), which is colored with a bright optimism, a spring-like freshness. There is a developing emotional subtlety, fed by a growing self-consciousness as a ragtime classicist: Joplin as "the King of Ragtime Writers," the slogan Stark used as early as 1900. After 1900 the idiomatic syncopations become more subdued, more implicit rather than explicit in the composer's rags. By 1901 he had already created a new masterpiece in a distinctly different style from "Maple Leaf Rag," which culminated in the great riches of the very early explosive rag playing of black midwestern pioneers. In contrast, "Easy Winners" is in a flowing legato style that was to become one of his compositional characteristics. By 1904 and "The Cascades," Joplin displayed a bolder use of the piano's total resources, and his rags became more thickly textured (compare the "Easy Winners" A section with the C section of "Cascades"—similar changes but very differently executed).

The second phase (from "The Sycamore" to "Pine Apple Rag") produced mature works by an assured Joplin who wrote chromatically and used the minor tonality distinctively. He expressed deeply felt emotions in his rags, but, more importantly, he expressed several varying moods within one rag. In this he was unique. For all other writers one emotion per rag was sufficient. A peak is reached with "Fig Leaf Rag," a quintessential Joplin masterpiece of majestic melodies possessing a deep, reflective quality.

His third and experimental period (from "Wall Street Rag" to "Magnetic Rag") is a moving and autobiographical one with an inconsistent development. This phase includes some of the most probative work in the idiom, epitomized by the expanded harmonics of "Euphonic Sounds." "Scott Joplin's New Rag," however, has older stylistic ideas combined with a stark melancholy, a marriage more successfully achieved in his most intense and personal ragtime essay, "Magnetic Rag," probably his last rag, and certainly his most affecting. Joplin was steeped in nineteenth-century romanticism, especially in his use of minor tonality to effect

## TO PLAY RAGTIME IN EUROPE

SCOTT JOPLIN.

Director Alfred Ernst of the St. Louis Choral Symphony Society believes that he has discovered, in Scott Joplin of Sedalia, a negro, an extraordinary genius as a composer of ragtime music.

So deeply is Mr. Ernst impressed with the ability of the Sedalian that he intends to take with him to Germany next summer copies of Joplin's work, with a view to educating the dignified disciples of Wagner, Liszt, Mendelssohn and other European masters of music into an appreciation of the real American ragtime melodies. It is possible that the colored man may accompany the distinguished conductor.

When he returns from the storied Rhine Mr. Ernst will take Joplin under his care and instruct him in the theory and harmony of music.

Joplin has published two ragtime pieces, "Maple Leaf Rag" and "Swipesey Cake Walk," which will be introduced in Germany by the St. Louis musician.

"I am deeply interested in this man," said Mr. Ernst to the Post-Dispatch. "He is young and undoubtedly has a fine future. With proper cultivation, I believe, his talent will develop into positive genius. Being of African blood himself, Joplin has a keener insight into that peculiar branch of melody than white composers. His ear is particularly acute.

"Recently I played for him portions of 'Tannhauser.' He was enraptured. I could see that he comprehended and appreciated this class of music. It was the opening of a new world to him, and I believe he felt as Keats felt when he first read Chapman's Homer.

"The work Joplin has done in ragtime is so original, so distinctly individual, and so melodious withal, that I am led to believe he can do something fine in compositions of a higher class when he shall have been instructed in theory and harmony.

"Joplin's work, as yet, has a certain crudeness, due to his lack of musical education, but it shows that the soul of the composer is there and needs but to be set free by knowledge of technique. He is an unusually intelligent young man and fairly well educated."

Joplin is known in Sedalia as "The Ragtime King." A trip to Europe in company with Prof. Ernst is the dream of his life. It may be realized.

Scott Joplin story.

a melancholy mood. All other rag composers used it merely for a change of color in a simpler, happier vein. But the Joplin hallmark was actually juxtaposing different deeply felt emotions in one rag, which he accomplished with attention to subtle details. He had a classical approach to composition, much as Beethoven and Chopin had, and also possessed a skill in handling both folk material and his own clearly developed musical ideas. The way he developed was highly individualistic, outside the mainstream of ragtime composition. In this sense he was much like Jelly Roll Morton.

There is a netherworld aura in Joplin's bittersweet music, an esoteric fantasy, a nostalgia that evokes imagery of the Old South, replete with Spanish moss and plantation oaks. But where the black Broadway musicals of Bert Williams and George Walker were spoofing plantation life, Joplin, in *Treemonisha*, was trying to convey a serious message set on that same plantation. Joplin's early ragtime influence—his great friend and companion, legendary Otis Saunders of Springfield, Missouri—undoubtedly encouraged him in his organization of folk elements (he claimed to have helped Joplin write the "Maple Leaf Rag" and "The Favorite," as well as Tom Turpin's "St. Louis Rag"). But Joplin's formal training at Smith College allowed him to write down his ideas in detail. Whereas the rags before, during, and after Joplin were simplified by schooled arrangers, Joplin's rags were published the way he conceived them. This was true not only because he could express himself accurately on paper, but also because Tin Pan Alley respected success, and Joplin's "Maple Leaf Rag" was the unquestioned success throughout his lifetime.

The definition of ragtime formulated by the author precludes consideration of certain works that fall outside this definition. Some of these, especially in the case of Joplin, are among his most revered pieces. These include the syncopated waltzes "Bethena," "Pleasant Moments," the Afro-American Intermezzo "Chrysanthemum," and the syncopated tango "Solace." The syncopated waltzes are basically adaptations to ragtime of an older idiom, and this is true also of the tango-rags, which also do not have an even, steady duple rhythm.

Joplin was a constant experimenter with the form, exploring it emotionally more than any other writer. The original impetus toward composition away from the piano, rather than the usual writing down of what was being played, stemmed from the fact that Joplin was not a good performer. And although he stopped performing, he recognized and appreciated superior players. In a letter, Joe Lamb recalled Joplin telling him that he, Joplin, had little hope for the success of his "School of Ragtime" exercises, recognizing that some players had a greater feel for playing ragtime than others. From interviews with fellow musicians who knew and heard him, the reports were all the same. Composer–conductor–arranger Will Vodery said, "Joplin was nervous, not literate. Made his music sort of academic, tried to be concert, strictly his own style. He felt he was above entertainment type of music." Sam Patterson, friend and colleague, remembered, "Joplin never played well. He couldn't play continuously." And Artie Matthews recalled, "All the players could beat Joplin in playing. All took delight in cutting him." So, Joplin devoted his life to making ragtime a classic in form and content. His thirty-eight rags constitute a major achievement in the history of popular music. Truly, "the King of Ragtime Writers."

## Ragtime Compositions

"Original Rags," March 15, 1899, Carl Hoffman, Kansas City, MO

"Maple Leaf Rag," September 18, 1899, John Stark & Son, Sedalia, MO

"Peacherine Rag," March 18, 1901, John Stark & Son, St. Louis

"The Easy Winners," October 10, 1901, Scott Joplin, St. Louis

"A Breeze from Alabama," December 29, 1902, John Stark & Son, St. Louis

"Elite Syncopations," December 29, 1902, John Stark & Son, St. Louis

"The Entertainer," December 29, 1902, John Stark & Son, St. Louis

"The Strenuous Life," not copyrighted, published 1902

"Weeping Willow," June 6, 1903, Val A. Reis Music, St. Louis

"Palm Leaf Rag," November 14, 1903, Victor Kremer Co., Chicago

"The Favorite," June 23, 1904, A. W. Perry Sons' Music, Sedalia, MO

"The Sycamore," July 18, 1904, Will Rossiter, Chicago

"The Cascades," August 22, 1904, John Stark & Son, St. Louis

"Leola," not copyrighted, published 1905, American Music Syndicate, St. Louis

"Eugenia," February 26, 1906, Will Rossiter, Chicago

"The Ragtime Dance," December 21, 1906, John Stark & Son, St. Louis

"Search Light Rag," August 12, 1907, Jos. W. Stern & Co., New York

"Gladiolus Rag," September 24, 1907, Jos. W. Stern & Co., New York

"Rose Leaf Rag," November 15, 1907, Jos. M. Daly Music, Boston

"Nonpareil," not copyrighted, published 1907, Stark Music Co., St. Louis

"Fig Leaf Rag," February 24, 1908, Stark Music Co., St. Louis

"Sugar Cane," April 21, 1908, Seminary Music, New York

"Pine Apple Rag," October 12, 1908, Seminary Music, New York

"Wall Street Rag," February 23, 1909, Seminary Music, New York

"Country Club," October 30, 1909, Seminary Music, New York

"Euphonic Sounds," October 30, 1909, Seminary Music, New York

"Paragon Rag," October 30, 1909, Seminary Music, New York

"Stoptime Rag," June 4, 1910, Jos. W. Stern & Co., New York

"Scott Joplin's New Rag," May 1, 1912, Jos. W. Stern, New York

"Silver Swan Rag," not copyrighted, published 1971, Maple Leaf Club, Los Angeles

"Magnetic Rag," July 21, 1914, Scott Joplin Music, New York

"Reflection Rag," December 4, 1917, Stark Music Co., St. Louis

# The Joplin Tradition

The term *Classic rag* has been as misused, abused, and misunderstood as the very word *ragtime*. A basic definition of *classic* is "best of its type." Ragtime publisher John Stark was the first to coin the phrase, and he used the term as an advertising gimmick to include every rag he published: Only he published the Classic rags. Other writers on ragtime have been equally absurd in using it to describe rags they liked and approved of. It is now clear that the term *Classic ragtime* refers to those compositions in the Joplin tradition of ragtime writing—a form with the style of musical composition created and developed by Scott Joplin, combining the folk music of the Missouri and Mississippi Valleys with the European tradition in classical music of the nineteenth century.

Although ragtime derived from the performance tradition of improvised styles, Joplin's idea was to develop the rag as a composed music with thoroughly worked-out harmonies, voice leadings, and other rhythmic considerations as equal partners with and frequently in contrast to the necessary syncopation. W. P. Stark had an interesting comment along these lines in a 1909 *St. Louis Post-Dispatch* article: "In ragtime of the past syncopation was carried to an extreme in which it overshadowed everything else. Rhythm was everything; melody of little importance. But many of the writers have made money enough to study harmony and counterpoint, and have themselves been affected by the spread of musical culture all over the country. . . Many of the recent compositions of ragtime writers plainly show an effort firmly to subdue the once masterful rhythm to its proper place, and to make it a means, instead of an end." It was to be played essentially as written to preserve the composer's detailed conception. It is this basic premise that characterizes Classic rags and sets them apart from all other rags.

It is known—through recordings of such pioneers as Brun Campbell and through early hand-played rolls—that the creative performers like Louis Chauvin, who could not read music, used many melodic and rhythmic embellishments as they played. Joplin made seven hand-played rolls that were issued, and, though he was a mediocre pianist, most of the rolls contain embellishments in the bass. When these rolls were played for Joplin's protégé Arthur Marshall, he verified this bass work as being part of Joplin's performing style, which was, of course, a departure from the printed admonition to play as written. The entire question of interpretation, though, rests with the individual nature of the composition. Those of simpler conceptions—most Popular rags—lend themselves to embellishments more than the more musically polished and fine constructed Classic rags.

If Joplin was the creator of the Classic rag, then Stark was its greatest fan and promoter. Stark became involved with Joplin by publishing the "Maple Leaf Rag" (there are conflicting anecdotes about how that happened), giving Joplin fifty dollars for it and a royalty of one cent for every copy sold, which was unheard of at that time. The initial printing, done by the firm of Westover in St. Louis, was five thousand copies, and by the end of 1909, according to Stark's personal ledger, "Maple Leaf Rag" had sold a total of half a million copies.

John Stillwell Stark was born on April 11, 1841, in Shelby County, Kentucky, but grew up on a farm in Gosport, Indiana. He joined the First Regiment of the Indiana Heavy Artillery Volunteers, in which he was bugler during the Civil War. While stationed in New Orleans, he met and married Sarah Ann Casey. They settled with their growing family on a farm near Maysville, Missouri. A little later, he gave up the farm and moved the family to Cameron, where he pioneered in the new business of making ice cream. To stimulate trade, he traveled around the countryside selling it from his Conestoga wagon. He soon outgrew Cameron and moved to Chillicothe, where he engaged in the piano and organ business. Looking for a more prosperous town, he finally moved to the railroad center of Sedalia around 1885, where he established his firm of John Stark & Son at 516 Ohio Street. His general music store was one of three, and about ten years later he bought out one of his competitors, J. W. Truxel, and with it the seven copyrights he owned. That was Stark's beginning as a publisher.

With the success of "Maple Leaf Rag," Stark moved his family and business once again in 1900 to St. Louis, where he purchased a printing plant at 210 Olive Street. He later moved to larger premises at 3804 Laclede Avenue. In August 1905 he set up editorial offices at 127 East 23rd Street in New York City while maintaining his printing plant in St. Louis. On August 15 he printed the following statement in trade journals: "We are here with the goods. We left our sombrero in St. Louis—and we have had our hair cut—and even now there is not one person in five who turns to take a second look at us when we have met them on the street. And more, we will soon be able to describe our prints in the native vernacular. We should shrink from the firing line were it not for the fact that our rag section is *different*." His son William ran the plant while Stark concentrated on selling and publicizing his music. And publicize he certainly did. He invented the term *Classic rag* to distinguish his music from that of the other publishers and helped to perpetuate the myth that these selections were the source and inspiration for all other ragtime; in his hyperbolic ads he insisted that the Stark rags were the "Simon-pure" and that everything else was a "pale imitation." The label *Classic rag* was an appropriate choice to proclaim the rags of the likes of Joplin, James Scott, and Joseph Lamb as truly immortal works. But the Classic rag form was also just one way of organizing folk materials and writing ragtime. From 1897 on, there were publishers all over the country who, like Stark, published the ragtime they believed in. Composers and performers everywhere were producing excellent ragtime, and much of it was more syncopated—more raggy—than the formal Classic rag. The ragtime world outside the Classic school was extremely variegated, and, with the exception of "Maple Leaf Rag," most people were unfamiliar with the Stark catalogue. While Tin Pan Alley was opening new branches in the larger cities, small publishers, both rural and urban, were exercising the last vestige of pioneer initiative in publishing fine works of local talent.

When Sarah Stark died late in 1910, John closed his Manhattan office and went back to St. Louis to live and work. He continued publishing the rags of Scott and Lamb as well as other, lesser-known composers until 1922. He lived to see Lottie Joplin renew the copyright on "Maple Leaf Rag" and sign it over to him on November 26, 1926. Retired from active business, Stark died in St. Louis on November 20, 1927 at age eighty-six.

No greater champion of the Classic rag existed, and it is to Stark's credit that his faith in Joplin's creation never faltered and that he continued to publish and publicize that ideal as expressed by Scott Hayden, Marshall, Louis Chauvin, Scott, and Lamb.

One of the few surviving pianists of the ragtime era was W. N. H. Harding, who plied his trade in ragtime's heyday from 1908 through 1914. Communicating in 1964 with the Ragtime Society, whose aim was "dedicated to the preservation of classical ragtime," he wrote a fascinating letter responding to what had previously been published and how differently he remembered the musical life. Part of his letter follows:

> ...your efforts to give an interesting picture of an attempt to revive what may be termed the Sedalia or St. Louis style of ragtime, for as Brunson Campbell points out, there were many styles of playing and this particular style seemed to have had a slow growth, and was largely of local interest. Ragtime certainly didn't reach Chicago, New York or vaudeville in that form. I speak from experience for in my youthful days I played in our big night spots.

> One summer season I played the opposite twenty minute shift to Mike Bernard, who was then admitted best performer in the country. He played rag solos and I played for the singers. In Chicago in those days, if you could only play what was printed you had little chance of a future. Rags as printed may have been used as the basis for the coloured boys who had to learn by ear and who were usually referred to as having a weak left hand. I heard many of them, and I think they played the *Maple Leaf Rag* more as Joplin wanted, than the rest of us did. Most Chicagoans, in fact most large city listeners, liked the brilliant verve that Mike put into his playing, and most piano players attempted to imitate him. In my day our big restaurants seated many hundreds, so in a special appearance with only a few minutes to make a showing, it was necessary to put on a sparkling performance. In the smaller places, the slow drags, bucks, and ragtime played largely as printed as possible, but I do not think that Joplin's "Not Too Fast" meant "To Be Played Slowly."

> In playing for the coon shouters, it was customary on the second chorus to rag up the number to a climax so the singer would get a good hand. For the ballad singers and others, everything was played straight. When Mike went back to New York, I took his place and played rags as well for the singers, while a twenty piece orchestra played the classics.

> I knew Percy Wenrich quite well before he went to New York. He was a fine piano player and his style of playing his numerous rags was hard to beat. I occasionally visited the Pekin Restaurant where Joe Jordan had a band, and their playing of ragtime was a long way from the Sedalia style. Jordan wrote a *Pekin Rag* in 1904 and it is strictly in Chicago style. In those days in the vaudeville houses there would usually be a ragtime player on the weekly bill, mostly white boys who featured their own stuff and who would never have dared to play in the more confined and restricted manner of Stark's arrangements. You may have noticed that Joplin's numbers issued by other publishers are very differently arranged. Even Stark's music in the 1910-16 period gives more latitude to the left hand.

> I don't recall hearing any rags by Lamb or Scott in those days and of Joplin, aside from the *Maple Leaf Rag* there were few that attained popularity. I played his *Pine Apple, Cascades* and a few others, but for the most part, it was the rags of Wenrich, Bernard, Snyder and similar composers that were used, and all our local boys had special numbers of their own.

# Joe Jordan

## (b. February 11, 1882, Cincinnati; d. September 9, 1971, Tacoma, Washington)

Jordan grew up in St. Louis where he heard the early greats of ragtime. He studied music formally at the Lincoln Institute at Jefferson, Missouri, became an orchestra leader in Chicago, and then wrote and arranged revues in New York City. Back in Chicago, he became musical director, arranger, and composer for the Pekin Theatre. Later he wrote pop songs; "Lovie Joe" gave Fannie Brice her start in show business. He dropped out of music and became a millionaire four times during a lengthy career in real estate and business. He wrote commemorative tunes in his final years.

Joe Jordan.

Jordan's rags are structured with remarkable consistency. With one exception, all contain three sections, modulating to the subdominant at the trio and ending with this C section. His use of the trio follows professional popular songwriting patterns where it was added to a verse–chorus song to create the instrumental version. In this case, the trio always moved to the subdominant, and this was probably the basic function of a trio. Most often, this is a very melodic strain.

## Ragtime Compositions

"Double Fudge," December 20, 1902, Jos. F. Hunleth Music, St. Louis

"Nappy Lee," December 15, 1903, James F. Agnew, Des Moines

"Pekin Rag," September 24, 1904, Jordan & Motts Pekin Pub., Chicago

"J. J. J. Rag," April 17, 1905, Pekin Pub., Chicago

"That Teasing Rag," December 24, 1909, Jos. W. Stern & Co., New York

"Darkey Todalo, a Raggedy Rag," November 15, 1910, Harry Von Tilzer Music, New York

Joe Jordan, c. 1960.

# "Jungle Time" (Eric Philip Severin)

## February 23, 1905, self, Moline

A rollicking rag by the trombonist–publisher. A has an octave interchange between the hands in sixteenths so that the left seems to be chasing the right. Section B uses the popular broken-chord figure of the "Maple Leaf Rag" B section, but is a more extended idea, running to twenty measures. C, also twenty measures long, is a lyrical trio.

# "Just Ask Me" (Charles Hunter)

## April 5, 1902, Frank G. Fite, Nashville

A is in the key of C major. Section B begins abruptly in the key of A flat and repeats eight measures. C contains the usual sixteen measures, also in A flat, and is somewhat reminiscent of "'Possum and 'Taters." D is a thirty-two-measure march-like section. The change from the key of C to A flat is a startling one but is very effective. Scott Joplin extended this idea in "Breeze from Alabama," published later the same year. It is based on the use of the lowered sixth chord (a change, for example, in the key of C, from C to A flat). This is a staple in Folk rags, which became a feature in later pop music.

# "Just Blue" (F. Wheeler Wadsworth and Victor Arden)

## September 21, 1918, McCarthy & Fisher, Inc., New York

Still another variation on the blues–rag pattern, this one has twelve-measure strains but does not have the blues changes as one might expect. Section C is twenty-four measures. Tonal color is achieved by the use of the lowered sixth (sometimes called the raised fifth) chord, a popular device in many of the rags called *blues* (here A flat in the key of C). The composer was one of the most brilliant pop pianists and was the partner of Phil Ohman—together they were the most popular piano duo of the twenties. Arden made dozens of fine piano rolls for QRS and others.

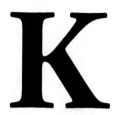

# K

## "Kalamity Kid" (Ferdinand Alexander Guttenberger)

### Not copyrighted, published 1909, self, Macon

Unusual placement of sections with an imaginative use of harmonies characterize this fine Folk rag. Dave Jasen first recorded it in 1977 (Folkways FG-3561).

## "Kansas City Rag" (James Scott)

### January 2, 1907, Stark Music Co., St. Louis

A beautiful A section flows directly into an imaginative B section, which teases with its insistent melody trying to escape from its confines. The C section is brilliantly original in phrasing, which creates one-measure breaks, such as jazz bands did on recordings ten years later.

## "Kansas City Stomp" (Jelly Roll Morton)

### August 20, 1923, Melrose Bros. Music Co., Chicago

It was first composed in 1919 and named after a bar in Tijuana, Mexico. It is probably Morton's best rag and best illustrates his concept of a piano sounding like a jazz band. Listen to his first piano solo recorded on July 18, 1923 (Gennett 5218), and contrast it with his "Red Hot Peppers" recording in 1928 (Victor V-38010). The introduction is tricky as it is a favorite syncopated waltz figure repeated four times. In the band version, it is done by a clarinet, then a trumpet, then a trombone, followed by a tuba. Thus, the feeling of a basic duple meter is suspended until the fourth measure. The trio alternates beautifully sustained chords with a ragged phrasing.

# "King Porter Stomp" (Jelly Roll Morton)

## December 6, 1924, Melrose Bros. Music Co., Chicago

Probably Morton's earliest stomp, he named it after a marvelous pianist from Florida, Porter King. There is a legend that Morton consulted Scott Joplin about it after he had finished it and that Joplin returned it with the comment that it needed no improvement. Although Morton only recorded it as a piano solo, it was Fletcher Henderson's arrangement that established Benny Goodman's orchestra and gave new life to the rag in the mid thirties. The B section uses the Joplinesque broken-chord pattern but, in typical Jelly Roll fashion, breaks away from A with a syncopation on a rest. The trio is a floating folk strain, recalled by St. Louis ragtime pianist Charles Thompson as "the Rush-On"—a musical interlude used by local pianists in contests between the tunes. The final section of variations is built on a favorite progression that Morton used in at least one other stomp, "Hyena Stomp."

# "Kinklets" (Arthur Marshall)

## December 10, 1906, Stark Music Co., New York

Originally called "Smokeville Kinklets," it was Marshall's own favorite and was named after John Stark first heard the rag; patting his foot, he remarked with admiration, "That tune's got plenty kinks in it." It flows beautifully throughout and is a graceful march-like Classic rag. Section A uses a pattern that became a standard one in later years (see Scott Joplin's "Paragon Rag"). C and D feature a Folk rag-style pattern.

# "Kismet Rag" (Scott Hayden with Scott Joplin)

## February 21, 1913, John Stark & Son, St. Louis

A lyrical collaboration with an unusual modulation at B that goes to the dominant. The final rhythmic theme appears to be built from a floating folk idea found with some modification in E. Harry Kelly's "Peaceful Henry," E. Warren Furry's early "Robardina Rag," and in one of the so-called rag medleys, "Bunch of Rags," arranged by Ben Jerome ("I Don't Like that Face You Wear" by Ernest Hogan).

# "Kitchen Tom" (Eubie Blake)

## October 20, 1962, *Sincerely, Eubie Blake,* self, 1975

Composed circa 1905. The third strain is one Blake heard played by an Atlantic City pianist. Such folk strains survive because of Blake's adaptation of these to his own style and tunes. He also did this when he cut pop blues rolls in the twenties (see *Eubie Blake, 1921,* Biograph BLP-1012Q).

# "Kitten on the Keys" (Zez Confrey)

## March 11, 1921, Jack Mills, Inc., New York

This is the "Maple Leaf Rag" of the Novelty rags. An instantaneous success, it spawned dozens of imitators. The basic ingredient is that ragtime cliché, the three-over-four pattern, but instead of single notes Confrey harmonizes and creates partial dissonance with the pattern in the right hand of an augmented fourth, a third, and then a single note against the steady, even duple rhythm of the left hand. To insure the proper kitten-on-the-keys effect, Confrey said to me of the third section, "Be sure to scramble up the octaves in the part which is supposed to sound like a cat bouncing down the keyboard. In other words, make a fist when simulating the cat running up and down, otherwise it won't sound real." The B section is a beauty. Confrey usually managed to have a ballad-like section, one that stressed melody, in at least one section of his rags.

# "Klondike Rag" (George Botsford)

## January 23, 1908, William R. Haskins Co., New York

More ambitious than later, more formulated rags, this has effective syncopation crossing the bar line, a good chromatic melody, and an orchestral concept in section C where the bass echoes the treble melody.

# "Knice and Knifty" (Charley Straight and Roy Bargy)

## February 7, 1922, Sam Fox Publishing Co., Cleveland

This was first composed by Straight, who made the piano roll (Imperial 512260) in December 1917. When he met Bargy in August 1919, he gave co-composer credit to him for this and "Rufenreddy." Bargy kept composing in this Novelty rag vein throughout the first half of the 1920s. His best roll version is on Melodee (204039).

# Max Kortlander

## (b. September 1, 1890, Grand Rapids; d. October 11, 1961, New York)

Kortlander was a composer of extraordinary rags, a brilliant piano-roll arranger of pop tunes of the day, and a magnificent performer of hand-played piano rolls. On finishing high school, he enrolled at Oberlin Conservatory for specialized music courses and the American Conservatory in Chicago for piano lessons.

Through a friend, he was introduced to Lee Roberts, composer and vice president of the QRS Music Company, the largest manufacturer of piano rolls, whose headquarters was in Chicago. Under the tutelage of Roberts in 1916, Kortlander became adept at arranging and performing for piano-roll recordings. He was well liked at QRS, and the public liked his hand-played arrangements so much that he had to resort to a pseudonym. "Ted Baxter" became Max's most well-known pen name, and many rolls can be found "played by Ted Baxter and Max Kortlander." He became general manager of the QRS recording laboratories by the late teens and became president of QRS in 1931, which he owned until his death.

## Ragtime Compositions

"Blue Clover," June 18, 1920, Jack Mills, Inc., New York

"Deuces Wild," November 17, 1923, Jack Mills, Inc., New York

"Funeral Rag," not copyrighted or published

"Hunting the Ball," June 12, 1922, unpublished

"Let's Try It," not copyrighted or published

"Li'l Joe," not copyrighted or published

"Red Clover," October 17, 1923, Jack Mills, Inc., New York

"Shimmie Shoes," October 17, 1923, Jack Mills, Inc., New York

# William Fred Krenz

## (b. February 23, 1899, Rock Island, Illinois; d. November 1980, Fort Lauderdale)

Krenz became interested in music and started taking piano lessons when he was eight years old. At thirteen he was a member of a piano-violin duo on a Mississippi riverboat, and, for the next ten years, he was part of a minstrel show. He toured with the Paul Biese Orchestra, recorded with the Jean Goldkette and Ray

Miller orchestras, appeared at the Trianon Ballroom with Arnold Johnson's orchestra, and conducted his own orchestras at many Chicago hotels and nightclubs. He was staff pianist and composer for the extraordinarily popular ABC radio show "Breakfast Club" from 1933 to 1962 when he retired. In the mid thirties, he composed six Novelty rags. In the fifties he composed and published rags in the Popular ragtime tradition. He was one of the great ragtime pianists.

## Ragtime Compositions

"Barber Shop Rag," January 19, 1953, Mills Music, New York

"Marita," December 14, 1934, M. M. Cole, Chicago

"Mud Cat Rag," November 24, 1953, Mills Music, New York

"Oh! Willie, Play that Thing," May 23, 1952, Mills Music, New York

"Pianola Rag," December 29, 1953, Mills Music, New York

"Poodle Rag," August 12, 1954, Mills Music, New York

"Ramblin' Rag," July 11, 1952, Mills Music, New York

"Rochelle," December 15, 1934, M. M. Cole, Chicago

"Showboat Rag" (with Tommy Filas), November 24, 1953, Mills Music, New York

"Sophisticated Rhythm," January 22, 1935, M.M. Cole, Chicago

"Yvonnette," February 1, 1935, M. M. Cole, Chicago

"Zephyr," February 12, 1935, M.M. Cole, Chicago

# L

## Joseph Francis Lamb

### (b. December 6, 1887, Montclair, New Jersey; d. September 3, 1960, Brooklyn)

The youngest son in a family of four children, Lamb grew up in an Irish Catholic neighborhood. His father, James, was born in Drogheda, Ireland, married Julia Henneberry of Kilkenny, and settled in Montclair in a home he built. A successful building contractor, he taught Lamb carpentry and mechanics. Lamb attended the Catholic grammar school attached to the Church of the Immaculate Conception. At about eight years of age he asked his older sisters to teach him the piano lessons they were taking. Katherine became a church organist and professional piano teacher. Anastasia was awarded a piano scholarship at St. Elizabeth's Convent. Aside from these infrequent lessons and studying a beginner's book, he was self-taught. On his father's death in 1900, he was sent to St. Jerome's College in Berlin, Ontario, where he enrolled as a preengineering student. His interest in music flourished, and he composed waltzes, songs, and other popular dance music the Harry H. Sparks Music Publishing Company of Toronto issued. He got a job as an office boy in a wholesale dry goods company in summer 1904 and never returned to school. He spent some time with his brother in San Francisco, returning home shortly before the earthquake of 1906, and then worked first for a clothing company and then a publishing house. He was attracted to Scott Joplin's ragtime, and in 1907 he went to the Stark office in Manhattan, where he purchased most of their rags. There he met Joplin, his ragtime idol, who liked his rags and got John Stark to publish them. After the first published rag, which listed Joplin as arranger, Stark took everything Lamb sent to him. Lamb formed the Clover Imperial Orchestra, which performed at church and lodge dances. In 1911 Joe married Henrietta Schultz and moved from Montclair to Brooklyn, where he also briefly entered the Tin Pan Alley world as an arranger for the J. Fred Helf Music Publishing Company. In April, 1914 he went to work for L. F. Dommerich & Company, Inc., which financed accounts of manufacturers and guaranteed their sales. He retired in December 1957. His wife died during the flu epidemic in early 1920, leaving him with a five-year-old son. In November 1922 Lamb married Amelia Collins and moved into a large house on East 21st Street in the Sheepshead Bay section of Brooklyn. Four more children were born to the couple, who became solidly entrenched in their neighborhood—so solidly, in fact, that when the local grammar school celebrated its fiftieth anniversary in May 1976, its name was changed from P. S. 206 to the Joseph F. Lamb School. Fame for the ragtimer came with the publication of *They All Played*

Joseph Lamb.

*Ragtime* (Knopf, 1950), when it was learned that he was still alive and living in Brooklyn. The ragtime revival of the forties and fifties brought him fan mail and visits from dedicated ragtimers. It also stimulated him to compose new rags and dust off older ones to complete or revise. Bob Darch arranged to have Lamb play at Club 76 in Toronto in October 1959, his first and only professional engagement. Earlier that summer, Sam Charters recorded Lamb for an album of reminiscences and playing (Folkways FG-3562). He died of a heart attack at home.

The strength of Joplin's ideas in ragtime is best exemplified by Lamb's rags. Rags written before 1907—which is to say before he became aware of the Joplin rags—recently found in manuscript form show a rather mediocre attempt at composing rags, using all of the overworked devices of the cakewalk, Popular rag, and song. From the twelve works published between 1908 and 1919, his rags are more predictable, as he synthesized the Joplinesque legato melody style with James Scott's expansive keyboard work. Then, Lamb replaced Joplin's phrase structure, making the first half of a section contrasting rather than parallel. He also avoided the short, motivic phrasing of Scott but used Scott's echo effect and rhythmic exuberance. Among Lamb's greatest original stylistic features are his use of sequences for developmental purposes and his diversity of texture, not only from light to heavy rags but also from section to section and even phrase to phrase, with the total eclipse of the four-measure phrase in three of his best rags: A sections of "American Beauty Rag," "Top Liner Rag," and "Cottontail Rag." Whereas Joplin preferred four-measure phrases and Scott two-measure ones, Lamb developed eight-measure phrases. These rags published by Stark can be placed in two groups: easy and hard. The easy-to-play ones are lighthearted and reflect Scott's expansive keyboard approach. The hard-to-play ones illustrate Lamb's deep understanding of Joplin's ideas. They have rich and unusual harmonies and varied yet exciting rhythms. In both types, however, his intuitive feeling for the Missouri folk sounds is not imitative, but imaginatively original. Lamb was the consummate ragtime composer, the genius who possessed the ability to synthesize the best from all the Folk, Classic, and Popular ragtime music worlds into stirring works of his own great originality.

For the sake of simplicity, the rags Stark published are listed first, and then the rest are grouped in alphabetical sequence. Many of these other works were written much earlier but were revised and rewritten during the 1950s. Some bear no date at all. It is certain that "Alaskan Rag" was a new one written to celebrate that territory's entrance into the United States in 1959.

## Ragtime Compositions

"Sensation Rag," October 8, 1908, Stark Music Co., New York

"Ethiopia Rag," not copyrighted, published 1909, Stark Music Co., New York

"Excelsior Rag," not copyrighted, published 1909, Stark Music Co., New York

"Champagne Rag," September 15, 1910, Stark Music Co., St. Louis

"American Beauty Rag," December 27, 1913, Stark Music Co., St. Louis

"Contentment Rag," January 10, 1915, Stark Music Co., St. Louis

"Ragtime Nightingale," June 10, 1915, Stark Music Co., St. Louis

"Cleopatra Rag," June 16, 1915, Stark Music Co., St. Louis

"Reindeer," not copyrighted, published 1915, Stark Music Co., St. Louis

"Top Liner Rag," January 4, 1916, Stark Music Co., St. Louis

"Patricia Rag," November 19, 1916, Stark Music Co., St. Louis

"Bohemia," February 17, 1919, Stark Music Co., St. Louis

"Alabama Rag," 1964, *Ragtime Treasures*, Mills Music, New York

"Alaskan Rag," 1966, *They All Played Ragtime*, Oak Publications, New York

"Arctic Sunset," 1964, *Ragtime Treasures*, Mills Music, New York

"Beehive," March 27, 1959, unpublished

"Bird-Brain Rag," 1964, *Ragtime Treasures*, Mills Music, New York

"Blue Grass Rag," 1964, *Ragtime Treasures*, Mills Music, New York

"Chasin' the Chippies," not published, written 1914, copyrighted 1961

"Cottontail Rag," 1964, *Ragtime Treasures*, Mills Music, New York

"Firefly Rag," 1964, *Ragtime Treasures*, Mills Music, New York

"Good and Plenty Rag," 1964, *Ragtime Treasures*, Mills Music, New York

"Greased Lightning," March 27, 1959, unpublished

"Hot Cinders," 1964, *Ragtime Treasures*, Mills Music, New York

"Jersey Rag," March 17, 1959, unpublished

"Joe Lamb's Old Rag," written 1908, originally titled "Dynamite Rag," copyrighted 1962, unpublished

"The Old Home Rag," 1964, *Ragtime Treasures*, Mills Music, New York

"Ragged Rapids Rag," written 1905, copyrighted 1962, unpublished

"Ragtime Bobolink," 1964, *Ragtime Treasures*, Mills Music, New York

"Ragtime Special," March 21, 1959, unpublished

"Rapid Transit Rag," March 17, 1959, unpublished

"Thoroughbred Rag," 1964, *Ragtime Treasures*, Mills Music, New York

"Toad Stool Rag," 1964, *Ragtime Treasures*, Mills Music, New York

"Walper House Rag," written 1903, copyrighted 1962, unpublished

# "Lazy Luke" (George J. Philpot)

## December 10, 1904, Walter Jacobs, Boston

Sections A and B seem to be a rehash of E. Harry Kelly's "Peaceful Henry," but it is the delightful and unforgettable C section that makes this rag outstanding.

# "Leola" (Scott Joplin)

## Not copyrighted, published 1905, American Music Syndicate, St. Louis

A graceful reworking of "Maple Leaf Rag." A foretaste of "Gladiolus."

# "Lily Queen" (Arthur Marshall)

## November 8, 1907, W. W. Stuart, New York

Although the name of Scott Joplin appears as collaborator, he did not write any part of it. In a letter to Rudi Blesh, Marshall explained, "Joplin told me he had a party that would publish that piece of music so I let him handle it. But for him having any part in the composing, he did not. Now he was the more popular as a composer and that is why his name was mentioned in the writing of *Lily Queen*. I got about $50 in all for it at the time. I was living in Chicago."

The D section of this march-style rag is one of the most moving climactic final strains in all of ragtime. It rolls along, sparked by repeated slurs in the treble, an explicit touch best described as funky. It is hardly ever found in the Classic rags but is one that was popular as a performance device (see Bowman's "11th Street Rag").

# "The Lily Rag" (Charles Thompson)

## Not copyrighted, published 1914, Syndicate Music Co., St. Louis

A masterpiece with which Thompson won cutting contests and became the ragtime champion of Missouri. The A section features contrasting syncopations skillfully juxtaposed. Section B is delicate and lyrical. C builds tension with sustained arpeggios on a circle of fifths, climaxed by a syncopated bass break in octaves. This break is not in the original score but was always included by Thompson, at least in his later years (American Music 527).

# "The Lion Tamer Rag" (Mark Janza)

## January 2, 1913, A. F. Marzian, Louisville

The most adventurous of the Ohio Valley rags, this is accurately subtitled "Syncopated Fantasia." It combines a circus pomposo air with surprises at every turn. Measures 15 and 16 in the trio are the most ambitious, creative use of an idea that dates from 1898 (see "Incandescent Rag"). Here the pattern is executed in the bass, combined with a three-over-four treble.

# "Little Bit of Rag" (Paul Pratt)

## Not copyrighted or published

This is another rag written solely for piano-roll issue (U. S. Music 8005). The tremolo effect, which became standard during the twenties, was usually arranged in the middle range of the piano carrying the melody, whereas in the upper treble there were syncopated embellishments. Such rolls were marketed as *saxo-rags, cello rags,* and even *jug band rags.* Interestingly, these arrangements were very much in the style of recorded ragtime group arrangements of the teens. The complex nickelodeon pianos, with such instruments as xylophone, flute pipes, and drums, went one step further in imitating the sound of these early ragtime groups.

# "Little Jack's Rag" (Arthur Marshall)

## 1976, published in *This Is Ragtime,* Hawthorne, 1976

One of Marshall's very finest, it was discovered posthumously as a complete manuscript by pianist–historian Terry Waldo (Stomp Off 1007) when visiting his daughter, Mildred Steward. The title is the affectionate nickname for Mildred. Marshall performed the C section in 1959 at an early Joplin Festival in Sedalia. It must have been one of his favorite themes; it is certainly one of his most inspired.

# Thomas Henry Lodge

## (b. February 9, 1884, Providence; d. February 16, 1933, West Palm Beach)

Lodge was the eldest of four brothers and one sister. His father had come from Manchester, England, and worked in a textile mill. His mother came from Maryland. There was no musical background in the family, but with an acquired piano Lodge took lessons when he was twelve. After school he obtained a job demonstrating and selling pianos at Meiklejohn's Music Store. In 1906 he married Sarah Agnes Mackie. Their only child, Mary, was born in 1907. In 1912 they moved to New York City, where he played piano in cabarets. He worked as pianist for Irene and Vernon Castle at Castle House, where they gave private dance instructions for very high fees. Lodge hung around the publishers' offices where he was hailed as a fine composer of Popular rags. His 1909 "Temptation Rag" was an outstanding success and was played most often in vaudeville. He led bands in vaudeville and in dance halls. He moved to Atlantic City, where his orchestra played on the Million Dollar Pier. In 1918 his wife died. In the early twenties he wintered in West Palm Beach, where his orchestra played for the wealthy. It was there he met and eventually married his second wife, Irene. They had three children: Sally, Arthur, and Theodore. He started writing background music for films and, in 1930, lived in Los Angeles while working for Universal and MGM. At the end of the year his family moved back to the New York area but continued to winter in West Palm Beach where he unexpectedly died in 1933.

The late rags from 1917 and 1918 are written in a more advanced style, using more complex tonal plans, odd harmonies, and surprising textures. Those called *blues* are rags with some emphasis on minor chords to

Henry Lodge.

effect a slightly melancholy aura and are far from the down-home blues style. They are a complete departure from his earlier rags, which are very danceable and are in the Popular ragtime format. In all his work, Lodge was fascinated with the minor tonality and made more creative use of it than any other composer. His predilection was for a pattern of three minors: Dm/Am/Gm. This became a staple of much later writing in pop music, especially during the rock era.

## Ragtime Compositions

"Temptation Rag," September 9, 1909, M. Witmark & Sons, New York

"Sure Fire Rag," March 15, 1910, Victor Kremer Co., Chicago

"Sneaky Shuffles," October 4, 1910, Jerome H. Remick & Co., New York

"Red Pepper, a Spicy Rag," December 19, 1910, M. Witmark & Sons, New York

"Black Diamond, a Rag Sparkler," February 5, 1912, M. Witmark & Sons, New York

"Tokio Rag," May 21, 1912, M. Witmark & Sons, New York

"Pastime Rag," April 28, 1913, M. Witmark & Sons, New York

"Moonlight Rag," May 5, 1913, M. Witmark & Sons, New York

"Oh You Turkey," January 20, 1914, Waterson, Berlin & Snyder Co., New York

"The Baltimore Blues," June 20, 1917, Jerome H. Remick & Co., New York

"Remorse Blues," July 30, 1917, Jerome H. Remick & Co., New York

"The Bounding Buck," March 1, 1918, M. Witmark & Sons, New York

"Hifalutin' Rag," March 28, 1918, M. Witmark & Sons, New York

"Misery Blues," May 1, 1918, M. Witmark & Sons, New York

# OUR FAMILY

## Intimate Glimpses of Our Authors and Composers

Mr. Pete Wendling

PETE WENDLING who was born in New York City in 1888 has been a real writer of hits, and of striking personality; besides one of the greatest piano players in existence. One of his early numbers was "Yaaka Hula Hickey Dula," the first real popular Hawaiian numbers published. Next came "I Wish I Could Sleep Until My Daddy Comes Home"; then the hits came in an avalanche, until the time of "Oh What A Pal Was Mary." This song netted Pete over one hundred thousand dollars for one hour's work. He is one of the best piano roll recording artists in the country and makes rolls for the Q.R.S. Rolls. "Dream Face" is his contribution to this issue for our magazine.

Mr. Henry Lodge

HENRY LODGE is the composer of the charming number "Just A Little Bit Of Lavender" and you will find it in this issue he hardly needs an introduction to the popular music buying public. Mr Lodge has long been known as one of the greatest writers of light instrumental compositions in the country. Some of his numbers such as "Temptation Rag," "Geraldine Waltz," "That Red Head Gal," and "My Bouquet of Memories," etc., have been wide world successes. Mr. Lodge, a native of New York City has long been identified with the music business.

Mr. Chas. Kenny

CHARLES KENNY was born on Long Island, New York State and then migrated to Canada; came back to United States and saw service in the U. S. Navy, has been leader of dance orchestras on Ocean going Liners; started writing poetry under the nom-de-plume "Ocean Duster." He has written such songs as "We're The Sunday Drivers," and "When The Robert E. Lee," etc. Mr. Kenny is a violinist of note and edits a popular column of verse and humor on one of the New York Papers called WEATHERVANE. He resides at Pleasant Plains, Staten Island, N. Y. Mr. Kenny wrote the lyric for our popular number "I Met Mary On the Merry-Go-Round."

Mr. Ben Gordon

BEN GORDON, was born in New York City and has been a number of years in the music business and all of its allied branches. Mr. Gordon has been in vaudeville for a number of years and has done concert work as well as being a Radio Broadcaster, having broadcasted over such stations as WEAF, WOR, and many others. Mr. Gordon is a vocalist of unusual ability. His songs are, "Howd'y Do Miss Spring-time" and "Can't Be Blue" and many others. Ben can sing a popular song probably as good as anyone in the business. He is a lyric writer of the number "Dream Face" appearing in this issue.

Mr. William Covell

WILLIAM COVELL was born in Tottenville, Staten Island, N. Y. He is a war veteran, also closely identified with the many phases of the amusement business. He is an excellent pianist, broadcasts over the radio, having appeared at the stations of WEAF, WMCA, and WNYC. He has been on the road in a vaudeville sketch entitled "Rebellion" and is also an arranger of music. Bill holds patents on several inventions and can play almost any instrument you want him to and play them well. He is diversification itself. Mr. Covell is the melody writer of "I Met Mary On The Merry-Go-Round."

Mr. Chas. L. Tarr

CHARLES L. TARR who wrote "To Be With You," published in this number of our magazine is a native of Absecon, New Jersey. Mr. Tarr came from a theatrical family, mother, father and six children, and made his appearance on the stage at the age of five years with Sol Smith Russell in a play "Edgewood Folks," later on in vaudeville and finally started writing songs. Mr. Tarr's numbers are distinctly of the operatic type, probably due to his long association with the stage. In 1925 and 1926 he wrote the score for the show called "Flirting Flapper," in 1927-1928 score for "Round the World" Revue, and at present he is working on a production for this Fall. He is an accomplished pianist.

Mr. Sidney Holden

SIDNEY HOLDEN has written another inspirational song in this issue. Both words and music belong to this gifted and talented composer and the title is "Just Keep On Hoping." Sydney's biographical sketch appeared in a previous issue. Sydney is Canadian born, an overseas veteran and a real likeable personality.

Mr. Lotus F. Brown

MR. BROWN is the writer of our prize song appearing in this issue entitled "Shady River." Mr. Brown is from Salem, Indiana, a real hoosier and a song writer in the amateur field whose writings promise a real career for him. We are glad to establish and welcome you to the field of popular song writers, Mr. Brown.

Henry Lodge and others.

# "Louisiana Glide" (Blind Leroy Garnett)

This is another Folk rag that was never published and only exists on record by its composer–performer (Paramount 12879). Like Sugar Underwood (see "Dew Drop Alley Stomp"), Garnett was an unknown black itinerant who had an incredible mastery of the piano and, in a seemingly effortless rendition of a common folk tune, transformed it into one of the greatest ragtime piano recordings ever made. This highly personal statement of a syncopated floating folk tune is filled with such great creativity and virtuosity that it justifies his composer credit. This same material was taken by Alonzo Yancey who truthfully called his version "Everybody's Rag."

# "Louisiana Rag" (Theodore Northrup)

## October 20, 1897, Thompson Music Co., Chicago

The first published ragtime composition done expressly for the piano—William H. Krell's *"Mississippi Rag"* was done as an orchestral cakewalk. Northrup is one of the important yet overlooked professional arrangers who not only helped codify syncopations but also made excellent contributions to the genre of rags. In this he is unique among the earliest arrangers. Section A weaves the aura of the lost South so prevalent in many early characteristic instrumentals. The bass movement here is extraordinary for such an early rag, and C is most heavily syncopated.

DESCRIPTION OF LOUISIANA NIGGERS
DANCING   (THE PAS MA LA RAG)

LOUISIANA RAG
(PAS MA LA)
TWO STEP

AUTHOR OF
A NIGHT ON THE
LEVEE
SAVANAH JUBILEE SCHOTTISCHE
& OVER THE FENCE SWEET
POLLY

COMPOSED BY
Theo. H. Northrup

5

PUBLISHED BY
THE THOMPSON MUSIC CO.
CHICAGO ILL

## "Louisiana Rag"  (Harry Austin Tierney)

### May 3, 1913, Jos. Krolage Music Co., Cincinnati

The trio is a blues (twelve measures with a reprise of the last four). This is a rare, idiomatic score with indications of ragtime performing conventions usually found only on rolls.

## "Lover's Lane Glide" (Calvin Woolsey)

### October 5, 1914, self, St. Joseph, MO

Certainly the most folksy glide ever published. The A section somewhat resembles the 1909 dance hit "The Cubanola Glide" but overall contains more ragtime elements than the dance tune. Section B is a magnificent example of well-scored Folk rag circle of fifths with a touch of bass syncopation. The trio is a collection of the composer's idiosyncratic licks, with the characteristic "Mashed Potatoes" bass. The fine variation of the trio is spiced with startling bass octave grace notes.

# M

## "Magnetic Rag" (Scott Joplin)

### July 21, 1914, self, New York

The final rag in the most distinguished series of rags by a single composer. Experimenting to the end, he begins with a section that combines the joyous Folk rag style with a bittersweet quality and follows with a B section in the relative minor that changes the rag to a melancholy mood. The twenty-four-measure C section is one of Joplin's most moving, incorporating down-home blues elements with much syncopation. The D section in the parallel minor of A (B flat minor) is the most somber in all of Joplin's rags. Joplin sensed that the rag could not end this way, so he repeated the A section twice. As if loath to say farewell to ragtime, he added a joyful coda with which to be remembered. In all, this is Joplin's most autobiographical rag and certainly one of the most moving in all of ragtime.

## "Mandy's Broadway Stroll" (Thomas E. Broady)

### Not copyrighted, published 1898, H. A. French, Nashville

Broady's first published tune occurred in 1896 in his hometown of Springfield, Illinois. This, the first Nashville rag in print, is one of the most melodious and forthright ragtime marches ever done. Basic cakewalk syncopations are beautifully combined with more sophisticated patterns such as the one found in the A section.

# "Maple Leaf Rag" (Scott Joplin)

## September 18, 1899, John Stark & Son, Sedalia, MO

The A section has always seemed to me to be an elongated introduction with the B section as the actual beginning of the rag. Joplin used the A section in "Cascades," "Sycamore," "Leola," "Gladiolus," and "Sugar Cane." As if to demonstrate the validity of the statement that the A section is really an introduction in extended form, Joplin took the A section for his prelude to act three of his folk opera, *Treemonisha*. The B section contains the pianistic syncopated pattern that was the most influential part of the rag and established the first ragtime cliché (e.g., the B section of James Scott's "Frog Legs Rag" and the B section of Joseph Lamb's "Contentment Rag"). Section C has a thicker texture and uses a counter-bass line of descending octaves, accentuating the more idiomatic syncopation of this section. The phrasing and syncopated figures in the D section (measures 3, 5, and 11) recall the B section of "Original Rags." It is with this D section that Joplin conceptually is most involved, with alternating bass patterns enriching the complexity of this great final section. The transition from the trio (in the key of D flat) back to the home key for the final section is done smoothly by opening with a D flat harmony, which then becomes the subdominant of the home key of A flat. Joplin made a similar change in "Original Rags," opening its E section on a $D_7$ (coming from a section in the key of D). In this rag, however, the $D_7$ becomes the dominant seventh of the last section (for this example in the key of G). With this rag, Joplin begins using his triumphant endings. Surely, this one is his greatest.

First edition cover of "Maple Leaf Rag."

***** Article of Agreement. *****

This agreement entered into this  10th day of August in the year of our Lord 1899 by and between John Stark and son party of the first part and Scott Joplin party of the second part both of the City of Sedalia and County of Pettis and State of Missouri.

Witnesseth: That whereas Scott Joplin has composed a certain piece of music entitled Maple Leaf Rag and has not funds sufficient to publish same it is hereby agreed with above parties of the first part that John Stark and son shall publish said piece of music and shall pay for all plates and for copy right and printing and whatevr may be necessary to publish said piece of music

It is further agreed by and between the parties hereto that John Stark an son shall have the exclusive right to said piece of music to publish and s sell and handle the same as they may seem fit and proper to their interest

It is further agreed by and between the parties hereto that Scott Joplins name shall appear in print on each and every piece of music as composer and John Stark and son as publishers.

It is further agreed by and between the parties hereto that Scott Joplin shall have free of charge ten copies of said piece of music as soon as published.

It is further agreed by and between said parties that Scott Joplin the composer of said music shall have and recieve a royalty of one cent per copy on each copy of said piece of musi sold by said Stark and son.

It is further agreed by and between said parties that the said Scott Joplin Shall be allowed to purchase and the said Stark and son agrees to sell to the said Joplin all the copies of said music he may want at the price of Five cents per copy, said copies shall not be sold for less than Twent-five cents per copy by said Joplin. It is further agreed that John Stark & son will not retail for less than Twenty five cents per copy.

Witness our hands and seals the day and year first above written.

John Stark & Son
Scott Joplin

Signed in presence of
R A Higdon

"Maple Leaf Rag" contract.

"Maple Leaf Rag" hand-played roll.

"Maple Leaf Rag" record label.

# Arthur Marshall

## (b. November 20, 1881, Saline County, Missouri; d. August 18, 1968, Kansas City, Missouri)

Marshall attended grade school and Lincoln High School with Scott Hayden in Sedalia. He was a protégé of Scott Joplin, who lived with the Marshall family when he first arrived in Sedalia. Marshall also took private classical lessons from Lillian Read and from Mrs. Teeter while in grade school. Under Joplin's influence, he played his first piano job at the Maple Leaf Club. Marshall then attended the George R. Smith College, studying music theory, and went to the Teacher's Institute, majoring in education and obtaining a teaching license. During this time he began his professional career as a ragtime pianist and played for dances at Liberty Park and for picnics and barbecues at Forest Park. He also worked in the parlors, where the official rate was $1.50 for the evening; with tips take-home pay was closer to $10.00. He joined McCabe's Minstrels in 1901 as an intermission pianist and marched in their parades playing cymbals. Marshall found lots of work in St. Louis during the World's Fair. He married Maude McMannes, joining Joplin's Drama Company along with Hayden. In a private interview, he recalled friendly, cutting contests among the pianists: "shootin' at one another—where it caused them to write some pretty good rags." He left for Chicago in 1906 where opportunities to earn a decent living as a pianist were more plentiful. Here he married Julia Jackson, who bore him two daughters and a son. He entered a ragtime contest around 1910 at the Booker T. Washington Theatre in St. Louis, run by Charlie Turpin, and won the top prize of five dollars. He then went to work for Tom Turpin at the Eureka on Chestnut Street and 22nd Avenue. His last piano job was playing at Henry Maroche's Moonshine Gardens, when his wife died in childbirth at the end of 1916. He went to Kansas City in 1917, retired from the music business, and married for a third and last time.

## Ragtime Compositions

"Swipesy Cakewalk" (with Scott Joplin), July 21, 1900, John Stark & Son, St. Louis

"Kinklets," December 10, 1906, Stark Music Co., New York

"Lily Queen," November 8, 1907, W. W. Stuart, New York

"Ham And!" February 24, 1908, Stark Music Co., New York

"The Peach," December 7, 1908, Stark Music Co., New York

"The Pippin Rag," December 7, 1908, Stark Music Co., New York

"Century Prize," 1966, published in *They All Played Ragtime*, 3d ed., Oak Publications, New York

"Missouri Romp," 1966, published in *They All Played Ragtime*, 3d ed., Oak Publications, New York

"Silver Rocket," 1966, published in *They All Played Ragtime*, 3d ed., Oak Publications, New York

"Little Jack's Rag," 1976, published in *This Is Ragtime*, Hawthorne, New York

# "Mashed Potatoes" (Calvin Woolsey)

## August 12, 1911, self, Braymer, MO

One of the most idiomatic Folk rag scores. Section A has ascending bass octaves scored with the middle note, a characteristic of folk playing, and much in evidence on early hand-played piano rolls. The middle note—the fifth of the chord—stays the same as the octaves ascend. This is a more harmonically correct way of using a funky bass pattern—usually with the middle note moving as well as the octave—thereby creating a dissonance, which is the sound associated with both Folk rag and blues players. C is built on an octave interchange in both hands that was apparently popular with pianists, encountered as early as 1907 in "That Rag" by Ted Browne. Section D is sparsely syncopated in the style of a straight march, a contrasting touch used in rag composition (also found in Chas. L. Johnson's "Blue Goose Rag"). Apparently *mashed potatoes* referred to playing ragtime; on another Woolsey tune he is advertised as "The 'Guy' that 'Mashed Potatoes' a la Piano."

# Artie Matthews

### (b. November 15, 1888, Braidwood, Illinois; d. October 25, 1958, Cincinnati)

Matthews moved to Springfield as a boy, where his father's job of sinking shafts for coal mines necessitated travel. Here he took piano lessons from his mother and then from a teacher. He did not learn to read music but was taught pieces. He first played ragtime around 1905 after he heard Banty Morgan, a dope addict. He played in wine rooms at the back of saloons where women could be found (women were not allowed to stand at bars). He settled in St. Louis around 1908 but traveled frequently to Chicago. There he heard and met Tony Jackson and Jelly Roll Morton. He thought Morton was better than Jackson, and he was, in turn, recalled by Jelly Roll as the best musician in town when Jelly visited St. Louis in the teens. He also considered Clarence Jones and Ed Hardin to be outstanding players. He arranged for John Stark and wrote much of the music with Tom Turpin for the Booker T. Washington Theatre shows. By that time he had not only learned to read music but also was considered the best sight reader of all the pianists in the district. Early in 1913 one of the Starks heard Matthews and offered him fifty dollars for each rag he turned in. Five eventually saw publication, but there had been more. He also arranged and wrote down music for other composers like Charley Thompson ("The Lily Rag") and Robert Hampton ("Cataract Rag"). He finally moved to Chicago in 1915, where he played at the Berea Presbyterian Church. At the end of the First World War he was offered the job of organist at the church in Cincinnati. He moved there permanently and in 1921 founded the Cosmopolitan School of Music, a conservatory where blacks could study classical music. He taught there until his death. The five "Pastimes" reveal his milieu in theater work; they are bold and dramatic, extraordinarily pianistic, and reflect the vaudeville side of ragtime, but within the polished Classic rag format. From the perspective of early Classic ragtime, these works are innovations in the idiom. However, some of the devices used in them were probably not new to the more articulate ragtime performers.

## Ragtime Compositions

"Pastime Rag No. 1," August 15, 1913, Stark Music Co., St. Louis

"Pastime Rag No. 2," not copyrighted, published 1913, Stark Music Co., St. Louis

"Pastime Rag No. 3," not copyrighted, published 1916, Stark Music Co., St. Louis

"Pastime Rag No. 5," not copyrighted, published 1918, Stark Music Co., St. Louis

"Pastime Rag No. 4," September 15, 1920, Stark Music Co., St. Louis

# Billy Mayerl

## (b. May 31, 1902, London; d. March 25, 1959, London)

A child prodigy, Mayerl was the son of an impoverished violinist. Formal training began at age five. He won a scholarship to Trinity College of Music, gave his first concert at age twelve at the Queen's Hall, and, after school, played evenings in movie houses accompanying the silent films. In 1920 he had his first work with an orchestra, where he came to the attention of American saxophonist Bert Ralton, who quickly hired him first as band pianist and then as solo pianist with the Savoy Havana Band, where Mayerl became famous. In 1923 he became involved with the musical theater as pianist, conductor, and finally composer. At the same time, he appeared on the British Broadcasting Corporation (BBC). In 1925 he began his recording career, which lasted almost until his death. In 1927 he started what was to become the most famous and successful undertaking of its kind: the Billy Mayerl School of Music, with branches all over the world. He published his own magazine and taught many thousands of pupils by the correspondence method. This included not only instruction booklets but recordings as well, where he personally demonstrated the various exercises and effects to be gained. In addition to his school and instruction books, Mayerl wrote in various music magazines for the amateur pianist over the years, giving tips for achieving professional competence.

> Syncopating on a piano is an art that cannot be picked up casually. It has got to be learned thoroughly. Maybe it seems funny to you that an hour or so playing scales and the good old exercises to be found in the tutors is a help for playing dance music. But it's more than a help. It's essential. But the embryo pianist won't always do this. He wants the fun without the work. Another grave fault of many embryo pianists is carelessness with the left hand. Most pianists play fairly accurately with the right hand. But the left is often a different proposition. So long as what they play in the bass doesn't actively interfere with the melody they rarely worry. Obviously they don't realize that a great deal of the effect of syncopated dance music is obtained with the left hand. The finest dance-band pianists have a wide span with the left, and can strike a chord of ten notes (or a "tenth" as it called technically) with ease and without any slurring. Would-be syncopated pianists should inscribe in large letters on a placard above their pianos: PRACTISE WITH YOUR LEFT HAND. There was once a young man who wrote to me: "How many weeks will it take me to learn to play jazz? I'm keen to become a famous dance-band pianist." Those of us who have been through the mill must find it a little amusing to encounter people coupling "weeks" and "fame" in one sentence! Because fame is something that's very illusory, anyway. Once I walked into a music store in a Northern town and asked for a copy of one of my compositions. Said the charming young assistant: "I've never heard of that title. You're mistaken." I assured her that there was no mistake. "Pardon me," she replied icily, 'but I stock all Mr. Mayerl's music." "Pardon me," I returned equally icily, "but I write all Mr. Mayerl's music!

He was a prolific composer with a predilection for naming his works after flowers. His most successful number, which became his theme song, was "Marigold," followed by "Hollyhock." Though his Novelty rags were called syncopated impressions and were patterned after Zez Confrey's enormous successes, Mayerl developed his own original phrases, harmonies, and rhythmical devices, as well as rich and beautiful melodies. During the Second World War he worked for the Light Music Unit of the BBC, broadcasting, recording, and composing. He died of a heart attack.

## Ragtime Compositions

"The Jazz Master," August 4, 1925, Keith-Prowse & Co., London

"All-of-a-Twist," August 21, 1925, Keith-Prowse & Co., London

"Eskimo Shivers," August 21, 1925, Keith-Prowse & Co., London

"The Jazz Mistress," September 25, 1925, Keith-Prowse & Co., London

"Virginia Creeper," October 12, 1925, Keith-Prowse & Co., London

"Jazzaristrix," November 4, 1925, Keith-Prowse & Co., London

"Antiquary," March 9, 1926, Keith-Prowse & Co., London

"Loose Elbows," March 9, 1926, Keith-Prowse & Co., London

"Jack-in-the-Box," July 15, 1926, Keith-Prowse & Co., London

"Sleepy Piano," July 15, 1926, Keith-Prowse & Co., London

"Puppets Suite" ("Punch," "Judy," "Golliwog"), June 1, 1927, Keith-Prowse & Co., London

"Honky Tonk," August 10, 1928, Keith-Prowse & Co., London

"Jasmine," August 23, 1929, Keith-Prowse & Co., London

# "Medic Rag" (Calvin Woolsey)

## April 13, 1910, Jerome H. Remick & Co., New York

Woolsey's most inspired piece and his most commercially successful. It is a memorable, thickly textured Folk rag in A flat and D flat. The trio contains his most complex use of syncopations, rarely encountered in the scores but sometimes found in the highly articulate and sophisticated ragtime performances of the Harlem Stride school.

# "Melodic Rag" (Eubie Blake)

## January 3, 1972, unpublished

Composed in October 1971, to furnish Blake with new material to perform at the annual Ragtime Society Bash (Eubie Blake Music EBM-1). This is one of his most sensitive and lyrical ragtime conceptions.

# "Melody Rag" (as Raymond Birch)

## January 3, 1911, Johnson Publishing Co., Kansas City, MO

Ragging the classics, based on Rubinstein's "Melody in F."

# "Meteor Rag" (Arthur C. Morse)

## Not copyrighted, published 1920, Walter Jacobs, Boston

An excellent rag with a most optimistic A section. However, section B is sparked by an extended descent of syncopated chromatic chords. Compare Dave Jasen's recording (Folkways FG-3561) with the piano-roll arrangement (Columbia 95129).

# "The Midnight Trot" (George L. Cobb)

## April 5, 1916, Will Rossiter, Chicago

Perhaps Cobb's best rag, with an inspired trio consisting of extremely adventurous key changes. For example, the second eight measures in section C, which is in the key of B flat, looks harmonically like this: B flat/ B flat/D/D-B$^7$/E$^7$/A$^7$/D-E flat$^{o7}$/C$^7$-F$^7$.

# Mills Music, Inc.

Jack Mills.

The most productive publishing house of the 1920s. The emergence of Jack Mills (1891–1979) in July 1919 at 152 West 45th Street, was due to his days as a song plugger in the Alley. Most recently, he had been professional manager of the McCarthy and Fisher Company. That experience spurred him to start his own firm. He established the genre of piano Novelty ragtime with his purchase of Zez Confrey's masterpiece, "Kitten on the Keys," in July 1921. This, along with nearly 100 other pieces in this idiom that he eventually issued, gave him preeminence as a publisher of Novelty rags. He also published many great blues and jazz numbers, such as "Down Hearted Blues," "I Just Want a Daddy I Can Call My Own," "Graveyard Dream Blues," "Farewell Blues," and "The Great White Way Blues."

In August 1928, the firm changed its name to Mills Music, Inc. The following year, in celebration of its tenth anniversary, Mills bought the catalogs of Gus Edwards Music, Stark and Cowan, Harold Dixon, McCarthy and Fisher, and Fred Fisher Music. In November 1931, Mills obtained the catalog of Waterson, Berlin and Snyder Company—minus the Berlin songs, which were already owned and published by Irving Berlin. From 1923 to 1932, the firm was located in the Mills Building, at 148–150 West 46th Street. Jack's brother, Irving, managed Duke Ellington, among other jazz performers, and the Mills firm published many of Ellington's compositions.

After World War II, the firm focused on classical music instructional publishing under the name of Belwin-Mills, Inc. Its back catalog is now part of Warner/Chappell Music.

Mills Music ad.

# "The Minstrel Man" (J. Russel Robinson)

## July 27, 1911, Stark Music Co., St. Louis

Section A is reminiscent of the A section in "Maple Leaf" but is a creative reworking of the phrasing. C and D are folk strains, with D's stomping finish especially reminiscent of Brun Campbell's playing.

# "Missouri Romp" (Arthur Marshall)

## 1966, published in *They All Played Ragtime*, 3d ed., 1966, Oak Publications

The soulful, spiritual overtones of Marshall's work were never stronger and reach a truly masterful height in the B section. The trio modulates to the key of C from E flat by way of an eight-measure interlude and a four-measure vamp, marked "clap hands."

# "Modesty Rag" (James Scott)

## September 15, 1920, Stark Music Co., St. Louis

Section A uses varied bass patterns to excellent effect. Starting with the sixth and eighth measures in the B section and continuing with the second, fourth, and tenth measures of the trio, Scott employs phrasing in the right hand that became popular in piano-roll performances of popular songs.

# "Modulations" (Clarence M. Jones)

## April 17, 1923, Will Rossiter, Chicago

A tour de force by one of the few black Novelty writers (Autograph). He was a thoroughly schooled musician and a popular piano-roll artist. Taught famous blues pianist–accompanist James Blythe.

# Max Morath

## (b. October 1, 1926, Colorado Springs)

As a pianist, singer, and actor Morath uses all of his talents to project his enthusiasm for the ragtime era. He is intrigued not only by ragtime but also by the dances and songs of the turn of the century. He is also fascinated by its humor as found in the columns of the daily newspaper. Putting all this together, he has spent his career selling the entire age to his fellow Americans. He plays college campuses, gives concerts, and makes up theatrical shows, shoving in plenty of social commentary to illumine the music. Morath is a superb showman and has brought his considerable skills to create a bygone time when ragtime was king. He was the first to embrace television and produced, wrote, and starred in *The Ragtime Era*, a twelve-part series for National Educational Television during the 1959–1960 season. It was so successful that he was asked to do another one of fifteen programs called *Turn of the Century,* which aired during the 1961–1962 season. He incorporated chunks for his off-Broadway show, *Max Morath at the Turn of the Century,* after which he toured the country for three years. Among his many record albums over the years, he put his show onto wax, which was a good seller for RCA Victor. Although Morath includes rags in his show and at ragtime festivals, he is by no means a ragtime pianist. When he entertains, almost like no one else he presents a world that includes ragtime. He is a most wonderful entertainer. In 1999, he finally brought it altogether in his remarkable self-published scrapbook, *The Road to Ragtime: The Book.*

# Ferdinand Joseph La Menthe (Jelly Roll Morton)

**(b. October 20, 1890, New Orleans;
d. July 10, 1941, Los Angeles)**

Jelly Roll Morton circa 1921

Brought to New Orleans as a child to live with his grandmother, Morton first learned guitar and then, at age ten, learned to play the piano at St. Joseph's Catholic School. In 1902, at age twelve, he played in the district known as Storyville and became one of the top "professors," earning a minimum of $100 a night. From 1904 on, beginning with the St. Louis World's Fair, he traveled around the country, having a good time, picking up local musical styles, playing pool, hustling for women, singing, appearing in vaudeville as part of a comedy team, and playing piano. He met and won the admiration of Artie Matthews in St. Louis in 1911 and impressed budding musicians in New York the same year. He then went to Chicago where he led his own band until 1915, moved to San Francisco and Los Angeles where he attended the Exposition and ran a club, and then moved on to Vancouver, Alaska, Wyoming, and Denver, frequented bars in Tijuana and San Diego, and finally returned to Chicago in 1923, where he made his first records. He became staff arranger and composer for the Melrose Brothers Music Company. He organized the Red Hot Peppers (one of the greatest jazz bands of all time) for the Victor Talking Machine Company and made a series of outstanding recordings. In 1928 he came to New York City, where he organized other bands for touring the East and Midwest. Morton made more recordings, accompanied singers, played in revues, and entered the cosmetic business to sell a hair preparation. He settled in Washington, D.C., at the end of 1936 and worked a dive variously

Jelly Roll Morton, 1938.

called Blue Moon Inn, Music Box, and Jungle Inn. From May through July 1938, he made an extraordinary series of recordings for the Folk Music Archive of the Library of Congress, talking, playing, and singing—an autobiography on disc, from which Alan Lomax wrote the best biography of Morton, *Mister Jelly Roll* (Duell, Sloan and Pearce, 1950). The recordings have been issued in several editions, the most recent (2005) appearing in eight CDs on the Rounder label. With the help of Roy Carew, he formed the Tempo Music Publishing Company to issue his songs and instrumental numbers. Looking for a comeback, he stayed in New York City from late 1938 until 1940, when he made his last recordings—both solo and with a band—and appeared on radio shows. Late in 1940 he made a final move to Los Angeles where he became chronically ill and died without making his dreamed-of comeback.

Morton was a unique figure in American music. Everything he did was sparked with originality. He created a style of playing that could encompass other individual jazz musicians' styles and could retain his own conception. He could also take a published piano rag and transform it into *Jelly Roll* style. His sound reflected his upbringing in cosmopolitan New Orleans, where folk music from Africa, the West Indies, Portugal, Spain, France, England, and Italy abounded, mixed with the blues and the syncopated sounds of ragtime. Two fine examples of this transformation exist on phonograph records. One is his version of Scott Joplin's "Maple Leaf Rag" ("They All Played the Maple Leaf Rag," Herwin 401), and the other is a swinging version of Joplin's "Original Rags" ("Black & White Piano Ragtime," Biograph BLP-12047).

Of all the ragtime composers, Morton had many more diverse moods in his works than anyone else. His use of sixths in the left hand, an old midwestern ragtime device, provided uncommon voicings that lent a touch of the unusual and thereby created greater interest for the listener. Morton was also the first ragtimer to consider the audience and to ensure continued interest in his performances by creating unexpected rhythmic patterns within a performance and by continually improvising the same section of a tune over and over. However, unlike later jazz musicians, Morton's variations were carefully built on each section in the rag.

He had definite ideas about his music and was the most articulate ragtimer and jazz musician of his time. He did nothing—either as composer or performer—that he could not explain. Nothing was haphazard or accidental. Every musical device he used was well thought out and deliberately done. He achieved his distinctive piano sound by trying not to sound like a typical pianist. His idea was to imitate an entire jazz band; his extraordinary left hand not only kept a steady rhythm, like a tuba or string bass, but also incorporated the counterpoint of a trombone. His right hand alternated the clear-cut melody line as played by the trumpet with the embellishments and flourishes of the clarinet. To complete the band, Morton in performance usually had a drumstick placed in his inner left shoe to beat against his bench or chair while playing.

A large body of recorded work, all available now on CD, clearly illustrates the magnitude of Morton's understanding of music and the wide scope of his interpretations. Especially interesting are the alternate takes of a tune that show just how creative he was as a performer. No less interesting is listening to the same rag recorded years apart. Morton matured musically as he got older, bringing new meaning and a fresh understanding to his older rags.

Because Morton did not write down his rags the way he played them, and since most of them were never published during his lifetime, copyright dates for these numbers reveal little. It really made no difference if he composed a rag in 1906, recorded it in 1923, and had it published a year or ten years later. That rag could not have been written by anyone else at any time because Morton's entire musical outlook was original and unique.

With the Novelty and Stride stages of ragtime, Morton combined his composition development with his performing style, giving uniformity to his entire work. It can be said that everything Morton played was his own creation, if not in melody—harmony–rhythm—then in interpretation. More than anyone else, Morton embodied ragtime, an original American art form, as it was conceived in performance. Morton created a way of arranging that encompassed other players' ideas yet retained his own conceptions. Morton's piano style was distinctive and, once heard, was never forgotten or confused with anyone else's. He had definite ideas about his music and was the most articulate jazz musician of his time.

Morton, playing and acting in a vaudeville comedy sketch, was the first jazz musician to travel extensively around the country, from the time he was fourteen until he settled in Chicago in 1923, at the age of thirty-three. There he became an arranger and composer for the newly formed Melrose Brothers Music Company. Although he had had one piece published earlier ("The 'Jelly Roll' Blues," Will Rossiter, September 1915), his steady publishing, recording, and performing careers dated from his arrival in Chicago. Encouraged by the sales of "Wolverine Blues" (1923), Walter Melrose set up recording sessions with Gennett Records of Richmond, Indiana. This company eventually recorded every major Dixieland jazz band—with the sole exception of the Original Dixieland Jazz Band—and most of the important individual jazz musicians of the 1920s.

Between July 1923 and June 1924, Morton recorded nineteen now-classic piano solos, sixteen of them his own compositions: All of these were eventually published by Melrose. The solo piano recordings were the start of his legend among his peers. His publications are important not only as vehicles for himself but also as permanent parts of the jazz repertoire. The majority of his work was published by Melrose between 1923 and 1928.

"King Porter Stomp" was recorded more often by Morton and others than any of his other compositions. It was the first piano solo (Gennett 5289) he recorded at his first solo session on July 17, 1923, and it was among the last (General 4005) he recorded in his last solo session on December 14, 1939. This work started the swing era, when Fletcher Henderson arranged it for Benny Goodman's band in 1935 (Victor

25090). It has the distinction of being in the ragtimer's repertoire as well as those of Dixieland bands and swing bands. Melrose published it in 1924.

"Milenberg Joys" led the eight Morton tunes published in 1925. Although it is a standard today and has been recorded by dance and jazz bands through the years, it is the only one not recorded by Morton himself. His famous rags "Kansas City Stomp" and "Grandpa's Spells," as well as "Chicago Break Down," "Shreveport Stomp," "New Orleans Blues," "London Blues," and "Tom Cat Blues," were all issued in that year.

Morton published six compositions in 1926. "Sweetheart O' Mine" was a reworking of his earlier "Frog-I-More Rag," the lead sheet of which was entered for copyright in 1918. "Stratford Hunch" was the last of his original piano solos to be issued. Melrose obtained a contract with the Victor Company for Morton to record with a seven-piece band of his choosing. It was to be an ideal band, for Morton was allowed to request his favorite musicians, those usually working for other leaders. In an unusual arrangement, Morton handpicked his band for recordings only and called his group the Red Hot Peppers. He did not have a performance band at the time. Even as the personnel of the Red Hot Peppers changed during its four years of recording, the group never failed to provide stimulating jazz. The remaining tunes published in the exciting year of 1926 came from the recordings of the Red Hot Peppers: "Black Bottom Stomp," "Sidewalk Blues," "Dead Man Blues," and "Cannon Ball Blues."

Two old solos and four new ones account for his 1927 output. "The Pearls," with its clever use of the rudimentary timekeeping of the left hand, and "Mr. Jelly Lord" were finally issued. "Billy Goat Stomp," "Jungle Blues," "Wild Man Blues," and "Hyena Stomp" were other Peppers tunes. In 1928, Melrose published "Boogaboo" and "Georgia Swing," a reworking of an earlier Melrose tune, Santo Pecora's "She's Crying for Me."

Morton reminisced, played, and sang his life story to Lomax for the Library of Congress during a six-week period in May and June 1938. His reminiscences stand as the greatest audio documentary of a jazz musician ever recorded. He made a few final recordings during the 1940s while living in New York but did not live to see the Dixieland revival of the post-World War II period.

## Ragtime Compositions

"Bert Williams," June 29, 1948, unpublished
"Chicago Breakdown," January 12, 1926, Melrose Bros., Chicago
"The Finger Breaker," November 23, 1942, unpublished
"Frances," January 10, 1931, unpublished
"Freakish," September 28, 1929, unpublished
"Frog-I-More Rag," May 15, 1918, unpublished
"Grandpa's Spells," August 20, 1923, Melrose Bros., Chicago

"Kansas City Stomp," August 20, 1923, Melrose Bros., Chicago
"King Porter Stomp," December 6, 1924, Melrose Bros., Chicago
"The Naked Dance," December 20, 1939, Tempo Music, Washington, D.C.
"The Pearls," August 20, 1923, Melrose Bros., Chicago
"Pep," January 10, 1931, unpublished
"Perfect Rag," not copyrighted or published

# "The Music Box Rag" (Luckey Roberts)

## October 23, 1914, Jos. W. Stern & Co., New York

Though supposedly an imitation of its name, it clearly illustrates Luckey's melodic flair and skill at writing for musical shows.

# "Muslin Rag" (Mel B. Kaufman)

## December 16, 1918, Forster Music Publisher, Chicago

A fine rag by a leading composer of dance tunes during the teens specializing in one-steps. The B section has a bizarre ending that sounds like a silent-movie accompaniment to a scene of sudden mayhem. The Columbia recording uses a slide whistle to heighten the effect (Columbia A-6084).

# "My Pet" (Zez Confrey)

## March 11, 1921, Jack Mills, Inc., New York

This is Confrey's first essay in what was to become the Novelty ragtime idiom. Ragtime's ebullient feelings are obtained compositionally in the major tonality; consider, then, Confrey's innovation of starting the first section in a minor mode, but with feelings that are happy and bright. In its final printed form, it appears as a rag in four sections. However, in the July 1918 roll version, five sections are found (QRS 100827). He dropped the original fourth section when printed and in all recordings on disc. A unique rag and the first in the Novelty ragtime style.

# N

## "The Naked Dance" (Jelly Roll Morton)

### December 20, 1939, Tempo Music Publishing Co., Washington, DC

This was written by Morton after Roy Carew recalled to him a "ratty strain" that Tony Jackson and other Storyville professors used to accompany the dances of the upstairs girls in the houses. It is Morton's most haunting and exotic recollection of Storyville (Circle JM 85). The later 1939 version (General 4002) evokes a sensuous mood that he achieved again only in his best syncopated tangos such as "Creepy Feeling."

## "Nappy Lee" (Joe Jordan)

### December 15, 1903, James E. Agnew, Des Moines

Named after a trombonist associate who was notorious for his unkempt hair. B opens with part of the chromatic descent that became famous in Louis Chauvin's "Heliotrope Bouquet" (1907). The C section recalls Tom Turpin in his use of bass triplets (see "Bowery Buck") and in the general melodic style.

## "New Era Rag" (James Scott)

### June 1, 1919, Stark Music Co., St. Louis

The B section is a reworking of the B section of Scott Joplin's "Cascades." The C section is a tour de force and is a fine contrast to B: an answer, in effect, to Joplin's pianistics. John Stark adapted an earlier cover for this tune, Ed Hallway's "Tango Tea," which accounts for the potted-palm dance salon of the title page.

## "The New Russian Rag" (George L. Cobb)

### May 16, 1923, Will Rossiter, Chicago

A more pyrotechnical conception of "Russian Rag," reflecting musical changes that occurred from the Advanced rag to the Novelty rag (see Buck Johnson's piano roll, Vocalstyle 50409).

## "Nickel in the Slot" (Zez Confrey)

### April 6, 1923, Leo Feist Inc., New York

A brilliant Novelty rag that imitates a nickelodeon—an automated player piano machine—that frequently breaks down. The third section is the beauty with a marvelous break. Compare Zez Confrey and his orchestra's July 1924 recording (Victor 19430) with Willie Eckstein's November 1923 piano solo (Okeh 40018).

## "Nonpareil" (Scott Joplin)

### Not copyrighted, published 1907, Stark Music Co., St. Louis

The A section is surprisingly gentle and flows into the B section, which contains a very busy left hand, interspersing rapid sixteenth notes between the conventional octave-chord-octave-chord approach. In an effort to unify this rag, Joplin used the same endings in both the B and D sections. Section D has a marvelously pretty melody and an infectious rhythm.

## "Nothin'" (Luckey Roberts)

### Not copyrighted or published

A great rag and the last word in cutting contest pieces from around 1908, Roberts dug it out of his archives just for the March 1958 recording session (Good Time Jazz M-12035). The C section is outstanding. The first time through he plays it lyrically punctuated with his famous quick and furious treble runs. The repeat is a whirling stride finish.

## Novelty Ragtime, 1918–1928

Novelty piano ragtime was the product of American pianists with classical music training who originally arranged and performed popular songs on piano rolls. The idea was developed from hand-played piano roll

Sid Reinherz.

artists who were ordered to make full, rich arrangements so the player-roll customers felt they had gotten their money's worth. Using their piano-roll tricks, they put together an extremely complex rhythmic and harmonic series of progressions that demanded the greatest technical skill to perform. Just as Advanced ragtime composers were ignoring the at-home amateur pianists, Novelty pianists similarly put forth their efforts for themselves as special material. The big surprise, then, was the astounding hit in Zez Confrey's warm-up exercise, "Kitten on the Keys," which, like the earlier ragtime hit, Joplin's "Maple Leaf Rag," established and maintained this latest development of ragtime. Decidedly not dance music, "Kitten on the Keys" in some strange fashion appealed to the piano-playing public, who avidly bought the sheet music, piano rolls, and recordings. It is among the top three rags in the number of recordings made. The pattern of the Novelty rag follows the Popular rag: Each has three sections. The distinctive sound of the Novelty rag is a combination of the influence of French Impressionists Claude Debussey and Maurice Ravel with contrasting rhythms as used by the roll arrangers. Chromaticism is at the heart of the Novelty tradition, and the use of the whole-tone scale may have evolved from this, as it appears within the chromatic scale: In a sequence of ascending chromatic major thirds the top note of every other interval forms the whole-tone scale. Probably the most striking hallmark of Novelty writing is the use of consecutive fourths in the melody voicing.

The two publishers who consistently published and urged this new ragtime on the public were Jack Mills and Jack Robbins. It was Jack Mills who was first given the opportunity to introduce the Novelty rag to the public when he was told about the extraordinary musician at QRS who had produced an amazing roll of his highly original rag and who had newly recorded it for the Brunswick label. And so on July 8, 1921, Jack Mills issued Confrey's "Kitten on the Keys." Within the year, it had sold over a million copies and became the prototype for all that was to follow throughout the 1920s. Mills did not present "Kitten" or the five other Confrey rags as either rags or popular music. Instead, he proudly presented them printed in stately grey with black rococo borders as classical pieces.

St. Louis was the center of ragtime at the beginning of the twentieth century, but Chicago took over with the advent of the Novelty rag. The two leading piano-roll companies, QRS and Imperial, had their offices and factories there. The two leading recording companies, Victor Talking Machine Company and Columbia Graphophone, had recording studios there, as well as the fledgling Brunswick–Balke–Collander Company, the experimental Autograph, and the on-the-move Okeh Record Company.

The Novelty rag's appearance coincided with the growth of the record industry. This is why so many rags appear only on recordings performed by their composers. The industry was now in the million-dollar category and could afford the high-priced vaudeville talent, and pianists began recording substantially.

The same could then be said of the player-piano rolls, for during the twenties the peak was reached in roll manufacture. Therefore, it is no surprise that many great Novelty rags appear only on piano rolls played mostly by their composers.

# O

## "Oh You Devil" (Ford T. Dabney)

### July 2, 1909, Maurice Shapiro, New York

A sophisticated rag with extensive use of nonchord tones. The trio harmony creates an unusual effect with a continued emphasis (in the key of C) on A in the melody—first as the sixth of tonic and then as a fifth combined with the ninth (E) over a $D^7$, then as a ninth over a $G^7$, and then again as the sixth of C. The home key of C is not stressed at all until the fifteenth measure.

## "Oh! Willie, Play that Thing" (Bill Krenz)

### May 23, 1952, Mills Music, New York

This was the first of Krenz's (1899–1980) rags during the 1950s. He recorded it in June 1952 (MGM 11264). He was a studio musician in Chicago, after having a career as a band pianist in the orchestras of the likes as Ray Miller, Paul Biese, and Jean Goldkette. His '50s compositions combine the easy listening of the melodious Tin Pan Alley rags with the breaks of the later and more complex Novelty rags.

## Philmore (Phil) Ohman

### (b. October 7, 1896, New Britain, Connecticut; d. August 8, 1954, Santa Monica)

After high school, Ohman became a piano demonstrator and then assistant organist in New York City. He arranged tunes and composed for QRS piano rolls in 1919 and made tours as accompanist with concert

Phil Ohman.

singers. He formed a wildly successful duo piano team with Victor Arden (Lewis J. Fuiks). They were perhaps the best-known duo in the business; they made rolls and recordings, were featured in early Gershwin Broadway musicals (as the entire orchestra), and appeared on their own radio show. From 1934 to 1946 Ohman led his own orchestra at various restaurants and cafes in Hollywood. A superb pianist who wrote brilliant rags, he employed an interesting compositional device that harked back to the Folk ragtime days; as a help in unifying a rag, he would bring back the last half of the first strain at various points.

## Ragtime Compositions

"Dixie Kisses," not copyrighted or published

"Try and Play It," August 5, 1922, Richmond-Robbins, New York

"Up and Down the Keys," September 30, 1922, Richmond-Robbins, New York

"Piano Pan," October 10, 1922, Richmond-Robbins, New York

"Sparkles," June 12, 1935, Robbins Music, New York

Ohman and Arden.

# "The Old Home Rag" (Joseph Lamb)

### *Ragtime Treasures,* 1964, Mills Music, Inc., New York

Another adventurous ragtime experiment predating the more orthodox Scott Joplin influence. Lamb draws on another Tin Pan Alley device as he climaxes the rag with a syncopated transformation of "Home Sweet Home."

# "The Old Professor" (Dick Hyman)

### April 18, 1955, Hollis Music, New York

This was one of several rags composed by Hyman during the 1950s. This one was published under his own name. Usually, for ragtime, Dick hid under several pseudonyms: Knuckles O'Toole, Willie "The Rock" Knox, and J. Gaines. He recorded this with his trio (MGM K-1195l).

## "Old Virginia Rag" (Clyde Douglass)

### December 19, 1907, W. C. Parker Music Co., New York

As scored, one of the great throwaways of ragtime, as only the trio is repeated.

## "Omeomy" (Roy Bargy)

### Not copyrighted or published

The A section is the reverse of "Pianoflage" and, like that great rag, is quite a remarkable achievement of composition. It is a pity it was never written down and published; it is available on a hand-played roll by the composer (Imperial 513980).

## "On the Pike" (James Scott)

### April 13, 1904, Dumars Music Co., Carthage, MO

The A section starts out like the B section of "At a Georgia Camp Meeting" but includes a vigorous left hand that is extended in an unusual C section of thirty-two measures. Of these first three rags published by Dumars, this one makes a more complete break with Scott Joplin and is the most original of the three, foretelling later Scott rags. This one was dedicated to visitors at the 1904 St. Louis World's Fair and was named after the amusement section of the fair where most of the ragtime pianists were playing.

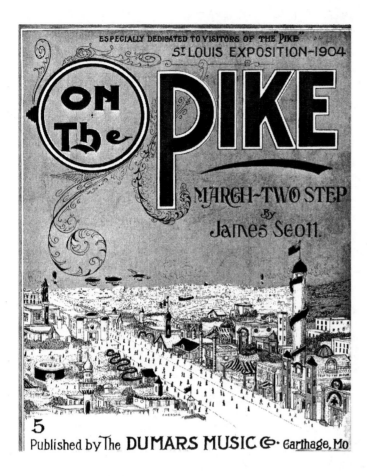

## "One o' Them Things!" (James Chapman and Leroy Smith)

### Not copyrighted, published 1904, Jos. Placht & Son, St. Louis

The most fascinating of all St. Louis rags published by small firms. Section A is the first scored twelve-bar blues found to date. B and C melodically and harmonically have an air of Scott Joplin, which is not surprising as both Joplin and John Stark were known to Chapman. The latter published his march, "Military Parade," for which Joplin did the orchestration. In one of his ledgers, Stark commented, "Its composer was a real genius but sad to say died suddenly while the piece was in press. This march was his idol but like many another he never saw the fruition of his hope." This last comment was probably a reflection on the many talents wasted in the sporting world. This rag was kept alive by its co-composer, Leroy Smith, who is listed as having performed it at a birthday party, as chronicled in the May 25, 1907, issue of the *St. Louis Palladium*.

## "Ophelia Rag" (James Scott)

### June 6, 1910, Stark Music Co., St. Louis

Scott made direct use of folk elements of pianistic ragtime. The chromatic ascent in the A section is identical with Tom Turpin's dramatic use of it in his "Ragtime Nightmare." The B section is outstanding both for its melody and for its variation of the B section of "Maple Leaf Rag." The C section has a most unusual left hand, which is not merely used as an arresting device as in "Great Scott Rag" but as an integral part of the melody.

# Orchestrated Ragtime

Orchestrated ragtime is as old as published ragtime. The 1897 cover of *Mississippi Rag*—the first published composition calling itself a rag—states, "The First Rag-Time Two-Step Ever Written and First Played by Krell's Orchestra, Chicago."

Brass bands flourished and became the staple of the musical life in the United States from the Civil War through World War I. These brass bands were sometimes called military bands. Every town and village had at least one such amateur organization that gave Sunday concerts in the village green, all dressed up in their smart and snappy uniforms. Among the outstanding professional concert bands were those conducted by Patrick Gilmore, John Philip Sousa, and Patrick Conway. When Sousa toured Europe at the beginning of the twentieth century, he featured the latest American music—cakewalks and rags—which in turn received wild approbation from audiences wherever he played.

The era of vaudeville (1892–1932) dominated the entertainment field, and everyone in vaudeville used this happy, zesty music, whether as a background for their acrobatics, juggling, and dancing or as the main ingredient to their act; they performed it on their particular instruments, especially as their walk-on and exit music.

Though ragtime was primarily piano music, the more popular rags were almost always immediately published in arrangements for mandolin, banjo, guitar, orchestra, and military band. The two largest recording companies, Victor and Columbia, had their house bands record rags as soon as they were available from the publishers. Sometimes Walter B. Rogers for Victor and Charles A. Prince for Columbia made special arrangements for their bands; others used the publishers' house arrangers. Sousa's opposition to making his own records and instead giving permission for some of his band members to do so under the Sousa name gave lead virtuoso Sousa trombonist Arthur Pryor (1870–1942) his start. Pryor not only conducted but also arranged the music to be recorded by the dozen members of the large Sousa organization. Within a few years, Pryor left Sousa to organize his own band, which recorded exclusively for the Victor Talking Machine Company.

The end of the First World War heralded the jazz age, which inaugurated the era of ballroom dancing. In big cities, fancy restaurants featured orchestras for listening while eating, and later at night for supper parties bands played for dancing.

Jazz bands from the start consisted of from five to nine pieces jamming together on a given tune that could be punctuated with solos of varying instruments. The basic five pieces consisted of cornet, trombone, clarinet, piano, and drums. To this was added a banjo, tuba, alto saxophone, and a tenor saxophone. It was when doubling and trebling of the same instruments came into vogue that arrangements were necessary so that each group of the same instrument or group of related instruments would not clash with each other. The famous dance and larger jazz bands hired their own arrangers to exploit the individual members of the band and also to create a unique band sound.

As ragtime was part of the popular music scene, it was only natural that the bands included ragtime in their repertoire. The recordings of dance and jazz bands illustrated how creative the band arrangers were in orchestrating the piano rags for their organizations.

# "Oriental Blues" (Jack Newlon)

## May 25, 1933, self, Glenside, PA

Considering ragtime composing and publishing was over by 1929, the publication of Newlon's 1933 rag was late. He was an organist at a local movie house and a piano teacher. What is so unusual about this late rag is that its first section is practically a direct steal of the first section from the Will Donaldson–George Gershwin "Rialto Ripples Rag" of 1917. However, this theme is better suited in this context and is a much neater and original rag overall. Its fabulously happy-go-lucky performance by Newlon's pupil, Philadelphia television studio musician Tony DeSimone, is the exact recording (Decca 29183) used by television comedian Ernie Kovacs as his theme song when he originated his NBC TV show from Philadelphia in the 1951–52 season. This rag was arranged for publication by pop songwriter Billy James.

# "Original Rags" (Scott Joplin, arr. Charles N. Daniels)

## March 15, 1899, Carl Hoffman, Kansas City, MO

A bewitching, irresistible rag that illustrates his genius with folk materials. Until this time, most rag medleys consisted of popular "coon" songs arranged for piano. He transformed this format in his debut publication from a coon song medley to a real piano ragtime medley, clearly establishing his higher musical ideals of syncopated composition. The A section has a decided cakewalk feeling mingled with the minstrel banjo pickings. The D section is remarkable for its harmonic similarity to H. O. Wheeler's "A Virginny Frolic" (A section), by a strange coincidence published in 1898 by Hoffman. Could Daniels have taken it and syncopated it, or did Scott Joplin?

# Vess L. Ossman

## (b. August 21, 1868, Hudson, New York; d. December 8, 1923, Minneapolis)

Ossman's father, of German extraction, owned a bakery and raised a large family. Ossman learned to play the five-string banjo when he was twelve years old, and by 1896 he was making cylinder recordings. A year later, when Emile Berliner started manufacturing flat discs, Ossman was among the first to record for the newly invented gramophone. Not only were his solo recordings popular, but his agreement to accompany Arthur Collins, one of the most famous and prolifically recorded tenors of the early days of recording, also gave him an even wider audience. With his tour of England in 1900 and again in 1903, his reputation and recordings became worldwide. He played for President Theodore Roosevelt as well as two command performances for King Edward VII of England. Fred Van Eps attested to the fact that Ossman was the finest banjoist of his time when he said, "Ossman had a certain rhythmic facility that I don't think any other banjoist has ever equaled."

Vess Ossman.

In October 1903 in the first issue of the English magazine *B.M.G.*, a journal devoted to the banjo, mandolin, and guitar, Ossman was interviewed and said that practice is what made him so good: "Ten hours a day for the first three years and at least four hours a day thereafter." He commented about recording techniques, "You have to pick hard and keep the same volume of tone all through a piece, combined with absolute accuracy. That makes a superb foundation on which to put light and shade for concert work and fairly kill nervousness. Most players prefer the keys of G and C; I do not. My favorite is F, and I always like to play in flats—they are not only softer, but higher. I also always like to employ octaves freely—of course, avoiding consecutive octaves in my harmonical progressions." When asked if he elevates his bass strings, he said, "Absolutely never. After reasonable practice it is just as easy to play octaves on a bass string tuned to C as to D, though I grant that the opinion of many of the best players differs from mine on this point. I have one habit which is in direct violation with conventional tenets: I make notes on the fifth string. I mean to say, I will play A, B, C above the clef and higher notes on the high G string. I am also addicted to grace notes and appogiatura, and for these, when I can, I like to use the fifth string. The snap comes especially clean from it, because it is technically so taut." Asked if he went in for double fingering, he replied, "I think it is imperative." He also complained that other banjoists neglected the metronome. "It is the playing of marches, two-steps, cake walks, etc. in unsuitable time which make them sound ridiculous."

Not being content with accompanying famous singers and recording banjo solos, Ossman formed trios, the most famous of which was the Ossman–Dudley Trio, which started recording in 1906. It consisted of Ossman, Audley Dudley on mandolin, and Roy Butin on harp-guitar. They were extremely successful, and their most popular recording was their version of "St. Louis Tickle" (Victor 16092).

Vess Ossman record label.

From 1910, Ossman concentrated on playing in hotels in the Midwest and touring Europe. As a result, he recorded less frequently than he previously had. Living in New York City made him available to record for the major labels, but when he moved to Indianapolis, he cut himself off from the companies he had contributed to for so long—Victor Talking Machine Co., Columbia Graphophone Co., and Edison. Of later years (1917–1923), he did not practice as much as he should have. Though he made a few solo recordings, the majority featured his Banjo Orchestra. He played vaudeville houses in the Midwest, collapsed while playing a charity show at a theater in Minneapolis and died a week later. He is buried in Valhalla Cemetery in St. Louis.

# P

## "Palm Leaf Rag" (Scott Joplin)

### November 14, 1903, Victor Kremer Co., Chicago

A fitting companion to "Weeping Willow," this one shares a grace and elegance along with a sophisticated use of anticipatory syncopation (most noticeable in the C section). Asymmetrical phrasing—found not only in the A section here but also in the D section of "Weeping Willow"—contributes to the darker emotions expressed here and contrasts nicely with the lighter content in the B and C sections.

## "Pan-Am Rag" (Tom Turpin)

### June 8, 1914, *They All Played Ragtime*, 3d ed., 1966, Oak Publications, New York

Arranged by Classic rag composer–pianist Arthur Marshall, who worked for Turpin at his Eureka Saloon. It has an eccentric format, highlighted by typical Turpin pianistics in section B in the form of quick arpeggios alternating between bass and treble. Written for the Pan-American Exposition of 1914, most of the rag has an implied Latin American tango rhythm and feeling.

## "Panama Rag" (Cy Seymour)

### August 15, 1904, Albright Music Co., Chicago

This is the composer's most popular rag. Measures 5–8 in section B come from the ragtime folkways, as they turn up in an obscure Florence, Alabama, 1913 rag by D. W. Batsell, "Sweety, Won't You Be Kind to Me."

# "Paragon Rag" (Scott Joplin)

## October 30, 1909, Seminary Music Co., New York

The A section harks back to the A section of "Weeping Willow Rag," reminiscent of the plantation era. Section B carries us on to the Sedalia ragtime days, adding a break in measures 3 and 4 that foreshadows a device used by the Novelty rag composers (see Zez Confrey's "Kitten on the Keys"). C section is interesting not only for its block-chorded left hand (similar to measures 9–16 of the A section of "Maple Leaf Rag") but also for using melodies called for in *Treemonisha*. Section D combines the flag-waving of the older days with a sophistication found from 1907 onward—a restrained but grandly triumphal ending.

# "Paramount Rag" (James Scott)

## November 24, 1917, Stark Music Co., St. Louis

A very ambitious rag that combines most features of the composer. Section A has a brassy, almost funky quality, making use of a pianistic device considered under "Paragon Rag" and "Kitten on the Keys." Section B takes Scott's echo one step further, with two repeats of the one measure idea, ranging high up the keyboard. These dramatic register shifts seem difficult for piano but are much easier for a multiple-keyboard theater organ such as one used by Scott. The C section is a surprise in its almost uninterrupted lyrical flow.

# "Pastime Rag No. 1" (Artie Matthews)

## August 15, 1913, Stark Music Co., St. Louis

An exposition of breaks, featured in all three sections. The unusual and delightful A section was bodily stolen by Muriel Pollock for her A section of "Rooster Rag." Section B is basically a Folk rag-style circle of fifths, but here it is arranged with the finesse characteristic of the composer. C is the climax, with a slurred effect in the right hand that is traded for a walking broken-octave bass pattern in the variation. Those broken octaves hint of the boogie-woogie bass, which would be prominently featured throughout the twenties.

# "Pastime Rag No. 2" (Artie Matthews)

## Not copyrighted, published 1913, Stark Music Co., St. Louis

This was probably used in one of the musical dance routines at the Booker T. Washington Theatre or Princess Roadhouse, for which Matthews composed the scores along with Tom Turpin. The A section features a break of chromatic descending triads as does the same section of "No.1." The bass line is largely in sixteenths, a variation on the regular ragtime bass pattern of octaves alternating with chords. The rest of the rag is lightly syncopated and suggests dancing. C has a stop-time pattern in which the pianist is instructed to clap hands—a popular performing trick with ragtime pianists.

# "Pastime Rag No. 3" (Artie Matthews)

## Not copyrighted, published 1916, Stark Music Co., St. Louis

A beautiful, reflective tango in section A climaxed with syncopated bass octaves. The B section is an interlude that complements the mood in the relative minor. C has thickly textured treble chords, rich harmonies, and a fine stop-time effect. Section D has a repeated rhythmic figure largely on tonic-dominant harmonies.

# "Pastime Rag No. 4" (Artie Matthews)

## September 15, 1920, Stark Music Co., St. Louis

The most advanced of the five, Stark held back on this until the last. Section A is the most arresting by the use of tone clusters; the major and minor seconds add much dissonance to a basic dominant-tonic harmony. B is dramatically pianistic with a descending series of sixteenths in triplet formation, complemented by the same phrasing in a long, chromatic, ascending bass run to cap the section. The chromaticism is climaxed in C as the melody rises in half steps from the bass register over a repeated low F pedal tone. Truly an innovative rag.

# "Pastime Rag No. 5" (Artie Matthews)

## Not copyrighted, published 1918, Stark Music Co., St. Louis

A section is a bright tango in the minor mode. Section B employs a mixture of standard Popular ragtime with the bird calls so loved by James Scott and Joseph Lamb. The C section is a development from B using a different minor at the sixth measure. Section D starts off as a variation of the A section of "Maple Leaf Rag" but continues the developmental feeling, beginning with tonic-dominant harmonies, as in sections B and C, but substituting a different idea in measures 6 through 9. It is the most heavily textured of the "Pastimes" and, in the fashion of many late rags, alternates the dotted rhythm with a straight one (here in D), simulating a looser swing (see J. Russel Robinson's "Eccentric Rag" for a varied use of this rhythm).

# "Patricia Rag" (Joseph Lamb)

## November 19, 1916, Stark Music Co., St. Louis

The A section is a clever working of its counterpart in the "Maple Leaf Rag." It also contains two of Joseph Lamb's creative devices: a use of sequences to develop the mood and a characteristic diminished seventh chord that appears in many of his best rags. The trio is especially original in measures 1, 2, and 3, which contain one descending melody line, but before completion an ascending melody line overlaps in a broad sweep.

# "Peace and Plenty Rag" (James Scott)

## December 1, 1919, Stark Music Co., St. Louis

A peculiar mixture of march-like features and typical late James Scott ragtime complexities. He even makes use of the old march-styled interlude or dogfight before the repeat of C.

# "Peaceful Henry" (Edward Harry Kelly)

## Not copyrighted, published 1901, Carl Hoffman Music Co., Kansas City, MO

An all-time favorite, it is a most richly folk-inspired Missouri rag with a fine cakewalk flavor. It was later purchased and published by Jerome H. Remick & Co.

# "The Peach" (Arthur Marshall)

## December 7, 1908, Stark Music Printing & Publishing Co., New York

The trio has a strong feeling of a spiritual, and section D maintains his high standard with an exceptional final section. In measure 8, he has a phrase of moving ambiguity in the treble, which is supported by a diminished chord but also has the feeling of a flatted blue third.

# "Peacherine Rag" (Scott Joplin)

## March 18, 1901, John Stark & Son, St. Louis

A totally different composition from "Maple Leaf Rag," it is nonetheless excitingly original. The fresh spring-like sounds of wonderment unfold reaching the apex in the C section, which Percy Wenrich took wholesale for his C section in "The Smiler." The most exotic effect in the C section comes at the thirty-second-note triplets, which have the effect of bluesy slurs. And instead of capitalizing on whirlwind climactic endings, this one shows a rare degree of musical sophistication in its conclusion of the development, and the piece comes to a logical and firm end.

# "Peaches and Cream" (Percy Wenrich)

## November 27, 1905, Jerome H. Remick & Co., New York

An important yet overlooked early rag that anticipated "Dill Pickles" with the three-over-four device.

# "Pear Blossoms" (Scott Hayden)

## November 1, 1960, published in *They All Played Ragtime,* 3d ed., 1966, Oak Publications, New York, arr. Bob Darch, ed. Donald Ashwander

Hayden wrote this while still in high school. The manuscript contains the complete melody line but only sketchy bass parts, which were completed by Bob Darch, who obtained the manuscript from Sedalia musician Tom Ireland.

# "The Pearls" (Jelly Roll Morton)

## August 20, 1923, Melrose Bros. Music Co., Chicago

The A section is an adventurous harmonic conception, sparked by an effective use of the lower VI chord (E flat seventh in the key of G here). The thirty-two-measure trio is one of Morton's most original strains, despite its reliance in the first few measures on the pop blues song "Go Back Where You Stayed Last Night." In the key of C, he creates a pedal-tone effect with G in the bass with repeated patterns of first C-G, then D-G. Over this he created a fascinating treble: a lyrical, constantly moving melodic line with great invention.

# "Peek-a-Boo Rag" (Charles L. Johnson)

## September 28, 1914, Forster Music Publisher, Chicago

A most lyrical rag, but one that stays in one key throughout (A flat). The C section is, nevertheless, marked "trio" and alternates a straight rhythm with a dotted-note pattern more typical of fox-trot writing, which began in 1914.

# "Pegasus" (James Scott)

## September 15, 1920, Stark Music Co., St. Louis

The trio uses the same harmonic progression found in such later popular songs as "Birth of the Blues" and "Tip Toe through the Tulips."

# "Pekin Rag" (Joe Jordan)

## September 24, 1904, Jordan & Motts Pekin Publishing Co., Chicago

The remarkable feature of this 1904 rag is the C section where Jordan applies anticipatory syncopation in an extended pattern throughout the entire section, giving the right hand a forward-moving, horizontal feeling, independent of the basic pulse—a texture usually associated with Advanced rags. The C section was later used as the chorus for his "Sweetie Dear."

# "Perfect Rag" (Jelly Roll Morton)

## Not copyrighted or published

In this June 1924 recording (Gennett 5486), Morton treats us to his adaptation of the ragtime formula demonstrating the positive effects in performing improvisations. Section A is laid out in typical ragtime fashion. B, however, is a series of breaks on a circle of fifths, but a different break is used each time. C is a lyrical trio typical to ragtime, repeated almost without variation. Instead of a D strain, Morton climaxes the rag with a brilliantly worked-out variation of C, which he plays and then repeats. An inspired and most creative transformation of an older ragtime formula.

# "Peroxide Rag" (Calvin Woolsey)

## May 3, 1910, self, Braymer, MO

A melodious rag with a varied bass pattern in the folksy B section. The cover shows the following prescription: "For Miss Peroxide Blonde-Hydrogen Peroxide…apply morning and night…Dr. Funny Bones."

# "Perpetual Rag" (Harry Thomas)

## May 29, 1911, Harry Thomas, Montreal

An explosive performance with triplets, breaks, dramatic tremolos, and walking bass. The perpetual effect comes from not resolving the melody in the final measure of the A section. A piano-roll-only performance by the composer (Uni-Record 203063).

## "Persian Lamb Rag" (Percy Wenrich)

### June 15, 1908, Walter Jacobs, Boston

He had a truly great flair for writing lyrical popular song melodies with a genuine folk flavor. Although he had heard the legendary ragtime pioneers in his youth play at the House of Lords, one of the most plush sporting emporiums, his total output of first-rate rags is less than one might expect. Only a few are in that category, but his forte was the pop song (e.g., "Put on Your Old Grey Bonnet," "When You Wore a Tulip"). The A section of "Persian Lamb" is reminiscent of an old fiddle tune known as "Whiskers," played in his hometown of Joplin, Missouri.

## "Petticoat Lane" (Euday Bowman)

### June 1, 1915, unpublished, August 14, 1915, transferred to J. W. Jenkins' Sons, Kansas City, MO

This is the composer's most ambitious rag, which combines his feeling for blues with a lyricism not present in his other rags. This is in the key of C and seems to allow a bit more freedom of movement. The thick treble chords are relieved by lighter, single-note lines. The rag ends triumphantly with a blazing, insistent motive in the right hand.

## "Piano Salad" (George L. Cobb)

### January 18, 1923, Walter Jacobs, Boston

Fine Novelty rag with an especially clever C section.

## "Pianoflage" (Roy Bargy)

### June 27, 1922, Sam Fox Publishing Co., Cleveland

This is Bargy's finest rag and his fifth excursion into the Novelty rag idiom. His piano-roll versions (Imperial 513130 and Melodee 204047) and his solo piano recording (Victor 18969) illustrate the differences between the two types of presentations.

# "Pickles and Peppers" (Adaline Shepherd)

## November 7, 1906, Jos. Flanner, Milwaukee

One of the most beloved rags, it defines a creative Folk rag. The most important feature, the key to its success as a popular Folk rag, is its developmental C to $C_1$ idea, which turns a straight cakewalk theme into a stomping syncopation.

# "Pine Apple Rag" (Scott Joplin)

## October 12, 1908, Seminary Music Co., New York

This is among the very finest rags ever written. An advanced way of handling folk material, the A section is one of his happiest and brightest. The B section is extremely pianistic with a solid use of rhythm as the major focal point of this section. The C section changes the emotional level to one of introspection. In keeping with this, note the use of the minor seventh in the trio, which is the only time Joplin used such an intense blues coloration. Changing moods once again for the last section, Joplin cleverly integrated the former mood while offering a more optimistic outlook. In the last two sections (C and D) the harmonies and use of bass lines are extremely adventurous. In a detailed analysis of ragtime composition, one characteristic becomes evident: the intermingling of pentatonicism, chromaticism, formal European traditions, and black folk materials produces moments of the richest beauty that sometimes defies a one-way analysis of what is heard. This ambiguity arises from the strength of incorporated traditions, a synthesis of both black and white sources and is at the same time one of the joys of ragtime's art. For example, the most moving idea in Joplin's trio of "Pine Apple Rag" comes with the melodic and harmonic coloration in the third measure, which can be heard three different ways. A jazz-oriented listener would hear this idea as a blue seventh on the subdominant. If the melody line alone is heard, one hears it as a flatted third. It can also appear as an enharmonically spelled German six chord (see also the commentary on Arthur Marshall's "The Peach").

# "Pink Poodle" (Charles L. Johnson)

## May 6, 1914, Forster Music Publisher, Chicago

One of his more ambitious rags. The first two sections alternate between the keys of C and A flat. Section B is a tango, first suggested in section A and also recalled in the imaginative twenty-four-measure trio (in the key of F).

# "The Pippin Rag" (Arthur Marshall)

## December 7, 1908, Stark Music Printing & Publishing Co., New York

In printing both "The Peach" and "Pippin," a mix-up occurred in the subtitles: On the cover of "Peach" the subtitle is "Ragtime Two Step," and on the "Pippin" cover is "A Sentimental Rag." On the inside, however, the subtitles are reversed. This is Marshall's most unusual conception, with a twenty-four-measure A section largely in F minor, which ends, however, on the relative major. The C section has effective call-and-response patterns and one of the most soulful endings in ragtime writing. The rag returns to the ambivalent minor-major A section to finish, trimmed to a regular sixteen-measure version.

# "Poison Rag" (Calvin Woolsey)

## May 3, 1910, self, Braymer, MO

Interesting device in section A that states a phrase and then echoes it in minor.

# "Poor Buttermilk" (Zez Confrey)

## July 22, 1921, Jack Mills, Inc., New York

Structurally akin to "Kitten," it is more like "Ivories" in atmosphere. The mysterious mood is more pronounced, as the introduction and A section are both in the minor mode. Section B is probably the most rhythmically complex of anything found in Novelty rags. An exotic and very typical Confrey sound here results from a series of ninth chords built on augmented triads, descending in intervals of a minor third. Section C harks back to Scott Joplin's flag-waving endings—but in the Novelty style. The ending is a rhythmic surprise and is found as an interlude on his QRS roll of "Putting on the Dog."

# "Poor Katie Red"
# ("Eubie's Slow Drag") (Eubie Blake)

## August 18, 1960, *Sincerely, Eubie Blake,* 1975, Eubie Blake Music, New York

Blake remarked that the A section was a folk melody played in St. Louis around the turn of this century, and indeed it is: It is his adaptation of the notorious "St. Louis Tickle" strain (see Theron Bennett).

# "The Pop Corn Man" (Jean Schwartz)

## December 15, 1910, Jerome H. Remick & Co., Detroit

The most lyrical of the Schwartz rags, with interpolated "steamboat whistle" in the A section and "pop" written above several afterbeats in the trio, commemorating the ubiquitous popcorn man of earlier years.

Jean Schwartz.

# Popular Ragtime, 1906–1912

Popular ragtime came into its own with the huge success of Charles L. Johnson's "Dill Pickles Rag." It was published by the Carl Hoffman Music Company of Kansas City, Missouri, the same firm that published Scott Joplin's "Original Rags." And the man who bought the Joplin number for the Hoffman firm was the same one who bought "Dill Pickles" for his new firm, the Jerome H. Remick Company of Detroit, Michigan. That man was famous composer–arranger–publisher Charles Neil Daniels, who made this rag the first Tin Pan Alley million-selling hit and established the form and device for most rags that followed.

Tin Pan Alley became the collective name for the popular sheet music publishers that made it their business to publicize, market, and distribute their wares on a large scale, concentrating on the national marketplace. Selling popular sheet music to the masses was a new idea in the early 1890s, and it worked mainly by means of song pluggers. These were men hired by the publishers to ensure that the firm's songs were being played and sung in saloons, vaudeville houses, restaurants, and music stores. Most of the time they had to play the songs themselves.

With the creation of Tin Pan Alley came the composer, a person hired at a stated salary and paid a weekly advance against future royalties for creating songs on demand. There was no waiting for the muse or inspiration, but rather a turning out of a product either for general popular consumption or for a specific performer or client. As ragtime became part of the pop music scene, publishers had their own composers write easy-to-play rags for the amateur pianist. Ragtime was now big business, with schools like Axel Christensen's, which advertised "Ragtime Taught in Ten Lessons." The large firms not only employed staff composers to

Charles Neil Daniels.

turn it out but also bought rags from outsiders. The demand was so great that everyone had an opportunity to be published—amateur and professional alike.

The most significant ragtime entrepreneur besides John Stark was Charles Neil Daniels, manager of Tin Pan Alley's largest firm, Jerome H. Remick & Company. Born in Leavenworth, Kansas, on April 12, 1878, Daniels grew up in Kansas City, Kansas, with his father, Alfred Edward from Ireland (the original surname was O'Daniels), his mother, Agnes Tholen from Hanover, Germany, and his sister, Elizabeth. Though not affluent, the Daniels family was comfortable because the father made a good living as a watch and jewelry repairperson. Daniels graduated from high school in Kansas City; this was the end of his academic training. During high school he accompanied singers and played piano in a dance orchestra. He could sight read well, play by ear, and improvise beautifully. It was also during this time that he learned music calligraphy. He was justly proud of his pen and ink manuscripts, which were among the most attractive ever seen. He studied harmony, composition, and arranging with Carl Pryor. On graduation he worked at the Carl Hoffman Music Company as a song demonstrator during the day and for the Kronberg Concert Company at night, accompanying the singers. In 1898 the Hoffman firm offered a prize of $25 for the best two-step by a local composer. Daniels, after much prodding by friends, finally competed for the prize, and his composition, "Margery," won. At that time John Phillip Sousa was playing at the Coats Opera House. He heard of the contest and offered to perform the work; much to everyone's amazement, it became an instant success. This led to a lasting friendship that came in handy for Daniels more than once. Though "Margery" sold 275,000 copies, Daniels had to be content with the prize money and some favorable publicity. But the tune's success led to a promotion to manager. In December 1898 he purchased Scott Joplin's "Original Rags." He still maintained two jobs, and, in the next year, he was accompanying Harry Haley, featured singer with Epperson's Minstrels. He wrote "You Tell Me Your Dream, I'll Tell You Mine" for Haley. The song became a bigger hit than "Margery." But this time he published it himself, starting the firm of Daniels, Russel and Boone. The following year he left Kansas City and moved the new firm to St. Louis, where he stayed for the next two years. By coincidence, Stark arrived in St. Louis during this same period. During his St. Louis days, Daniels managed the sheet music department of the Barr Dry Goods Company. In 1901 the firm published his new Indian tune, "Hiawatha," which became another success when Sousa was prevailed upon to perform and record it. The firm of Daniels, Russel and Boone was purchased by the Detroit-based publishing house of Whitney–Warner so that they could have "Hiawatha." Daniels was paid $10,000 for it, which created a sensation in the music world; it was the highest sum then paid for a song. With it went an offer to head up the company as manager. Daniels accepted and moved to Detroit in 1902. The following year words were added, and sales zoomed into the millions, thus starting the trend toward Indian songs, which were extremely popular during the first decade of this century. For many of his songs, he used the pseudonym of Neil Moret. He also used the names of L' Albert, Lamonte C. Jones, Jules Lemare, Charlie Hill, and Sidney Carter. He married Pearl Hamlin on New Year's Eve 1904. A son, Neil Moret Daniels, was born in 1907, and a daughter, Dana Agnes Daniels was born the following year. Because Dana was in poor health, Daniels was advised to move to the West Coast, which he did in 1912. He gave up his position in Detroit with Remick, as Whitney–Warner became the Jerome H. Remick Company in 1905, and created his own firm, this time in partnership with Weston Wilson. The new firm was known as Daniels and Wilson, Inc. Most notably, in 1918 they published the Daniels song commissioned by Mack Sennett for his movie, *Mickey,* starring Mabel Normand. This was the first motion picture theme song. From 1924 to 1931 Daniels was president of Villa Moret, Inc. Sensing that the movies, with their new soundtracks, and commercial radio were cutting into sheet music sales, he decided to withdraw from active management in the music business. After a lengthy illness, he died of kidney failure in Los Angeles on January 23, 1943. During the years he owned his own firms, he composed many popular hit songs selling into the millions: "Moonlight and Roses," "Mello Cello," "Song of the Wanderer," "Chloe," "She's Funny that Way," "In Monterey," and "Sweet and Lovely." A pioneering music publisher and manager of the largest music publishing firm in the United States, Daniels contributed greatly during the boom years of ragtime, which he helped to create and maintain. His thorough knowledge of the business and of the public's taste helped him to sustain the popularity of ragtime for many years. He encouraged his staff to compose rags by accepting unsolicited manuscripts and by purchasing small-town publishers' rags. Daniels, heretofore, has been remembered by ragtime scholars as the arranger of "Original Rags," but that was only the beginning. He nurtured ragtime until it was a flourishing and significant part of the popular sheet music industry.

For the most part, the rags created by Tin Pan Alley were done by professional tunesmiths, not particularly dedicated to the art of ragtime. They created their rags for the seemingly insatiable market that made ragtime a fad.

"Dill Pickles Rag" was the next big hit after "Maple Leaf Rag," written by composer–publisher Charles L. Johnson. It is interesting to see how Johnson adapted Joplin's framework of a rag to suit his own work style. Keeping the essence of Joplin's structure of a five-part rag, Johnson made a slight but commercially important change. Instead of the AA BB A CC DD formula, Johnson created a three-section rag and substituted a repeat of either the first or second section, which saved him from having to write a fourth section. The Johnson formula, therefore, looked like this: AA BB A CC AA or AA BB A CC BB. For this particular rag, however, the structure he used was INTRO AA B A CC B.

The chief device that made "Dill Pickles Rag" such a hit was what is known as the three-over-four pattern (discussed under "12th Street Rag"). This configuration was then used so much that it became the first of several musical clichés in ragtime writing. The public seemed not to tire of it, because they made substantial hits of "Black and White Rag," "Spaghetti Rag," "Crazy Bone Rag," "Grizzly Bear Rag," "Hungarian Rag," and, the most widely known of them all, "12th Street Rag."

Recordings from this period feature the military band, the five-string banjo—accompanied by either piano or military band—or some other percussive or high-pitched instrument like the piccolo, accordion, and xylophone. The first known ragtime piano recording occurred on December 2, 1912, when Mike Bernard recorded Wallie Herzer's popular rag *Everybody Two Step* for Columbia (*Ragtime Piano Interpretations,*

Folkways RBF-24). Bernard was the orchestra leader and chief accompanist at Tony Pastor's Music Hall, the leading variety and vaudeville showplace in New York. Bernard won the major ragtime piano contest on January 23, 1900, that was sponsored by the *Police Gazette* at Tammany Hall in New York. He got a diamond-studded medal proclaiming him as the "Ragtime King of the World." This got him the position at Pastor's. Perhaps the greatest display of his talents on record appears in his own April 1918 composition, "Blaze Away," which Columbia also originally issued (Columbia A-2577) and reissued on *Ragtime Piano Originals* (Folkways RBF-23).

Player-piano rolls were still not true recordings but were conceived by arrangers away from any recording piano. The catalogs from the major roll companies detail ragtime's popularity as it kept pace with the ballads and comic songs of the day.

With the concentration of publishing houses in the large cities, most of the working composers lived there. New York was the leading center, offering employment not only to composers of popular songs but also work for people in the musical theater as well. Such composers as Albert Gumble, Jean Schwartz, Harry Tierney, Ford Dabney, and Ted Snyder—who also functioned as a publisher, first as Seminary Music, which issued several Joplin rags, then as Ted Snyder Company, and then as Waterson, Berlin & Snyder—all wrote popular rags. In Chicago, always right behind New York, rags from the gifted pens of Egbert Van Alstyne, Bernie Adler, and Percy Wenrich were being published. With prolific composer and publisher Johnson headquartered in Missouri, Kansas City became a ragtime center where Johnson's success, particularly as a ragtime composer, served as an on-the-spot example for others like Ed Kuhn, Maude Gilmore, and Charles A. Gish. Although hardly a Tin Pan Alley area, Indianapolis became a center of ragtime publishing through the efforts of John H. Aufderheide, a pawnbroker-turned-publisher, issuing rags by his daughter, May, and her similarly minded ragtime composing friends Julia Lee Niebergall, Cecil Duane Crabb, Will Morrison, and Paul Pratt.

The best of the ragtime composers of Popular ragtime were not the hacks found in the back rooms in Tin Pan Alley but were dedicated craftsmen who took pains to produce quality work yet managed to please the public time and again, as their output demonstrates, with easily playable works that convey the happy sprightliness inherent in ragtime's charm.

# "Popularity" (George Michael Cohan)

## August 27, 1906, F. A. Mills, New York

An instrumental composed for Cohan's show of the same name, it was an extremely popular rag. It has a cakewalk flavor, but with much more syncopation and imaginative use of harmonies.

# "Pork and Beans" (Theron Bennett)

## January 26, 1909, Victor Kremer Co., Chicago

A more conventional rag in three sections that combine the three-over-four pattern with a melodic cakewalk style of construction. The more rambunctious A and B sections contrast with the more genteel trio, marked "cantabile," which seems ideally suited for a mellow string band treatment.

# "Pork and Beans" (Luckey Roberts)

## June 24, 1913, Jos. W. Stern & Co., New York

Named after a favorite sandwich combination, it is unique and stands out in ragtime literature for its originality. It was the first rag to go back and forth from the minor to the parallel major modes. Between Wally Rose's 1964 performance (Fantasy 5016) and Roberts's own (Circle 1027), the difference can be heard between the printed score—which Rose follows—of a rag and a performance by its creator. That ragtime is mainly a performer's tradition, the Joplin School notwithstanding, is proved, thanks to the recordings by these composers.

# "'Possum and 'Taters, a Ragtime Feast"
# (Charles Hunter)

## April 20, 1900, Henry A. French, Nashville

The score is prefaced by a setting of the scene: "Just after the first severe frost in the Fall...the persimmons are full ripe and the possums are all fat...possum hunts are of nightly occurrence...sweet potatoes are an invariable...accompaniment...to a possum feast...always an occasion for a general gathering and great rejoicing. The title was suggested by the composer's having been a witness at one of these joyful occasions." (The term *witness* here, unless applied carelessly, may indicate that the composer was not totally blind). This is Hunter's most moving rag; it is carefully marked with dynamics. The joyous C section has surprising and beautiful harmonies. At the end of the last C, there is what will become a characteristic pause—the last note is a dotted half note in cut time—that he was to use between strains or midway into one. This idiosyncrasy marks a separation between sections indicating a contrast and usually implies a change of dynamics.

# "Powder Rag" (as Raymond Birch)

## August 20, 1908, Chas. L. Johnson & Co., Kansas City, MO

A popular hit scored in 4/4 instead of the usual 2/4. Thickly textured using octaves instead of single notes. Favorite with bands for its strutting, folksy nature. In Birch's happiest vein.

# Paul Charles Pratt

## (b. November 1, 1890, New Salem, Indiana; d. July 7, 1948, Indianapolis)

Pratt was a vaudeville pianist who made a few piano rolls under the name Paul Parnell, a name he also used as conductor of musical shows on the road. In December 1908 he became general manager of J. H. Aufderheide Publishing Co. The firm did well under his direction, and in 1911 he went to Chicago to open a branch office. There he married Beatrice Harcourt. Unfortunately, she died a few months later in the great flu epidemic of 1918. He collaborated briefly with Will Callahan on popular songs. He married Edythe Lee in 1943, and they had a daughter, Sharon Gaye. From 1934 until his death he owned and operated the Pratt Photo Studio in Indianapolis. Among his other compositions are "Everybody Tango," "'Mid the Purple Tinted Hills of Tennessee," and "Dreamy Days of Long Ago."

## Ragtime Compositions

"Vanity Rag," April 11, 1909, J. H. Aufderheide, Indianapolis

"Colonial Glide," January 13, 1910, J. H. Aufderheide, Indianapolis

"Walhalla," January 13, 1910, J. H. Aufderheide, Indianapolis

"Hot House Rag," July 27, 1914, Stark Music Co., St. Louis

"Spring-Time Rag," January 4, 1916, Stark Music Co., St. Louis

"On the Roural Route," May 10, 1917, Stark Music Co., St. Louis

"Little Bit of Rag," not copyrighted or published

"Prattles," not copyrighted or published

"Wailana Rag," not copyrighted or published

# "Pride of the Smoky Row"
# ("Q Rag") (J. M. Wilcockson)

## February 5, 1911, self, Hammond, IN

A less familiar structure that ends the rag with a lyrical trio rather than the more rhythmic D, a great folk strain in the circle-of-fifths pattern. The subtitle is still a mystery but may be a reference to *bar-b-que*.

# "Prosperity Rag" (James Scott)

## March 10, 1916, Stark Music Co., St. Louis

This rag is to "Grace and Beauty" as "Gladiolus Rag" is to the "Maple Leaf Rag." Each section reflects its companion, but with advanced conception and writing. An interesting touch is the restatement of B at the end with a change of bass. The original line is much like that described in C of "Ophelia," but for the finish Scott adopts the traditional octave-chord pattern, giving the rag a stronger finish.

# Q

## "Quality" (James Scott)

### July 27, 1911, Stark Music Co., St. Louis

A graceful and characteristic rag with an unusual adaptation of Scott Joplin's C section of "Maple Leaf Rag" in this C section—it is usually the B section that is borrowed.

## "Queen of Love-Two-Step" (Charles Hunter)

### June 21, 1901, Henry A. French, Nashville

Note the designation *two-step* instead of *rag*. This is actually a lightly syncopated cakewalk-march, somewhat reminiscent of "Tickled to Death." Sections A and C are thirty-two-measure strains each.

# R

## "Race Track Blues" (Les Copeland)

### Not copyrighted or published

Though Copeland later wrote at least one midwestern-style blues in a twelve-bar format ("Texas Blues," 1917), this solo contains three sections of sixteen measures each of blues influence, all in one key, E flat. Here, rag and blues elements are mixed with the true vigor of a gifted Folk rags artist, outdistancing the more hybridized blues-rags Tin Pan Alley was turning out during the teens.

## "Rag-a-Bit" (Charley Straight)

### March 1918

One of Straight's original Novelty rags and written especially as a piano roll (Imperial 511760) and issued March 1918. The B section is a neat variation of the A section of his earlier rag "Rufenreddy." The C section is the main theme of Jelly Roll Morton's "Wolverine Blues."

## "Rag Doll" (Nacio Herb Brown)

### March 20, 1928, Sherman, Clay & Co., San Francisco

An extremely popular follow-up to "Doll Dance." Edna Fischer had the most ebullient arrangement (Victor 21384).

# "Rag Picker's Rag" (Robert J. O'Brien)

## October 19, 1901, Union Music Co., Cincinnati

Section C best illustrates restlessness through syncopation; it begins as a straight march and then for contrast ends with a riotously syncopated sixteen measures.

# "Rag Sentimental" (James Scott)

## Not copyrighted, published 1918, Stark Music Co., St. Louis

The fascinating A section uses the minor mode, but a major key feeling dominates the rag. This is the more usual use of the minor tonality in ragtime, as a change in color, unlike Scott Joplin's use to affect a melancholy mood.

# Rag Song

In collecting circles, the designation *rag song* is given to a pop song with the word *rag* or *ragtime* in the title. It does not have to have syncopated melody, and it is not otherwise distinguished in form from a regular pop song, both having two parts, whether tearjerker or coon song, was the same throughout its first decade: There was a verse that nobody knew and a chorus that everybody knew. Though the verse might be any length, the chorus was usually either sixteen or thirty-two measures long. During the ragtime age, the tearjerker gave way to the pleasant love song: "On a Sunday Afternoon," "In the Good Old Summertime," "Meet Me in St. Louis, Louis," "Wait Till the Sun Shines, Nellie," "By the Light of the Silvery Moon," and "Let Me Call You Sweetheart." Peppier songs used the word *rag* or *ragtime* in their titles and have come to be known as rag songs. As a musical fact, however, they are constructed exactly like other popular songs: with a verse that nobody knows and a chorus that everybody knows. Such titles during this time were "That _____ Rag": Fill in the blank with, for example, *African, Beautiful, College, Devil, Epidemic, Fussy, Gossiping, Hypnotizing, Indian, Kleptomaniac, London, Moving Picture, Nightmare, Operatic, Puzzlin', Raggedy, Shakespearian, Teasin', Whistling, X-Ray,* or *Yodeling.* Then there are "Ragging the Baby to Sleep," "The Ragtime Boardinghouse," and "Rag, Rag, Rag"—not forgetting the most famous rag song of all, "Alexander's Ragtime Band."

# "Ragging the Scale" (Edward B. Claypoole)

## April 2, 1915, Broadway Music Corp., New York

One of the most popular rag hits of this era, it has a clever use of syncopated scale patterns. The trio is the highlight in which the scale ascends then descends as a whole-note melody while the rest of the right hand executes a syncopated fill-in figure.

## "The Raggy Fox Trot" (Laurence E. Goffin)

### October 20, 1915, Jerome H. Remick & Co., New York

A good and clever rag, it includes some very early tricks that would later be used in the Novelty rags of the twenties.

## "Ragman's Exercise" (Harry D. Squires)

### April 3, 1922, Jack Mills, New York

This Novelty rag is a clever way to demonstrate various components of a Novelty rag. It is an excellent example of how to practice novelty runs and breaks. Squires (1897–1961) had it published, and its only recording took place a year later by British pianist and dance band leader Stanley C. Holt ([E] Homocord 434).

# Ragtime

Ragtime, the joyous syncopated piano music from the Midwest, had its first publication in 1897. It was not until 1899 that John Stark and Son published Scott Joplin's "Maple Leaf Rag" in Sedalia, Missouri. From there, Stark moved to St. Louis, where the rag eventually sold more than one million copies of sheet music, thus establishing ragtime as a solid genre of popular music nationally and, during its first decade, internationally. Joplin was its leading composer, and such was his brilliance that seventy-two years after he published "The Entertainer," it became a hit all over again on a recording selling more than two million copies on the soundtrack for the film *The Sting* (Universal, 1973). Of the approximately 2,000 rags issued in sheet music, most were published in small towns far from Tin Pan Alley. Of all popular music, it was ragtime that attracted women to compose in the pop idiom, which is not surprising since they were the ones who took piano lessons.

# Ragtime as a Form and a Fad

Ragtime is a musical composition for the piano comprising three or four sections containing sixteen measures each that combines a syncopated melody accompanied by an even, steady duple rhythm. If there is one incontestable statement to be made about ragtime, it is that ragtime is a paradoxical art form with a perplexing history. In an age of rigid racial divisions, ragtime appeared as a racially ambiguous commodity whose earliest composers had neither a common racial identity nor the desire to promote their music under an ethnic banner.

Though ragtime constitutes a concrete musical idiom with more tangible structural features than jazz, its distinguishing musical characteristics were lost on its early promoters and contemporary listening audience and, thanks to a long tradition of erroneous commentary on the subject, remain muddled to this day. Although ragtime's compositional history must be discerned mostly through musty sheet-music scores, it began as a performance medium. Early ragtime leaders viewed such scores as a point of musical departure, if they were able to read them at all. Though ragtime's commercial history is inseparable from mainstream American popular music, where it played a prominent role between 1906 and the First World War, the composer who developed ragtime into a profitable commodity—Scott Joplin—seemed curiously innocent of crass commercial impulses and remote from ragtime's lively tradition as a performing art.

By all rights, ragtime should have enjoyed little popularity, for it was far more complex than the competing pop music of its day and demanded rhythmic techniques that lay beyond the grasp of the amateur pianist for whom sheet music was tailored. Yet it not only became a staple of Tin Pan Alley—the clannish New York publishing houses that monopolized the music industry between 1890 and 1930—but proved so popular that the very word *ragtime* quickly became an indiscriminate label used to confer commerciality on just about any music. But this is yet another paradox, for the original meaning of the word *ragtime* remains undiscoverable: An early Bert Williams song, "Oh, I Don't Know, You're Not So Warm!," used the word in 1896, a year before the publication of the first rag. As early as April 1, 1899, an etymology of the word appeared in a Boston *Musical Record* article on ragtime by Rupert Hughes' entitled "A Eulogy of Ragtime": "Negroes call their clog dancing 'ragging' and the dance a 'rag,' a dance largely shuffling." It cannot be demonstrated that this or any other derivation is trustworthy, and by the time ragtime—usually printed as "rag-time"—became a recognizable musical form, it had little utility as dance music.

Before ragtime appeared in sheet music, ragtime's origins were lost in an undocumented lower-class tradition of saloon and whorehouse piano playing, a tradition composed of talented freelance itinerants. Because the nineteenth-century saloon was invariably equipped with a piano, it offered ready employment to any roving pianist who could entertain the all-male saloon audiences of the times. Hence, the saloon became ragtime's earliest performance setting. In early vaudeville, the piano was used only to accompany vocalists and thus offered little opportunity for early ragtime pianists to develop. The typical saloon pianist was hired to provide a pleasant, nondescript background diversion and was expected to honor requests. It is inconceivable that any of these musicians were restricted to a ragtime repertoire; this would have invited professional suicide. In reality, such now-celebrated ragtime pianists as Eubie Blake were all-purpose entertainers. They are not remembered as such now, not because ragtime was their only performing vehicle but because their other period pieces are less interesting to modern listeners. By the same token, few early composers worked strictly within a ragtime format.

Although ragtime's early detractors made much of its lowly social origins and even used its presumed racial origins as a means of dismissing the music as an art form, a ragtime that had emerged as a polite parlor pastime would have enjoyed little more prestige. "Ragtime that is different...played by the culture of all nations and...welcomed in the drawing rooms and boudoirs of good taste" were Classic rag publisher John Stark's blurbs, obviously aimed at the parlor pianists of polite society. However, outside of St. Louis, it is questionable whether Stark's efforts to establish his publications as ragtime's crème de la crème ever superseded his one great success, "Maple Leaf Rag," sheet-music sales of which supported the rest of the catalog. Both its chilly academic reception and the lack of data about ragtime's historical beginnings followed from the fact that it grew in an age when only classical music was considered worthy of serious scrutiny. Most of the written commentary ragtime inspired before its demise as popular music turned solely on the question of ragtime's musical legitimacy, expressing either the writer's individual distaste or, in some instances, enthusiasm for the form.

Ironically, the pompous prejudices that once rejected ragtime largely because it was a pleasurable form of popular entertainment are now responsible for ragtime's current reception as a hallowed art form; the music is now solemnly embraced by classicists precisely because it is construed as something more exalted and serious than mere entertainment. Yet of all ragtime composers, only Joplin had any classical pretensions, and even he was primarily concerned with achieving what he termed a "weird and intoxicating effect" on the listener.

It was ragtime's relentless syncopation that made the music so striking and unsettling to a public accustomed to a sentimental musical diet of dreary ballads and buffoonish depictions of "darkies." So completely did ragtime mesmerize its turn-of-the-century audience that the word *ragtime* soon acquired a figurative meaning, synonymous with merry or lively. A definition of ragtime given in the fifth volume of Farmer and Henley's *Slang and Its Analogues* (1902) listed *rag-time girl* as a term for a sweetheart or harlot.

As well as creating a new sense of euphoria in American popular music, ragtime represented an unprecedented compositional format. As a musical entity ragtime was, and is, an instrumental work in 2/4 time composed for the piano that combines a syncopated series of melodies accompanied by an even, steady rhythm. Despite the fact that ragtime proved to be a popular recording vehicle for both brass bands and banjos during the first decade of the century, it was seldom conceived for nonpiano presentations and was generally ill-suited for it. The most sophisticated solo banjo rendition of a ragtime composition could produce only a one-dimensional melodic rhythm instead of the contrasting melodic and accompaniment rhythms made by the piano. By virtue of the fact that ragtime's melodies are too abstract and pianistic to be vocalized or even hummed and its syncopations too elaborate to lend themselves to dancing, ragtime renounces these two basic components of American pop music and black folk music. The customary view of ragtime as a kind of musical hybrid created by someone with a Caucasian cortex and an African central nervous system shortchanges the significance of this renunciation, which Tin Pan Alley sought to obscure by labeling ragtime as dance music. Most frequently, a ragtime composition was called a two-step.

A ragtime composition typically contains three or four distinct sections, each consisting of sixteen measures and each a self-contained entity. In its serial presentation of melody, ragtime resembles the waltz or march rather than classical or jazz music, which give freer play to thematic development and variations. Structurally, the rag most resembles the march, which likewise consists of three or four sections. A march-like rhythm is produced by the left hand of the ragtime pianist, which accents the first and third notes of a measure in contrast with the syncopated right hand. This march-like flavor was undoubtedly a self-conscious device on the part of the earliest ragtime pianists, probably reflecting the fact that marches, such as John Philip Sousa's famous 1889 "Washington Post," were often published for piano and formed a basic part of the nineteenth-century popular piano repertoire. The syncopation for which ragtime was chiefly noted, on the other hand, cannot be attributed to any one source. As a musical device, syncopation had an age-old association with black music and had long since been appropriated by minstrel banjoists by the time the first ragtime composition was published in 1897. An anonymously published instrumental, "The Bonja Song" (1818), contains the earliest documented instance of syncopation in American music. But the syncopated patterns appearing in most subsequent ragtime were of a nonbanjoistic character, which is not surprising considering the fact that the piano had no place within the minstrel show. Moreover, ragtime presented a unique approach to syncopation that was found nowhere in the realm of previously published music or even in the black folk music belatedly recorded in the 1920s. It was not a syncopated treatment of a straight-laced song, but a music whose melodies were conceived as fully syncopated. The distinction between ragtime and other styles of music containing syncopated elements was thus qualitative, not quantitative.

The now familiar ordering of ragtime's strains was copied from Joplin's 1899 "Maple Leaf Rag." In 1906, when "Maple Leaf Rag" had sold nearly a half-million copies, the publication of Charles Leslie Johnson's "Dill Pickles—a New Rag" was destined to inspire the pattern for the hundreds of popular Tin Pan Alley rags. The new qualities were a shortened format from four to three sections and the use of the three-over-four pattern of syncopation. Ironically, the three-over-four pattern was used in the opening section of one of the first rags, "Roustabout Rag" by Paul Sarabresole of New Orleans. But the idea did not catch on until "Dill Pickles" became successful. Two years later, a similar rag hit, George Botsford's "Black and White Rag," ensured that this pattern would become a favorite device.

The carefully wrought framework of "Maple Leaf Rag" was new for its time and brought a measure of stability and precision to a form that had been previously marked by capricious key changes and an unschematic presentation of different sections. It amounted to five parts, with all but the third consisting of a sixteen-measure melody repeated once: AA BB A CC DD. Each part except the third was thus given the thirty-two-measure value of the typical pop song chorus. The return to the initial strain (A) in the third part derived from familiar dance forms like the polka and the Schottische. This subdominant section (cc), which became a basic ragtime harmonic ingredient, is commonly termed the *trio* after march vocabulary.

Under the homogenizing influence of Tin Pan Alley, ragtime was not only given a predictable format but was also invariably simplified, particularly in the left hand, to make it accessible to amateur pianists. Had ragtime been a purely compositional medium, its Tin Pan Alley presentation would have had a blighting effect on the form. But only mediocre ragtime performers who lacked the capacity to create their own individual flourishes were ever limited by ragtime sheet music. Even Joplin, who took a strict view of ragtime as an unalterable written form, was willing to add bass embellishments to the seven rags he produced as piano rolls, thus leaving his own performance signature for posterity. All piano rolls that were hand played are open to question as accurate and faithful records of a performance. Unlike phonograph recordings, notes could be added or subtracted to a master roll after the initial performance. However, in 1959 Trebor Tichenor played two of the Joplin hand-played rolls for Arthur Marshall, Joplin's close friend and fellow ragtimer from the Sedalia and early St. Louis days. When his attention was called to the quick octave embellishments in the bass, Marshall responded, "That was his style." His protégé S. Brun Campbell would recall thus in his autobiography in *Jazz Report* (1971), "None of the original pianists played ragtime that way it was written. They played their own style…if you knew the player and heard him a block away, you could name him by his ragtime style." A similar observation was offered by Axel Christensen, a Chicagoan who began teaching ragtime to amateurs in 1903 and who authored a series of best-selling instruction books on the subject: "In 1902 and 1903 there was no accepted method or system of playing ragtime…no two pianists ever played syncopated numbers alike," he told Rudi Blush in *They All Played Ragtime* (Knopf, 1950).

Unfortunately for the music historian, this emphasis on individuality makes it impossible for modern-day ragtime musicians to convincingly recreate the lost styles of legendary ragtime figures; when an artist like Jelly Roll Morton offers pianistic impressions of his idol Tony Jackson, he scarcely suppresses his own distinct musical personality in the process. Because commercial record companies ignored piano ragtime—preferring band and banjo renditions—the true diversity of the form can no longer be fully appreciated.

If Tin Pan Alley tunesmiths and arrangers ultimately converted ragtime into a cut-and-dried formula and obliterated much of its performing intricacy, it was nevertheless Tin Pan Alley's very promotion of the form that proved decisive in keeping it before the public. As a continuing vogue, ragtime was almost single-handedly fostered by the largest Tin Pan Alley publishing house, Jerome H. Remick and Company, which issued more ragtime compositions than its next ten competitors combined. The pivotal figure behind this commercial commitment to ragtime was Remick's manager, Charles N. Daniels, a highly successful songwriter whose sponsorship of the form actually preceded its emergence as pop music. While managing the Kansas City publishing firm of Carl Hoffman, Daniels had accepted Joplin's early ragtime manuscript, "Original Rags," in December 1898. On becoming the head of Remick's predecessor, Whitney–Warner of Detroit, he arranged for the company's acquisition of both "Original Rags" and another previously published Hoffman rag, the 1901 hit "Peaceful Henry" by E. Harry Kelly. After transferring to Remick, Daniels acquired "Dill Pickles" from Hoffman. Thereupon he seems to have indiscriminately accepted nearly every ragtime composition submitted to him before leaving the company in 1912, and his successor at Remick, Mose Gumble, followed the same policy over the next five or six years until ragtime went the way of all fads. Remick issued some 500 rags, or roughly a sixth of the entire published ragtime output.

Tin Pan Alley's largest output was vocal music, so it was inevitable that rag songs would appear once instrumental ragtime assumed fad-like proportions. The so-called ragtime song was a genre whose very name was a contradiction in terms. Like the bona fide ragtime it pretended and was popularly taken to be, the ragtime song enjoyed huge popularity, resulting in such successes as Ted Snyder's 1908 "Wild Cherries Rag," which had originally sold nearly a million copies in instrumental form; Percy Wenrich's "Red Rose Rag," a 1911 composition that could have passed muster as a three-theme ragtime instrumental had it not been vocalized; and such Irving Berlin favorites as "That Mesmerizing Mendelssohn Tune," a syncopated treatment of Felix Mendelssohn's "Spring Song" appearing in 1909, "The Grizzly Bear," another work of instrumental origin, coauthored with George Botsford in 1910, "Ragtime Violin" (1911), and "That Mysterious Rag" (1911). The hack-like, hokum nature of the typical ragtime song was not lost on the composers, as the lyrics of Louis A. Hirsch's "The Bacchanal Rag" (1912) indicate:

Take some music,

Start to fake some music in a lag time

Then you have some ragtime.

Steal from the masters any classic you see

Rag it a little bit with his melody

Don't try at all to hide

Call it the Gaby Glide

No matter what it may be

Other writers will give brother writers inspiration

Handy op'ra will be dandy just for syncopation.

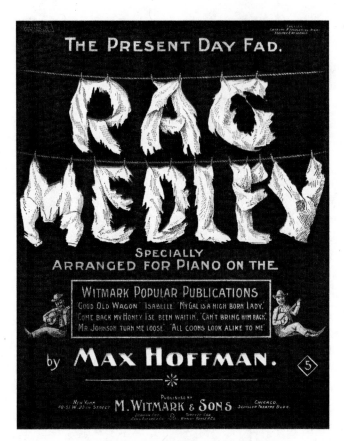

Indeed, it was the oversimplified view of ragtime as a musical synonym of syncopation that gave rise to the ragtime song and inspired the popular game of "ragging" the classics. Yet the notion that ragtime could be created merely by giving a syncopated bounce to any preexistent melody had been used as an arranging gimmick by Tin Pan Alley even before the first published ragtime composition appeared in 1897. In 1896 Max Hoffman, an orchestrator for the firm Witmark and Sons, had furnished the company with what he termed *rag accompaniment* sections for choruses of various then-popular coon songs, including Ernest Hogan's "All Coons Look Alike to Me" and W. T. Jefferson's "My Coal Black Lady." The following year Witmark issued a Hoffman-arranged "Rag Medley" composed of six such song choruses and a complete version of Ben Harney's "Mister Johnson, Turn Me Loose," all rendered as syncopated instrumentals designed for the amateur pianist. A similar Hoffman compilation containing nine songs, *Ragtown Rags,* appeared in 1898. *Ben Harney's Ragtime Instructor* (Sol Bloom, 1897) carried this notion of syncopated transformations even further by converting a semiclassical tune, "Annie Laurie," a hymn, "Come Thou Fount," and a show tune, "The Man that Broke the Bank at Monte Carlo," into ragtime. In this collection the unsyncopated original was set before its ragtime equivalent. In a similar vein, Detroit composer Fred Stone produced a syncopated waltz, "Silks and Rags" (1901), which began in conventional waltz rhythm.

It is sometimes supposed that ragtime arose through a similar patchwork process of looping together and instrumentalizing various strains of black folk music. But this idea rests largely on an unsupported folk etymology of the word *ragtime,* with its prefix being taken as an analogy to bits of tattered cloth. The only black pianist known to have created such a composite was John W. "Blind" Boone (1864–1927), a renowned virtuoso from Columbia, Missouri, whose concert career was built on classical music and Boone's amazing ability to imitate other pianists who played for him. In 1912, Boone recorded several hand-played piano rolls for the QRS Company in Chicago that not only represent the earliest hand-played rolls but afford one of the earliest glimpses of black folk music as interpreted by a black musician. As Boone was nearly fifty at the time of his QRS recordings, his playing was probably in the style of the nineteenth century. His treatment of folk material is astonishingly different from his romantic works, like "Woodland Murmurs" and "Sparkling Spring," as well as Victorian parlor pieces like "When You and I Were Young, Maggie." It is even more startling that two instrumental adaptations of such material should be offered as ragtime: "Rag Medley #1" (subtitled "Strains from the Alleys") and "Blind Boone's Southern Rag Medley #2" (subtitled "Strains from Flat Branch," invoking a Columbia neighborhood). The first of these was originally published in 1908 by Boone's manager, Wayne Allen of Columbia. Both contained strains that were common to early jazz and blues musicians and remained in the black song tradition well into the 1920s: "I'm Alabama Bound," which appeared in the "Flat Branch" medley, and "Make Me a Pallet on the Floor," part of the "Alleys" medley. "Alabama Bound," which Morton claimed to have written in 1901–02, appeared in 1909 as the work of another New Orleans composer, Bob Hoffman. W. C. Handy recalled hearing "Pallet on the Floor" as early as 1892. Though Boone did not syncopate this material in the manner of Max Hoffman's "Rag Medley," his loose timing and idiosyncratic rhythm techniques give the impression of ragged time that some dictionaries see as the semantic source of the word *ragtime*. In one four-measure section of his "Flat Branch" medley, for example, he uses a 5/4 right-hand pattern set against a 4/4 bass. His use of suspension foreshadows a device used, though much less extravagantly, by Harlem stride pianists like James P. Johnson.

Whether Boone's instrumental medleys represent the kind of potpourri approach that eventually blossomed into ragtime or are the products of an eccentric folk artist remains a moot point. Nor is it possible to perceive the direct predecessor of ragtime in isolated nineteenth-century piano compositions such as those of Boone's predecessor, Blind Thomas Greene Bethune, the eccentric slave genius, even though there are noteworthy instances of syncopation, such as Louis M. Gottschalk's "La Bamboula" (1847), W. K. Batchelder's "Imitation of the Banjo" (1854), Otto Gunnar's "New Coon in Town" (1884), and George Lansing's "Darkies Dream" (1889). With the exception of Gottschalk's work—a depiction of a black festival dance performed in New Orleans to drum accompaniment—these pieces derived their syncopated patterns from minstrel banjo. "Imitation of the Banjo," a jig-like exercise played cross-handed fashion that was dedicated to the famous minstrel banjoist Tom Briggs, features a marked accent on the second half of the first beat. "New Coon in Town," an instrumental with both folk and classical overtones, has an accent mark on the last afterbeat. In "Southern Jollification" by Charles Kunkel (1890), the last afterbeat is divided into two eighth notes. "Darkies Dream," which became a staple among vaudeville banjoists, mixes a Schottische rhythm with a syncopated pattern.

But in such pieces syncopation is not used as a compositional principle. Rather, it is coyly summoned as a flourish suggesting the imagined quaintness of "darky" music. Lest the parlor pianist failed to appreciate this, the St. Louis publisher of "Southern Jollification" obligingly provided a visual scenario:

> Synopsis: Darkies gathering at twilight after a day of cotton picking in the fields. Uncle Joshua leads off with his favorite song "I'm a happy little Nig" which is responded to by all the darkies in a grand "Hallelujah." Then follow the irresistible "Break Down" and Banjo Solo, while the dusky queens are up and tripping light fantastic step...("Break down" was the conventional nineteenth-century term for a black dancing party).

In the same spirit of facile and probably a far-fetched depiction of Negro life, the coon song and the cakewalk were developed in the mid 1890s. In the process, rudimentary syncopation entered mainstream popular music. Though it cannot be demonstrated that either of these Tin Pan Alley confections directly influenced the development of ragtime, their earlier vogues undoubtedly did much to enhance ragtime's commercial prospects.

The coon song, the comic counterpart of the 1890s tearjerker ballad, became a craze with the publication of Hogan's "All Coons Look Alike to Me" (1896) and remained standard fare in vaudeville and musical revues throughout the early 1900s. The ragtime song was a twentieth-century carryover of the coon song tradition and, had the rag song not acquired more desirable commercial connotations, such ragtime favorites as Hughie Cannon's "Bill Bailey, Won't You Please Come Home?" (1902), Berlin's "Alexander's Ragtime Band" (1911), and Shelton Brooks's "Darktown Strutters' Ball" (1917) would have been called coon songs. Both genres used lilting melodies and simple syncopation to create a happy-go-lucky quality.

Although the coon song lyric was grounded in crude racial stereotypes and portrayed blacks in either a contemptuous or condescending manner, the music that typically accompanied it represented an enlightened rhythmic departure from the straight-laced waltz time of the popular ballad. Most coon songs contained slight syncopation in both their vocal and accompaniment, though some, such as the 1894 offering "Coon from the Moon," featured no syncopation whatsoever, whereas others bore either a regularly accented vocal melody set against a lightly syncopated accompaniment or a syncopated vocal line set against a straight chordal accompaniment. Some coon songs contrasted a syncopated chorus with an unsyncopated verse. A popular coon song gimmick, found in such works as "My Coal Black Lady," "Good Morning, Carrie," and "My Lady Hottentot," was to speed up the tempo in the chorus after a slow, ballad-style beginning. Some of the early instrumental coon song medleys such as Hoffman's "Ragtown Rags" (1898) indicated a slower tempo for certain tunes with the "C" or "cut-time" marking.

The coon song's frequent confusion with ragtime is largely attributable to the fanciful self-billing of one of its most gifted composers, Benjamin R. Harney (1871–1938), a Kentucky-bred mulatto who promoted himself in 1896 as the originator of ragtime while appearing at Tony Pastor's Music Hall, a New York theater considered the country's leading vaudeville house. Soon afterward, two Harney compositions, "You've Been a Good Old Wagon but You Done Broke Down" (1894) and "Mister Johnson, Turn Me Loose" (1896), were acquired by M. Witmark and Sons from smaller publishing firms and became celebrated hits. Though Harney is even today credited with popularizing ragtime among vaudeville audiences, his known musical portfolio did not include a single authentic ragtime composition. Even the arrangements for his *Ragtime Instructor* were devised by another musician, Theodore Northrup, and probably issued under Harney's banner for reasons of commercial expediency.

If the original impulse that in 1896 led Harney to declare himself the founder of ragtime remains puzzling, it is not difficult to understand why such a pretension was readily accepted: As much of the public—and many commentators on the subject—likewise did, he construed ragtime as a synonym for syncopation per se. Though most of Harney's published output did not fall within even this ill-conceived definition of ragtime, the syncopation found in his "Good Old Wagon"—a black folk air that appeared the same year as "Possumala" by Irving Jones and published by Willis Woodward—far surpassed its coon song contemporaries in complexity. Its score alternated between straight rhythm patterns and dotted-note phrasing, with many staccato notes, a mixture reminiscent of both E. B. Hunt's piano instrumental, "The Darky Tickle" (1892) and Les Copeland's "Invitation Rag" (1911). The concluding forty-measure dance segment of the piece, which was divided into three sections and was built on stop-time features, used a sophisticated clash of two syncopated rhythms, one in the bass and one in the treble. Harney's quasi-instrumental "The Cake Walk in the Sky" (1899) ended with a syncopated sixteen-measure chorus using interpolated nonsense syllables but was primarily an exercise in cakewalk rhythm patterns. This composition was issued in two versions, both copyrighted in 1899. One version in the key of F arranged by F. W. Meacham is a simplified version of the other in E flat, which also has lyrics, including a "chorus in Ragtime—Words ad lib," Harney's famous style of adding syllables to the words; this survives on Gene Greene's recording, "King of the Bungaloos" (Victor 18266 and *Ragtime Entertainment,* Folkways RBF-22). The chorus is the first notation of the notorious Mississippi Valley folk song (known as "Funky-Butt") that became famous as the second section of "St. Louis Tickle" in 1904.

It was the cakewalk that had the distinction of being the first syncopated style of music to become popular in America, and its influence would be felt in some of the earliest published rags. Just as the coon song foreshadowed the ragtime song, so did the cakewalk anticipate the Tin Pan Alley dance song of the next decade, which was embodied by such hits as "The Cubanola Glide" (1909), "The Grizzly Bear," and the

Irving Berlin turkey trot, "Everybody's Doin' It" (1911). The early convention of labeling ragtime as dance music was probably fostered by the practice of billing cakewalks as two-step pieces.

When not intended for dancing, the cakewalk had a descriptive character, purporting to depict a slow, high-kicking improvisatory black dance, done by couples competing for a prize cake. Though believed to be of plantation origin, the dance became familiar to the general American public through stage representations, beginning with Ned Harrigan and Tony Hart's "Walking for Dat Cake" (1877). Some two decades later it became a vaudeville sensation owing to its Broadway presentation by Bert Williams and George Walker, the country's best-known black entertainers, whose likenesses appear on the first edition of the "Maple Leaf Rag" sheet music. Soon the cakewalk was a high-society pastime, both here and abroad. Among blacks it remained less respectable. W. E. B. DuBois, writing in the *Philadelphia Negro,* an 1899 sociological study, relegated it to the bottom third of black society, and remarked of local cakewalk gatherings: "they are accompanied by much drinking, and are attended by white and black prostitutes."

As a Tin Pan Alley product, the cakewalk undoubtedly bore little resemblance to whatever music blacks contrived to accompany their own cakewalks. Blacks who published cakewalks, like Fred S. Stone, wrote within the Tin Pan Alley format. In their Tin Pan Alley form, they were 2/4 instrumentals, with occasional vocal trios, founded on a simple march framework and using simple syncopation in a single rhythm pattern. Compositionally, they were unpianistic pieces, involving single-note, easily remembered melody lines one could sketch out on piano with a single finger without disturbing their harmony. Recognizing this distinction, Stark wrote in his ledger: "... the truth is that the St. Louis article of ragtime is a distinctive feature of twentieth century creation. It is not a coon song nor a cakewalk." Though cakewalks were often arranged for piano—as were marches—their sheet-music covers typically displayed other instruments, like trombones, and they were customarily performed by marching or circus bands as well as string bands deploying a violin, banjo, and string bass. The earliest cakewalk hits were popularized by Sousa, who was responsible for the cakewalk's European popularity.

The cakewalk's true predecessor was Fred Neddermeyer's "Happy Hottentots" (1889), a banjo imitation piece that contained scattered syncopation, mixing a Schottische rhythm pattern with conventional accenting. Three years later, Neddermeyer produced the first self-proclaimed cakewalk, "Opelika Cake Walk," published by Schott of New York. It featured a then-conventional rhythm pattern of two long beats followed by busier phrasing, possibly in emulation of a banjo.

The first truly syncopated cakewalk was "Rastus on Parade," which was published as a "two-step march" in 1895 by its composer Kerry Mills (1869–1948), a classically trained violinist. It established what soon became a cakewalk harmonic cliché by beginning in a minor key and moving to the relative major, a construction that cakewalk writers later followed with a subdominant section. Mills's cakewalk of 1897, "At a Georgia Camp Meeting," was likewise self-published, after being rejected by every firm to which it was submitted. Its instantaneous success ushered in the cakewalk as a Tin Pan Alley rage. Mills is said to have taken up the cakewalk as a musical protest against the vulgar racial stereotypes projected in the coon songs, and his sheet-music description of "At a Georgia Camp Meeting" sought to place the music in a genteel, decorous social setting:

> This march was not intended to be part of the Religious Exercises…when the young folks got together, they felt as if they needed some amusement. A cake walk was suggested, and held in a quiet place near by—hence this music.

As a sheet-music hit, "At a Georgia Camp Meeting" enjoyed a five- or six-year life span and was still popular at the time of the First World War, when Mills helped ignite a brief cakewalk revival with "Kerry Mills' Cake Walk" (1915). Other early cakewalk successes included Sadie Koninsky's "Eli Green's Cake Walk" (1898), Abe Holzmann's "Smokey Mokes" (1899) and "Bunch o' Blackberries" (1900), J. Bodewalt Lampe's "Creole Belles" (1900), and Arthur Pryor's "Coon Band Contest" (1900). Pryor, who had produced Sousa's cakewalk arrangements while working as a trombone soloist in Sousa's band, wrote one of the last cakewalk hits, "Razzazza Mazzazza," for his own highly successful band in 1906.

The cakewalk craze precipitated by Mills had only recently erupted when ragtime made its debut in sheet-music form. Though some early ragtime composers drew on cakewalk rhythms, most cakewalk writers never tackled the ragtime form, even after it had replaced their specialty in popularity. Mills wrote a single rag, "Wyoming Prance" (1910), whereas Lampe, who was the chief arranger for Remick, composed two rags under the pseudonym Ribe Danmark: "Glad Rag" (1910) and "Turkey Trot-Rag Two Step" (1912). By a process of semantic juggling, however, cakewalks like Sherman Swisher's "King of Rags" (1908) and Mills's "Ragtime Dance" (1909) were fobbed off as ragtime to a public that made no real distinctions between the two genres, except to regard the latter as more fashionable. Even before ragtime became popular and the cakewalk passé, the two terms were used capriciously by the music industry. Thus, in 1898 a Harry Von Tilzer coon song was titled "Rastus Thompson's Rag Time Cake Walk," whereas in 1899 Pryor published "Southern Hospitality Rag Time Cake Walk." A cakewalk of the same year by the black Detroit songwriter Fred S. Stone was titled "Bos'n Rag." The first three published rags, in fact, were cakewalks: William Krell's "Mississippi Rag" (January 1897), William Beebe's "Ragtime March" (published three days afterward), and R. J. Hamilton's "Ragtime Patrol." Though Krell's orchestral composition was labeled by its publisher, S. Brainard's Sons of Chicago, as "the first rag-time two step ever written," it presented no departure whatsoever from established cakewalk convention, beginning in the customary minor key and presenting a slightly syncopated, single-note melody. If either the composer or the publisher attached any musical significance to the term *rag-time,* it could only have meant *syncopation.* Even as a syncopated two-step, however, "Mississippi Rag" was not novel in any respect but belonged in the same category as Mills's "Rastus on Parade."

It was not until October 1897 that the first true ragtime composition was published. Like its predecessor rags, it bore the imprint of a Chicago publishing house. It has been suggested that ragtime's early publishing association with Chicago was a delayed reaction to the Columbian Exposition held there in 1893, which was attended by Harney and Joplin. This composition was "Louisiana Rag" by Theodore H. Northrup, who worked as an arranger for the firm that issued the piece, Thompson Music Company. Northrup seemed to have had a special interest in syncopation. His first entry was as early as 1891 with an instrumental, "Two Happy Coons." In 1897, Thompson published two more: "Night on the Levee," subtitled "Rag Dance," contrasts cakewalk devices with surprisingly ambitious syncopation; "Plantation Echoes" is similar but drops most of the cakewalk flavor in favor of more fully textured and pianistic syncopation. Both pieces were steps toward his full-fledged piano rag, "Louisiana Rag."

"Louisiana Rag" was a truly unconventional offering even within the context of later ragtime. Though its opening section had a pronounced cakewalk rhythm, it used three different rhythm patterns that removed it from the sphere of dance music. The second section inverted the typical ragtime attack by setting a strong left-hand syncopation against a more steady right hand, a device later associated with Harlem stride pianists. The end of the second section contained an unusual suggestion of Latin rhythm, perhaps reflecting the influence of "Trocha," a Latin-flavored piece composed the previous year by a West Indian, William Tyers.

The four sections of "Louisiana Rag" were unraveled in a pattern later used in Joplin's "The Chrysanthemum" (1904): AABBA/CCDDC. Unlike the latter, however, "Louisiana Rag" closed with a recapitulation of the first section.

Northrup was never recognized as ragtime's earliest composer of record, and his publishers made no historic claims on behalf of the work. Rather, they seemed determined to cash in on the popularity of an 1895 Hogan coon song title by printing the legend "Pas Ma La" on its cover; the "Pas Ma La" was a black dance step featured in another song title of the period, Paul Rubens's "Rag-Time Pasmala" (1899). Neither this gimmick nor the subsequent appearance of "Louisiana Rag" as a piano roll—issued by the Universal Music Company—rescued it from almost total commercial failure. It was Northrup who provided the syncopated arrangements for Harney's *Ragtime Instructor* (1897). In 1898, Northrup's "On a Bayou," a ragtime two-step, was issued by the American Musical Association in Chicago, and his name appears as the arranger of a 1901 coon song by Brown and Allen, "Every Darky Had a Raglan On." Though a pioneering publication endeavor, "Louisiana Rag" plainly echoed an already established piano tradition that wanted less for composers than promoters. The separate publication of five other rags in 1897 by scattered publishing firms in New Orleans, Cincinnati, and St. Louis indicated the spread of both this tradition across the South and Midwest and its early compositional uncertainties. Were it not for the presence among them of Tom Turpin's relatively elegant "Harlem Rag," one would be tempted to explain the vagaries of this early ragtime in terms of an unfocused tradition rather than the ineptitude of the typical 1897 composer, who was generally preoccupied with syncopation at the expense of other musical qualities. Two Cincinnati concoctions by Robert S. Roberts, a professional arranger—"Pride of Bucktown" and "A Bundle of Rags," both published by Philip Kussel—alternate between cakewalk rhythm patterns and erratic, eccentric syncopated piano figures. Walter Starck's equally ungainly but more engaging "Darktown Capers—An Original Southern Rag," published by Shattinger Music of St. Louis and later brought out by Joplin's publisher, Starck is virtually monothematic, alternating between eight- and sixteen-measure sections in the key of A flat. Besides "Harlem Rag," the first published product of a black composer, the most compositionally noteworthy of these early entries was Paul Sarebresole's "Roustabout Rag," published by Gruenewald of New Orleans. It featured the three-over-four rhythm pattern that became ragtime's most conspicuous element after 1905: a sequence of three different notes placed within a four-beat measure, which resulted in the accenting of a new note whenever the phrase was repeated.

By 1898 the word *ragtime* had become a sheet-music catch phrase, randomly employed in the title or subtitle of over a dozen compositions issued that year by various publishers in New York, Chicago, Detroit, St. Louis, Kansas City, and even San Francisco. But if the word had suddenly acquired sales value in the eyes of music publishers and songwriters—perhaps mindful of Harney's vaudeville success, or merely desperate for novel musical labels—the ragtime form had not. An indication that the music had no commercial status is seen by the fact that the ragtime instruction books of Max Hoffman and Harney were actually vehicles to promote coon songs. With these publications the technical problems of scoring ragtime syncopation were disposed of. Ragtime compositions as such, however, played almost no part in the sheet music of 1898 and had no impact on the world of popular music until Joplin's masterful "Maple Leaf Rag" appeared the following year. It was Joplin's genius that gave ragtime its self-conscious compositional character and provided a framework that later composers could readily assimilate. Yet for years to come numerous ragtime composers continued to work within the naive, untutored tradition of pre-"Maple Leaf" ragtime, all but oblivious to Joplinesque refinement. These were the so-called Folk ragtime composers.

## "The Ragtime Betty" (James Scott)

### October 5, 1909, Stark Music Co., St. Louis

Scott's most complex essay of 1909, it contains all his hallmarks in a more demanding and involved format than in the preceding rags. Section C has short one-measure runs of single-note lines that Scott made greater use of later on.

# "Ragtime Bobolink" (Joseph Lamb)

### *Ragtime Treasures,* 1964, Mills Music, Inc., New York

Intricate, challenging Lamb rag in his most advanced Classic rag style.

# "Ragtime Chimes" (Egbert Van Alstyne)

### October 16, 1900, Will Rossiter, Chicago

The first rag published to use the chimes effect that subsequently became a popular device. Van Alstyne later became a famous popular composer, best known for his songs.

# "Ragtime Chimes" (Percy Wenrich)

### July 26, 1911, Jerome H. Remick & Co., New York

A clever chimes effect on a very pianistic figure in section A.

# "The Ragtime Dance" (Scott Joplin)

### December 21, 1906, John Stark & Son, St. Louis

Originally written as a folk ballet with lyrics, it was performed at Wood's Opera House in Sedalia before the turn of the twentieth century. Published in this form by Stark in 1902, it was a commercial failure. In an effort to recoup his losses, he issued this instrumental version, which eliminated a thirty-two-measure verse. This is a joyous work and, in keeping with his other rags written in Sedalia, a most beautiful ragtime number.

# "Ragtime Fantasy for Piano & Orchestra" (Dick Hyman)

### March 15, 1976, Eastlake Music, Inc., New York

This is a marvelous synthesis of ragtime highlights of Scott Joplin, Jelly Roll Morton, Eubie Blake, James P. Johnson, and Zez Confrey—in a delightfully original manner. By far, the most ambitious use of ragtime materials, it is artfully done. The piece, commissioned by the Austin Symphony Society and performed by the Austin Symphony Orchestra with the composer at the piano on January 30, 1976, is suitable for ballet.

# "Ragtime Nightingale" (Joseph Lamb)

## June 10, 1915, Stark Music Co., St. Louis

One of the all-too-rare descriptions of how a great rag was inspired and set about is Lamb's story of how he was inspired by James Scott's "Ragtime Oriole" and the concept of a bird-call rag. He did not know what a nightingale sounded like but took a bit from Chopin's "Revolutionary Etude" and another bit from Ethelbert Nevin's "Nightingale Song." Highlight comes in section A, which sets a majestic mood, largely in C minor.

# "A Ragtime Nightmare" (Tom Turpin)

## April 13, 1900, Robt. De Yong & Co., St. Louis

"A Ragtime Nightmare" was used as a subtitle for Ben Harney's "Cakewalk in the Sky" of 1899, but here Turpin is effecting a musical contrast most widely popularized in a banjo instrumental recorded by Vess L. Ossman and Fred Van Eps. The performance is based on a very popular prerag character piece, "Darkies Dream," by George Lansing, one of several whimsical compositions that achieve a rustic sound through the use of the old Schottische rhythm. However, a later version by the banjoists included a second part in fast march style called "Darkies Awakening," contrasting to the slow dream opening. Here in "Nightmare," Turpin condenses the idea, opening with an eight-measure Schottische introduction that changes suddenly to the even rhythm of the A strain as the real "Ragtime Nightmare" begins. This was the last of the Turpin–De Yongs that went almost immediately to Rossiter. The A section is spiced with a chromatic run, a bit of Turpin's dramatic pianistics, and one that Classic rag composer James Scott used ten years later in the same context ("Ophelia Rag"). C is the busy single-note line here, a tradition that harks back to virtuoso fiddle and banjo playing.

# "Ragtime Oriole" (James Scott)

## December 10, 1911, Stark Music Co., St. Louis

An outstanding rag that pioneered the use of bird calls in ragtime. Among the greatest syncopated masterpieces, the unity of feeling is superb. The A section looks ahead to what was going to happen in the Novelty rags. The C section is, of course, another way of stating the C and bits of B from the "Maple Leaf Rag." The D section illustrates the high degree of musicianship that Scott possessed; he took a midwestern blues device and reshaped it on an ascending circle of fifths connected with chromatic runs.

# Ragtime Performance

Though ragtime, as a form of music, necessarily makes the composition of prime importance, in the professional playing of it, the performer and its performance assumes greater interest. Playing any kind of music usually means reading the notes in a desultory fashion. This is something that is done at home, during practice sessions. Performing a piece requires an understanding of the music, not just the ability to get through it. It further demands a personal interpretation by the performer that derives from his understanding of the composition. In ragtime performance, the performer's ideal is to combine the piece's flavor while establishing, and maintaining, his own musical identity throughout. One develops certain stylistic tricks to sustain interest in the performance. One, over time, also develops a personal performing sound; for example, Jelly Roll Morton even extended his personal playing sound to his compositions, all immediately identifiable as belonging to him.

# The Ragtime Pianist

Contrary to popular belief, the ragtime pianist is a product of the mid fifties onward. It was during the first ragtime revival that this phenomenon surfaced. Heretofore, pianists who performed ragtime in public—in houses of ill repute, in vaudeville, as part of dance bands and jazz bands—also performed other popular music of the day. It was not until the first ragtime revival that ragtime caught the attention of pianists of jazz and popular dance music that some of them wanted to play ragtime exclusively. That meant that venues other than nightclubs and bars needed to be found to satisfy the needs of their audiences. Loud talking and drinking in smoke-filled rooms did not allow the listeners to fully hear either the compositions or the interpretations of the rags being played. During the 1960s, ragtime festivals came into existence allowing the fans to create a listening environment in which to appreciate the rags and performances. From this to formal concerts in halls became the norm for the fans to hear their favorite performers. During this time, the performers who became steady favorites at festivals and all-ragtime concerts started to make long-playing recordings that were offered to fans attending these specialized venues. Most composers of new rags were also their own performers. Pianists now concentrate on a repertoire of rags in various combinations, from all-Joplin (or any one composer's rags) to a wide variety of ragtime periods (Folk rags, Tin Pan Alley rags, Advanced rags, Stride rags, Novelty rags, contemporary rags) or one type of rag or even rags composed in a geographic area (e.g., St. Louis, Indianapolis, New York City). During the past fifty years, the ragtime pianist has come into his own, and as ragtime festivals flourish in different parts of the country, so are the ragtime pianists encouraged to stick with this musical specialty.

# Ragtime Publications

The first publication devoted to the various musics hiding under the ragtime ruberic was Axel Christensen's *The Ragtime Review,* a monthly magazine started in Chicago in December 1914. It lasted until the January 1918 issue, whereupon Christensen continued with a monthly column in Boston publisher Walter Jacobs's *Melody* magazine throughout the twenties. It was not until 1961 that Trebor Tichenor and Russ Cassidy wrote and published their publication *The Ragtime Review* in honor of Christensen's pioneer periodical. Their first issue, however, was dated January 1962. This one did better, lasting through the April 1966 issue. This was followed by *The Ragtimer,* the journal of the Canadian-based Ragtime Society, which also started publishing with their January 1962 issue and ended with their 1986 publication. Dick Zimmerman, a cofounder of the Maple Leaf Club in Los Angeles, became editor of *The Rag Times* at its inception on May 15, 1967, and has continued to research, write, and edit it throughout its lengthy career, sporadically during the millenium, its latest issue dated July 2003. Since its first issue, it has contained the latest news, reviews of books and records, the latest research on relevant topics and people in ragtime, and important historical reprints

# THE RagTime Review

Special Issue Summer, 1965    Vol. 4 No. 3A    St. Louis, Mo. Bicentennial

# GOLDENROD SHOWBOAT PRESENTS BICENTENNIAL RAGTIME MUSIC FESTIVAL ON ST. LOUIS RIVERFRONT, WEEKEND OF AUGUST 13-15

**Musical Greats of the Nation Featured with "St. Louis Ragtimers" Band in Nite Performances Fri. & Sat., Matinee Sat., & Special "On the Levee" Concert Sun.; Ragtime and Classic Jazz.**

Ragtime — the foot-tapping music that flourished under St. Louis leadership during the city's glorious steamboat and turn-of-the-century days — highlights a unique musical treat on the weekend of August 13th through 15th, as an official St. Louis Bicentennial public program on the levee at the Gateway Arch.

Centering appropriately about the historic St. Louis riverfront and the famed Goldenrod Showboat, the Festival of "music of the good old days" spotlights the authentic ragtime renditions of the nationally-known St. Louis Ragtimers, regular entertainers on the Goldenrod Showboat.

### Ragtime A St. Louis Music Form

A wealth of other widely acclaimed musicians and recording artists join the festivities in a spectacular gathering of talent and virtuoso presentations of the Ragtime and classic Jazz music of that nostalgic era. Familiar old melodic favorites mix with all-time classic numbers of Ragtime music that was born and nurtured in Missouri and St. Louis on its way to national popularity.

### Friday & Saturday Nights, 10:30

Aboard the air-conditioned Goldenrod Showboat, the St. Louis Ragtimers

*GOLDENROD SHOWBOAT — air conditioned home of old-time melodrama, and saloon-deck haunt of St. Louis Ragtimers.*

and guest artists hold forth on Friday and Saturday nights, beginning at 10:30 p.m. after the presentation of the "Old Time Melodrama" which runs from 8:15 to 10 p.m.

On Saturday night at 10:30, with admission $1.50, the Ragtimers and guest artists present a more intimate preview version of the wide-ranging program of Sunday afternoon on the levee.

#### Saturday Matinee, 2 to 5 p.m.

On Saturday afternoon at 2:00, with admission $3.00, the Ragtimers and famed musicians present a "Concert in Ragtime", aboard the Goldenrod. The artists vie in authentic flourishes of interpretation on old favorites, classics, and new compositions in the great old-time Ragtime musical form.

A word to the wise: since Goldenrod seating is necessarily limited, call GA 1-8675 for reservations to enjoy the special Saturday afternoon session.

**Free Bicentennial Concert Sunday, Aug. 15, 3 p.m., On the Levee Climaxes Ragtime Festival**

On the historic St. Louis levee beside the Goldenrod Showboat, all St. Louisans are invited to enjoy a free concert of St. Louis-centered Ragtime and other old-time music, as an official Bicentennial program in sight of the Gateway Arch and riverfront development.

The unique concert on Sunday, August 15, at 3 p.m., climaxes the Ragtime Festival with the St. Louis Ragtimers and guest artists presenting a wide range of cakewalks, ragtime, and classic jazz from a special bandstand beside the Goldenrod.

The Showboat is located just south of the Admiral landing at the foot of Washington Ave. below Eads Bridge. Parking is available on the levee and at the riverfront lot on Washington just south of Eads Bridge above the levee. As with other outdoor levee entertainments, small folding chairs or blankets for sitting are recommended.

# BLIND BOONE
## LINK TO RAGTIME ORIGINS

From an article by

PATRICIA RICE

in the

ST LOUIS POST DISPATCH

RAGTIME is keeping feet tapping again. Disk jockeys are spinning ragtime records and ragtime albums are in demand at record shops. The movie, "The Sting," used Scott Joplin's ragtime music on its soundtrack. One of the best-selling albums last year was the New England Conservatory Ragtime Ensemble's renditions.

On the levée, the St. Louis Ragtimers are playing to more attentive, knowledgeable audiences

The audiences are asking more questions, and one of the questions is where did ragtime come from. Lots of ragtime was played in St. Louis - in the "tenderlóin" along Morgan Street (Delmar) and Franklin Avenue. The black piano player was paid good money to play the exciting music in the garish bordellos.

Ragtime's musical origins are harder to pin down. One of the links with where the music began is the ragtime music of Blind Boone.

Boone wasn't a stereotype piano player wearing sleeve garters and pounding away on a bordello upright.

Boone was a debonair black pianist who played in the finest halls here and in Europe. He was considered an outstanding musician by his peers and won acclaim from Paderewski and Rachmaninoff. His repertoire was vast and he had the near-genius gift of being able to imitate anything he heard after one or two hearings.

When Mrs. Irene Cortinovis, assistant director of archives and manuscripts at the University of Missouri at St. Louis, interviewed 20 old Mississippi Riverboat musicians, she found that Boone was one of their heroes.

Boone, a black man who had made it in the white European tradition of classical music, loved ragtime. He used to get lost from time to time and go to bordello districts where he played ragtime.

He may have been one of the first musicians to play ragtime before an audience of white men and women in a serious music concert hall. When his audience would become restless after a number of concertos he would stop and say: "We are going to put the cookies on the lower shelf now," and he would burst out in a rag.

The rag the audience heard was not like the rag you buy in the record shop today - even if what you are buying is a recording of 1900 piano rolls. Boone re-

**NEXT MEET APRIL 2 AT THE MAYFAIR**

Our next Extravaganza of Syncopation will be one week later than usual since Easter falls on the last Sunday in March. Join us April 2 at the Mayfair Music Hall, 214 Santa Monica Blvd. in Santa Monica from 1:30 until 4:30. Who knows, maybe someone will play "April Fool Rag!" As always admission is free. Snacks and spirits will also be available.

DEDICATED TO THE
PRESERVATION OF
CLASSICAL RAGTIME

of articles throughout the ragtime years. For most of its life, it was a bimonthly that kept the ragtime community informed of all ragtime events. It has lately been published as time permits but is eagerly awaited nevertheless. The closest publication is Leslie Johnson's *The Mississippi Rag*, named after the first musical composition called a rag but shares articles and reviews with the band music known as traditional jazz. It started as a monthly newspaper with the November 1973 issue in Minneapolis and until October 2006, continued as the only regular source for news and reviews of ragtime in the world. Although its print publication stopped, it can be found on the Internet as of January 2007.

# The Ragtime Revival, 1941–1978

Shortly after Jelly Roll Morton's death, interest in ragtime was renewed, first by musicians and then by critics and listeners—people dissatisfied with the contemporary big band swing sounds who yearned for the older forms of American popular music.

The spread of ragtime from the 1940s on was mainly accomplished with the vital help of the record industry. Lu Watters's Yerba Buena Jazz Band was formed in 1941 in San Francisco, and they made their first recordings by the end of that year. Their local fans were vociferous and loyal, but it was not until they made some records that they influenced countless pianists and other young traditional jazz bands. Their repertoire included piano rags, many discovered by the trombonist Turk Murphy. As their pianist Wally Rose recalled, in their set of first recordings, their version of George Botsford's "Black and White Rag" sold well enough to pay for the entire recording venture. Radio stations picked up their records and played them over and over. The original sound the band created was perfect for the rags being rediscovered. Rose had to adapt the rags to his conditions, which included a heavy rhythm section: banjo, tuba, and drums. He had to thicken them so that he could be heard in the clubs. As a result, his versions have a unique and satisfying sound. All of his recordings with the band are available on Good Time Jazz (12001, 12002, 12003, 12007, 12024), Homespun (101, 102, 103, 104, 105, 106), and Fairmont (101, 102).

Ragtime Revival, Joplin.

Ragtime Revival, The Sting.

During the forties two major jazz magazines published the majority of articles concerning ragtime: *The Record Changer* and *Jazz Journal.* The former was started in 1942 in Virginia, and the latter began publication in 1949 in London. With rags appearing on records, the critics now had something to pick apart. The critical wrangling led to chapters on ragtime being included in the jazz histories that came out during this decade. Because the writers of the jazz histories were the same ones writing the articles on ragtime for the magazines, their comments on ragtime were terribly uninformed and often wrong. All of them placed ragtime as jazz's antecedent and looked on ragtime as the beginning of jazz. Their assumption in linking ragtime with jazz bands was logical—from their viewpoint—because most ragtime was being played in the forties within traditional jazz bands, either by the bands in toto or else, as in the case of the Yerba Buena Jazz Band, by the piano with full rhythm accompaniment. At the end of the forties, the ragtime-jazz association was further cemented by jazz pianists such as Don Ewell, Ralph Sutton, Marvin Ash, Paul Lingle, and Dick Wellstood, all of whom made piano ragtime recordings in a jazzy, swingy manner.

The Dixieland bands, wanting variety in their repertoire, and in imitation of the Yerba Buena Jazz Band, included rags not only in their club dates but for their recording sessions as well. The outstanding bands of that time were Pete Daily and his Chicagoans, Pee Wee Hunt and his orchestra (actually five men), and the great playing-for-kicks band from the Walt Disney studio, The Firehouse Five Plus Two.

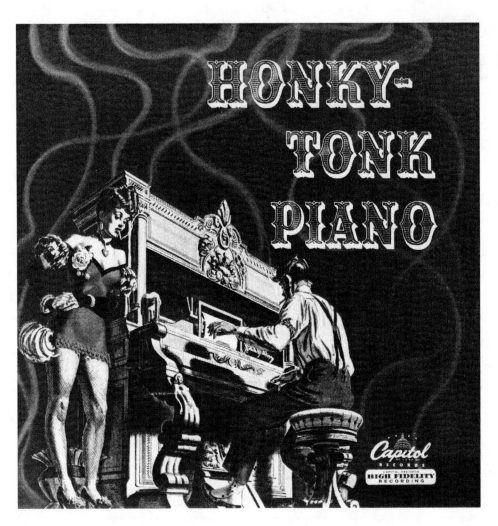

Ragtime Revival, Honky-Tonk.

The importance of the jazz magazines to the ragtime revival is apparent by the many articles devoted to the subject. Another stimulus came from the record reviews given to ragtime recordings. The ragtime movement was helped by so many jazz musicians playing and recording rags. In publications sympathetic to ragtime, old timers started reminiscing in print about the days when ragtime was new. And not only were these people being given opportunities to write about the old days, but some also discovered even older ragtime composers and performers. New companies were formed to record these pioneers, rather late in their lives. One consideration in evaluating these recordings is that even though many years had passed, the pioneer composer–performers were playing the rags in their original manner. Their playing shows that they retained the original flavor and optimism of ragtime's happily infectious sounds. They put their creations permanently onto disc, enabling future generations to hear their ideas and styles. Luckey Roberts, Euday Bowman, James P. Johnson, and Charles Thompson were among those pioneers who recorded during this decade—some for the first time. And Morton's fabled set for the Library of Congress was made available in a limited collector's edition during the late forties. *Piano Ragtime of the Forties* (Herwin 403) makes many of the best of these recordings available on LP.

The fifties was the most creative and active period for piano ragtime since ragtime's early era of explosive popularity. There were significant differences in both the sound of the piano and in the players. Starting in 1950, ragtime appeared to the public through the publication of *Mister Jelly Roll*, Morton's autobiography, and

*They All Played Ragtime* (a social history and the first book devoted entirely to ragtime), Riverside Records' recordings of ragtime piano rolls, and Capitol Records' worldwide promotion of ragtime with such piano artists as Joe "Fingers" Carr as well as Dixieland jazz band interpretations. Ragtime was once again a popular music form, not only in America but now all over the world. This was no flash-in-the-pan popularity but rather a steady development that increased with the years. More ragtime was recorded during this decade by more people than during any other decade in history. And it was ragtime of the widest variety, the entire spectrum from Folk to Novelty. It was more than a revival. Rags were being newly composed, published, and recorded. They were bright, fresh rags that evoked the golden age of ragtime while using more modern harmonies.

This was an age when jazz musicians continued to play rags, giving them a performer's swing not found in their printed form. They added a new dimension to the music that attracted more fans. Professional studio musicians were pressed into service by the large recording companies to satisfy the demand for honky tonk music, the pop music from the 1890s through the 1920s played on slightly out-of-tune pianos with a tinny sound, recalling the old saloon days. But when these professional musicians—Bill Krenz, Lou Busch, Sid Nierman, Ray Turner, Billy Rowland, Buddy Weed, and Dick Hyman—recorded, usually with rhythm sections, they also recorded real rags, building up the weaker ones by clever new arrangements. They also composed their own rags.

It was also a time when pseudonyms masked these professional musicians (e.g., Joe "Fingers" Carr, Knuckles O'Toole, Pete Handy), and it is a mistake to dismiss them without studying their sparkling originality, for they added significantly to ragtime's ever-growing repertoire. Their musical tastes and skill created a highly polished series of performances that has not been equaled since. A sampling may be found on *Piano Ragtime of the Fifties* (Herwin 404).

The major jazz magazine established during the fifties was *Record Research,* devoted to the art of discography. Piano-roll scholar Mike Montgomery presented a series of rollographies, which coincided with renewed interest in new player pianos and the QRS Company's release of rolls of reissued Classic ragtime from their vast catalog.

The first all-ragtime long-playing disc came from Capitol Records, whose phenomenally successful late forties recording of Hunt's version of "12th Street Rag" prompted that company under the brilliant leadership of James Conkling to go all out promoting ragtime. They recorded and developed such groups as Pete Daily, Nappy Lamare, Hunt, Chuck Thomas, and Red Nichols's Five Pennies and transformed the outstanding arranger–conductor–pianist–composer, Busch, into the most well-known international favorite, Carr.

That first all-ragtime LP was incorrectly called *Honky Tonk Piano* (Capitol H-188), but its cover made a lasting impression. The LP featured three fine pianists who grew up during the teens and twenties and well remembered the old ragtime performances. Marvin Ash was a jazz musician who had played in bands and soloed throughout the West and Midwest. Ray Turner, born in St. Joseph, Missouri, played with Paul Whiteman's orchestra and became the film industry's greatest pianist, playing entire scores for the imaginative life stories of great composers in which Hollywood indulged throughout the forties and fifties. He had a prodigious technique and tremendous affection for the Novelty rags, which he recorded for the album. The third member of this truly epoch-making LP was none other than Busch, who, in addition to creating a unique overall ragtime sound, composed an original rag for this album. At this time he adopted his world-famous pseudonym, Joe "Fingers" Carr, under which he recorded a greater number of rags—most for the first time—than anybody up to his time. He also composed more original rags than anyone since the original ragtime years.

The fifties also saw the rise of the ragtime entertainers. Coming from the South and Southwest, their forte was playing in clubs away from the major musical centers and building an incredible following. Del Wood came to prominence from her native Nashville with her recording of "Down Yonder." This led to her appearance on the *Grand Old Opry* network radio show and her marvelous composition, "Ragtime Melody." Johnny Maddox made the first 78 rpm recording for the Dot Record Company in his hometown of Gallatin,

Tennessee. His 10" LP, *Authentic Ragtime* (Dot DLP-102), was filled with the down-home flavor of the pioneers like Brun Campbell, because Maddox was taught by his great-aunt who had lived and performed in the ragtime era. Bob Darch, from Detroit, left the army and started playing and singing ragtime solos and syncopated songs in Alaska and throughout the West. Passing through Colorado, he influenced another like-minded actor-turned-entertainer, Max Morath, who developed an appreciation for the entire age. Morath developed his love of theater and music and combined them doing stage shows, with appropriate scenery, costumes, song slides, and authentic stories and jokes from the turn of the century. He had the first television series devoted to ragtime over the educational stations at the end of the fifties.

In the sixties the first modern-day journal dedicated to ragtime, the *Ragtime Review,* was established (edited by Russell Cassidy and Trebor Jay Tichenor). This publication featured the first serious attempt at analyzing Classic rags and contributing articles exhibiting first-class scholarship. The *Review* was quickly joined by the *Ragtimer,* the journal of the Canadian-based Ragtime Society, the first organization devoted to the appreciation of ragtime. The society was the first to reprint the long-forgotten rags, and the *Ragtimer* kept readers informed of ragtime activities around the world, reviewed recordings of ragtime, and reprinted the early articles on ragtime. Later, the society started a recording company to produce albums by contemporary pianists performing ragtime. In 1964 it also initiated a bash, an annual get-together in Toronto during a weekend usually in late October or early November. This enabled the membership to join together in a meeting of good fellowship, listening, talking and playing ragtime. It was one of the major ragtime events each year.

In 1967 Zimmerman started the Maple Leaf Club for ragtime fans on the West Coast, holding an all-day meeting once every two months. He issues a bimonthly journal called the *Rag Times.* In addition to describing the meetings and reviewing recordings, publications, and news stories pertaining to ragtime, he also published for the first time a sheet-music version of the sensational discovery of Joplin's "Silver Swan Rag." Dave Bourne's Dawn of the Century Ragtime Orchestra (Arcane AR-601, 602, 603) was composed of members who attended the bimonthly meetings. It was probably the best of the ragtime orchestras, playing authentic arrangements from the ragtime age. In the early sixties, John W. "Knocky" Parker was the first to record the complete works of Joplin and Scott, mostly omitting the repeats and improvising on the sections. Later in the decade he made four albums called *The Golden Treasury of Ragtime,* a chronological gathering from 1895 to 1913. Most of those rags had never been recorded previously.

It was a time when only one jazz musician—a modern jazz pianist at that—recorded an album of rags. Hank Jones, a versatile musician, became intrigued with ragtime and produced an incredibly understanding series of ragtime performances with taste and great skill (*This Is Ragtime Now,* ABC-Paramount 496) in 1964.

In St. Louis, "the cradle of ragtime," a trio was formed comprising Trebor Jay Tichenor on piano, Al Stricker on banjo, and Don Franz on tuba and called the St. Louis Ragtimers. As their popularity grew from playing at Gaslight Square, they added cornetist Bill Mason and finally clarinetist Glen Meyer. Their unusual repertoire is based on Tichenor's vast resources in ragtime piano rolls and music sheets. Since 1965, the Ragtimers have been hosts at the annual National Ragtime Festival aboard the Goldenrod Showboat, a registered historic landmark, and the largest showboat ever built. Usually taking place in mid June, the festival lasted an entire week and featured the best of the active ragtime pianists.

The sixties saw the surfacing of composer–pianists who came to ragtime in the late forties and early fifties, growing up with the recordings of the past, collecting sheet music and piano rolls, and interviewing pioneer ragtime composers, performers, and publishers. Recording for small, specialist LP labels, Dave Jasen, Tichenor, Tom Shea, Charlie Rasch, John Arpin, and Donald Ashwander were promoted throughout the world and appeared at the St. Louis Ragtime Festival and at the Ragtime Society's Ragtime Bash.

In the seventies an unprecedented awareness of Joplin arose through recordings by Joshua Rifkin, who played the Joplin rags in a classical music manner (Nonesuch H-71248, 71264, 71305). He influenced an entirely new audience—students of classical music, studying in conservatories and universities.

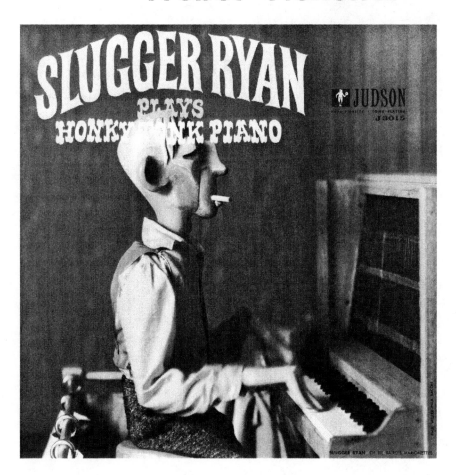

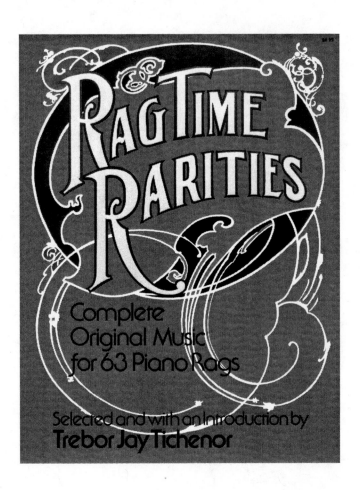

The next big event was the publication by the New York Public Library of a two-volume set of *The Collected Works of Scott Joplin,* meticulously edited by Vera Brodsky Lawrence. It is the definitive edition of Joplin's works, and it prompted the staging of Joplin's folk opera, *Treemonisha,* which had its world premiere in Atlanta, Georgia, in January 1972 and its Broadway premiere in 1975.

The explosion in the ragtime world came with the motion picture, *The Sting* (Universal Studios, 1974), which used six Joplin rags as background music. The arrangements were orchestrated by Marvin Hamlisch, who also played piano on the soundtrack. His version of "The Entertainer" put that 1902 Joplin rag on top of the Hit Parade and made it the number-one recording for 1974. It was a genuine pop hit, and millions of people around the world became conscious of classic ragtime.

The Joplin rage was further stimulated by the first complete recording of Joplin's works done by Zimmerman (Murray Hill 931079). Its success spurred RCA to ask Hyman to record the piano works for their classical Red Seal label (RCA CRL5-1106).

The seventies produced significant activities designed to ensure the posterity of ragtime performances on record and piano roll through their issuance on long-playing albums for record companies who specialized in jazz and ragtime. The first of the reissues coincided with the Lawrence edition of Joplin's works and was, appropriately, an album devoted to Joplin's "Maple Leaf Rag" (*They All Played the Maple Leaf Rag,* Herwin 401), performed by the greatest ragtime exponents over a sixty-year span. Biograph, Folkways, Eubie Blake Music, and Yazoo, as well as Herwin, have produced the finest ragtime reissues on LP.

Publications have been an important part of the ragtime scene in the 1970s. First came Dave Jasen's ragtime discography for 78 rpm discs called *Recorded Ragtime* (Archon, 1973). Then came William Schafer and Johannes Riedel's *The Art of Ragtime* (Louisiana State University Press, 1973) and then Terry Waldo's fine

Neville Dickie.

ragtime history, *This Is Ragtime* (Hawthorne, 1976). Quality folios of reprinted ragtime sheet music complemented the reissued recordings. The finest of these was issued by Dover (*Classic Piano Rags,* 0-486-20469-3
and *Ragtime Rarities,* 0-486-23157-7), the Charles Hanson folio, *A Tribute to Scott Joplin and the Giants of
Ragtime* (R049), and *The Big 3* ("100 Greatest Ragtime Hits," Vol. 1-B3-3262; Vol. 2-B3-3263).

To climax thirty-five years of the ragtime revival, a bicentennial concert was staged at the C. W. Post
Center of Long Island University in Brookville, Long Island, New York, on October 30, 1976. It was called
"Rags to Riches" and featured the greatest collection of ragtime stylists on the same stage in one evening,
the first such gathering since Mike Bernard won the National Ragtime Piano Contest at Tammany Hall on
January 23, 1900. This ragtime spectacular included Carr, who came out of retirement to perform his first
engagement on the East Coast; Neville Dickie, making his debut in the United States; Bob Seeley; the St.
Louis Ragtimers; Dick Wellstood; Hyman; and Jasen. The concert was a huge success, and *New York Times*
critic John S. Wilson's headline for the review stated, "Ragtime Program with 7 on the Piano Hits Its Stride
Well." (*New York Times,* November 1, 1976)

# "Ragtime Special" (Joseph Lamb)

## March 27, 1959, unpublished

"Respectfully dedicated to my friend, Scott Joplin." A curious Lamb reflection on the earliest Folk rag style
compilations, this seems almost a medley of various ideas, although it is finely put together. Sections C and
E contain only eight measures each, and the tonal plan of the entire rag keeps moving as in the early rags—it
begins in the key of G, goes to C, and finally to F.

## "Ramshackle Rag" (Ted Snyder)

### March 10, 1911, self, New York

A good rag with clever phrasing in the introduction and ambitious harmonies in the interlude.

## "Rapid Transit Rag" (Joseph Lamb)

### March 17, 1959, unpublished

A rag of motion, beginning with a minor strain, but one that could be used for chase scenes in the silent movies. The rest of the rag rolls along merrily in the major tonality.

## "Red Pepper, a Spicy Rag" (Henry Lodge)

### December 19, 1910, M. Witmark & Sons, New York

No less ingenious and more of a rouser than "Temptation." The idea of A is an unusually long series of sixteenths. B has the following pattern combined with the three-over-four and chromatic descents in the form of one-measure

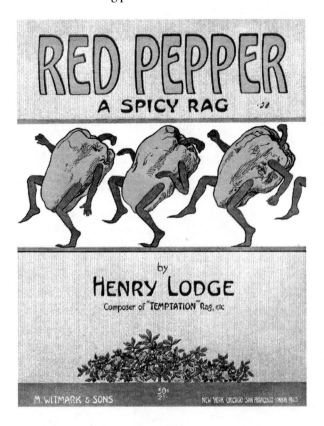

breaks. C is one of the most joyous strains in ragtime and combines syncopations from A and B. The interlude is in minor and cleverly written to lead back into C, which also begins on minor but ends in the relative major. Another popular Lodge hit, helped originally by the Fred Van Eps recording at the end of 1911 (Victor 17033).

# "Reflection Rag" (Scott Joplin)

## December 4, 1917, Stark Music Co., St. Louis

Posthumous publication of a work John Stark had bought before 1908. In a blurb when this was issued, Stark mentioned two more unpublished Joplin manuscripts owned by him. These were destroyed during the 1930s when the family moved their plant. "Reflection" is a pleasant rag with a characteristic final section that winds up Scott Joplin's ragtime with a strong, optimistic feeling.

# "Reindeer" (Joseph Lamb)

## Not copyrighted, published 1915, Stark Music Co., St. Louis

One of Lamb's light cakewalk-march inspired rags. In contrast to his more serious legato rags, part of A is marked to be played staccato. The tempo marking is a quarter-note equals 100. The B section has a most beautifully flowing melody.

# Jerome H. Remick and Company

Publisher Jerome H. Remick (1869–1931), a Detroit businessman, bought the old-line Detroit firm of Whitney Warner Publishing Company, with offices at 10 Witherell Street, in 1902. It did not take him long to determine that most of the publishing action was in New York City. At the end of 1902, Remick purchased Charles N. Daniels's Indian intermezzo, "Hiawatha," for the then unheard-of sum of $10,000 and installed Daniels in Detroit as his general manager. The following year, he bought out Louis Bernstein's half of Shapiro, Bernstein and Company to become a partner with Maurice Shapiro in Shapiro, Remick and Company, also proprietors of the Whitney Warner Company, located at 45 West 28th Street in New York.

At the end of 1904, Jerome Remick bought out Maurice Shapiro with the stipulation that Shapiro not engage in music publishing in the United States for two years. The beginning of 1905 saw the establishment of Jerome H. Remick and Company. Remick retained Fred E. Belcher (1869–1919) of the Whitney Warner staff in Detroit to look after his office in New York during the partnership with Shapiro. On establishing his own company, Remick kept Belcher in charge of the New York office, where his duties included overseeing the more than fifty retail stores Remick owned around the country. Moses Edwin Gumble (1871–1947), composer and plugger supreme, who had worked in 1902 as branch manager in Chicago for Shapiro, was brought to New York and put in charge of Remick's professional department, becoming the number-two man in the office after Belcher.

Jerome Remick, largest publisher of ragtime sheet music.

Remick kept his editorial headquarters in Detroit. Under the direction of composer Charles N. Daniels (usually writing under the pseudonym of Neil Moret), the firm prospered. It not only published over 100 rags but also established an enormous catalog of every kind of popular song with many hits. So large was his output that Remick was forced to buy a printing plant in 1907. His volume of published songs remained the largest of any Tin Pan Alley firm until the end of World War I. Like other major firms—Leo Feist, M. Witmark, Joseph W. Stern, and Shapiro—the Remick Company had a branch office in theater-filled Chicago, managed for years by Harry Werthan. When Daniels left Detroit in 1912 to move to the West Coast, the Remick editorial office moved to 219–221 West 46th Street in New York City under the guidance of Gumble. Fred Belcher became vice president and secretary of the Remick Company, supervising the empire from its new office. The firm took a twenty-year lease.

The first million-selling rag issued by Remick was Charles L. Johnson's "Dill Pickles Rag," which had first been published in 1906 by Carl Hoffman in Kansas City. Daniels, who had previously worked for Hoffman, bought the copyright in 1907, launched an extensive plugging campaign, and made it a huge success. The company's next million-selling rag was George Botsford's "Black and White Rag," in 1908. And so they continued until the end of the war.

About 2,000 rags were published, most of them originating from ragtime's regional, small-town roots. For all the influence that ragtime had on the popular music business, the form developed and took root far from New York City. While major publishers Stern, Snyder, Rossiter, Forster, Kremer, Vandersloot, Witmark, Mentel Bros., and Jenkins all issued more rags than the rest of the other publishers and had their share of ragtime hits, the total output of these nine firms did not equal the combined number of rags published by Stark and Remick.

The Remick firm was purchased by Warner Brothers Pictures in 1929 and merged with their other music holdings. Its back catalog is now part of Warner/Chappell Music, Inc.

Jerome Remick in his office.

Jerome H. Remick and Company (1904–1928)
1905–1908: 45 West 28th Street
1908–1911: 131 West 41st Street
1912–1931: 219–221 West 46th Street
1931–1935: 1657 Broadway (Hollywood Building, owned by Warner Bros.)

# Harry Reser

## (b. January 17, 1896, Piqua, Ohio;
## d. September 27, 1965, New York)

Reser was truly the greatest banjoist in the world. Unlike other banjo virtuosi, Reser first learned the guitar at the age of five, playing on one specially built as his hands were very small for his age. He learned the banjo many years later.

Harry showed his love for stringed instruments early on. As he was progressing on the guitar, he learned to play the violin and cello. It was not until he found that the banjo was popular on Broadway, in cafes, and dance halls that he investigated that instrument. Inspired by the artistry of Vess L. Ossman and Fred Van Eps, Harry, at the age of sixteen, mastered the intricacies first of the five-string and then of the plectrum and finally the tenor banjo.

Coming to New York City in 1921, he quickly joined such diverse recording groups as those headed by Joe Samuels, Milo Rega, Mike Markel, and Nathan Glantz. His first solos were recorded in 1922 and were of his newly minted Novelty rags. The final development of ragtime composition at the start of the '20s was known as Novelty ragtime. It was created and developed by hand-played piano-roll artists who had to make full, rich arrangements of the rather thin-sounding pop songs then in vogue. Taking their unusual tricks, they put together an extremely complex rhythmic and harmonic series of progressions that demanded the greatest technical skill to perform. Reser quickly challenged these piano masters as he composed equally difficult ragtime solos, but for the tenor banjo, which was normally regarded as basically a rhythm instrument. His technique was overwhelming, and he created the impression of playing two banjos at the same time—with the melody on one and keeping an even, steady rhythm with the other. Of his twenty-three original compositions for tenor banjo, Reser recorded ten of his Novelty rags, over an eight-year period.

Finding quick acceptance in the recording studios, he spent most of his time recording with many dance bands and then becoming leader of a group that recorded for several companies under a variety of names. Toward the end of 1925, he began what was to become a ten-year association with the Clicquot (pronounced klee-ko) Club Company. This Massachusetts-based firm manufactured carbonated soft drinks and used an Eskimo as the company symbol. When the company wanted to advertise on the newly developed radio and the newer-still concept of a radio network—independent radio stations agreeing to carry a program simultaneously—they went to the National Broadcasting Company and asked them to create a radio program they could sponsor.

Reser was asked for suggestions, and he came up with an orchestra featuring his banjo sound that resembled the fizz and sparkle of the soft drinks it was to represent. He composed their theme song, "The Clicquot Club March," produced the show, and directed the orchestra, which he called the Clicquot Club Eskimos. The studio audiences were treated to seeing the orchestra wearing Eskimo-type costumes. Both Reser and the company enjoyed unparalleled recognition and identification as a result of this weekly half-hour network radio program. From the mid thirties to the late fifties, he traveled extensively touring the world, playing in hotels, dance halls, and night clubs as well as for the Armed Forces and playing concerts. He managed to write ten instruction books for the banjo, guitar, and ukulele. He appeared on television as banjoist on Sammy Kaye's ABC network show, *Music from Manhattan.*

His last engagement was as guitarist—finishing as he started—in the orchestra for the hit Broadway musical *Fiddler on the Roof.* He never missed a performance of the show since its opening on September 22, 1964. On the evening of September 27, 1965, Reser went to the pit early to tune up. He was found there by fellow orchestra members with the guitar in his hands, dead of a heart attack. His unique and superb recorded performances and published compositions remain with us for our enjoyment.

# "Ripples of the Nile" (Luckey Roberts)

## Not copyrighted or published

Only syncopated section is C. A, from which was taken "Moonlight Cocktail," and B, which develops from A, are ballad-type material.

# Robbins Music Corporation

A new company was formed on January 1, 1922, when Maurice Richmond, a major jobber and a minor publisher who had bought the F. A. Mills catalog in 1915, created a firm with his nephew and general manager,

Jack Robbins.

John J. Robbins (1894–1959), whose nickname was Jack, to form Richmond–Robbins at 1658 Broadway. When Robbins became a partner with Harry Engel two years later (Robbins–Engel), the new firm stayed at the same address. From 1927 to 1935, when Robbins sold out to MGM, the firm was known as Robbins Music Corporation at 799 Seventh Avenue.

Robbins loved the Novelty rags as performed by the talented '20s band pianists. He bought and published almost as many as Mills Music. Included in his publications are "In a Mist," "Raindrops," "Pianogram," "The Birds Carnival," "One Finger Joe," "Up and Down in China," and "Bluin' the Black Keys."

In 1935, MGM formed The Big Three, including the holdings of Leo Feist, Miller Music, and Robbins.

# Charles Luckeyth Roberts

## (b. August 7, 1887, Philadelphia;
## d. February 5, 1968, New York)

Roberts began his show business career at five years old in Gus Seekes's *Pickaninnies,* which toured the country in vaudeville. He became an expert tumbler in addition to being a singer and dancer, and he traveled to Europe as part of Mayne Remington's *Ethiopian Prodigies.* He started learning piano at age five and quickly became New York's premier performer, playing at the Little Savoy Club in 1910. Roberts was unusually short, at four feet ten inches, but had long arms and massive hands that could stretch fourteen keys. He taught James P. Johnson and George Gershwin. Eubie Blake, with the same finger span, quickly became his friend. He studied counterpoint, fugue, and composition in private lessons. Roberts wrote musical revues and Broadway shows. He made his first recordings, which were never released, in 1916. He was the first of the Harlem stride ticklers to be published. He found his niche as an orchestra leader playing for the socialites in

Lucky Roberts.

Lucky Roberts label.

Palm Beach, Newport, and New York. When the Second World War put an end to the big parties, Roberts purchased a restaurant, the Rendezvous, in Harlem and ran it with singing waiters from 1942 till 1954 when he retired. He recorded solo piano sets in 1946 for Circle Sound and once more in 1958 for Good Time Jazz. He composed special material for radio, stage, and screen. His most popular songs include "Rosetime and You," "Railroad Blues," and "Moonlight Cocktail," taken from one section of his rag "Ripples of the Nile." His piano roll of "Mo'Lasses" (QRS 2306) is one of the greatest of all hand-played rolls and can be heard on Parlor Piano (Biograph BLP-1001Q).

## Ragtime Compositions

"The Junk Man Rag," May 26, 1913, Jos. W. Stern & Co., New York

"Pork and Beans," June 24, 1913, Jos. W. Stern & Co., New York·

"The Music Box Rag," October 23, 1914, Jos. W. Stern & Co., New York

"Shy and Sly," May 7, 1915, G. Ricordi & Co., New York

"Bon Ton," May 7, 1915, G. Ricordi & Co., New York

"Ripples of the Nile," not copyrighted or published

"Nothin'," not copyrighted or published

# J. Russel Robinson

## (b. July 8, 1892, Indianapolis; d. September 30, 1963, Palmdale, California)

Robinson attended Shortridge High School. Always fooling around the piano as a youngster, he finally took lessons and concentrated on reading. During high school he and his brother, John, a drummer, played for lodge dances and other social functions. From 1905 to 1909 the family accompanied the Famous Robinson Brothers as they toured the South, settling in Macon, Georgia, where they accompanied the silent movies. His first composition was "Sapho Rag," which was published by John Stark. During his stay in Macon he became acquainted with Ferd Guttenberger, a fine pianist and co-owner of the local music store. Robinson arranged and wrote down two of Guttenberger's rags, "Kalamity Kid" and "Log Cabin Rag." He wrote rags first, he remembered, because there was no demand for songs. In 1910 the family went to New Orleans to play at the Alamo Theatre and the Penny Wonderland. He was not impressed with the pianists there and called them fakers; they could not read music. The following year the brothers played in Montgomery, Alabama, where two more rags were written. He heard W. C. Handy's band at Memphis and said that they, too, were fakers. By 1912 the family had returned to Indianapolis, where "That Eccentric Rag" was written during a short walk with the publisher to his music store. At the store Robinson played it for him, wrote it down, and sold it for $25: "I don't know which made me most excited, the money or the prospect of getting another song in print…probably the latter." From 1917 to 1925 he worked for the Imperial Company and QRS—he was introduced by QRS in their catalog as "the White Boy with the colored fingers"—making two rolls a month and getting $50 apiece. During the day he worked as a demonstrator for Leo Feist, Inc. in Chicago. In 1918 he played at the Starr Theatre and began recording for Gennett. He wrote the words and music to "Singin' the Blues," which became a hit song in 1921. Finally, in late 1918 he went to New York, where he became Handy's personal manager. He met Al Bernard, lyric writer and blackface singer, and formed the famous vaudeville team called the Dixie Stars. They recorded for Columbia, Brunswick, Cameo, and Okeh. Robinson joined the famous Original Dixieland Jass Band in 1919 and went to London with

J. Russel Robinson.

them. He returned home at the end of the year but rejoined the group in mid 1920 and persuaded them to add the alto saxophone virtuoso, Bennie Krueger. He also accompanied Lou Holtz, Kate Smith, and Marian Harris in vaudeville. Robinson wrote such great pop song hits during the twenties as "Margie" (earlier song in different tempo called "Lullaby Blues"), "Aggravatin' Papa," "Rhythm King" (as Joe Hoover), "Mary Lou," "Palesteena," and "Beale Street Mama." He went to the West Coast to freelance as composer.

## Ragtime Compositions

"Sapho Rag," October 5, 1909, Stark Music Co., St. Louis

"Dynamite Rag," October 1, 1910, Southern California Music, Los Angeles

"The Minstrel Man," July 27, 1911, Stark Music Co., St. Louis

"Whirl Wind," December 11, 1911, Stark Music Co., St. Louis

"That Erratic Rag," not copyrighted, published 1911, Stark Music Co., St. Louis

"Erratic," October 17, 1923, Jack Mills, Inc., New York

"That Eccentric Rag," January 22, 1912, I. Seidel Music, Indianapolis

"Eccentric," October 17, 1923, Jack Mills, Inc., New York

"Rita" (with Bernie Cummins), May 20, 1929, Vincent Youmans Music, New York

# "Rocky Mountain Fox" (Les Copeland)

## Not copyrighted or published

A stomping Folk rag that begins with a tinge of the blues but evolves into a more typical rag after the introduction to section B. The composer made the piano roll (Universal 202725).

# Wally Rose

## (b. October 2, 1913, Oakland; d. January 12, 1997, San Francisco)

Rose made his first ragtime recording on December 19, 1941. When it was released in January 1942, it started a revival of ragtime, an interest in its compositions, composers, and performers that is still very much going on today. Rose could be considered the first of the second generation of ragtime performers and a considerable influence on the third generation. Though Rose's personal influence had been largely maintained in the San Francisco area, especially among their pianists, his highly developed musical taste in ragtime has dominated the choice of repertoire for at least two generations of ragtime pianists through the rags he chose to record, giving them widespread popularity and thereby encouraging other pianists to perform them. Rose's taste in rags spanned the entire spectrum from Folk to Novelty. His approach, however, was always within the confines of his own musical personality. His playing was unique and immediately identifiable.

Except for a brief five years when his family lived in Honolulu, Rose spent his formative years in Oakland. When he was nine years old, he started taking classical piano lessons, which continued for the next fourteen years. At the same time, he was captivated by the family player piano and the current pop tunes as arranged on the rolls. During his high school summer months, he started what was to become a way of life for the next ten years—working as pianist on board liners for pleasure cruises.

From the start of Lu Watters's Yerba Buena Jazz Band in 1941 until its demise nearly a decade later, Rose was its sole pianist and driving inspiration. Thanks to both Watters and trombonist Turk Murphy's interest in ragtime, Rose began to be featured in spots devoted to his ragtime piano backed by the strong Yerba Buena Jazz Band rhythm section, both on the job and on recordings. With the ragtime feature becoming a favorite of the band's patrons, Rose and company had to dig up more rags. As a result of this activity, he rediscovered and recorded for the first time some of what are now accepted classics in this genre. When the Watters band broke up, two groups emerged, and Rose first played with Bob Scobey's and then finally with Murphy's Jazz Band. In 1954, Rose wanted to pursue other types of music, but instead of leaving Murphy's band cold he devoted considerable time to one of his classical pupils, Pete Clute, so that he could step in and replace Rose without disturbing the fine balance Murphy had created. In 1982 Rose was playing intermission piano at Murphy and Clute's Club in San Francisco, called Earthquake McGoon's. He continued to perform in San Francisco until his death.

## "Rose Leaf Rag" (Scott Joplin)

### November 15, 1907, Jos. M. Daly Music Publishing Co., Boston

Section A is a study in contrary motion in ragtime. Section B shows a highly developed syncopation pattern for the piano. C section works in the folk idiom with sophisticated harmonies. D section follows the other 1907 rags with a strong and happy finish.

## "Rubber Plant Rag" (George L. Cobb)

### June 14, 1909, Walter Jacobs, Boston

The B section has rapid harmonic rhythm, where the chord changes come quickly, creating a silent-movies aura, foretelling his later extensive music writing for the motion pictures.

## "Rufenreddy" (Charley Straight and Roy Bargy)

### November 14, 1921, Sam Fox Publishing Co., Cleveland

A great Novelty rag, this turned out to compete with QRS rival Zez Confrey's. Straight and Bargy were fine pianists and roll arrangers who created rags not imitative of Confrey but distinctive in themselves. Straight made his first piano roll of it in December 1917 (Imperial 511360), whereas Bargy made his first roll arrangement in 1922 (Medodee 204027).

## "Russian Rag" (George L. Cobb)

### April 27, 1918, Will Rossiter, Chicago

This is the famous adaptation of Sergei Rachmaninoff's Prelude in C Sharp Minor; it was a hit for many years and the vaudeville virtuoso's favorite. Joe "Fingers" Carr made his recording in August 1950 (Capitol 1311).

# S

## "S.O.S."

## ("Musician's Distress") (K. W. Bradshaw and Joe McGrade)

### Not copyrighted, published 1919, Stark Music Co., St. Louis

Perhaps the title reflected the oncoming change in popular music taste. The highlight is the experimental trio harmony. The arranged roll was issued at the time of publication (Keynote 1174).

## "Sapho Rag" (J. Russel Robinson)

### October 5, 1909, Stark Music Co., St. Louis

Named after a popular New Orleans dancer, this is an impressive first rag of five sections. It is a folksy composition with a bucolic flavor effected by the use of a dotted rhythm and phrasing that suggests a country Schottische. C has a pattern that Folk rag performer Brun Campbell used.

## "Satisfied" (Theron Bennett)

### January 2, 1904, Victor Kremer Co., Chicago

Originally published in Pierce City, Missouri, by Bennett–Kreyer Music Co. under the alias of Bruce Raymond. This is a combination of ragtime and cakewalk song features. Instead of ending with a simple repeat of B, Bennett created a fine variation to finish it.

# "Scandalous Thompson" (Charles L. Johnson)

## May 27, 1899, J. W. Jenkins' Sons, Kansas City, MO

A marvelously polished and original rag concept for 1899. The A strain was quoted ten years later by Classic rag composer James Scott in his A section of "Great Scott Rag." C is the most clever use of stop-time in a piano rag, making it difficult for the ear to perceive just where C begins and ends; thus, the CC part of the rag one hears as a seamless continuum. The overall structure was in the march–cakewalk tradition, which was not frequently used in rags, probably because it is rather lengthy.

# Arthur Schutt

## (b. November 21, 1902, Reading, Pennsylvania; d. January 28, 1965, San Francisco)

Schutt started his career at age thirteen playing for silent movies. From 1918 to 1924 he was pianist and arranger for Paul Specht's orchestra. He established himself in New York as one of the top pianist–arrangers and was in great demand for recording and radio work. He regularly appeared on disc with such bands as Mike Markel's, Vincent Lopez's, The Georgians, Roger Wolfe Kahn's, Fred Rich's, and Nat Shilkret's, and he played with such jazz greats as Bix Beiderbecke, Benny Goodman, Red Nichols, Frankie Trumbauer, and the Dorseys. During the forties and fifties he worked in Hollywood for the major studios. For the last few years of his life, he was ill and played sporadically.

## Ragtime Compositions

"Syncopating the Scales," November 3, 1922, Jack Mills, Inc., New York

"The Ghost of the Piano," March 5, 1923, Jack Mills, Inc., New York

"Teasing the Ivories," January 18, 1924, Francis, Day & Hunter, London

"Bluin' the Black Keys," February 24, 1926, Robbins–Engel, New York

"Rambling in Rhythm," November 5, 1927, Jack Mills, Inc., New York

"Piano Puzzle," not copyrighted or published

# James Sylvester Scott

## (b. February 12, 1885, Neosho, Missouri; d. August 30, 1938, Kansas City, Kansas)

The second child in a family of six, Scott was gifted with perfect pitch. He was given piano lessons by local pianist John Coleman, who was able to give him a thorough grounding in both playing and theory. His parents, James Sr. and Molly Thomas Scott, were former slaves who tried to find work to support their large family. They moved to Carthage in 1901 where Scott completed his schooling at the segregated Lincoln

School and took further lessons from Emma Johns, a Carthage piano teacher. He started playing at the famed Lakeside Park—both piano and steam calliope—and obtained a job in 1902 with the Dumars Music Store, owned by Charlie Dumars, the director of the Carthage Light Guard Band. He started out as window washer and store sweeper, but it was not long before he was demonstrating music, plugging songs, and playing his own tunes. Demand for Scott's music induced Dumars to publish his work. He took a trip to St. Louis in 1906 where he met Scott Joplin, who took his work to John Stark. Fortunately, the first rag Stark bought, "Frog Legs Rag," was a hit. Thus encouraged, Stark kept on publishing whatever Scott sent until 1922 when Stark stopped publishing new works. Scott left Carthage and the Dumars firm in 1914 when he went to Kansas City, Kansas. He married Nora Johnson, who predeceased him; they had no children. One of his cousins was the famed vaudeville blues singer Ada Brown, who also lived in Kansas City. He taught piano and organ and played at moving picture theaters. At first he played at the keyboard for the Panama Theatre; then he formed an eight-piece band for which he acted as arranger. Scott played at the Lincoln and finally the Eblon. During the last years of his life he was in poor health, but kept on composing, although nothing further was published.

The only Missourian of the Big Three, Scott's rags reflect his activity as a professional pianist and theater organist. As with most ragtime composers, Scott wrote in one sustained mood. Joplin was the only one to use moods of varying intensity in one composition. Whereas Joplin synthesized nineteenth-century European classicism with Mississippi Valley Afro-American folk roots, Scott synthesized the folk tradition with his professional career in popular and jazz music. This resulted in a developmental feeling in his rags, a spirit more characteristic of twentieth-century music to come, and one step farther away from the oldest concept of ragtime, that of a patchwork of various different musical ideas. He was undoubtedly the best keyboard man of the classic ragtimers and loved to punctuate his lyrical melodies with short, abrupt phrases. Toward the

James Scott.

end of his published writing career, his rags became more thickly textured with much varied bass work. Scott, much more than Joplin, was concerned with exploring the form pianistically more than emotionally.

## Ragtime Compositions

"A Summer Breeze," M arch 14, 1903, Dumars Music, Carthage, MO

"The Fascinator," September 23, 1903, Dumars Music, Carthage, MO

"On the Pike," April 13, 1904, Dumars Music, Carthage, MO

"Frog Legs Rag," December 10, 1906, John Stark & Co., New York

"Kansas City Rag," January 2, 1907, Stark Music Co., St. Louis

"Great Scott Rag," August 18, 1909, Allen Music Co., Columbia, MO

"The Ragtime Betty," October 5, 1909, Stark Music Co., St. Louis

"Sunburst Rag," not copyrighted, published 1909, Stark Music Co., St. Louis

"Ophelia Rag," June 6, 1910, Stark Music Co., St. Louis

"Hilarity Rag," September 15, 1910, Stark Music Co., St. Louis

"Quality," July 27, 1911, Stark Music Co., St. Louis

"Ragtime Oriole," December 10, 1911, Stark Music Co., St. Louis

"Princess Rag," not copyrighted, published 1911, Stark Music Co., St. Louis

"Climax Rag," March 5, 1914, Stark Music Co., St. Louis

"Evergreen Rag," not copyrighted, published 1915, Stark Music Co., St. Louis

"Prosperity Rag," March 10, 1916, Stark Music Co., St. Louis

"Honey Moon Rag," August 15, 1916, Stark Music Co., St. Louis

"Efficiency Rag," January 10, 1917, Stark Music Co., St. Louis

"Paramount Rag," November 24, 1917, Stark Music Co., St. Louis

"Rag Sentimental," not copyrighted, published 1918, Stark Music Co., St. Louis

"Dixie Dimples," not copyrighted, published 1918, Will L. Livernash Music, Kansas City, MO

"Troubadour Rag," February 7, 1919, Stark Music Co., St. Louis

"New Era Rag," June 1, 1919, Stark Music Co., St. Louis

"Peace and Plenty Rag," December 1, 1919, Stark Music Co., St. Louis

"Modesty Rag," September 15, 1920, Stark Music Co., St. Louis

"Pegasus," September 15, 1920, Stark Music Co., St. Louis

"Don't Jazz Me Rag" ("I'm Music"), September 18, 1921, Stark Music Co., St. Louis

"Victory Rag," not copyrighted, published 1921, Stark Music Co., St. Louis

"Broadway Rag," January 3, 1922, Stark Music Co., St. Louis

"Calliope Rag," 1966, published in *They All Played Ragtime*, 3d ed., Oak Publications, New York

# "Scott Joplin's New Rag" (Scott Joplin)

## May 1, 1912, Jos. W. Stern & Co., New York

A magnificent rag combining the sparkling effervescence of his youth with the understanding and maturity gained from his experiments. An extended interlude of minor and diminished chords leading to a repeat of the A section is quite out of character for this rag but would be appropriate, for example, in "Euphonic Sounds."

# "Search Light Rag" (Scott Joplin)

## August 12, 1907, Jos. W. Stern & Co., New York

Optimistic and strutting, the A section looks forward to the brilliant "Pine Apple Rag." The C section is unusual for Joplin, as he switches the syncopation from right to left and back to the right hand. The D section is in the old socko finish tradition with which he ended his earliest works and that becomes a feature of all the 1907–08 rags.

# "Sensation Rag" (Joseph Lamb)

## October 8, 1908, Stark Music Co., New York

The most interesting aspect of the rag is the way popular harmonic devices were used to construct a Classic rag.

# "Shamrock Rag" (Euday Bowman)

## January 21, 1916, self, Fort Worth

As is the case with most of Bowman's rags, this one is in the key of E flat. The introduction and A section total eighteen measures combined, giving the piece an asymetrical feeling. Though each section makes use of the three-over-four pattern made famous in "12th Street Rag," he mixes it with several others, adding a welcome variety to the rag. Each section is a fresh idea, sustaining interest while keeping the entire piece in the same key.

# "Shave 'Em Dry" (Sam Wishnuff)

## May 10, 1917, Stark Music Co., St. Louis

A characteristic late rag mixture (one section is straight blues), very pianistic, with the three-over-four device featuring Novelty-style breaks.

# Thomas William Shea

## (b. November 14, 1931, Mattoon, Illinois; d. March 12, 1982, Raleigh)

Shea studied piano as a child for seven years. He became interested in ragtime about 1960 and learned the "Maple Leaf Rag" from *They All Played Ragtime*. He found a collection of rags on a piano roll album, learned some by ear, and then started composing his own rags. He went to the St. Louis Ragtime Festival starting in 1962 and met many contemporary performers as well as Jim Kinnear, secretary of the Ragtime Society, who wanted to publish Shea's originals. He became the Detroit editor for *The Ragtimer*, wrote articles, edited submissions by others, coined the title "Sounds Familiar" for columnist Roger Hankins, interviewed surviving members of early bands, and recorded two albums for the society. He founded Mother's Boys with

Thomas Shea.

clarinetist Walt Gower, a traditional jazz band that recorded for Audiophile. In 1970 he moved to North Carolina, where he played with the Carolina Foot Warmers. He worked as an executive with a pharmaceutical company.

## Ragtime Compositions

"Black Mike's Curse," not copyrighted or published
"Brun Campbell Express," 1966, *They All Played Ragtime,*
    3d. ed., Oak Publications, New York.
"Corinthian Rag," not copyrighted or published
"Hasty Pudding," not copyrighted or published
"Johnny Walker Rag," not copyrighted or published
"Oliver Road Rag," not copyrighted or published
"Pegtown Patrol," not copyrighted or published
"Prairie Queen," June 28, 1963, Ragtime Society, Ontario

"R. F. D.," not copyrighted or published
"Rosebud Rag," not copyrighted or published
"Spasm Rag," March 21, 1963, Ragtime Society,
    Ontario
"The Storyville Sport," not copyrighted or published
"Trillium Rag," 1964, *Max Morath's Guide to Ragtime,*
    Hollis Music, New York
"Venial Sin," not copyrighted or published

# "Shimmie Shoes" (Max Kortlander)

## October 17, 1923, Jack Mills, Inc., New York

Many of the Kortlander rolls were created for dancing the one-step and foxtrot. They are brilliant pianistic conceptions whether they are lightly syncopated dance tunes or the more heavily syncopated rags selected here. An interesting feature is that nearly all end with a repeat of section A.

# "The Shovel Fish" (Harry L. Cook)

## October 4, 1907, self, Louisville

Cook was a professional clown who later worked with the Six Brown Brothers, a popular vaudeville saxophone group who recorded for the Victor Talking Machine Co. He manages to create a unified work from six sections that avoids the feeling of a medley.

# "Shy and Sly" (Luckey Roberts)

## May 7, 1915, G. Ricordi & Co., New York

Except that the A section closely resembles Charles L. Johnson's "Southern Beauties" B section, this is a great example of taking one idea and fitting perfectly with developing ideas. A well-constructed rag.

# "Slipova" (Roy Bargy)

## November 14, 1921, Sam Fox Publishing Co., Cleveland

This marvelous rag incorporates several Novelty embellishments, used by the more imaginative arrangers in rolls, in the melody proper. The composer's October 1922 roll arrangement (Melodee 203999) is a sheer delight.

# "Silver Rocket" (Arthur Marshall)

## 1966, published in *They All Played Ragtime*, 3d. ed., Oak Publications, New York

Excellent strutting rag with extended twenty-measure D section. John Arpin made a memorable recording (Jazzology JCE 52).

# "Silver Swan Rag" (Scott Joplin)

## Not copyrighted, published 1971, Maple Leaf Club, Los Angeles

Found on a piano roll in 1970, "Silver Swan" was issued both by QRS and National in 1914. Dick Zimmerman and Donna McCluer then transcribed it and had it published. It is a serious work, definitely done in his last working period. The C section sounds as though it consists of three fragments put together, with the third a folksy rhythmic idea usually done at the beginning of a section; its use here at the end gives the effect of a seamless thirty-two-measure section.

# "Sleepy Hollow Rag" (Clarence Woods)

## Not copyrighted, published 1918, Will L. Livernash Music Co., Kansas City, MO

The title refers to a black community just outside Carthage. A most unusual and expressive rag. Section A is built around a tremolo effect. B has written fill-ins in small notes to be executed lightly above the sustained chord. C has a lyrical, other-worldly aura, intensified in C$^1$ with a return to the delicate tremolo.

# "Slippery Elm Rag" (Clarence Woods)

## December 2, 1912, Bush & Gerts Piano Co., Dallas

Section A combines three features: the three-over-four, an even flow of sixteenth notes, and the syncopation. A and B are chromatic melodically, and C has a fine and unusual break that, with the indicated slurs, achieves a blues quality. The whole composition balances chromaticism and blues writing to become one of the most original rags ever written.

# "Smart Alec" (Zez Confrey)

## December 27, 1933, Mills Music, Inc., New York

Written ten years after "Dizzy Fingers," it is in that same tradition and a puzzler for the student going through several Novelty patterns.

# "The Smiler Rag" (Percy Wenrich)

## January 2, 1907, Arnett–Delonais Co., Chicago

His best rag with four strong sections of varying character. A has a fine folk flavor, B features a break, C has a Scott Joplin lyricism since it is stolen from his "Peacherine Rag" trio, and D is highlighted by treble runs.

## "Smiles and Chuckles" (Frank Henri Klickman)

### October 8, 1917, Frank K. Root & Co., Chicago

Klickman's main vocation was as an arranger for several publishers, although he composed many pieces. As a sideline, he was the arranger for the Zez Confrey Orchestra recordings on Victor.

## William Henry Joseph Bonaparte Berthloff (Willie "The Lion" Smith)

### (b. November 25, 1897, Goshen, New York; d. April 18, 1973, New York)

Taught by his mother who played both organ and piano, Smith claimed to have developed his left hand by playing Johann Sebastian Bach. He started playing in Newark in the early teens. He joined the 350th Field Artillery in November 1916 and saw active service in France, where he served with distinction and earned his nickname of the Lion. He accompanied Mamie Smith on "Crazy Blues," the first blues record. Throughout the

Willie the Lion.

twenties and early thirties, he made many recordings in bands and played nightly as a featured pianist at Pod's and Jerry's in Harlem. With James P. Johnson and Fats Waller, he was a favorite at rent parties. Famed for his red vest, a tilted derby, and a cigar clenched at the side of his mouth, he had the highest opinion of himself as a pianist. He toured Europe in the late forties and fifties and appeared in major jazz festivals during the sixties and early seventies. Perhaps he was not the great pianist he thought he was, but his compositions are among the finest written, with an originality that ranks him as a leader. Of all the Harlem composers, he made the most use of bass syncopation. He was not satisfied with just varying the octave–chord accompaniment but went on to create jagged, restless bass syncopations in more complex patterns than the other composers. In contrast to his usual *fortissimo* stride, he wrote remarkably reflective pieces, such as "Echo of Spring." He won recognition as a composer from such jazz musicians as Duke Ellington, Count Basie, and Dizzy Gillespie. He made a two-album set of reminiscences, singing and playing in 1968 (*The Memoirs of Willie the Lion Smith*, RCA Victor LSP-6016), and wrote his autobiography, *Music on My Mind,* with George Hoefer (Doubleday, 1964).

## Ragtime Compositions

"Keep Your Temper," September 19, 1925, Clarence Williams Music, New York

"Finger Buster," October 15, 1934, Clarence Williams Music, New York

"Echo of Spring," April 4, 1935, Clarence Williams Music, New York

"In the Groove," August 18, 1936, Mills Music, New York

"Sneak Away," August 21, 1937, Mills Music, New York

"Keep Fingering," March 11, 1938, Mills Music, New York

"Cuttin' Out," not copyrighted or published

"Rippling Waters," not copyrighted or published

Willie the Lion.

# "S'more" (Charley Straight)

## Not copyrighted or published

This performance (QRS 100409) highlights one of his favorite bass patterns. In the June 7, 1919, *Music Trade Indicator* he was referred to as the man "who is putting pep into piano rolls."

# "Snappin' Turtle Rag" (Charles L. Cooke)

## October 27, 1913, Jerome H. Remick & Co., New York

The title is descriptive of the grace note used again and again here.

# "Sneaky Shuffles" (Henry Lodge)

## October 4, 1910, Jerome H. Remick & Co., New York

An odd rag with unexpected harmonies in section B, followed by a clever trio involving syncopation in both hands, but in a lyrical and original format.

# "Sneeky Peet" (Charles L. Johnson)

## January 10, 1907, J. W. Jenkins' Sons Music Co., Kansas City, MO

Eubie Blake used the B section in his song "You're Lucky to Me."

# "Snookums" (Charles L. Johnson)

## February 9, 1916, Forster Music Publisher, Chicago

A beautiful finale to the Johnson rags, this one is more in the style of his older rags, with imaginative harmonies in the A section, a very country-sounding B, and a trio that is in the late teens one-step pattern. Terry Waldo featured it in his 1974 recording (Dirty Shame 1237).

# "Snuggle Pup" (George L. Cobb)

## March 4, 1929, Walter Jacobs, Boston

Clever Novelty rag taken from "Doll Dance."

# "Some Blues for You All" (Theron Bennett)

## January 8, 1916, Joe Morris Music Co., New York

One of the most fascinating of the rag–blues mixtures of the teens. A fitting compositional end as the A section recalls the opener of his earlier small masterwork "Sweet Pickles." A comparison between the two reveals the evolution in musical styles. In "Sweet Pickles" the first phrase featured, ironically, is a flatted third: a true blue note. Here, the melodic emphasis is on sixths and ninths, with the blues effect on a flatted sixth. A more idiomatic, down-home blues develops in the last half of the tune.

# "Something Doing" (Scott Hayden with Scott Joplin)

## February 24, 1903, Val A. Reis Music Co., St. Louis

This masterwork is totally original. Its rich inspiration is reflected in its eternal springtime freshness that is so characteristic of the early Classic rags. It is largely in flowing melodic lines, with a final D section that features anticipatory syncopation—notable in the 1903 rags of Scott Joplin.

## "Soup and Fish Rag" (Harry Jentes with Pete Wendling)

### December 11, 1913, George W. Meyer Music Co., New York

A wandering labyrinth of strange harmonies. The B strain is an experiment in chromatic writing. It has a four-measure sequence on a previous four, with the same melodic intervals, only one half step higher; but in character with the rest of the tune, there is a clever modulation back to the home key as soon as the feeling of a new key becomes established.

## "Sour Grapes" (Will B. Morrison)

### November 11, 1912, self, Indianapolis

A rather athletic A strain melody precedes an imaginative B section of involved syncopation.

## "Southern Beauties" (Charles L. Johnson)

### October 12, 1907, Jerome H. Remick & Co., Detroit

Harks back to the cakewalk and uses common syncopated figures. However, the B section was used by Luckey Roberts for his A section in "Shy and Sly."

# "Spaghetti Rag" (George Lyons and Bob Yosco)

## April 11, 1910, Maurice Shapiro, New York

This was composed by an unlikely vaudeville duo that featured mandolin and harp. Only a modest success in its day, it became a favorite during the fifties revival of ragtime interest.

# "Spring Fever" (Rube Bloom)

## June 21, 1926, Triangle Music Publishing Co., New York

A brilliant original; one of the most ebullient Novelty rags with a fine jazz flavor and lyrical flair that requires great technical skill. This is perhaps Bloom's finest ragtime composition. Though it was copyrighted and published on June 21, 1926, Bloom first recorded it in March 1926 (Harmony l64-H) and then a year later in another splendid version in April 1927 (Cameo 1153).

# "Spring-Time Rag" (Paul Pratt)

## January 4, 1916, Stark Music Co., St. Louis

Pratt's most lilting rag, and the finest creative use in ragtime of Felix Mendelssohn's "Spring Song," a favorite of Tin Pan Alley writers.

# "St. Louis Rag" (Tom Turpin)

## November 2, 1903, Sol Bloom, New York

This was written to celebrate the Louisiana Purchase Exposition, better known as the St. Louis World's Fair, scheduled originally for 1903 but realized a year later. This is the most orthodox of the Turpins, with the usual Classic rag key change to the subdominant at section C, which is a typical melodic trio. However, A does not return after B in the most frequent Classic rag pattern. It features typical Turpin fireworks, beginning with a beautifully syncopated and very pianistic A section. There are breaks in both B and C sections—another pioneering feature in ragtime by the composer. D is the final display, sparked with a blaze of ascending chromatic runs, a fitting overture to "that splendid summer" in St. Louis. This is the first Turpin rag without D. S. DeLisle indicated as arranger.

# "St. Louis Tickle" (Theron Bennett credited to Barney and Seymore)

## August 20, 1904, Victor Kremer Co., Chicago

This was probably written by Bennett, as a note in the Pierce City newspaper in late 1903 reports him going to Chicago and wowing them with his tunes, including "The Tickle." Kremer published much music in commemoration of the 1904 St. Louis World's Fair. This was a hit at the fair and became one of the most beloved rags of all time. The tune is a natural for strings; Bennett had a mandolin orchestra. Several of his other tunes have similar strains, especially "Pudnin' Tame." Its second section was a notorious bit of musical low life. One old-timer remembered getting his face slapped as a kid for whistling it. Another reported that in small Missouri towns someone could be jailed for whistling it. Another remembered the original set of lyrics, which began, "Been to the East, Been to the West, I found my honey can do it the best." It is generally credited to New Orleans cornetist Buddy Bolden, but it appears in several early rags and was well known in Missouri as "Funky Butt." More polite words were written for the song version, brought out by Kremer in 1905. The phrase "take it away" survived in the O'Dea version from the original bawdy lyrics.

# John Stark

## (b. April 11, 1841, Shelby County, Kentucky; d. November 20, 1927, St. Louis)

Stark was born in Kentucky but grew up on a farm in Gosport, Indiana. He joined the 1st Regiment of the Indiana Heavy Artillery Volunteers, in which he was bugler during the Civil War. While stationed in New Orleans, he met and married Sarah Ann Casey. They settled with their growing family on a farm near Maysville, Missouri. A little later, he gave up the farm and moved his family to Cameron, where he pioneered in the new business of making ice cream. To stimulate trade, he traveled around the countryside selling it from his Conestoga wagon. He soon outgrew Cameron and moved to Chillicothe, where he engaged in the piano and organ business. Looking for a more prosperous town, he finally moved to the railroad center of

John Stark, founder of the Stark Music Co.

Sedalia around 1885, where he established his firm of John Stark & Son at 516 Ohio Street. His general music store was one of three, and about ten years later he bought out one of his competitors, J. W. Truxel, and with it the seven copyrights he owned. That was Stark's beginning as a publisher.

    With the success of "Maple Leaf Rag," Stark moved his family and business in 1900, this time to St. Louis, where he purchased a printing plant at 210 Olive Street. He later moved to larger premises at 3804 Laclede Avenue. In August 1905 he set up editorial offices at 127 East 23rd Street in New York City while maintaining his printing plant in St. Louis. On August 15 he printed the following statement in an advertisement in trade journals: "We are here with the goods. We left our sombrero in St. Louis—and we have had our hair cut—and even now there is not one person in five who turns to take a second look at us when we have met them on the street. And more, we will soon be able to describe our prints in the native vernacular. We should shrink from the firing line were it not for the fact that our rag section is *different*." His son, William, ran the plant while Stark concentrated on selling and publicizing his music. And publicize he certainly did. He invented the term *Classic rag* to distinguish his music from that of the other publishers and helped to perpetuate the myth that these selections were the source and inspiration for all other ragtime; in his hyperbolic ads he insisted that the Stark rags were the "Simon-Pure" and that everything else was a "pale imitation." The label *Classic rag* was an appropriate choice to proclaim the rags of the likes of Scott Joplin, James Scott, and Joseph Lamb, among others, as truly immortal works. But the Classic rag form was also just one way of organizing folk materials and writing ragtime. From 1897 on, local publishers all over the country published the ragtime they believed in in idiosyncratic form. Composers and performers everywhere were producing excellent ragtime, and much of it was more syncopated—more raggy—than the formal Classic rag. The ragtime world outside the Classic school was extremely variegated, and, with the exception of "Maple Leaf Rag," most people were unfamiliar with the Stark catalog. While Tin Pan Alley was opening new branches in the larger cities, small publishers, both rural and urban, were exercising the last vestige of pioneer initiative in publishing fine works of local talent.

When his wife died late in 1910, Stark closed the Manhattan office and went back to St. Louis to live and work. He continued publishing the rags of Scott and Lamb as well as other, lesser-known composers until 1922. He lived to see Lottie Joplin renew the copyright on "Maple Leaf Rag" and sign it over to him on November 26, 1926. Retired from active business, Stark died the following year in St. Louis at age eighty-six. No greater champion of the Classic rag existed, and it is to Stark's credit that his faith in Joplin's creation never faltered and that he continued to publish and publicize that ideal as expressed by Scott Hayden, Arthur Marshall, Louis Chauvin, Scott, and Lamb.

# "Steeplechase Rag" (James P. Johnson)

## Not copyrighted or published, composed around 1914, recorded as "Over the Bars"

Johnson played this at an extremely fast tempo in the spirit suggested by the titles (Universal 203179). The A section in minor has a typical silent-movie air. The driving trio features a favorite climactic stride figure in the treble, which is repeated for nearly the entire strain.

# "Stompin' 'Em Down" (Alex Hill)

This was Hill's only rag, which exists solely on his record (Vocalion 1270). This tour de force places the Little Rock-born pianist–composer–arranger–conductor in the forefront of ragtimers. Shortly after making this recording, Hill moved permanently to California, where he became the arranger for Paul Howard's Quality Serenaders. The versatile musician also arranged for such diverse orchestras as those led by Claude Hopkins, Paul Whiteman, and Duke Ellington.

# "Stop It" (James P. Johnson)

## August 21, 1917, F. B. Haviland Publishing Co., New York

This roll (Universal 203205) has a rhythmic feeling characteristic of much black ragtime playing where subtle syncopations are achieved by the use of suspensions and quarter-note triplets in 4/4 time. Though Johnson favored octaves in the bass, this roll featured tenths with added harmonic notes. He breaks these from the bottom as harmonic fifths, followed by the upper notes. This bass playing along with his treble phrasing created a loose, jangling quality—an intricate texture that suggests the two hands working independently of each other. This feeling of detachment is the key to the more subtle and complex striding syncopations.

# "Stoptime Rag" (Scott Joplin)

## June 4, 1910, Jos. W. Stern & Co., New York

This appears in one sense to be a throwback to the earlier "Ragtime Dance" in which musical breaks are provided so the dancers' stomping feet could be heard. The stop effects are indicated in the scores of both numbers. Another unusual feature is that there are seven different melodies of eight measures each rather than the usual three or four sections containing sixteen measures each. Truly an experiment—one that worked. The C section is used as a contrast with long lyrical melody lines in the traditional sixteen-measure section. Once again Joplin combines the major and minor tonalities in one piece, and for once the performer is permitted to play "fast or slow."

# Charley Straight

## (b. January 16, 1891, Chicago; d. September 21, 1940, Chicago)

Straight spent his whole life in Chicago; he was born and died there. In between, he was responsible for lots of good music as composer, arranger, pianist, orchestra leader, accompanist, and musical director of the Imperial Player Roll Company.

After graduating from Wendell Philips High School, Straight entered the world of vaudeville in 1909 as the partner of singing comedian Gene Greene. With Straight accompanying on piano, Greene sang their own songs, which comprised their act. Their first hit was also the first song recorded by them, "King of the Bugaloos." What put it over was Greene's funny put-on growly voice and the fact that it was the first ragtime song featuring nonsense syllables with those syllables vocally taking the place of the pianistic syncopations. Straight and Greene made a series of what has become very rare recordings for Pathe. Greene went on to record for Victor, Emerson, and Columbia.

After the team broke up, Straight joined Imperial, supervised their entire popular song program as well as arranged and performed his own rags on rolls. In a most unusual move, at the same time he was musical director for Imperial he also recorded for rival QRS. And what he recorded for both of them at first were his own Novelty rags. Just prior to that in 1916, he adopted the pseudonym of "Billie King" for the Rudolph Wurlitzer company's Rolla Artis label, where he performed his own novelty rags as well as a few pop songs. Combining the two, his first rag roll was "My Baby's Rag" (Rolla Artis 50297), which was a takeoff of Tony Jackson's sensational hit "Pretty Baby."

Charley Straight.

In August 1919, he met, auditioned, and hired Roy Bargy to edit the song rolls for Imperial and to perform his own Novelty rags. To get him started, Straight gave Bargy cocomposer credit for "Rufenreddy" and "Knice and Knifty," both of which Straight recorded as piano rolls and claimed sole composer credit for in December 1917 (Imperial 511360 and Imperial 512260, respectively).

From 1920 on, Straight's own orchestra took up most of his time, as he arranged its numbers, signed recording contracts, and handled the bookings, which frequently took him touring throughout the Midwest. The orchestra recorded for Paramount and Brunswick, companies with their headquarters and main studios in Chicago. His was not a studio band but was featured nightly, when not on tour, at the top hotels and nightclubs in Chicago. His career came to an abrupt end when he was killed in an automobile accident.

## Ragtime Compositions

"Humpty Dumpty," January 13, 1914, M. Witmark & Sons, New York

"Let's Go," December 30, 1915, Jerome H. Remick & Co., New York

"Red Raven Rag," December 30, 1915, Jerome H. Remick & Co., New York

"Hot Hands," February 16, 1916, Jerome H. Remick & Co., New York

"Sweet Pickin's Rag," April 30, 1918, Forster Music, Chicago

"Blue Grass Rag," November 11, 1918, Joe Morris Music Co., New York

"Black Jack Rag," not copyrighted or published

"A Dippy Ditty," not copyrighted or published

"Fastep," not copyrighted or published

"ItsIt," not copyrighted or published

"Knice and Knifty" (with Roy Bargy) (see Roy Bargy)

"Lazy Bones," not copyrighted or published

"Mitinice," not copyrighted or published

"Mow 'Em Down," not copyrighted or published

"Nifty Nonsense," not copyrighted or published

"Out Steppin'," not copyrighted or published

"Playmor," not copyrighted or published

"Rag-a-Bit," not copyrighted or published

"Rufenreddy" (with Roy Bargy) (see Roy Bargy)

"S'more," not copyrighted or published

"Try Me," not copyrighted or published

"Universal Rag" (with McKay), not copyrighted or published

# "The Strenuous Life" (Scott Joplin)

## Not copyrighted, published 1902, John Stark & Son, St. Louis

Very march-like, it echoes President Theodore Roosevelt's advocacy of a strenuous life. The A section is similar in feeling to its counterpart in the "Easy Winners." The C section features an unusual bass rhythm of octave-chord-chord-octave instead of the usual octave-chord-octave-chord. However, the final section is a strong one maintaining the martial feeling created at the beginning.

# Stride Ragtime

Stride ragtime was the name given to that style created and developed by the black New York ticklers who, when they traveled around the country, wanted to be distinctive and be recognized as the finest in the country.

The word stride means the syncopation alternating between the right and left hands and the counter-melodies created by a moving bass line. This was putting a new twist on the regular way to play ragtime; alternating the syncopation between both hands made it twice as difficult to perform, thereby enabling the performers to win contests. It not only sounded harder to do, but it also was in fact harder to do. And unlike the rest of ragtime, Stride was conceived by and originally performed solely by black artists.

It was thought to have been created by Luckey Roberts and his pupil Richard (Abba Labba) McLean, but as James P. Johnson pointed out in an interview with Tom Davin, "I was getting around town and hearing everybody. If they had anything I didn't have, I listened and stole it…I was born with absolute pitch and could catch a key that a player was using and copy it—even Luckey's…In 1914 in Atlantic City, Eubie [Blake] had a couple of rags. One, *Troublesome Ivories,* was very good. I caught it." And so it was that this giant of the New York scene, Johnson, developed the Stride sound and became the major influence of the great jazz pianists—Willie "The Lion" Smith, Duke Ellington, Count Basie, Fats Waller, Cliff Jackson, Hank Duncan, Joe Sullivan, Teddy Weatherford, Don Lambert, Ralph Sutton, Dick Wellstood, Art Tatum, and Thelonious Monk—through his many piano rolls, recordings and live performances in cafes and dance halls, and, most of all, at rent parties. And though Luckey, Blake, and Johnson were composing rags during the teens, it was not until 1921 that the Stride sound became definitely established. Stride rags, as composed and performed by these men, were cast in the same mold as the Popular rag. Most of the evidence comes not only from the sheet music but also from some hand-played piano rolls of the teens. In 1921 there was a startling change in performance and, simultaneously, in conception of composition. It seems as though the new Novelty ragtime was an additional challenge to the New Yorkers, and they responded.

They viewed their rags not as polished compositions as Scott Joplin did but as special material for their exclusive use as performers. As a consequence, most Stride rags were not published. Stride ragtime was a framework on which they could make changes as various ideas and tricks came to them in the immediacy of performance. As with the Novelty rag, Stride ragtime became a style of playing as well as a type of composition. The pianists, most of whom did not compose original pieces, learned many of the idiomatic tricks in this style and placed them within pop songs, hymns, marches, and even classical compositions. Blake once said, "I don't play any better than any real pianist, but it's the tricks I know. I know tricks that the average guy don't know. Because I've been playing all this time, I had to play against this guy, that guy—the finest pianists, see?"

Because the performing aspect assumed greater importance, it is essential to listen to the performer playing the same rag at different times to fully appreciate Stride ragtime. And it is fortunate that the major composer–performers recorded their rags at different times during their careers.

Being in New York, the heart of Tin Pan Alley and the Broadway musical, meant that outlets were plentiful. And so it is not surprising to find that many of the leading Stride ragtimers also created hit pop songs and wrote scores for musical comedies.

# "Sugar Cane" (Scott Joplin)

## April 21, 1908, Seminary Music Co., New York

John Stark objected to Joplin's reuse of the "Maple Leaf Rag" format, as expressed in his personal ledger. These remarks were probably intended for advertising blurbs or for use in his *Intermezzo* magazine: "No one will perhaps ever surpass Joplin's *Maple Leaf, Sunflower* or *Cascades* but alas like all composers do sooner or later, Joplin is verging to the sear and yellow leaf. His muse seems to have been pumped into inocuous (sic) desuetude, and his labored efforts are but a rehash of *Maple Leaf* or some of his first numbers that no self respecting publisher would print. Joplin's case is pitiful. When he hawks a manuscript around and finally sells it for a few dollars—the next publisher he strikes tells him, 'Why I would have given you $500 for that'—this keeps Joplin miserable and thinking that his last publisher is cheating him. We have several Joplin manuscripts that were written before the spring of inspiration had run dry which we will bring out from time to time." A most interesting variation of "Maple Leaf Rag" that contrasts nicely with "Gladiolus" but even more illustrates just how fine an improvisor Joplin was. To tie the sections together, as in "Nonpareil," he uses the same ending for B and D. The point about the A section in "Maple Leaf" is here amply demonstrated. In the C section, the device in the third measure was borrowed by Joseph Lamb for his "Ragtime Nightingale." The D section, as in the last few rags, has a cheery and vital ending.

# "A Summer Breeze" (James Scott)

## March 14, 1903, Dumars Music Co., Carthage, MO

This first Scott work is greatly influenced by Scott Joplin's work. Though the format is identical, the first three sections indicate a general appreciation of Joplin's ideas, but the D section is an outright steal from the B section of "Elite Syncopations." Nevertheless, there is an indication of originality, especially in the trio, which has a brassy but artistic use of parallelism.

# "Sunburst Rag" (James Scott)

## Not copyrighted, published 1909, Stark Music Co., St. Louis

One of the great joys of Classic ragtime. The intensely pianistic C section has an ascending break of triads that foretells Novelty ragtime. Scott uncannily predicted specific tunes in much later popular music. This trio, for instance, is identical to a Herb Albert tune called "Spanish Flea."

# "Sunflower Slow Drag" (Scott Hayden with Scott Joplin)

## March 18, 1901, John Stark & Son, St. Louis

Though Hayden and Joplin worked together on this piece, the trio is by Joplin alone and the rest primarily by Hayden. This rag once rivaled the popularity of "Maple Leaf Rag" and was one of the very first Classic rags available on piano rolls. John Stark advertised it as "the twin sister of *Maple Leaf*" and told of Joplin's writing of the trio during his courtship of Belle Hayden. The A section is very ingenious and extremely pianistic; Brun Campbell recalled that Hayden was one of the best players locally. The trio uses a wider range of keys and is dramatically marked, beginning *pianissimo* and achieving a fine lyricism. As is true of the "Swipesy" trio, this one is also heavily pentatonic. The D section caps the lyricism with a delicate melody that nevertheless assures the firm ending of the rag.

# "Swanee Ripples" (Walter E. Blaufuss)

## December 27, 1912, Frank Clark Music Co., Chicago

Arranged by another rag composer, Harry Thompson, this is a most imaginative rag with an ambitious syncopated B strain and dotted-note phrasing much like an advanced rag. Blaufuss was a Milwaukee-born musician whose first rag appeared in 1899: "Chicago Rag," named after the Chicago Musical College, the training ground for many of the ragtime composers. He went on to become music director for the popular radio program *Don McNeil's Breakfast Club* (also see Bill Krenz).

# "Sweet and Tender" (Roy Bargy)

## April 17, 1923, Will Rossiter, Chicago

Though this Novelty rag was Bargy's last published rag, it was the first piano rag roll done by Bargy in September 1919 (Imperial 512980). Most of Bargy's ragtime output was issued by Sam Fox during 1921 and 1922. The first disc recording taken from the sheet music can be found on Dave Jasen's *Rip-Roarin' Ragtime* LP (Folkways FG-3561), which was recorded in 1977. A comparison of Jasen's performance with the Bargy Imperial roll indicates a substantial change in Bargy's musical thinking between the time he made his roll and the issuance of the sheet music. One difference is immediately apparent as the introduction, as performed on the roll, shifts the syncopated accents. Then the A section is treated in the major mode whereas the sheet music is in the minor. The C section on the roll starts with a tremolo in thirds, placing the real melody line inside, which changes the voicings and creates a different impression.

# "Sweet Pickles" (credited to George E. Florence)

## October 23, 1907, Victor Kremer Co., Chicago

The first printing and the copyright stated the author as appears above. On subsequent editions Theron Bennett has been given sole credit. This is his most original folk-inspired rag. Section A is eight measures repeated and also serves as the last half of B, a regular sixteen-measure section. This idea was used in a few other Folk rags, such as "Cotton Patch," and the principle was adapted to the Classic rag form by Scott Joplin in his use of the same four-measure ending for two different sections in the same rag, such as "Easy Winners" and "Sugar Cane." Another highlight is the sense of tonality that is an ambivalent C minor/E flat feeling from section C to the final D. The ending of C has a surprising descent of consecutive fourths, in a sequence pattern, much like later Novelty rag patterns, whereas section E develops the sequence idea in phrases of two measures in C minor, modulating to E flat at the end. D consists of a busy, brisk, and winding melody in single notes with an unexpected one-measure break.

# "Swipesy Cakewalk" (Arthur Marshall with Scott Joplin)

## July 21, 1900, John Stark & Son, St. Louis

The title was suggested by a local Sedalia newsboy whose photo is on the original cover and who, Stark said, "looked like he just swiped something." This has a simple folk spirit suggested by the "cakewalk" title but is a polished Classic rag in form and ideas, having little to do with the cakewalk tradition. An important highlight is the lyrical Scott Joplin trio, brought in with abrupt sixteenth-note bass octaves, much like the embellishments on the hand-played Joplin rolls. The final section is a quintessential Folk rag style stomper—Marshall at his best.

# "The Sycamore" (Scott Joplin)

## July 18, 1904, Will Rossiter, Chicago

The most notable development is the treatment Joplin gives his A section, which is a breakthrough in the A section of "Maple Leaf." The C section is a foretaste of a song in *Treemonisha*. The D section is unusual for its time with its changing harmonies and use of a diminished chord within such a happy framework. Joplin experiments with textures of sound here and developed it in later rags.

# "Sycamore Saplin'" (Theron Bennett)

## April 9, 1910, Jerome H. Remick & Co., New York

One of his most inspired and certainly one of his most folksy rags. The overall construction is rarely used—identical to Scott Joplin's "Chrysanthemum"—wherein C becomes the featured strain in the last half and the D in relative minor has the effect of an interlude. The final C section has a different and more varied bass structure, a development from an idea set forth in section A.

# T

## "Talk of the Town" (Elijah W. Jimerson and Marietta Cranston)

**Not copyrighted, published 1919, Syndicate Music Co., St. Louis**

A late hybrid containing a blues strain as its B section.

## "Teasing the Cat" (Charles L. Johnson)

**August 19, 1916, Forster Music Publisher, Chicago**

A later-style rag, almost entirely in dotted rhythm.

## "Teddy in the Jungle" (Edward J. Freeberg)

**February 8, 1910, Rinker Music Co., Lafayette, IN**

The title is a reference to Theodore Roosevelt's hunting days, which section A describes by using the minor tonality and numerous grace notes, suggesting the exotic jungle atmosphere.

## "Temptation Rag" (Henry Lodge)

**September 9, 1909, M. Witmark & Sons, New York**

A unique rag. The overall tonal plan rejects the classic splitting in half in favor of one major key and its relative minor. This, combined with Lodge's flair for long lyrical lines, results in an unusually cohesive and forward-moving rag. But the internal element that makes it a success is a masterful use of varied syncopated patterns for each section. The B section introduces a different idea from A. Section C begins with still another yet also recalls that of B. D functions as an interlude of largely unsyncopated staccato sixteenths; however, its one syncopation is derived from the opening C pattern. This all lends a developmental air to the rag and contributes to its unity. His greatest success and one of the biggest rag hits of its day, it was appropriately most often performed by a band. Although Lodge composed at the piano, he was, from all accounts, a good performer, but his rags did not become pianistic until 1917.

## "Ten Penny Rag" (Clarence E. Brandon and Billy Smythe)

### December 6, 1911, self, St. Louis

A heavily textured rag voiced almost entirely in treble octaves over an octave-chord-chord-octave bass. John Stark later took over this rag. Both active musicians in St. Louis, Brandon wrote the first "I Ain't Got Nobody," which he published in 1911, years before the Warfield–Williams hit to which it bears some similarity.

## "A Tennessee Jubilee" (Thomas E. Broady)

### Not copyrighted, published 1899, H. A. French, Nashville

This is a good study of a conventional cakewalk developing into a full-fledged piano rag.

# "A Tennessee Tantalizer" (Charles Hunter)

## November 19, 1900, Henry A. French, Nashville

Most of the syncopation is affected by delayed entrance of the right hand extended to the bass in quick one measure comments or answers to the treble. The C section is a true thirty-two-measure musical thought. It does not split into parallel eight-measure periods. The last sixteen measures of C, however, split into four measures plus twelve and are further spiced with a blue seventh.

# "Tent Show Rag" (Brun Campbell)

## Not copyrighted or published

This is Campbell's version of the last part of the verse of "Memphis Blues." The title commemorates the Turpin brothers' tent shows in St. Louis, which came before their Booker T. Washington Theatre was built.

# "Texas Rag" (Callis Welborn Jackson)

## June 5, 1905, self, Dallas

This is a study in contrasting syncopations. A and B are constructed of typical broken-octave syncopation, and C enters on the subdominant and is a complete change of pace: It is march-like with the bass written in two quarter-note octaves instead of the usual four eighth-note pattern. Section D moves up another fourth and combines features of all the previous sections in a masterful, beautifully melodic inspiration. This section returns to the regular 2/4 pattern of four eighth notes in the bass. The rag ends with a return to section C twice, written out as a thirty-two-measure section.

# "That Demon Rag" (Russell Smith)

## January 27, 1911, I. Seidel, Indianapolis

An original conception by a black Indianapolis composer who also worked in vaudeville and minstrelsy. C is especially beautiful as the syncopated patterns alternate between the bass and treble, rejecting the traditional ragtime bass. Section D breaks away with a burst of sixteenths—a fine touch.

# "That Futuristic Rag" (Rube Bloom)

## April 9, 1923, Jack Mills, Inc., New York

Incredibly fine and, indeed, futuristic. He predicted that a distinctive national school of music was being born in the United States.

# "That Rag" (Ted Browne)

## April 6, 1907, Thiebes–Stierlin Music Co., St. Louis

"Dedicated to the lovers of ragtime." This entire piece may well be a collection of floating folk strains: The B section has an interesting octave interchange between the hands that forms part of a section in Calvin Woolsey's "Mashed Potatoes." C has an eccentric idea in dotted rhythm. The thirty-two-measure E section was the best remembered. Marked "Chicago Slow Drag," it is a pure ragtime delight and remained popular enough to be included in Gene Rodemich's 1920s band recording of "St. Louis Tickle" as an interlude.

# "That Teasin' Rag" (Joe Jordan)

## December 24, 1909, Jos. W. Stern & Co., New York

Section C contains thirty-two measures and is by far the best known of all trios. This was due to the Original Dixieland Jazz Band using it as their trio in "The Original Dixieland One Step" (Victor 18255).

# "That's a Plenty" (Lew Pollack)

## February 25, 1914, Joe Morris Music Co., New York

The title reflects the popularity of "Too Much Mustard." Television comedian Jackie Gleason used this as his "And awaaaay we go" traveling music. Although it started out as a rag, it is now a permanent part of the Dixieland repertoire. An interesting and dramatic feature is the variation on A, which changes four quarter-note octaves into triplets.

# Charles Hubbard Thompson

## (b. June 19, 1891, St. Louis; d. June 13, 1964, St. Louis)

A professional pianist at age twenty in 1911, Thompson teamed with a white player, Rudy Gibson, touring Ohio and Indiana and playing duets and solos. By 1916 he was back in St. Louis, where he entered a mammoth ragtime piano competition lasting eight weeks in which sixty-eight contestants were eliminated before he was declared winner. Shortly thereafter, in a special contest with the Missouri State Champion, Thompson defeated none other than Tom Turpin. Thompson was a solo pianist aboard riverboats and played in such local bands as Charles Creath's Jazz-O-Maniacs and with the Dewey Jackson organization. In 1919, in Toledo he met James P. Johnson, whose unique style influenced his own. A quiet, unassuming musical illiterate, he nonetheless created original and unique rags. His rags are an original blend of late Missouri ragtime and Harlem stride influences. In true midwestern style he also had a great flair for the blues, which he preferred up tempo and mixed with his ragtime licks. He was a black key player, preferring A flat, D flat, and G flat. Early in his career he abandoned playing in the easier keys such as C because, as he commented, "you run all over yourself." His playing had a bounce and sprightliness to be found nowhere else. After the

St. Louis district shut down, he became a chef at the famous Greenbriar Resort, where his specialty was preparing pheasants and guinea hens. During the Depression he worked as a chef on the Pennsylvania railroad. In October 1945 he opened his own cafe and ran it until he retired. In the late '50s, Thompson regularly played at the St. Louis Jazz Club. In 1960 he joined old-timers Eubie Blake and Joe Jordan in Bob Darch's *Reunion in Ragtime* project for Stereoddities.

## Ragtime Compositions

"The Lily Rag," not copyrighted, published 1914, Syndicate Music Co., St. Louis
"Delmar Rag," not copyrighted or published

# "Thoroughbred Rag" (Joseph Lamb)

## *Ragtime Treasures,* 1964, Mills Music, Inc., New York

Section A recalls "Excelsior Rag" but, in typical Lamb fashion, the texture changes with the B section to a thinner, more intricate one. D is a dramatic ending.

# Three over Four

The most popular and ultimately, the most rewarding ragtime cliché used throughout the publishing life of ragtime compositions. The pattern was a sequence of three different notes placed within a four-beat measure, which resulted in the accenting of a new note whenever the phrase was repeated. It was the mainstay of four of the most popular rags: "Dill Pickles," "Black and White," "Twelfth Street," and "Kitten on the Keys."

# "The Thriller" (May Aufderheide)

## September 4, 1909, J. H. Aufderheide, Indianapolis

This has a very chromatic melody and a Classic rag style change in section A with the introduction of the minor of the dominant. Sections B and C are more orchestral with the B section a remarkable blend of chromaticism and the use of blue thirds and sevenths, with a call-and-response phrasing in C. It is a companion to "Dusty Rag" and a fine example of blending both black and white folk music materials in a ragtime composition.

# Trebor Jay Tichenor

## (b. January 28, 1940, St. Louis)

Tichenor was named by his father, who inverted his own name, Robert, into Trebor. He first heard Novelty rags and popular music played by his mother, whose band—Letty's Collegiate Syncopators—was active in the St. Louis area in the thirties. He began taking piano lessons at age five with John Gross and studied with Bernell Fiegler until age thirteen, when he discovered ragtime through recordings by Lou Busch. He began

collecting ragtime piano rolls and sheet music and learned to play rags. He was influenced during contacts with Dr. Hubert S. Pruett, whose pioneer collection of sheet music and rolls stimulated Tichenor's own collecting efforts. He resumed classical piano studies for two more years with Gross, at his father's suggestion. In 1958 he graduated cum laude from St. Louis Country Day School and received an AB degree from Washington University in St. Louis in 1963. He heard Ragtime Bob Darch perform in Joplin, Missouri, in 1959. Tichenor met ragtime pianists Knocky Parker and Pete Clute in 1960, and they inspired him to become a professional performer. He began composing his own rags in the folk idiom in 1961. Also in 1961, in collaboration with the late Russ Cassidy, he formed the *Ragtime Review,* the first regular publication devoted exclusively to ragtime since Axel Christensen's earlier magazine of the same name appeared in 1915. He helped form and played in a four-piece band, the St. Louis Ragtimers, in 1961 and played with this group in St. Louis' Gaslight Square at the Natchez Queen and at Bustle and Bowes. He has remained with the group ever since. The Ragtimers have appeared on the Goldenrod Showboat continuously since 1965. He owns the largest private collection of ragtime piano rolls—including Pruett's collection—in the country and has an authoritative library of original ragtime sheet music. He married Jeanette Taft Jordan in 1966, and they have two children, Virginia and Andrew. His weekly radio program called *Ragophile,* heard in St. Louis, is the oldest show of its kind in the nation. He has appeared in concerts in California, Missouri, Toronto, and New York and was seen with the Ragtimers on the *Today Show's* "Salute to Missouri" in January 1976. He

House of Lords.

Market St.

teaches ragtime history at Washington University and collaborated with collector and piano-roll historian Mike Montgomery to produce six definitive LPs on the Biograph label of the piano-roll music of Scott Joplin and James Scott. Tichenor has recorded two record albums of piano solos and appears on five additional LPs with the St. Louis Ragtimers. He has contributed ragtime articles to magazines and furnished original sheet music to several publishers for reprint projects during the seventies. He edited and selected the rags for two major folios for Dover Publications.

## Ragtime Compositions

"Big Ben—a Rag for Ben Conroy," not copyrighted or published

"Boom Town Echoes—a Gold Camp Fracas," not copyrighted or published

"Bucksnort Stomp—an Arkansas Hell-Raiser," not copyrighted or published

"Chestnut Valley Rag," 1966, *They All Played Ragtime*, 3d ed., Oak Publications, New York

"Cottonwood Rag," not copyrighted or published

"Days beyond Recall," not copyrighted or published

"Glen Arbor Rag," 1994, Trebor J. Tichenor, St. Louis

"Goldenrod Stomp," not copyrighted or published

"Hickory Smoked Rag," not copyrighted or published

"It's a Long Way Back Home," not copyrighted or published

"The Last Cake Walk," not copyrighted or published

"The Last Trip down from Hannibal," not copyrighted or published

"Market St. Rag—a Rosebud Club Revelry," not copyrighted or published

"The Mississippi Valley Frolic," not copyrighted or published

"Missouri Autumn Rag," not copyrighted or published

"A Missouri Breeze—Ragtime Two Step," not copyrighted or published

"Missouri Rambler," not copyrighted or published

"Old Levee Days," not copyrighted or published

"Olive St. Rag—a Gaslight Square Delight," not copyrighted or published

"Ozark Rag," not copyrighted or published

"Pierce City Rag," not copyrighted or published

"Ragtime in the Hollow," not copyrighted or published

"St. Louis Days," not copyrighted or published

"Sappington Memories," not copyrighted or published

"The Show-Me Rag—a Missouri Defiance," 1977, *The Ragtime Current*, Edward B. Marks Music, New York

"Wine Room Rag," not copyrighted or published

# "Tickled to Death" (Charles Hunter)

## May 11, 1901, first appeared in 1899, Frank G. Fite, Nashville

A joyous, stomping debut. It is a typical Nashville rag in that it combines very ambitious syncopation with simpler cakewalk figures. This became a popular and standard rag and remained available on piano roll into the twenties. The C section is scored as thirty-two measures in the tradition of a march. The thirty-two-bar strain, whether derived from the pop song or the march, persisted in ragtime through the Novelty rags of the twenties. Usually the section could be scored as sixteen measures with two different endings of four measures each. In early rags, the thirty-two-bar strain is almost never repeated until after an interlude is played. In later ragtime it was repeated immediately. Some of these double sixteen-measure sections have different ideas in each of their last eight measures. In two of the Hunter rags, in fact, they are even more asymmetrical in phrasing, as well as in the total concepts. In these, the basic concept overall is indeed thirty-two measures.

# "Tiddle-De-Winks" (Melville Morris)

## September 16, 1916, Jerome H. Remick & Co., New York

This rag uses the parallel minor; see Luckey Roberts's "Pork and Beans" and Henry Lodge's "Temptation Rag."

# Harry Austin Tierney

## (b. May 21, 1890, Perth Amboy, New Jersey; d. March 22, 1965, New York)

Tierney's musical education began with his mother and continued with Nicholas Morrissey. He subsequently attended the Virgil Conservatory of Music in New York City. Tierney toured the country as a concert pianist. He went to London in 1916, where he wrote music for a show and revue and returned the following year to embark on a career in popular music. He joined the publishing firm of Jerome H. Remick & Co. and, in 1919, wrote the complete score to *Irene,* which had the longest run for a musical comedy up to that time on Broadway; the most famous tune from the show was the lovely waltz "Alice Blue Gown." He wrote for several Ziegfeld Follies and, in 1927, again composed the entire score for a smash musical comedy, *Rio Rita,* which, in addition to the title song also contained a clever syncopated number, "The Kinkajou." He went to Hollywood in 1931 under contract to RKO.

Featured by
Edwards, Ryan and Tierney

Harry A. Tierney.

## Ragtime Compositions

"The Bumble Bee," November 24, 1909, Ted Snyder Co., New York

"The Fanatic Rag," February 15, 1911, Ted Snyder Co., New York

"Uncle Tom's Cabin," March 14, 1911, Jos. W. Stern & Co., New York

"Dingle Pop Hop," April 12, 1911, Ted Snyder Co., New York

"Black Canary," May 5, 1911, Ted Snyder Co., New York

"Checkerboard," May 13, 1911, Ted Snyder Co., New York

"Crimson Rambler," May 19, 1911, Ted Snyder Co., New York

"William's Wedding," June 23, 1911, Ted Snyder Co., New York

"Rubies and Pearls," June 24, 1911, Ted Snyder Co., New York

"Fleur de Lis," August 16, 1911, Jos. W. Stern & Co., New York

"Cabaret Rag," not copyrighted or published

"Variety Rag," July 1, 1912, George W. Meyer Music, New York

"Louisiana Rag," May 3, 1913, Jos. Krolage Music, Cincinnati

"Chicago Tickle" (a.k.a. "The Tierney Rag"), August 8, 1913, not published

"1915 Rag," August 8, 1913, not published

# Tin Pan Alley Steals from Ragtime Composers

There were many kinds of instrumental piano music published at the same time rags were popular: marches, waltzes, intermezzos, and characteristics. Ragtime composer Charles L. Johnson had a massive hit with his Indian intermezzo "Iola," originally published in 1904. It was so successful that Jerome Remick bought it and had James O'Dea write lyrics in 1906. Della Fox popularized it in vaudeville. It was a million-selling hit that remained in the national consciousness for a couple of decades. It was, therefore, astonishing to find Saxie Dowell claiming copyright credit when what he claimed was his "Playmates" climbed to the number-two position on the 1940 Billboard charts. Charley Johnson could also cry foul when his 1902 novelette "A Whispered Thought," with very little alteration, became the 1949 evergreen "Rudolph the Red-Nosed Reindeer." The trio of another 1902 publication, "Siamese Patrol," by German composer Paul Lincke was taken by Cole Porter for his "You Do Something to Me," and its opening melody was closely adapted by Anton Karas for his 1950 "Third Man Theme." The phenomenal World War II hit, "Don't Sit under the Apple Tree," was taken bodily from J. Bodewalt Lampe's 1905 hit characteristic "Happy Heine." His 1915 idyll, "The Glad Girl," was used in 1950 for "Music! Music! Music!" In 1951, Del Wood used the trio of Max Hoffman's 1904 rag "Yankee Land" as the chorus for her song "Ragtime Melody." And ragtime composer Percy Wenrich had published "Flower Girl" as an intermezzo in 1907, which could have figured in Mack David's suit against Jerry Herman when David claimed that Herman stole his 1948 "Sunflower" (a top hit) for "Hello Dolly" in 1964. Wenrich had them both beat and could have won twice.

# "Tin Pan Rag" (Lou Busch)

## March 5, 1952, Chatsworth Music, New York

Busch (1910–1979) used the name Joe "Fingers" Carr to record ragtime. Though he published this rag in his 1952 folio, *Bar Room Piano Solos*, he did not record it until the end of the '50s, and then it was only released in Holland (Warner Bros. 5149). It typifies the atmosphere of joy that was Busch's basic ragtime ingredient.

# "Toad Stool Rag" (Joseph Lamb)

## *Ragtime Treasures*, 1964, Mills Music, Inc., New York

The trio is a beautiful reflection on Scott Joplin's "Cascades" trio. Section D is an eight-measure conception repeated.

# "Tom and Jerry Rag" (Jerry Cammack)

## Not copyrighted, published 1913, St. Louis Publishing Co., St. Louis

Cammack was a professional musician (1890–1963) who began his career as a ragtime pianist but later did most of his keyboard work on the organ for circuses. This rag was written in 1906 when he was living in Marion, Indiana, where he had heard Scott Joplin demonstrating his rags on a sidewalk piano in 1903.

# "Too Much Raspberry" (Sydney K. Russell)

## September 6, 1916, Charles N. Daniels, San Francisco

A very fine rag with unusual left hand in the A section. This is perhaps the most successful rag using unexpected harmonies and retains a cohesiveness despite its harmonic wanderings (e.g., C-E-A flat$_7$-C-A$_7$-D$_7$-G$_7$-C). It was first recorded by Dave Jasen in June 1977 (Folkways FG-3561).

# "Top Liner Rag" (Joseph Lamb)

## January 4, 1916, Stark Music Co., St. Louis

Undoubtedly Lamb's greatest rag and among the three greatest rags of all time. In its construction and development, it is a perfect rag. Lamb consistently returned to this rag as his own favorite, and the 1958 Wally Rose recording (Good Time Jazz M-12034) was Lamb's favorite recording of all of his rags.

# "Torpedo Rag" (George Oscar Young)

## June 5, 1917, Daniels & Wilson, San Francisco

A rather difficult, heavily textured rag abounding in treble octaves, triplet breaks, and chromatic harmonies. The composer later recorded with the Georgia Melodians for Edison.

# "A Totally Different Rag" (May Aufderheide)

## July 16, 1910, J. H. Aufderheide, Indianapolis

The title is descriptive of unusual melodic construction of section B, achieved partially by a suspended fourth, another feature of Ohio Valley rags after 1908.

# "Town Talk" (Elmer Olson)

## November 27, 1917, E. F. Bickhart's Song Shop, Minneapolis

An expansive rag spiced with flatted fifths and major sevenths. The introduction begins with a Confrey-like voicing on an augmented triad.

# "Triangle Jazz Blues" (Irwin P. Leclere)

## February 21, 1917, Triangle Music Publishing Company, New Orleans

A great and very original conception of late ragtime (all sections contain sixteen measures) with much jazz coloration—flatted thirds, breaks, slurs, and minor seconds. Named after a theater in New Orleans where the

Leclere takes a rare turn at the piano. (States-item photo by Ronald LeBoeuf.)

composer performed in vaudeville, it was also the name of Leclere's publishing company. Wally Rose made a much-admired recording in May 1953 (Columbia CL-6260).

## "Trilby Rag" (Carey Morgan)

### May 11, 1915, Jos. W. Stern & Co., New York

An inspired rag written with a strong one-step feeling. The trio has a blues quality, which is perhaps why it attracted Charles "Cow Cow" Davenport, a blues pianist who transformed it into "Atlanta Rag" and "Texas Shout"—claiming composer credit with each retitling. This transformation idea was a later Folk rag development that involved popular published rags, or parts thereof, being turned into Folk rag performances.

## "Troubadour Rag" (James Scott)

### February 7, 1919, Stark Music Co., St. Louis

A typical late-Scott rag; heavily textured. Unusual feature is the dotted-note writing for part of the A section. The rag includes variations of his familiar devices but beautifully articulated.

# "Troublesome Ivories"
# (also known as "Ragtime Rag") (Eubie Blake)

## May 14, 1971, *Giants of Ragtime,* Edward B. Marks Music Corp., New York

This has a favorite Blake bass pattern and also one of his favorite tricks done on a diminished chord to punctuate a phrase.

# Thomas M. J. Turpin

## (b. 1873, Savannah; d. August 13, 1922, St. Louis)

Pioneer ragtime pianist and composer whose first saloon was at 9 Targee Street, a notorious area recalled by W. C. Handy when he passed through St. Louis in 1893 as "so crowded it was a luxury to sit down in one of the many pool halls there." Before he ran his own saloon, Turpin played piano at Babe Connors's world-renowned Castle Club in St. Louis, where several popular songs of the 1890s originated in versions later expurgated for polite society: "Hot Time in the Old Town," "Ta-Ra-Ra-Boom-Der-A," and "Bully of the Town." All were introduced by the famous New Orleans octoroon entertainer, Mama Lou, and a chorus line of girls who wore only skirts and danced on a mirrored floor. In 1900 Turpin opened at 2220 Market Street in the heart of the St. Louis District, then developing around Union Station, the new train depot. This area,

Tom Turpin ad.

The Rosebud Bar.

centering around Market and Chestnut Streets, became known as Chestnut Valley but was referred to by the clergy as Death Valley. Most outraged was Father Koffee, who tried to get a law passed in 1893 removing the pianos from the wine rooms. Turpin's saloon became the Rosebud Bar, the mecca for all underground ragtime musicians. Turpin is referred to in the black newspaper of the time, the *St. Louis Palladium*, as "President of the Rosebud Club," a group of ragtime pianists. He and his brother, Charlie, controlled the Booker T. Washington Theatre where music was composed and arranged at various times by Turpin, Joe Jordan, and Artie Matthews. The brothers were the first black politicians in town and ran gambling houses, dance halls, and sporting houses. Turpin was so heavy that his piano was raised on blocks so that he could play it standing up; his stomach got in the way when he was seated.

The Turpin rags are vibrant, energetic rags, stamped with a distinct personality and with the spontaneity of a creative performance. They are mostly linear and always in one of the following keys: C, F, or G. The rags have what is called a "jumpy," urban flavor mixed with a Mississippi Valley folk-roots flavor, and they are intensely pianistic overall. They are creative transformations of folk backgrounds into early idiomatic rag scores for piano—not very bucolic, as with many small-town Folk rags, but rather with a restlessness and gaiety of Old St. Louis, itself evolving from a countrified atmosphere to a metropolitan center.

## Ragtime Compositions

"Harlem Rag," December 17, 1897, Robt. De Yong & Co., St. Louis

"Bowery Buck," March 6, 1899, Robt. De Yong & Co., St. Louis

"Ragtime Nightmare," April 13, 1900, Robt. De Yong & Co., St. Louis

"St. Louis Rag," November 2, 1903, Sol Bloom, New York

"The Buffalo Rag," November 2, 1904, Will Rossiter, Chicago

"Pan-Am Rag," June 8, 1914, *They All Played Ragtime*, 3d ed., 1966, Oak Publications, New York

# "Twelfth Street Rag" (Euday L. Bowman)

## January 30, 1914, August 24, 1914, January 2, 1915, self, Fort Worth

This was the most recorded rag during the 78 rpm era. Since it was composed in 1914, it has been a favorite of dance bands, jazz bands, pianists, and all other instrumentalists. "Twelfth Street Rag," except for its sixteen-measure introduction (see "Maple Leaf Rag"), is a scored thirty-two-measure theme and variations. Published variations are not common (e.g., Tom Turpin's "Harlem Rag," James E. C. Kelly's "Bully Rag"), but there is no other example of a published rag that has one section with variations throughout. It is also a magnificent example of what has become the major standard musical cliché in ragtime: the three-over-four pattern, which is a sequence of three different notes placed within a four-beat measure resulting in the accenting of a new note whenever the phrase was repeated. The first edition and Bowman's own recording (Bowman 11748) confirm that this rag was written on the order of the Folk school of improvisatory playing.

The biggest selling ragtime recording in history is the one that Pee Wee Hunt and his Orchestra (Capitol 15105) recorded in May 1948. This recording, which was an accident, took place informally after a session that recorded a transcribed radio program. The engineer, having some acetate left on the disc, asked them to play anything they wanted for a couple of minutes. Inadvertently, the tune was left on the disc, and when it was broadcast listeners called their radio stations asking what that unannounced last tune was. A demand was created that forced Capitol Records to issue this strictly-for-fun effort as a single. From its release in fall

12th Street Rag.

"12th Street Rag" recorded by Pee Wee Hunt and his Orchestra, the biggest selling ragtime recording in history.

1948, it ultimately sold over three million copies. It also established the "doo-wacka-doo" chorus as a must-play feature in every rendition since. It featured leader Hunt on trombone, Frank Bruno on trumpet, Rosy McHargue on clarinet, Carl Fischer on piano, Harvey Chermak on bass, and Glenn Walker on drums.

# "Twist and Twirl" (Les Copeland)

## Not copyrighted or published

Perhaps Copeland's finest and most original rag, presented in a simple linear format. Section A recalls "38th Street Rag" and features slurs in the right hand. B is the most melodic of the three. C is a tour de force, a high point in Folk rag performance wherein Copeland in 1917 executes a quick bass descent in straight octaves that melt suddenly into a funkier broken octave bass, an inspired bit of good humor (Universal 202755).

# U

## "Uncle Tom's Cabin" (Harry Austin Tierney)

### March 14, 1911, Jos. W. Stern & Co., New York

A good rag with a truly exceptional trio. The initial C states a great lyrical melody. $C_1$ thickens the texture with octaves in the treble. $C_2$ is a ragged transformation.

## "Universal Rag" (George Botsford)

### February 14, 1913, self, New York

A rouser apparently written exclusively for issue on Universal piano rolls (see Scott Joplin's "Silver Swan").

## "Universal Rag" (Charley Straight with McKay)

### Not copyrighted or published

Straight had an infectious swing on his early QRS Autograph rolls that added great style and personality to the tunes he performed on that series. The B section has a characteristic descending treble figure that he loved to use. It breaks up a chord into the pattern of a single note followed by a harmonic interval of, for example, a third or fourth (QRS 100801).

# "Up and Down in China" (Willard Robison)

## September 14, 1926, Robbins–Engel Inc., New York

A sense of the exotic far-off lands pervades much Novelty writing since the idiom coincided with a rage for such pseudooriental tunes as "Sahara," "Karavan," and "Cairo," of which Zez Confrey made a specialty during his brilliant series of rolls for QRS in 1919. Native Missourian Robison displays an original flair for such exotica here (Autograph 601).

# V

## "Valentine Stomp" (Thomas "Fats" Waller)

### December 26, 1929, Southern Music Publishing Co., New York

Fats had a predilection for bass tenths and a flair for impeccable voicings. His chords seem to melt into each other. He had an ease in his swing that was incomparable, as well as the most sensitive dynamics of all the Harlem pianists. His mastery is best displayed in this rag, which is highlighted in the A section by a flowing descent of eighth-note triplets in the right hand—a favorite Waller device (Victor V-38554).

## Fred Van Eps

### (b. December 30, 1878, Somerville, New Jersey; d. November 22, 1960, Burbank)

Van Eps's father was a watchmaker of Dutch origin. His mother's family came from Norway. At his father's insistence, he was given violin lessons when he was seven. At the magical age of twelve—the same as Vess Ossman—Van Eps heard a railroad conductor playing the banjo and started taking lessons from him. From there, he bought a cylinder machine and many cylinders, especially Ossman's, and learned the pieces by ear. He wrote out the part, practiced it, and then played it. With his cylinder phonograph, he made his own recordings, as cylinder machines were able to record as well as to play back. At this time, his parents moved to Plainfield, New Jersey, which was close to Newark, where the United States Phonograph Company was located. They manufactured cylinders as early as 1893—three years before Edison. In 1897, Van Eps thought he was good enough to record professionally and went to the Edison studios in West Orange, New Jersey. In an interview, he recalled, "I got a job for every Wednesday afternoon making forty cylinders, one after the other. They paid me the usual rate—$1 for each round." He was only making $16 a week helping his father repair watches, and $40 was considerable—for one afternoon's work.

Fred Van Eps.

Van Eps remembered his first disc being a duet with fellow banjoist Bill Bowen made around 1903. This was a direct result of their working for Ossman that summer, filling engagements Ossman obtained from his booking office. When Ossman decided to give up recording work to tour, Van Eps began his recording career in earnest. From 1910 until 1926, Van Eps was the premier recording banjo virtuoso. He worked for Zon-O-phone, Victor, Columbia, and Edison, as well as for dozens of small companies that appeared and disappeared with alarming frequency.

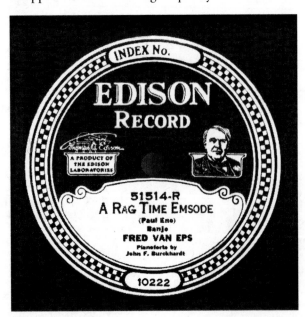

Fred Van Eps record label.

Van Eps was making disc recordings on a freelance basis for a minimum of $100 a recording, getting much more from Victor and Columbia. As social dancing was the new craze by the second decade of the twentieth century, Van Eps formed a trio both for recording and for playing dances. The first trio had Van Eps on lead banjo, his brother, Bill, playing second banjo, and Felix Arndt on piano. Victor wanted Van Eps to drop his brother and substitute Eddie King on drums. Because King was Victor's artist and repertoire director, that was the new line-up of the Van Eps Trio. But, as soon as Van Eps recorded with a different combination for Pathe Records, Victor insisted on this new sounding trio for their own recordings. So, from 1916 on, the trio consisted of Van Eps on banjo, Nathan Glantz on alto saxophone, and Frank Edgar Banta on piano. Around 1918, Van Eps joined the Eight Famous Victor Artists, who toured the United States and Canada for several months during each year. He left the troupe in 1922 to market a banjo he developed. Going from that to manufacturing his inventions that simplified the recording process was but a step. During the last quarter of his life, long after his recording career ended, he developed and perfected a new technique for playing the five-string banjo. With recordings made in 1951, he issued three discs on his own Five String Banjo label, featuring his solos using the new technique, accompanied by his son, Robert, on piano. At the end of his life, he moved to California to be with his children and remained there until his death.

# "Variety Rag" (Harry Austin Tierney)

## July 1, 1912, George W. Meyer Music Co., New York

The introduction is scored as seven measures with an introductory measure to A. This same measure is used again to bring back A after B.

# "Victory Rag" (James Scott)

## Not copyrighted, published 1921, Stark Music Co., St. Louis

Has the most involved and varied bass work of any of Scott's rags. Section B contains a left hand alternating between a regular ragtime bass and single-note runs.

# "Vivacity Rag" (Frank C. Keithley)

## February 5, 1910, New York and Chicago Music Publishing House, Chicago

Nice variation on "Maple Leaf Rag" and "The Naked Dance."

# "Wall Street Rag" (Scott Joplin)

## February 23, 1909, Seminary Music Co., New York

This begins Joplin's experimental period and an attempt to continue his programmatic music, which he began with "The Cascades." He labeled each section, intimating a musical description: The A section is titled "Panic in Wall Street, Brokers Feeling Melancholy"; the B section is called "Good Times Coming"; the C section—the most happily syncopated in the entire rag—is titled "Good Times Have Come"; and the D section is in the fine tradition of having a splendid and victorious ending, using tone clusters and deliberately creating a Folk rag atmosphere for its "Listening to the Strains of Genuine Negro Ragtime, Brokers Forget Their Cares."

# Thomas Wright (Fats) Waller

## (b. May 21, 1904, New York; d. December 15, 1943, Kansas City, Kansas)

Waller was the most well known of all of the Stride pianists. He made piano rolls and over 500 records (mostly for RCA Victor), had his own weekly network radio program, performed in Europe and England, and was featured in such motion pictures as *Hooray for Love* (RKO, 1935), *King of Burlesque* (TCF, 1935), and *Stormy Weather* (TCF, 1943). He began piano studies at six, played in a high school orchestra, won a talent contest playing "Carolina Shout," whereupon he became a protégé of James P. Johnson. This relationship turned into friendship, and Johnson became his close companion, introducing Waller to the world of piano rolls (QRS) and records, playing at rent parties, and becoming resident organist at the Lincoln Theatre in Harlem. He wrote scores to such musical comedies as *Keep Shufflin'*, *Hot Chocolates*, and *Early to Bed*. He wrote many other successful pop songs, among them "Squeeze Me," "My Fate Is in Your Hands," "I've Got a Feeling I'm Falling," "Honeysuckle Rose," "Blue Turning Grey over You," "Keepin' out of Mischief Now," "I'm Crazy 'bout My Baby," and "Ain't Misbehavin'." He spent most of his professional life on the road

Thomas Waller.

touring and playing nightclubs throughout this country. He died of pneumonia on a train to New York. In 1966 his manager, Ed Kirkeby, wrote his biography, *Ain't Misbehavin'*.

## Ragtime Compositions

"Wild Cat Blues" (with Clarence Williams), September 24, 1923, Clarence Williams Music, New York

"Hog Maw Stomp," November 5, 1928, unpublished

"Gladyse," December 26, 1929, Southern Music, New York

"Valentine Stomp," December 26, 1929, Southern Music, New York

"Harlem Fuss," December 17, 1930, Southern Music, New York

"Handful of Keys," December 29, 1930, Southern Music, New York

"Smashing Thirds," March 23, 1931, Southern Music, New York

"African Ripples," April 20, 1931, Joe Davis, Inc., New York

# "Walper House Rag" (Joseph Lamb)

## Written 1903, copyrighted 1962, unpublished

Lamb's first rag. Folksy and rambunctious, using a simple cakewalk pattern. Not an immortal work.

# "Water Wagon Blues" (George L. Cobb)

## Not copyrighted, published 1919, Walter Jacobs, Boston

It is a fine example of humor and prohibition affecting ragtime as the C section quotes "How Dry I Am" in a very effective blues-tinged ragtime style.

# "The Watermelon Trust" (Harry C. Thompson)

## May 25, 1906, Barron & Thompson Co., New York

One of the most lyrical works that makes inspired use of nonchord tones in the melody to produce a sensitive rag.

# "Weeping Willow" (Scott Joplin)

## June 6, 1903, Val A. Reis Music Co., St. Louis

The first two sections seem like a happy, carefree romp during a lazy, sunny afternoon in the South. Beautifully melodic and with clever use of syncopation it evokes different images—just what Joplin intended. A wonderfully constructed rag; the various sections bring out differing emotions. Section C begins with a favorite black folk strain, best remembered in "'Tain't Nobody's Business If I Do."

# Percy Wenrich

## (b. January 23, 1880, Joplin, Missouri; d. March 17, 1952, New York)

Wenrich was born and raised in the mining town of Joplin, Missouri, which featured an abundance of saloons and sporting houses. He joined an amateur minstrel group where he learned coon songs and cakewalks. His entire family played the piano. He paid Chicago publisher Sol Bloom to publish his two-step "L'Inconnu" in 1897, which he then personally peddled from door to door in and around his hometown. He left for Chicago in 1901, where he attended the Chicago Musical College and began his career as a professional songwriter. He had a truly great flair for writing lyrical popular song melodies with a genuine folk flavor. Although he had heard the legendary ragtime pioneers in his youth play at the House of Lords, one of the most plush sporting emporiums—bar on the ground floor, gambling on the second, and sporting house on the third—his total output of first-rate rags is less than might be expected. Only a few are in that category. His forte was the pop song, and his biggest hits included "Moonlight Bay," "When You Wore a Tulip," and

Percy Wenrich.

"Put On Your Old Gray Bonnet." Hollywood celebrated his songwriting career with the Doris Day film *On Moonlight Bay* (Warner, 1951), which featured the best of his songs.

## Ragtime Compositions

"Ashy Africa," October 29, 1903, Buck & Carney, Chicago

"Chasing the Fox," June 5, 1922, Forster Music, Chicago

"Chestnuts," November 7, 1906, Arnett–Delonais, Chicago

"Crab Apples," January 27, 1908, Brehm Brothers, Erie

"Dixie Blossoms," July 16, 1906, Jerome H. Remick & Co., Detroit

"Dixie Kicks," September 14, 1908, McKinley Music, Chicago

"Egyptian Rag," November 16, 1910, Jerome H. Remick & Co., New York

"Fun Bob," March 30, 1907, Arnett–Delonais, Chicago

"Made in Germany" (as Karl Schmidt), 1906, Frank K. Root, Chicago

"Noodles," August 21, 1906, Arnett–Delonais, Chicago

"Peaches and Cream," November 27, 1905, Jerome H. Remick & Co., New York

"Pennant Rag," September 12, 1913, Charles I. Davis, Cleveland

"Persian Lamb Rag," June 15, 1908, Walter Jacobs, Boston

"Rag Time Chimes," July 26, 1911, Jerome H. Remick & Co., New York

"Ragtime Ripples," September 14, 1908, McKinely Music, Chicago

"Smiler Rag," January 2, 1907, Arnett–Delonais, Chicago

"Southern Symphony," April 13, 1910, Jerome H. Remick & Co., New York

"Sunflower Rag," July 26, 1911, Jerome H. Remick & Co., New York

"Sunflower Tickle" (as Dolly Richmond), September 14, 1908, McKinley Music, Chicago

"Sweetmeats," February 18, 1907, Arnett–Delonais, Chicago

"Whipped Cream," January 18, 1913, Wenrich–Howard, New York

# "West Coast Rag" (Will Ezell)

Chicago-based itinerant pianist Ezell made very few recordings, and it demonstrates how the traveling player picked up ideas in different locations and somehow glued the several themes together. This one is a hodge-podge of printed ragtime themes along with improvised rag licks (Paramount 12549).

# "Whitewash Man" (Jean Schwartz)

## September 8, 1908, Cohan & Harris Publishing Co., New York

A prolific songwriter and composer of show tunes, Schwartz had a flair for smooth harmonic changes, frequently with the bass moving downward adding interesting color in an orthodox tonal format.

# "Whittling Remus" (Thomas E. Broady)

## April 20, 1900, H. A. French, Nashville

Broady's best, with a fine melodious A section, a rousing B, and capped with a trio that is a highpoint of Nashville ragtime, where there are twenty rags known to have been published.

# "Who Let the Cows Out, a Bully Rag" (Charles Humfeld)

## March 10, 1910, Howard & Browne Music Co., St. Louis

A whimsical rag by a prominent St. Louis pianist who called himself Humpy and the Musical Architect. A one-measure break challenges the pianist to "make a noise like a cow."

# "Whoa! Nellie" (George Gould)

## June 4, 1925, not copyrighted, published 1915, Charles N. Daniels, San Francisco

This is typical of many Advanced rags, which are expansive and expressive, making more demands on the performer by enlarging on but retaining a basically older rag style and flavor. The D section is pure joy.

# "Why We Smile" (Charles Hunter)

## September 28, 1903, Frank G. Fite, Nashville

The title may have been taken from the original caption of an advertisement used on the cover of "Tickled to Death" of three happy children smiling.

# "Wild Cherries" (Ted Snyder)

## September 23, 1908, self, New York

The A section starts off with a descending progression that is a floating folk strain also used in James P. Johnson's "Carolina Shout," Jelly Roll Morton's "Perfect Rag," and Joe Sullivan's "Little Rock Getaway." The B section cleverly uses bass octaves affecting harmonic changes. C section is climaxed by a sustained low-ered sixth, or raised fifth, chord. This was such a popular number that years later, comedian-Pianist Jimmy Durante remembered playing it nightly in Coney Island.

# H. Clarence Woods

## (b. June 19, 1888, Blue Earth, Ohio;
## d. September 30, 1956, Davenport, Iowa)

Woods grew up in Carthage, Missouri, where he and James Scott took piano lessons from the same teacher, Emma Johns. He spent many early years as a pianist with a traveling drama troupe, a silent film pianist, and an accompanist and soloist in vaudeville throughout Texas and Oklahoma; he became a theater manager, an organist in movie houses, an orchestra leader, and a radio entertainer and finally ended his career as a professional musician as chief organist, composer, and arranger for the Ringling Brothers and Barnum & Bailey Circus.

### Ragtime Compositions

"Slippery Elm Rag," December 2, 1912, Bush & Gerts Co., Dallas
"Sleepy Hollow Rag," not copyrighted, published 1918, Will L. Livernash Music, Kansas City, MO
"Black Satin Fox Trot," not copyrighted or published

# Calvin Lee Woolsey

## (b. December 26, 1884, Tinney's Point, Missouri;
## d. November 12, 1946, Braymer, Missouri)

Woolsey was a small-town physician who served in the First World War. He did his postgraduate work at Harvard University Medical School, specializing in mental hygiene. He was also an accomplished gourmet

cook, carpenter, and builder of radios. He played ragtime piano and published his own rags, which reflect his own playing style, with many elements found in the Folk rags of the turn of the century when these were probably first written.

## Ragtime Compositions

"Funny Bones," July 17, 1909, Jerome H. Remick & Co., New York

"Medic Rag," April 13, 1910, Jerome H. Remick & Co., New York

"Poison Rag," May 3, 1910, C. L. Woolsey, Braymer, MO

"Peroxide Rag," May 3, 1910, C. L. Woolsey, Braymer, MO

"Mashed Potatoes," August 12, 1911, C. L. Woolsey, Braymer, MO

"Lover's Lane Glide," October 5, 1914, C. L. Woolsey, St. Joseph, MO

# Y

## "Yankee Land" (Max Hoffman)

**August 31, 1904, Rogers Bros. Music Publishing Co., New York**

Most of Hoffman's early original work such as that contained in the Witmark *Pioneer Ragtime Folio* is mediocre—restless syncopes that ignore the need for some measure of lyricism and melody. This one, however, is a sturdy composition with a trio that became more famous as the chorus of Del Wood's "Ragtime Melody" and the reverse of the trio of George Botsford's "Black and White Rag."

# "You Tell 'Em Ivories" (Zez Confrey)

## July 19, 1921, Jack Mills, Inc., New York

The A section begins with a sweeping, cheerful melodic line largely in consecutive fourths, which creates a faintly mysterious atmosphere. Section B fulfills that mysterious promise with the forthright bunch of triplets found in "Kitten." The C section combines the rhythmic contrasts of the first two sections, giving a sense of completion.

# Z

## Dick Zimmerman

**(b. August 11, 1937, Charleston, West Virginia)**

Zimmerman is an all-in-one ragtimer who has literally spread the ragtime word around the world. With his sometime performing partner, Ian Whitcomb, he has spent time giving concerts in England, Europe, and all over the United States. He delights in discovering obscure rags with which to challenge other pianists to "name that rag." He is also a consummate showman who puts together ragtime festivals and then emcees the various and varied concerts. Though most performers record single albums of rags, Zimmerman put together two five-disc packages: *Complete Works of Scott Joplin* (Murray Hill 931079) and *The Collector's History of Ragtime* (Murray Hill 60556/5). He was one of the founders of the Los Angeles Maple Leaf Club and the sole editor of its sensational bimonthly journal the *Rag Times*. Not only does it feature all of the happenings of the ragtime world and reviews of books and recordings, but it also publishes original research, much of which Zimmerman does himself, as well as reprints articles of interest from the original ragtime era. He is also responsible for compiling and publishing folios of specialized interest, such as *Gems of St. Louis Ragtime* and *Gems of Texas Ragtime.*

# APPENDIX 1

## Rags on Record:
## A Discography

Since music is primarily an aural art, the examples of a form of music can best be preserved on the reproducing medium of phonograph recordings. It is significant that the commercial availability of the phonograph record came simultaneously with the explosive popularity of ragtime, thus documenting from the start the development of this art form. As American technology made rapid advances with lightness of material and the ability to put more tunes on one disc, the 45 rpm and 33 1/3 rpm records finally replaced the 78 rpm disc. With the advent of the compact disc and the passing of 78s, 45s, and LPs, it becomes imperative to gather together a complete list of those recordings pertaining to ragtime.

The intention of this discography is to identify all commercially released discs of 78s, 45s, and LPs throughout the world since the beginning of ragtime recording in 1897. Only first-issued recordings are listed, with reissues or dubs excluded. Exceptions are made for recordings reissued on the Victor and Columbia labels from 1900 to 1910 because of their widespread availability.

As ragtime is primarily concerned with the compositions, this discography lists the compositions alphabetically with the name of the composer under the title. The second column lists the performers alphabetically. A small (m) by the performer's name indicates that the composition is part of a medley and does not take up the entire track. The third column lists the record speed. The fourth column lists the record company and its record number. If there is no other identification here, it is assumed that the record company comes from the United States; otherwise, either the country of origin or an abbreviation precedes it in parentheses. The final column shows the year and month of recording, unless preceded by an r, which stands for the year and month of that disc's release date for sale to the public.

| Composition | Performer | Record Speed | Record Company/No. | Year-Month |
|---|---|---|---|---|
| ACORN STOMP | | | | |
| | East Texas Serenaders | 78 | Brunswick 282 | 28-11 |
| AFFINITY RAG | | | | |
| Cozad, Irene | Elliott Adams | LP | Stomp Off 1198 | 1988 |
| THE AFRICAN 400 | | | | |
| Roberts, Charles J. | Arthur Pryor's Band | 78 | Victor 16444 | 09-12 |
| | Zonophone Concert Band | 78 | Zonophone 5531 | r. 09-10 |
| AFRICAN PAS' | | | | |
| Kirwin, Maurice | Chrysanthemum Ragtime Band | LP | Stomp Off 1196 | 1988 |
| | London Ragtime Orchestra | LP | GHB 199 | 87-2 |
| | Johnny Maddox | 45 | Dot 45-15028 | c.1952 |
| | New Orleans Ragtime Orchestra | LP | Vanguard VSD-69/70 | 1971 |
| AFRICAN RAG (see SOUNDS OF AFRICA) | | | | |
| AFRICAN RIPPLES | | | | |
| Waller, Thomas | Judy Carmichael | LP | Progressive 7072 | 1983 |
| | Louis Mazetier | LP | Stomp Off 1182 | 88-7 |
| | Ralph Sutton | LP | Riverside RLP-12-212 | 52-6 |
| | Fats Waller | 78 | Victor 24830 | 34-11 |
| AGGRAVATION RAG | | | | |
| Cobb, George L. | George Foley | LP | Stomp Off 1088 | 1984 |
| AGITATION RAG | | | | |
| Hampton, Robert | W. Arlington Piano Roll | LP | Biograph 1006Q | |
| | Bill Mitchell | LP | Ethelyn 1750 | 1972 |
| | Richard Zimmerman | LP | Murray Hill 60556/5 | 1981 |
| ALABAMA JIGGER | | | | |
| Claypoole, Ed | Elite Syncopators | LP | Jazzology JC-102 | r. 1989 |
| | Max Morath | LP | Vanguard VSD-39/40 | 1967 |
| ALABAMA RAG | | | | |
| Lamb, Joseph | John Jensen | LP | Genesis 1045 | 1974 |
| | Milton Kaye | LP | Golden Crest 31035 | 1974 |
| ALASKAN RAG | | | | |
| Lamb, Joseph | John Arpin | LP | (Canada) Scroll 103 | 1966 |
| | Philip Gammon | LP | CRD 1029 | 1976 |
| | Lou Hooper | LP | (Canada) Radio Canada Int. 380 | 1973 |
| | Jazzou Jones | LP | High Water 101 | 1983 |
| | Milton Kaye | LP | Golden Crest 4127 | 1974 |
| | David Laibman | LP | Rounder 3040 | r. 1981 |
| | Joseph Lamb | LP | Folkways FG-3562 | 59-8 |
| ALKALI IKE | | | | |
| Perfect, Albert | Waldo's Ragtime Orchestra | LP | Stomp Off 1007 | 80-10 |
| ALL OF A TWIST | | | | |
| Mayerl, Billy | Billy Mayerl | 78 | (England) HMV B-2130 | 25-8 |

| Composition | Performer | Record Speed | Record Company/No. | Year-Month |
|---|---|---|---|---|
| **ALLIGATOR CRAWL** | | | | |
|   Waller, Fats | Neville Dickie | LP | Stomp Off 1176 | 88-2 |
| | Down Home Jazz Band | LP | Stomp Off 1190 | 88-8 |
| | Tomas Irnberg's Blue Five | LP | Stomp Off 1043 | 82-3 |
| | Steve Waddell's Creole Bells | LP | Stomp Off 1173 | 87-11 |
| | Watergate Seven Plus One | LP | Stomp Off 1165 | 87-7 |
| | Dick Wellstood | 10″LP | Riverside RLP-2506 | 54-10 |
| | Fess Williams Orchestra | 78 | Vocalion 1117 | 27-6 |
| **ALL-OF-A-TWIST** | | | | |
|   Hersom, Frank E. | Richard Zimmerman | LP | Murray Hill 60556/5 | 1981 |
| **ALONG THE TAR** | | | | |
|   Shea, Tom | Tom Shea | LP | Stomp Off 1022 | 1981 |
| **AMAZON RAG** | | | | |
|   Hahn, Teddy | David Thomas Roberts | LP | Stomp Off 1132 | 1983 |
| **AMERICAN BEAUTY RAG** | | | | |
|   Lamb, Joseph | Marc Bercovic | LP | (France) Promophone Rom-1 | 1973 |
| | Brian Dykstra | LP | Century Advent 5075 | 1974 |
| | Patrick Gogerty | LP | Sounds Current | 1976 |
| | John Jensen | LP | Genesis 1045 | 1974 |
| | Milton Kaye | LP | Golden Crest 4127 | 1974 |
| | Max Kortlander Piano Roll | LP | Folkways RBF-43 | |
| | Joseph Lamb | LP | Folkways FG-3562 | 59-8 |
| | Max Morath | LP | Vanguard VSD-39/40 | 1967 |
| | Roland Nadeau | LP | VQR 2625 | 1979 |
| | Knocky Parker & Bill Coffman | LP | Jazzology JCE-81 | r. 1979 |
| | Piano Roll | 78 | Century 4024 | |
| | Piano Roll | 10″LP | Riverside RLP-1006 | |
| | Mike Polad | LP | Jazzology JCE-77 | r. 1975 |
| | Wally Rose | LP | Blackbird 12010 | 71-6 |
| | Ton Van Bergeyk | LP | Kicking Mule 114 | 1976 |
| | Dick Wellstood | LP | (England) 77 SEU-12/51 | 74-1 |
| | Paul Zukofsky & Robert Dennis | LP | Vanguard SRV-350 | 1975 |
| **ANGEL FOOD RAG** | | | | |
|   Marzian, Al | Joe "Fingers" Carr | LP | Capitol T-280 | c. 1952 |
| | Richard Zimmerman | LP | Murray Hill 60556/5 | 1981 |
| **ANNIE'S RAG** | | | | |
|   Smith, Eddie | Eddie Smith | 78 | King 1019 | 51-11 |
| **ANOMA RAG** | | | | |
|   Dabney, Ford | W. Axtmann Piano Roll | LP | Biograph 1006Q | |
| | Piano Roll (aka Watermelon Rebels) | LP | Dot DLP-25478 | |
| | Richard Zimmerman | LP | Murray Hill 60556/5 | 1981 |
| **ANTIQUARY** | | | | |
|   Mayerl, Billy | Billy Mayerl | 78 | (England) Columbia 3926 | 26-3 |

| Composition | Performer | Record Speed | Record Company/No. | Year-Month |
|---|---|---|---|---|
| APPLE JACK | | | | |
| Johnson, Charles L. | Chrysanthemum Ragtime Band | LP | Stomp Off 1079 | 1984 |
| | Red Nichols Five Pennies | LP | Capitol ST-2065 | 63-10 |
| | Knocky Parker | LP | Audiophile AP-91 | |
| | Richard Zimmerman | LP | Murray Hill 60556/5 | 1981 |
| APPLE SASS | | | | |
| Belding, Harry | Chrysanthemum Ragtime Band | LP | Stomp Off 1196 | 1988 |
| ARCTIC SUNSET | | | | |
| Lamb, Joseph | Milton Kaye | LP | Golden Crest 4127 | 1974 |
| ARIZONA STOMP | | | | |
| Williams, Daniel H. | East Texas Serenaders | 78 | Decca 5375 | 37-2 |
| THE ARM BREAKER | | | | |
| Rose, Fred | Clarence M. Jones & Orchestra | 78 | Okeh 8404 | 26-6 |
| | Richard Zimmerman | LP | Murray Hill 60556/5 | 1981 |
| ARNOLD WILEY RAG | | | | |
| Wiley, Arnold | Arnold Wiley | 78 | Brunswick 7113 | 29-7 |
| AT A GEORGIA CAMP MEETING | | | | |
| Mills, Kerry | Sidney Bechet & Band | 78 | Commodore 638 | 50-4 |
| | Graeme Bell & Band | 78 | (Australia) Swaggie 2 | 50-3 |
| | Bell-Monsbourgh Group | 78 | (Australia) Amerpsand 5 | 45-11 |
| | Carolina Mandolin Orchestra | 78 | Okeh 45191 | 28-3 |
| | Castle Jazz Band | 78 | Castle 2 | 47-12 |
| | Columbia Orchestra | 78 | Columbia 406, A-315 | 01-10 |
| | Cullen & Collins | 78 | Berliner 477 | 97-10 |
| | Pete Daily & Band | 78 | Capitol 15434 | 49-10 |
| | Joe Daniels & Band | 78 | (England) Parlophone F-2458 | |
| | Down Home Jazz Band | LP | Stomp Off 1171 | 87-11 |
| | Grammavox Military Band | 78 | (England) Grammavox 58 | |
| | Milt Herth Trio | 78 | Decca 2964 | 39-10 |
| | Jumbo Military Band | 78 | (England) Jumbo 331 | 09-5 |
| | Leake County Revelers | 78 | Columbia 15409-D | 29-4 |
| | London Orchestra | 78 | (England) Cinch 5164 | 13-6 |
| | McLaughlin's Old Time Band | 78 | Victor 21286 | 28-2 |
| | Metropolitan Orchestra | 78 | Berliner 1472 | 97- |
| | Musical Avaloes | 78 | (England) Zonophone 46752 | 02- |
| | New York Military Band | 78 | Edison 50636 | 19-11 |
| | Kid Ory Band | 78 | Columbia 38957 | 50-6 |
| | Sid Phillips & Band | 78 | (England) HMV BD-6159 | 53-12 |
| | Prince's Band | 12"78 | Columbia A-5691 | 15-5 |
| | Ragtime Orchestra | LP | (Czechoslovakia) Supraphon 1115.1965 | 1976 |
| | Royal London Orchestra | 78 | (England) Da Capo 277 | |
| | Sousa's Band | 78 | Berliner 136 | 99-5 |
| | Sousa's Band | 78 | Victor 315 | 00-10 |
| | Sousa's Band | 78 | Victor 16402 | 08-10 |
| | Southern Jazz Group | 78 | (Australia) Wilco 0–107 | 49-5 |

| Composition | Performer | Record Speed | Record Company/No. | Year-Month |
|---|---|---|---|---|
| AT A GEORGIA CAMP MEETING (continued) | Harry Taft | 78 | Berliner 435 | 97-9 |
| | John Terrell | 78 | Berliner 1903 | |
| Mills, Kerry | Ernest Thompson & Connie Sides | 78 | Columbia 15002-D | 24-9 |
| | Lu Watters & YBJB | 78 | Jazz Man 4 | 41-12 |
| | William Whitlock | 78 | (England) Zonophone 41751 | 04-6 |
| ATLANTA RAG (see also TRILBY RAG) | | | | |
| | Cow Cow Davenport | 78 | Gennett 6869 | 29-4 |
| ATLANTA RAG | | | | |
| Morgan, Carey | Ton Van Bergeyk | LP | Kicking Mule 114 | r. 1976 |
| AUNT JEMIMA'S BIRTHDAY | | | | |
| Bloom, Rube | Rube Bloom | 78 | Victor 25227 | 34-12 |
| BACHELOR'S BUTTON | | | | |
| Powell, W. C. | Chrysanthemum Ragtime Band | LP | Stomp Off 1047 | 1983 |
| BACK TO LIFE | | | | |
| Hunter, Charles | David Thomas Roberts | LP | Stomp Off 1021 | 1981 |
| A BAG OF RAGS | | | | |
| McKanlass, W. R. | Marvin Ash | 78 | Capitol 15841 | 49-12 |
| | Paul Lingle | LP | Euphonic 1227 | 1951 |
| | Wilbur Sweatman & Orchestra | 78 | Pathe 20167 | 17-4 |
| | Terry Waldo | LP | Stomp Off 1002 | 80-7 |
| | Mark Wetch | LP | Wilson Audio 8417 | |
| BALTIMORE RAG (aka THAT CERTAIN PARTY) | | | | |
| Kelley, Tom | Joe "Fingers" Carr's Ragtime Band | LP | Capitol T-443 | c. 1953 |
| | Jack Fina Orchestra | 78 | MGM 10869, 30676 | 50-4 |
| BALTIMORE TODALO | | | | |
| Blake, Eubie | Eubie Blake | LP | Columbia C2S-847 | 69-3 |
| | George Hicks | LP | Folkways FS-3165 | 1983 |
| | Moonlight Ragtime Band | LP | National Geographic 07817 | 1979 |
| | Richard Zimmerman | LP | Murray Hill 60556/5 | 1981 |
| BANANA PEEL RAG | | | | |
| Winkler, Gus | Roger's Band | 78 | Paroket 95 | r. 17-4 |
| | Sharkey Bonano Jazz Band | 78 | Capitol 1735 | 51-6 |
| BANJO RAG | | | | |
| Lee, Chauncey | Chauncey Lee | 78 | Okeh 40321 | 25-2 |
| BANJOKES | | | | |
| Smeck, Roy | Roy Smeck & Art Kahn | 78 | Columbia 1127-D | 27-6 |
| BANJOMANIA | | | | |
| Mandell, Pete | Michael Danzi | 78 | (Germany) Gloria G0-27298 | 36-1 |
| | Maya Danzie | 78 | (Germany) Homochord 4-3307 | 29-8 |
| | Phil Russell (Mandell) | 78 | (England) Edison Bell Winner 4591 | 26-9 |
| BANJOVIALITY | | | | |
| Fillis, Len & Bright, Sid | Len Fillis w/ Sid Bright | 78 | (England) Columbia 4643 | 27-2 |

| Composition | Performer | Record Speed | Record Company/No. | Year-Month |
|---|---|---|---|---|
| BANTAM STEP | | | | |
| Jentes, Harry | Conway's Band | 78 | Victor 18141 | 16-10 |
| | Dave Jasen | LP | Folkways FG-3561 | 77-6 |
| | Daryl Ott | LP | Dirty Shame 1238 | 1978 |
| | Pathe Dance Orchestra | 78 | Pathe 29171 or 35029 | 16-8 |
| | Prince's Band | 78 | (England) Regal G-5826 | 16-7 |
| | Trebor Tichenor | LP | Folkways FS-3164 | 1979 |
| | Richard Zimmerman | LP | Murray Hill 60556/5 | 1981 |
| THE BARBARY RAG | | | | |
| Prince, Charles A. | Prince's Band | 78 | (England) Regal G-6727 | 13-9 |
| BARBER POLE RAG | | | | |
| Johnson, Chares L. | Queen City Ragtime Ensemble | LP | Stomp Off 1138 | 1986 |
| BARBERSHOP RAG | | | | |
| Campbell, Brun | Brun Campbell | LP | Euphonic 1201 | 45-6 |
| | David Thomas Roberts | LP | Stomp Off 1132 | 1983 |
| BARKY-ROLL STOMP | | | | |
| Busch, Louis F. | Joe "Fingers" Carr | 78 | Capitol 3201 | 55- |
| BARTENDER'S RAG | | | | |
| Gordon–Trace | Sid Nierman | 78 | Wing 90012 | 55- |
| BEEDLE-UM-BO | | | | |
| Birch, Raymond | George Foley | LP | Stomp Off 1088 | 84-3 |
| BEES AND HONEY RAG | | | | |
| Copeland, Les | Les Copeland Piano Roll | LP | Herwin 407 | |
| BEHAVE YOURSELF | | | | |
| Bargy, Roy | Roy Bargy Piano Roll | LP | Folkways RF-35 | |
| BELL HOP RAG | | | | |
| Bryan, Fred M. | Pathe Dance Orchestra | 78 | Pathe 70128 | 15-9 |
| BELLE OF THE PHILIPPINES | | | | |
| Stone, Fred S. | Ophelia Ragtime Orchestra | LP | Stomp Off 1108 | 1985 |
| | Zonophone Concert Orchestra | 78 | Zonophone 109 | |
| BERT WILLIAMS | | | | |
| Morton, Jelly Roll | Jelly Roll Morton | 12"78 | Circle JM-45 | 38-5 |
| | Knocky Parker | LP | Audiophile AP-105 | |
| | Ray Smith | LP | Stomp Off 1012 | 1981 |
| | Butch Thompson | LP | Center 9 | 68-6 |
| | Butch Thompson & Hal Smith | LP | Stomp Off 1075 | 84-3 |
| | Tex Wyndham | LP | Yerba Buena Jazz 201 | r. 1989 |
| BIG BEN | | | | |
| Tichenor, Trebor | St. Louis Ragtimers | LP | SLR TS-80-46/47 | 1979 |
| BILLY'S RAG | Billy Hamilton | 78 | Kappa 127 | |
| Hamilton, Billy | | | | |

| Composition | Performer | Record Speed | Record Company/No. | Year-Month |
|---|---|---|---|---|
| BIRD-BRAIN RAG | | | | |
| Lamb, Joseph | John Arpin | LP | (Canada) Scroll 101 | 1965 |
| | John Jensen | LP | Genesis 1045 | 1974 |
| | Max Morath | LP | Vanguard SRV-351 | r. 1976 |
| BLACK & BLUE RAG | | | | |
| Nichols, Hal G. | Graeme Bell | 78 | (Australia) Swaggie 4504 | 50-9 |
| | Georgie's Varsity Five | LP | HiFi R-805 | 1959 |
| | Paul Lingle | LP | Euphonic 1217 | 1951 |
| | San Francisco Harry | LP | Fantasy 3270 | 1958 |
| BLACK & WHITE RAG | | | | |
| Botsford, George | American Symphony Orchestra | Cylinder | Edison Standard 100 | |
| | Winifred Atwell | 78 | (England) Decca F-9790 | 51-6 |
| | Ray Bauduc JB | LP | Cap T-877 | 1957 |
| | Graeme Bell | LP | (Australia) Festival L-45545/6 | 74-8 |
| | Graeme Bell | 78 | (England) Par R-3390 | 51-2 |
| | Graeme Bell & Ragtime Four | 78 | (England) Parlophone R-3390 | 51-2 |
| | Albert Benzler | LP | Herwin 405 | c. 1910 |
| | Albert Benzler | Cylinder | US Everlasting 380 | c. 10- |
| | Barney Bigard JB | LP | Crescent Jazz 2 | 1974 |
| | Bindsouw Jazzmen | EP | (Denmark) Storyville SEP-405 | 1961 |
| | Owen Bradley & Band | 78 | Coral 60236 | 50-3 |
| | Harry Breuer Orchestra | LP | Audio Fidelity DFM-3001 | 1960 |
| | Milton Brown & Brownies | 78 | Decca 5129 | 35-1 |
| | Joe "Fingers" Carr | LP | Cap T-760 | |
| | Mannie Carstens Band | LP | (Denmark) Olufsen 5082 | 1987 |
| | Cave Stompers | LP | (Sweden) Storyville SLP-182 | 1966 |
| | Jerry Colonna JB | LP | Wing MGW-12153 | 1958 |
| | Gil Dech | 78 | (Australia) Regal G-21662 | 33-3 |
| | Dixie Stompers | 10"LP | Delmar DL-113 | 1954 |
| | El Cota w/Orchestra | 78 | Columbia A-1118 | 11-12 |
| | Doc Evans JB | 10"LP | Soma 1208 | 1957 |
| | Joe Glover's Cotton Pickers | LP | Epic LN-3581 | |
| | Erwin Halletz & Orchestra | 78 | (Austria) Austroton 58374 | 50- |
| | Hellman's Angels | LP | Plus 8 | 86-1 |
| | Humphries Brothers | 78 | Okeh 45464 | 30-6 |
| | Martin Jager | LP | (Germany) Gold 11034 | 77-11 |
| | Nappy Lamare & Orchestra | 78 | D.J. 100 | 49-12 |
| | Walter Larsson's Band | 78 | (Sweden) Columbia DS-2035 | 52-6 |
| | Alain Lesire | LP | (Belgium) Jazz Cats 6983003 | 1982 |
| | London Orchestra | 78 | (England) Cinch 5245 | 13-5 |
| | Geoff Love Band | LP | (Canada) Quality 753 | 1974 |
| | Luciano's Jazz Sextet | EP | (Uruguay) Sondor 45074 | 1959 |
| | Fess Manetta | LP | Jazzology JCE-6 | 57-5 |
| | Bob Milne | LP | Jim Taylor Presents 113 | 1979 |
| | Turk Murphy JB | LP | Solo 107 | 1958 |

| Composition | Performer | Record Speed | Record Company/No. | Year-Month |
|---|---|---|---|---|
| BLACK & WHITE RAG | New Orleans Ragtime Orchestra | LP | Arhoolie 1058 | 71-5 |
| (continued) | New York Military Band | 78 | Edison 50116 | 14-2 |
| Botsford, George | Red Nichols Five Pennies | LP | Cap ST-2065 | 63-10 |
| | Odeon Dance Orchestra | 78 | (Germany) Odeon A-41170 | 22- |
| | Orchestra | 78 | Silvertone 4117 | 22- |
| | Knuckles O'Toole | LP | Grand Award 33-373 | |
| | Palais de Danse Orchestra | 78 | (Germany) Beka 14362 | 13-2 |
| | Papa Bue's JB | 10"LP | (Denmark) Storyville SLP-191 | 62-1 |
| | Brooke Pemberton | LP | Warner Bros. W-1235 | 1958 |
| | Frank Petty Trio | 78 | MGM 11186 | 52-1 |
| | Prince's Orchestra | 78 | Columbia A-711 | 07-12 |
| | Trevor Richards Trio | LP | Crescent CJP-4 | 75-3 |
| | Riverboat Dandies | LP | Cap T-877 | |
| | Wally Rose | LP | Dawn Club 12003 | 42-3 |
| | Wally Rose | LP | Fairmont 102 | 47-8 |
| | Sao Paulo JB | LP | (Brazil) Phonodisc 0-30-404-023 | 75-9 |
| | Sammy Spear Orchestra | LP | Mercury MG-20116 | 1954 |
| | Ralph Sutton | 78 | Down Home 9 | 49-11 |
| | Tailgate Ramblers | LP | Valon LPC-504 | 62-10 |
| | Ray Turner | 78 | Capitol 1046 | 50- |
| | Victor Orchestra | 78 | Victor 16350 | 09-6 |
| | Lu Watters & YBJB | 78 | Jazz Man 1 | 41-12 |
| | Mark Wetch | LP | Wilson Audio 8417 | |
| | Albert White Orchestra | LP | Barbary Coast 33008 | 1958 |
| | White Eagle JB | LP | (Germany) Biton 2123 | 74-10 |
| | Leo Wijnkamp | LP | Kicking Mule 108 | 1974 |
| | Bill Williams & Band | 78 | Albert 725-4 | 49-12 |
| | Johnny Wittwer | 10"LP | Stinson SLP-58 | 1945 |
| | Richard Zimmerman | LP | Murray Hill 60556/5 | 1981 |
| BLACK BEAUTY RAG | | | | |
| Schwartz, Jean | Piano Roll (aka: Keystone Kapers) | LP | Dot DLP-25478 | |
| | Wally Rose | LP | Stomp Off 1057 | 1982 |
| BLACK CAT RAG | | | | |
| Andrews | Sid Phillips & Band | 78 | (England) HMV BD-6141 | 52-12 |
| BLACK DIAMOND RAG | | | | |
| Lodge, Henry | Knocky Parker | LP | Audiophile AP-92 | |
| | Prince's Band | 78 | Columbia A-1140 | 12-2 |
| | Fred Van Eps w/Orchestra | 78 | Victor 17168 | 12-5 |
| | Fred Van Eps w/Orchestra | 78 | Zonophone 5905 | r. 12-6 |
| BLACK HAND RAG | | | | |
| Norton, George | Queen City Ragtime Ensemble | LP | Stomp Off 1138 | 1986 |
| BLACK JACK RAG | Charley Straight Piano Roll | LP | Folkways RBF-44 | |
| Straight, Charley | Richard Zimmerman | LP | Murray Hill 60556/5 | 1981 |

| Composition | Performer | Record Speed | Record Company/No. | Year-Month |
|---|---|---|---|---|
| BLACK MOUNTAIN RAG | | | | |
| Tichenor, Trebor | St. Louis Ragtimers | LP | Audiophile AP-81 | 1964 |
| BLACK SATIN RAG | | | | |
| Woods, Clarence | Piano Roll | LP | Herwin 407 | |
| BLACK SMOKE | | | | |
| Johnson, Charles L. | Terry Waldo | LP | Dirty Shame 1237 | 1974 |
| THE BLACKTHORNS | | | | |
| Morris, George E. | George E. Morris w/Orchestra | 78 | (England) Decca F-1686 | 30-2 |
| BLAME IT ON THE BLUES | | | | |
| Cooke, Charles | Albion JB | LP | Stomp Off 1206 | 90-3 |
| | Pierre Atlan's Piccadilly Revelers | LP | Stomp Off 1181 | 88-11 |
| | Steen Christensen | LP | (Denmark) LB 1 | 1972 |
| | Max Collie's Rhythm Aces | LP | (Holland) Beerendonk 9996 | 80-1 |
| | Paul Furniss Band | LP | (Australia) Swaggie 1368 | 74-10 |
| | Eric Gemsa | LP | (France) Cezanne 1002 | 1975 |
| | Hager's Dance Orchestra | 78 | Rex 5248 | |
| | William Headon | 78 | Dootone 427 | |
| | Lou Hooper | LP | (Canada) Radio Canada Int. 380 | 1973 |
| | Dave Jasen | LP | Blue Goose 3002 | 1974 |
| | Paul Lingle | LP | GTJ L-12025 | 52-2 |
| | Paul Lingle | LP | Euphonic 1227 | 1951 |
| | Turk Murphy JB | LP | Merry Makers 105 | 1970 |
| | New Black Eagle JB | LP | Stomp Off 1224 | 90-6 |
| | New Ragtime Band | LP | (Switzerland) Evasion 100.208 | 73-5 |
| | Piano Roll | LP | (England) Saydisc SDL-117 | |
| | Prince's Band | 12"78 | Columbia A-5675 | 15-5 |
| | Alan Rogers | LP | (England) VJM LC-4 | 1965 |
| | Willie the Lion Smith | LP | Dot 3094 | 57-11 |
| | Willie the Lion Smith | LP | (France) Jazz Odyssey 006 | 72-2 |
| | Victor Military Band | 78 | Victor 17764 | 15-4 |
| | Richard Zimmerman | LP | Murray Hill 60556/5 | 1981 |
| BLAZE AWAY | | | | |
| Bernard, Mike | Mike Bernard | 78 | Columbia A-2577 | 18-4 |
| BLIND BOONE'S SOUTHERN RAG MEDLEY #2 | | | | |
| Boone, Blind | Queen City Ragtime Ensemble | LP | Stomp Off 1138 | 1986 |
| BLOOEY BLUES | | | | |
| Jentes, Harry | Harry Jentes | 78 | Okeh 4868 | 23-3 |
| BLOOIE-BLOOIE | | | | |
| Baker, Edythe | Edythe Baker Piano Roll | LP | Herwin 407 | |
| BLUE BLACK BOTTOM | | | | |
| Waller, Fats | Fats Waller | LP | RCA-Victor LPV-516 | 27-2 |
| BLUE CLOVER MAN | | | | |
| Kortlander, Max | Max Kortlander Piano Roll | LP | Folkways RF-43 | |

| Composition | Performer | Record Speed | Record Company/No. | Year-Month |
|---|---|---|---|---|
| BLUE GOOSE RAG | | | | |
| Birch, Raymond | Hall Bros. Jazz Band | LP | Stomp Off 1031 | 81-9 |
| | Dave Jasen | LP | Blue Goose 3002 | 1974 |
| | Majestic Military Band | 78 | Majestic 176 | 17-1 |
| | Melodograph Dance Band | 78 | Melodograph 217 | |
| | Tony Parenti's Ragtime Gang | LP | Jazzology J-21 | 66-4 |
| | Roger's Band | 78 | Paroquette 72 | r. 17-3 |
| | Wally Rose | LP | Blackbird 12010 | 71-6 |
| BLUE GRASS RAG | | | | |
| Lamb, Joseph | John Jensen | LP | Genesis 1045 | 1974 |
| | Milton Kaye | LP | Golden Crest 4127 | 1974 |
| BLUE GRASS RAG | | | | |
| Straight, Charley | Paul Lingle | LP | Euphonic 1227 | 1951 |
| BLUE RAG IN 12 KEYS | | | | |
| Blake, Eubie | Eubie Blake | LP | Columbia C2S-847 | 69-2 |
| A BLUE STREAK | | | | |
| Bargy, Roy | Roy Bargy Piano Roll | LP | Folkways RF-35 | |
| BLUIN' THE BLACK KEYS | | | | |
| Schutt, Arthur | Tony Caramia | LP | Stomp Off 1209 | 1989 |
| | George Hicks | LP | Folkways FS-3165 | 1983 |
| BOOGIE RAG | | | | |
| Sweatman, Wilbur | Chrysanthemum Ragtime Band | LP | Stomp Off 1047 | 83-1 |
| BOHEMIA RAG | | | | |
| Lamb, Joseph | John Arpin & Catherine Wilson | LP | (Canada) Fanfare 9023 | r. 1986 |
| | Chris Barber JB | LP | (England) Col. 33SX-1245 | 1960 |
| | Bill Coffman & Kathy Craig | LP | OTMH 101 | r. 1980 |
| | Dave Dallwitz Ensemble | LP | Stomp Off 1098 | 84-8 |
| | Dawn of the Century Orchestra | LP | Arcane 602 | 1972 |
| | Neville Dickie | LP | (England) Major Minor SMCP-5039 | 1969 |
| | Brian Dykstra | LP | Advent 5021 | 1976 |
| | Patrick Gogerty | LP | Sounds Current | 1976 |
| | Steve Hancoff | LP | Dirty Shame 4553 | 1977 |
| | Paul Hersh & David Montgomery | LP | RCA ARL1-0364 | 1974 |
| | Dave Jasen | LP | Blue Goose 3002 | 1974 |
| | Hank Jones | LP | ABC-Paramount 496 | 64-4 |
| | Milton Kaye | LP | Golden Crest 4127 | r. 1974 |
| | Original Prague Syncopated Orchestra | LP | (Czechoslovakia) Supraphon 1115.1965 | 1976 |
| | Knocky Parker & Bill Coffman | LP | Jazzology JCE-82 | c. 1979 |
| | Scat Cats | LP | (Holland) Feel the Jazz 5556 | 84-3 |
| | Roger Shields | LP | Turnabout 34579 | 1974 |
| | Szeged Old Timers | LP | (Holland) Beerendonk 99919 | 84-1 |
| BOLO RAG | | | | |
| Gumble, Albert | Bill Mitchell | LP | Ethelyn 1750 | 1972 |

| Composition | Performer | Record Speed | Record Company/No. | Year-Month |
|---|---|---|---|---|
| BOMBSHELL RAG<br>Confare, Thomas &<br>Silver, Morris | Elliott Adams | LP | Stomp Off 1198 | 1988 |
| BON TON ONE STEP<br>Roberts, Charles Luckeyth | Conway's Band | 78 | Victor 17851 | 15-8 |
| BONE HEAD BLUES<br>Gordon, Leo | Terry Waldo Orchestra | LP | Stomp Off 1069 | 83-6 |
| BOOGIE WOOGIE RAG<br>Busch, Louis F. | Joe "Fingers" Carr | 78 | Capitol 2187 | 52-7 |
| BOOM TOWN ECHOES<br>Tichenor, Trebor | Trebor Tichenor | LP | Dirty Shame 2001 | 1973 |
| BOOMERANG RAG<br>Botsford, George | Band<br>Charlie Rasch | 78<br>LP | Little Wonder 473<br>(Canada) Ragtime Society 4 | 16-<br>1966 |
| BOOSTER RAG<br>Lake, M. L. | Terry Waldo Orchestra | LP | Stomp Off 1069 | 1983 |
| THE BOSTON TROT<br>Reinherz, Sid | Sid Reinherz | 78 | Gennett 5330 | 23-12 |
| BOWERY BUCK<br>Turpin, Tom | Trebor Tichenor | LP | (Canada) Scroll 102 | 1966 |
| BRANDON BOUNCE<br>Dickie, Neville | Neville Dickie | 45 | (England) Major Minor MM-644 | 1969 |
| BRANDY AND SODA<br>Elizalde, Fred | Fred Elizalde | 78 | (England) Brunswick 161 | 28-1 |
| BREAKIN' THE PIANO<br>James, Billy | Vee Lawnhurst<br>Isadore Maurice | 78<br>78 | Arto 9193<br>(England) Aco G-15190 | r. 23-1<br>23-2 |
| A BREEZE FROM ALABAMA<br>Joplin, Scott | Ann Charters<br>Dick Hyman<br>Max Morath<br>Knocky Parker<br>Piano Roll<br>Sigi Schwab<br>Southland Stingers<br>Dick Zimmerman | LP<br>LP<br>LP<br>LP<br>LP<br>LP<br>LP<br>LP | (England) Sonet 661<br>RCA CRL5-1106<br>Vanguard SRV-310<br>Audiophile AP-71/72<br>Biograph 1013Q<br>(Germany) Jupiter 6.24831<br>Angel S-36074<br>Murray Hill 931079 | 1974<br>1975<br>r.1974<br>1960<br><br>c. 1985<br>1974<br>1974 |
| BRING UP BREAKDOWN<br>Schutt, Arthur | Arthur Schutt | LP | Folkways RBF-41 | 34-9 |
| BRITANNIA RAG<br>Atwell, Winifred | Winifred Atwell | 78 | (England) Decca F-10015 | 52-10 |

| Composition | Performer | Record Speed | Record Company/No. | Year-Month |
|---|---|---|---|---|
| BRITTWOOD RAG | | | | |
| Blake, Eubie | Eubie Blake | LP | Columbia C2S-847 | 68-12 |
| | Oliver Jackson Quartet | LP | (France) Black & Blue 33180 | 82-9 |
| | Dave Jasen | LP | Blue Goose 3001 | 1972 |
| | Max Morath | LP | Vanguard 79418 | 1979 |
| BROADWAY RAG | | | | |
| Powell, W. C. | Bob Wilson Varsity Rhythm Boys | LP | Reader's Digest 70-01-05 | 1968 |
| BROADWAY RAG | | | | |
| Scott, James | John Jensen | LP | Genesis 1044 | 1974 |
| | Max Morath | LP | Vanguard SRV-310 | r. 1974 |
| | Knocky Parker | LP | Audiophle AP-76/77 | 1962 |
| BRUN CAMPBELL EXPRESS | | | | |
| Shea, Tom | Brian Dykstra | LP | Century Advent 5075 | 1974 |
| | St. Louis Ragtimers | LP | Conservatory | 1982 |
| | Tom Shea | LP | Jazzology JCE-52 | c.1967 |
| | Tom Shea | LP | Stomp Off 1022 | 1981 |
| BUBBLES | | | | |
| Nash, M.M. | Hager's Orchestra | 78 | Zonophone 159 | r. 05-6 |
| | Red Wing Blackbirds Ragtime Band | LP | Stomp Off 1018 | 1981 |
| BUCKET OF BLOOD | | | | |
| Ezell, Will | Will Ezell | 78 | Paramount 12773 | 29-2 |
| BUCKSNORT STOMP | | | | |
| Tichenor, Trebor | St. Louis Ragtimers | LP | Audiophile AP-81 | 1964 |
| BUFFALO BLUES | | | | |
| (see MISTER JOE) | | | | |
| | Johnny Dunn & Band | 78 | Columbia 14306-D | 28-3 |
| BUFFALO RAG | | | | |
| Turpin, Thomas | Elliott Adams | LP | Stomp Off 1198 | 1988 |
| | Milton Kaye | LP | Golden Crest 31032 | 1974 |
| | New Orleans Ragtime Orchestra | LP | (Sweden) Sonet 709 | 76-3 |
| | Vess L. Ossman w/Orchestra | 78 | Columbia 3360, A-218 | 05-12 |
| | Vess L. Ossman w/Orchestra | 78 | Victor 4628 | 06-1 |
| | Vess L. Ossman w/pno | 78 | Victor 16779 | 06-1, 09-3 |
| | Ton Van Bergeyk | LP | Kicking Mule 114 | r. 1976 |
| BUGLE CALL RAG | | | | |
| Blake, Eubie & Morgan, Carey | John Arpin | LP | Eubie Blake Music 10 | 1976 |
| | Metropolitan Military Band | 78 | Emerson 549 | 16- |
| | Pathe Dance Orchestra | 78 | Pathe 29157 or 30430 | r. 16-6 |
| | Victor Military Band | 12″78 | Victor 35533 | 16-1 |
| BULL DOG RAG | | | | |
| Dobyns, Geraldine | Richard Zimmerman | LP | Murray Hill 60556/5 | 1981 |
| BULL TROMBONE | | | | |
| Fillmore, Henry | Turk Murphy Jazz Band | LP | (Australia) Jazz & Jazz 6357.903 | 78-12 |
| BURNT SUGAR | | | | |
| Gideon, Melville | Melville Gideon | 78 | (England) Zonophone 2231 | 22-5 |

| Composition | Performer | Record Speed | Record Company/No. | Year-Month |
|---|---|---|---|---|
| BUSINESS IN TOWN | | | | |
| Ashwander, Donald | Donald Ashwander | LP | Jazzology JCE-52 | c. 1967 |
| BUSYBODY | | | | |
| Dickie, Neville | Neville Dickie | 45 | (England) Major Minor MM-685 | 1970 |
| BUTTER SCOTCH | | | | |
| White, Willy | Willy White | 78 | Pathe 021102 | r. 24-2 |
| BUTTERFINGERS | | | | |
| Fillis, Len & Bright, Sid | Len Fillis w/Sid Bright | 78 | (England) Columbia 4920 | |
| BUZZER RAG | | | | |
| Aufderheide, May | Chrysanthemum Ragtime Band | LP | Stomp Off 1196 | 1988 |
| | Piano Roll | LP | (England) Saydisc SDL-132 | |
| CABARET RAG | | | | |
| Tierney, Harry Austin | Prince's Band | 78 | Columbia A-1164 | 12-3 |
| CALICO RAG | | | | |
| Johnson, Nat | Frank Banta & Howard Kopp | 78 | Columbia A-2241 | 17-3 |
| | Graeme Bell | LP | (Australia) Parlophone PMD-7501 | 53-4 |
| | Vera Guilaroff | 78 | Pathe 21178 | 26-7 |
| | Andrew Setaro | 78 | Rex D-5355 | |
| | Uptown Lowdown Jazz Band | LP | Uptown Lowdown 303 | 1978 |
| | Richard Zimmerman | LP | Murray Hill 60556/5 | 1981 |
| CALLIOPE RAG | | | | |
| Scott, James | Donald Ashwander | LP | Jazzology JCE-52 | c. 1967 |
| | Philip Gammon | LP | CRD 1029 | 1976 |
| | John Jensen | LP | Genesis 1044 | 1974 |
| | Jazzou Jones | LP | High Water 101 | 1983 |
| | Morton Gunnar Larsen | LP | (Sweden) Sonet 1450 | 1978 |
| | LeRoy Larson | LP | Banjar 1781 | 1973 |
| | Ophelia Ragtime Orchestra | LP | Stomp Off 1108 | 85-2 |
| | Paul Zukofsky & Robert Dennis | LP | Vanguard SRV-350 | 1975 |
| CANADIAN CAPERS | | | | |
| Chandler, Gus; White, Bert Cohen, Henry | Victor Arden & Phil Ohman | 78 | Victor 22608 | 30-12 |
| | Burt Bales | 78 | Good Time Jazz 10 | 49-12 |
| | Ballyhooligans | 78 | (England) HMV BD-5094 | 36-7 |
| | Lloyd Barber & Orchestra | 78 | Gennett 4852 | r. 22-5 |
| | Paul Biese Trio | 78 | Columbia A-3470 | r.21-11 |
| | Jimmy Blade's Music | 78 | Rondo R-104 | |
| | Claude Bolling | LP | Philips 70341 | 1966 |
| | Cabrelli | 78 | (England) Regal-Zonophone MR-1484 | |
| | Joe "Fingers" Carr | LP | Warner Bros. W-1386 | 1960 |
| | Joe "Fingers" Carr's Ragtime Band | LP | Cap. T-443 | |
| | Frankie Carle | 78 | Columbia 37315 | |
| | Casino Dance Orchestra | 78 | Pathe A-20619 | r. 21-9 |
| | Chrysanthemum Ragtime Band | LP | Stomp Off 1168 | 1987 |
| | H. Robinson Cleaver | 78 | (England) Parlophone F-1636 | |

| Composition | Performer | Record Speed | Record Company/No. | Year-Month |
|---|---|---|---|---|
| CANADIAN CAPERS (continued) | Dick Contino | 78 | Horace Heidt 501 | |
| Chandler, Gus; White, Bert | Damon's Orchestra | 78 | Okeh 4421 | r.21-11 |
| Cohen, Henry | Joe Daniels & Hotshots | 78 | (England) Parlophone F-1514 | 39-6 |
| | Doris Day & Orchestra | 78 | Columbia 38595 | |
| | Neville Dickie | LP | (England) Major Minor SMCP-5039 | 1969 |
| | Reginald Dixon | 78 | (England) Regal-Zonophone MR-1432 | |
| | Tommy Dorsey Orchestra | 78 | Victor 25887 | 37-7 |
| | Vic Filmer | LP | Jazzology JCE-58 | 1970 |
| | Jack Fina | 78 | MGM 10289 | 47-9 |
| | Green Bros. Novelty Orchestra | 78 | Cardinal 2047 | 21-8 |
| | Milt Herth Trio | 78 | Decca 4118 | 41-12 |
| | Homochord Dance Orchestra | 78 | (England) Homochord H-294 | |
| | Lou Hooper | LP | (Canada) Radio Canada Int. 380 | 1973 |
| | Claude Hopkins & Orchestra | 78 | Columbia 2747-D | 33-1 |
| | Dick Hyman | LP | Cadence CR-2001 | 1974 |
| | Kern & Sloop | 78 | Tempo 994 | |
| | Keyboard Capers | 78 | (Denmark) HMV X-6815 | 1941 |
| | Bernie Leighton | LP | Cameo 1005 | 1958 |
| | Nisse Lind Hot Trio | 78 | (Sweden) Decca SF-44068 | 32-12 |
| | Guy Lombardo Orchestra | 78 | Decca 24624 | 49-3 |
| | Charles Magnante Quartet | 78 | Silverstone 219 | |
| | Bobby Mickleburgh's Bobcats | 78 | (England) Esquire 10-429 | 54-12 |
| | Art Mooney Orchestra | 78 | MGM 10466 | 49-9 |
| | Russ Morgan & Orchestra | 78 | Brunswick 7902 | 37-5 |
| | Red Nichols Five Pennies | LP | Capitol T-2065 | 61-2 |
| | Jimmy O'Keefe (1) | 78 | Puritan 11066 | |
| | Jimmy O'Keefe (2) | 78 | Bluebird 20066 | |
| | Oregon JB | LP | OJB 1005 | 1967 |
| | Knuckles O'Toole | LP | Grand Award 33-373 | |
| | Palm Beach Players | 78 | Regal 9133 | |
| | Pennsylvania Hotel Orchestra | 78 | Emerson 10449 | r.21-10 |
| | Sid Phillips & Band | 78 | (England) HMV B-10015 | 50-10 |
| | Cesar Poggi | LP | (Italy) Dire FO-344 | 1979 |
| | Ben Pollack Orchestra | 78 | Savoy XP-8027 | 52-8 |
| | Ben Pollack Californians | 45 | Savoy XP-8027 | 52-8 |
| | Harry Raderman's Orchestra | 78 | Edison 50802 | 21-8 |
| | Ritz-Carlton Orchestra | 78 | Olympic 15121 | r. 21-9 |
| | Billy Rowland | LP | RCA Victor LPM-1872 | 1958 |
| | Harry Roy Orchestra | 78 | (England) Parlophone R-1505, F-1919 | 33-4 |
| | Joseph Samuels Orchestra | 78 | Grey Gull 1088 | |
| | Santa Anita Band | 78 | (Argentina) Vic 60-2208 | 52-2 |
| | Arthur Schutt & Jack Cornell | 78 | (England) Brunswick 01134 | 31-4 |
| | Bob Scobey JB | 78 | Down Home 1000 | 56-3 |
| | Selvin's Dance Orchestra | 78 | Vocalion 14217 | r. 21-8 |
| | Selvin's Orchestra | 78 | Brunswick 2164 | r.21-12 |

| Composition | Performer | Record Speed | Record Company/No. | Year-Month |
|---|---|---|---|---|
| CANADIAN CAPERS (continued) | Six Keyboard Kings | 78 | (England) Regal-Zonophone MR-1226 | |
| Chandler, Gus; White, Bert | | | | |
| Cohen, Henry | Harry Snodgrass | 78 | Brunswick 3137 | 26-3 |
| | Lew Stone Orchestra | 78 | (England) Decca F-3839 | 34-1 |
| | The Three Suns | 78 | Victor 20-2818 | 47-10 |
| | Ray Turner | 78 | Capitol 2095 | 52-3 |
| | Ted Weems Orchestra | 78 | Mercury 5287 | |
| | Lawrence Welk Orchestra | 45 | Mercury 1406 | 1950 |
| | Lawrence Welk Orchestra | 78 | Decca 3726, 25316 | 41-3 |
| | Paul Whiteman Orchestra | 78 | Victor 18824 | 21-10 |
| | Jay Wilbur Band | 78 | (England) Rex 8485 | 35-5 |
| CANDIED SWEETS | | | | |
| Johnson, James P. | James P. Johnson | LP | Jazzology JCE-1003 | 44-6 |
| THE CANDY | | | | |
| Jones, Clarence | David Thomas Roberts | LP | Stomp Off 1132 | 1981 |
| CANHANIBALMO RAG | | | | |
| Pryor, Arthur | Arthur Pryor's Band | 78 | Victor 16883 | 11-5 |
| CANNED CORN RAG | | | | |
| Cobb, George L. | George Foley | LP | Stomp Off 1088 | 1984 |
| CANNON BALL RAG | | | | |
| Northrup, Joseph C. | Marvin Ash | 78 | Capitol 15435 | 49-12 |
| | William Axtmann Piano Roll | LP | Biograph 1006Q | |
| | Ben Bernie Orchestra | 78 | Brunswick 4042 | 28-7 |
| | Harry Breuer Orchestra | LP | Audio Fidelity AFSC-5912 | 1960 |
| | Chrysanthemum Ragtime Band | LP | Stomp Off 1196 | 1988 |
| | Home Guards Band | 78 | (England) Zonophone 74 | 08-9 |
| | Armand Hug | 10"LP | Circle L-411 | 1951 |
| | Dink Johnson | LP | Euphonic 1201 | c. 1948 |
| | Hank Jones | LP | ABC-Paramount 496 | 64-4 |
| | Alain Lesire | LP | (Belgium) Jazz Cats 6983003 | 1982 |
| | Guy Lombardo Orchestra | 78 | Columbia 1451-D | 28-3 |
| | Max Morath | LP | Vanguard VSD-39/40 | 1967 |
| | Knuckles O'Toole | LP | Grand Award 33-373 | |
| | Piano Roll | 10"LP | (England) London AL-3542 | |
| | Wally Rose | LP | Blackbird 12007 | 1968 |
| | Fred Sokolow | LP | Kicking Mule 212 | c. 1982 |
| | Roy Spangler | 78 | Rex 5024 | c. 13- |
| | Tanz Palast Orchestra | 78 | (Germany) Grammophon 13152 | 14- |
| | Merle Travis | 78 | Capitol 2245 | |
| CAPRICE RAG | | | | |
| Johnson, James P. | Marc Bercovic | LP | (France) Promophone Rom-1 | 1973 |
| | Dick Hyman | LP | Col. M-33706 | 75-5 |
| | James P. Johnson | 12"78 | Blue Note 26 | 43-12 |
| | James P. Johnson | LP | Chiaroscuro 113 | 44-8 |
| | James P. Johnson | LP | Euphonic 1226 | 1944 |

| Composition | Performer | Record Speed | Record Company/No. | Year-Month |
|---|---|---|---|---|
| CAPRICE RAG (continued) | James P. Johnson | LP | (England) Rarities 33 | 47-3 |
| Johnson, James P. | James P. Johnson Piano Roll | LP | Biograph 1009Q | |
| | Morton Gunnar Larsen | LP | (Norway) Flower 439 | 75-11 |
| | Cesare Poggi | LP | (Italy) Dire FO-344 | 1979 |
| | Willie the Lion Smith | LP | Blue Circle 1500-33 | 53-8 |
| | Smithsonian Jazz Ensemble | LP | Smithsonian 21 | 1979 |
| | Ken Werner | LP | Finnedar SR-9019 | r. 1982 |
| CAR BARLIC ACID | | | | |
| Wiley, Clarence | Bob Darch | LP | United Artists UAL-3120 | 1960 |
| | Max Morath | LP | Vanguard 79440 | 1981 |
| | Daryl Ott | LP | Dirty Shame 1238 | 1978 |
| | Red Wing Blackbirds | LP | Stomp Off 1018 | 1981 |
| CAROLINA BALMORAL | | | | |
| Johnson, James P. | Dick Hyman Band | LP | Columbia M-33706 | 75-5 |
| | James P. Johnson | 12″78 | Blue Note 25 | 43-11 |
| CAROLINA FOX TROT | | | | |
| Vodery, Will H. | Victor Military Band | 12″78 | Victor 35415 | 14-10 |
| CAROLINA SHOUT | | | | |
| Johnson, James P. | Eddie Bernard | 78 | (France) Blue Star 56 | 47-10 |
| | Johan Bijkerk | LP | (Holland) Hot Dogs 0002 | 76-6 |
| | Claude Bolling | LP | (France) CY 733.607 | c. 1980 |
| | Canadian Brass | LP | RCA XRL1-3212 | 1979 |
| | Judy Carmichael | LP | Progressive 7072 | 1983 |
| | Henri Chaix | LP | (Switzerland) Philips 843813 | 1969 |
| | Neville Dickie | LP | (England) Col. SCX-6445 | 1970 |
| | Neville Dickie | LP | Euphonic ESR-1206 | 1966 |
| | Neville Dickie | LP | Stomp Off 1096 | 83-4 |
| | Hank Duncan | LP | Hot Piano BS-6913 | |
| | Hank Duncan | LP | (Switzerland) 88 UR-001 | c. 1960 |
| | Hank Duncan | LP | (Switzerland) Ri-Disc 4 | c. 1948 |
| | Keith Dunham | LP | Master Jazz MJR-8117 | 71-7 |
| | Don Ewell (m) | LP | Chiaroscuro 106 | 70-8 |
| | Fenix JB | LP | Stomp Off 1129 | c. 1986 |
| | Chuck Folds | LP | Jazzways 106/4 | 1974 |
| | Henry "Thins" Francis | LP | Mephistopheles 101 | c. 1980 |
| | Gabriel Garvanoff | LP | (France) Black & Blue 59.216 | 70-11 |
| | John Gill | LP | Stomp Off 1066 | 1983 |
| | Joe Glover's Cotton Pickers | LP | Epic LN-3581 | |
| | Steve Hancoff | LP | Out of Time 920 | 85-4 |
| | Stephen Henderson | LP | Euphonic 1226 | c. 1945 |
| | Dick Hyman Orchestra | LP | Col. M-33706 | 75-5 |
| | Cliff Jackson | LP | (England) Black Lion BLP-30136 | 61-12 |
| | Cliff Jackson | LP | Fat Cat's Jazz 107 | 68-11 |
| | Cliff Jackson | LP | (Switzerland) Ri-Disc 5 | 65-7 |
| | James P. Johnson | 78 | Decca 24885 | 44-8 |
| | James P. Johnson | LP | (Italy) FDC 1012 | 47-4 |

| Composition | Performer | Record Speed | Record Company/No. | Year-Month |
|---|---|---|---|---|
| CAROLINA SHOUT (continued) | James P. Johnson | LP | Jazzology JCE-1001 | 44-5 |
| Johnson, James P. | James P. Johnson | 78 | Okeh 4495 | 21-10 |
| | James P. Johnson | LP | Vanguard VSD-47/48 | 38-12 |
| | James P. Johnson Piano Roll | LP | Biograph BLP-1003Q | |
| | James P. Johnson Piano Roll | LP | Biograph 1009Q | |
| | Jimmy Johnson's Jazz Boys | 78 | Arto 9096 | 21-10 |
| | Dill Jones | 78 | (England) Nixa NJ-2021 | 57-10 |
| | Katia & Marielle Labeque | LP | Angel S-37980 | 1982 |
| | Donald Lambert | LP | Pumpkin 104 | 1960 |
| | Mike Lipskin & Willie the Lion Smith | LP | Flying Dutchman FD-10140 | 1970 |
| | Louis Mazetier & Francois Rilhac | LP | Stomp Off 1218 | 89-11 |
| | Tom McDermott | LP | Stomp Off 1024 | 82-1 |
| | Keith Nichols Ragtime Orchestra | LP | (England) EMI One up 2135 | 1976 |
| | Charlie Rasch | LP | CK 3204 | 73-4 |
| | Zutty Singleton Trio | 78 | (France) Eko 6 | 52- |
| | Willie the Lion Smith | 10"LP | Blue Circle 1500-33 | 53-8 |
| | Willie the Lion Smith | LP | Dot DLP-3094 | 1957 |
| | Willie the Lion Smith | 78 | (France) Royal Jazz 745 | 49-12 |
| | Willie the Lion Smith | LP | RCA Victor LSP-6016 | 67-4 |
| | Smithsonian Jazz Ensemble | LP | Smithsonian 21 | 1979 |
| | Duncan Swift | LP | (England) Big Bear 28 | 88-3 |
| | Duncan Swift | LP | (England) Black Lion 12123 | 69-8 |
| | Keith Taylor | LP | Sami 1002 | r. 1984 |
| | Butch Thompson | LP | Prairie Home Companion 34817 | 1979 |
| | Jim Turner | LP | Euphonic 1222 | 1981 |
| | Joe Turner | LP | (France) Black & Blue 33031 | 71-8 |
| | Joe Turner | LP | (Switzerland) Tell LP-542 | 1955 |
| | Waldo's Syncopators | LP | Stomp Off 1036 | 81-8 |
| | Fats Waller | 78 | Victor 27563 | 41-5 |
| | Dick Wellstood | LP | Audiophile AP-120 | 75-10 |
| | Dick Wellstood | LP | Fat Cat's Jazz FCJ-158 | 74-4 |
| | Dick Wellstood | LP | Jazzology JCE-73 | 1971 |
| CARPET RAGS | | | | |
| Connor, Raymond W. | Hager's Orchestra | 78 | Zonophone 817 | r. 07-8 |
| CARR'S HOP | | | | |
| Busch, Louis F. | Joe "Fingers" Carr | 78 | Capitol 15725 | c. 1952 |
| | Joe "Fingers" Carr | LP | Capitol T-280 | |
| CASCADE PLUNGE | | | | |
| Ashwander, Donald | Donald Ashwander | LP | Upstairs 1 | 1973 |
| CASCADES | | | | |
| Joplin, Scottt | E. Power Biggs | LP | Col. M-33205 | 1974 |
| | William Cerny | LP | University of Notre Dame | 1975 |
| | Concert Arban | LP | (France) Arion ARN-33786 | 1985 |
| | Eddy Davis | LP | Pa Da 7402 | 1974 |

| Composition | Performer | Record Speed | Record Company/No. | Year-Month |
|---|---|---|---|---|
| CASCADES (continued) | Eden Electronic Ensemble | LP | (England) Pye 12101 | 1975 |
| Joplin, Scottt | Raymond Fonseque | LP | (France) Promophone 4 | 73-10 |
| | David Andrew Frost | LP | MHS 3201 | 1975 |
| | Joe Glover's Cotton Pickers | LP | Epic LN-3581 | |
| | Dick Hyman | LP | RCA CRL5-1106 | 1975 |
| | Imperial JB | LP | Signature BFW-40112 | 1985 |
| | Hank Jones | LP | ABC-Paramount 496 | 64-4 |
| | Milton Kaye | LP | Golden Crest 31032 | 1974 |
| | Bill Knopf | LP | First Inversion 001 | r. 1983 |
| | James Levine | LP | RCA ARL1-2243 | 1976 |
| | London Ragtime Orchestra | LP | GHB 199 | 87-2 |
| | Stan Mendelson | LP | Land of Jazz 2674 | 1974 |
| | Molnar Dixieland Band | LP | (Hungary) Radioton SLPX-37343 | 1988 |
| | David Montgomery & Cecil Lytle | LP | Klavier KS-533 | 1974 |
| | Moonlight Ragtime Band | LP | National Geographic 07817 | 1979 |
| | Max Morath | LP | Vanguard VSD-39/40 | 1967 |
| | Turk Murphy JB | LP | Atlantic 1613 | 71-9 |
| | N.O. Ragtime Orchestra | LP | Pearl 7 | 67-9 |
| | New England Conservatory | LP | Angel 36060 | 1973 |
| | Keith Nichols | LP | (England) EMI OU-2035 | 1974 |
| | Knocky Parker | LP | Audiophile AP-71/72 | 1960 |
| | Piano Roll | LP | Biograph 1008Q | |
| | Piano Roll | 10″LP | Riverside RLP-1025 | |
| | Piano Roll | LP | Sounds 1201 | |
| | Mike Polad | LP | Jazzology JCE-77 | r. 1975 |
| | Joshua Rifkin | LP | Nonesuch H-71305 | 1974 |
| | William Neil Roberts | LP | Klavier 516 | 1973 |
| | Wally Rose | LP | Fairmont 102 | 47-8 |
| | Wally Rose | 10″LP | GTJ L-3 | 53-2 |
| | Wally Rose | LP | GTJ M-12034 | 58-12 |
| | Wally Rose | 78 | Good Time Jazz 27 | 50-6 |
| | Royal Ballet Orchestra | LP | CRD 1029 | 1976 |
| | Sigi Schwab | LP | (Germany) Jupiter 6.24831 | c. 1985 |
| | Janice Scroggins | LP | Flying Hearts 334 | 87-9 |
| | Fred Sokolow | LP | Kicking Mule 212 | c. 1982 |
| | St. Louis Ragtimers | LP | Audiophile AP-122 | 1977 |
| | St. Louis Ragtimers | LP | Ragophile TSLR-007 | 1986 |
| | Chris Stone | LP | ABC 823 | 1974 |
| | Ralph Sutton | 78 | Down Home 10 | 49-11 |
| | Ralph Sutton | LP | Verve MCV-1004 | 1949 |
| | Bob Tryforous | LP | Puritan 5002 | r. 1976 |
| | Dick Wellstood | LP | Pickwick SPC-3376 | 1974 |
| | Dick Zimmerman | LP | Murray Hill 931079 | 1974 |
| CASTLE DOGGY | | | | |
| Europe, James Reese | Piano Roll | LP | Herwin 407 | |

| Composition | Performer | Record Speed | Record Company/No. | Year-Month |
|---|---|---|---|---|
| CASTLE HOUSE RAG | | | | |
| Europe, James Reese | T. J. Anderson Orchestra | LP | Smithsonian 001 | 1975 |
| | Black Music Repertory Ensemble | LP | CBMR 001 | 1989 |
| | Budapest Ragtime Orchestra | LP | (Czechoslovakia) Krem SLPX-17794 | 1984 |
| | Europe's Society Orchestra | 12"78 | Victor 35372 | 14-2 |
| | Paul Hersh & David Montgomery | LP | RCA Victor ARL1-0364 | 1974 |
| | Knocky Parker & Bill Coffman | LP | Jazzology JCE-82 | c. 1979 |
| | Phoenix Ragtime Ensemble | LP | World Jazz 12 | 77-6 |
| | Wally Rose | 10"LP | Columbia CL-6260 | 53-5 |
| | Roger Shields | LP | Turnabout 34579 | 1974 |
| | South Frisco Jazz Band | LP | Alpha 2002 | 1981 |
| THE CAT AND THE DOG | | | | |
| Reser, Harry | Harry Reser | 78 | Columbia 1537-D | 28-7 |
| THE CAT'S PAJAMAS | | | | |
| Jentes, Harry | Stanley C. Holt | 78 | (England) Homochord H-492 | 23-9 |
| | Harry Jentes | 78 | Arto 9221 | 23-4 |
| | Harry Jentes | 78 | Okeh 4850 | 23-2 |
| CATARACT RAG | | | | |
| Hampton, Robert | Kenny Ball JB | LP | Kapp KL-1314 | 1963 |
| | Claude Bolling | LP | (France) Philips 70341 | 1966 |
| | Dave Brennan JB | LP | (England) VJM LC-205 | 1973 |
| | Tony Caramia | LP | Stomp Off 1209 | 1989 |
| | Ann Charters | LP | Folkways FG-3563 | 1961 |
| | Ken Colyer's Jazz Band | 78 | (England) Decca F-10504 | 53-11 |
| | Ken Colyer's Jazzmen | 10"LP | (England) Decca FL-1152 | 1953 |
| | Ken Colyer's Jazzmen | LP | (England) Joy S-194 | 1974 |
| | Brian Dykstra | LP | Century Advent 5075 | 1974 |
| | Paul Hersh & David Montgomery | LP | RCA ARL1-0364 | 1974 |
| | Hitch's Happy Harmonists | 78 | Gennett 5633 | 25-1 |
| | Glenn Jenks | LP | Bonnie Banks 103 | 1983 |
| | Lawson–Haggart JB | 10"LP | Decca DL-5456 | 53-1 |
| | London Ragtime Orchestra | LP | GHB 199 | 87-2 |
| | Merseysippi JB | 10"LP | (England) Esquire 20-088 | 57-8 |
| | New England Conservatory Ensemble | LP | Golden Crest 31042 | 1975 |
| | Tony Parenti JB | LP | Jazzology J-11 | 1961 |
| | Ragpickers | 78 | Circle 1054 | 49-1 |
| | Royal Ballet Orchestra | LP | CRD 1029 | 1976 |
| | Roger Shields | LP | Turnabout 34579 | 1974 |
| | Ralph Sutton | 78 | Down Home 7 | 49-11 |
| | Ralph Sutton | LP | Down Home MGD-4 | 1949 |
| | Keith Taylor | LP | Sami 1001 | 1974 |
| | Vintage JB | LP | (Australia) VJS 2 | 78-2 |
| | Terry Waldo Orchestra | LP | Stomp Off 1069 | 83-6 |
| CAULDRON RAG | | | | |
| Christensen, Axel W. | Axel Christensen (m) | 78 | Puritan 11239 | |

| Composition | Performer | Record Speed | Record Company/No. | Year-Month |
|---|---|---|---|---|
| CELESTIAL RAG | | | | |
| Glover, Joe | Joe Glover's Cotton Pickers | LP | Epic LN-3581 | |
| CENTENNIAL RAG | | | | |
| Arpin, John | John Arpin | LP | (Canada) Scroll 101 | 1965 |
| CENTENNIAL RAG | | | | |
| Thompson, Charley | Charley Thompson | LP | Euphonic 1221 | c. 1960 |
| CEONOTHUS RAG | | | | |
| Williams, Quentin | Quentin Williams | LP | (England) Saydisc 118 | 1966 |
| CHAMPAGNE RAG | | | | |
| Lamb, Joseph | Dave Jasen | LP | Folkways FG-3561 | 77-6 |
| | Paul Lolax | LP | Titanic 13 | r. 1981 |
| | Original Prague Syncopated Orchestra | LP | (Czechoslovakia) Supraphon 1115.1965 | 1976 |
| CHARLESTON CAPERS | | | | |
| Green, George Hamilton | George Hamilton Green | 78 | Columbia 977-D | 26-2 |
| CHARLESTON RAG | | | | |
| Blake, Eubie | William Albright | LP | Music Masters 20033 | 80-12 |
| | Amherst Saxophone Quartet | LP | MHS 4368 | 80-12 |
| | Eubie Blake | LP | 20th Century Fox 3039 | 1958 |
| | Eubie Blake | LP | Col. C2S-847 | 69-2 |
| | Eubie Blake | LP | Col. KCZ-37100 | 1981 |
| | Eubie Blake | LP | EBM 2 | 1971 |
| | Eubie Blake | LP | (France) RCA FXM1-7157 | 1974 |
| | Eubie Blake Piano Roll | LP | Biograph 1011Q | |
| | Boston Pops Orchestra | LP | Polydor PD-6033 | 1974 |
| | George Foley | LP | Century Advent 778 | 1977 |
| | Jim Hession | LP | Tam 1 | 1979 |
| | Dick Hyman | LP | Project 3 PR-5080 | 1973 |
| | Dick Hyman | LP | Sine Qua Non 71017 | 1984 |
| | Imperial JB | LP | Signature BFW-40112 | 1985 |
| | Dave Jasen | LP | Blue Goose 3001 | 1972 |
| | Jazzou Jones | LP | High Water 101 | 1983 |
| | Morton Gunnar Larsen | LP | (Sweden) Sonet 1450 | 78-10 |
| | Al McDearmon | LP | NGJB 6 | 85-8 |
| | Max Morath | LP | Vanguard VSD-79391 | 1977 |
| | Max Morath Quintet | LP | Normacks 100 | c. 1981 |
| | New England Conservatory Ensemble | LP | Golden Crest 31042 | 1975 |
| | Butch Thompson Trio | LP | Triangle Jazz 109 | 87-3 |
| | Terry Waldo | LP | Conservatory | 82-6 |
| | Terry Waldo | LP | Fat Cat's Jazz 151 | 74-1 |
| CHASIN' THE CHIPPIES | | | | |
| Lamb, Joseph | Milton Kaye | LP | Golden Crest 31035 | 1974 |
| CHASING THE CHICKENS | | | | |
| Walker, Raymond & Olman, Abe | Six Brown Bothers | 78 | Victor 18476 | 18-6 |

| Composition | Performer | Record Speed | Record Company/No. | Year-Month |
|---|---|---|---|---|
| CHATTERBOX RAG | | | | |
| Botsford, George | Steen Christensen | LP | (Denmark) Louis Barnewitz 1 | 1972 |
| | Joe Glover's Cotton Pickers | LP | Epic LN-3581 | |
| | Red Nichols Five Pennies | LP | Broadway Intermission 130 | 51-7 |
| | Knocky Parker | LP | Audiophile AP-92 | |
| | Piano Roll (aka: Take It Easy) | LP | Dot DLP-25478 | |
| | Tanz Palast Orchestra | 78 | (Germany) Grammophon 13152 | 14- |
| | Fred Van Eps w/Orchestra | 78 | Zonophone 5828 | r.11-12 |
| | Richard Wayne's Bearcats | LP | Reader's Digest RDA-70-01-05 | 1968 |
| CHEESE & CRACKERS | | | | |
| Denney, Homer | John Hancock | LP | Stomp Off 1025 | 1982 |
| CHESTNUT STREET IN THE 90'S | | | | |
| Campbell, Brun | Brun Campbell | 78 | West Coast 113 | 46-12 |
| | David Thomas Roberts | LP | Stomp Off 1132 | 1983 |
| | Trebor Tichenor | LP | (Canada) Scroll 102 | 1966 |
| CHESTNUT VALLEY RAG | | | | |
| Tichenor, Trebor | Trebor Tichenor | LP | Audiophile AP-81 | 1964 |
| | Trebor Tichenor | LP | Jazzology JCE-52 | 1967 |
| CHEVY CHASE | | | | |
| Blake, Eubie | Amherst Saxophone Quartet | LP | MHS 4368 | 80-12 |
| | Concert Arban | LP | (France) Arion 33786 | 1985 |
| | John Arpin | LP | (Canada) Scroll 103 | 1966 |
| | John Arpin & Catherine Wilson | LP | (Canada) Fanfare 9023 | r. 1986 |
| | Marc Bercovic | LP | (France) Promophone ROM-1 | 1973 |
| | Eubie Blake | LP | Col. C2S-847 | 68-12 |
| | Lee Erwin | LP | Angel S-36075 | 1974 |
| | Glenn Jenks | LP | Bonnie Banks 104 | 1985 |
| | Al McDearmon | LP | NGJB 5 | 82-7 |
| | Turk Murphy JB | LP | (Australia) Jazz & Jazz 6437.157 | 1980 |
| | Keith Nichols | LP | (England) EMI One Up 2135 | 1976 |
| | Ophelia Ragtime Orchestra | LP | Stomp Off 1108 | 85-2 |
| | Pathe Dance Orchestra | 78 | Pathe 70130 | r. 15-9 |
| | Ragtime Society of Frankfurt | LP | (Germany) Joke JLP-217 | 81-10 |
| | Charlie Rasch | LP | CK 8301-3900 | 71-8 |
| | Willie the Lion Smith | 10"LP | Dial 305 | 1950 |
| | Willie the Lion Smith | LP | RCA Victor LSP-6016 | 67-4 |
| | James Tyler Orchestra | LP | Desto 7181 | 1979 |
| | Terry Waldo | LP | Stomp Off 1002 | 80-7 |
| | Zinn's Ragtime String Quartet | LP | Music Minus One 13 | 1974 |
| CHICAGO BREAKDOWN | | | | |
| Morton, Jelly Roll | Louis Armstrong & Hot Seven | 78 | Columbia 36376 | 27-5 |
| | Dick Wellstood | 78 | Rampart 15 | 49-8 |
| CHICAGO TICKLE | | | | |
| Tierney, Harry Austin | Prince's Band | 78 | (England) Regal G-6845 | 13-7 |

| Composition | Performer | Record Speed | Record Company/No. | Year-Month |
|---|---|---|---|---|
| CHICKEN AND ALMONDS | | | | |
| Bell, Graeme | Graeme Bell & Jazz Band | 78 | (Australia) Parlophone A-7724 | 49-3 |
| CHICKEN CHARLIE | | | | |
| Ballou, Ashley | Pryor's Band | 78 | Victor 5011, 16274 | 06-5 |
| | Zonophone Concert Band | 78 | Zonophone 271 | r.05-11 |
| CHICKEN CHOWDER | | | | |
| Gibbin, Irene M. | Ossman–Dudley Trio | 78 | Columbia 3591, A-220 | 07-1 |
| | Victor Orchestra | 78 | Victor 4715, 16091 | 06-7 |
| CHILI PEPPER | | | | |
| Longshaw, Fred | Fred Longshaw | 78 | Columbia 14080-D | 25-6 |
| CHIMES | | | | |
| Denney, Homer | J.H. Squire's Orchestra | 78 | (England) Guardsman 894 | 19- |
| CHIMES | | | | |
| Pastalley, V. & Viladomat, J. | Willie Eckstein | 78 | Okeh 4899 | r.23-10 |
| CHIMES RAG | | | | |
| Denney, Homer | John Hancock | LP | Stomp Off 1025 | 1982 |
| | Jazzou Jones | LP | High Water 101 | 1983 |
| CHO-PIANO | | | | |
| Lange, Henry | Henry Lange | 78 | Okeh 4809 | 21-11 |
| | Henry Lange | 78 | Pathe 020671 | 21-10 |
| CHOPSTICKS | | | | |
| Mayerl, Billy | Billy Mayerl | 78 | (England) Columbia 4677 | 27-10 |
| CHROMATIC CAPERS | | | | |
| Cobb, George L. | George Foley | LP | Stomp Off 1088 | 1984 |
| CHROMATIC RAG | | | | |
| Held, Will | Ralph Sutton | 78 | Down Home 8 | 49-11 |
| | Ralph Sutton | LP | Down Home MGD-4 | 1949 |
| | Keith Taylor | LP | Sami 1001 | 1974 |
| CLASSIC RAG | | | | |
| Peterson, H. | Miss Holsom | 78 | (England) Victory 234 | 29-7 |
| CLASSICAL RAG | | | | |
| Blake, Eubie | Eubie Blake | LP | Columbia M-34504 | 1977 |
| | Eubie Blake | LP | Eubie Blake Music 2 | 1971 |
| | Eubie Blake | LP | (France) RCA FXM1-7157 | 1974 |
| | Max Morath | LP | Vanguard SRV-351 | r. 1976 |
| A CLASSICAL SPASM | | | | |
| Thomas, Harry | Harry Thomas | 78 | Victor 18229 | 16-12 |
| CLASSICANA | | | | |
| Lange, Henry | Alan Moran & Walter Feldkamp | 78 | Columbia 434-D | 25-7 |
| | Al Siegel | 78 | (England) Zonophone 2945 | 27-2 |
| CLEOPATRA RAG | | | | |
| Lamb, Joseph | Joe "Fingers" Carr & Tiny Little | LP | Coral CRL-7-57444 | 63-7 |
| | Jazz Fiddlers | LP | (Czechoslovakia) Supraphon 1150904 | 70-4 |

| Composition | Performer | Record Speed | Record Company/No. | Year-Month |
|---|---|---|---|---|
| CLEOPATRA RAG (continued) | Paul Hersh & David Montgomery | LP | RCA Victor ARL1-0364 | 1974 |
| Lamb, Joseph | Milton Kaye | LP | Golden Crest 4127 | 1974 |
| | Joseph Lamb | LP | Folkways FG-3562 | 59-8 |
| | New Orleans Ragtime Orchestra | LP | Vanguard VSD-69/70 | 1971 |
| | Ragtime Society of Frankfurt | LP | (Germany) Joke JLP-217 | 81-10 |
| | Wally Rose | LP | Blackbird 12010 | 71-6 |
| CLEVER FELLER | | | | |
| Monsbourgh, Adrian | Southern Jazz Group | 78 | (Australia) Parlophone A-7749 | 50-6 |
| CLIMAX RAG | | | | |
| Scott, James | Chris Barber JB | LP | (England) Col. 33SX-1158 | 1959 |
| | Paul Barnes Quartet | LP | Nola LP-17 | 1974 |
| | Acker Bilk Band | 10"LP | (England) 77 LP-23 | 1957 |
| | Black Eagle JB | LP | (Canada) Onward OHF-1001 | 1964 |
| | Eric Brooks | 78 | (England) Poydras 17 | 50- |
| | Kid Chapman's JB | LP | GHB 36 | 1966 |
| | Doc Evans Band | 10"LP | Soma MG-1211 | 57-8 |
| | Capt. John Handy Band | LP | Polydor 623222 | 65-8 |
| | Hird Family | LP | (Australia) Stomperphone SPR-61 | 79-6 |
| | Kid Howard Band | 10"LP | Icon 8 | 1962 |
| | Percy Humphreys Band | LP | Riverside 378 | 61-1 |
| | John Jensen | LP | Genesis 1044 | 1974 |
| | Max Kortlander Piano Roll | LP | Folkways RBF-43 | |
| | La Vida JB | LP | (Holland) Polydor 2441086 | 79-1 |
| | George Lewis' Stompers | 78 | Climax 101 | 43-5 |
| | Magnolia Jazz Group | LP | (Holland) CNR SKLP-4271 | 68-2 |
| | Stan Mendelson | LP | Land O' Jazz 2674 | 74-6 |
| | Max Morath | LP | Epic LN-24106 | 1964 |
| | Jelly Roll Morton's Jazzmen | 78 | Bluebird 10442 | 39-9 |
| | Turk Murphy JB | LP | Atlantic 1613 | 71-9 |
| | Louis Nelson Band | LP | GHB 241 | 88-4 |
| | New Black Eagle JB | LP | Stomp Off 1054 | 82-9 |
| | New Orleans Express | 7"LP | (England) Bootleg 006 | 1981 |
| | New Orleans Joymakers | LP | (Italy) Memories 03 | 78-12 |
| | Red Nichols Five Pennies | LP | Cap. ST-2065 | 63-10 |
| | Original East Side Stompers | LP | TAM 8035 | 81-11 |
| | Papa Bue's Viking JB | LP | (Denmark) Storyville SLP-121 | 60-5 |
| | Papa Tom's Band | LP | (Holland) RCS 489 | 82-3 |
| | Knocky Parker | LP | Audiophile AP-49 | 1958 |
| | Knocky Parker | LP | Audiophile AP-76/77 | 1962 |
| | Alcide "Slow Drag" Pavageau Band | LP | Jazz Crusade 2005 | 65-4 |
| | Mike Peters Band | EP | (England) 77 EP-11 | 57-8 |
| | Piano Roll | LP | Biograph BLP-1016Q | |
| | Ragtime Society of Frankfurt | LP | (Germany) Joke JLP-217 | 81-10 |
| | Ranier JB | LP | Triangle Jazz 104 | 1981 |
| | Trevor Richards Trio | LP | Stomp Off 1222 | 90-6 |
| | Wally Rose w/YBJB Rhythm | 78 | West Coast 116 | 46-5 |

| Composition | Performer | Record Speed | Record Company/No. | Year-Month |
|---|---|---|---|---|
| CLIMAX RAG (continued) | Emanuel Sayles Band | LP | (Italy) Big Lou SBL-1004 | 1969 |
| Scott, James | Jabbo Smith Joymakers | LP | (France) Memories MEO-3 | 78-12 |
| | Ralph Sutton | 78 | Down Home 8 | 49-11 |
| | Duncan Swift | LP | (England) Black Lion 12123 | 69-8 |
| | Yarra Yarra JB | EP | (Australia) Crest CRT-7-EP-006 | 1962 |
| | Zenith Six | 78 | (England) Tempo A-145 | 56-5 |
| CLOCKWORK | | | | |
| Mayerl, Billy | Billy Mayerl (m) | 78 | (England) Columbia 4975 | 28-5 |
| COAXING THE PIANO | | | | |
| Confrey, Zez | Ray Allen | 78 | (Germany) Vox 6265 | 24-5 |
| | Tony Caramia | LP | Stomp Off 1209 | 1989 |
| | Zez Confrey | 78 | Brunswick 2167 | r. 22-3 |
| | Max Darewski | 78 | (England) Zonophone 2469 | 24-2 |
| | Willie Eckstein | 78 | Pathe 20944 | 23-1 |
| | Frank Herbin | 78 | (England) HMV B-1774 | 24-1 |
| | Stanley C. Holt | 78 | (England) Homochord H-477 | 23-4 |
| | Dick Hyman | LP | RCA XRL1-4746 | 1983 |
| | John Jensen | LP | Genesis 1051 | 1974 |
| | Milton Kaye | LP | Golden Crest 31040 | 1974 |
| | Arthur Kleiner | LP | Golden Crest 2004 | c. 1967 |
| | Bill Krenz | 78 | MGM 11264, 30704 | 52- |
| | Isadore Maurice | 78 | (England) Aco G-15171 | 23-2 |
| | Russ Morgan & Eddie Wilser | 78 | Decca 30615 | 58-2 |
| | Ray Turner | 78 | Capitol 2097 | 52-3 |
| | Tom Waltham | 78 | (France) Pathe 9608 | 23-10 |
| | Frank Westphal | 78 | Columbia A-3800 | 22-12 |
| | Harold Willoughby | 78 | (England) Columbia 3219 | 22-12 |
| COLE SMOAK | | | | |
| St. John, Clarence | Chris Barber Jazz Band | LP | (England) Columbia 33SX-1245 | 1960 |
| | David Thomas Roberts | LP | Stomp Off 1021 | 1981 |
| COLLEGE RAG | | | | |
| Hunter, William | Olly Oakley w/Orchestra | 78 | Pathe 20091 | r.16-11 |
| | Olly Oakley w/pno | 78 | (England) Zonophone 1060 | 13-3 |
| COLONIAL GLIDE | | | | |
| Pratt, Paul | Glenn Jenks | LP | Bonnie Banks 103 | 1983 |
| | Wally Rose | LP | Stomp Off 1057 | 1982 |
| CONTENTMENT RAG | | | | |
| Lamb, Joseph | Patrick Gogerty | LP | Sounds Current | 1976 |
| | Dave Jasen | LP | Blue Goose 3002 | 1974 |
| | Dave Jasen | LP | Euphonic ESR-1206 | 1966 |
| | Hank Jones | LP | ABC-Paramount 496 | 64-4 |
| | Milton Kaye | LP | Golden Crest 31035 | 1974 |
| | David Laibman | LP | Rounder 3040 | r. 1981 |
| | Joseph Lamb | LP | Folkways FG-3562 | 59-8 |
| | Alain Lesire | LP | (Belgium) Jazz Cats 6983003 | 1982 |

| Composition | Performer | Record Speed | Record Company/No. | Year-Month |
|---|---|---|---|---|
| CONTENTMENT RAG (continued) | New Orleans Ragtime Orchestra | LP | Pearl 7 | 67-9 |
| | Steve Williams Piano Roll | LP | Folkways RBF-17 | |
| Lamb, Joseph | Johnny Wittwer | 10"LP | Stinson 58 | 1945 |
| COON BAND PARADE | | | | |
| Europe, James Reese | Red Wing Blackbirds | LP | Stomp Off 1018 | 1981 |
| COON CAN RAG | | | | |
| Vessey, G.B. | London Orchestra | 78 | (England) Cinch 5118 | 13-5 |
| CORN ON THE COB | | | | |
| Hess, Cliff | Frank Banta & Cliff Hess | 78 | Okeh 4825 | r. 23-6 |
| | Banta–Hess w/ Selvin's Orchestra | 78 | Vocalion 14671 | r.23-11 |
| CORN SHUCKS RAG | | | | |
| Kuhn, Ed | Harry Breuer Orchestra | LP | Audio Fidelity AFSC-5912 | 1960 |
| CORNCRACKER RAG | | | | |
| Shea, Tom | Jack Rummel | LP | Stomp Off 1118 | 1985 |
| | Tom Shea | LP | Stomp Off 1022 | 1981 |
| CORONATION RAG | | | | |
| Atwell, Winifred | Winifred Atwell | 78 | (England) Decca F-10110 | 53-3 |
| CORSICA RAG | | | | |
| Jordan, Joe | Terry Waldo (m) | LP | Stomp Off 1002 | 80-7 |
| COTTON | | | | |
| Von Tilzer, Albert | Vess L. Ossman w/pno | 78 | Nassau B-77 | |
| | Arthur Pryor's Band | 78 | Victor 16044 | |
| | Zonophone Concert Band | 78 | Zonophone 1038 | r. 08-5 |
| COTTON BOLLS | | | | |
| Hunter, Charles | Bill Mitchell | LP | Ethelyn 1750 | 1972 |
| | Tom Shea | LP | Stomp Off 1022 | 1981 |
| | Trebor Tichenor | LP | Folkways FS-3164 | 1979 |
| COTTON PATCH RAG | | | | |
| | John Dilleshaw & String Marvel | 78 | Okeh 45328 | 29-3 |
| COTTON TIME | | | | |
| Daniels, Charles N. | Chrysanthemum Ragtime Band (m) | LP | Stomp Off 1123 | 1985 |
| | Dawn of the Century Orchestra | LP | Arcane 602 | 1972 |
| | Piano Roll (aka The Sneak) | LP | Dot DLP-25478 | |
| COTTONTAIL RAG | | | | |
| Lamb, Joseph | Brian Dykstra | LP | Orion 83449 | 82-7 |
| | Patrick Gogerty | LP | Sounds Current | 1976 |
| | Glenn Jenks | LP | Bonnie Banks 104 | 1985 |
| | John Jensen | LP | Genesis 1045 | 1974 |
| | Jazzou Jones | LP | High Water 101 | 1983 |
| | Milton Kaye | LP | Golden Crest 31035 | 1974 |
| | David Laibman | LP | Rounder 3040 | r. 1981 |
| | Joseph Lamb | LP | Folkways FG-3562 | 59-8 |
| | Max Morath | LP | Vanguard VSD-39/40 | 1967 |
| | New Orleans Ragtime Orchestra | LP | (Sweden) Sonet 709 | 76-3 |

| Composition | Performer | Record Speed | Record Company/No. | Year-Month |
|---|---|---|---|---|
| COTTONTAIL RAG (continued) | Mike Polad | LP | Jazzology JCE-77 | r. 1974 |
| Lamb, Joseph | Queen City Ragtime Ensemble | LP | Zeno 99 | 1976 |
| | Ragtime Orchestra | LP | (Czechoslovakia) Supraphon | 1976 |
| | | | 1115.1965 | 1976 |
| COTTONWOOD RAG | | | | |
| Tichenor, Trebor | Trebor Tichenor | LP | Folkways FS-3164 | 1979 |
| COUNTRY CLUB | | | | |
| Joplin, Scott | Claude Bolling | LP | (France) CY 733.607 | c. 1980 |
| | Ann Charters | LP | Sierra Wave 101 | 1974 |
| | Dick Hyman | LP | RCA CRL5-1106 | 1975 |
| | Morton Gunnar Larsen | LP | (Sweden) Sonet 1450 | 1978 |
| | Max Morath | LP | Vanguard VSD-39/40 | 1967 |
| | Pacific Coast Ragtimers | LP | Circle CLP-137 | r. 1988 |
| | Knocky Parker | LP | Audiophile AP-71/72 | 1960 |
| | Piano Roll | LP | Biograph 1014Q | |
| | Joshua Rifkin | LP | Nonesuch 71305 | 1974 |
| | Dick Zimmerman | LP | Murray Hill 931079 | 1974 |
| CRAB APPLES | | | | |
| Wenrich, Percy | Trebor Tichenor | LP | Folkways FS-3164 | 1979 |
| CRACKER JACK | | | | |
| Reser, Harry | Howard Alden | LP | Stomp Off 1200 | 1988 |
| | Harry Reser | 78 | (England) Brunswick 1069 | 30-10 |
| CRADLE ROCK | | | | |
| Frankl, Abe & Kornheiser, Phil | Charley Straight Piano Roll | LP | Folkways RBF-44 | |
| THE CRAVE | | | | |
| Morton, Jelly Roll | Jelly Roll Morton | 12"78 | Circle JM-31 | 38-5 |
| | Jelly Roll Morton | 78 | General 4003 | 39-12 |
| | Duncan Swift | LP | (England) Black Lion 12123 | 69-8 |
| | Uptown Lowdown Jazz Band | LP | Stomp Off 1030 | 81-10 |
| CRAZY BONE RAG | | | | |
| Johnson, Charles L. | Frankie Carle | LP | Victor LPM-2491 | 1962 |
| | Goon-Bones Trio | 78 | Mercury 5498 | 50- |
| | Johnny Maddox | 78 | Dot 1005 | 50-5 |
| | Knocky Parker | LP | Audiophile AP-92 | |
| | Steve Pistorious | LP | Jazzology JCE-78 | 1975 |
| | U.S. Marine Band | 12"78 | Victor 35380 | 14-3 |
| CRAZY CHORD RAG | | | | |
| Morton, Jelly Roll | Knocky Parker | LP | Audiophile AP-104 | |
| CRAZY JO' | | | | |
| Reser, Harry | Harry Reser | 78 | Okeh 4571 | r. 22-5 |
| | Harry Reser | 78 | Brunswick 2308 | r. 22-9 |
| | Harry Reser | 78 | (England) Columbia 3317 | 23-6 |
| | Royale Trio | 78 | Pathe 020896 | r. 23-3 |
| | Terry Waldo's Band | LP | Stomp Off 1201 | 89-3 |

| Composition | Performer | Record Speed | Record Company/No. | Year-Month |
|---|---|---|---|---|
| CRAZY ORGAN RAG (aka MAPLE LEAF RAG) | | | | |
| Joplin, Scott & Woody, Dave | Lenny Dee | 45 | Coral 9-29579 | |
| CRAZY OTTO | | | | |
| | Hoagy Carmichel | 78 | Coral 61384 | |
| | Crazy Otto | 78 | (Germany) Polydor 22009 | 55-3 |
| | Hugo & Luigi | 78 | Mercury 70563 | 55- |
| | Murray Kaufman | 78 | Fraternity 714 | |
| | Joe Loss Orchestra | 78 | (England) HMV BD-6200 | |
| | Johnny Maddox (Billy Rowland) | 78 | Dot 15325 | 55- |
| CRAZY RAG (see DILL PICKLES) | | | | |
| | Texas Night Hawks | 78 | Okeh 45363 | 29-6 |
| CREOLE BELLES | | | | |
| Lampe, J. Bodewalt | Graeme Bell's Dixieland Band | 78 | (Australia) Ampersand 1201 | 47-6 |
| | Charles H.H. Booth | 78 | Victor 1079 | 01-11 |
| | Budapest Ragtime Orchestra | LP | (Czechoslovakia) Krem SLPX-17794 | 1984 |
| | Columbia Orchestra | 78 | Columbia 330, A-171 | 01-8 |
| | London Orchestra | 78 | (England) Cinch 5182 | 13-5 |
| | London Ragtime Orchestra | LP | Stomp Off 1081 | 1984 |
| | Louisiana Repertory Jazz Ensemble | LP | Stomp Off 1197 | 87-9 |
| | Metropolitan Orchestra | 78 | Victor 1023 | 01-10 |
| | New York Military Band | 78 | Edison 50514 | 19-5 |
| | Olly Oakley | 78 | (England) HMV GC-6426 | 04-11 |
| | Vess L. Ossman | 78 | Columbia 465 | 01-11 |
| | Vess L. Ossman w/pno | 78 | Imperial 44826 | r.06-11 |
| | Vess L. Ossman w/pno | 78 | Victor 1291 | 02-2 |
| | Alexander Prince | 78 | (England) Zonophone 49112 | 07-7 |
| | Tom Shea | LP | Stomp Off 1022 | 1981 |
| | Erik Silk & Southern Jazz Band | 78 | (England) Esquire 10-469 | 55-11 |
| | Sousa's Band | 78 | Victor 1182 | 02-1 |
| | Sousa's Band | 78 | Victor 17252 | 12-12 |
| | South Frisco Jazz Band | LP | Stomp Off 1035 | 81-7 |
| | Uptown Lowdown Jazz Band | LP | Stomp Off 1030 | 81-10 |
| | Watergate Seven Plus One | LP | Stomp Off 1165 | 87-7 |
| | Lu Watters YBJB | 78 | West Coast 102 | 46-6 |
| CROOKED NOTES | | | | |
| Paques, Jean | Jean Paques | 78 | (England) Edison Bell Winner 4932 | 29-7 |
| CROSS CORNERS | | | | |
| Green, George Hamilton | George Hamilton Green | 78 | Columbia 265-D | 24-12 |
| | Nexus | LP | (Canada) Umbrella 2 | 1976 |
| CUBIST | | | | |
| Griselle, Thomas | Frank Banta | 78 | Gennett 4735 | 21-5 |
| CUM BAC RAG | | | | |
| Johnson, Charles L. | Dave Jasen | LP | Euphonic ESR-1206 | 1966 |
| | New Sunshine Jazz Band | LP | Flying Dutchman 1-0549 | 1972 |
| | Knocky Parker | LP | Audiophile AP-92 | |
| | Charlie Rasch | LP | (Canada) Ragtime Society 4 | 1966 |

| Composition | Performer | Record Speed | Record Company/No. | Year-Month |
|---|---|---|---|---|
| THE CUTTER | | | | |
| McClure, Elma Ney | Elliott Adams | LP | Stomp Off 1198 | 1988 |
| A CYCLONE IN DARKTOWN | | | | |
| Barnard, George D. | Arthur Pryor's Band | 78 | Victor 17040 | 11-11 |
| DAILY RAG | | | | |
| Daily, Pete & Smith, Warren | Pete Daily's Dixieland Band | 78 | Capitol 805 | 49-10 |
| DAINTINESS RAG | | | | |
| Johnson, James P. | Neville Dickie | LP | (England) Saydisc SDL-118 | 1966 |
| | James P. Johnson | LP | Folkways FJ-2850 | 42-4 |
| | James P. Johnson | 78 | (France) Blue Star 198 | 47-6 |
| | James P. Johnson Piano Roll | LP | Biograph 1009Q | |
| | Donald Lambert | LP | Pumpkin 104 | 1960 |
| | Knocky Parker | LP | Audiophile AP-49 | 1958 |
| | Willie the Lion Smith | LP | Blue Circle 1500-33 | 53-8 |
| | Ken Werner | LP | Finnadar SR-9019 | 1978 |
| DAINTY DOLL | | | | |
| Barnes, Bernard | Anton & Orchestra (m) | 78 | (England) HMV BD-570 | |
| | Reginald Dixon (m) | 78 | (England) Regal Zonophone MR-3385 | |
| | Ivor Moreton & Dave Kaye (m) | 78 | (England) Parlophone F-550 | |
| | Bert Read | 78 | (England) Decca F-3977 | 34-6 |
| | Harry Robbins (m) | 78 | (England) Columbia FB-1355 | |
| | Jack Wilson (m) | 78 | (England) Regal-Zonophone MR-1825 | |
| DAINTY DOLLY | | | | |
| Seeboeck, W. C. E. | Pryor's Band | 78 | Victor 16073 | 08-9 |
| DAINTY MISS | | | | |
| Barnes, Bernard | H. Robinson Cleaver | 78 | (England) Parlophone F-892 | |
| | Charles Cooksey | 78 | (England) Octacros 1089 | |
| | Raie Da Costa | 78 | (England) Parlophone R-3534 | 28-3 |
| | Murray Kellner's Orchestra | 78 | Edison 52122 | 27-10 |
| | Constance Mering & Muriel Pollock | 78 | Columbia 1211-D | 27-11 |
| | Pattman | 78 | (England) Columbia 4659 | |
| | Rawicz & Landauer | 78 | (Austria) HMV AM-1794 | 28- |
| | Nat Shilkret & Orchestra | 78 | Victor 21037 | 27-10 |
| | King Solomon & His Miners | 78 | (England) Brunswick 3628 | |
| | Lawrence Welk & Orchestra | 78 | Coral 83006 | 53-5 |
| | Duke Yellman | 78 | Edison 52033 | r. 27-7 |
| DALLAS RAG | | | | |
| | Dallas String Band | 78 | Columbia 14290-D | 27-12 |
| DANCE OF THE WITCH HAZELS | Paul Lingle | LP | Euphonic 1217 | 1951 |
| Lingle, Paul | Ray Skjelbred | LP | Stomp Off 1124 | 85-8 |
| DANCING DEACON | | | | |
| Bryan, Frederick M. | Ford Dabney's Band | 78 | Aeolian-Vocalion 12217 | 19-9 |
| | Jim Europe's Hellfighters | 78 | Pathe 22167 | 19-4 |

| Composition | Performer | Record Speed | Record Company/No. | Year-Month |
|---|---|---|---|---|
| DANCING SHADOWS | | | | |
|   Golden, Ernie | Jimmy Andrews | 78 | Banner 6116 | 27-8 |
| | Raie DaCosta | 78 | (England) Parlophone R-335 | |
| | Galla-Rini | 78 | Brunswick 3873 | |
| DANCING TAMBOURINE | | | | |
|   Polla, William C. & Ponce, Phil | Pauline Alpert | 78 | Victor 21252 | 27-11 |
| | Don Baker | 78 | Columbia 36624 | |
| | Harry Bidgood's Orchestra | 78 | (England) Broadcast 193 | 27-12 |
| | Bert Block & Bell Music | 78 | Okeh 4087 | 38-2 |
| | Rube Bloom | 78 | Okeh 40901 | 27-9 |
| | Paul Bolognese | 78 | Radiex 1456 | |
| | Frankie Carle | 78 | Decca 1641, 25145 | 38-1 |
| | Freeman Clark & Frank Chidester | 78 | Linden 43 | |
| | Corn Cob Crushers | 78 | Champion 16373 | 31-12 |
| | Jesse Crawford | 78 | Victor 21171 | 27-11 |
| | Fred Elizalde | 78 | (England) Brunswick 130 | 27-8 |
| | Geoffrey Gelder & Orchestra | 78 | (England) Regal G-8997 | 27-10 |
| | Jack Hylton's Orchestra | 78 | (England) HMV B-5362 | 27-9 |
| | Dick Hyman | LP | Cadence CR-2001 | 1974 |
| | Louis Katzman & Kittens | 78 | Brunswick 3655 | |
| | Sam Lanin's Dance Orchestra | 78 | Banner 6083 | 27-8 |
| | Piccadilly Revels Band | 78 | (England) Columbia 4604 | 27-10 |
| | The Radiolites | 78 | Columbia 1114-D | 27-9 |
| | B.A. Rolfe Orchestra | 78 | Edison 52094 | 27-9 |
| | Rudy Starita w/Syd Bright | 78 | (England) Columbia 4622 | |
| | Three Suns | 78 | Victor 20-2815 | 47-10 |
| | WMCA Broadcasters | 78 | Harmony 493-H | 27-9 |
| | Ted Weems Orchestra | 78 | Mercury 5287 | 49- |
| | Paul Whiteman Orchestra | 78 | Victor 20972 | 27-9 |
| DARKEY TODALO | | | | |
|   Jordan, Joe | Lois Delano | LP | (Canada) Arpeggio 1205 | 1968 |
| | Knocky Parker | LP | Audiophile AP-91 | |
| DAVE'S RAG | | | | |
|   Jasen, David A. | Dave Jasen | LP | Euphonic ESR-1206 | 1966 |
| | Dave Jasen | LP | Blue Goose 3001 | 1972 |
| DAYS BEYOND RECALL | | | | |
|   Tichenor, Trebor | Trebor Tichenor | LP | Folkways FS-3164 | 1979 |
| DEIRO RAG | | | | |
|   Deiro, Guido | Guido Deiro | 78 | Columbia A-1229 | 12-8 |
| DELCAMP RAG | | | | |
|   Delcamp, J. Milton | J. Milton Delcamp | LP | Folkways RF-23 | 1920 |
| DELIRIOUS RAG | | | | |
|   Eckstein, Willie & Thomas, Harry | Harry Thomas | 78 | Victor 18229 | 16-12 |

| Composition | Performer | Record Speed | Record Company/No. | Year-Month |
|---|---|---|---|---|
| DELIRIUM TREMENS | | | | |
| Klickmann, F. Henri | Mitch Parks | LP | (Canada) CBC LM-430 | 75-11 |
| DELMAR RAG | | | | |
| Sullivan, Joe | Max Kaminsky Jazz Band | LP | Jazztone 1009 | 1954 |
| | Joe Sullivan | 78 | Commodore 538 | 41-3 |
| DELMAR RAG | | | | |
| Thompson, Charles | Charles Thompson | 78 | American Music 528 | 49-8 |
| | Charley Thompson | LP | Euphonic 1221 | c. 1960 |
| | Charley Thompson | LP | Stereoddities C-1900 | 1962 |
| DESECRATION RAG | | | | |
| Arndt, Felix | Felix Arndt | 78 | Victor 17608 | 14-3 |
| DETROIT RAGS | | | | |
| Lee, Dewey | Tom Shea | LP | Stomp Off 1022 | 1981 |
| DEUCES WILD | | | | |
| Kortlander, Max | Max Kortlander Piano Roll | LP | Folkways RBF-43 | |
| DEUCES WILD RAG | | | | |
| Bauersachs, Hubert | Hubert Bauersachs & Orchestra | 78 | Victor QB-1851 | 22- |
| | Terry Waldo Orchestra | LP | Stomp Off 1069 | 83-6 |
| DEW DROP ALLEY STOMP | | | | |
| Underwood, Sugar | Sugar Underwood | 78 | Victor 21538 | 27-8 |
| DICTY'S ON SEVENTH AVENUE | | | | |
| Blake, Eubie | Amherst Saxophone Quartet | LP | Musical Heritage Society 4368 | 80-12 |
| | Eubie Blake | LP | Eubie Blake Music 1 | 1971 |
| | Eubie Blake | LP | Stereoddities C-1900 | 1962 |
| | Dick Hyman | LP | Cadence CR-2001 | 1974 |
| | Charley Thompson | LP | Euphonic 1221 | c.1960 |
| | Terry Waldo | LP | Eubie Blake Music 8 | 1974 |
| DIGBETH & MILK STREET | | | | |
| Foxley, Ray | Ray Foxley | 78 | (England) Tempo A-29 | 49-6 |
| DILL PICKLES | | | | |
| Johnson, Charles L. | Winifred Atwell | 78 | (England) Decca F-10161 | 53- |
| | Winifred Atwell | 78 | (England) Phillips PB-266 | |
| | Burt Bales | 78 | Good Time Jazz 9 | 49-12 |
| | Ballyhooligans (m) | 78 | (England) HMV BD-5130 | 36-10 |
| | Len Barnard JB | 45 | (Australia) Swaggie 4514 | 58-12 |
| | Dr. Humphrey Bate & Possum Hunters | 78 | Brunswick 243 | 28-3 |
| | J. Brady | 78 | (England) Beka 843 | 14-1 |
| | Harry Breuer Orchestra | LP | Audio Fidelity AFSC-5912 | 1960 |
| | Chuck Cabot | 78 | Jubilee 5228 | |
| | Joe "Fingers" Carr's Brass Band | LP | Warner Bros. W-1456 | 1962 |
| | Chris Chapman | 78 | Victor 5560, 16678 | 08-7 |
| | Steen Christensen | LP | (Denmark) Louis Barnewitz 1 | 1972 |
| | Freeman Clark (m) | 78 | Linden 09 | |

| Composition | Performer | Record Speed | Record Company/No. | Year-Month |
|---|---|---|---|---|
| DILL PICKLES (continued) | Eddie Condon Orchestra | 78 | Decca 24987 | 50-3 |
| Johnson, Charles L. | Corn Cob Crushers | 78 | Champion 16373 | 31-12 |
| | Jim Couch | 78 | Okeh 40467 | |
| | Graeme Coyle | 45 | (Australia) Swaggie 4514 | 55-12 |
| | Crooks | LP | (Sweden) Opus 3 Nr.7916 | 1979 |
| | Farres Dansorkester | 78 | (Sweden) Pathe H-6017 | 21-12 |
| | Bob Darch | LP | United Artists UAL-3120 | 1960 |
| | Guido Deiro | 78 | Columbia A-1051 | 11-6 |
| | Neville Dickie | LP | (England) Contour 2870-190 | 1972 |
| | Dukes of Dixieland | LP | Audio Fidelity AF-1840 | 1956 |
| | Elite Syncopators | LP | Jazzology JC-102 | |
| | Empire Military Band | 78 | (England) Beka 41552 | 11- |
| | Pee Wee Erwin JB | LP | United Artists UAL-4010 | 58-10 |
| | Doc Evans JB | LP | Audiophile XL-329 | 1955 |
| | Chuck Folds | LP | Jazzways 106/4 | 1974 |
| | Four Pickled Peppers | 78 | Bluebird 8518 | 39-8 |
| | Frog Joseph JB | LP | Nobility LP-704 | 64-2 |
| | Georgie's Varsity Five | LP | HiFi R-805 | 1959 |
| | Hager's Orchestra | 78 | Zonophone 856 | r.07-10 |
| | Roy Hogsed | 78 | Capitol 57-40220 | |
| | Pee Wee Hunt & Orchestra | 78 | Capitol 57-773 | 49-1 |
| | Hurtado Bros. Royal Marimba Band (m) | 12"78 | Victor 35557 | 16-4 |
| | Kessinger Brothers | 78 | Brunswick 315 | 29-2 |
| | Merle Koch | LP | TAB 1002 | |
| | Bill Krenz | 10"LP | MGM E-184 | 1952 |
| | Bill Krenz | 78 | MGM 30707 | 52- |
| | LeRoy Larson | LP | Banjar 1781 | 1973 |
| | Johnny Maddox | 78 | Dot 1057 | 50- |
| | McLaughlin's Old Time Melody Makers | 78 | Victor 21286 | 28-2 |
| | Billy Milton | 78 | Gennett 6318 | |
| | Marvin Montgomery | LP | Audiophile AP-83 | c. 1969 |
| | Max Morath | LP | Vanguard 79440 | 1981 |
| | New Orleans Ragtime Orchestra | LP | GHB 210 | 87-1 |
| | Nexus | LP | (Canada) Umbrella 2 | 1976 |
| | Keith Nichols | LP | (England) EMI OU-2035 | 1974 |
| | Odeon Tanz Orchestra | 78 | (Germany) Odeon UAA-57584 | |
| | Knuckles O'Toole | LP | Grand Award 33-373 | |
| | Knocky Parker | LP | Audiophile XL-329 | |
| | Arthur Pryor's Band | 78 | Victor 16482 | 09-2 |
| | Ragtime Banjo Commission | LP | GHB 154 | 80-8 |
| | Ragtime Society of Frankfurt | LP | (Canada) Joke JLP-205 | 78-2 |
| | Razzberrie Ragtimers | LP | Razzberrie 32888 | 1979 |
| | Alex Read | LP | (Canada) RCA CTLS-1097 | 67-12 |
| | Harry Roy Orchestra | 78 | (England) Parlophone F-460 | 36-5 |
| | Scala Military Band | 78 | (England) Scala 216 | 12- |

| Composition | Performer | Record Speed | Record Company/No. | Year-Month |
|---|---|---|---|---|
| DILL PICKLES (continued) | Rick Schoenberg | LP | Kicking Mule 107 | r. 1976 |
| Johnson, Charles L. | Smith's Georgia Fiddle Band | 78 | Vocalion 5306 | |
| | Olle Sundh JB | 78 | (Sweden) Odeon 5598 | 51-4 |
| | Ralph Sutton | 78 | Circle 1053 | 49-1 |
| | Swift Jewel Cowboys | 78 | Vocalion 05309 | |
| | Keith Taylor | LP | Sami 1002 | r. 1984 |
| | Tiny Little | LP | Brunswick BL-54030 | |
| | Fred Van Eps w/Orchestra | 78 | Remington 5002 | |
| | Waldo's Ragtime Orchestra | LP | Stomp Off 1007 | 80-10 |
| | Ron Weatherburn | LP | (England) Rediffusion 0100170 | 74-3 |
| | Mark Wetch | LP | Wilson Audio 808 | 1980 |
| | Eddie Zack | 78 | Decca 46245 | 50-5 |
| DITTO | | | | |
| Bargy, Roy | Roy Bargy Piano Roll | LP | Folkways RF-35 | |
| DIXIE BLOSSOMS | | | | |
| Wenrich, Percy | Dave Dallwitz Ensemble | LP | Stomp Off 1098 | 84-8 |
| | Dawn of the Century Orchestra | LP | Arcane 601 | 1971 |
| | Elite Syncopators | LP | Jazzology 102 | r. 1989 |
| | Thomas Mills | 78 | Columbia 3628, A-224 | r. 07-5 |
| DIXIE DIMPLES | | | | |
| Scott, James | Knocky Parker | LP | Audiophile AP-76/77 | 1962 |
| DIXIE KISSES | | | | |
| Ohman, Phil | Phil Ohman Piano Roll | LP | Herwin 407 | |
| DIXIE QUEEN | | | | |
| Hoffman, Robert | Trebor Tichenor | LP | Folkways FS-3164 | 1979 |
| DIZZY DIGETS | | | | |
| Fillis, Len | Len Fillis | 78 | (England) Decca F-2379 | 30-11 |
| DIZZY FINGERS | | | | |
| Confrey, Zez | William Albright | LP | Music Masters 20033 | 80-12 |
| | Jan August | 78 | Mercury 5654 | 51- |
| | Moissaye Boguslawski | 78 | Autograph 500 | 26- |
| | Carmen Cavallero & Orchestra | 78 | Decca 29912 | 56-1 |
| | Tony Caramia | LP | Stomp Off 1209 | 1989 |
| | Zez Confrey Orchestra | 78 | Victor 20777 | 27-6 |
| | J. Lawrence Cook | 78 | Abbey 15040 | |
| | Max Darewski | 78 | (England) Zonophone 2432 | 24-2 |
| | Willie Eckstein | 78 | Okeh 40076 | r. 24-5 |
| | Bernard Ette Orchestra | 78 | (Germany) Vox 8403 | 27-1 |
| | Sal Franzella Quartet | 78 | Swan 7514 | 46-8 |
| | Lud Gluskin | 78 | (France) Pathe 8527 | 28-2 |
| | Benny Goodman & Orchestra | 78 | Capitol 439 | 47-6 |
| | Frank Herbin | 78 | (England) HMV B-1770 | 24-1 |

| Composition | Performer | Record Speed | Record Company/No. | Year-Month |
|---|---|---|---|---|
| DIZZY FINGERS (continued) | Dick Hyman | LP | Cadence CR-2001 | 1974 |
| Confrey, Zez | Dick Hyman | LP | RCA XRL1-4746 | 1983 |
| | Herb Inskip | LP | Hi GSR-4147 | 74-10 |
| | John Jensen | LP | Genesis 1051 | 1974 |
| | Milton Kaye | LP | Golden Crest 31040 | 1974 |
| | Arthur Kleiner | LP | Golden Crest 2004 | c. 1967 |
| | Bernie Leighton | LP | Cameo 1005 | 1958 |
| | Charles Magnante | 78 | Brunswick 7691 | |
| | Charles Magnante | 78 | Columbia 36088 | |
| | Charles Magnante Quartet | 78 | Silvertone 219 | |
| | Magnante-Carlino Lange Trio | 78 | Edison 52126 | 27-12 |
| | Major and Minor | 78 | (England) Regal G-21397 | 32- |
| | Silvia Marie | 78 | Web 1061 | |
| | Max Morath | LP | Vanguard VSD-79391 | 1977 |
| | Ivor Moreton & Dave Kaye | 78 | (England) Parlophone F-1987 | |
| | Russ Morgan & Eddie Wilser | LP | Decca DL-8746 | 1958 |
| | Keith Nichols | LP | (England) EMI One Up-2085 | 1975 |
| | Phil Ohman & Victor Arden w/ Orchestra | 78 | Brunswick 3305 | r. 26-9 |
| | Muriel Pollock & Vee Lawnhurst | 78 | Decca 164 | 34-9 |
| | Steve Race w/Orchestra | 78 | (England) Columbia DB-2937 | 51-2 |
| | Henri Rene Orchestra | 78 | Victor 20-3166 | 47-10 |
| | Savoy Orpheans | 78 | (England) HMV B-5105 | 26-7 |
| | Bill Snyder | 78 | Decca 27907 | 51-11 |
| | Three Suns | 78 | Victor 20-2816 | |
| | Ray Turner | 78 | Capitol 2096 | 52-3 |
| | Two Octaves | 78 | (Australia) Regal G-21397 | 32-5 |
| | Robert Wasmuth | 78 | (Germany) Telefunken A-10421 | 41-11 |
| | Bob Wilbur JB | LP | Audiophile AP-187 | 80-8 |
| | Jack Wilson (m) | 78 | (England) Regal Zonophone MR-1694 | 1934 |
| DIZZY KEYS | | | | |
| | Jay Wilbur | 78 | (England) Victory 252 | 30-6 |
| DOCTOR BROWN | | | | |
| Irvin, Fred | Charley Straight Piano Roll | LP | Folkways RBF-44 | |
| | Richard Zimmerman | LP | Murray Hill 60556/5 | 1981 |
| DOG ON THE PIANO | | | | |
| Shapiro, Ted | Arcadia Peacock Orchestra | 78 | Okeh 40272 | 24-11 |
| | Devonshire Restaurant Band | 78 | (England) Zonophone 5059 | c. 1925 |
| | Isham Jones Orchestra | 78 | Brunswick 2646 | 24-4 |
| | Percival Mackay's Band | 78 | (England) Columbia 3822 | 25-11 |
| | Cecil Norman | 78 | (England) Homochord DO-929 | 26- |
| DOING THE DOMINEOS | | | | |
| Gourlay, Ronald | Ronald Gourlay | 78 | (England) Edison Bell Electron 0222 | |

| Composition | Performer | Record Speed | Record Company/No. | Year-Month |
|---|---|---|---|---|
| DOLL DANCE | | | | |
| Brown, Nacio Herb | Pauline Alpert | 78 | Victor 21252 | 27-11 |
| | Jimmy Andrews (Frank Banta) | 78 | Banner 6116 | 27-8 |
| | Anton & Orchestra (m) | 78 | (England) HMV BD-570 | |
| | Sara Berner | 78 | Vocalion VL7-3921 | 53-5 |
| | Harry Bidgood & Orchestra | 78 | (England) Broadcast 163 | |
| | Rube Bloom | 78 | Okeh 40842 | 27-6 |
| | Paul Bolognese & Orchestra | 78 | Grey Gull 1441 | |
| | Brother Bones & His Shadows | 78 | Tempo 668 | c. 1948 |
| | Earl Burnett & Orchestra | 78 | Columbia 934-D | r. 27-5 |
| | Frankie Carle | 78 | Decca 1623, 25146 | 38-1 |
| | Coldstream Guards Band | 78 | (England) HMV B-8960 | |
| | Willie Creager's Rhythm Aces | 78 | Gennett 6083 | 27-3 |
| | Herman Darewski & Band (m) | 78 | (England) Parlophone F-1573 | |
| | Reginald Dixon (m) | 78 | (England) Regal-Zonophone MR-3385 | |
| | Bernard Ette Orchestra | 78 | (Germany) Vox 8532 | 27-6 |
| | Gus Farney | LP | Warner Brothers Y-1425 | 1961 |
| | Carl Fenton Orchestra | 78 | Brunswick 3519 | 27-3 |
| | Bert Firman's Orchestra | 78 | (England) Zonophone 2998 | |
| | Jan Garber Orchestra | 78 | Dot 15202 | |
| | Hank "Sugarfoot" Garland | 78 | Decca 27426 | 50-10 |
| | Georgia Collegians | 78 | Champion 15242 | |
| | Lou Gold Orchestra | 78 | Harmony 415-H | 27-5 |
| | Ken Harvey | 78 | (England) HMV BD-248 | |
| | Dick Hyman | LP | Cadence CR-2001 | 1974 |
| | Imperial Dance Orchestra | 78 | Banner 1981 | r. 27-6 |
| | Imperial Dance Orchestra | 78 | (England) Imperial 1805 | |
| | Julius Jackobsen & Bengt Hallberg | LP | (Sweden) Phontastic 7542 | 82-12 |
| | Russell Jones | EP | (Australia) Century EPC-3 | 56-3 |
| | Bert Kaplan & Collegians | 78 | Emerson 3134 | r. 27-5 |
| | Murray Kellner's Ensemble | 78 | Edison 52009 | r. 27-6 |
| | Sam Lanin Orchestra | 78 | Perfect 14800 | 27-3 |
| | Bernie Leighton | LP | Cameo 1005 | 1958 |
| | Guy Lombardo Orchestra | 78 | Decca 23768 | 44-2 |
| | Mike Markel's Orchestra | 78 | Okeh 40805 | 27-4 |
| | Robert Maxwell | 78 | MGM 11671 | 53-12 |
| | Constance Mering & Muriel Pollack | 78 | Columbia 1004-D | 27-5 |
| | Billy Milton / Billy Mayerl | 78 | (England) Broadcast 158 | |
| | Ivor Moreton & Dave Kaye (m) | 78 | (England) Parlophone F-550 | |
| | Russ Morgan & Eddie Wilser | LP | Decca DL-8746 | 1958 |
| | Russ Morgan Orchestra | 78 | Decca 27704 | 51-7 |
| | New Mayfair Novelty Orchestra(m) | 78 | (England) HMV BD-683 | |
| | Keith Nichols | LP | (England) EMI One Up-2085 | 1975 |
| | Pattman | 78 | (England) Columbia 4649 | |
| | Eddie Peabody | 78 | Victor 20698 | 27-5 |

| Composition | Performer | Record Speed | Record Company/No. | Year-Month |
|---|---|---|---|---|
| DOLL DANCE (continued) | Radio City Music Hall Orchestra(m) | 78 | Decca DA-23519 | 45-4 |
| Brown, Nacio Herb | Harry Robbins (m) | 78 | (England) Columbia FB-1355 | |
| | B.A. Rolfe Orchestra | 78 | Edison 52013 | r. 27-6 |
| | Savoy Orpheans | 78 | (England) HMV B-5290 | 27-5 |
| | Nat Shilkret Orchestra | 78 | Victor 20503 | 27-3 |
| | Freddie Slack Orchestra | 78 | Capitol 113 | 42-5 |
| | Debroy Somers Band | 78 | (England) Columbia 4462 | |
| | Claude Thornhill & Orchestra | 78 | Harmony 1038 | 40-9 |
| | Three Suns | 78 | Victor 20-2817 | |
| | Lawrence Welk Orchestra | 78 | Coral 61207 | 53-5 |
| | Jack Wilson (m) | 78 | (England) Regal-Zonophone MR-1825 | |
| DOLLAR DANCE | | | | |
| Wellstood, Dick | Dick Wellstood | LP | Jazzology JCE-73 | 1971 |
| | Dick Wellstood | LP | (Switzerland) 88 UpRight 005 | 76-1 |
| DOLLY DIMPLES | | | | |
| Alter, Louis | Michael Danzi | 78 | (Germany) Telefunken A-1721 | 34-6 |
| | Murray Kellner's Ensemble | 78 | Edison 52252 | 28-5 |
| | Fred Rich & Orchestra | 78 | (England) Columbia 4786 | 28-2 |
| | Paul Whiteman & Orchestra | 78 | Victor 21301 | 28-1 |
| DON'T JAZZ ME | | | | |
| Scott, James | Elliott Adams | LP | Stomp Off 1198 | 1988 |
| | Knocky Parker | LP | Audiophile AP-76/77 | 1962 |
| DON'T YOU HIT THAT LADY DRESSED IN GREEN | | | | |
| Smith, Willie the Lion | Willie the Lion Smith | 10"LP | Dial 305 | 1950 |
| DOO-WACKY RAG | | | | |
| Busch, Louis F. | Joe "Fingers" Carr & Band | 78 | Capitol 2359 | |
| DOROTHY | | | | |
| Banta, Frank E. | Frank Banta | 78 | Victor 21821 | 28-10 |
| DOUBLE FUDGE | | | | |
| Jordan, Joe | Steen Christensen | LP | (Holland) Jazz Crooner 155.771 | 1977 |
| | Lois Delano | LP | (Canada) Arpeggio 1205 | 1968 |
| | Knocky Parker | LP | Audiophile AP-89 | |
| DOWN HOME RAG | | | | |
| Sweatman, Wilbur | Apex JB | LP | (Canada) World A-7710-2101 | |
| | Chris Barber JB | LP | (England) Col. 33 SX-1321 | 1960 |
| | Sidney Bechet w/Luter Orchestra | 78 | (France) Vogue 5068 | 50-10 |
| | Black Bottom Stompers | LP | (England) VJM 23 | 1974 |
| | Joe "Fingers" Carr's Band | LP | Warner Bros. W-1389 | 1960 |
| | Joe "Fingers" Carr's Brass Band | LP | Warner Bros. W-1456 | 1962 |
| | Joe "Fingers" Carr's Ragtime Band | LP | Cap. T-443 | |
| | Climax JB | LP | (Canada) Tormax 33001 | 1973 |
| | Climax JB | LP | (Germany) CJB F-65311 | 1974 |

| Composition | Performer | Record Speed | Record Company/No. | Year-Month |
|---|---|---|---|---|
| DOWN HOME RAG (continued) | Larry Clinton Orchestra | 78 | Vic. 26414 | 39-11 |
| Sweatman, Wilbur | Max Collie's Rhythm Aces | LP | (Holland) Beerendonk 9997 | 80-1 |
| | Ken Colyer's Jazzmen | LP | (England) 77LEU 12/10 | 1964 |
| | Creole Rice JB | LP | Stomp Off 1170 | 1987 |
| | Pete Daily's Chicagoans | 78 | Cap. 57-760 | 49-9 |
| | Dave Dallwitz Ensemble | LP | (Australia) Swaggie S-1393 | |
| | John Defferary JB | LP | (England) VJM LC-7 | c. 1966 |
| | Clyde Doerr Orchestra | 78 | Cameo 1120 | 27-2 |
| | Tommy Dorsey Orchestra | 78 | Vic. 26097 | 38-10 |
| | Down Home JB | LP | Stomp Off 1190 | 88-8 |
| | Europe's Society Orchestra | 12″78 | Vic. 35359 | 13-12 |
| | Willie Farmer Orchestra | 78 | Bluebird B-7813 | 38-9 |
| | Wally Fawkes Rhythm Kings | LP | Stomp Off 1060 | 82-11 |
| | John Gill's Sunset Five | LP | Stomp Off 1126 | 85-8 |
| | Joe Glover's Cotton Pickers | LP | Epic LN-3581 | |
| | Benny Goodman Orchestra | 78 | Col. 3033-D | 35-1 |
| | Edmond Hall Quintet | LP | (Denmark) Storyville SLP-192 | 66-12 |
| | Capt. John Handy Band | LP | Polydor 623222 | 65-8 |
| | Clancy Hayes JB | LP | ABC-Paramount 591 | 1966 |
| | Dick Hyman | LP | Cadence CR-2001 | 1974 |
| | Herb Kern | 78 | Decca 24913 | 50-1 |
| | Lawson–Haggart JB | 10″LP | Decca DL-5456 | 53-1 |
| | Paul Lingle | LP | Euphonic 1227 | 1951 |
| | London Orchestra | 78 | (England) Cinch 5066 | 13-5 |
| | Humphrey Lyttelton Band | 78 | (England) Par R-3413 | 51-5 |
| | Rod Mason JB | LP | (Germany) Happy Bird 5008 | 74-2 |
| | Billy May Orchestra | LP | Cap. T-677 | 55-11 |
| | Milan College Jazz | EP | (Italy) Combo EP-10078 | 59-3 |
| | Turk Murphy JB | LP | Dawn Club 12019 | 58-12 |
| | Orange Peels | LP | Inter-Varsity 1201 | c. 1960 |
| | Kid Ory's JB | 78 | Crescent 4 | 45-9 |
| | Kid Ory's JB | LP | GTJ L-12041 | 56-6 |
| | Brooke Pemberton | LP | Warner Bros. W-1235 | 1958 |
| | Picadilly Six | LP | (Switzerland) Elite Special SOLP-526 | 76-2 |
| | Charlie Rasch | LP | (Canada) Ragtime Society 4 | 1966 |
| | Harry Roy Orchestra | 78 | (England) Par. F-1132 | 37-12 |
| | Six Brown Brothers | 78 | Vic. 17834 | 15-7 |
| | South Frisco JB | LP | Stomp Off 1143 | 84-11 |
| | Sammy Spear Orchestra | LP | Jubilee JLP-110 | c. 1952 |
| | Monty Sunshine JB | LP | (England) Philips 6459221 | 61-10 |
| | Ralph Sutton | LP | Down Home 4 | 49-11 |
| | Wilbur Sweatman JB | 7″78 | Emerson 7161 | 16-12 |
| | Butch Thompson | LP | (Denmark) CSA 1014 | 74-9 |
| | Uptown Lowdown JB | LP | Yerba Buena Jazz 101 | c. 1985 |
| | Van Eps Banjo Orchestra | 78 | Pathe 70090 | |
| | Harry Walton JB | LP | (England) Saga XID-5041 | 58-9 |

| Composition | Performer | Record Speed | Record Company/No. | Year-Month |
|---|---|---|---|---|
| DOWN HOME RAG (continued) | Lu Watters YBJB | 78 | Down Home 4 | 50-1 |
| Sweatman, Wilbur | Lu Watters YBJB | LP | Fairmont 101 | 1946 |
| | Lu Watters YBJB | 78 | West Coast 105 | 46-4 |
| | Richard Wayne's Bearcats | LP | Reader's Digest RDA-70-01-05 | 1968 |
| | Chick Webb Orchestra | 78 | Decca 785 | 35-6 |
| DOWN TOWN RAG | | | | |
| Signorelli, Frank & | H.B. Headley | 78 | (England) Homochord H-512 | 23-10 |
| Carrazza, George | Stanley C. Holt | 78 | (England) Homochord H-564 | 23-9 |
| | Three Barbers | 78 | Pathe 11165 | 26-2 |
| DUSTING THE KEYS | | | | |
| Blythe, James & Burton, Buddy | Jimmy Blythe & W.E. Burton | 78 | Gennett 6502 | 28-4 |
| DUSTING THE KEYS | | | | |
| Claypoole, Edward | Joseph Samuels & Orchestra | 78 | Pathe 021045 | 23-7 |
| | Harry Snodgrass | 78 | Brunswick 2852 | r. 25-6 |
| | Frank Westphal | 78 | Columbia A-3930 | 23-5 |
| DUSTING THE KEYS | | | | |
| O'Neil, Walker | Tony Caramia | LP | Stomp Off 1209 | 1989 |
| | Cecil Norman | 78 | (England) Homochord H-545 | 23-12 |
| | Walker O'Neil | 78 | (England) Homochord H-675 | 24-2 |
| | Walker O'Neil | 78 | (England) HMV B-1806 | 24-3 |
| | Walker O'Neil & Ray Allen | 78 | (Germany) Vox 6217 | 24-5 |
| | Al Siegel | 78 | (England) Zonophone 5056 | 27-2 |
| DUSTY RAG | | | | |
| Aufderheide, May | Freeman Clark (m) | 78 | Linden 09 | |
| | Ken Colyer's Jazzmen | LP | (England) Col. 33SX-1220 | 1959 |
| | Crane River Jazz Band | 78 | Crane River Jazz | 51-4 |
| | Frank Gillis | LP | Raintree 701 | 1981 |
| | Bunk Johnson's Jazz Band | 78 | Jazz Information 14 | 42-10 |
| | Turk Murphy JB | LP | Atlantic 1613 | 71-9 |
| | New Iberia Stompers | LP | (Italy) Rusty LPO-403 | 68-4 |
| | New Orleans Ragtime Orchestra | LP | GHB 210 | 87-1 |
| | New Orleans Ragtime Orchestra | LP | Pearl 8 | 1970 |
| | Old Merrytale Jazzband | LP | (Germany) Br. LPM-87906 | 60-8 |
| | Knocky Parker | LP | Audiophile AP-91 | |
| | Ragtime Society of Frankfurt | LP | (Germany) Joke JLP-205 | 78-2 |
| | Red Rose Ragtime Band | LP | Stomp Off 1128 | 1986 |
| | Red Wing Blackbirds | LP | Stomp Off 1018 | 1981 |
| | Pixie Roberts Trio | 78 | (Australia) Swaggie S-1004 | 49-8 |
| | Ken Sims JB | EP | (England) Polydor EPH-21598 | 1961 |
| | Zenith Six | 10"LP | (England) Decca LK-4100 | 55-1 |
| DYNAMITE RAG | | | | |
| Robinson, J. Russel | Grammophon Orchestra | 78 | (Germany) Grammophon 12801 | |
| | Tony Parenti's Ragtime Gang | LP | Jazzology J-21 | 66-4 |
| | Peerless Orchestra | 78 | (England) Zonophone 999 | 12-12 |
| | Salt City Five | 10"LP | Jubilee 13 | 1955 |

| Composition | Performer | Record Speed | Record Company/No. | Year-Month |
|---|---|---|---|---|
| DYNAMITE RAG | | | | |
| Beise, Paul & Klickmann, Henri | Albert White Orchestra | LP | Fantasy 3292 | |
| EASY GOIN' | | | | |
| Reser, Harry | Howard Alden | LP | Stomp Off 1200 | 88-12 |
| | Harry Reser w/pno | 78 | Okeh 40092 | 23-12 |
| | Harry Reser w/pno | 78 | Paramount 20330 | 24-5 |
| EASY WINNERS | | | | |
| Joplin, Scott | Marden Abadi | LP | Sine Qua Non 2020 | c. 1979 |
| | Concert Arban | LP | (France) Arion 33786 | 1985 |
| | John Arpin & Catherine Wilson | LP | (Canada) Fanfare 9023 | r. 1986 |
| | E. Power Biggs | LP | Col. M-32495 | 1973 |
| | William Bolcom | LP | Nonesuch 71257 | 1971 |
| | Sune Borg | LP | (Sweden) Sumpen SB-1001 | 1977 |
| | Boston Pops | LP | Polydor PD-6033 | 1974 |
| | Canadian Brass | LP | (Canada) Boot 3004 | 1974 |
| | Jo Ann Castle | LP | Reader's Digest RDA-70-01-05 | 1968 |
| | William Cerny | LP | University of Notre Dame | 1975 |
| | Eddie Erickson & Randy Morris | LP | House of Ragtime 1001 | 1974 |
| | Myron Floren | LP | Ranwood 8127 | 1974 |
| | Raymond Fonseque Band | LP | (France) Promophone 4 | 73-10 |
| | David Andrew Frost | LP | MHS 3201 | 1975 |
| | Nap Hayes & Matthew Prater | 78 | Okeh 45314 | 28-2 |
| | Dick Hyman | LP | RCA CRL5-1106 | 1975 |
| | Milton Kaye | LP | Golden Crest 31032 | 1974 |
| | Bill Knopf | LP | First Inversion 001 | r. 1983 |
| | James Levine | LP | RCA ARL1-2243 | 1976 |
| | Mimi & Russell | LP | Mumpus 791 | r. 1979 |
| | Bill Mitchell | LP | Ethelyn 1750 | 1972 |
| | Moonlight Ragtime Band | LP | National Geographic 07817 | 1979 |
| | Max Morath | LP | Epic LN-24106 | 1964 |
| | Max Morath Quintet | LP | Normacks 100 | c. 1981 |
| | Max Morath | LP | RCA Victor LSO-1159 | 69-4 |
| | Max Morath | LP | Vanguard SRV-351 | r. 1976 |
| | Roland Nadeau | LP | VQR 2625 | 1979 |
| | New England Conservatory | LP | Angel 36060 | 1973 |
| | Keith Nichols | LP | (England) EMI One UP 2035 | 1974 |
| | Knocky Parker | LP | Audiophile AP-71/72 | 1960 |
| | Itzhak Perlman & Andre Previn | LP | Angel S-37113 | 1975 |
| | Phoenix Symphony Ensemble | LP | World Jazz 12 | 77-6 |
| | Piano Roll | LP | Biograph 1013Q | |
| | Ronnie Price | LP | (England) Embassy 31043 | c. 1973 |
| | The Ragtimers | LP | RCA Camden ACL1-0599 | 74-5 |
| | William Neil Roberts | LP | Klavier 510 | 1972 |
| | Wally Rose | LP | Fairmont 102 | 47-8 |
| | Wally Rose | 10″LP | GTJ LP-3 | 53-2 |
| | Wally Rose | LP | GTJ M-12034 | 58-12 |

| Composition | Performer | Record Speed | Record Company/No. | Year-Month |
|---|---|---|---|---|
| EASY WINNERS (continued) | Wally Rose | 78 | Good Time 28 | 50-6 |
| Joplin, Scott | Sigi Schwab | LP | (Germany) Jupiter 6.24831 | c. 1985 |
| | Janice Scroggins | LP | Flying Hearts 334 | 87-9 |
| | Ray Smith | LP | (Holland) Timeless 538 | 86-12 |
| | Fred Sokolow | LP | Kicking Mule 212 | c. 1982 |
| | Chris Stone | LP | ABC 823 | 1974 |
| | Roy Sturgis | 78 | (England) Melodisc 1028 | 51-6 |
| | Swingle II | LP | Col. PC-34194 | 1975 |
| | Butch Thompson | LP | MPR PHC-505 | 81-7 |
| | Lu Watters & YBJB | 78 | West Coast 113 | 47-2 |
| | Dick Wellstood | LP | Pickswick SPC-3376 | 1974 |
| | Leo Wijnkamp (m) | LP | Kicking Mule 108 | 1974 |
| | Dick Zimmerman | LP | Murray Hill 931079 | 1974 |
| | Zinn's Ragtime String Quartet | LP | Music Minus One 13 | 1974 |
| | Paul Zukofsky & Robert Dennis | LP | Vanguard SRV-350 | 1975 |
| ECHO OF SPRING | | | | |
| Smith, Willie "The Lion" | Claude Bolling | LP | (France) Philips 6332087 | 1972 |
| | Ralph Burns | 10"LP | Period SLP-1105 | 1955 |
| | John Eaton | LP | Chiaroscuro 174 | 77-9 |
| | Morton Gunnar Larsen | LP | (Norway) Hot Club 6 | 1983 |
| | Cesare Poggi | LP | (Italy) Dire FO-357 | 79-7 |
| | Willie the Lion Smith | 78 | Commodore 521 | 39-1 |
| | Willie the Lion Smith | LP | Commodore FL-30.003 | 50-12 |
| | Willie the Lion Smith | LP | Dot DLP-3094 | 57-11 |
| | Willie the Lion Smith | LP | Flying Dutchman 10140 | 1970 |
| | Willie the Lion Smith | 78 | (France) Royal Jazz 730 | 49-12 |
| | Willie the Lion Smith | LP | Grand Award 33-368 | 57-8 |
| | Willie the Lion Smith | LP | Jazum 73 | 44-7 |
| | Willie the Lion Smith | LP | Urania UJ-1207 | 1954 |
| | Willie the Lion Smith & His Cubs | 78 | Decca 7090 | 35-5 |
| | Ralph Sutton | LP | (Italy) FDC 3002 | 79-5 |
| | Ralph Sutton | LP | Project 3 5040 | 69-5 |
| | Ralph Sutton | LP | Roulette R-25232 | 1962 |
| | Ralph Sutton | LP | (Switzerland) 88 Upright 004 | 75-11 |
| | Joe Turner | LP | (France) Black & Blue 33102 | 76-5 |
| EFFICIENCY RAG | | | | |
| Scott, James | John Arpin | LP | (Canada) Scroll 101 | 1965 |
| | William Bolcom | LP | Nonesuch 71299 | 1974 |
| | Brian Dykstra | LP | Orion 83449 | 82-7 |
| | Knocky Parker | LP | Audiophile AP-76/77 | 1962 |
| | Piano Roll | LP | Biograph 1016Q | |
| EIGHT O'CLOCK RUSH RAG | | | | |
| Rudisill, Bess | Chrysanthemum Ragtime Band | LP | Stomp Off 1047 | 1983 |
| ELEPHANT RAG | | | | |
| Franklin, Malvin | Knocky Parker | LP | Audiophile AP-92 | |

| Composition | Performer | Record Speed | Record Company/No. | Year-Month |
|---|---|---|---|---|
| ELITE SYNCOPATIONS | | | | |
| Joplin, Scott | Chris Barber JB | LP | (England) Col. 33SX-1245 | 1960 |
| | E. Power Biggs | LP | Col. M-32495 | 1973 |
| | Eubie Blake | LP | EBM 6 | 1973 |
| | Ann Charters | LP | Portents 3 | |
| | Eden Electronic Ensemble | LP | (England) Pye 12101 | 1975 |
| | Dick Hyman | LP | RCA CRL5-1106 | 1975 |
| | Dave Jasen | LP | Blue Goose 3001 | 1972 |
| | Jazzou Jones | LP | High Water 101 | 1983 |
| | Katia & Marielle Labeque | LP | Angel 37980 | 1982 |
| | James Levine | LP | RCA ARL1-2243 | 1976 |
| | London Ragtime Orchestra | LP | GHB 199 | 87-2 |
| | Mando Boys | LP | Red House 10 | 86-6 |
| | Bob Milne | LP | Jim Taylor Presents 113 | 1979 |
| | Mimi & Russell | LP | Mumpus 791 | r. 1979 |
| | Max Morath | LP | Vanguard VSD-39/40 | 1967 |
| | Mr. Joe's Ragtime Group | LP | (Denmark) LBS 1 | 1972 |
| | New England Conservatory Ensemble | LP | Golden Crest 31031 | 1973 |
| | New Orleans Ragtime Orchestra | LP | ABC AA-1076 | 1977 |
| | New Orleans Ragtime Orchestra | LP | Pearl 8 | 1970 |
| | Knocky Parker | LP | Audiophile AP-71/72 | 1960 |
| | Itzhak Perlman & Andre Previn | LP | Angel S-37113 | 1975 |
| | Piano Roll | LP | Biograph 1014Q | |
| | Ronnie Price | LP | (England) Embassy 31043 | c. 1973 |
| | Ragtime Orchestra | LP | (Czechoslovakia) Supraphon 1115.1965 | 1976 |
| | Ragtime Society of FrankFurt | LP | (Canada) Joke JLP-217 | 81-10 |
| | Joshua Rifkin | LP | Nonesuch 71264 | 1972 |
| | William Neil Roberts | LP | Klavier 510 | 1972 |
| | Wally Rose | LP | Blackbird 12007 | 1968 |
| | Royal Ballet Orchestra | LP | CRD 1029 | 1976 |
| | Janice Scroggins | LP | Flying Hearts 334 | 87-9 |
| | Southland Stingers | LP | Angel S-36078 | 1974 |
| | Chris Stone | LP | ABC 823 | 1974 |
| | Roy Sturgis | 78 | (England) Melodisc 1028 | 51-6 |
| | Swingle II | LP | Col. PC-34194 | 1975 |
| | Mary Lou Williams | LP | NYPL SJ | 71-10 |
| | Dick Zimmerman | LP | Murray Hill 931079 | 1974 |
| EMU STRUT | | | | |
| Dallwitz, Dave | Southern Jazz Group | 78 | (Australia) Parlophone A-7749 | 50-6 |
| THE ENTERTAINER | | | | |
| Joplin, Scott | Mardsen Abadi | LP | Sine Qua Non 2020 | c. 1979 |
| | Chris Barber JB | LP | (England) Col. 33SX-1245 | 1960 |
| | Johnny Bastable | LP | (England) Joy 214 | 1971 |
| | Marc Bercovic | LP | (France) Promophone ROM-1 | 1973 |
| | E. Power Biggs | LP | Col. M-33205 | 1974 |
| | Peter Bocage Orchestra | LP | Riverside RLP-379 | 1960 |
| | Sune Borg | EP | (Sweden) Scam EPS-001 | 1974 |

| Composition | Performer | Record Speed | Record Company/No. | Year-Month |
|---|---|---|---|---|
| THE ENTERTAINER (continued) | Hans-Jurgen Bock | LP | (Germany) Intercord 26454 | 1971 |
| Joplin, Scott | Boston Pop Orchestra | LP | Poloydor PD-6033 | 1974 |
| | Canadian Brass | LP | (Canada) Boot 3004 | 1974 |
| | Mutt Carey's New Yorkers | 78 | Century 4007 | 47-11 |
| | Mannie Carstens Band | LP | (Denmark) Olufsen 5082 | 87- |
| | Jo Ann Castle | LP | Reader's Digest RDA-70-01-05 | 1968 |
| | Cave Stompers | EP | (Sweden) Karusell KSEP-3170 | 1959 |
| | William Cerny | LP | University of Notre Dame | 1975 |
| | Climax JB | LP | (Canada) United Artists UALA-254-D | 1974 |
| | Max Collie's Rhythm Aces | LP | (England) Reality 106 | 1973 |
| | Ken Colyer's Jazzmen | 45 | (England) Decca F-10519 | 55-4 |
| | Cotton City JB | LP | (Belgium) Flamingo 2004 | 77-6 |
| | Darktown JB | LP | (Germany) Darktown Jazz SP1/74 | 74-7 |
| | Eddy Davis | LP | Pa Da 7402 | 1974 |
| | Brian Dykstra | LP | Century Advent 5075 | 1974 |
| | Eden Electronic Ensemble | LP | (England) Pye 12101 | 1975 |
| | Percy Faith Orchestra | LP | Col. KC-33006 | 1974 |
| | Myron Floren | LP | Ranwood 8127 | 1974 |
| | Flower Street JB | LP | (Germany) JLO 0401 | 80-12 |
| | Ray Foxley | LP | (Germany) Jeton 100.3301 | 79-3 |
| | David Andrew Frost | LP | Musical Heritage Society MHS-3201 | 1975 |
| | Earl Fuller's Orchestra | 78 | Col. A-2907 | 1920 |
| | John Gill's Original Sunset Five | LP | Stomp Off 1126 | 1985 |
| | Gotfried & Lonzo | LP | (Germany) Telefunken 6.22312 | 75-6 |
| | Hall Bros. JB | 10"LP | GHB 11 | 1964 |
| | Marvin Hamlisch | LP | MCA 2115 | 1974 |
| | Harbour JB | LP | (Holland) Omega 444.059 | 74-6 |
| | Hellman's Angels | LP | Plug 8 | 86-1 |
| | Paul Hersh & David Montgomery | LP | RCA Victor ARL1-0364 | 1974 |
| | Dick Hyman | LP | Project 3 PR-5080 | 1973 |
| | Dick Hyman | LP | RCA CRL5-1106 | 1975 |
| | Imperial JB | LP | Signature BFW-40112 | 1985 |
| | Herb Inskip | LP | Inskip GSR-4147 | 74-10 |
| | Glenn Jenks | LP | Bonnie Banks 103 | 1983 |
| | Bunk Johnson Band | LP | Col. GL-520 | 47-12 |
| | Bunk Johnson Band | LP | Col. ML-4802 | 47-12 |
| | Bill Knopf | LP | First Inversion 001 | r. 1983 |
| | Paul Kosmala | LP | Mark 5560 | 1979 |
| | Dick Kroeckel | LP | Ragtime GRU-1930 | 1977 |
| | Dick Kroeckel (m) | LP | Ragtime GRU-1930 | c. 1977 |
| | Katia & Marielle Labeque | LP | Angel S-37980 | 1982 |
| | Steve Lane's Stompers | EP | (England) Vortex 1001 | 1957 |
| | Alain Lesire | LP | (Belgium) Jazz Cats 6983003 | 1982 |
| | James Levine | LP | RCA ARL1-2243 | 1976 |
| | Jack Lidstrom's Hep Cats | EP | (Denmark) Storyville SEP-510 | 58-4 |
| | Paul Lolax | LP | Titanic 13 | r. 1981 |

| Composition | Performer | Record Speed | Record Company/No. | Year-Month |
|---|---|---|---|---|
| THE ENTERTAINER (continued) | London Ragtime Orchestra | LP | GHB 199 | 87-2 |
| Joplin, Scott | Geoff Love Ragtime Band | LP | (Canada) Quality 753 | 1974 |
| | Johnny Maddox | LP | Blythewood 103 | r. 1988 |
| | Rod Mason JB | LP | (Germany) Happy Bird 5008 | 74-2 |
| | Melbourne JB | EP | (Australia) Swaggie S-4529 | 60-4 |
| | Moonlight Ragtime Orchestra | LP | National Geographic 07817 | 1979 |
| | Max Morath | LP | Vanguard VSD-39/40 | 1967 |
| | New England Conservatory | LP | Angel 36060 | 1973 |
| | New Orleans Jazz Babies | LP | Biton 2113 | 74-11 |
| | New Orleans Ragtime Orchestra | LP | Arhoolie 1058 | 71-5 |
| | New Orleans Rascals | LP | (Japan) RCA RVL-5517 | 1975 |
| | Old Merrytale JB | LP | (Germany) Polydor 2371534 | 74-10 |
| | Original East Side Stompers | LP | (England) VJM LC-21 | 72-8 |
| | Darryl Ott | LP | Uplift R-0180 | 1980 |
| | Papa Benny Band | EP | (Denmark) Metronome MEP-1720 | 58-11 |
| | Papa Bue's JB | EP | (Denmark) Storyville SEP-356 | 58-1 |
| | Knocky Parker | LP | Audiophile AP-71/72 | 1960 |
| | Roy Pellett JB | LP | (Germany) Polydor 2377308 | 74-7 |
| | Itzhak Perlman & Andre Previn | LP | Angel S-37113 | 1975 |
| | Phoenix Ragtime Ensemble | LP | World Jazz 12 | 77-6 |
| | Piano Roll | LP | Biograph 1013 | |
| | Piano Roll | 78 | Jazz Classics 534 | |
| | Piano Roll | 10"LP | Riverside RLP1006 | |
| | Cesare Poggi | LP | (Italy) Dire FO-344 | 1979 |
| | Portena JB | LP | (Arg) Trova XT-80029 | 70-11 |
| | Prague Television Orchestra | LP | (Czechoslovakia) Supraphon 1115.1965 | 1976 |
| | Ray Price | LP | (Australia) Dixie RPQ-001 | 1974 |
| | Ronnie Price | LP | (England) Embassy 31043 | c. 1973 |
| | Ragtime Banjo Commission | LP | GHB 154 | 80-8 |
| | Ragtime Ensemble of Turino | LP | (Italy) Carosello 20144 | 78-10 |
| | Ragtime Society of Frankfurt | LP | (Germany) Joke JLP-205 | 78-2 |
| | Ragtime Specht Groove | LP | (Germany) Intercord 130001 | c. 1972 |
| | Ragtimers | LP | RCA ANL1-2818 | 74-5 |
| | The Ragtimers | LP | RCA Camden ACL1-0599 | 1974 |
| | Jean-Pierre Rampal | LP | CBS 37818 | 1982 |
| | Joshua Rifkin | LP | Nonesuch 71248 | 1970 |
| | William Neil Roberts | LP | Klavier 516 | 1973 |
| | Myron Romanul | LP | Angel 36060 | 1973 |
| | Tom Schmutzler & Harry Malfas | LP | Fleet Street 80-01 | 1980 |
| | Sigi Schwab | LP | (Germany) Jupiter 6.24831 | c. 1985 |
| | Janice Scroggins | LP | Flying Hearts 334 | 87-9 |
| | Roger Shields | LP | Turnabout 34579 | 1974 |
| | Yannick Singery | LP | (France) Swing SLD-928 | c. 1975 |
| | Fred Sokolow | LP | Kicking Mule 212 | c. 1982 |
| | Southern Stompers | EP | (England) Vortex 1001 | 1957 |
| | Chris Stone | LP | ABC 823 | 1974 |
| | Duncan Swift | LP | (England) Black Lion 12123 | 69-8 |

| Composition | Performer | Record Speed | Record Company/No. | Year-Month |
|---|---|---|---|---|
| THE ENTERTAINER (continued) | Szeged Old Timers | LP | (Holland) Beerendonk BR-99919 | 84-1 |
| Joplin, Scott | Keith Taylor | LP | Sami 1001 | 1974 |
| | Bob Tryforous | LP | Puritan 5002 | r. 1976 |
| | Vistula River Band | LP | (Poland) Muza SX-1479 | 1977 |
| | Terry Waldo | LP | Fat Cat's Jazz 151 | 74-1 |
| | Ron Weatherburn | LP | (England) Alpha LPX-32 | 62-1 |
| | Ray Weatherburn | LP | (England) Rediffusion 0100170 | 1974 |
| | Dick Wellstood | LP | (Canada) Unisson 1003 | 85-5 |
| | Dick Wellstood | LP | Fat Cat's Jazz FCJ-158 | 74-4 |
| | Dick Wellstood | LP | Pickwick SPC-3376 | 1974 |
| | White Eagle JB | EP | (Germany) Studio 102 | 74-7 |
| | Leo Wijnkamp | LP | Kicking Mule 108 | 1974 |
| | Bob Wilbur & Dick Wellstood | LP | Parkwood 103 | 84-5 |
| | Dick Zimmerman | LP | Murray Hill 931079 | 1974 |
| ENTERTAINER'S RAG | | | | |
| Roberts, Jay | Claude Bolling | LP | (France) Philips 70341 | 1966 |
| | Joe "Fingers" Carr | LP | Cap. T-760 | |
| | Joe "Fingers" Carr's Brass Band | LP | Warner Bros. W-1456 | 1962 |
| | Chrysanthemum Ragtime Band | LP | Stomp Off 1168 | 1987 |
| | Billy Hamilton's Rag Pickers | 78 | Kappa 127 | |
| | Red Nichols & Orchestra | 78 | Capitol 1763 | |
| | Brooke Pemberton | LP | Warner Bros. W-1235 | 1958 |
| | Piano Roll | 10"LP | (England) London AL-3542 | |
| | Cesare Poggi | LP | (Italy) Dire FO-357 | 79-7 |
| | Ragpickers | 78 | Circle 1054 | 49-1 |
| | Ray Turner | 78 | Capitol 15437, 1046 | 50- |
| | Waldo's Syncopators | LP | GHB 55 | 70-4 |
| | Richard Zimmerman | LP | Murray Hill 60556/5 | 1981 |
| ESKIMO SHIVERS | | | | |
| Mayerl, Billy | Hans Bund & Herbert Jager | 78 | (Germany) Telefunken A-1376 | 33-2 |
| | Billy Mayerl | 78 | (England) HMV B-2130 | 25-8 |
| ESSAY IN RAGTIME | | | | |
| Campbell, Brun | Brun Campbell | LP | Euphonic 1201 | |
| | Brun Campbell | 78 | West Coast 114 | 46-8 |
| | Trebor Tichenor | LP | Folkways FS-3164 | 1979 |
| ESTELLE | | | | |
| Carle, Frankie | Frankie Carle | 78 | Columbia 35571 | |
| | Frank Froeba | 78 | Hit 8008 | 42-7 |
| | Bill Krenz | 78 | MGM 30707 | 52- |
| | Bill Krenz | 10"LP | MGM E-184 | 1952 |
| ETHIOPIA RAG | | | | |
| Lamb, Joseph | William Bolcom | LP | Nonesuch 71257 | 1971 |
| | Ann Charters | LP | Folkways FG-3563 | 1961 |
| | Patrick Gogerty | LP | Sounds Current | 1976 |
| | John Jensen | LP | Genesis GS-1045 | 1974 |
| | Milton Kaye | LP | Golden Crest 31035 | 1974 |

| Composition | Performer | Record Speed | Record Company/No. | Year-Month |
|---|---|---|---|---|
| ETHIOPIA RAG (continued) | David Laibman | LP | Rounder 3040 | r. 1981 |
| Lamb, Joseph | New Orleans Ragtime Orchestra | LP | Stomp Off 1213 | 1989 |
| | Keith Nichols Ragtime Orchestra | LP | (England) EMI One Up 2135 | 1976 |
| EUGENIA | | | | |
| Joplin, Scott | Lee Erwin | LP | Angel S-36075 | 1974 |
| | Dick Hyman | LP | RCA CRL5-1106 | 1975 |
| | Hank Jones | LP | ABC-Paramount 496 | 64-4 |
| | New Orleans Ragtime Orchestra | LP | GHB 210 | 87-1 |
| | Knocky Parker | LP | Audiophile AP-71/72 | 1960 |
| | Piano Roll | LP | Biograph 1014Q | |
| | Mike Polad | LP | Jazzology JCE-77 | r. 1975 |
| | Ragtime Banjo Commission | LP | GHB 154 | 80-8 |
| | Joshua Rifkin | LP | Nonesuch 71264 | 1972 |
| | Fred Sokolow | LP | Kicking Mule 212 | c. 1982 |
| | Southland Stingers | LP | Angel S-36078 | 1974 |
| | James Tyler Orchestra | LP | Desto 7181 | 1979 |
| | Dick Zimmerman | LP | Murray Hill 931079 | 1974 |
| EUPHONIC SOUNDS | | | | |
| Joplin, Scott | William Albright | LP | Music Masters 20033 | 80-12 |
| | Canadian Brass | LP | (Canada) Boot 3004 | 1974 |
| | Ann Charters | LP | Portents 1 | 1958 |
| | Eddy Davis | LP | Pa Da 7401 | 1974 |
| | Raymond Fonseque | LP | (France) Promophone 4 | 73-10 |
| | Dick Hyman | LP | RCA CRL5-1106 | 1975 |
| | Herb Inskip | LP | Repertoire 7177 | c. 1977 |
| | James P. Johnson | 12"78 | Asch 551-1 | 44-6 |
| | James P. Johnson (tk 2) | LP | (England) Xtra 1024 | 1945 |
| | James P. Johnson (tk 1) | LP | Folkways FJ-2850 | 1945 |
| | James P. Johnson | LP | Jazzology JCE-1009 | 44-9 |
| | Max Morath | LP | Epic LN-24106 | 1964 |
| | Max Morath | LP | Vanguard VSD-39/40 | 1967 |
| | Turk Murphy JB | LP | Atlantic 1613 | 71-9 |
| | New England Conservatory Ensemble | LP | Golden Crest 31031 | 1973 |
| | Knocky Parker & Bill Coffman | LP | Euphonic 1216 | 77-4 |
| | Knocky Parker | LP | Audiophile AP-49 | 1958 |
| | Knocky Parker | LP | Audiophile AP-71/72 | 1960 |
| | Piano Roll (m) | LP | Biograph 1010Q | |
| | Joshua Rifkin | LP | Nonesuch 71248 | 1970 |
| | Wally Rose | LP | GTJ M-12034 | 58-12 |
| | Wally Rose | 78 | Good Time Jazz 51 | 51-7 |
| | Tom Shea | LP | (Canada) Ragtime Society 1 | 1963 |
| | Bob Tryforus | LP | Puritan 5002 | r. 1976 |
| | Uptown Lowdown JB | LP | UL 303 | 1978 |
| | Dick Zimmerman | LP | Murray Hill 031079 | 1974 |

| Composition | Performer | Record Speed | Record Company/No. | Year-Month |
|---|---|---|---|---|
| **EVERGREEN RAG** | | | | |
| Scott, James | Brian Dykstra | LP | Century Advent 5075 | 1974 |
| | John Jensen | LP | Genesis 1044 | 1974 |
| | Max Morath | LP | Vanguard SRV-351 | r. 1976 |
| | Knocky Parker | LP | Audiophile AP-76/77 | 1962 |
| | Piano Roll | LP | Biograph 1016Q | |
| | Piano Roll | 10″ LP | Riverside RLP-1025 | |
| **EVERYBODY TWO STEP** | | | | |
| Herzer, Wallie | Mike Bernard | 78 | Columbia A-1266 | 12-12 |
| | Chrysanthemum Ragtime Band | LP | Stomp Off 1168 | 1987 |
| | Frisco Syncopators | 78 | Clarion 1119 | |
| | Johnny Gibbs Band | LP | Reader's Digest RDA-70-01-05 | 1968 |
| | Johnny Maddox | LP | Paragon 102 | c. 1978 |
| | National Military Band | 78 | Phono Cut 5024 | |
| | Peerless Orchestra | 78 | (England) Zonophone 1000 | 12-12 |
| | Rega Dance Orchestra | 78 | Okeh 4452 | 21-8 |
| | Roane County Ramblers | 78 | Columbia 15398-D | 29-4 |
| | Victor Military Band | 78 | Victor 17271 | 13-1 |
| **EVERYBODY'S RAG** | | | | |
| Goldsmith, Dan & | Queen City Ragtime Ensemble | LP | Stomp Off 1138 | 1986 |
| Sharp, Robert | San Francisco Harry | LP | Fantasy 3270 | 1958 |
| | Richard Zimmerman | LP | Murray Hill 60556/5 | 1981 |
| **EVERYBODY'S RAG** | | | | |
| Jasen, Dave & | Dave Jasen | LP | Blue Goose 3001 | 1972 |
| Yancey, Alonzo | Alonzo Yancey | 78 | Session 10-015 | 43-12 |
| **EVOLUTION RAG** | | | | |
| Allen, Thomas S. | Piano Roll | LP | Herwin 407 | |
| **EXCELSIOR RAG** | | | | |
| Lamb, Joseph | John Arpin | LP | (Canada) Scroll 103 | 1966 |
| | Patrick Gogerty | LP | Sounds Current | 1976 |
| | John Jensen | LP | Genesis 1045 | 1974 |
| | Milton Kaye | LP | Golden Crest 31035 | 1974 |
| | Joseph Lamb | LP | Folkways FG-3562 | 59-8 |
| | Piano Roll | 78 | Circle 5004 | |
| **EYE OPENER** | | | | |
| Zurke, Bob & Matlock, Julian | Bob Crosby Orchestra w/ Zurke | 78 | Decca 2282 | 39-1 |
| **FAIR AND WARMER** | | | | |
| Reser, Harry | Howard Alden | LP | Stomp Off 1200 | 1988 |
| | Harry Reser | 78 | Columbia 1537-D | 28-7 |
| **FANCY FINGERS** | | | | |
| Knowles, Burn | Tony Caramia | LP | Stomp Off 1209 | 1989 |
| **FASCINATING RAG** | | | | |
| Hug, Armand and | Larry Fotine Band | LP | Bel Canto SR-1009 | |
| Fotine, Larry | Armand Hug | LP | Golden Crest CR-3064 | 1959 |
| | Armand Hug | 78 | Okeh 6950 | 50- |
| | Yannick Singery | LP | (France) Swing SLD-928 | c. 1975 |

| Composition | Performer | Record Speed | Record Company/No. | Year-Month |
|---|---|---|---|---|
| THE FASCINATOR | | | | |
| Scott, James | Knocky Parker | LP | Audiophile AP-76/77 | 1962 |
| FASHION RAG | | | | |
| Cohen, Charles | Herb Inskip | LP | Inskip 4147 | 74-10 |
| | Charlie Rasch | LP | (Canada) Ragtime Society 4 | 1966 |
| FASHIONETTE | | | | |
| Glogau, Jack & King, Robert A. | Victor Arden & Phil Ohman | 78 | Victor 21902 | 29-2 |
| | Joe Candullo Orchestra | 78 | Harmony 888-H | 29-4 |
| | Raie Da Costa w/Orchestra | 78 | (England) Parlophone R-335 | 29-3 |
| | Mario De Pietro | 78 | (England) Sterno 605 | |
| | Bert Firman & Rhythmic Eight | 78 | (England) Zonophone 5305 | 29-2 |
| | Murray Kellner's Ensemble | 78 | Edison 52421 | 28-10 |
| | Piccadilly Players | 78 | (England) Columbia 5465 | |
| FAST AND FURIOUS | | | | |
| Ellington, Duke | Duke Ellington & Orchestra | 78 | Brunswick 6355 | 32-5 |
| THE FAVORITE | | | | |
| Joplin, Scott | Chris Barber JB | LP | (England) Col. 33SX-1245 | 1960 |
| | Canadian Brass | LP | (Canada) Boot 3004 | 1974 |
| | Ann Charters | LP | (England) Sonet SNTF-661 | 1974 |
| | Climax JB | LP | (Canada) Tormax 33007 | 1979 |
| | Dick Hyman | LP | RCA CRL5-1106 | 1975 |
| | Mouldy Five | 10″LP | GHB 181 | 66-9 |
| | Knocky Parker | LP | Audiophile AP-71/72 | 1960 |
| | Piano Roll | LP | Biograph 1008Q | |
| | Jean-Pierre Rampal | LP | CBS 37818 | 1982 |
| | Sigi Schwab | LP | (Germany) Jupiter 6.24831 | c. 1985 |
| | Southland Stingers | LP | Angel S-36074 | 1974 |
| | Trebor Tichenor | LP | (Canada) Scroll 102 | 1966 |
| | Vistula River Band | LP | (Poland) Poljazz PSJ-105 | c. 1981 |
| | Dick Zimmerman | LP | Murray Hill 931079 | 1974 |
| FELICITY RAG | | | | |
| Hayden, Scott & Joplin, Scott | E. Power Biggs | LP | Col. M-33205 | 1974 |
| | Bill Bolcom | LP | Music Master 0149 | 1981 |
| | Ann Charters | LP | Sierra Wave 101 | 1974 |
| | Steen Christensen | LP | (Denmark) LB 1 | 1972 |
| | George Foley | LP | Stomp Off 1187 | 1988 |
| | Dick Hyman | LP | RCA CRL5-1106 | 1975 |
| | Mouldy Five | 10″LP | GHB 181 | 66-9 |
| | Knocky Parker | LP | Audiophile AP-71/72 | 1960 |
| | Piano Roll | LP | Biograph 1008Q | |
| | Ton Van Bergeyk | LP | Kicking Mule 114 | 1976 |
| | Dick Zimmerman | LP | Murray Hill 931079 | 1974 |
| | Paul Zukofsky & Robert Dennis | LP | Vanguard SRV-350 | 1975 |
| FESTIVAL RAG | | | | |
| Jasen, David A. | Dave Jasen | LP | Blue Goose 3001 | 1972 |
| | Dave Jasen | LP | Euphonic ESR-1206 | 1966 |

| Composition | Performer | Record Speed | Record Company/No. | Year-Month |
|---|---|---|---|---|
| FIDDLESTICKS RAG | | | | |
| Coney, Al B. | Peerless Orchestra | 78 | (England) Zonophone 1049 | 13-2 |
| FIDGETY FINGERS | | | | |
| Elholm, Norman | Stanley G. Holt | 78 | (England) Homochord 434 | 1923 |
| FIG LEAF RAG | | | | |
| Atkins, Chet | Chet Atkins | 78 | Victor 20-5181 | 52-10 |
| FIG LEAF RAG | | | | |
| Joplin, Scott | Hans-Jurgen Bock | LP | (Germany) Intercord 28535 | 1973 |
| | Canadian Brass | LP | (Canada) Boot 3004 | 1974 |
| | Ann Charters | LP | Portents 1 | 1958 |
| | Ken Colyer's Jazzmen | EP | (England) Decca DFE-6466 | 1958 |
| | Ken Colyer's Jazzmen | LP | (England) Joy S-194 | 1974 |
| | Leonine Consort | LP | (Australia) KGC KL-20026 | 1978 |
| | Hugh Crozier | LP | (England) VJM LC-33 | 1978 |
| | Dick Hyman | LP | RCA CRL5-1106 | 1975 |
| | Dave Jasen | LP | Folkways FG-3561 | 77-6 |
| | New Orleans Ragtime Orchestra | LP | Vanguard VSD-69/70 | 1971 |
| | Knocky Parker | LP | Audiophile AP-49 | 1958 |
| | Knocky Parker | LP | Audiophile AP-71/72 | 1960 |
| | Piano Roll | LP | Biograph 1008Q | |
| | Piano Roll | 78 | Jazz Classics 533 | |
| | Piano Roll | 10"LP | Riverside RLP-1006 | |
| | Ragtime Specht Groove | LP | (Germany) Intercord 130005 | c. 1973 |
| | Joshua Rifkin | LP | Nonesuch 71248 | 1970 |
| | Myron Romanul | LP | Golden Crest 31042 | 1975 |
| | Ron Weatherburn | LP | (England) Rediffusion 0100170 | 74-3 |
| | Dick Wellstood | LP | Fat Cat's Jazz 159 | 74-4 |
| | Dick Wellstood | LP | Jazzology JCE-73 | 1971 |
| | Dick Wellstood | LP | Pickwick SPC-3376 | 1974 |
| | Leo Wijnkamp | LP | Kicking Mule 108 | 1974 |
| | Dick Zimmerman | LP | Murray Hill 931079 | 1974 |
| FINE FEATHERS | | | | |
| Briers, Larry | Larry Briers | 78 | Gennett 9453 | 23-4 |
| | Willie Eckstein | 78 | Okeh 40076 | 23-11 |
| FINESSE | | | | |
| Maltin & Doll | New Mayfair Dance Orchestra | 78 | (England) HMV B-5737 | 29-10 |
| | Muriel Pollock & Vee Lawnhurst | 78 | Decca 164 | 34-9 |
| FINGER BUSTER | | | | |
| Morton, Jelly Roll | John Arpin | LP | Eubie Blake Music 10 | 1976 |
| | Peter Fahrenholtz | LP | (Poland) Polijazz ZSX-0638 | 1977 |
| | John Gill | LP | Stomp Off 1066 | 1983 |
| | Dick Hyman | LP | Columbia M-32587 | 73-12 |
| | Dick Hyman Band | LP | Smithsonian N-006 | 78-2 |
| | Morton Gunnar Larsen | LP | Stomp Off 1009 | 81-1 |
| | Jelly Roll Morton | 78 | Jazz Man 12 | 38-12 |
| | Knocky Parker | LP | Audiophile AP-105 | |
| | Ron Weatherburn | LP | (England) Alpha 32 | 62-1 |

| Composition | Performer | Record Speed | Record Company/No. | Year-Month |
|---|---|---|---|---|
| FINGER BUSTER | | | | |
| Smith, Willie the Lion | Neville Dickie | LP | Stomp Off 1096 | 83-4 |
| | John Gill | LP | Stomp Off 1066 | 1983 |
| | Dick Hyman | LP | Project 3 PR-5080 | 1973 |
| | Willie the Lion Smith | 78 | Commodore 522 | 39-1 |
| | Willie the Lion Smith | LP | Commodore FL-30.003 | 50-12 |
| | Willie the Lion Smith | LP | Dot DLP-3094 | 1957 |
| | Willie the Lion Smith | LP | IAJRC 45 | 56-7 |
| | Willie the Lion Smith | LP | Jazz Kings 1207 | |
| | Willie the Lion Smith | LP | Merritt 4 | 34-5 |
| | Willie the Lion Smith | LP | Urania UJ-1207 | 1954 |
| FINGER TRICKS | | | | |
| De Pietro, Mario | Louis Revel w/pno (Mario De Pietro) | 78 | (England) Piccadilly 568 | 30-5 |
| FINGERS MEDLEY | | | | |
| Busch, Louis F. | Joe "Fingers" Carr | 78 | Capitol 3883 | 56- |
| FIRE CRACKERS | | | | |
| Thorne, Donald | Donald Thorne | 78 | (England) Columbia 5155 | 28-6 |
| FIRESIDE FUSILIERS | | | | |
| Mayerl, Billy | Billy Mayerl | 78 | (England) Decca F-8271 | 43-1 |
| FIZZ WATER | | | | |
| Blake, Eubie | Amherst Saxophone Quartet | LP | Musical Heritage Society 4368 | 80-12 |
| | T. J. Anderson Orchestra | LP | Smithsonian 001 | 1975 |
| | Eubie Blake | LP | Eubie Blake Music 1 | 1971 |
| | Emerson Military Band | 78 | Emerson 9144 | 19-4 |
| | Hall Brothers Jazz Band | LP | Stomp Off 1062 | 1981 |
| | New Leviathan Orchestra | LP | Camel Race 19325 | r. 1975 |
| | New Sunshine Jazz Band | LP | Fat Cat's Jazz 115 | 70-6 |
| | Pathe Dance Orchestra | 78 | Pathe 70127 | r. 15-9 |
| | Phoenix Ragtime Ensemble | LP | World Jazz 12 | 77-6 |
| | Mike Polad | LP | Jazzology JCE-77 | 1975 |
| | Ragtime Society of Frankfurt | LP | (Germany) Joke 217 | 81-10 |
| FLAPPER RAG | | | | |
| Penrose, Billy | Sid Phillips & Band | 78 | (England) HMV BD-6149 | 53-8 |
| FLAPPERETTE | | | | |
| Greer, Jesse | Harry Breuer | 78 | Vocalion 15723 | |
| | Frankie Carle | 78 | Decca 1641, 25145 | 38-1 |
| | Continental Dance Orchestra | 78 | Banner | 27-8 |
| | Gil Dech | 78 | (Australia) Columbia 0881 | 27-12 |
| | Harmonicats | 78 | Mercury 5756 | 51- |
| | Dick Hyman | LP | Cadence CR-2001 | 1974 |
| | Victor Irwin & Orchestra | 78 | Harmony 493-H | 27-9 |
| | Herb Kern & Lloyd Sloop | 78 | Tempo 1066 | |
| | Harold Leonard Orchestra | 78 | Brunswick 3255 | r. 26-8 |

| Composition | Performer | Record Speed | Record Company/No. | Year-Month |
|---|---|---|---|---|
| FLAPPERETTE (continued) | Magnante–Carlino–Lange Trio | 78 | Edison 52126 | 27-11 |
| Greer, Jesse | Russ Morgan & Eddie Wilser | LP | Decca DL-8746 | 1958 |
| | Ronnie Munroe & Orchestra | 78 | (England) Parlophone E-5953 | |
| | Cecil Norman | 78 | (England)Homochord D-1153 | 27-6 |
| | Jean Paques | 78 | (England) Edison Bell Radio 804 | 28-1 |
| | Knocky Parker & Patrick Gogerty | LP | Euphonic 1215 | 77-4 |
| | Piccadilly Revels Orchestra | 78 | (England) Columbia 4339 | |
| | Harry Reser | 78 | (England) Brunswick 01069 | 30-10 |
| | Fred Rich & Orchestra | 78 | (England) Imperial 1833 | |
| | Willard Robison | 78 | Perfect 14836 | 27-7 |
| | Schutt & Cornell | 78 | (England) Brunswick 01134 | 31-4 |
| | Nat Shilkret Orchestra | 78 | Victor 20503 | 27-1 |
| | Paul Weston Orchestra | 78 | Columbia 39666 | |
| | Jack Wilson (m) | 78 | (England) Regal-Zonophone MR-1694 | 1934 |
| FLORIDA RAG | | | | |
| Lowry, George L. | Bob Darch | LP | United Artists UAL-3120 | 1960 |
| | Morton Gunnar Larsen | LP | Stomp Off 1009 | 81-1 |
| | Vess L. Ossman w/Orchestra | 78 | Victor 5058 | 07-2 |
| | Vess L. Ossman w/pno | 78 | Columbia 3644, A-224 | 07-4 |
| | Knocky Parker | LP | Audiophile AP-90 | |
| | Piano Roll | LP | (England) Saydisc SDL-132 | |
| | Fred Van Eps | 78 | Pathe 29032 | |
| | Van Eps Trio | 78 | Victor 17308 | 12-7 |
| FLYING FINGERS | | | | |
| Clark, Valerie | Bill Snyder | 78 | Decca 27907 | 51-11 |
| FOURTH MAN RAG | | | | |
| Hamilton, Dick & Leland, Jill | Pee Wee Hunt & Orchestra | 78 | Capitol 1091 | 50-4 |
| FRANCES | | | | |
| Morton, Jelly Roll | Burt Bales | LP | Euphonic 1210 | 1957 |
| | James Dapogny | LP | Smithsonian 003 | 1976 |
| | Jelly Roll Morton | 78 | Victor V-38627 | 29-7 |
| | Knocky Parker | LP | Audiophile AP-104 | |
| | David Thomas Roberts | LP | Mardi Gras 1002 | 1978 |
| | Ray Smith | LP | Stomp Off 1012 | 81-3 |
| FREAKISH | | | | |
| Morton, Jelly Roll | Jelly Roll Morton | 12″78 | Circle JM-71 | 38-5 |
| | Jelly Roll Morton | 78 | Victor 27565 | 29-7 |
| FRECKLES RAG | | | | |
| Buck, Larry | Chrysanthemum Ragtime Band | LP | Stomp Off 1079 | 1984 |
| FREDDY | | | | |
| Cook, J. Lawrence | J. Lawrence Cook | 78 | Abbey 15060 | c. 49- |
| FRENCH PASTRY RAG | | | | |
| Copeland, Les | Trebor Tichenor | LP | Folkways FS-3164 | 1979 |

| Composition | Performer | Record Speed | Record Company/No. | Year-Month |
|---|---|---|---|---|
| FRIDAY NIGHT | | | | |
| Ashwander, Donald | Donald Ashwander | LP | Jazzology JCE-52 | c. 1967 |
| | Royal Ballet Orchestra | LP | CRD 1029 | 1976 |
| FRIDAY NIGHT STOMP | | | | |
| Maddox, Johnny | Johnny Maddox | 78 | Dot 15014 | |
| FRIED CHICKEN RAG | | | | |
| Day, Ella Hudson | Elliott Adams | LP | Stomp Off 1198 | 1988 |
| FRISCO RAG | | | | |
| Armstrong, Harry | San Francisco Harry | LP | Fantasy 3270 | 1958 |
| | Wayne & Geraldi | LP | Reader's Digest RDA-70-01-05 | 1968 |
| FRIVOLOUS JOE | | | | |
| De Pietro, Mario | Mario De Pietro | 78 | (England) HMV B-2820 | 28-3 |
| FROG LEGS RAG | | | | |
| Scott, James | Marc Bercovic | LP | (France) Promophone Rom-1 | 1973 |
| | Peter Bocage Orchestra | LP | Riverside RLP-379 | 1960 |
| | Neville Dickie | LP | (England) Contour 2870-190 | 1972 |
| | John Hasse | LP | Sunflower 501 | 1980 |
| | John Jensen | LP | Genesis 1044 | 1974 |
| | Love–Jiles Ragtime Orchestra | 10"LP | Riverside RLP-9379 | 60-6 |
| | Max Morath | LP | Vanguard SRV-310 | r. 1974 |
| | New England Conservatory Ensemble | LP | Golden Crest 31042 | 1975 |
| | Knocky Parker | LP | Audiophile AP-49 | 1958 |
| | Knocky Parker | LP | Audiophile AP-76/77 | 1962 |
| | Sid Phillips & Band | 78 | (England) HMV BD-6198 | 55-4 |
| | Phoenix Ragtime Ensemble | LP | World Jazz 12 | 77-6 |
| | Piano Roll | LP | Biograph 1016Q | |
| | Piano Roll | 10"LP | (England) London 3542 | |
| | Wally Rose | 10"LP | GTJ LP-3 | 53-2 |
| | Wally Rose | LP | GTJ M-12034 | 58-12 |
| | Wally Rose | 78 | Good Time Jazz 25 | 50-6 |
| | Yannick Singery | LP | (France) Swing SLD-928 | c. 1975 |
| | Ralph Sutton | 78 | Down Home 9 | 49-11 |
| FROGGIE MOORE (see FROG-I-MORE RAG) | | | | |
| FROG-I-MORE RAG | | | | |
| Morton, Jelly Roll | Len Barnard JB | LP | (Australia) Swaggie S-1221 | 1952 |
| | Len Barnard JB | LP | (Australia) Swaggie S-1238 | 1968 |
| | Roger Bell JB | LP | (Australia) Swaggie S-1351 | 76-6 |
| | Adrian Bentzen | 10"LP | (Denmark) Sonet DLP-1 | 1954 |
| | Hans Blaas | LP | (Holland) Cat LP-52 | 84-6 |
| | Black Bottom Stompers | LP | (Switzerland) Elite Special SJLP-6321 | 1976 |
| | Jean-Francois Bonnel | LP | Stomp Off 1131 | 1985 |
| | Canal Street JB | LP | Stomp Off 1005 | 1978 |

| Composition | Performer | Record Speed | Record Company/No. | Year-Month |
|---|---|---|---|---|
| FROG-I-MORE RAG (continued) | Charleston JB | LP | (Holland) Harbour Jazz HJL-008 | 1981 |
| Morton, Jelly Roll | Rod Cless Quartet | 78 | Black & White 29 | 44-9 |
| | Climax JB | LP | (Canada) Tormax 33008 | 1981 |
| | Max Collie's Rhythm Aces | LP | (Holland) Beerendonk 9996 | 80-1 |
| | Graham Coyle | EP | (Australia) Swaggie S-4507 | 55-12 |
| | Jim Cullum JB | LP | Jazzology J-132 | 82-6 |
| | James Dapogny | LP | Smithsonian 003 | 1976 |
| | Delta JB | LP | (Argentina) Tondisc 1033 | 71-10 |
| | Dixieland Reunie | LP | (Holland) Discofoon 6957.110 | 71-10 |
| | Dutch Swing College Band | 10"LP | (Holland) Philips P-10042 | 53-7 |
| | Doc Evans JB | 10"LP | Audiophile AP-50 | 1958 |
| | Evergreen JB | LP | Stomp Off 1202 | 89-6 |
| | Don Ewell | LP | Windin' Ball 103 | 52-11 |
| | Flower Street JB | LP | (Germany) JLO 0401 | 80-12 |
| | Ray Foxley | LP | (Germany) Jeton 100.3301 | 79-3 |
| | Ray Foxley Trio | EP | (England) Tempo EXA-24 | 1955 |
| | Frog Island JB | LP | (England) Stomp ROBB-004 | 70-12 |
| | Hall Bros. JB | 10"LP | GHB 46 | 1966 |
| | Harlem Ramblers | LP | (Sweden) Polydor 2377336 | 80-12 |
| | Ray Heitger JB | LP | Spittune 6189-90 | 77-4 |
| | Hot Cotton JB | LP | GHB 168 | c. 1980 |
| | Armand Hug | LP | (Australia) Swaggie 1296 | 71-6 |
| | Armand Hug | LP | (Australia) Swaggie 1365 | 1975 |
| | Armand Hug | 78 | Good Time Jazz 20 | 50-6 |
| | Dink Johnson | LP | Euphonic 1202 | |
| | Connie Jones JB | LP | Crescent City LP-1212 | c. 1982 |
| | King Oliver's Creole Jazz Band | 78 | Gennett 5135 | 23-4 |
| | Cy Laurie's Band | EP | (England) Melodisc EPM 7-89 | 1957 |
| | Lawson–Haggert Jazz Band | 78 | Decca 28490 | 52-3 |
| | Martin Litton | LP | (England) Black Lion 51108 | 86-8 |
| | Louisiana Jazz Ensemble | LP | Stomp Off 1140 | 86-6 |
| | Claude Luter JB | 78 | (France) Pathe OC54-16028 | 48-2 |
| | Humphrey Lytellton Jazz Band | 78 | (England) Parlophone R-3292 | 50-4 |
| | Rod Mason's Hot Seven | LP | (England) Black Lion 51114 | 86-4 |
| | Memphis Nighthawks | LP | Delmark DS*216 | 1977 |
| | Midge Town JB | LP | (Holland) JS 7769 | 1977 |
| | Jelly Roll Morton | 78 | Steiner-Davis 103 | 24-4 |
| | Jelly Roll Morton | 78 | Vocalion 1019 | 26-4 |
| | Turk Murphy JB | LP | GHB 92 | 72-4 |
| | Natural Gas JB | LP | NGJB 6 | 85-8 |
| | New Black Eagle JB | LP | Stomp Off 1065 | 83-12 |
| | New Sunshine JB | LP | Flying Dutchman 1-0549 | 1972 |
| | New Yankee Rhythm Kings | LP | Stomp Off 1015 | 81-7 |
| | Ib K. Olson Jazzband | LP | (Denmark) LB Specialty 2 | 64-4 |
| | Original Eastside Stompers | LP | (England) VJM LC-37 | 85-2 |
| | Knocky Parker | LP | Audiophile AP-102 | |
| | Bent Persson JB | LP | (Sweden) Kenneth KS-2045 | 79-8 |

| Composition | Performer | Record Speed | Record Company/No. | Year-Month |
|---|---|---|---|---|
| FROG-I-MORE RAG (continued) | Peruna Jazzmen | LP | Stomp Off 1020 | 80-7 |
| Morton, Jelly Roll | Platte River JB | LP | PRJB 33014 | 1978 |
| | Port of Dixie Band | LP | P.O.D. 101 | 76-5 |
| | Portena JB | LP | (Argentina) Trova TL-6 | 66-11 |
| | Reunion JB | LP | (Holland) Artone 3121 | 67-11 |
| | Wally Rose | LP | Col. CL-559 | 53-9 |
| | Royal Garden Ramblers | LP | (Switzerland) Elite Special 52584 | 79-3 |
| | Bob Scobey JB | LP | Verve MG V-1009 | 57-2 |
| | Soprano Summit II | LP | World Jazz S-13 | 77-12 |
| | South Frisco JB | LP | (Holland) Mark Town 15875 | 77-5 |
| | Storyville Creepers | EP | (Sweden) Polydor EPH-10707 | 1955 |
| | Storyville Creepers | EP | (Sweden) Polydor EPH-10707 | 1956 |
| | Duncan Swift | LP | (England) Black Lion 12123 | 69-8 |
| | Duncan Swift | LP | (England) Big Bear 34 | 90-7 |
| | Swiss Dixie Stompers | LP | (Switzerland) Newland 891 | 89-3 |
| | Butch Thompson | LP | Stomp Off 1037 | 82-4 |
| | Ron Weatherburn | LP | (England) Rediffusion 0100170 | 74-3 |
| | Bob Wilbur JB | LP | GHB 201 | 81-5 |
| | Bob Wilbur & Wildcats | 78 | Rampart 7 | 47-12 |
| | Zenith Hot Stompers | LP | Stomp Off 1191 | 1988 |
| FROSTED CHOCOLATE | | | | |
| Reser, Harry | Howard Alden | LP | Stomp Off 1200 | 1988 |
| | Harry Reser w/pno | 78 | Brunswick 3821 | 28-4 |
| FUCALLIA | | | | |
| Wellstood, Dick | Dick Wellstood | LP | Chiaroscuro 109 | 70-11 |
| FUN BOB RAG | | | | |
| Wenrich, Percy | Zonophone Orchestra | 78 | Zonophone 5603 | r. 10-3 |
| FUNERAL RAG | | | | |
| Kortlander, Max | Max Kortlander Piano Roll | LP | Folkways RBF-43 | |
| FUNNY BONES | | | | |
| Woolsey, Calvin Lee | David Thomas Roberts | LP | Stomp Off 1132 | 1981 |
| FUSSIN' | | | | |
| Smith, Willie the Lion | Ralph Sutton | LP | (England) Ace of Hearts AH-39 | 1953 |
| FUSSY DOREEN | | | | |
| Foxley, Ray | Ray Foxley | 78 | (England) Tempo A-29 | 49-6 |
| FUZZY WUZZY RAG (see MAPLE LEAF RAG) | | | | |
| Morton, Al | Handy's Orchestra from Memphis | 78 | Columbia A-2421 | 17-9 |
| GASLIGHT JAZZ | | | | |
| Watts, Cyril | Cy Watts & Jazzman | 78 | (Australia) Jazzart 12 | 49-1 |
| GASOLINE RAG | | | | |
| Mentel, Louis | Dave Jasen | LP | Folkways FG-3561 | 77-6 |

| Composition | Performer | Record Speed | Record Company/No. | Year-Month |
|---|---|---|---|---|
| GEORGIA CAKE WALK (see AT A GEORGIA CAMP MEETING) | | | | |
| | Doc Evans Band | 78 | Art Floral 101 | 49-2 |
| | Art Hodes & Orchestra | 78 | Decca 18437 | 42-3 |
| | Ma Rainey | 78 | Paramount 12590 | 27-12 |
| | Freddy Randall Band | 78 | (England) Tempo A-45 | 49-9 |
| GEORGIA GRIND | | | | |
| Dabney, Ford | Len Barnard Jazz Band | 78 | (Australia) Swaggie S-1011 | 52-11 |
| | Mannie Carstens Band | LP | (Denmark) Olufsen 5082 | 1987 |
| | Signor Grinderino | 78 | Victor 17884 | 15-10 |
| | Dick Kroeckel | LP | Ragtime GRU-1930 | 1977 |
| | Johnny Maddox | LP | Redstone 101 | r. 1978 |
| | Metropolitan Military Band | 78 | Emerson 527 | |
| | New Sunshine Jazz Band | LP | Flying Dutchman 1-0549 | 1972 |
| | Pathe Dance Orchestra | 78 | Pathe 70129 | 15-9 |
| | Prince's Band | 12"78 | Columbia A-5687 | 15-7 |
| | Red Rose Ragtime Band | LP | Stomp Off 1128 | 1986 |
| | Wally Rose | LP | Stomp Off 1057 | 1982 |
| | St. Louis Ragtimers | LP | Paseo DF-102 | 1968 |
| GEORGIA RAG | | | | |
| Gumble, Albert | Dave Jasen | LP | Blue Goose 3002 | 1974 |
| | Piano Roll (aka: Tennessee Centennial Rag) | LP | Dot DLP-25478 | |
| GEORGIA RAINBOW | | | | |
| Gordon, Leo | Cynthia Sayer | LP | New York Jazz 008 | 1987 |
| GERALDINE RAG | | | | |
| Dickie, Neville | Neville Dickie | LP | Euphonic ESR-1206 | 1966 |
| | Neville Dickie | LP | (England) Major Minor 5054 | 1970 |
| GERTRUDE HOFFMAN GLIDE | | | | |
| Hoffman, Max | Victor Military Band | 78 | Victor 17292 | 13-2 |
| GET GOIN' | | | | |
| Mandell, Pete | Pete Mandell w/pno | 78 | (England) Duo D-523 | 28-9 |
| | Pete Mandell w/Savoy Orpheans | 78 | (England) HMV B-5035 | 26-3 |
| | Phil Russell (Pete Mandell) | 78 | (England) Edison Bell Winner 4591 | 26-9 |
| GET UP, BESSIE | | | | |
| Wilson, Garland | Garland Wilson | 78 | (France) Brunswick A-500220 | 32-11 |
| GHOST OF THE BANJO | | | | |
| Smeck, Roy | Roy Smeck & Art Kahn | 78 | Columbia 1127-D | 27-6 |
| GHOST OF THE PIANO | | | | |
| Schutt, Arthur | Arthur Schutt | 78 | (England) Regal G-8032 | 23-7 |
| THE GIGGLER | | | | |
| Haines, Chauncey | Victor Orchestra | 78 | Victor 4520 | 05-10 |

| Composition | Performer | Record Speed | Record Company/No. | Year-Month |
|---|---|---|---|---|
| GINGER SNAP RAG | | | | |
| Campbell, Brun | Brun Campbell | LP | Euphonic 1202 | 1947 |
| | Trebor Tichenor | LP | Dirty Shame 2001 | 1973 |
| GINGER SNAPS | | | | |
| Bourdon, Rosario | Victor Novelty Orchestra | 78 | Victor 22201 | 29-11 |
| GINGER SNAPS | | | | |
| Reser, Harry | Howard Alden | LP | Stomp Off 1200 | 1988 |
| GLAD RAG | | | | |
| Danmark, Ribe | Piano Roll | 10"LP | (England) London AL-3542 | |
| GLAD RAGS | | | | |
| Bryan, J. Wallace | Victor Military Band | 78 | Victor 17808 | 15-8 |
| GLADIOLUS RAG | | | | |
| Joplin, Scott | William Albright | LP | Music Masters 20033 | 80-12 |
| | John Arpin | LP | (Canada) Scroll 103 | 1966 |
| | John Arpin & Catherine Wilson | LP | (Canada) Fanfare 9023 | r. 1986 |
| | Acker Bilk Band | LP | (England) Nixa 513 | 58-3 |
| | Claude Bolling | LP | (France) CY 733.607 | c. 1980 |
| | William Cerny | LP | University of Notre Dame | 1975 |
| | Ann Charters | LP | Portents 1 | 1958 |
| | Brian Dykstra | LP | Advent 5021 | 1976 |
| | Flower Street JB | LP | (Germany) JLO 0401 | 80-12 |
| | Steve Hancoff | LP | Dirty Shame 4553 | 1977 |
| | Dick Hyman | LP | RCA CRL5-1106 | 1975 |
| | Glenn Jenks | LP | Bonnie Banks 104 | 1985 |
| | Paul Kosmala | LP | Mark 5660 | 1979 |
| | David Laibman | LP | Rounder 3040 | r. 1981 |
| | Max Morath | LP | Vanguard VSD-39/40 | 1967 |
| | New England Conservatory Ensemble | LP | Golden Crest 31031 | 1973 |
| | Keith Nichols | LP | (England) EMI OU-2035 | 1974 |
| | Knocky Parker | LP | Audiophile AP-71/72 | 1960 |
| | Pathe Dance Orchestra | 78 | Pathe B-8030, 29050 | c. 15-1 |
| | Piano Roll | LP | Biograph 1013Q | |
| | Ronnie Price | LP | (England) Embassy 31043 | c. 1973 |
| | Ragtime Orchestra (m) | LP | (Czechoslovakia) Supraphon 1115.1965 | 1976 |
| | The Ragtimers | LP | RCA Camden ACL1-0599 | 74-5 |
| | Joshua Rifkin | LP | Nonesuch 71248 | 1970 |
| | Wally Rose | 10"LP | GTJ LP-3 | 53-2 |
| | Wally Rose | LP | GTJ M-12034 | 58-12 |
| | Wally Rose | 78 | Good Time Jazz 25 | 50-6 |
| | Southland Stingers | LP | Angel S-36074 | 1974 |
| | Lee Stafford | 78 | Castle 11 | 51-1 |
| | Bob Tryforous | LP | Puritan 5002 | r. 1976 |
| | James Tyler Orchestra | LP | Desto 7181 | 1979 |
| | Dick Wellstood | LP | Pickwick SPC-3376 | 1974 |
| | Dick Zimmerman | LP | Murray Hill 931079 | 1974 |

| Composition | Performer | Record Speed | Record Company/No. | Year-Month |
|---|---|---|---|---|
| GLADYSE | | | | |
| Waller, Thomas | Neville Dickie | LP | (England) Columbia SCX-6445 | 1970 |
| | Fats Waller | 78 | Victor V-38554 | 29-8 |
| GLORIA | | | | |
| Wiedoeft, Rudy | Rudy Wiedoeft Trio | 78 | Brunswick 3103 | 26-1 |
| GLORIA | | | | |
| Hager, Fred and Ring, Justin | Tony Caramia | LP | Stomp Off 1209 | 1989 |
| | Vincent Lopez Orchestra | 78 | Okeh 4921 | 23-8 |
| | Percival Mackay Orchestra | 78 | (England) Columbia 4083 | 26-4 |
| GO! GO! | | | | |
| Colicchio, Ralph | Maya Danzi | 78 | (Germany) Homochord 4-3307 | 29-8 |
| | Michael Danzi | 78 | (Germany) Telefunken A-1660 | 34-6 |
| | Michael Danzi | 78 | (Germany) Gloria G0-27298 | 36-1 |
| GOLD BAR RAG | | | | |
| Morath, Max | Max Morath | 10″LP | Gold Camp KCMS-1091 | 1956 |
| GOLDEN SLIPPER RAG | | | | |
| | Eddie Hawks | 78 | Mercury 6368 | 1951 |
| GOLDEN SPIDER RAG | | | | |
| Johnson, Charles L. | Piano Roll (aka: Get Hot Rag) | LP | Dot DLP-25477 | |
| GOLDENROD STOMP | | | | |
| Tichenor, Trebor | St. Louis Ragtimers | LP | Audiophile AP-122 | 1977 |
| GOOD AND PLENTY RAG | | | | |
| Lamb, Joseph | Milton Kaye | LP | Golden Crest 31035 | 1974 |
| GOOD GRAVY RAG | | | | |
| Belding, Harry | Dave Jasen | LP | Blue Goose 3002 | 1974 |
| | Paul Lingle | LP | Euphonic 1217 | 1951 |
| | Turk Murphy Jazz Band | LP | (Australia) Jazz & Jazz 6437.157 | 1980 |
| | Turk Murphy Jazz Band | LP | Motherlode 104 | 1964 |
| | Alex Read | LP | (Canada) RCA CTLS-1097 | 67-12 |
| | Terry Waldo Orchestra | LP | Stomp Off 1069 | 83-6 |
| GOOD GRAVY RAG | | | | |
| Hug, Armand | Armand Hug | 78 | Good Time Jazz 19 | 50-6 |
| GOOFY DUST | | | | |
| Moten, Bennie | Bennie Moten's Kansas City Orchestra | 78 | Okeh 8184 | 24-11 |
| GOTHENBURG RAG | | | | |
| Lundberg, Peter | Peter Lundberg | LP | Jazzology JCE-52 | c. 1967 |
| | Jack Rummel | LP | Stomp Off 1118 | 1985 |
| GRACE & BEAUTY | | | | |
| Scott, James | T.J. Anderson Orchestra | LP | Smithsonian N-001 | 1975 |
| | W. Arlington Piano Roll | LP | Biograph 1006Q | |
| | Wilda Baughn | LP | Sacramento Jazz 16 | 1981 |
| | Eric Brooks | 78 | (England) Poydras 16 | 50- |
| | Ken Colyer's Jazzmen | LP | (England) Joy S-194 | 1974 |

| Composition | Performer | Record Speed | Record Company/No. | Year-Month |
|---|---|---|---|---|
| GRACE & BEAUTY (continued) | Eddie Condon Orchestra | 78 | Decca 27408 | 50-10 |
| Scott, James | Neville Dickie | LP | (England) Saydisc SDL-118 | 1966 |
| | Dukes of Dixieland | LP | Audio Fidelity AF1928, AF-5928 | 1959 |
| | John Jensen | LP | Genesis GS-1044 | 1974 |
| | Dink Johnson | 78 | American Music 515 | 46-3 |
| | Frank Johnson JB | 7"LP | (Australia) Swaggie JCS-3372 | 52-2 |
| | Jazzou Jones | LP | High Water 101 | 1983 |
| | Vladimir Klusak | LP | (Czechoslovakia) Supraphon 1115.1965 | 1976 |
| | Lawson–Haggart JB | LP | Decca DL-8199 | 1954 |
| | London Ragtime Orchestra | LP | GHB 199 | 87-2 |
| | Bill Mitchell | LP | Ethelyn 1750 | 1972 |
| | Max Morath | LP | Vanguard VSD-39/40 | 1967 |
| | Turk Murphy | LP | Atlantic 1613 | 71-9 |
| | Roland Nadeau | LP | VQR 2625 | 1979 |
| | New England Conservatory Ensemble | LP | Golden Crest 31042 | 1975 |
| | New Orleans Ragtime Orchestra | LP | Pearl 7 | 67-9 |
| | New Orleans Ragtime Orchestra | LP | Vanguard VSD-69/70 | 1971 |
| | Keith Nichols | LP | (England) EMI One Up-2035 | 1974 |
| | Parenti's Ragtime Band | 78 | Circle 1030 | 47-11 |
| | Knocky Parker | LP | Audiophile AP-76/77 | 1962 |
| | Knocky Parker | 78 | Paradox 8 | 49-4 |
| | Knocky Parker & Bill Coffman | LP | Jazzology JCE-81 | r.1979 |
| | Bent Persson JB | LP | (Sweden) Kenneth KS-2046 | 85-7 |
| | Phoenix Ragtime Ensemble | LP | World Jazz 12 | |
| | Piano Roll | LP | Biograph 1016Q | 77-6 |
| | Piano Roll | 78 | Century 4022 | |
| | Piano Roll | LP | Sounds 1201 | |
| | Cesare Poggi | LP | (Italy) Dire FO-344 | 1979 |
| | Ralph Sutton | 78 | Down Home 10 | 49-11 |
| | Fred Van Eps w/Frank Banta | 78 | Pathe 021088 | 23-9 |
| | Fred Van Eps w/John F. Burkhardt | 78 | Edison 51324 | 24-2 |
| | Terry Waldo's Syncopators | LP | Stomp Off 1032 | 81-6 |
| | Ron Weatherburn | LP | (England) Rediffusion 0100170 | 74-3 |
| | Leo Wijnkamp | LP | Kicking Mule 100 | 1972 |
| | Richard Zimmerman | LP | Murray Hill 60556/5 | 1981 |
| GRAMOPHONE RAG | | | | |
| Daily, Pete & Esterhahl, Lennie | Pete Daily's Dixieland Band | 78 | Capitol 2302 | 51-5 |
| GRANDPA'S SPELLS | | | | |
| Morton, Jelly Roll | Pete Allen | LP | (England) ARB 831 | 83-10 |
| | Burt Bales | LP | Euphonic 1210 | 1957 |
| | Len Barnard | LP | (Australia) Swaggie S-1222 | 54-1 |
| | Barrelhouse JB | | (Germany) Intercord 145038 | 1980 |
| | Acker Bilk JB | LP | (England) Col. 33SX-1456 | 62-6 |
| | Black Bottom Stompers | LP | (England) Sunshine SM-5 | 1977 |
| | Harry Blons Band | LP | Audiophile XL-329 | 1955 |

| Composition | Performer | Record Speed | Record Company/No. | Year-Month |
|---|---|---|---|---|
| GRANDPA'S SPELLS (continued) | Hans-Jergen Bock | LP | (Germany) Intercord 28535 | 1973 |
| Morton, Jelly Roll | Boll Weevil JB | LP | GHB 34 | 1964 |
| | Canadian Brass | LP | RCA XRL1-3212 | 1979 |
| | Joe "Fingers" Carr's Brass Band | LP | Warner Bros. W-1456 | 1962 |
| | Max Collie's Rhythm Aces | LP | (England) Reality R-105 | 1971 |
| | Graham Coyle | EP | (Australia) Swaggie 4507 | 55-12 |
| | Charles Creath's Jazz-O-Maniacs | 78 | Okeh 8257 | 25-11 |
| | Devil Mountain JB | LP | Jazznut 707 | 1983 |
| | Dixieland Rhythm Kings | LP | Red Onion 1 | 1968 |
| | Dukes of Dixieland | LP | Audio Fidelity AF-1928, AF-5928 | 1959 |
| | Pee Wee Erwin Dixieland Band | LP | United Artists UAL-4010 | 58-10 |
| | European Classic Jazzband | LP | Stomp Off 1070 | 83-12 |
| | Doc Evans JB | LP | Audiophile XL-329 | 1955 |
| | Fenix JB | LP | Stomp Off 1129 | c.1986 |
| | Bob Greene & Peruna JB | LP | Fat Cat's Jazz 139 | 72-1 |
| | Bob Greene's Red Hot Peppers | LP | RCA ARL1-0504 | 1973 |
| | Marvin Hamlisch | LP | MCA 2115 | 1974 |
| | Lance Harrison Band | 10"LP | (Canada) CBC RM-50 | 61-11 |
| | Paul Hersh & David Montgomery | LP | RCA Victor ARL1-0364 | 1974 |
| | Art Hodes | LP | (Denmark) Storyville SLP-221 | 1970 |
| | Art Hodes | LP | Euphonic 1207 | 72-4 |
| | Art Hodes Band | EP | EmArcy EP1-6004 | 54-4 |
| | Armand Hug | LP | (Australia) Swaggie 1365 | 1975 |
| | Dick Hyman Band | LP | Smithsonian N-006 | 78-2 |
| | Dick Hyman Orchestra | LP | Col. M-32587 | 73-12 |
| | Ken Ingram Syncopators | LP | (England) Stomp ROBB-006 | 71-6 |
| | Jazz O'Maniacs | LP | (Germany) Teldec 22634 | 1980 |
| | Merle Koch | LP | Carnival 102 | 1959 |
| | Merle Koch | LP | Jump J-12 | 83-1 |
| | David Laibman | LP | Kicking Mule 107 | r.1976 |
| | Lawson–Haggart JB | LP | Decca DL-8182 | c.1954 |
| | Claude Luter Quartet | LP | (France) Vogue LDA-20228 | 1976 |
| | Rod Mason's Hot Seven | LP | (England) Black Lion 51114 | 86-4 |
| | Merseysippi JB | EP | (England) Esquire EP-130 | 55-6 |
| | Minstrels of Annie Street | LP | (Holland) Spronk 52735 | 1980 |
| | Bill Mitchell | LP | Euphonic 1203 | 1962 |
| | Jelly Roll Morton | 78 | Gennett 5218 | 23-7 |
| | Jelly Roll Morton & Red Hot Peppers | 78 | Victor 20431 | 26-12 |
| | Jelly Roll Morton Piano Roll | LP | Biograph 1004Q | 24-9 |
| | Turk Murphy Band | 78 | Good Time Jazz 8 | 49-5 |
| | Natural Gas JB | LP | NGJB 2 | 77-5 |
| | New Black Eagle JB | LP | (Holland) Philips 9198.784 | 78-1 |
| | New Bull Moose Party Band | LP | Antler 8356-1 | 80-8 |
| | New England Conservatory Ensemble | LP | Golden Crest 31042 | 1975 |
| | New Orleans Jazz Party Band | LP | (England) Rarities 62 | 58-8 |

| Composition | Performer | Record Speed | Record Company/No. | Year-Month |
|---|---|---|---|---|
| GRANDPA'S SPELLS (continued) | Original Salty Dogs | LP | (Australia) Jazz & Jazz 6437128 | 79-6 |
| Morton, Jelly Roll | Paramount JB | 10"LP | (Australia) Par. PMDO-7507 | 56-1 |
| | Knocky Parker | LP | Audiophile AP-102 | |
| | Knocky Parker | LP | (England) London HA-U2008 | 52-4 |
| | Knocky Parker | 78 | Paradox 7 | 49-5 |
| | Knocky Parker Trio | LP | GHB 19 | 1949 |
| | Bent Persson JB | LP | (Sweden) Kenneth KS-2046 | 83-10 |
| | Peruna Jazzmen | LP | Fat Cat's Jazz 139 | 72-1 |
| | Polites–Coyle Jelly Rollers | LP | (Australia) Col. 330SX-7618 | 58-12 |
| | Queen City Ragtime Ensemble | LP | Stomp Off 1138 | 1986 |
| | Ragtime Specht Groove | LP | (Germany) Intercord 130005 | c.1973 |
| | Billy Rowland | LP | RCA Victor LPM-1872 | 1958 |
| | Duncan Swift | LP | (England) Black Lion 12123 | 69-8 |
| | Swingle II | LP | Col. PC-34194 | 1975 |
| | Uptown Lowdown JB | LP | Stomp Off 1030 | 81-10 |
| | Verinary Street JB | LP | (Switzerland) Elite Special 30220 | 1988 |
| | Westend Stompers | LP | (England) Sweet & Country 083 | 78-8 |
| GRANDPA'S STOMP | | | | |
| Campbell, Brun | Brun Campbell | LP | Euphonic 1202 | 1947 |
| | Brun Campbell | 78 | Echoes 1 | |
| GREAT SCOTT RAG | | | | |
| Scott, James | John Arpin | LP | (Canada) Scroll 101 | 1965 |
| | William Bolcom | LP | Nonesuch 71299 | 1974 |
| | Bill Coffman & Kathy Craig | LP | OTMH 101 | r. 1980 |
| | Morton Gunnar Larsen | LP | (Norway) Flower 439 | 75-11 |
| | Knocky Parker | LP | Audiophile AP-76/77 | 1962 |
| | Piano Roll | LP | Biograph 1016Q | |
| | Fred Sokolow | LP | Kicking Mule 212 | c. 1982 |
| GREEN LIGHT RAG | | | | |
| Daily, Pete & McHargue, Rosy | Pete Daily's Dixieland Band | 78 | Capitol 57-728 | 49-3 |
| GREENWICH WITCH | | | | |
| Confrey, Zez | Ray Allen | 78 | (Germany) Vox 06217 | 24-5 |
| | Zez Confrey | 78 | Brunswick 2167 | r. 22-3 |
| | Zez Confrey | 78 | Emerson 10523 | 22-2 |
| | Stanley C. Holt | 78 | (England) Homochord H-406 | 23-3 |
| | John Jensen | LP | Genesis 1051 | 1974 |
| | Isham Jones Orchestra | 78 | Brunswick 2365 | r. 23-1 |
| | Milton Kaye | LP | Golden Crest 31040 | 1974 |
| | Arthur Kleiner | LP | Golden Crest 2004 | c.1967 |
| | Bill Krenz | 78 | MGM 30705 | 52- |
| | Percival Mackey Orchestra | 78 | (England) Columbia 3230 | 23-1 |
| | Isadore Maurice | 78 | (England) Aco G-15190 | 23-2 |
| | Russ Morgan & Eddie Wilser | 78 | Decca 30615 | 58-2 |
| | Vi Palmer (Zez Confrey) | 78 | Banner 2059 | 22-2 |
| | Ernest L. Stevens | 78 | Edison 51209 | r.23-10 |
| | Ray Turner | 78 | Capitol 2097 | 52-3 |
| | Frank Westphal & Orchestra | 78 | Columbia A-3786 | 22-12 |

| Composition | Performer | Record Speed | Record Company/No. | Year-Month |
|---|---|---|---|---|
| THE GRIZZLY | | | | |
| Roth-Roberts, arr. | Pryor's Band | 78 | Victor 17111 | 12-4 |
| GRIZZLY BEAR RAG | | | | |
| Botsford, George | Alexander's Jazz Band | 78 | Trilon 222 | 47-12 |
| | Appollo Military Band | 78 | (England) Appollo 10001 | 13-4 |
| | Ballyhooligans (m) | 78 | (England) HMV BD-5131 | 36-10 |
| | Black Diamonds Band | 78 | (England) Zonophone 801 | 11-8 |
| | Teresa Brewer | 78 | London 794 | |
| | Jack Charman w/ Olly Oakley | 78 | (England) Edison Bell Winner 2142 | 12-5 |
| | Chrysanthemum Ragtime Band | LP | Stomp Off 1168 | 1987 |
| | Arthur Collins & Orchestra | 78 | Sonora 5051 | r. 10-9 |
| | Arthur Collins | 78 | Columbia A-844 | |
| | Gottlieb's Orchestra | 78 | (England) HMV B-134 | 11-10 |
| | Irish Guards Band | 78 | (England) Da Capo 446 | 12-9 |
| | Max Morath | LP | Epic LN-24066 | 1963 |
| | Billy Murray & American Quartet | 78 | Victor 16681 | 10-11 |
| | Piano Roll | LP | (England) Saydisc 132 | |
| | Piano Roll | 10″LP | Riverside RLP-1025 | |
| | Pryor's Band | 78 | Victor 5802 | 10-9 |
| | Red Wing Blackbirds | | Stomp Off 1018 | 1981 |
| | Wally Rose | LP | Columbia CL-782 | 1955 |
| | Royal Court Orchestra | LP | (England) Edison Bell Winner 2136 | 12- |
| | Royal Military Band | 78 | (England) Diploma A-61 | 13-2 |
| | Royal Victory Band | 78 | (England) Victory A-18 | 22-11 |
| | Tanz Palast Orchestra | 78 | (Germany) Grammophon 12489 | 14- |
| | Ton Van Bergeyk | LP | Kicking Mule 114 | r.1976 |
| | Mark Wetch | LP | Wilson Audio 808 | 1980 |
| | Albert White Orchestra | LP | Fantasy 3292 | |
| GULBRANSON RAG | | | | |
| Willet, Herb | Piano Roll | LP | Herwin 407 | |
| GUT STOMP | | | | |
| Johnson, James P. & Smith, Willie the Lion | James P. Johnson | 12″78 | Blue Note 24 | 43-11 |
| HALLEY'S COMET RAG | | | | |
| Lincoln, Harry J. | St. Louis Ragtimers | LP | Ragophile 007 | 1986 |
| HAM AND! | | | | |
| Marshall, Arthur | Elite Synocopators | LP | Jazzology 102 | r.1989 |
| | John Hancock | LP | Stomp Off 1025 | 1982 |
| | Milton Kaye | LP | Golden Crest 31032 | 1974 |
| | Knocky Parker | LP | Audiophile AP-91 | |
| | Trebor Tichenor | LP | (Canada) Scroll 102 | 1966 |
| HAM BONES | | | | |
| Denney, Homer | John Hancock | LP | Stomp Off 1025 | 1982 |
| HAM TROMBONE | | | | |
| Fillmore, Henry | Spokane Falls Brass Band | LP | Folkways FTS-32325 | 83-12 |

| Composition | Performer | Record Speed | Record Company/No. | Year- Month |
|---|---|---|---|---|
| HAMPSTEAD HUNCH | | | | |
| Foxley, Ray | Ray Foxley Trio | 78 | (England) Tempo A-118 | 55- |
| HANDFUL OF KEYS | | | | |
| Waller, Thomas | John Arpin | LP | (Canada) Harmony 6026 | 1970 |
| | Canadian Brass | LP | RCA XRL1-3212 | 1979 |
| | Judy Carmichael | LP | Progressive 7065 | 1980 |
| | Eddie Condon Orchestra (m) | LP | Queen 031 | 49-5 |
| | Martha Davis & Spouse | LP | ABC-Paramount 213 | c. 1959 |
| | Frank Denke | LP | Doric 1408 | 1976 |
| | Neville Dickie | LP | (England) Col. SCX-6445 | 1970 |
| | Hank Duncan | LP | (England) Pianola BS-6913 | |
| | Hank Duncan | LP | (Switzerland) Ri Disc 4 | c. 1948 |
| | Don Ewell | LP | (England) 77 SEU-12/42 | 71-2 |
| | Don Ewell | LP | Stomp Off 1077 | 1957 |
| | Don Ewell (m) | LP | Pumpkin 120 | 66-12 |
| | Don Ewell & Dick Wellstood | LP | Fat Cat's Jazz 218 | 79-12 |
| | Henry "Thins" Francis | LP | Mephistopheles 101 | c. 1984 |
| | Benny Goodman Quartet | 78 | Victor 25705 | 37-7 |
| | Bobby Henderson | LP | Vanguard VRS-8511 | 56-11 |
| | Mark Hess | LP | American Jazz 123 | 1975 |
| | Gene Krupa Orchestra | 78 | Victor 20-3734 | 50-3 |
| | Humphrey Lyttelton Band | 78 | (England) Par. MD-1035 | 55-10 |
| | Red Roseland Cornpickers | LP | Stomp Off 1133 | 86-3 |
| | Smithsonian Jazz Ensemble | LP | Smithsonian 21 | 1979 |
| | Ralph Sutton | LP | (Holland) Riff 659.009 | 75-10 |
| | Duncan Swift | LP | (England) Big Bear 28 | 88-3 |
| | Jack Teagarden Sextet | LP | Roulette R-25243 | 61-2 |
| | Fats Waller | LP | RCA Victor LPV-543 | 35-3 |
| | Fats Waller | 78 | Victor V-38508 | 29-3 |
| | Dick Wellstood | LP | Chiaroscuro 109 | 70-11 |
| | Dick Wellstood | LP | (Germany) MRC 006-32-859 | 77-1 |
| | Dick Wellstood | LP | Smithsonian N-021 | 79-6 |
| | Teddy Wilson | LP | (England) Black Lion BLP-30156 | 74-1 |
| HAPPY RAG | | | | |
| Gradi, R. G. | George Bruns Jazz Band | LP | Disneyland WDL-3009 | 1957 |
| | Neville Dickie | LP | Stomp Off 1096 | 83-4 |
| HARLEM RAG | | | | |
| Turpin, Tom | Albion JB | LP | Stomp Off 1206 | 90-3 |
| | Chris Barber JB | LP | (England) Black Lion 57007 | 1980 |
| | Eric Brooks | 78 | (England) Poydras 16 | 50- |
| | Cave Stompers | EP | (Sweden) Storyville SEP-519 | 1962 |
| | Ann Charters | LP | Folkways FG-3563 | 1961 |
| | Steen Christensen | LP | (Denmark) LB 1 | 1972 |
| | Bill Coffman & Kathy Craig | LP | OTMH 101 | r.1980 |
| | Ken Colyer's Jazzmen | 78 | (England) Decca F-10241 | 53-11 |
| | Ken Colyer's Jazzmen | LP | (England) Joy S-194 | 1974 |

| Composition | Performer | Record Speed | Record Company/No. | Year-Month |
|---|---|---|---|---|
| HARLEM RAG (continued) | Ken Colyer's Jazzmen | 10"LP | Decca FL-1152 | 1953 |
| Turpin, Tom | Concert Arban | LP | (France) Arion 33786 | 1985 |
| | Dave Jasen | LP | Blue Goose 3002 | 1974 |
| | Milton Kaye | LP | Golden Crest 31032 | 1974 |
| | Midge Town JB | EP | (Holland) Cat EP-1 | 66-6 |
| | Turk Murphy JB | LP | Merry Makers 106 | 71-8 |
| | Turk Murphy JB | LP | GHB 93 | 72-4 |
| | New England Conservatory Ensemble | LP | Golden Crest 31042 | 1975 |
| | Wally Rose | LP | Fairmont 102 | 47-8 |
| | Wally Rose | LP | GTJ M-12034 | 58-12 |
| | Wally Rose | 78 | Good Time Jazz 51 | 51-7 |
| | Wally Rose w/YBJB Rhythm | 78 | West Coast 107 | 46-6 |
| | Roger Shields | LP | Turnabout 34579 | 1974 |
| | St. Louis Ragtimers | LP | Ragophile | 1961 |
| | Ralph Sutton | LP | Down Home 4 | 49-11 |
| | Trebor Tichenor | LP | Dirty Shame 2001 | 1973 |
| | Ton Van Bergeyk | LP | Kicking Mule 114 | r.1976 |
| | Zenith Hot Stompers | LP | Stomp Off 1191 | 1988 |
| | Richard Zimmerman | LP | Murray Hill 60556/5 | 1981 |
| | Zinn's Ragtime String Quartet | LP | Music Minus One 13 | 1974 |
| HARLEM STRUT | | | | |
| Johnson, James P. | Claude Bolling | EP | (France) Philips 424292 | 1962 |
| | Neville Dickie | LP | (England) Pizza Express 5507 | 81-3 |
| | Neville Dickie | LP | Stomp Off 1176 | 1988 |
| | Dick Hyman | LP | Project 3 PR-5080 | 1973 |
| | James P. Johnson | 78 | Black Swan 2026 | c. 21-8 |
| | Donald Lambert | LP | IAJRC 23 | c.1962 |
| | Donald Lambert | LP | Pumpkin 110 | c.1961 |
| | Louis Mazetier | LP | Stomp Off 1182 | 88-7 |
| | Wally Rose | LP | Stomp Off 1057 | 1982 |
| | Joe Turner | LP | (France) Black & Blue 33064 | 74-5 |
| | Joe Turner | 78 | (Swiss) Columbia SCMZ-3019 | 50-3 |
| HARMONY RAG | | | | |
| Nichols, Hal G. | Pete Daily's Dixieland Band | 78 | Capitol 1588 | 51-5 |
| | Eddie Erickson and Randy Morris | LP | House of Ragtime 1001 | 1974 |
| | Sexette From Hunger | 78 | MacGregor 1015 | 50- |
| HARPSICHORD RAG | | | | |
| Weed, Buddy | Buddy Weed | 78 | Coral 61404 | 55-3 |
| HAUNTING RAG | | | | |
| Lenzberg, Julius | The Ballyhooligans (m) | 78 | (England) HMV BD-5131 | 36-10 |
| | Vic Filmer | LP | Jazzology 58 | 1970 |
| | Mandell Novelty Concert Band | LP | Reader's Digest RDA-70-01-05 | 1968 |
| | Red Wing Blackbirds | LP | Stomp Off 1018 | 1981 |
| | Harry Roy Orchestra (m) | 78 | (England) Parlophone F-338 | 35-11 |
| | Fred Van Eps | 78 | Rex 5044 | |
| | Victor Military Band | 78 | Victor 17319 | 13-3 |

| Composition | Performer | Record Speed | Record Company/No. | Year-Month |
|---|---|---|---|---|
| **HEEBIE JEEBIES** | | | | |
| Reser, Harry | Howard Alden | LP | Stomp Off 1200 | 1988 |
| | Harry Reser | 78 | Columbia 409-D | 25-6 |
| | Harry Reser | 78 | Edison 52269 | r. 28-5 |
| | Harry Reser | 78 | Vocalion 15136 | r. 25-11 |
| **HELIOTROPE BOUQUET** | | | | |
| Joplin, Scott & Chauvin, Louis | Marc Bercovic | LP | (France) Promophone ROM-1 | 1973 |
| | William Bolcom | LP | Nonesuch 71257 | 1971 |
| | Ann Charters | LP | Portents 1 | 1958 |
| | Ken Colyer's Jazzmen | EP | (England) Decca DFE-6466 | 1958 |
| | Ken Colyer's Jazzmen | LP | (England) Joy S-194 | 1971 |
| | Brian Dykstra | LP | Advent 5021 | 1976 |
| | Chuck Folds | LP | Jazzways 106/4 | 1974 |
| | Ray Foxley Trio | EP | (England) Tempo EXA-24 | 1955 |
| | Bob Greene | LP | ABC AA-1076 | c. 1978 |
| | Marvin Hamlisch | LP | MCA 2115 | 1974 |
| | Steve Hancoff | LP | Dirty Shame 4553 | 1977 |
| | Armand Hug | LP | (Australia) Swaggie 1361 | 75-2 |
| | Armand Hug | 10"LP | Circle L-411 | 1951 |
| | Dick Hyman | LP | RCA CRL5-1106 | 1975 |
| | Dave Jasen | LP | Euphonic ESR-1206 | 1966 |
| | Glenn Jenks | LP | Bonnie Banks 103 | 1983 |
| | Milton Kaye | LP | Golden Crest 31032 | 1974 |
| | Morton Gunnar Larsen | LP | (Sweden) Sonet SLP-1450 | 1978 |
| | Paul Lolax | LP | Titanaic 13 | r. 1981 |
| | Max Morath | LP | Vanguard VSD-79391 | 1977 |
| | New England Conservatory Ensemble | LP | Golden Crest 31042 | 1975 |
| | New Orleans Ragtime Orchestra | LP | ABC AA-1076 | 1977 |
| | Knocky Parker | LP | Audiophile AP-28 | 1956 |
| | Knocky Parker | LP | Audiophile AP-71/72 | 1960 |
| | Knocky Parker & Bill Coffman | LP | Jazzology JCE-81 | r. 1979 |
| | Piano Roll | | Biograph 1014Q | |
| | Cesare Poggi | LP | (Italy) Dire FO-357 | 79-7 |
| | Queen City Ragtime Ensemble | LP | Zeno 99 | 1976 |
| | Ragtime Banjo Commission | LP | GHB 154 | 80-8 |
| | Ragtime Society of Frankfurt | LP | (Germany) Joke JLP-205 | 78-2 |
| | William Neil Roberts | LP | Klavier 510 | 1972 |
| | Lalo Schifrin Orchestra | 45 | MCA 52175 | 1982 |
| | Yannick Singery | LP | (France) Swing SLD-928 | c. 1975 |
| | Southland Stingers | LP | Angel SDS-36078 | 1974 |
| | Lee Stafford | 78 | Castle 10 | 50-1 |
| | Chris Stone | LP | ABC 823 | 1974 |
| | Duncan Swift | LP | (England) Black Lion 12123 | 69-8 |
| | Swingle II | LP | Col. PC-34194 | 1975 |
| | James Tyler Orchestra | LP | Desto 7181 | 1979 |
| | Ron Weatherburn | LP | (England) Rediffusion 0100170 | 74-3 |
| | Zenith Hot Stompers | LP | Stomp Off 1191 | 1988 |
| | Dick Zimmerman | LP | Murray Hill 931079 | 1974 |
| | Zinn's Ragtime String Quartet | LP | Music Minus One 13 | 1974 |

| Composition | Performer | Record Speed | Record Company/No. | Year-Month |
|---|---|---|---|---|
| HEY, TAXI | | | | |
| De Bie, Ivon | Leroy Holmes & Tug Boat Eight | 78 | MGM 12408 | 56-12 |
| HICKORY SMOKED RAG | | | | |
| Tichenor, Trebor | Trebor Tichenor | LP | Folkways FS-3164 | 1979 |
| HILARITY RAG | | | | |
| Scott, James | Peter Bocage Orchestra | LP | Riverside RLP-379 | 1960 |
| | Dave Brennan JB | LP | (England) VJM LC-12 | 1971 |
| | Eric Brooks | 78 | (England) Poydras 69 | 50- |
| | Ken Colyer's Jazzmen | LP | (England) Col. 33SC-1220 | 1959 |
| | Peter Davis | LP | (England) Saydisc SDL-118 | 1966 |
| | John Jensen | LP | Genesis 1044 | 1974 |
| | Bunk Johnson Band | LP | Col. ML-4802 | 47-12 |
| | London Ragtime Orchestra | LP | GHB 199 | 87-2 |
| | Love–Jiles Ragtime Orchestra | 10″LP | Riverside RLP-9379 | 60-6 |
| | Mandell Novelty Concert Band | LP | Reader's Digest RDA-70-01-05 | 1968 |
| | Max Morath | LP | Vanguard VSD-39-40 | 1967 |
| | Roland Nadeau | LP | VQR 2625 | 1979 |
| | New England Conservatory Ensemble | LP | Golden Crest 31042 | 1975 |
| | Knocky Parker | LP | Audiophile AP-76/77 | 1962 |
| | Piano Roll | LP | Biograph 1016Q | |
| | Piano Roll | 78 | Circle 5003 | |
| | Leo Wijnkamp | LP | Kicking Mule 156 | 78-11 |
| HOBBLE RAG | | | | |
| Morrissey, Will | Wally Rose | LP | Blackbird 12010 | 71-6 |
| HOBO RAG | | | | |
| Yancey, Alonzo | Alonzo Yancey | 78 | Seesion 10-003 | 43-12 |
| HOBSON STREET BLUES | | | | |
| Zurke, Bob | Neville Dickie | LP | (England) Pizza Express 5507 | 81-3 |
| | Ralph Sutton | LP | Roulette R-25232 | c. 1963 |
| | Bob Zurke | LP | MIS 4 | 1937 |
| | Bob Zurke & Delta Rhythm Band | 78 | Victor 26317 | 39-7 |
| HOG MAW STOMP | | | | |
| Waller, Thomas | Thomas Waller | 78 | Victor 21525 | 27-2 |
| HOLD 'ER NEWT | | | | |
| Shaw, Theodore | Theodore Shaw | 78 | Vaughan 825 | 24-4 |
| HOLLYHOCK | | | | |
| Mayerl, Billy | Raie Da Costa | 78 | (England) Parlophone R-189 | 28-7 |
| | Billy Mayerl | 78 | (England) Columbia 4783 | 27-10 |
| | Billy Mayerl (m) | 78 | (England) Columbia FB-1438 | 27-10 |
| | Jack Wilson (m) | 78 | (England) Regal Zonophone MR-1547 | 34-9 |
| HOLY MOSES | | | | |
| Seymour, Cy | Knocky Parker | LP | Audiophile AP-90 | |
| | David Thomas Roberts | LP | Stomp Off 1021 | 1981 |

| Composition | Performer | Record Speed | Record Company/No. | Year-Month |
|---|---|---|---|---|
| HOMESPUN RAG | | | | |
| Allen, Thomas S. | | 78 | Phono Cut 5169 | |
| HONEY RAG | | | | |
| Van Alstyne, Egbert | Neville Dickie | LP | (England) Contour 2870-190 | 1972 |
| | Neville Dickie | LP | Stomp Off 1096 | 83-4 |
| | San Francisco Harry | LP | Fantasy 3270 | 1958 |
| HONEYMOON RAG | | | | |
| Scott, James | John Jensen | LP | Genesis 1044 | 1974 |
| | Knocky Parker | LP | Audiophile AP-76/77 | 1962 |
| | Piano Roll | LP | Biograph 1016Q | |
| HONEYSUCKLE RAG | | | | |
| Botsford, George | Knocky Parker | LP | Audiophile AP-92 | |
| HONKY TONK | | | | |
| Mayerl, Billy | Billy Mayerl | 78 | (England) Columbia 5154 | 28-10 |
| HONKY TONK RAG | | | | |
| Rees | Sid Phillips & Band | 78 | (England) HMV BD-6178 | 54-8 |
| HOOK AND LADDER RAG | | | | |
| Busch, Louis F. | Joe "Fingers" Carr's Ragtime Band | LP | Capitol T-527 | |
| HOOSIER RAG | | | | |
| Jergensen, Sophus | Piano Roll | LP | Indiana Historical Society 1001 | |
| HOOSIER RAG | | | | |
| Niebergall, Julia Lee | Max Morath Band | LP | Vanguard VSD-79402 | 1977 |
| HOP SCOTCH | | | | |
| Cobb, George L. | George Foley | LP | Stomp Off 1088 | 1984 |
| HOR D'OEUVRES | | | | |
| Comer, David | Ambrose & Orchestra | 78 | (England) Decca F-5375 | 33-12 |
| | Joe "Fingers" Carr | LP | Capitol T-345 | c.1952 |
| | Neville Dickie | LP | (England) Major Minor 5054 | 1970 |
| | Marty Grosz's Orphan Newsboys | LP | Stomp Off 1225 | 90-6 |
| | Merle Koch | LP | Carnival 102 | 1959 |
| | Murray's Ragtime Quartet | 78 | (England) Edison Bell Winner 2871 | 15-10 |
| | Murray's Ragtime Trio | 78 | (England) HMV C-399 | 15-4 |
| | Keith Nichols | LP | (England) EMI One-Up-2085 | 1975 |
| | Pathe Dance Orchestra | 78 | (England) Pathe 20986 | 18-10 |
| | Peerless Orchestra | 78 | (England) Zonophone 1485 | 15-3 |
| | Sid Phillips & Orchestra | 78 | (England) HMV BD-6053 | 49-6 |
| | Royal Military Band | 78 | (England) Coliseum 760 | 14-3 |
| | J. H. Squire's Dance Orchestra | 78 | (England) Guardsman 2083 | 19- |
| | Richard Zimmerman | LP | Murray Hill 60556/5 | 1981 |
| HORSESHOE RAG | | | | |
| Niebergall, Julia Lee | Knocky Parker | LP | Audiophile AP-92 | |
| | Wally Rose | LP | Stomp Off 1057 | 1982 |
| | Keith Taylor | LP | Sami 1002 | r. 1984 |

| Composition | Performer | Record Speed | Record Company/No. | Year-Month |
|---|---|---|---|---|
| HOT CABBAGE | | | | |
| Denney, Homer | John Hancock | LP | Stomp Off 1025 | 1982 |
| HOT CHOCOLATE RAG | | | | |
| Franklin, Malvin and Lange, Arthur | Dave Jasen | LP | Blue Goose 3002 | 1974 |
| | Knocky Parker | LP | Audiophile AP-91 | |
| | Pathe Dance Orchestra | 78 | Pathe 5041, 29038 | |
| | Wally Rose | 10"LP | Columbia CL-6260 | 53-5 |
| HOT CINDERS | | | | |
| Lamb, Joseph | Milton Kaye | LP | Golden Crest 4127 | 1974 |
| HOT FINGERS | | | | |
| Gold, Joe | Tony Caramia | LP | Stomp Off 1209 | 1989 |
| HOT FINGERS | | | | |
| Frosini | Frosini | 78 | Decca 211 | 34-9 |
| HOT HANDS | | | | |
| Straight, Charley | George Foley | LP | Stomp Off 1088 | 1984 |
| | Piano Roll | LP | Dot DLP-25321 | |
| HOT HOUSE RAG | | | | |
| Pratt, Paul | Scott Anthony | LP | Dawson & Chambers 001 | 1981 |
| | Chris Barber Jazz Band | LP | (England) Columbia 33SX-1158 | 1959 |
| | John Hasse | LP | Sunflower 501 | 1980 |
| | Max Morath | LP | Vanguard SRV-351 | r.1976 |
| | Red Nichols Five Pennies | LP | Capitol ST-2065 | 63-10 |
| | Wally Rose | 10"LP | Columbia CL-6260 | 53-5 |
| | Wally Rose | LP | Fairmont 102 | 1946 |
| | Wally Rose | LP | Stomp Off 1057 | 1982 |
| | Wally Rose w/ YBJB Rhythm | 78 | Jazz Man 17 | 42-3 |
| | Royal Ballet Orchestra | LP | CRD 1029 | 1976 |
| HOT IVORIES | | | | |
| Sinatra, Ray | Tony Caramia | LP | Stomp Off 1209 | 1989 |
| HOT PIANO | | | | |
| Paques, Jean | Jean Paques | 78 | (England) Edison Bell Radio 804 | 28-1 |
| HOT POTATOES | | | | |
| Busch, Louis F. | Joe "Fingers" Carr (m) | 78 | Capitol 3883 | |
| HOT SCOTCH RAG | | | | |
| Fischler, H. A. | Marc Herouet | LP | (Belgium) Snow LN-1001 | c. 1980 |
| HUGGIN' THE KEYS | | | | |
| Hug, Armand | Armand Hug | LP | (Australia) Swaggie 1361 | 75-2 |
| | Armand Hug | 78 | Capitol 863 | 49-10 |
| | Armand Hug | LP | Dulai 804 | 1968 |
| HUMPTY DUMPTY | | | | |
| Straight, Charley | National Promenade Band | 78 | Edison 50180 | 14-10 |
| | Victor Military Band | 12"78 | Victor 35419 | 14-10 |
| | Tex Wyndham | LP | Yerba Buena Jazz 201 | r. 1989 |

| Composition | Performer | Record Speed | Record Company/No. | Year-Month |
|---|---|---|---|---|
| HUNGARIAN RAG | | | | |
| Lenzberg, Julius | Eubie Blake Trio | 78 | Pathe 20326 | 17-8 |
| | Harry Breuer Orchestra | LP | Audio Fidelity AFSC-5912 | 1960 |
| | Conway's Band | 78 | Victor 17392 | 13-7 |
| | Guido Deiro | 78 | Columbia A-1720 | r. 15-6 |
| | Pietro Deiro | 78 | Victor 17609 | 14-3 |
| | Joe Glover's Cotton Pickers | LP | Epic LN-3581 | |
| | Mayfair Dance Orchestra | 78 | (England) HMV B-216 | 13-10 |
| | New York Military Band | 78 | Edison 50123 | 13-11 |
| | Original Excentric Band | 78 | (Germany) Homocord 15992 | 19-12 |
| | Brooke Pemberton | LP | Warner Brothers W-1235 | 1958 |
| | Prince's Band | 12"78 | Columbia A-5541 | r. 14-5 |
| | Royal Court Orchestra | 78 | (England) Edison Bell Winner 2522 | 14- |
| | Keith Taylor | LP | Sami 1001 | 1974 |
| | Ray Turner | LP | Capitol T-188 | |
| | Richard Zimmerman | LP | Murray Hill 60556/5 | 1981 |
| HUNTING THE BALL | | | | |
| Kortlander, Max | Max Kortlander Piano Roll | LP | Folkways RBF-43 | |
| | Richard Zimmerman | LP | Murray Hill 60556/5 | 1981 |
| HURRICANE RAG | | | | |
| Glover, Joe | Joe Glover's Cotton Pickers | LP | Epic LN-3581 | |
| | Zinn's Ragtime String Quartet | LP | Music Minus One 13 | 1974 |
| HY 'N DRY | | | | |
| Wadsworth, Wheeler & Arden, Victor | All Star Trio | 78 | Victor 18675 | 20-1 |
| HYACINTH RAG | | | | |
| Botsford, George | Colonial Military Band | 78 | Phonocut 5161 | |
| | Dawn of the Century Orchestra | LP | Arcane 602 | 1972 |
| | Knocky Parker | LP | Audiophile AP-92 | |
| HYSTERICS RAG | | | | |
| Biese, Paul and Klickman, Henri | Papa Bue's Jazz Band | LP | (Denmark) Storyville SLP-150 | 61-6 |
| | First Life Guards Band | 78 | (England) Edison Bell Winner 3104 | 16-6 |
| | Merseysippi Jazz Band | 10"LP | (England) Esquire 20-093 | 58-5 |
| | Parenti's Ragtimers | 78 | Circle 1029 | 47-11 |
| | Red Onion Jazz Band | LP | (Australia) Swaggie S-1260 | 69-10 |
| I'M ALABAMA BOUND | | | | |
| Hoffman, Robert | Prince's Band | 78 | Columbia A-901 | 09-11 |
| I'VE GOT MY FINGERS CROSSED | | | | |
| Reinherz, Sid | Sid Reinherz | 78 | Gennett 5439 | 24-4 |
| IN A MIST | | | | |
| Beiderbecke, Bix | Len Barnard JB | LP | (Australia) Swaggie S-1302 | 1968 |
| | Bix Beiderbecke | 78 | Okeh 40916 | 27-9 |
| | Bunny Berigan & Orchestra | 78 | Victor 26123 | 38-11 |

| Composition | Performer | Record Speed | Record Company/No. | Year-Month |
|---|---|---|---|---|
| IN A MIST (continued) | Claude Bolling | LP | (France) CY 733.607 | c. 1980 |
| Beiderbecke, Bix | Dick Cathcart JB | LP | Warner Bros. W-1275 | 1958 |
| | Ry Cooder | LP | Warner Bros. BSK-3197 | 1978 |
| | Lillian Crawford | 78 | Champion 16817 | 34-2 |
| | Sal Franzella Quintet | LP | Blue Heaven 7-701 | c. 1945 |
| | Dave Frishberg | LP | Concord Jazz 37 | 77-1 |
| | Harry Gibson | LP | Jazum 10 | 44-7 |
| | Mel Henke | LP | Contemporary 5003 | 55-10 |
| | Mel Henke | 78 | Vita 5 | 46- |
| | Lou Hooper | LP | (Canada) Radio Canada Int. 380 | 1973 |
| | Armand Hug | LP | Dulai 805 | 1968 |
| | Dick Hyman | LP | Cadence CR-2001 | 1974 |
| | Harry James Orchestra | 78 | Columbia 38902 | 49-12 |
| | Dill Jones | LP | Chiaroscuro 112 | c. 1972 |
| | Frank Mazzola | LP | (Italy) Carosello 21051 | 81-12 |
| | Jimmy McPartland Band | 78 | Prestige 302 | 49-3 |
| | Metropolitan Jazz Octet | 10"LP | Argo LP-659 | 59-8 |
| | Keith Nichols | LP | (England) Col. EMI One Up-2085 | 1975 |
| | Red Norvo | 78 | Brunswick 6906, 8236 | 33-11 |
| | Jess Stacy Trio | 10"LP | Col. CL-6147 | 1950 |
| | Wilbur Stump | LP | B & W 1178 | 1978 |
| | Ralph Sutton | 78 | Commodore 1525 | 50-3 |
| | Ralph Sutton | LP | Project 3 PR-5040 | 69-5 |
| | Ralph Sutton | LP | Roulette R-25232 | 1962 |
| | Swingle II | LP | Col. PC-34194 | 1975 |
| | Tommy Talbert Orchestra | LP | Atlantic 1250 | 1956 |
| | Frankie Trumbauer Orchestra | 78 | Brunswick 6997 | 34-2 |
| | Vintage JB | LP | (Australia) VJS 2 | 78-2 |
| | Ken Werner | LP | Finnadar SR-9019 | 1978 |
| | Bob Wilbur JB | LP | (Italy) RCA PL-74766 | 90-5 |
| IN THE GROOVE | | | | |
| Smith, Willie the Lion | Neville Dickie | LP | Stomp Off 1176 | 1988 |
| INCANDESCENT RAG | | | | |
| Botsford, George | George Foley | LP | Stomp Off 1187 | 1988 |
| IRISH CONFETTI | | | | |
| Cobb, George L. | George Foley | LP | Stomp Off 1088 | 1984 |
| IT'S A PEACH | | | | |
| Franklin, Malvin | Malvin Franklin | 78 | Emerson 7122 | r. 17-2 |
| ITCHING FINGERS | | | | |
| Smeck, Roy | Roy Smeck | 78 | Edison 52287 | 28-6 |
| | Roy Smeck & Art Kahn | 78 | Banner 7097 | 28-2 |
| | Roy Smeck & Art Kahn | 78 | Victor 21277 | 27-6 |
| ITSIT | | | | |
| Straight, Charley | Charley Straight Piano Roll | LP | Folkways RBF-44 | |

| Composition | Performer | Record Speed | Record Company/No. | Year-Month |
|---|---|---|---|---|
| IVORY RAG | | | | |
| Busch, Louis F. & Elliott, Jack | Graeme Bell | EP | (Australia) Magna Sound MEP-11 | 53-6 |
| | Joe "Fingers" Carr | 78 | Capitol 962 | 50-3 |
| | Joe "Fingers" Carr's Swinging Strings | LP | Capitol T-1217 | |
| | Joe "Fingers" Carr & Tiny Little | LP | Coral CRL-7-57444 | 63-7 |
| | Billy Cotton | 78 | London 1128 | |
| | Fernand Coppoeters | LP | (Belgium) Victory 9386 | 1951 |
| | Tiny Little | LP | Brunswick 54030 | |
| | Ivor Moreton & Dave Kaye | 78 | (England) Parlophone F-2468 | 51-1 |
| | Norrie Paramar Orchestra | 78 | (England) Columbia DB-2898 | 51-1 |
| | Sid Phillips & Band | 78 | (England) HMV BD-6100 | 51-6 |
| | Semprini (m) | 78 | (England) HMV B-10123 | 51-1 |
| | Lawrence Welk Orchestra | 78 | Coral 60677 | 52-3 |
| | Kurt Widmann & Orchestra | 78 | (Germany) Odeon 0-28287 | 51-12 |
| J.J.J. | | | | |
| Jordan, Joe | Lois Delano | LP | (Canada) Arpeggio 1205 | 1968 |
| JACK IN THE BOX | | | | |
| Confrey, Zez | Zez Confrey Orchestra (Nat Shilkret Orchestra) | 78 | Victor 21845 | 29-1 |
| | John Jensen | LP | Genesis 1051 | 1974 |
| | Milton Kaye | LP | Golden Crest 31040 | 1974 |
| | Russ Morgan and Eddie Wilser | LP | Decca DL-8746 | 1958 |
| | Arthur Schutt | 78 | Harmony 860 | 28-1 |
| JACK IN THE BOX | | | | |
| Mayerl, Billy | Bidgood & Wendell | 78 | (England) Broadcast 957 | 33-3 |
| | Billy Mayerl | 78 | (England) Columbia 4115 | 26-8 |
| JAMAICA JINGER | | | | |
| Van Alstyne, Egbert | Wally Rose | LP | Blackbird 12007 | 1968 |
| | Wally Rose | LP | Stomp Off 1057 | 1982 |
| JAMES P. AND ME | | | | |
| Parrish, Terry | Elite Syncopators | LP | Jazzology 102 | r. 1989 |
| JAPANESE BREAKDOWN | | | | |
| | Scottdale String Band | 78 | Okeh 45509 | 30-12 |
| JASMINE | | | | |
| Mayerl, Billy | Billy Mayerl | 78 | (England) Columbia 5671 | 29-9 |
| | Jack Wilson (m) | 78 | (England) Regal Zonophone MR-1547 | 34-9 |
| JAY WALK | | | | |
| Confrey, Zez | Zez Confrey Piano Roll | LP | Folkways RF-28 | |
| | John Jensen | LP | Genesis 1051 | 1974 |
| | Milton Kaye | LP | Golden Crest 31040 | 1974 |
| JAZZ MASTER | | | | |
| Mayerl, Billy | Claude Bolling | LP | (France) CY 733.607 | c. 1980 |
| | Billy Mayerl | 78 | (England) HMV B-2131 | 25-8 |
| | Jack Wilson (m) | 78 | (England) Regal Zonophone MR-1547 | 34-9 |

| Composition | Performer | Record Speed | Record Company/No. | Year-Month |
|---|---|---|---|---|
| JAZZ MISTRESS | | | | |
| Mayerl, Billy | Billy Mayerl | 78 | (England) HMV B-2131 | 25-11 |
| JAZZARISTRIX | | | | |
| Mayerl, Billy | Billy Mayerl | 78 | (England) HMV B-2203 | 25-8 |
| JERSEY RAG | | | | |
| Lamb, Joseph | Elite Syncopators | LP | Jazzology 102 | r. 1989 |
| JIM JAMS | | | | |
| Bargy, Roy | John Arpin | LP | Eubie Blake Music 10 | 1976 |
| | Roy Bargy | 78 | Victor 19537 | 24-3 |
| | Roy Bargy Piano Roll | LP | Folkways RF-35 | |
| | The Duchess | 78 | (England) Decca F-10140 | |
| | George Hicks | LP | Folkways FS-3165 | 1983 |
| | Ray Turner | 78 | Capitol 15437 | 50- |
| | Dick Wellstood | LP | Chiaroscuro 139 | 1975 |
| | Dick Wellstood | LP | Fat Cat's Jazz 158 | 74-4 |
| JINGLES | | | | |
| Johnson, James P. | John Gill | LP | Stomp Off 1066 | 1983 |
| | Dick Hyman Band | LP | Columbia M-33706 | 75-5 |
| | James P. Johnson | 78 | Brunswick 4762 | 30-1 |
| | Clarence Williams & Orchestra | 78 | Paramount 12587 | 27-10 |
| JOHNSON RAG | | | | |
| Hall, Guy & Kleinkauf, Henry | Pud Brown JB | LP | Jazzology J-166 | 1988 |
| | Joe "Fingers" Carr's Brass Band | LP | Warner Bros. W-1456 | 1962 |
| | Joe "Fingers" Carr's Ragtime Band | LP | Cap. T-527 | |
| | Larry Clinton Orchestra | 78 | Vic. 26414 | 39-11 |
| | Lee Collins Jazzola Six | LP | (England) Rarities RA-31 | 1953 |
| | Warren Covington Orchestra | LP | Decca DL-4352 | c. 1963 |
| | Peter Daily's Chicagoans | 78 | Cap. 1370 | 50-12 |
| | Gene Dersin Orchestra | 78 | (Belgium) Decca 9155 | 44-4 |
| | Jimmy Dorsey Orchestra | 78 | Col. 38649 | 49-11 |
| | Dukes of Dixieland | LP | Audio Fidelity AF-1928 | 1959 |
| | Hank Duncan | LP | Hot Piano BS-6913 | |
| | Ray Eberle Orchestra | LP | Design DCF-1023 | |
| | Nat Gonella's Georgians | 78 | (England) Col. FB-2638 | 41-5 |
| | Jerry Gray Orchestra | LP | Viking 1013 | c. 1960 |
| | Connie Jones JB | LP | Crescent City LP-1212 | c. 1982 |
| | Nappy Lamare Band | 78 | Dixieland Jubilee 101 | 49-12 |
| | Syd Lawrence Orchestra | LP | (England) Fontana 6438041 | 70-12 |
| | Lawson–Haggart JB | 10″LP | Decca DL-5456 | 53-1 |
| | Geoff Love Ragtime Band | LP | (Canada) Quality 753 | 1974 |
| | Bob Mandell's Wolverines | LP | Reader's Digest RDA-70-01-05 | 1968 |
| | Russ Morgan Orchestra | 78 | Decca 2778 | 39-9 |
| | Albert Nichols Band | 10″LP | (France) Col. FPX-142 | 57-6 |
| | Rune Ofwerman | LP | (Sweden) Sonet SLP-2606 | 77-9 |
| | Oregon JB | LP | OJB 1002 | 64-1 |
| | Original Sloth Band | LP | (Canada) Woodshed 003 | 1974 |

| Composition | Performer | Record Speed | Record Company/No. | Year-Month |
|---|---|---|---|---|
| JOHNSON RAG (continued) | Sid Phillips Band | 10″LP | (England) HMV DLP-1206 | 50-3 |
| Hall, Guy & Kleinkauf, Henry | Red Nichols Five Pennies | LP | Broadway Intermission 130 | 59-8 |
| | Jerry Smith | LP | Ranwood R-8126 | 1974 |
| | Claude Thornhill Orchestra | 78 | Victor 20-3604 | 49-11 |
| | Orchester van t'Hoff | 78 | (Holland) Grammophon 4721 | 41-2 |
| | Richard Zimmerman | LP | Murray Hill 60556/5 | 1981 |
| JOVIAL JASPER | | | | |
| Green, George Hamilton | George Hamilton Green | 78 | Columbia 977-D | 26-1 |
| | Nexus | LP | (Canada) Umbrella 2 | 1976 |
| JOY RAG | | | | |
| Roberts, Jay | Chrysanthemum Ragtime Band | LP | Stomp Off 1196 | 1988 |
| JUBILATION RAG | | | | |
| Bowsher, Stan | Harry Roy Orchestra | 78 | (England) Parlophone F-158 | 35-5 |
| JUBILEE RAG | | | | |
| Atwell, Winifred | Winifred Atwell | 78 | (England) Decca F-9841 | |
| | Geoff Love Ragtime Band | LP | (Canada) Quality 753 | 1974 |
| THE JUGGLER | | | | |
| Groitzsch, G. | Jack Bund Orchestra | 78 | (England) Parlophone R-1364 | 32-10 |
| | Commodore Grand Orchestra | 78 | (England) Regal Zonophone MR-1276 | 34-4 |
| | Charlie Kunz & Tony Blade | 78 | (England) Sterno 1434 | 34- |
| | Ragamuffin Syncopators | 78 | (England) Bosworth 1072 | |
| JUGGLING THE IVORIES | | | | |
| Jentes, Harry | George Foley | LP | Stomp Off 1187 | 1988 |
| JUGGLING THE PIANO | | | | |
| Perry, Sam | Tony Caramia | LP | Stomp Off 1209 | 1989 |
| JUMPING JACK | | | | |
| Bloom, Rube, Seaman, Bernie & Smolev, Marvin | Zez Confrey Orchestra (Nat Shilkret) | 78 | Victor 21845 | 28-12 |
| | Deep River Orchestra | 78 | Perfecct 15030 | 28-8 |
| | Willie Eckstein | 78 | (Canada) Apex 26127 | 28-10 |
| | Sam Lanin Orchestra | 78 | Okeh 41121 | 28-9 |
| | Varsity Four | 78 | Brunswick 4075 | 28-9 |
| JUNGLE TIME | | | | |
| Severin, E. Philip | Piano Roll | 10″LP | Riverside RLP-1025 | |
| | Jack Rummel | LP | Stomp Off 1118 | 1985 |
| JUNK MAN RAG | | | | |
| Roberts, Luckey | T. J. Anderson Orchestra | LP | Smithsonian 001 | 1975 |
| | Concert Arban | LP | (France) Arion 33786 | 1985 |
| | Lionel Belasco | 78 | Victor 67685 | 15-8 |
| | Eubie Blake | LP | Eubie Blake Music 2 | 1971 |
| | Steen Christensen | LP | (Holland) Jazz Crooner 155.771 | 1977 |
| | Hank Duncan | LP | (Switzerland) Ri-Disc 4 | c. 1948 |
| | Vladimir Klusak | LP | (Czechoslovakia) Supraphon 1115.1965 | 1976 |

| Composition | Performer | Record Speed | Record Company/No. | Year-Month |
|---|---|---|---|---|
| JUNK MAN RAG (continued) | Steve Lane's Stompers | LP | (England) 77LEU-12/3 | 61-7 |
| Roberts, Luckey | New Orleans Ragtime Orchestra | LP | Stomp Off 1213 | 1989 |
| | Pathe Dance Orchestra | 78 | Pathe 29050 | |
| | Phoenix Ragtime Ensemble | LP | World Jazz 12 | 77-6 |
| | Luckey Roberts | 78 | Circle 1026 | 46-5 |
| | Wally Rose | LP | Blackbird 12007 | 1968 |
| | Willie the Lion Smith | LP | (England) Black Lion BLP-30123 | 66-11 |
| | Fred Van Eps | 78 | Columbia A-1417 | 13-9 |
| | Victor Dance Orchestra | 12"78 | Victor 35429 | 14-12 |
| | Victor Military Band | 78 | Victor 17489 | 13-11 |
| JUST ASK ME | | | | |
| Hunter, Charles | Tom McDermott | LP | Stomp Off 1024 | 82-1 |
| | Trebor Tichenor | LP | Dirty Shame 2001 | 1973 |
| JUSTIN-TYME | | | | |
| Bargy, Roy | Roy Bargy | 78 | Victor 19537 | 24-3 |
| | Roy Bargy Piano Roll | LP | Folkways RF-35 | |
| KALAMITY KID | | | | |
| Guttenberger, Ferd | Dave Jasen | LP | Conservatory | 82-6 |
| | Dave Jasen | LP | Folkways FG-3561 | 77-6 |
| | Knocky Parker | LP | Audiophile AP-91 | |
| | David Thomas Roberts | LP | Stomp Off 1021 | 1981 |
| | Tex Wyndham | LP | Fat Cat's Jazz 168 | 1975 |
| KANGAROO HOP | | | | |
| Morris, Melville | Prince's Band | 12"78 | Columbia 5738 | 15-10 |
| | Wally Rose | LP | Blackbird 12010 | 71-6 |
| KANSAS CITY RAG | | | | |
| Scott, James | Knocky Parker | LP | Audiophile AP-76/77 | 1962 |
| | Piano Roll | LP | Biograph 1016Q | |
| | Max Morath | LP | Vanguard 79440 | 1981 |
| KANSAS CITY STOMP | | | | |
| Morton, Jelly Roll | John Arpin | LP | (Canada) Scroll 103 | 1966 |
| | Burt Bales | LP | Euphonic 1210 | 1957 |
| | Kenny Ball JB | LP | (England) Pye NJL-42 | 1962 |
| | Len Barnard JB | LP | (Australia) Swaggie S-1221 | 1952 |
| | Len Barnard JB | EP | (Australia) Swaggie S-4507 | 58-12 |
| | Graeme Bell | LP | (Italy) Raretone 5006 | 51-9 |
| | Black Bottom Stompers | LP | (Switzerland) Elite Special SJLP-6328 | 1979 |
| | Hans-Jurgen Bock | LP | (Germany) Intercord 26454 | 1971 |
| | Boll Weevil JB | LP | GHB 33 | 1963 |
| | Eric Brooks | 78 | (England) Poydras 92 | 50- |
| | George Bruns JB | LP | Disneyland WDL-3009 | 1957 |
| | Canal Street JB | LP | (Norway) Herman 1002 | 1979 |
| | Ernie Carson JB | LP | Pearl 4 | 1964 |
| | Castle JB | LP | GTJ L-10030 | 1957 |

| Composition | Performer | Record Speed | Record Company/No. | Year-Month |
|---|---|---|---|---|
| KANSAS CITY STOMP (continued) Morton, Jelly Roll | Castle Jazz Band | 78 | Castle 3 | 48-1 |
| | Graeme Coyle | EP | (Australia) Swaggie 4507 | 55-12 |
| | Hugh Crozier | LP | (England) VJM LC-34 | 1980 |
| | Mike Daniels JB | LP | Stomp Off 1203 | 89-9 |
| | James Dapogny | LP | Smithsonian 003 | 1976 |
| | Eddy Davis | LP | Pa Da 7402 | 1974 |
| | Neville Dickie | LP | Euphonic ESR-1206 | 1966 |
| | Neville Dickie | LP | Stomp Off 1096 | 83-4 |
| | Doktor Jazz & Co. | LP | (Holland) Eurosound ES-46.408 | 79-2 |
| | Dukes of Dixieland | LP | Audio Fidelity AF-1928, 5928 | 1959 |
| | Dutch Swing College Band | LP | (Holland) Philips P-08005 | 56-12 |
| | Pee Wee Erwin Dixieland Band | LP | United Artists UAL-4010 | 58-10 |
| | Doc Evans Band | 10"LP | Audiophile AP-33 | 1956 |
| | Don Ewell | LP | Pumpkin 120 | 66-12 |
| | Fortified Few | LP | (Australia) Jazznote 016 | 76-11 |
| | Ray Foxley & Orchestra | 78 | (England) Tempo A-24 | 49-6 |
| | Frog Island JB | LP | (England) Stomp ROBB-004 | 70-12 |
| | Johnny Gibbs Band | LP | Reader's Digest RDA-70-01-05 | 1968 |
| | Bob Greene w/Peruna JB | LP | Fat Cat's Jazz 139 | 72-1 |
| | Bob Greene's Red Hot Peppers | LP | RCA ARL1-0504 | 1973 |
| | Mike Hallam's Hot Six | LP | (Australia) Janda Jazz 001 | 79-11 |
| | Happy Jazz & Co. | EP | (Germany) Happy Jazz 100 | 70-10 |
| | Hot Frogs | LP | (England) Ribbet 4905 | c. 1980 |
| | Armand Hug | 78 | Good Time Jazz 19 | 50-6 |
| | Dick Hyman | LP | Project 3 PR-5080 | 1973 |
| | Conrad Janis JB | 10"LP | Circle L-404 | 50-11 |
| | Conrad Janis Band | 78 | Circle 1076 | 50-11 |
| | Dink Johnson | LP | Euphonic 1201 | c. 1948 |
| | Deane Kincaide Band | LP | RCA Victor LPM-1325 | 1956 |
| | Merle Koch | LP | Carnival CLP-102 | 1959 |
| | Merle Koch | LP | Jump J-12 | 83-1 |
| | Cy Laurie's Band | 78 | (England) Esquire 10-480 | 55-6 |
| | Lawson–Haggart JB | LP | Decca DL-8182 | 51-6 |
| | Lawson–Haggart Jazz Band | 78 | Decca 27791 | 51-6 |
| | Leicester Jazz Band | 78 | (England) Talent 144 | 49-11 |
| | Rod Mason JB | LP | (England) Black Lion 51114 | 86-4 |
| | Stanley Mendelson | LP | Land O'Jazz 2674 | 74-6 |
| | Merseysippi JB | 10"LP | (England) Esquire 20-088 | 57-8 |
| | Jelly Roll Morton | 78 | Gennett 5218 | 23-7 |
| | Jelly Roll Morton | 12"78 | Circle JM-18/19 | 38-5 |
| | Jelly Roll Morton & Red Hot Peppers | 78 | Victor V-38010 | 28-6 |
| | Turk Murphy JB | LP | Merry Makers 114 | 85-2 |
| | New Orleans Hot Lips Orchestra | LP | (Holland) Megaphone 2008 | 79-6 |
| | New Orleans Seven | EP | (Holland) RCA CID-75175 | 56-1 |
| | New Yankee Rhythm Kings | LP | Stomp Off 1015 | 81-7 |
| | Original Salty Dogs | LP | (Australia) Jazz & Jazz 6437158 | 79-6 |

| Composition | Performer | Record Speed | Record Company/No. | Year-Month |
|---|---|---|---|---|
| KANSAS CITY STOMP | Knocky Parker | LP | Audiophile AP-102 | |
| (continued) | Bent Persson JB | LP | (Sweden) Kenneth KS-2045 | 76-5 |
| Morton, Jelly Roll | Peruna Jazzmen | LP | Fat Cat's Jazz 139 | 72-1 |
| | Peruna Jazzmen | LP | Stomp Off 1105 | 84-8 |
| | Ragtime Specht Groove | LP | (Germany) Intercord 130001 | c.1972 |
| | Charlie Rasch | LP | CK 8301-3900 | 71-8 |
| | Reunion JB | LP | (Holland) Artone 3121 | 67-11 |
| | Riverboat Jazzband | LP | (Holland) Mirasound 5001 | 71-2 |
| | Rivertown JB | EP | (Sweden) Metronome MEP-1732 | 58-10 |
| | David Thomas Roberts | LP | Mardi Gras 1002 | 1978 |
| | Wally Rose | LP | Col. CL-559 | 53-9 |
| | Bob Scobey JB | LP | Victor LPM-2086 | 59-7 |
| | Smith Street JB | LP | Fat Cat's Jazz 211 | 80-12 |
| | South Frisco JB | LP | Stomp Off 1035 | 81-7 |
| | St. Louis Ragtimers | LP | Ragophile | 1961 |
| | Benny Strickler & YBJB | 78 | Good Time Jazz 21 | 42-8 |
| | Wilbur Stump | LP | B & W 1178 | 1978 |
| | Swingle II | LP | Columbia PC-34194 | 1975 |
| | Tennessee Tooters | 78 | Vocalion 15022 | 25-4 |
| | Butch Thompson | LP | Center 9 | 68-6 |
| | Two Beat Stompers | EP | (Germany) Brunswick EPB-10054 | 1956 |
| | Two Beat Stompers | LP | (Germany) Brunswick LPBM-87901 | 56-4 |
| | Vistula River Band | LP | (Poland) Muza SX-2404 | 82-5 |
| | Alex Welsh Dixielanders | 10″ LP | (England) Nixa 516 | 58-2 |
| | George Zack | 78 | Commodore 597 | 44-4 |
| KATER STREET RAG | | | | |
| Moten, Bennie | Dave Carey Band | 78 | (England) Tempo A-122 | 55-7 |
| | Humphrey Lyttelton & Band | 78 | (England) Parlophone R-3734 | 53-6 |
| | Bennie Moten's Kansas City Orchestra | 78 | Okeh 8277 | 25-5 |
| KEE TO KEE RAG | | | | |
| Platzmann, Eugene & Eastwood, Ted | Fred Van Eps & Boudini | 78 | Emerson 7399, 957 | r. 18-9 |
| KEEN KUT-UPS | | | | |
| Muth, Armand | Armand Muth Piano Roll | LP | Herwin 407 | |
| KEEP FINGERING | | | | |
| Smith, Willie the Lion | Neville Dickie | LP | Stomp Off 1176 | 1988 |
| KEEP OFF THE GRASS | | | | |
| Johnson, James P. | William Albright | LP | MHS 4880 | c. 1981 |
| | Eddie Erickson & Randy Morris | LP | House of Ragtime 1001 | 1974 |
| | Stephen Henderson | LP | Euphonic 1226 | c. 1945 |
| | Dick Hyman | LP | Project 3 PR-5080 | 1973 |
| | Dick Hyman & Dick Wellstood | LP | (Canada) Unisson 1006 | 86-7 |
| | Cliff Jackson | LP | Fat Cat's Jazz 107 | 68-11 |
| | James P. Johnson | 78 | Decca 24883 | 44-8 |
| | James P. Johnson | 78 | Okeh 4495 | 21-10 |

| Composition | Performer | Record Speed | Record Company/No. | Year-Month |
|---|---|---|---|---|
| KEEP OFF THE GRASS (continued) Johnson, James P. | Donald Lambert | LP | Pumpkin 104 | 61-3 |
| | Louis Mazetier & Francois Rilhac | LP | Stomp Off 1218 | 89-11 |
| | Willie the Lion Smith | LP | (France) Jazz Odyssey 009 | 72-6 |
| | Butch Thompson | LP | Prairie Home Companion 34817 | 1979 |
| | Jim Turner | LP | Euphonic 1222 | 1981 |
| | Joe Turner | LP | (France) Black & Blue 33064 | 74-5 |
| KEEP YOUR TEMPER Smith, Willie the Lion | Blue Rhythm Orchestra | 78 | Perfect 14545 | 25-11 |
| | Neville Dickie | LP | Stomp Off 1052 | 82-11 |
| | George Foley | LP | Stomp Off 1088 | 1984 |
| | Golf Coast Seven | 78 | Columbia 14107-D | 25-11 |
| | Don Lambert | LP | Pumpkin 110 | c. 1961 |
| | Donald Lambert | LP | IAJRC 23 | c. 1962 |
| | Willie the Lion Smith | LP | (France) Jazz Odyssey 006 | 72-2 |
| | Willie the Lion Smith | LP | RCA Victor LSP-6016 | 67-4 |
| | Ralph Sutton | 78 | Columbia 39457 | 50-7 |
| KEY STONE RAG Anderson, Willie | Tex Wyndham | LP | Yerba Buena Jazz 201 | r. 1989 |
| KEYBOARD KAPERS Steele, Henry | Mario De Pietro | 78 | (England) HMV B-2475 | 27-3 |
| | Henry Steele | 78 | (England) Piccadilly 446 | 29-12 |
| KING OF RAGS Swisher, Sherman | Mario Pezzotta Jazz Band | 78 | (Italy) Fonit 15595 | 57-1 |
| | Pryor's Band | 78 | Victor 5301, 16821 | 07-9 |
| | Sammy Spear Orchestra | LP | Mercury MG-20116 | 1953 |
| | Zonophone Concert Band | 78 | Zonophone 853 | r. 07-10 |
| KING PORTER STOMP Morton, Jelly Roll | Allotria JB | LP | (Germany) Ariola 86561 | 72-11 |
| | Ray Anthony Orchestra | LP | Cap. T-663 | 54-8 |
| | John Arpin | LP | (Canada) Scroll 101 | 1965 |
| | Burt Bales | LP | ABC-Paramount 181 | 1957 |
| | Burt Bales | LP | Cavalier 5007 | 1954 |
| | Burt Bales | LP | Euphonic 1210 | 1957 |
| | Barrelhouse JB | LP | (Germany) Inercord 145038 | 1980 |
| | Count Basie Orchestra | LP | Jazz Archive JA-16 | 1937 |
| | Sidney Bechet & Dutch College Orchestra | 78 | (Holland) Decca M-33199 | 51-5 |
| | Claude Bolling Orchestra | LP | (France) CFD HF-107 | 1957 |
| | Claude Bolling Orchestra | LP | (France) Philips 6332087 | 1972 |
| | Sune Borg | LP | (Sweden) Sumpen SB-1001 | 1977 |
| | Sandy Brown | 78 | (England) S & M | 52-5 |
| | Sandy Brown JB | EP | (England) Esquire EP-28 | 53-7 |
| | Teddy Bunn | 78 | Blue Note 503 | 40-3 |
| | Casa Loma Orchestra | LP | Cap. T-1506 | 1960 |
| | Jo Ann Castle | LP | Reader's Digest RDA-70-01-05 | 1968 |
| | George Cates Orchestra | LP | Dot DLP-3400 | |
| | Ken Colyer's Jazzmen | LP | (England) 77 LEU 12/10 | 1964 |

| Composition | Performer | Record Speed | Record Company/No. | Year-Month |
|---|---|---|---|---|
| KING PORTER STOMP | Chas. Creath's Jazz-O-Maniacs | 78 | Okeh 8210 | 25-3 |
| (continued) | Crescent City JB | LP | (Holland) Crescent City 100180 | 1979 |
| | Bob Crosby Orchestra | 78 | Decca 4390 | 42-1 |
| Morton, Jelly Roll | Dr. Dixie Jazzband | LP | (Italy) Pathos 1980 | 1978 |
| | Mike Daniels JB | LP | (England) Col. 33SX-1256 | 60-3 |
| | Eddy Davis | LP | Pa Da 7402 | 1974 |
| | Doktor Jazz & Co. | LP | (Holland) Kimball 6818.003 | 83-5 |
| | Jimmy Dorsey Orchestra | 78 | Coral 60259 | 43-10 |
| | Al "Spider" Dugan | LP | Warner Bros. W-1329 | 1959 |
| | Dutch Swing College Band | 78 | (Holland) Decca M-33199 | 51-5 |
| | Doc Evans JB | LP | Audiophile AP-68 | 59-8 |
| | Doc Evans JB | LP | Soma MG-101 | 54-2 |
| | Doc Evans Band | 78 | Soma 1025 | |
| | Gil Evans Orchestra | LP | World Pacific 1246 | 58-4 |
| | Don Ewell | LP | Fat Cat's Jazz 194 | 1975 |
| | Buddy Featherstonhaugh Sextet | 78 | (England) HMV B-9361 | 44-1 |
| | Fenix JB | LP | (Argentina) RCA Victor AVS-4671 | 79-11 |
| | Four City Seven Plus One | LP | (Holland) Fontana 63430031 | 72-11 |
| | Dave Frishberg | LP | Concord Jazz 37 | 77-1 |
| | Matt Fuchs | LP | Riverside RLP-12-261 | 57-8 |
| | Benny Goodman & Orchestra | 78 | Columbia 39564 | 51-4 |
| | Benny Goodman & Orchestra | 78 | Victor 25090 | 35-7 |
| | Grant–Lyttelton Band | 78 | (England) Parlophone R-3566 | 52-6 |
| | Bob Greene | LP | ABC AA-1076 | c. 1978 |
| | Bob Greene | LP | (Denmark) Storyville SLP-221 | 70-8 |
| | Harbour JB | LP | (Holland) Imperial 50052-24302 | 70-4 |
| | Herbie Harper Quintet | LP | Archive of Jazz 507 | 1953 |
| | Erskine Hawkins Orchestra | 78 | Bluebird 7839 | 38-9 |
| | Hazy-Gate Bellhops | LP | (Holland) Kimball 6802753/4 | 71-5 |
| | Ted Heath Band | LP | (England) Decca PFS-4357 | 1976 |
| | Fletcher Henderson Orchestra | 78 | Columbia 1543-D | 28-3 |
| | Fletcher Henderson Orchestra | 78 | Okeh 41565 | 32-12 |
| | Fletcher Henderson Orchestra | 78 | Vocalion 2527 | 33-8 |
| | Paul Hersh  David Montgomery | LP | RCA Victor ARL1-0364 | 1974 |
| | Teddy Hill Orchestra | 78 | Bluebird 6988 | 37-5 |
| | Earl Hines Band | LP | (England) Jazz Panorama 7 | 61-7 |
| | Claude Hopkins & Orchestra | 78 | Decca 184 | 34-9 |
| | Hot Owls | LP | (Germany) WAM 5483 | 73-5 |
| | Hot Shots | LP | (Germany) Happy Bird 90123 | 83-4 |
| | Peanuts Hucko Orchestra | 10"LP | Grand Award 33-331 | 1953 |
| | Dick Hyman Band | LP | Smithsonian 006 | 78-2 |
| | Dick Hyman Orchestra | LP | Col. M-32587 | 73-12 |
| | Chuck Israels Orchestra | LP | Chiaroscuro 151 | 1976 |
| | Franz Jackson's All Stars | LP | Riverside RLP-406 | 61-9 |
| | Harry James Orchestra | 78 | Brunswick 8366 | 39-4 |
| | Kansas City Stompers | LP | (Argentina) Opus 20006 | 60-11 |

| Composition | Performer | Record Speed | Record Company/No. | Year-Month |
|---|---|---|---|---|
| KING PORTER STOMP (continued) | King Oliver w/Jelly Roll Morton | 78 | Autograph 617 | 24-12 |
| | Merle Koch | LP | TAB 1006 | |
| Morton, Jelly Roll | Steve Lane's Stompers | EP | (England) VJM VEP-5 | 61-2 |
| | Lanin's Red Heads | 78 | Columbia 327-D | 25-2 |
| | Morton Gunnar Larsen | LP | (Sweden) Sonet SLP-1450 | 78-10 |
| | Lawson–Haggart JB | LP | Decca DL-8182 | 51-6 |
| | Lawson–Haggart Band | 78 | Decca 27788 | 51-6 |
| | Limehouse Seven | LP | (Holland) Cat LP-1 | 72-4 |
| | Lawrence Lucie Combo | LP | Toy T-1005 | c. 1978 |
| | Claude Luter Orchestra | LP | (France) Vogue SLD-804 | 1971 |
| | Manhattan Jazz Septet | LP | Coral CRL-57090 | 56-6 |
| | Rod Mason's Hot Seven | LP | (England) Black Lion 51114 | 86-4 |
| | Jimmy Maxwell Band | LP | Circle CLP-50 | 77-4 |
| | John Mehegan | LP | Perspective PR-1 | 1952 |
| | Merseysippi JB | LP | (England) Ribbet KM-4904 | 79-10 |
| | Metronome All Stars | 78 | Columbia 35389 | 40-2 |
| | Glenn Miller Orchestra | 78 | Bluebird 7853 | 38-9 |
| | Mills Brothers | 78 | Decca 29897 | 56-3 |
| | Merrill Moore | 78 | Capitol 3397 | |
| | Jelly Roll Morton | 12"78 | Circle JM-23/73 | 38-5 |
| | Jelly Roll Morton | 78 | General 4005 | 39-12 |
| | Jelly Roll Morton | 78 | Gennett 5289 | 23-7 |
| | Jelly Roll Morton | 78 | Vocalion 1020 | 26-4 |
| | Jelly Roll Morton Piano Roll | LP | Biograph 1004Q | |
| | Jelly Roll Morton w/Chamber Music Society | LP | (Australia) Swaggie S-1213 | 40-7 |
| | Turk Murphy JB | LP | Motherlode M-0104 | 1964 |
| | Turk Murphy JB | LP | Stomp Off 1155 | 87-1 |
| | New Delta Jazzmen | LP | (England) VJM SLC-28 | 76-8 |
| | New Leviathan Orchestra | LP | Hump 19329 | 1988 |
| | Orpheon Celesta | LP | (France) Manusic LP-2 | c. 1982 |
| | Matty Matlock Paducah Patrol | LP | Warner Bros. W-1202 | 1958 |
| | Knocky Parker | LP | Audiophile AP-103 | |
| | Pasadena Jazz Society | 78 | Tournament 2501 | 46-1 |
| | Leonardo Pederson Band | EP | (Denmark) CSA CEP-103 | 68-6 |
| | Andre Persiany Orchestra | 10"LP | (France) Pathe ST-1042 | 54-6 |
| | Bent Persson JB | LP | (Sweden) Kenneth 2045 | 79-6 |
| | Portena JB | LP | (Argentina) Trova TL-4 | 66-3 |
| | RAI Big Band | LP | (Germany) FMP SAJ-31 | 80-5 |
| | Charlie Rasch | LP | CK 3204 | 73-4 |
| | Red & Brown Brothers | LP | (Holland) Fontana 680500 | 56-12 |
| | Red Hot Hottentots | LP | (Germany) Biton 2104 | 76-8 |
| | Ed Reed's Riverboat Five | LP | Mercury MG-20629 | 61-1 |
| | Trevor Richards Trio | LP | Stomp Off 1222 | 90-6 |
| | Wally Rose | 10"LP | GTJ LP-3 | 53-2 |
| | Wally Rose | LP | GTJ M-12034 | 58-12 |
| | Wally Rose | 78 | Good Time Jazz 28 | 50-6 |

| Composition | Performer | Record Speed | Record Company/No. | Year-Month |
|---|---|---|---|---|
| KING PORTER STOMP (continued) | Harry Roy Orchestra | 78 | (England) Parlophone F-1158 | 37-12 |
| | Pete Rugolo & Orchestra | 78 | Columbia 40519 | 54-4 |
| Morton, Jelly Roll | Santa Maria Band | LP | (Argentina) Redondel SL-10515 | 76-10 |
| | Maxim Saury Band | 10″LP | (France) Vega 16329 | 72-1 |
| | Peter Schilperoort Combo | EP | (Holland) Fontana 463158 | 59-7 |
| | Doc Severinsen Band | LP | Amherst 3311 | 86-8 |
| | Mike Simpson Band | LP | Mercury MG-20697 | 1962 |
| | Zutty Singleton & Orchestra | 78 | Decca 18093 | 40-5 |
| | Jess Stacy Band | LP | Atlantic LP-1225 | 1955 |
| | Rex Stewart JB | 10″LP | Jazztone J-1285 | 57-11 |
| | Storyville Jazzmen | LP | (Australia) World Record Club R-02168 | 74-12 |
| | Johnny Sylvester Orchestra | 78 | Pathe 036211 | 25-2 |
| | Jack Teagarden Orchestra | LP | Bethlehem BCP-32 | 54-11 |
| | Jack Teagarden Orchestra | LP | Period SPL-1110 | 1954 |
| | Butch Thompson | LP | Center 9 | 68-6 |
| | Two Beat Stompers | LP | (Germany) Brunswick LPBM-87901 | 57-2 |
| | Al Turk's Princess Orchestra | 78 | Olympic 1463 | 24-10 |
| | Ton Van Bergeyk | LP | Kicking Mule 114 | r. 1976 |
| | Chick Webb Orchestra | LP | (Germany) Polydor 423248 | 36-2 |
| | Alex Welsh Dixielanders | 10″LP | (England) Nixa 516 | 58-3 |
| | West End JB | LP | Stomp Off 1042 | 82-8 |
| | Teddy Wilson Trio | 10″LP | Col. CL-1442 | 59-12 |
| | Windy City Jazzband | LP | (Holland) Munich BM-150233 | 81-5 |
| KINKLETS | | | | |
| Marshall, Arthur | T.J. Anderson Orchestra | LP | Smithsonian 001 | 1975 |
| | Kid Chapman's JB | LP | (Canada) Allied 14 | 1969 |
| | Max Collie's Rhythm Aces | LP | (Holland) Timeless TTD-504 | 1982 |
| | Ken Colyer's Jazzmen | EP | (England) Decca DFE-6466 | 1958 |
| | Ken Colyer's Jazzmen | LP | (England) Joy S-194 | 1974 |
| | Neville Dickie | LP | Euphonic ESR-1206 | 1966 |
| | Jazzin' Jacks | LP | (Sweden) Four Leaf 5106 | 88-11 |
| | Bunk Johnson Band | LP | Col. ML-4802 | 47-12 |
| | Milton Kaye | LP | Golden Crest 31032 | 1974 |
| | Alain Lesire | LP | (Belgium) Jazz Cats 6983003 | 1982 |
| | London Ragtime Orchestra | LP | GHB 199 | 87-2 |
| | Max Morath | LP | Vanguard SRV-310 | r. 1974 |
| | New Black Eagle JB | LP | Dirty Shame 2002 | 73-6 |
| | New England Conservatory Ensemble | LP | Golden Crest 31042 | 1975 |
| | New Orleans Ragtime Orchestra | LP | Vanguard VSD-69/70 | 1971 |
| | Papa Bue JB | 10″LP | (Denmark) Storyville SLP-121 | 60-5 |
| | Knocky Parker | LP | Audiophile AP-90 | |
| | Ragtime Society of Frankfurt | LP | (Germany) Joke JLP-205 | 78-2 |
| | Ragtime Ensemble of Torino | LP | (Italy) Carosello 20144 | 78-10 |

| Composition | Performer | Record Speed | Record Company/No. | Year-Month |
|---|---|---|---|---|
| KINKLETS (continued) | Ricardo's Jazzmen | LP | (Denmark) EMI C058-39129 | 1971 |
| Marshall, Arthur | Ray Smith | LP | Stomp Off 1012 | 80-11 |
| | Richard Zimmerman | LP | Murray Hill 60556/5 | 1981 |
| KINKY | | | | |
| Bernard, Mike | Prince's Band | 12"78 | Columbia A-5702 | r. 15-8 |
| KISMET RAG | | | | |
| Joplin, Scott and | Ann Charters | LP | Sierra Wave 101 | 1974 |
| Hayden, Scott | Steen Christensen | LP | (Denmark) LBS 1 | 1972 |
| | Dick Hyman | LP | RCA CRL5-1106 | 1975 |
| | Knocky Parker | LP | Audiophile AP-71/72 | 1960 |
| | Piano Roll | LP | Biograph 1010Q | |
| | Piano Roll | LP | Sounds 1201 | |
| | Trebor Tichenor | LP | Dirty Shame 2001 | 1973 |
| | Dick Zimmerman | LP | Murray Hill 931079 | 1974 |
| KITCHEN RAG | | | | |
| Baron | Billy Cotton & Orchestra | 78 | London 1473 | |
| | Sid Phillips & Band | 78 | (England) HMV BD-6149 | 53-8 |
| KITCHEN TOM | | | | |
| Blake, Eubie | Eubie Blake | LP | Columbia C2S-847 | 69-3 |
| | Eubie Blake | LP | Eubie Blake Music 8 | 1974 |
| | Ophelia Ragtime Orchestra | LP | Stomp Off 1108 | 85-2 |
| KITTEN ON THE KEYS | | | | |
| Confrey, Zez | Scott Anthony | LP | Dawson & Chambers 001 | 1981 |
| | Garcia Badenes | 78 | Discolux DF-519 | 32-3 |
| | Frank Banta & Jack Austin | 78 | Columbia A-3687 | 22-7 |
| | Claude Bolling | LP | (France) Philips 70341 | 1966 |
| | Jack Bund & Orchestra | 78 | (England) Parlophone R-1391 | 32-11 |
| | Lou Busch | 78 | Capitol 15436 | |
| | Tony Caramia | LP | Stomp Off 1209 | 1989 |
| | Frankie Carle | 78 | Decca 1740, 25144 | 38-1 |
| | Joe "Fingers" Carr | LP | Cap. T-345 | |
| | Zez Confrey | 78 | Brunswick 2082 | r. 21-4 |
| | Zez Confrey | 78 | Edison 50898 | 22-1 |
| | Zez Confrey | 78 | Emerson 10486 | 21-9 |
| | Zez Confrey | 78 | Arto 9082 | r. 21-10 |
| | Zez Confrey & Orchestra | 78 | Victor 18900 | 22-5 |
| | Zez Confrey & Orchestra | 78 | Victor 20777 | r. 27-8 |
| | J. Lawrence Cook | 78 | Abbey 15021 | |
| | Bill Davies Dixieland Band | 78 | Top Ten 471 | |
| | Neville Dickie | LP | (England) Major Minor 5054 | 1970 |
| | Reginald Dixon | 78 | (England) Columbia FB-3624 | |
| | The Duchess | 78 | London 1338 | |
| | Brian Dykstra | LP | Orion 83449 | 82-7 |
| | Willie Eckstein | 78 | (Canada) Apex 605 | 23-2 |
| | Embassy Dance Orchestra | 78 | (England) Zonophone 2310 | |
| | Bernard Ette & Orchestra | 78 | (Germany) Vox 01502 | 24-4 |

| Composition | Performer | Record Speed | Record Company/No. | Year-Month |
|---|---|---|---|---|
| KITTEN ON THE KEYS (continued) Confrey, Zez | Bernard Ette & Orchestra | 78 | (Germany) Vox 1573 | 24-5 |
| | Carl Fenton Orchestra | 78 | Brunswick 2261 | r. 22-5 |
| | Jack Fina | 78 | Mercury 5047 | 47-2 |
| | George Fishberg | 78 | (England) Edison Bell Winner 3771 | 22-11 |
| | Raymond Fonseque Band | LP | (France) President KVP-231 | 1969 |
| | Stan Freeman | 78 | Rainbow 10009 | |
| | H. B. Headley | 78 | (England) Imperial 1075 | 22- |
| | Armand Hug | LP | Dulai 804 | 1968 |
| | Dick Hyman | LP | Cadence CR-2001 | 1974 |
| | Dick Hyman | LP | RCA XRL1-4746 | 1983 |
| | Herb Inskip | LP | Hi GSR-4147 | 74-10 |
| | Dave Jasen | LP | Blue Goose 3001 | 1972 |
| | John Jensen | LP | Genesis GS-1051 | 1974 |
| | Milton Kaye | LP | Golden Crest 31040 | 1974 |
| | Keyboard Capers | 78 | (Denmark) HMV X-6815 | 1941 |
| | Arthur Kleiner | LP | Golden Crest 2004 | c. 1967 |
| | Paul Kosmala | LP | Mark 5560 | 1979 |
| | Bill Krenz | 78 | MGM 30706 | 52- |
| | Henry Lange | 78 | Pathe 020671 | 21-10 |
| | LeRoy Larson | LP | Banjar 1781 | 1973 |
| | Jimmy Leach & Harry Farmer | 78 | (England) Columbia FB-2850 | |
| | Jimmy Leach & Organolians | 78 | (Italy) Columbia FB-40288 | |
| | Bernie Leighton | LP | Cameo 1005 | c. 1958 |
| | Vincent Lopez | 78 | International 260 | |
| | Vincent Lopez | 78 | Silvertone 46 | |
| | Isadore Maurice | 78 | (England) Aco G-15131 | 22-12 |
| | Lindsay McPhail | 78 | Olympic 18112 | 21-8 |
| | Lindsay McPhail | 78 | Pathe A-20623 | r. 21-10 |
| | Dalton Marshall | 78 | (England) Homochord H-366 | 22-12 |
| | Billy Mayerl & Orchestra | 78 | (England) Decca F-8006 | |
| | Rafael Mendez & Orchestra | 78 | Pan American 112 | 45- |
| | Mister Mystery | LP | (Belgium) Palette MPZ-1003 | 1960 |
| | Ivor Moreton & Dave Kaye (m) | 78 | (England) Parlophone R-1797 | 34-3 |
| | Russ Morgan & Eddie Wilser | LP | Decca DL-8746 | 1958 |
| | Musical Bell Hops | 78 | Jewel 627 | |
| | New England Conservatory Ensemble | LP | Golden Crest 31042 | 1975 |
| | Keith Nichols | LP | (England) EMI OU-2085 | 1975 |
| | Noller–Straub Duo | 78 | Rondo 100 | |
| | Novelty Orchestra | 78 | (England) Decca F-5819 | |
| | Jimmy O'Keefe (1) | 78 | Puritan 11066 | |
| | Jimmy O'Keefe (2) | 78 | Bluebird 20066 | |
| | Okeh Trio | 78 | Okeh 4596 | r. 22-6 |
| | Joe "Fingers" O'Shay | LP | Golden Tone 4009 | c. 1956 |
| | Knuckles O'Toole | LP | Grand Award 33-373 | |
| | Vi Palmer (Zez Confrey) | 78 | Banner 2049 | 21-9 |
| | Harry Parella & Raymond Turner | 78 | (England) HMV B-2322 | 26-4 |

| Composition | Performer | Record Speed | Record Company/No. | Year-Month |
|---|---|---|---|---|
| KITTEN ON THE KEYS (continued) | Brooke Pemberton | LP | Warner Bros. W-1235 | 1958 |
| Confrey, Zez | Sid Phillips & Band | 78 | (England) HMV B-9930 | 50-4 |
| | Cesare Poggi | LP | (Italy) Dire FO-357 | 79-7 |
| | Phillip Porter | 78 | (England) Guardsman 1245 | |
| | Reiser Trio | 78 | Gennett 4906 | r. 22-7 |
| | Harry Robbins | 78 | (England) Columbia FB-1160 | |
| | Savoy Havana Band | 78 | (England) Columbia 3185 | 22-10 |
| | Ervin Schulhoff | 78 | (Czechoslovakia) Polydor 95197 | c. 1925 |
| | Semprini | 78 | (England) HMV B-10078 | |
| | Six Keybroad Kings | 78 | (England) Regal Zonophone MR-1226 | |
| | Freddie Slack Trio | 78 | Decca 4043, 25278 | 41-6 |
| | Freddie Slack & Orchestra | 78 | Capitol 20032, 15155 | 45-2 |
| | Hans Sommer | 78 | (Germany) Star 5998 | 25- |
| | Max Tak | 78 | (Holland) Pathe 30349 | c. 1922 |
| | Keith Taylor | LP | Sami 1001 | 1974 |
| | Three Town Ragtime Quartet | LP | (Holland) Beerendonk 99916 | 1982 |
| | John Scott Trotter Orchestra | 78 | Decca 4216 | 41-7 |
| | Ray Turner | 78 | Capitol 2094 | 52-3 |
| | Two Octaves | 78 | (Australia) Regal G-21397 | 32-5 |
| | Tom Waltham | 78 | (France) Pathe 9609 | 23-10 |
| | Dick Wellstood | LP | Chiaroscuro 109 | 70-11 |
| | Dick Wellstood | LP | Jazzology JCE-73 | 1971 |
| | Jack Wilson (m) | 78 | (England) Regal Zonophone MR-1694 | 1934 |
| | Arthur Young Orchestra | 78 | Decca 1011 | 35-5 |
| | Victor Young Concert Orchestra w/ Ray Turner | 78 | Decca 23952 | 44-10 |
| KLASSICLE RAG | | | | |
| Crabb, C. Duane | Piano Roll | LP | Indiana Historical Society 1001 | |
| KLU LUKUM RAG | | | | |
| Williams, Carl T. & Christopher, Claude P. | Elliott Adams | LP | Stomp Off 1198 | 1988 |
| KNAVE OF DIAMONDS | | | | |
| Steele, Henry | Jack Bund & Orchestra | 78 | (England) Parlophone R-1364 | 32-10 |
| | Bund & Jager | 78 | (Germany) Telefunken A-1386 | 32-12 |
| | Alfredo Campoli & Orchestra | 78 | (England) Decca F-6120 | |
| | H. Robinson Cleaver | 78 | (England) Parlophone F-999 | |
| | Commodore Grand Orchestra | 78 | (England) Regal Zonophone MR-1240 | 34-3 |
| | Pall Mall Revellers | 78 | (England) Bosworth BC-1079 | |
| KNICE AND KNIFTY | | | | |
| Bargy, Roy & Straight, Charley | Roy Bargy | 78 | Victor 18969 | 22-8 |
| | Roy Bargy Piano Roll | LP | Folkways RF-35 | |
| | Willie Eckstein | 78 | Pathe 20944 | r. 23-5 |
| | Fred Steamer | 78 | (Germany) Acme 2060 | 24-11 |
| | Ernest L. Stevens | 78 | Edison 51209 | 23-8 |
| | Charley Straight Piano Roll | LP | Folkways RF-44 | |

| Composition | Performer | Record Speed | Record Company/No. | Year-Month |
|---|---|---|---|---|
| KNOCKOUT DROPS | | | | |
| Klickmann, F. Henri | New Sunshine Jazz Band | LP | Fat Cat's Jazz 115 | 70-6 |
| | Zema Randale Piano Roll | LP | Folkways RBF-50 | |
| | Sammy Spear Orchestra | LP | Mercury MG-20116 | 1953 |
| | Waldo's Ragtime Orchestra | LP | Stomp Off 1007 | 80-10 |
| LASSUS TROMBONE | | | | |
| Fillmore, Henry | Danny Alvin's Band | 78 | Rondo 236 | 50-5 |
| | Harry Blons JB | 10"LP | Audiophile AP-1 | 1950 |
| | Harry Breuer Orchestra | LP | Audio Fidelity DFM-3001 | 1960 |
| | Teddy Buckner JB | 10"LP | Dixieland Jubilee DJ-504 | 1956 |
| | Canadian Brass | LP | (Canada) Boot 3004 | 1974 |
| | Columbia Orchestra | 78 | Columbia A-2825 | 18-9 |
| | Concert Arban | LP | (France) Arion 33786 | 1985 |
| | Ford Dabney's Band | 78 | Aeolian 12119 | 19-2 |
| | Jack Daniels Original Band | LP | Spring Branch 29403 | 81-6 |
| | Dixieland Bear Cats | LP | (France) Riviera R-0039 | c. 1968 |
| | Larry Dubin's Big Muddys | LP | (Canada) Capitol T-6074 | 64-6 |
| | Dukes of Dixieland | LP | Audio Fidelity AF-1851 | 1956 |
| | Pee Wee Erwin JB | 10"LP | Brunswick BL-54011 | 53-9 |
| | Firehouse Five Plus Two | LP | GTJ L-12048 | 62-7 |
| | Raymond Fonseque Band | LP | (France) President KVP-231 | 1969 |
| | Frog Joseph JB | LP | Nobility LP-704 | 64-2 |
| | Charlie Galbraith Band | EP | (England) VJM VEP-8 | c. 1962 |
| | Eddie Howard & Orchestra | 78 | Majestic 1178 | |
| | Eddie Howard & Orchestra | 78 | Mercury 5439 | 47-9 |
| | Pee Wee Hunt Band | LP | Cap. T-312 | 1956 |
| | Franz Jackson's All Stars | LP | Pinnacle 108 | 1966 |
| | Spike Jones & Orchestra | 78 | Victor 20-1983 | 46-5 |
| | Kid Ory JB | LP | Verve MGV-1026 | 60-12 |
| | Kings of Dixieland | LP | Crown 5129 | 59-7 |
| | Mandell Novelty Concert Band | LP | Reader's Digest RDA-70-01-05 | 1968 |
| | Buddy Morrow Orchestra | 78 | Victor 20-4543 | 52-1 |
| | Turk Murphy JB | LP | (Germany) MPS 22097 | 73-6 |
| | Red Nichols Five Pennies | LP | Cap. T-1163 | 58-10 |
| | New Orleans Ragtime Orchestra | LP | (Sweden) Sonet 709 | 76-3 |
| | Ragtime Society of Frankfurt | LP | (Germany) Joke JLP-217 | 81-10 |
| | Salt City Five | 10"LP | Jubilee 13 | 1955 |
| | Maxim Saury Band | EP | (France) Pathe EG-1019 | 1962 |
| | Kirby Stone Quartet | 78 | Coral 61538 | 55-5 |
| | Synco JB | 78 | Pathe 22117 | 19-3 |
| | Trombone Trio | 78 | Tempo 576 | |
| | Trombones Inc. | LP | Warner Bros. WB-1272 | 58-12 |
| | Albert White Orchestra | LP | Barbary Coast SLP-33002 | |
| | Spiegle Willcox Slidemen | LP | Fat Cat's Jazz 196 | 78-12 |
| LAST TRIP DOWN FROM HANNIBAL | | | | |
| Tichenor, Trebor | Trebor Tichenor | LP | Dirty Shame 2001 | 1973 |

| Composition | Performer | Record Speed | Record Company/No. | Year-Month |
|---|---|---|---|---|
| LAUGHING JIM (see THE BLACKTHORNES) | | | | |
| | George Clinton (George Morris) | 78 | (England) Victory 176 | 29-12 |
| LAZY LUKE | | | | |
| Philpot, George | Turk Murphy Jazz Band | LP | Stomp Off 1155 | 87-1 |
| LEICESTER SQUARE RAG | | | | |
| Roy, Harry | Eddie Miller Trio | 78 | Rainbow 140 | |
| | Harry Roy Orchestra | 78 | (England) Decca F-9145 | 49-1 |
| | Harry Roy Orchestra | 78 | (England) Parlophone F-2387 | 49-10 |
| | Three Suns | 78 | Victor 20-3768 | 49-12 |
| LEOLA | | | | |
| Joplin, Scott | John Arpin | LP | (Canada) Scroll 101 | 1965 |
| | Dick Hyman | LP | RCA CRL5-1106 | 1975 |
| | Knocky Parker | LP | Audiophile AP-71/72 | 1960 |
| | Joshua Rifkin | LP | Nonesuch 71264 | 1972 |
| | Charley Thompson | LP | Euphonic 1221 | c. 1960 |
| | Dick Zimmerman | LP | Murray Hill 931079 | 1974 |
| LES COPELAND'S RAG | | | | |
| Copeland, Les | Band (aka 39th Street Rag) | 5"78 | Little Wonder | |
| LET'S TRY IT | | | | |
| Kortlander, Max | Max Kortlander Piano Roll | LP | Folkways RBF-43 | |
| LIGHTNING FINGERS | | | | |
| Light, Ben | Ben Light | 78 | Tempo 684 | |
| LILY QUEEN | | | | |
| Marshall, Arthur | William Bolcom | LP | Music Masters 0149 | 1981 |
| | Ann Charters | LP | Sierra Wave 101 | 1974 |
| | Dick Hyman | LP | RCA CRL5-1106 | 1975 |
| | Keith Nichols | LP | (England) EMI One Up 2035 | 1974 |
| | Knocky Parker | LP | Audiophile AP-71/72 | 1960 |
| | Piano Roll | LP | Biograph 1014Q | |
| | Steve Pistorious | LP | Jazzology JCE-78 | 1975 |
| | William Neil Roberts | LP | Klavier 516 | 1973 |
| | Yannick Singery | LP | (France) Swing SLD-928 | c. 1975 |
| | Southland Stingers | LP | Angel S-36078 | 1974 |
| | Dick Zimmerman | LP | Murray Hill 931079 | 1974 |
| LILY RAG | | | | |
| Thompson, Charles | John Arpin | LP | (Canada) Harmony 6026 | 1970 |
| | George Foley | LP | Stomp Off 1187 | 1988 |
| | Dave Jasen | LP | Euphonic ESR-1206 | 1966 |
| | Keith Nichols | LP | (England) EMI One Up-2035 | 1974 |
| | Ragpickers | 78 | Circle 1056 | 49-1 |
| | Charles Thompson | 78 | American Music 527 | 49-8 |
| | Charles Thompson | LP | Euphonic 1221 | c. 1960 |
| | Charles Thompson | LP | Stereoddities C-1900 | 1962 |
| | Richard Zimmerman | LP | Murray Hill 60556/5 | 1981 |

| Composition | Performer | Record Speed | Record Company/No. | Year-Month |
|---|---|---|---|---|
| LION TAMER RAG | | | | |
|   Janza, Mark | George Hicks | LP | Folkways RF-3165 | 1983 |
| | Daryl Ott | LP | Dirty Shame 1238 | 1978 |
| LIPSTICK | | | | |
|   Rosoff, Charles & Murray, Ted | Lou Calabrese & Band | 78 | Gennett 6421 | 28-3 |
| | Muriel Pollock | 78 | Edison 52267 | 28-4 |
| LITTLE BIT OF RAG | | | | |
|   Pratt, Paul | Piano Roll | LP | Indiana Historical Society 1001 | |
| | Piano Roll | LP | Herwin 407 | |
| LITTLE JACK'S RAG | | | | |
|   Marshall, Arthur | Waldo's Ragtime Orchestra | LP | Stomp Off 1007 | 80-10 |
| LITTLE JOHN'S RAG | | | | |
|   Murphy, Turk | Turk Murphy Band | 78 | Good Time Jazz 45 | 50-5 |
| | Turk Murphy Jazz Band | LP | Atlantic 1613 | 71-9 |
| LITTLE ROCK GETAWAY | | | | |
|   Sullivan, Joe | Harry Blons JB | LP | Zephyr 12008 | 1956 |
| | Sandy Brown | 78 | S & M | 52-5 |
| | Joe "Fingers" Carr & Tiny Little | LP | Coral CRL-57444 | 63-7 |
| | Casa Loma Orchestra | LP | Capitol ST-1506 | 1960 |
| | Dick Cathcart JB | LP | Mercury MG-2009 | 1961 |
| | Eddie Condon Orchestra | LP | Pumpkin 106 | 44-12 |
| | Confederate Colonels of Jazz | LP | Golden Crest 3063 | 59-8 |
| | Bob Crosby Orchestra | LP | Dot DLP-3278 | 60-2 |
| | Bob Crosby Orchestra | 78 | Decca 1552 | 37-11 |
| | Jim Cullen JB | LP | Connecticut Trad Club SLP-18 | 81-6 |
| | Darktown JB | LP | (Germany) DJB 150001 | 80-5 |
| | Frank Denke | LP | Doric 1408 | c. 1976 |
| | Neville Dickie | LP | (England) Major Minor 5054 | 1970 |
| | Pee Wee Erwin JB | 10"LP | Cadence CLP-1011 | 1956 |
| | Don Ewell (m) | LP | Chiaroscuro 106 | 70-8 |
| | Rene Faure & Orchestra | 78 | Varsity 8236 | 40-3 |
| | Pete Fountain JB | LP | Coral CRL-57419 | 59-10 |
| | John Gill | LP | Stomp Off 1066 | 1983 |
| | Joe Glover Cotton Pickers | LP | Epic LN-3581 | |
| | Harry Gold Pieces of Eight | LP | (England) Lake 5011 | 88-5 |
| | Mel Henke | LP | Contemporary 5003 | 55-10 |
| | Mel Henke | 78 | Tempo 1232 | |
| | Hot Cotton JB | LP | GHB 168 | c. 1980 |
| | Armand Hug | LP | (Australia) Swaggie 1361 | 75-2 |
| | Armand Hug | LP | Chiaroscuro CR-112 | c. 1972 |
| | Armand Hug | LP | Dulai 805 | 1968 |
| | Armand Hug | 78 | Okeh 6802 | 50- |
| | Dill Jones | LP | Land O'Jazz 3475 | 75-4 |
| | Dill Jones | 78 | (England) Nixa NJ-2021 | 57-10 |
| | Dill Jones | LP | Keynote 100 | 70-11 |
| | Jeanette Kimball | LP | New Orleans 7208 | 80-2 |

| Composition | Performer | Record Speed | Record Company/No. | Year-Month |
|---|---|---|---|---|
| LITTLE ROCK GETAWAY (continued) | Light Crust Doughboys | 78 | Okeh 06016 | 39-7 |
| Sullivan, Joe | Paul Lingle | LP | Euphonic 1220 | 1951 |
| | Art Maiste | LP | (Canada) RCA CTLM-1085 | 66-11 |
| | Billy Maxted Band | LP | Seeco 458 | 1959 |
| | Hazy Osterwald Orchestra | LP | (Germany) Polydor LPHM-46329 | 58-9 |
| | Matty Matlock Paducah Patrol | LP | Warner Bros. W-1202 | 1958 |
| | Marty Paich Orchestra | LP | RCA Victor LPM-2251 | 60-6 |
| | Singleton Palmer Band | LP | Paddlewheel 001 | c. 1967 |
| | Les Paul | 78 | Capitol 1316 | |
| | Red Onion JB | LP | Biograph 12012 | 69-2 |
| | Maurice Rocco & Orchestra | 78 | Decca 8544 | 41-3 |
| | Saints & Sinners | LP | (Germany) Saba MPS-15174 | 68-4 |
| | Ray Skjelbred | LP | Stomp Off 1097 | 84-8 |
| | June Smalley Quintet | LP | Circle CLP-6 | 80-2 |
| | Joe Sullivan | 78 | Decca 600 | 35-8 |
| | Joe Sullivan | 78 | (England) Parlophone R-2006 | 33-9 |
| | Joe Sullivan | LP | (England) Rarities RA-31 | 1953 |
| | Joe Sullivan Trio | LP | Riverside RLP-12-202 | 1951 |
| | Ralph Sutton Quartet | LP | Chazjazz CJ-102 | 79-10 |
| | Frankie Trumbauer Orchestra | 78 | Varsity 8236 | 40-2 |
| | Ron Weatherburn | LP | (England) Alpha LPX-32 | 62-1 |
| | Bob Zurke | LP | MIS 4 | 1937 |
| LITTLE WABASH SPECIAL | | | | |
| Shea, Tom | David Thomas Roberts | LP | Stomp Off 1132 | 1983 |
| | Tom Shea | LP | Stomp Off 1022 | 1981 |
| LIVE WIRES RAG | | | | |
| Shepherd, Adeline | Knocky Parker | LP | Audiophile AP-92 | |
| THE LIZARD | | | | |
| Bell, Graeme | Graeme Bell & Band | 78 | (Australia) Regal Zonophone G-25115 | 47-4 |
| LOLLY-POPS | | | | |
| Reser, Harry | Howard Alden | LP | Stomp Off 1200 | 1988 |
| | Michael Danzi | 78 | (Germany) Homokord 4-1988 | 26-10 |
| | Michael Danzi | 78 | (Germany) Telefunken A-1660 | 34-6 |
| | Mario De Pietro | 78 | (England) Decca F-1894 | 30-8 |
| | Max Morath Quintet | LP | Normacks 100 | c. 1981 |
| | Michele Ortuso | 78 | (England) HMV B-3651 | 29-11 |
| | Paramount Theatre Orchestra | LP | Stomp Off 1089 | 84-7 |
| | Harry Reser | 78 | Okeh 40092 | 23-12 |
| | Harry Reser | 78 | Paramount 20330 | 24-5 |
| | Harry Reser | 78 | Victor 20439 | 26-10 |
| | Harry Reser | 78 | Edison 52269 | r. 28-5 |
| | Tuxedo Orchestra | 78 | Vocalion 14988 | r. 25-4 |
| LONDON RAG | | | | |
| Jasen, David A. | Dave Jasen | LP | Blue Goose 3001 | 1972 |

| Composition | Performer | Record Speed | Record Company/No. | Year-Month |
|---|---|---|---|---|
| LONG JOHN STOMP | | | | |
| Gold, Harry | Harry Gold's Pieces of Eight | 78 | (England) Decca F-9456 | 50-5 |
| LOONEY LOUIE | | | | |
| Busch, Louis F. | Joe "Fingers" Carr (m) | 78 | Capitol 3883 | |
| LOOSE ELBOWS | | | | |
| Mayerl, Billy | John Arpin | LP | Eubie Blake Music 10 | 1976 |
| | Billy Mayerl | 78 | (England) Columbia 3926 | 26-3 |
| LOOSE FINGERS | | | | |
| Swerdlow, Maurice | Hans Bund & Herbert Jager | 78 | (Germany) Telefunken A-1387 | 33-2 |
| LOOSE FINGERS | | | | |
| Holt, Stanley C. | Stanley C. Holt | 78 | (England) Homochord 425 | 23-2 |
| LOUISIANA GLIDE | | | | |
| Garnett, Blind Leroy | Blind Leroy Garnett | 78 | Paramount 12879 | 29-10 |
| LOUISIANA RAG | | | | |
| Block, Leon | Paul Lingle | LP | Euphonic 1217 | 1951 |
| | Paul Lingle | 78 | Good Time Jazz 88 | 52-2 |
| | Steve Pistorious | LP | Jazzology 78 | 1975 |
| LOUISIANA RAG | | | | |
| Northrup, Theo | Vladimir Klusak | LP | (Czechoslovakia) Supraphon 1115.1965 | 1976 |
| | Richard Zimmerman | LP | Murray Hill 60556/5 | 1981 |
| M. I. STOMP | | | | |
| Dickie, Neville | Neville Dickie | LP | (England) Major Minor SMCP-5039 | 1969 |
| MACADAMIAN SCUFFLE | | | | |
| Jasen, David A. | Dave Jasen | LP | Folkways FG-3561 | 77-6 |
| MAG'S RAG | | | | |
| Shea, Tom | Tom Shea | LP | Stomp Off 1022 | 1981 |
| MAGIC NOTES | | | | |
| Steininger, F. | Deauville Dance Band | 78 | (England) Edison Bell Winner 5415 | 31-11 |
| MAGNETIC RAG | | | | |
| Joplin, Scott | E. Power Biggs | LP | Columbia M-33205 | 1974 |
| | Cave Stompers | LP | (Sweden) Gazell GMG-1252 | 1976 |
| | Ann Charters | LP | Folkways FG-3563 | 1961 |
| | Ann Charters | LP | Sierra Wave 101 | 1974 |
| | Eddy Davis | LP | Pa Da 7401 | 1974 |
| | Brian Dykstra | LP | Century Advent 5075 | 1974 |
| | Raymond Fonseque Band | LP | (France) Promophone 4 | 73-10 |
| | Steve Hancoff | LP | Out of Time 920 | 85-4 |
| | Dick Hyman | LP | RCA CRL5-1106 | 1975 |
| | Scott Joplin Piano Roll | LP | Biograph 1006Q | |
| | Katia & Marielle Labeque | LP | Angel S-37980 | 1982 |
| | David Laibman | LP | Rounder 3040 | r. 1981 |
| | Mimi & Russell | LP | Mumpus 791 | r. 1979 |
| | Max Morath | LP | Vanguard SRV-351 | r. 1976 |

| Composition | Performer | Record Speed | Record Company/No. | Year-Month |
|---|---|---|---|---|
| MAGNETIC RAG (continued) | New England Conservatory Ensemble | LP | Golden Crest 31031 | 1973 |
| Joplin, Scott | New Leviathan Orchestra | LP | Carmel Race 19325 | 1975 |
| | Knocky Parker | LP | Audiophile AP-71/72 | 1960 |
| | Itzak Perlman & Andre Previn | LP | Angel S-37113 | 1975 |
| | Piano Roll | LP | Biograph 1010Q | |
| | Piano Roll | 10″LP | (England) London AL-3542 | |
| | Cesare Poggi | LP | (Italy) Dire FO-344 | 1979 |
| | Joshua Rifkin | LP | Nonesuch 71248 | 1970 |
| | Joshua Rifkin | LP | NYPL SJ | 71-10 |
| | William Neil Roberts | LP | Klavier 516 | 1973 |
| | Eric Rogers | LP | London Phase 4 21105 | 1974 |
| | Yannick Singery | LP | (France) Swing SLD-928 | c. 1975 |
| | Southland Stingers | LP | Angel S-36078 | 1974 |
| | Bob Tryforous | LP | Puritan 5002 | r. 1976 |
| | Terry Waldo | LP | Stomp Off 1002 | 80-7 |
| | Ron Weatherburn | LP | Stomp Off 1107 | 84-10 |
| | Leo Wijnkamp (m) | LP | Kicking Mule 108 | 1974 |
| | Dick Zimmerman | LP | Murray Hill 931079 | 1974 |
| | Paul Zukofsky & Robert Dennis | LP | Vanguard SRV-350 | 1975 |
| MAH JONG | | | | |
| Reinherz, Sid | Bernard Ette & Orchestra | 78 | (Germany) Vox 1772 | 25-4 |
| | Sid Reinherz | 78 | Gennett 5330 | 23-12 |
| MAKE BELIEVE RAG | | | | |
| Jasen, David A. | Dave Jasen | LP | Blue Goose 3001 | 1972 |
| MAMA NITA | | | | |
| Morton, Jelly Roll | Jelly Roll Morton | 12″78 | Circle JM-25 | 38-5 |
| | Jelly Roll Morton | 78 | Gennett 5632 | 24-6 |
| | Jelly Roll Morton | 78 | Paramount 11216 | 24-4 |
| MANDOLIN KING RAG | | | | |
| | Hinsley & Taylor | 78 | Vocalion 02640 | 34-1 |
| | Original Sloth Band | LP | (Canada) Woodshed 003 | 1974 |
| MANDY'S BROADWAY STROLL | | | | |
| Broady, Thomas | David Thomas Roberts | LP | Stomp Off 1132 | 1981 |
| | Trebor Tichenor | LP | Folkways FS-3164 | 1979 |
| MAPLE LEAF RAG | | | | |
| Joplin, Scott | Marden Abadi | LP | Orion 76217 | r. 1977 |
| | Marden Abadi | LP | Sine Qua Non 2020 | c. 1979 |
| | Danny Alvin Band | 78 | Rondo 236 | 50-5 |
| | Scott Anthony | LP | Dawson & Chambers 001 | 1981 |
| | Victor Arden & Phil Ohman | 78 | Victor 22608 | 30-12 |
| | Lil Armstrong | 78 | (France) Vogue 5169 | 53-5 |
| | Marvin Ash | 78 | Capitol 15435 | 49-12 |
| | Winifred Atwell | LP | London LL-1573 | |
| | Burt Bales | LP | Euphonic 1210 | 1957 |
| | Johnny Bastable | LP | (England) Joy 234 | 1972 |
| | Sidney Bechet w/Claude Luter Orchestra | 78 | (France) Vogue 5039 | 49-12 |

| Composition | Performer | Record Speed | Record Company/No. | Year-Month |
|---|---|---|---|---|
| MAPLE LEAF RAG (continued)<br>Joplin, Scott | Sidney Bechet & New Orleans Feetwarmers | 78 | Victor 23360 | 32-9 |
| | Graeme Bell | LP | (Australia) Festival L-45545/6 | 74-8 |
| | Graeme Bell | 78 | (Australia) Swaggie 4 | 50-3 |
| | Graeme Bell | 78 | (Australia) Swaggie 1002 | 50-6 |
| | Graeme Bell | LP | (England) Parlophone PMD-07501 | 53-4 |
| | Graeme Bell & Ragtime 4 | 78 | (Austrialia) Parlophone A-7824 | 53-4 |
| | Roger Bell Band | LP | (Australia) Swaggie S-1351 | 76-6 |
| | Marc Bercovic | LP | (France) Promophone ROM-1 | 1973 |
| | E. Power Biggs | LP | Columbia M-32495 | 1973 |
| | Eubie Blake | LP | 20th Century Fox 3003 | 1958 |
| | Eubie Blake | 10"LP | Circle L-407 | 1951 |
| | Eubie Blake | LP | Columbia C2S-847 | 69-2 |
| | Eubie Blake | LP | Herwin 401 | 1969 |
| | Bluebird Military Band | 78 | Bluebird 3201 | 38-8 |
| | Hans-Jurgen Bock | LP | (Germany) Intercord 26584 | 1975 |
| | William Bolcom | LP | New York Public Library | 1971 |
| | Boll Weevil Jazz Band | LP | GHB-61 | 1970 |
| | Claude Bolling | LP | (France) Philips 70.341 | 1966 |
| | Sune Borg | EP | (Sweden) Efel EF-7201 | 1971 |
| | Sune Borg | 78 | (Sweden) Gazell 3001 | 49-10 |
| | Sune Borg | LP | (Sweden) Sumpen | |
| | Boston Pops | LP | Polydor PD-6033 | 1974 |
| | Dave Brennan Jazz Band | LP | (England) VJM LC-205 | 1973 |
| | Sandy Brown | LP | S & M 1004 | 1952 |
| | Budapest Ragtime Orchestra | 78 | (Czechoslovakia) Krem SLPX-17794 | 1984 |
| | Brun Campbell | 78 | Brun 1 | 52- |
| | Brun Campbell | LP | Euphonic ESR-1201 | 1945-46 |
| | Brun Campbell | 78 | West Coast 112 | 45-6 |
| | Frankie Carle | LP | RCA LPM-2491 | 1962 |
| | Frankie Carle & Orchestra | 78 | Victor 20-3805 | 50-5 |
| | Joe "Fingers" Carr | LP | Capitol T-760 | |
| | Joe "Fingers" Carr & Band | 78 | Capitol 2665 | 53-8 |
| | Joe "Fingers" Carr's Brass Band | LP | Warner Bros. W-1456 | 1962 |
| | Jo Ann Castle | LP | Dot DLP-3249 | |
| | Jo Ann Castle | LP | Reader's Digest RDA-70-01-05 | 1968 |
| | William Cerny | LP | University of Notre Dame | 1975 |
| | Ann Charters | LP | Portents 1 | 1958 |
| | Ken Colyer's Jazzmen | 78 | (England) Columbia DB-4783 | 61-11 |
| | Eddie Condon Orchestra | 78 | Decca 27035 | 50-3 |
| | Corcoro Steel Band | LP | (France) Pragmaphone PRGLP-12 | 1973 |
| | Bob Darch | LP | United Artists UAL-3120 | 1960 |
| | Kenny Davern Trio | LP | Fat Cat's Jazz 207 | 79-12 |
| | Trump Davidson Band | LP | (Canada) Chateau 1009 | 1961 |
| | Rev. Gary Davis | LP | Prestige 14033 | 64-3 |
| | Pete Davis | LP | (England) Saydisc 118 | 1966 |
| | Wild Bill Davison Band | LP | Rarities 35 | 47-4 |

| Composition | Performer | Record Speed | Record Company/No. | Year-Month |
|---|---|---|---|---|
| MAPLE LEAF RAG (continued) | John Deffaray Jazz Band | LP | (England) VJM-7 | c. 1966 |
| Joplin, Scott | Wolff Delbruck | LP | (Germany) Telefunken 28090 | c. 1973 |
| | Neville Dickie | LP | (England) Contour 2870-190 | 1972 |
| | Neville Dickie | LP | Stomp Off 1096 | 1983 |
| | Vic Dickinson JB | LP | Jazzways 106/3 | 74-2 |
| | Dixieland Rhythm Kings | LP | Riverside RLP-12-259 | 53-12 |
| | Tommy Dorsey Orchestra | 78 | Victor 25496 | 36-10 |
| | Dukes of Dixieland | LP | Audio Fidelity AF-1928, AF-5928 | 1959 |
| | Hank Duncan | LP | 88 UR-001 | 1957-63 |
| | Hank Duncan | LP | (England) Pianola BS-6913 | r. 1972 |
| | Hank Duncan | LP | (Swiss) Ri-Disc 4 | c. 1948 |
| | Hank Duncan Trio | 78 | Black & White 31 | 44-6 |
| | Dutch Swing College Band | LP | (Holland) DSC PA-1022 | 78-12 |
| | Brian Dykstra | LP | Century Advent 5075 | 1974 |
| | Brian Dykstra | LP | Orion 83449 | 82-7 |
| | Willie Eckstein | 78 | Okeh 40018 | 23-11 |
| | Electrecord Ensemble | LP | (Roumania) Electrecord STM-EDE 01000 | 1977 49-2 |
| | Don Ewell | 78 | Jazz Limited 101 | |
| | Al Fairweather Band | LP | (England) Col. 33SX-1159 | 59-1 |
| | Firestone Dixieland Band | LP | (Germany) Metronome MLP-15021 | 58-10 |
| | Ray Foxley | LP | (Germany) Jeton 100.3301 | 79-3 |
| | Henry "Thins" Francis | LP | Mephistopheles 102 | 1986 |
| | David Andrew Frost | LP | Musical Heritage Society 3201 | 1975 |
| | Marco Fumo | LP | (Italy) Fonit-Cetra FDM-0004 | 83-2 |
| | Marta Garay | LP | (Hungary) Krem SLPX-179678 | 84-6 |
| | Eric Gemsa | LP | (France) Cezanne 1002 | 1975 |
| | Joe Glover's Cotton Pickers | LP | Epic LN-3581 | |
| | Gotfried und Lonzo | LP | (Germany) Telefunken 6.22312 | 75-6 |
| | Vera Guilaroff | LP | Biograph BLP-12047 | 26-5 |
| | Vera Guilaroff | 78 | Pathe 21178 | 26-7 |
| | W. G. Haenschen's Banjo Band | 78 | Personal M-61071 | 10- |
| | Halfway House Orchestra | 78 | Columbia 476-D | 25-9 |
| | Billy Hamilton's Rag Pickers | 78 | Vega 114 | |
| | Marvin Hamlisch | LP | MCA 2115 | 1974 |
| | Harlem Ramblers | LP | (Switzerland) Polydor 266448 | 80-12 |
| | John Hasse | LP | Sunflower 501 | 1980 |
| | Marc Herouet's Ragtime Cats | LP | (Belgium) Snow 1001 | r. 1981 |
| | Paul Hersh & David Montgomery | LP | RCA Victor ARL 1-0364 | 1974 |
| | Earl Hines & Orchestra | 78 | Decca 218 | 34-9 |
| | Art Hodes & Orchestra | 12"78 | Blue Note 505 | 44-3 |
| | Paul Hoffman | 78 | (Germany) Polydor | 27-9 |
| | Stig Holm & Arvid Sundin | 78 | (Germany) Telefunken 15050 | |
| | Hotcha Mundharmonika-Trio | 78 | (Germany) Phillips P-17155 | 53-2 |
| | Armand Hug | LP | Dulai 804 | 1968 |
| | Armand Hug | LP | Golden Crest 3064 | 1959 |
| | Dick Hyman | LP | Project 3 PR-5070 | 1972 |

| Composition | Performer | Record Speed | Record Company/No. | Year-Month |
|---|---|---|---|---|
| MAPLE LEAF RAG (continued) | Dick Hyman | LP | RCA CRL5-1106 | 1975 |
| Joplin, Scott | Imperial JB | LP | Signature BFW-40112 | 1985 |
| | Herb Inskip | LP | Hi GSR-4147 | 74-10 |
| | Franz Jackson's All Stars | LP | Pinnacle 108 | 1966 |
| | Dave Jasen | LP | Blue Goose 3001 | 1972 |
| | The Jazz Kings | 78 | (Germany) Tri-Ergon TE-5064 | 27-8 |
| | Glenn Jenks | LP | Bonnie Banks 103 | 1983 |
| | James P. Johnson | LP | Folkways 2841 | 46-9 |
| | James P. Johnson | 10″LP | Wax 201 | 47-2 |
| | Hank Jones | LP | ABC-Paramount 496 | 64-4 |
| | Jazzou Jones | LP | Riverboat Days 207018 | c. 1983 |
| | Scott Joplin Piano Roll | LP | Biograph 1006Q | r. 1972 |
| | Bob Kerr | LP | (England) Whoopee 101 | 1976 |
| | Arthur Kleiner | LP | Golden Crest CR-2004 | c. 1967 |
| | Willie "The Rock" Knox | 10″LP | Waldorf 33-147 | 1955 |
| | Merle Koch | LP | Tab 1002 | |
| | Dick Kroeckel | LP | Ragtime GRU-1930 | r. 1978 |
| | Katia & Marielle Labeque | LP | Angel S-37980 | 1982 |
| | Morton Gunnar Larsen | LP | Stomp Off 1009 | 81-1 |
| | Lawson–Haggart Jazz Band | 10″LP | Decca DL-5456 | 53-1 |
| | Bernie Leighton | LP | Cameo 1005 | 1958 |
| | James Levine | LP | RCA ARL-2243 | 1976 |
| | Paul Lingle | LP | Euphonic ESR-1203 | 1951 |
| | Paul Lingle | LP | Herwin 401 | 1958 |
| | Tiny Little | LP | Brunswick BL-54030 | |
| | Peter Lofthouse Band | LP | Windsor 4677 | |
| | Paul Lolax | LP | Titanic 13 | r. 1981 |
| | Charlie Love Jazz Band | LP | Folkways FA-2464 | 52-9 |
| | Geoff Love Band | LP | (Canada) Quality 753 | 1974 |
| | Art Lund & Orchestra | 78 | MGM 10713 | 50-4 |
| | Humphrey Lyttelton Band | 78 | (England) Parlophone R-3257 | 49-11 |
| | G. G. McBrayer | 78 | Gennett 20335 | 28-6 |
| | Clyde McCoy & Orchestra | 78 | Decca 681 | 35-7 |
| | Art Maiste | LP | (Canada) CBC RC-1398 | 70-2 |
| | Tony Marcus | LP | Kicking Mule 107 | r. 1976 |
| | Paul Mares & Friars Society Orchestra | 78 | Okeh 41574 | 35-1 |
| | | | | 52-6 |
| | Fabio Mataloni | 78 | (Italy) Parlophone TT-9580 | |
| | John Mehegan | LP | Perspective PR-1 | 1952 |
| | Mimi & Russell | LP | Mumpus 791 | r. 1979 |
| | Bill Mitchell | LP | Ethelyn 1750 | 1972 |
| | Deke Moffitt & His 29ers | 78 | King 1340 | 53-12 |
| | Monster Concert | LP | Columbia M-31726 | 1973 |
| | Moonlight Ragtime Band | LP | National Geographic 07817 | 1979 |
| | Max Morath | LP | Epic LN-24066 | 1963 |
| | Max Morath | 78 | Gold Camp 105 | 54-5 |
| | Max Morath | LP | RCA Victor LSO-1159 | 69-4 |

| Composition | Performer | Record Speed | Record Company/No. | Year-Month |
|---|---|---|---|---|
| MAPLE LEAF RAG (continued) | Max Morath | LP | Vanguard SRV-310 | r. 1974 |
| Joplin, Scott | Jelly Roll Morton | 12"78 | Circle JM-21 | 38-5 |
| | Jelly Roll Morton | 12"78 | Circle JM-22 | 38-5 |
| | Mr. Joe's Ragtime Group | LP | (Denmark) LBS-1 | 1972 |
| | Turk Murphy JB | LP | Stomp Off 1161 | 80-5 |
| | Turk Murphy's Jazz Band | LP | Motherlode M-0104 | 1964 |
| | Turk Murphy's Jazz Band | LP | Atlantic 1613 | 71-9 |
| | Roland Nadeau | LP | VQR 2625 | 1979 |
| | Ozzie Nelson & Orchestra | 78 | Bluebird 7726 | 38-7 |
| | New Black Eagle JB | LP | Stomp Off 1091 | 84-6 |
| | New England Conservatory Ragtime Ensemble | LP | Angel 36060 | 1973 |
| | New Orleans Ragtime Orchestra | LP | Arhoolie 1058 | 1971 |
| | New Orleans Rhythm Kings | 78 | Gennett 5104 | 23-3 |
| | Red Nichols & Five Pennies | LP | Capitol ST-2065 | 63-10 |
| | Red Nichols & Five Pennies | LP | Cap. T-775 | 56-9 |
| | Old Time Band | 78 | Bluebird 7816 | 38-8 |
| | Oregon JB | LP | OJB 1002 | 64-1 |
| | Kid Ory's Jazz Band | LP | GTJ-12004 | 54-8 |
| | Kid Ory's Jazz Band | 78 | Crescent 8 | 45-11 |
| | Vess L. Ossman | 78 | Imperial 45600 | 07-5 |
| | Vess L. Ossman w/ Prince's Band | 78 | Columbia 3626, A-228 | 07-3 |
| | Papa Bue's JB | EP | (Denmark) Storyville SEP-413 | 60-5 |
| | Tony Parenti Ragtime Gang | LP | Jazzology J-21 | 66-4 |
| | Tony Parenti Trio | LP | Jazztone J-730 | 55-8 |
| | Tony Parenti's All Stars | LP | Concert Hall 1215 | 55-8 |
| | Knocky Parker | LP | Audiophile AP-71 | 1960 |
| | Knocky Parker | LP | (England) London HA-U2008 | 52-4 |
| | Knocky Parker Trio | 78 | Texstar 200 | 49 |
| | Brooke Pemberton | LP | Warner Bros. W-1235 | 1958 |
| | Bent Persson JB | LP | (Sweden) Kenneth KS-2046 | 82-7 |
| | Phoenix Symphony Ragtime Ensemble | LP | World Jazz 12 | 77-6 |
| | Piano Roll | LP | Biograph 1010Q | r. 1973 |
| | Piano Roll | 78 | Circle 5003 | |
| | Piano Roll | LP | Dot DLP-25321 | |
| | Piano Roll | LP | (England) Saydisc SDL-117 | c. 1966 |
| | Piano Roll | 10"LP | Riverside RLP-1025 | |
| | Piano Roll | LP | Sounds 1201 | |
| | Nat Pierce Orchestra | LP | Coral CRL-57091 | 56-6 |
| | Cesare Poggi | LP | (Italy) Dire FO-344 | 1979 |
| | Prague Dixieland | LP | (Czechoslovakia) Supraphon DV-10168 | 64-10 |
| | Ray Price Quintet | LP | (Australia) Dixie RPQ-003 | 75-11 |
| | Ronnie Price | LP | (England) Embassy 31043 | c. 1973 |
| | Ike Ragon & Orchestra | 78 | Vocalion 03513 | 37-3 |
| | Ragtime Ensemble of Torino | LP | (Italy) Carosello 20144 | 78-10 |

| Composition | Performer | Record Speed | Record Company/No. | Year-Month |
|---|---|---|---|---|
| MAPLE LEAF RAG (continued) | Ragtime Society of Frankfurt | LP | (Germany) Joke 205 | 78-2 |
| Joplin, Scott | Ragtime Specht Groove | LP | (Germany) Intercord 130003 | 75-11 |
| | The Ragtimers | LP | RCA Camden ACL1-0599 | 74-5 |
| | Jean-Pierre Rampal | LP | CBS 37818 | r. 1983 |
| | Charlie Rasch | LP | C. K. 3204 | 73-4 |
| | Alex Read | 45 | (Canada) CTL 1012 | 62-11 |
| | Joshua Rifkin | LP | Nonesuch 71248 | 70-9 |
| | William Neil Roberts | LP | Klavier 510 | 1972 |
| | J. Russell Robinson | 78 | Eagle 900 | r. 47-9 |
| | Eric Rogers | LP | London Phase 4 - 21105 | 1974 |
| | Roman New Orleans Jazz Band | LP | (Italy) RCA A10V0-105 | 57-5 |
| | Wally Rose | LP | Columbia JZ-1 | 53-5 |
| | Harry Roy & Orchestra | 78 | (England) Parlophone F-1133 | 37-12 |
| | Harry Roy & Orchestra (m) | 78 | (England) Parlophone F-1568 | 39-2 |
| | Jack Rummel | LP | Stomp Off 1118 | 1985 |
| | Julian Russell Trio | LP | (New Zealand) TJF PRA-833/4 | 1977 |
| | Slick Salzer Quartet | LP | (Switzerland) Elite Special XZLP-5113 | 78-12 |
| | San Francisco Harry | LP | Fantasy 3270 | 1958 |
| | Elmer Schoebel's Dixieland | 78 | National 9113 | |
| | Sigi Schwab | LP | (Germany) Jupiter 6.24831 | c. 1985 |
| | Bob Scobey JB | LP | Jansco 6250 | 1956 |
| | Janice Scroggins | LP | Flying Hearts 334 | 1987 |
| | Ted Shafer JB | LP | Merry Makers 104 | c. 1970 |
| | Roger Shields | LP | Turnabout 34579 | 1974 |
| | Frank Signorelli | LP | Kapp KL-1005 | 1955 |
| | Yannick Singery | LP | (France) Swing 928 | c. 1975 |
| | Slugger Ryan | LP | Judson 3015 | 1958 |
| | Ethel Smith | 78 | Decca 27051 | 50-5 |
| | Willie the Lion Smith | 10"LP | Dial 305 | 1950 |
| | Willie the Lion Smith | 10"LP | Grand Award GA-33-368 | 1957 |
| | Harry Snodgrass | 78 | Brunswick 3239 | 26-6 |
| | Fred Sokolow | LP | Kicking Mule 212 | c. 1982 |
| | South JB | LP | (Holland) Telstar Parade 89622 | 74-9 |
| | St. Louis Ragtimers | LP | Audiophile AP-75 | 1962 |
| | Danny Stevenson Trio | LP | Great Lakes VC-907 | c. 1968 |
| | Chris Stone | LP | ABC 823 | 1974 |
| | Ralph Sutton | LP | Roulette 25232 | 1962 |
| | Ralph Sutton | 78 | (Swiss) E. S. 9114 | 52-7 |
| | Duncan Swift | LP | (England) Black Lion 301 | 1977 |
| | Keith Taylor | LP | Sami 1001 | 1974 |
| | Thai Internationals | LP | (Australia) Poodle 21179 | 79-11 |
| | Butch Thompson | LP | Stomp Off 1037 | 1982 |
| | Three Town Ragtime Quartet | LP | (Holland) Beerendonk 99916 | 1982 |
| | John Scott Trotter & Orchestra | 78 | Decca 4217 | 41-7 |
| | Bob Tryforous | LP | Puritan 5002 | r. 1976 |
| | U. S. Marine Band | 78 | Victor 4911 | 06-10 |

| Composition | Performer | Record Speed | Record Company/No. | Year-Month |
|---|---|---|---|---|
| MAPLE LEAF RAG (continued) | U. S. Marine Band | 78 | Victor 16792 | 09-2 |
| Joplin, Scott | Fred Van Eps w / Orchestra | 78 | Zonophone 5917 | r. 12-6 |
| | Fred Van Eps w/ pno | 78 | V-1 | 52-3 |
| | Benny Vasseur Orchestra | LP | (France) Festival 128 | 58-5 |
| | Benny Vasseur–Andre Paquinet Orchestra | LP | (France) Festival FLP-123 | 1958 |
| | Vistula River Band | LP | (Poland) EWP 1 | 78-11 |
| | Terry Waldo | LP | Fat Cat's Jazz 151 | 74-1 |
| | Lu Watters YBJB | LP | Verve 1008 | |
| | Lu Watters YBJB | LP | Homespun 106 | 1950 |
| | Lu Watters YBJB | LP | Homespun H-107 | 1941 |
| | Lu Watters YBJB | 78 | Jazz Man 1 | 41-12 |
| | Lu Watters YBJB | 78 | West Coast 114 | 47-2 |
| | Ron Weatherburn | LP | (England) Alpha LPX-32 | 62-1 |
| | Ron Weatherburn | LP | (England) Marble Arch 1293 | 1968 |
| | Ron Weatherburn | LP | (England) Rediffusion 0100170 | 74-3 |
| | Teddy Weatherford | 78 | Swing 315 | 37-6 |
| | Moe Wechsler | LP | Roulette R-25069 | 1960 |
| | Dick Wellstood | LP | Fat Cat's Jazz 159 | 74-4 |
| | Dick Wellstood | LP | Fat Cat's Jazz 207 | 78-12 |
| | Dick Wellstood | LP | (Germany) MRC 006-32-859 | 77-1 |
| | Dick Wellstood | LP | Pickwick SPC-3376 | 1974 |
| | Alex Welsh Dixielanders | LP | (England) Lake 5008 | 55-1 |
| | Albert White Orchestra | LP | Barbary Coast 33008 | 1958 |
| | Jerry White | LP | Monument MLP-8016 | c. 1964 |
| | Herb Wiedoeft's Orchestra | 78 | Brunswick 2795 | 24-9 |
| | Bob Wilbur JB | LP | (Italy) RCA PL-74766 | 90-5 |
| | Bill Williams & Band | 78 | Albert 725-1 | 49-12 |
| | Yorkshire Jazz Band | 78 | (England) Esquire 32-015 | 56-7 |
| | Dick Zimmerman | LP | Murray Hill 931079 | 1974 |
| | Richard Zimmerman | LP | Murray Hill M-60556/5 | 1981 |
| | Zinn's Ragtime String Quartet | LP | Music Minus One 13 | 1974 |
| MARIGOLD | | | | |
| Mayerl, Billy | Tony Bennett | 78 | (England) Dominion 262 | 29-4 |
| | W. Harris | 78 | (England) Duo D-522 | 28-9 |
| | Quentin MacLean | 78 | (England) Columbia FB-1846 | |
| | Billy Mayerl | 78 | (England) Decca F-7945 | 41-7 |
| | Billy Mayerl | 78 | (England) Columbia 4783 | 27-10 |
| | Billy Mayerl (m) | 78 | (England) Columbia FB-1438 | 27-10 |
| | Billy Mayerl & Wife | 78 | (England) Columbia FB-1161 | 34-8 |
| | Keith Nichols | LP | (England) EMI One Up-2085 | 1975 |
| | Jack Wilson (m) | 78 | (England) Regal Zonophone MR-1547 | 34-9 |
| MARITA | | | | |
| Krenz, Bill | Bill Krenz | 45 | Cole 90500 | 35-12 |
| MARKET STREET RAG | | | | |
| Tichenor, Trebor | Trebor Tichenor | LP | Folkways FS-3164 | 1979 |

| Composition | Performer | Record Speed | Record Company/No. | Year-Month |
|---|---|---|---|---|
| MASHED POTATOES | | | | |
| Woolsey, C. L. | David Thomas Roberts | LP | Stomp Off 1021 | 1981 |
| MATCH PARADE | | | | |
| Wehle, Karl | Raie Da Costa | 78 | (England) HMV B-3888 | 31-6 |
| MEADOW LARK RAG | | | | |
| Pitts, Tom | John Arpin | LP | (Canada) Scroll 103 | 1966 |
| | Scott Fogelsong | LP | Stomp Off 1168 | 1987 |
| | Richard Zimmerman | LP | Murray Hill 60556/5 | 1981 |
| MELODEE RAG | | | | |
| Stover, Harry | Harry Stover Piano Roll | LP | Herwin 407 | |
| MELODIC RAG | | | | |
| Blake, Eubie | Eubie Blake | LP | Eubie Blake Music 1 | 1971 |
| | Eubie Blake | LP | Chiaroscuro 170 | 1972 |
| MELODY RAG | | | | |
| Deiro, Pietro | Pietro Deiro | 78 | Victor 17895 | 15-10 |
| MELROSE RAG | | | | |
| Bauersachs, Hubert | Hubert Bauersachs & Orchestra | 78 | Victor QB-1850 | 22- |
| | Sybil Court Piano Roll | LP | Folkways RBF-50 | |
| MEMPHIS STOMP | | | | |
| | Blue Boys | 78 | Okeh 45314 | 28-2 |
| MERRY WIDOW RAG | | | | |
| Blake, Eubie | John Gill | LP | Stomp Off 1066 | 1983 |
| MERRYDOWN RAG | | | | |
| Barber, Chris | Chris Barber & Band | 78 | (England) Decca F-10417 | 54-7 |
| METEOR RAG | | | | |
| Morse, Arthur C. | Dave Jasen | LP | Folkways FS-3561 | 77-6 |
| MIDNIGHT TROT | | | | |
| Cobb, George L. | Dave Jasen | LP | Folkways FG-3561 | 77-6 |
| MIDNIGHT WHIRL RAG | | | | |
| Hein, Silvio | Victor Military Band | 12″78 | Victor 35431 | 14-11 |
| MINEOLA RAG | | | | |
| | East Texas Serenaders | 78 | Brunswick 562 | 30-11 |
| MINSTREL MAN | | | | |
| Robinson, J. Russell | Barrelhouse JB | LP | (Germany) Intercord 145017 | 1978 |
| | Bindsouw Jazzmen | EP | (Denmark) Storyville SEP-405 | 1961 |
| | Ken Colyer's Jazzmen | LP | (England) Joy S-194 | 1974 |
| | Neville Dickie | LP | Euphonic ESR-1206 | 1966 |
| | Indiana U. Orchestra | LP | IHS 1001 | 1981 |
| | Bunk Johnson Band | LP | Col. ML-4802 | 47-12 |
| | London Ragtime Orchestra | LP | Stomp Off 1081 | 84-8 |
| | Love–Jiles Ragtime Orchestra | LP | Sounds of New Orleans 1 | 59-6 |
| | New Orleans Ragtime Orchestra | LP | (Sweden) Sonet 709 | 76-3 |
| | Tony Parenti's Ragtime Gang | LP | Jazzology J-21 | 66-4 |
| | Knocky Parker | LP | Audiophile AP-92 | |

| Composition | Performer | Record Speed | Record Company/No. | Year-Month |
|---|---|---|---|---|
| MINSTREL MAN (continued) | J. Russell Robinson | 78 | Eagle 902 | r. 47-9 |
| Robinson, J. Russell | Keith Smith JB | LP | (England) 77LEU 12/9 | |
| MISERY RAG | | | | |
| Colby, Carlton | Piano Roll | LP | Herwin 407 | |
| | Waldo's Ragtime Orchestra | LP | Stomp Off 1069 | 83-6 |
| MISS TROMBONE | | | | |
| Fillmore, Henry | Chrysanthemum Ragtime Band | LP | Stomp Off 1079 | 1984 |
| | Columbia Orchestra | 78 | Columbia A-2825 | 18-9 |
| | Ford Dabney's Band | 78 | Aeolian 12167 | 19-5 |
| MISS VIXEN | | | | |
| Bowers, R. H. | Conway's Band | 12"78 | Victor 35502 | 15-9 |
| MISSISSIPPI SHIVERS | | | | |
| Confrey, Zez | Zez Confrey & Orchestra | 78 | Victor 19430 | 24-7 |
| | Dick Hyman | LP | RCA XRL1-4746 | 1983 |
| | Sid Williams | 78 | Gennett 6353 | 27-6 |
| MISSISSIPPI VALLEY FROLIC | | | | |
| Tichenor, Trebor | Trebor Tichenor | LP | (Canada) Scroll 102 | 1966 |
| MISSOURI RAG | | | | |
| Powell, W. C. | Steen Christensen | LP | (Holland) Jazz Crooner 155.771 | 1977 |
| | Knocky Parker | LP | Audiophile AP-90 | |
| MISSOURI RAMBLER | | | | |
| Tichenor, Trebor | Trebor Tichenor | LP | Folkways FS-3164 | 1979 |
| MISSOURI ROMP | | | | |
| Marshall, Arthur | Milton Kaye | LP | Golden Crest 31032 | 1974 |
| | Max Morath | LP | Jazzology 52 | c. 1967 |
| MISTER JOE | | | | |
| Morton, Jelly Roll | Burt Bales | LP | Euphonic 1210 | c. 1960 |
| | Burt Bales | 10"LP | Good Time Jazz LP-19 | 49-10 |
| | Hall Bros. Jazz Band | LP | Stomp Off 1062 | 1981 |
| | Jelly Roll Morton | 78 | General 4004 | 39-12 |
| | Knocky Parker | LP | Audiophile AP-49 | 1958 |
| | Knocky Parker | LP | Audiophile AP-105 | |
| | Butch Thompson | LP | (Denmark) CSA 1014 | 74-9 |
| | Richard Zimmerman | LP | Murray Hill 60556/5 | 1981 |
| MITINICE | | | | |
| Straight, Charley | Charley Straight Piano Roll | LP | Folkways RBF-44 | |
| MIXED UP RAG | | | | |
| Ezell, Will | Will Ezell | 78 | Paramount 12688 | 28-9 |
| MIXIN' IT UP | | | | |
| Grant, Mel | Professor Ragtime | 78 | Joco 109 | 50-4 |
| MIZZOURA MAG'S CHROMATIC RAG | David Thomas Roberts | LP | Stomp Off 1021 | 1981 |
| Farris, H. H. | | | | |

| Composition | Performer | Record Speed | Record Company/No. | Year-Month |
|---|---|---|---|---|
| MOBILE RAG | | | | |
| Blake, Eubie | Eubie Blake | LP | 20th Century Fox 3003 | 1958 |
| MODESTY RAG | | | | |
| Scott, James | William Bolcom | LP | Nonesuch 71299 | 1974 |
| | John Jensen | LP | Genesis 1044 | 1974 |
| | Knocky Parker | LP | Audiophile AP-76/77 | 1962 |
| MODULATION | | | | |
| Jones, Clarence M. | Clarence M. Jones | 78 | Autograph | 23-1 |
| MONKEY BLUES | | | | |
| Darewski, Max | Max Darewski | 78 | (England) Zonophone 2350 | 23-5 |
| MONKEY BUSINESS | | | | |
| Reinherz, Sid | Sid Reinherz | 78 | Gennett 5439 | 24-4 |
| MONOGRAMS | | | | |
| Denney, Homer | John Hancock | LP | Stomp Off 1025 | 1982 |
| MOONLIGHT RAG | | | | |
| Lodge, Henry | New York Military Band | 78 | Edison 50135 | 14-3 |
| MOW-EM-DOWN | | | | |
| Straight, Charley | Charley Straight Piano Roll | LP | Folkways RBF-44 | |
| MR. CRUMP RAG | | | | |
| Crump, Jesse | Jesse Crump | 78 | Gennett | 23-7 |
| MR. FREDDY'S RAG | | | | |
| Shayne, J. H. | J. H. Shayne | 78 | Circle 1011 | 46-2 |
| MR. FROGGIE (see FROG-I-MORE RAG) | Henry Starr | 78 | Flexo 148 | 28-3 |
| MUD CAT RAG | | | | |
| Krenz, Bill | George Foley | LP | Stomp Off 1187 | 1988 |
| MUFFIN MAN | | | | |
| Mayerl, Billy | Billy Mayerl (m) | 78 | (England) Columbia 4975 | 28-5 |
| MULE WALK | | | | |
| Johnson, James P. | Judy Carmichael | LP | Statiras 8078 | 1985 |
| | Neville Dickie | LP | (England) Pizza Express 5507 | 81-3 |
| | Chuck Folds | LP | Jazzways 106/4 | 1974 |
| | Jim Hession | LP | EBM 6 | 1973 |
| | James P. Johnson | 12"78 | Blue Note 27 | 43-12 |
| | James P. Johnson | LP | Col. CL-1780 | 39-6 |
| | James P. Johnson | LP | Vanguard VSD-47/48 | 38-12 |
| | Mike Lipskin | LP | Flying Dutchman FD-10140 | 1970 |
| | Louis Mazetier & Francois Rilhac | LP | Stomp Off 1218 | 89-11 |
| | Tom McDermott | LP | Stomp Off 1024 | 82-1 |
| | Willie the Lion Smith | LP | Blue Circle 1500-33 | 53-8 |
| | Dick Wellstood | LP | Audiophile AP-120 | 75-10 |
| | Dick Wellstood | 10"LP | Riverside RLP-2506 | 54-10 |
| | Dick Wellstood | LP | (Switzerland) 88 Up Right 005 | 76-1 |

| Composition | Performer | Record Speed | Record Company/No. | Year-Month |
|---|---|---|---|---|
| MUSIC BOX RAG | | | | |
| Roberts, Luckey | Marvin Ash | 10"LP | Jazz Man 335 | 1954 |
| | Paul Hersh & David Montgomery | LP | RCA ARL1-0364 | 1974 |
| | Jaudas Society Orchestra | 78 | Edison 50261 | 15-8 |
| | Pathe Dance Orchestra | 78 | Pathe 70127 | r. 15-9 |
| | Luckey Roberts | 78 | Circle 1027 | 46-5 |
| | Victor Military Band | 12"78 | Victor 35429 | 14-12 |
| | Zinn's Ragtime String Quartet | LP | Music Minus One 13 | 1974 |
| MUSLIN RAG | | | | |
| Kaufman, Mel B. | Prince's Band | 12"78 | Columbia A-6084 | r. 19-1 |
| MY BABY'S RAG | | | | |
| Straight, Charley | Charley Straight Piano Roll | LP | Folkways RBF-44 | |
| MY PET | | | | |
| Confrey, Zez | John Arpin | LP | Eubie Blake Music 10 | 1976 |
| | Claude Bolling | LP | (France) CY 733.607 | c. 1980 |
| | Zez Confrey | 78 | Brunswick 2082 | r. 21-4 |
| | Zez Confrey Piano Roll | LP | Folkways RF-28 | |
| | George Hicks | LP | Folkways FS-3165 | 1983 |
| | Stanley C. Holt | 78 | (England) Homochord H-477 | 23-3 |
| | Dick Hyman | LP | RCA XRL1-4746 | 1983 |
| | John Jensen | LP | Genesis 1051 | 1974 |
| | Milton Kaye | LP | Golden Crest 31040 | 1974 |
| | Arthur Kleiner | LP | Golden Crest 2004 | c. 1967 |
| | Percival Mackey Band | 78 | (England) Columbia 3230 | 23-1 |
| | Russ Morgan & Eddie Wilser | LP | Decca DL-8746 | 1958 |
| | Wayne & Geraldi | LP | Reader's Digest RDA-70-01-05 | 1968 |
| | Sid Williams | 78 | Vocalion 15691 | 28-4 |
| | Richard Zimmerman | LP | Murray Hill 60556/5 | 1981 |
| THE NAKED DANCE | | | | |
| Morton, Jelly Roll | Len Barnard JB | LP | (Australia) Swaggie S-1287 | 1961 |
| | Peter Fahrenholtz | LP | (Holland) Jazz Crooner 275761/62 | 76-5 |
| | Vic Filmer | LP | Jazzology JCE-58 | 1970 |
| | Adrian Ford | LP | (Australia) Festival L-25119 | 73-12 |
| | Eric Gemsa | LP | (France) Cezanne 1002 | 1975 |
| | Jelly Roll Morton | 12"78 | Circle JM-85 | 38-5 |
| | Jelly Roll Morton | 78 | General 4002 | 39-12 |
| | Jelly Roll Morton (tk. 2) | LP | Commodore XFL-14942 | 39-12 |
| | Knocky Parker | LP | Audiophile AP-105 | |
| | Knocky Parker Trio | 10"LP | (England) London H-BU 1044 | 1949 |
| | David Thomas Roberts | LP | Mardi Gras 1002 | 1978 |
| | Slugger Ryan | LP | Judson 3015 | 1958 |
| | Tom Shea | LP | Stomp Off 1022 | 1981 |
| | Duncan Swift | LP | (England) Black Lion 12123 | 69-8 |
| | Butch Thompson | LP | Center 4 | 66-8 |
| | Trebor Tichenor | LP | (Canada) Scroll 102 | 1966 |
| | Ron Weatherburn | LP | (England) Alpha 32 | 62-1 |

| Composition | Performer | Record Speed | Record Company/No. | Year- Month |
|---|---|---|---|---|
| NANETTE | | | | |
| Carroll, Adam | Wally Rose | LP | Stomp Off 1057 | 1982 |
| NAPPY LEE | | | | |
| Jordan, Joe | Lois Delano | LP | (Canada) Arpeggio 1205 | 1968 |
| | Milton Kaye | LP | Golden Crest 31032 | 1974 |
| NEW ERA RAG | | | | |
| Scott, James | William Bolcom | LP | Nonesuch 71299 | 1974 |
| | Knocky Parker | LP | Audiophile AP-76/77 | 1962 |
| | Wally Rose | LP | Blackbird 12007 | 1968 |
| | Royal Garden Ramblers | LP | (Germany) Intercord 661462 | 76-6 |
| NEW GOOFY DUST RAG | | | | |
| Moten, Bennie | Bennie Moten & Orchestra | 78 | Victor V-38091 | 29-7 |
| NEW ORLEANS RAG | | | | |
| Hyman, Dick | Willie the Rock Knox | LP | Waldorf 33-147 | c. 1955 |
| NEW RAGTIME LP'S | | | | |
| 19 Ragtime 70 | Hugh Crozier | LP | (England) Stomp Robb 002 | 1970 |
| Albright Plays Albright | William Albright | LP | Musical Heritage Society 4253 | 1973 |
| Bolcom Plays His Own Rags | William Bolcom | LP | Jazzology JCE-72 | |
| Classic & Modern Rags | Tom Shea | LP | Ragtime Society 1 | 1963 |
| Cleveland Rags | George Foley | LP | Century Advent 62778 | 1977 |
| Days Beyond Recall | Trebor Tichenor | LP | Folkways FS-3164 | |
| Little Wabash Special | Tom Shea | LP | Stomp Off 1022 | 1981 |
| Mississippi Motion | John Hancock | LP | Stomp Off 1025 | 1982 |
| New Rags | Tom McDermott | LP | Stomp Off 1024 | 1982 |
| Original Rags | David R. Lee | LP | (Canada) Jazz Studies 4 | 1976 |
| Pinelands Memoir | David Thomas Roberts | LP | Euphonic Sounds 1224 | c. 1983 |
| Prairie Ragtime | Tom Shea | LP | Ragtime Society 2 | 1974 |
| Ragtime Alchemy | Glenn Jenks | LP | Stomp Off 1179 | 1987 |
| Ragtime: A New View | Donald Ashwander | LP | Jazzology JCE-71 | |
| Ragtime Here and Now | Nurit Tilles | LP | Jazzology JCE-87 | 1983 |
| Rhythms in Ragtime | Gale Foehner | LP | Stomp Off 1023 | 1981 |
| Something Like a Rag | Brian Dykstra | LP | Advent 5021 | |
| Sunshine & Shadow | Donald Ashwander | LP | Upstairs 2 | 1979 |
| Through the Bottomlands | David Thomas Roberts | LP | Stomp Off 1072 | 1981 |
| Turnips | Donald Ashwander | LP | Upstairs 1 | 1974 |
| NEW RUSSIAN RAG | | | | |
| Cobb, George | George Foley | LP | Century Advent 778 | 1977 |
| NICKEL IN THE SLOT | | | | |
| Confrey, Zez | Zez Confrey Orchestra | 78 | Victor 19430 | 24-7 |
| | Willie Eckstein | 78 | Okeh 40018 | 23-11 |
| | Frank Herbin | 78 | (England) HMV B-1770 | 24-1 |
| | Dick Hyman | LP | RCA XRL1-4746 | 1983 |
| | Dave Jasen | LP | Blue Goose 3002 | 1974 |
| | Harry Jordan | 78 | (England) Columbia 3724 | 25-8 |
| | David Thomas Roberts | LP | Stomp Off 1132 | 1981 |

| Composition | Performer | Record Speed | Record Company/No. | Year- Month |
|---|---|---|---|---|
| NIGGER'S HOP | | | | |
| Batten, Joseph | Joseph Batten | 78 | (England) Popular P-656 | 12- |
| NIGHTINGALE RAG BLUES (see THE RAGTIME NIGHTINGALE) | Hitch's Happy Harmonists | 78 | Gennett 5633 | 25-1 |
| 1915 RAG | | | | |
| Tierney, Harry Austin | Mike Bernard | 78 | Columbia A-1427 | 13-6 |
| | Piano Roll | LP | (England) Saydisc 132 | |
| NOBODY'S RAG | | | | |
| Jasen, David A. | Dave Jasen | LP | Blue Goose 3002 | 1974 |
| NONPAREIL | | | | |
| Joplin, Scott | Ann Charters | LP | GNP Crescendo 9032 | 1974 |
| | Dick Hyman | LP | RCA CRL5-1106 | 1975 |
| | Knocky Parker | LP | Audiophile AP-71/72 | 1960 |
| | Piano Roll | LP | Biograph 1008Q | |
| | Joshua Rifkin | LP | Nonesuch 71305 | 1974 |
| | Southland Stingers | LP | Angel S-36078 | 1974 |
| | Bob Tryforous | LP | Puritan 5002 | r. 1976 |
| | Dick Zimmerman | LP | Murray Hill 931079 | 1974 |
| | Zinn's Ragtime String Quartet | LP | Music Minus One 13 | 1974 |
| NONSENSE RAG | | | | |
| Grady, R. G. | Nick Polites Quartet | LP | (Australia) Swaggie S-1205 | 61-7 |
| | Ragpickers | 78 | Circle 1055 | 49-1 |
| | Wally Rose | 10″LP | Columbia CL-6260 | 53-5 |
| NOTHIN' | | | | |
| Roberts, Luckey | Keith Nichols | LP | (England) EMI One Up-2085 | 1975 |
| | Luckey Roberts | LP | Good Time Jazz M-12035 | 58-3 |
| NOTORIETY RAG | | | | |
| Widmer, Kathryn L. | Band | 78 | Little Wonder 33 | |
| | Joe "Fingers" Carr's Brass Band | LP | Warner Bros. W-1456 | 1962 |
| | Chrysanthemum Ragtime Band | LP | Stomp Off 1047 | 1983 |
| | Prince's Band | 78 | Columbia | 14- |
| | Van Eps Trio | 78 | Victor 17601 | 14-3 |
| NOVELTY RAG | | | | |
| Blake, Eubie | Eubie Blake | LP | Eubie Blake Music 1 | 1971 |
| OH WILLIE PLAY THAT THING | Bill Krenz | 78 | MGM 11264, 30704 | 52- |
| Krenz, Bill | Mitch Parks | LP | (Canada) CBC LM-430 | 75-11 |
| OH YOU DEVIL | | | | |
| Dabney, Ford | Chrysanthemum Ragtime Band | LP | Stomp Off 1196 | 1988 |
| | Willie the Lion Smith | 10″LP | Dial 305 | 50-1 |
| | Willie the Lion Smith | LP | MPS/BASF 5055 | 66-11 |

| Composition | Performer | Record Speed | Record Company/No. | Year-Month |
|---|---|---|---|---|
| OLD FOLKS RAG | | | | |
| Sweatman, Wilbur | Metropolitan Military Band | 78 | Emerson 730 | |
| | Van Eps Banjo Orchestra | 12"78 | Columbia A-5618 | 14-7 |
| | Van Eps Trio | 12"78 | Victor 35400 | 14-9 |
| OLD HOME RAG | | | | |
| Lamb, Joseph | John Jensen | LP | Genesis 1045 | 1974 |
| | Milton Kaye | LP | Golden Crest 31035 | 1974 |
| THE OLD NORTH STATE | | | | |
| Shea, Tom | Tom Shea | LP | Stomp Off 1022 | 1981 |
| OLD PROFESSOR | | | | |
| Hyman, Dick | Dick Hyman Trio | 45 | MGM K-11951 | |
| OMEOMY | | | | |
| Bargy, Roy | Roy Bargy Piano Roll | LP | Folkways RF-35 | |
| ON THE PIKE | | | | |
| Scott, James | Marco Fumo | LP | (Italy) Fonit Cetra 0004 | 83-2 |
| | Knocky Parker | LP | Audiophile AP-76/77 | 1962 |
| | Rosebud Ragtime Ensemble | LP | Potomac River 001 | 84-6 |
| ONE O'THEM THINGS | | | | |
| Chapman, James & | David Thomas Roberts | LP | Stomp Off 1132 | 1981 |
| Smith, Leroy | Richard Zimmerman | LP | Murray Hill 60556/5 | 1981 |
| OPERA HOUSE RAG | | | | |
| Darch, Bob | Bob Darch | LP | Stereoddities C-1901 | 1962 |
| AN OPERATIC NIGHTMARE | | | | |
| (arr. Arndt, Felix) | Felix Arndt | 78 | Victor 18056 | 16-5 |
| | Frank Banta | 78 | Victor 20667 | 26-10 |
| OPERATIC RAG | | | | |
| Lenzberg, Julius | Joseph Moskowitz | 78 | Victor 17978 | 16-2 |
| | Sodero's Band | 78 | Edison 50217 | 15-2 |
| | Albert White Orchestra | LP | Fantasy 3292 | |
| OPHELIA RAG | | | | |
| Scott, James | Budapest Ragtime Orchestra | LP | (Czechoslovakia) Krem SLPX-17794 | 1984 |
| | Dave Jasen | LP | Folkways FG-3561 | 77-6 |
| | London Ragtime Orchestra | LP | Stomp Off 1081 | 84-8 |
| | New England Conservatory Ensemble | LP | Golden Crest 31042 | 1975 |
| | Knocky Parker | LP | Audiophile AP-76/77 | 1962 |
| | Piano Roll | LP | Biograph 1016Q | |
| ORANGE BLOSSOM RAG | | | | |
| Lada, Anton, Nunez, Al & Cawley, Joe | Louisiana Five | 78 | Emerson 9150 | 19-1 |
| ORIENTAL BLUES | | | | |
| Newlon, Jack | Jan August | 78 | Mercury 5725 | 51- |
| | Bill Davies Band | 78 | Top Tune 475 | |
| | Tony De Simone Trio | 78 | Decca 29183 | 54-5 |
| | Tony De Simone Trio | 78 | Epic 9059 | |
| | Leroy Holmes Orchestra | 78 | MGM 12408 | 56-12 |

| Composition | Performer | Record Speed | Record Company/No. | Year-Month |
|---|---|---|---|---|
| ORIGINAL RAGS | | | | |
| Joplin, Scott | John Arpin | LP | (Canada) Harmony 6026 | 1970 |
| | Burt Bales | LP | Cavalier 5007 | 1954 |
| | Burt Bales | LP | Euphonic ESR-1210 | 1957 |
| | E. Power Biggs | LP | Columbia M-32495 | 1973 |
| | Sune Borg | 78 | (Sweden) Gazell 3001 | 49-10 |
| | Budapest Ragtime Orchestra | LP | (Czechoslovakia) Krem SLPX-17794 | 1984 |
| | Ann Charters | LP | Portents 3 | |
| | Bill Coffman & Kathy Craig | LP | OTMH 101 | r. 1980 |
| | Bob Darch | LP | United Artists UAL-3120 | 1960 |
| | Eddy Davis | LP | Pa Da 7401 | 1974 |
| | Neville Dickie | LP | (England) Saydisc SDL-118 | 1966 |
| | Lee Erwin | LP | Angel S-36075 | 1974 |
| | Tom Gilfellon | LP | Kicking Mule 107 | r. 1976 |
| | Dick Hyman | LP | RCA CRL5-1106 | 1975 |
| | Jazz Fiddlers | LP | (Czechoslovakia) Supraphon 1150904 | 70-4 |
| | James Levine | LP | RCA ARL1-2243 | 1976 |
| | Paul Lingle | LP | Euphonic 1220 | 1951 |
| | Paul Lolax | LP | Titanic 13 | r. 1981 |
| | Humphrey Lyttelton Band | LP | (England) Calligraph 013 | 86-7 |
| | Merseysippi JB | 10"LP | (England) Esquire 20-093 | 58-5 |
| | Max Morath | LP | Epic LN-24106 | 1964 |
| | Max Morath | LP | Vanguard VSD-39/40 | 1967 |
| | Jelly Roll Morton | 78 | General 4001 | 39-12 |
| | Turk Murphy JB | LP | Atlantic 1613 | 71-9 |
| | Turk Murphy JB | LP | GHB 91 | 72-4 |
| | Natural Gas JB | LP | NGJB 2 | 77-5 |
| | New England Conservatory Ensemble | LP | Golden Crest 31031 | 1973 |
| | New Orleans Ragtime Orchestra | LP | Pearl 7 | 67-9 |
| | New Orleans Ragtime Orchestra | LP | Vanguard VSD-69/70 | 1971 |
| | Papa Bue's Viking JB | EP | (Denmark) Storyville SEP 413 | 61-12 |
| | Knocky Parker | LP | Audiophile AP-71/72 | 1960 |
| | Knocky Parker Trio | 10"LP | (England) London H-BU1044 | 1949 |
| | Piano Roll | LP | Biograph 1010Q | |
| | Piano Roll | 78 | Jazz Classics 534 | |
| | Piano Roll | 10"LP | Riverside RLP-1006 | |
| | Cesare Poggi | LP | (Italy) Dire FO-344 | 1979 |
| | Ronnie Price | LP | (England) Embassy 31043 | c. 1973 |
| | Queen City Ragtime Ensemble | LP | Zeno 99 | 1976 |
| | Ragtime Banjo Commission | LP | GHB 154 | 80-8 |
| | Ragtime Society of Frankfurt | LP | (Germany) Joke JLP-205 | 78-2 |
| | Jean-Pierre Rampal | LP | CBS 37818 | 1982 |
| | Red Rose Ragtime Band | LP | Red Rose 001 | 1983 |
| | Joshua Rifkin | LP | Nonesuch H-71305 | 1974 |
| | William Neil Roberts | LP | Klavier 516 | 1973 |

| Composition | Performer | Record Speed | Record Company/No. | Year-Month |
|---|---|---|---|---|
| ORIGINAL RAGS (continued) | Wally Rose & Rhythm | 78 | West Coast 112 | 47-2 |
| Joplin, Scott | Tom Shea | LP | (Canada) Ragtime Society 1 | 1963 |
| | Duncan Swift | LP | (England) Black Lion 12123 | 69-8 |
| | Butch Thompson | LP | Center 9 | 68-6 |
| | Ton Van Bergeyk | LP | Kicking Mule 114 | r. 1976 |
| | Waldo's Syncopators | LP | GHB 55 | 70-4 |
| | Ron Weatherburn | LP | (England) Alpha LPX-32 | 1962 |
| | Ron Weatherburn | LP | (England) Rediffusion 0100170 | 74-3 |
| | Dick Zimmerman | LP | Murray Hill 931079 | 1974 |
| ORINOCO | | | | |
| Crabb, C. Duane | Elliott Adams | LP | Stomp Off 1198 | 1988 |
| | Piano Roll | LP | Indiana Historical Society 1001 | |
| OUT OF THE SOUTH | | | | |
| Robison, Willard | Willard Robison | 78 | Autograph 601 | 24-9 |
| OUT STEPPIN' | | | | |
| Straight, Charley | Charley Straight Piano Roll | LP | Folkways RBF-44 | |
| OVER THE BARS (aka STEEPLECHASE RAG) | | | | |
| Johnson, James P. | John Arpin | LP | Eubie Blake Music 10 | 1976 |
| | James P. Johnson | 78 | Decca 24884 | 44-9 |
| | James P. Johnson | LP | Pumpkin 117 | 49-9 |
| | Max Morath Quintet | LP | Normacks 100 | c. 1981 |
| OZARK RAG | | | | |
| Marsh | East Texas Serenaders | 78 | Brunswick 538 | 30-11 |
| PAGE PADEREWSKI | | | | |
| Samuels, Joseph, Briers, Larry & Wendling, Pete | Harry Reser w/ Henry Lange, pno | 78 | (England) Columbia 3334 | 23-7 |
| | Joseph Samuels Orchestra | 78 | Perfect 14163 | 23-6 |
| | Pete Wendling | 78 | Okeh 4984 | 23-5 |
| PALM BEACH RAG | | | | |
| Roberts, Luckey | Van Eps–Banta Trio | 78 | Emerson 10206 | r. 20-7 |
| | Van Eps Trio | 78 | Melodisc 701 | |
| PALM LEAF RAG | | | | |
| Joplin, Scott | William Cerny | LP | University of Notre Dame | 1975 |
| | Ann Charters | LP | Portents 1 | 1958 |
| | Steen Christensen | LP | (Denmark) LB 1 | 1972 |
| | Bill Coffman & Kathy Craig | LP | OTMH 101 | r. 1980 |
| | Dick Hyman | LP | RCA CRL5-1106 | 1975 |
| | Moonlight Ragtime Band | LP | National Geographic 07817 | 1979 |
| | Max Morath | LP | Vanguard SRV-310 | r. 1974 |
| | New England Conservatory Ensemble | LP | Golden Crest 31031 | 1973 |
| | Knocky Parker | LP | Audiophile AP-71/72 | 1960 |
| | Knocky Parker & Bill Coffman | LP | Euphonic 1216 | 77-4 |
| | Piano Roll | LP | Biograph 1010Q | |
| | Southland Stingers | LP | Angel S-36074 | 1974 |
| | Dick Zimmerman | LP | Murray Hill 931079 | 1974 |

| Composition | Performer | Record Speed | Record Company/No. | Year-Month |
|---|---|---|---|---|
| PAN-AM RAG | | | | |
| Turpin, Tom | John Arpin | LP | Jazzology 52 | c. 1967 |
| | Milton Kaye | LP | Golden Crest 31032 | 1974 |
| PANAMA RAG | | | | |
| Seymour, Cy | Chrysanthemum Ragtime Band | LP | Stomp Off 1079 | 1984 |
| | Jazzou Jones | LP | High Water 101 | 1983 |
| | New Orleans Ragtime Orchestra | LP | Pearl 8 | 1970 |
| | Piano Roll | LP | (England) Saydisc 132 | |
| PARAGON RAG | | | | |
| Joplin, Scott | E. Power Biggs | LP | Col. M-33205 | 1974 |
| | Neville Dickie | LP | (England) Saydisc SDL-118 | 1966 |
| | Brian Dykstra | LP | Orion 83449 | 82-7 |
| | David Andrew Frost | LP | MHS 3201 | 1975 |
| | Steve Hancoff | LP | Dirty Shame 4553 | 1977 |
| | Dick Hyman | LP | RCA CRL5-1106 | 1975 |
| | James Levine | LP | RCA ARL1-2243 | 1976 |
| | Mimi & Russell | LP | Mumpus 791 | r. 1979 |
| | Max Morath | LP | Vanguard SRV-351 | r. 1976 |
| | Knocky Parker | LP | Audiophile AP-71/72 | 1960 |
| | Piano Roll | LP | Biograph 1014Q | |
| | Piano Roll (aka: Rag Pickers Rag) | LP | Dot DLP-25478 | |
| | Joshua Rifkin | LP | Nonesuch 71264 | 1972 |
| | William Neil Roberts | LP | Klavier 516 | 1973 |
| | Eric Rogers | LP | London Phase 4 21105 | 1974 |
| | Bob Tryforous | LP | Puritan 5002 | r. 1976 |
| | Dick Zimmerman | LP | Murray Hill 931079 | 1974 |
| PARAMOUNT RAG | | | | |
| Scott, James | John Jensen | LP | Genesis 1044 | 1974 |
| | Knocky Parker | LP | Audiophile AP-76/77 | 1962 |
| PARLOR SOCIAL | | | | |
| Ewell, Don | Don Ewell | EP | Good Time Jazz 1004 | 1946 |
| | Don Ewell | LP | Good Time Jazz L-12021 | 1956 |
| | Ray Smith | LP | Stomp Off 1162 | 1987 |
| PASSION RAG | | | | |
| Dallwitz, Dave | Southern Jazz Group | 78 | (Australia) Jazzart 39 | 49-12 |
| PASTIME RAG | | | | |
| Lodge, Henry | National Promenade Band | 78 | Edison 50158 | 14- |
| | Pacific Coast Ragtimers | LP | Circle CLP-137 | r. 1988 |
| PASTIME RAG #1 | | | | |
| Matthews, Artie | William Bolcom | LP | Nonesuch 71299 | 1974 |
| | Claude Bolling | LP | (France) CY 733.607 | c. 1980 |
| | Steen Christensen | LP | (Holland) Jazz Crooner 155.771 | 1977 |
| | Milton Kaye | LP | Golden Crest 31032 | 1974 |
| | New Orleans Ragtime Orchestra | LP | Pearl 7 | 67-9 |
| | Knocky Parker and Bill Coffman | LP | Jazzology 82 | c. 1979 |
| | Terry Waldo | LP | Dirty Shame 1237 | 1974 |

| Composition | Performer | Record Speed | Record Company/No. | Year-Month |
|---|---|---|---|---|
| PASTIME RAG #2 | | | | |
| Matthews, Artie | William Bolcom | LP | Nonesuch 71299 | 1974 |
| | Claude Bolling | LP | (France) CY 733.607 | c. 1980 |
| | Hall Brothers Jazz Band | LP | Stomp Off 1062 | 1981 |
| | Milton Kaye | LP | Golden Crest 31032 | 1974 |
| | Knocky Parker and Bill Coffman | LP | Jazzology 82 | c. 1979 |
| | Cesare Poggi | LP | (Italy) Dire FO-357 | 79-7 |
| | Terry Waldo | LP | Dirty Shame 1237 | 1974 |
| PASTIME RAG #3 | | | | |
| Matthews, Artie | William Bolcom | LP | Nonesuch 71299 | 1974 |
| | Ann Charters | LP | Folkways FG-3563 | 1961 |
| | Evergreen Classic Jazz Band | LP | Stomp Off 1202 | 89-6 |
| | Milton Kaye | LP | Golden Crest 31032 | 1974 |
| | Paul Lingle | LP | Euphonic 1227 | 1951 |
| | Paul Lingle | LP | Good Time Jazz L-12025 | 52-2 |
| | Knocky Parker and Bill Coffman | LP | Jazzology 82 | c. 1979 |
| | Terry Waldo | LP | Dirty Shame 1237 | 1974 |
| PASTIME RAG #4 | | | | |
| Matthews, Artie | William Bolcom | LP | Nonesuch 71299 | 1974 |
| | Claude Bolling | LP | (France) CY 733.607 | c. 1980 |
| | Dave Dallwitz Ensemble | LP | Stomp Off 1098 | 84-8 |
| | Glenn Jenks | LP | Bonnie Banks 103 | 1983 |
| | Milton Kaye | LP | Golden Crest 31032 | 1974 |
| | New England Conservatory Ensemble | LP | Golden Crest 31042 | 1975 |
| | Knocky Parker & Bill Coffman | LP | Jazzology JCE-82 | c. 1979 |
| | Wally Rose | LP | Blackbird 12007 | 1968 |
| | Cynthia Sayer Band | LP | New York Jazz 008 | 1987 |
| | Roger Shields | LP | Turnabout 34579 | 1974 |
| | Terry Waldo | LP | Dirty Shame 1237 | 1974 |
| PASTIME RAG #5 | | | | |
| Matthews, Artie | William Bolcom | LP | Nonesuch 71299 | 1974 |
| | Milton Kaye | LP | Golden Crest 31032 | 1974 |
| | LeRoy Larson | LP | Banjar 1784 | 1977 |
| | New Orleans Ragtime Orchestra | LP | (Sweden) Sonet 709 | 76-3 |
| | Knocky Parker and Bill Coffman | LP | Jazzology JCE 82 | c. 1979 |
| | Robbie Rhodes | LP | Stomp Off 1180 | 87-9 |
| | Wally Rose | LP | Fairmont 102 | 47-8 |
| | Wally Rose & Rhythm | 78 | West Coast 118 | 46-6 |
| | James Tyler Orchestra | LP | Desto 7181 | 1979 |
| | Terry Waldo | LP | Dirty Shame 1237 | 1974 |
| | Richard Zimmerman | LP | Murray Hill 60556/5 | 1981 |
| PATRICIA RAG | | | | |
| Lamb, Joseph | Brian Dykstra | LP | Orion 83449 | 82-7 |
| | Patrick Gogerty | LP | Sounds Current | 1976 |
| | John Jensen | LP | Genesis 1045 | 1974 |

| Composition | Performer | Record Speed | Record Company/No. | Year-Month |
|---|---|---|---|---|
| PATRICIA RAG (continued) | Milton Kaye | LP | Golden Crest 31035 | 1974 |
| Lamb, Joseph | Joseph Lamb | LP | Folkways FG-3562 | 59-8 |
| | Max Morath | LP | Vanguard VSD-39/40 | 1967 |
| | Tony Parenti's Ragtime Gang | LP | Jazzology 21 | 66-4 |
| PEACE & PLENTY RAG | | | | |
| Scott, James | William Albright | LP | Music Masters 20033 | 80-12 |
| | John Jensen | LP | Genesis 1044 | 1974 |
| | Morton Gunnar Larsen | LP | (Norway) Flower 439 | 75-11 |
| | Knocky Parker | LP | Audiophile AP-76/77 | 1962 |
| | Piano Roll | LP | Biograph 1016Q | |
| | Wally Rose | LP | Blackbird 12007 | 1968 |
| PEACEFUL HENRY | | | | |
| Kelly, E. Harry | Chrysanthemum Ragtime Band | LP | Stomp Off 1196 | 1988 |
| | Columbia Orchestra | 78 | Columbia 155, A-144 | |
| | Dawn of the Century Orchestra | LP | Arcane 601 | 1971 |
| | Burt Earle w/ Orchestra | 78 | (England) Odeon 0178 | 06-11 |
| | Burt Earle w/ pno | 78 | (England) Favorite 1-64002 | 06-11 |
| | King's Colonial Band | 78 | (England) Bell Disc 182 | 10-2 |
| | King's Colonial Band | 78 | (England) Bell Disc 305 | 11-6 |
| | Louisiana Symphony Orchestra | 78 | (England) Edison Bell Winner 2029 | 11-12 |
| | Vess L. Ossman w/ pno | 78 | Columbia 1620 | 04-1 |
| | Vess L. Ossman | 78 | Victor 578 | 03-10 |
| | Daryl Ott | LP | Conservatory | 82-6 |
| | Daryl Ott | LP | Dirty Shame 1238 | 1978 |
| | Alexander Prince | 78 | (England) Regal G-8160 | 21- |
| THE PEACH | | | | |
| Marshall, Arthur | Chris Barber Jazz Band | LP | (England) Columbia 33SX-1245 | 1960 |
| | Keith Nichols | LP | (England) EMI One-UP 2035 | 1974 |
| | Knocky Parker | LP | Audiophile AP-91 | |
| | Trebor Tichenor | LP | Dirty Shame 2001 | 1973 |
| PEACHERINE RAG | | | | |
| Joplin, Scott | E. Power Biggs | LP | Columbia M-32495 | 1973 |
| | William Cerny | LP | University of Notre Dame | 1975 |
| | Ann Charters | LP | Sierra Wave 101 | 1974 |
| | Dick Hyman | LP | RCA CRL5-1106 | 1975 |
| | Dave Jasen | LP | Blue Goose 3001 | 1972 |
| | New England Conservatory Ensemble | LP | Golden Crest 31031 | 1973 |
| | Knocky Parker | LP | Audiophile AP-71/72 | 1960 |
| | Piano Roll | LP | Biograph 1008Q | |
| | William Neil Roberts | LP | Klavier 510 | 1972 |
| | Mark Wetch | LP | Wilson Audio 8417 | |
| | Dick Zimmerman | LP | Murray Hill 931079 | 1974 |
| PEACHES AND CREAM | | | | |
| Wenrich, Percy | Hager's Orchestra | 78 | Zonophone 759 | r. 07-5 |
| | Red Wing Blackbirds | LP | Stomp Off 1018 | 1981 |

| Composition | Performer | Record Speed | Record Company/No. | Year-Month |
|---|---|---|---|---|
| PEANUT CACKLE | | | | |
| Herbin, Frank | Frank Herbin | 78 | (England) HMV B-1774 | 24-3 |
| PEAR BLOSSOMS | | | | |
| Hayden, Scott | Bob Darch | LP | United Artists UAL-3120 | 1960 |
| PEARL HOUSE RAG | | | | |
| Ash, Marvin | Marvin Ash | 78 | Capitol 855 | 49-11 |
| | Marvin Ash | LP | Jump J12-9 | 1947 |
| PEARL OF THE HAREM | | | | |
| Guy, Harry P. | Vess L. Ossman | 78 | Columbia 1059 | 02- |
| | Vess L. Ossman | 78 | Victor 1659 | 02-10 |
| | Fred Van Eps | 78 | Columbia A-1063 | 11-7 |
| | Fred Van Eps w/ Orchestra | 78 | Columbia A-1989 | 16-3 |
| | Fred Van Eps w/ pno | 78 | Pathe 20091 | r. 16-11 |
| | Fred Van Eps w/ pno | 78 | Pathe 30262 | r. 15-9 |
| | Fred Van Eps w/ pno | 78 | Victor 16969 | 11-1 |
| | Van Eps Banjo Band | 78 | Par-O-Ket 104 | r. 17-5 |
| | Van Eps Trio | 78 | Gennett 7610 | r. 17-10 |
| THE PEARLS | | | | |
| Morton, Jelly Roll | Lil Armstrong | 78 | (France) Vogue 5157 | 53-5 |
| | Burt Bales | LP | Euphonic 1210 | 1957 |
| | Barrelhouse JB | LP | (Germany) Intercord 145038 | 1980 |
| | Jim Beatty JB | LP | GHB 225 | 1988 |
| | Eric Brooks | 78 | (England) Poydras 70 | 50- |
| | Hans Carling JB | EP | (Sweden) Discus Celeste DCEP-105 | 1963 |
| | Judy Carmichael | LP | Statiras 8078 | 85-9 |
| | Ernie Carson JB | LP | Pearl 4 | 1964 |
| | Ry Cooder | LP | Warner Bros. BSK-3197 | c. 1978 |
| | Graham Coyle | LP | (Australia) World Record Club 2 | 1959 |
| | Mike Daniels JB | LP | (England) Col. 33SC-1256 | 60-3 |
| | James Dapogny | LP | Smithsonian 003 | 1976 |
| | Eddy Davis | LP | Pa Da 7402 | 1974 |
| | Wilbur DeParis JB | LP | Atlantic 1233 | 52-9 |
| | Downtown JB | LP | (Holland) EMI 1A054-26321 | 79-4 |
| | Don Ewell | LP | Pumpkin 120 | 66-12 |
| | Don Ewell | LP | Stomp Off 1077 | 1957 |
| | Don Ewell & Bob Greene | LP | Fat Cat's Jazz 110 | 1969 |
| | Don Ewell & Dick Wellstood | LP | Fat Cat's Jazz 218 | 81-11 |
| | Adrian Ford | LP | (Australia) Festival L-25119 | 73-12 |
| | Henry "Thins" Francis | LP | Mephistopheles 101 | c. 1984 |
| | Frank Gillis | LP | Raintree 701 | 1981 |
| | Bob Greene & Peruna JB | LP | Fat Cat's Jazz 139 | 72-1 |
| | Hall Bros. JB | 10"LP | GHB 46 | 1966 |
| | Steve Hancoff | LP | Out of Time 920 | 85-4 |
| | Happy JB | LP | Audiophile AP-86 | 64-9 |
| | Art Hodes | LP | (Canada) Sackville 3032 | 83-11 |
| | Hot Jazz Orchestra | LP | Revelation 28 | 77-8 |

| Composition | Performer | Record Speed | Record Company/No. | Year-Month |
|---|---|---|---|---|
| THE PEARLS (continued) | Dick Hyman | LP | Project 3 PR-5080 | 1973 |
| Morton, Jelly Roll | Dick Hyman Band | LP | Columbia M-32587 | 73-12 |
| | Dick Hyman Band | LP | Smithsonian N-006 | 78-2 |
| | Merle Koch | LP | Carnival 102 | 1959 |
| | Paul Kosmala | LP | Mark 5660 | 1979 |
| | Steve Lane's Stompers | LP | (England) 77 LEU 12/3 | 60-9 |
| | Cy Laurie Band | EP | (England) Esquire EP-200 | 54-7 |
| | Lawson–Haggart JB | LP | Decca DL-8182 | c. 1954 |
| | Claude Luter Sextet | LP | (France) Vogue 502606 | 79-6 |
| | Rod Mason's Hot Seven | LP | (England) Black Lion 51114 | 86-4 |
| | Midnight Stompers | EP | (Sweden) Col. SEG-22 | 56-6 |
| | Bill Mitchell | LP | Euphonic 1203 | 1962 |
| | Jelly Roll Morton | LP | (Australia) Swaggie S-1213 | 38-8 |
| | Jelly Roll Morton | 78 | Gennett 5323 | 23-7 |
| | Jelly Roll Morton | 78 | Vocalion 1020 | 26-4 |
| | Jelly Roll Morton | 12"78 | Circle JM-41/42 | 38-5 |
| | Jelly Roll Morton & Red Hot Peppers | 78 | Victor 20948 | 27-6 |
| | Turk Murphy JB | LP | (Australia) Jazz & Jazz 6357.903 | 78-12 |
| | Turk Murphy JB | LP | Dawn Club 12018 | 58-11 |
| | Turk Murphy JB | LP | GHB 93 | 72-4 |
| | Turk Murphy JB | LP | (Germany) MPS 22097 | 73-6 |
| | Turk Murphy JB | LP | Motherlode 0103 | 1967 |
| | New Delta Jazzmen | LP | (England) VJM SLC-28 | 76-8 |
| | New Orleans Rascals | LP | (Japan) RCA RVL-5517 | 1975 |
| | Keith Nichols Orchestra | LP | (England) EMI One-Up-2135 | 1976 |
| | Knocky Parker | LP | Audiophile AP-49 | 1958 |
| | Knocky Parker | LP | Audiophile AP-102 | |
| | Knocky Parker | LP | (England) London HA-U2008 | 52-4 |
| | Bent Persson JB | LP | (Sweden) Kenneth KS-2044 | 79-1 |
| | Peruna Jazzmen | LP | Fat Cat's Jazz 139 | 72-1 |
| | Portena JB | LP | (Argentina) RCA AVS-4634 | 78-10 |
| | RAI Big Band | LP | (Germany) FMP SAJ-31 | 80-5 |
| | David Thomas Roberts | LP | Mardi Gras 1002 | 1978 |
| | Wally Rose | LP | Columbia CL-559 | 53-1 |
| | Wally Rose | LP | Fairmont 102 | 47-8 |
| | Wally Rose | 78 | Good Time Jazz 26 | 50-6 |
| | Wally Rose | 10"LP | GTJ L-3 | 53-2 |
| | Wally Rose | LP | GTJ M-12034 | 58-12 |
| | Bob Scobey JB | LP | RCA Victor LPM-2086 | 59-7 |
| | Ray Smith | LP | Stomp Off 1162 | 87-8 |
| | South Frisco JB | LP | (Holland) Mark Town 15875 | 77-5 |
| | South Frisco JB | LP | Stomp Off 1035 | 81-7 |
| | Duncan Swift | LP | (England) Black Lion 12123 | 69-8 |
| | Jack Teagarden Orchestra | LP | Roulette R-25177 | 61-2 |
| | Jack Teagarden Sextet | LP | Roulette R-25177 | 1961 |
| | Butch Thompson | LP | MPR PHC-505 | 81-7 |

| Composition | Performer | Record Speed | Record Company/No. | Year-Month |
|---|---|---|---|---|
| THE PEARLS (continued) | Frank Traynor JB | LP | (Australia) W & G B-1546 | 62-12 |
| Morton, Jelly Roll | Uptown Lowdown JB | LP | Yerba Buena Jazz 101 | c. 1985 |
| | Vistula River Band | LP | (Poland) Muza SX-2404 | 82-5 |
| | Terry Waldo | LP | Dirty Shame 1237 | 1974 |
| | Weatherbird JB | LP | (Sweden) Kenneth KS-2044 | 79-1 |
| | Ron Weatherburn | LP | (England) Rediffusion 0100170 | 74-3 |
| | Mary Lou Williams | 78 | Decca 2796 | 38-9 |
| | Tex Wyndham | LP | Fat Cat's Jazz 168 | 1974 |
| PEEK-A-BOO | | | | |
| Johnson, Charles L. | Dick Zimmerman | LP | Stomp Off 1049 | 82-8 |
| PEGASUS RAG | | | | |
| Scott, James | William Bolcom | LP | Nonesuch 71257 | 1971 |
| | Brian Dykstra | LP | Orion 83449 | 82-7 |
| | John Jensen | LP | Genesis 1044 | 1974 |
| | Knocky Parker | LP | Audiophile AP-76/77 | 1962 |
| PEKIN RAG | | | | |
| Jordan, Joe | Lois Delano | LP | (Canada) Arpeggio 1205 | 1968 |
| | Glenn Jenks | LP | Bonnie Banks 104 | 1985 |
| | New Orleans Ragtime Orchestra | LP | Vanguard VSD-69/70 | 1971 |
| | Red Rose Band | LP | RedRose 001 | 1983 |
| PEP | | | | |
| Morton, Jelly Roll | Jelly Roll Morton | 12"78 | Circle JM-43 | 38-5 |
| | Jelly Roll Morton | 78 | Victor V-38627 | 29-7 |
| PEPPER SAUCE RAG | | | | |
| Fischler, H. A. | Chrysanthemum Ragtime Band | LP | Stomp Off 1047 | 1983 |
| | Piano Roll (aka: Southern Tantalizer Rag) | LP | Dot DLP-25478 | |
| PERFECT RAG | | | | |
| Morton, Jelly Roll | Len Barnard JB | EP | (Australia) Swaggie 4507 | 58-12 |
| | Len Barnard JB | LP | (Australia) Swaggie S-1011 | 53-11 |
| | Claude Bolling | LP | (France) Philips 70341 | 1966 |
| | Graham Coyle | EP | (Australia) Swaggie 4507 | 55-12 |
| | Hugh Crozier | LP | (Holland) Harbour Jazz Club 13 | 1982 |
| | Dr. Dixie Jazzband | LP | (Italy) Speedy CNR-101 | 1977 |
| | John Gill | LP | Stomp Off 1066 | 1983 |
| | Dick Hyman Orchestra | LP | Smithsonian N-006 | 78-2 |
| | Dick Hyman Trio | LP | Columbia M-32587 | 73-12 |
| | Merle Koch | LP | TAB 1006 | |
| | Morton Gunnar Larsen | LP | (Norway) Flower 439 | 75-11 |
| | Jelly Roll Morton | 78 | Gennett 5486 | 24-6 |
| | New Orleans Rascals | LP | (Japan) Philips FX-8529 | 73-6 |
| | Paramount Theatre Orchestra | LP | Stomp Off 1089 | 84-5 |
| | Knocky Parker | LP | Audiophile AP-103 | |
| | Portena JB | LP | (Argentina) Trova TL-4 | 66-4 |
| | Butch Thompson | LP | Center 4 | 66-8 |
| | Butch Thompson | LP | Stomp Off 1048 | 81-7 |
| | Uptown Lowdown JB | LP | GHB 159 | c. 1980 |
| | Ron Weatherburn | LP | (England) Alpha 32 | 62-1 |

| Composition | Performer | Record Speed | Record Company/No. | Year-Month |
|---|---|---|---|---|
| PERPETUAL RAG | | | | |
| Thomas, Harry | Harry Thomas Piano Roll | LP | Herwin 407 | |
| PERSIAN LAMB RAG | | | | |
| Wenrich, Percy | Gibson String Trio | 78 | Gennett 6618 | 28-8 |
| | Vess L. Ossman w/ pno | 78 | Victor 16127 | 08-10 |
| | Bob Roberts Trio | 78 | MGM 11414 | 52- |
| | Victor Militiary Band | 78 | Victor | 10-4 |
| | Richard Zimmerman | LP | Murray Hill 60556/5 | 1981 |
| | Zonophone Orchestra | 78 | Zonophone 1150, 5320 | 08-6 |
| PERSONALITY | | | | |
| Rowland, William | George Hicks | LP | Folkways FS-3165 | 1983 |
| PHANTOM RAG | | | | |
| Ginsburg, Sol and Brown, Al | Charlie Booty | LP | Dirty Shame 1239 | r. 1980 |
| PIANJO RAG | | | | |
| Cramer, Floyd | Floyd Cramer | 78 | MGM 12059 | 55-7 |
| PI-ANN-A RAG | | | | |
| Lally | Sid Phillips & Band | 78 | (England) HMV BD-6156 | 53-11 |
| PIANO MAN RAG (see NIGGER'S HOP) Batten, Joseph | Joe Bolton (Joe Batten) | 78 | (England) Edison Bell Winner 3771 | 22-11 |
| PIANO MARMALADE | | | | |
| Smith, Willie the Lion | Neville Dickie | LP | Stomp Off 1176 | 1988 |
| PIANO PUZZLE | | | | |
| Reichenthal, Ralph | Stanley C. Holt | 78 | (England) Homochord H-425 | 23-4 |
| | Ralph Reichenthal | 78 | Arto 9193 | r. 23-1 |
| PIANO PUZZLE | | | | |
| Schutt, Arthur | Arthur Schutt | 78 | Okeh 41243 | 29-3 |
| PIANOFLAGE | | | | |
| Bargy, Roy | Roy Bargy | 78 | Victor 18969 | 22-8 |
| | Roy Bargy Piano Roll | LP | Folkways RF-35 | |
| | George Hicks | LP | Folkways FS-3165 | 1983 |
| | Henry Lange | 78 | Brunswick 2344 | 22-9 |
| | Fate Marable's Orchestra | 78 | Okeh 40113 | 24-3 |
| | Ivor Moreton & Dave Kaye | 78 | (England) Parlophone F-2485 | |
| | Keith Nichols | LP | (England) EMI One-Up-2085 | 1975 |
| | Cecil Norman | 78 | (England) Homochord H-545 | 23-12 |
| | Patricia Rossborough | 78 | (England) Parlophone R-1599 | 33-7 |
| | Arthur Schutt | 78 | (England) Regal G-8046 | 23-7 |
| | Ray Turner | 78 | Capitol 2094 | 52-3 |
| PIANOLA | | | | |
| Westphal, Frank | Frank Westphal | 78 | Columbia A-3930 | 23-5 |
| PIANOTES | | | | |
| Paques, Jean | Jean Paques | 78 | (England) Edison Bell Winner 4932 | 29-7 |
| PICCADILLY RAG | | | | |
| Busch, Louis F. | Joe "Fingers" Carr | 78 | Capitol 2834 | 53-8 |

| Composition | Performer | Record Speed | Record Company/No. | Year-Month |
|---|---|---|---|---|
| PICKIN'S | | | | |
| Reser, Harry | Howard Alden | LP | Stomp Off 1200 | 1988 |
| | Keith Nichols | LP | (England) EMI One-Up-2085 | 1975 |
| | Harry Reser w/ Orchestra | 78 | Brunswick 2308 | r. 22-9 |
| | Harry Reser w/ pno | 78 | (England) Columbia 3317 | 23-6 |
| | Royale Trio | 78 | Pathe 020896 | r. 23-3 |
| | Terry Waldo's Band | LP | Stomp Off 1120 | 84-4 |
| PICKING THE GUITAR | | | | |
| Lucas, Nick | Nick Lucas | 78 | Brunswick 2536 | 23-11 |
| | Nick Lucas | 78 | Brunswick 6508 | 32-12 |
| | Nick Lucas | 78 | Pathe 020794 | 22-6 |
| PICKLES AND PEPPERS | | | | |
| Shepherd, Adaline | Max Morath | LP | Vanguard VSD-79402 | 1977 |
| | Turk Murphy Jazz Band | LP | Atlantic 1613 | 71-9 |
| | New Orleans Ragtime Orchestra | LP | Stomp Off 1213 | 1989 |
| | Piano Roll | LP | Sounds 1201 | |
| | Pryor's Band | 78 | Victor 5713 | 09-3 |
| | Wally Rose | LP | Blackbird 12007 | 1968 |
| | Uptown Lowdown Jazz Band | LP | Uptown Lowdown 303 | 1978 |
| | Richard Zimmerman | LP | Murray Hill 60556/5 | 1981 |
| | Zonophone Concert Band | 78 | Zonophone 839 | r. 07-9 |
| PIERCE CITY RAG | | | | |
| Tichenor, Trebor | St. Louis Ragtimers | LP | Ragophile | 1961 |
| | Trebor Tichenor | LP | Folkways FS-3164 | 1979 |
| PIFFLE RAG | | | | |
| Yelvington, Gladys | Max Morath | LP | Vanguard VSD-79402 | 1977 |
| PINEAPPLE RAG | | | | |
| Joplin, Scott | Marden Abadi | LP | Sine Qua Non 2020 | c. 1979 |
| | T. J. Anderson Orchestra | LP | Smithsonian 001 | 1975 |
| | John Arpin & Catherine Wilson | LP | (Canada) Fanfare 9023 | r. 1986 |
| | Graeme Bell | LP | (Australia) Festival L-45545/6 | 74-8 |
| | E. Power Biggs | LP | Columbia M-32495 | 1973 |
| | Sune Borg | LP | (Sweden) Sumpen 1001 | 1977 |
| | William Cerny | LP | University of Notre Dame | 1975 |
| | Steen Christensen | LP | (Denmark) LB 1 | 1972 |
| | Neville Dickie | LP | (England) Contour 2870-190 | 1972 |
| | David Andrew Frost | LP | MHS 3201 | 1975 |
| | John Hasse | LP | Sunflower 501 | 1980 |
| | Hellman's Angels | LP | Plug 8 | 86-1 |
| | Marc Herouet's Cats | LP | (Belgium) Snow 1001 | r. 1981 |
| | Dick Hyman | LP | RCA CRL5-1106 | 1975 |
| | James Levine | LP | RCA ARL1-2243 | 1976 |
| | Donny McDonald Band | LP | Pine Street 1 | 75-4 |
| | Turk Murphy JB | LP | Columbia CL-793 | 1955 |
| | Turk Murphy JB | LP | Dawn Club 12018 | 58-11 |
| | New England Conservatory Ensemble | LP | Golden Crest 31031 | 1973 |

| Composition | Performer | Record Speed | Record Company/No. | Year-Month |
|---|---|---|---|---|
| PINEAPPLE RAG (continued) | New Orleans Ragtime Orchestra | LP | Vanguard VSD-69/70 | 1971 |
| Joplin, Scott | Palm Court Orchestra | LP | (Australia) K-Tel NA-628 | r. 1986 |
| | Knocky Parker | LP | Audiophile AP-71/72 | 1960 |
| | Knocky Parker | LP | (England) London HA-U2008 | 52-4 |
| | Knocky Parker & Bill Coffman | LP | Euphonic 1216 | 77-4 |
| | Itzhak Perlman & Andre Previn | LP | Angel S-37113 | 1975 |
| | Piano Roll | LP | Biograph 1010Q | |
| | Piano Roll | LP | Biograph 1013Q | |
| | Steve Pistorious | LP | Jazzology JCE-78 | 1975 |
| | Cesare Poggi | LP | (Italy) Dire FO-357 | 79-7 |
| | Ronnie Price | LP | (England) Embassy 31043 | c. 1973 |
| | Ragtime Orchestra (m) | LP | (Czechoslovakia) Supraphon 1115.1965 | 1976 |
| | The Ragtimers | LP | RCA Camden ACL1-0599 | 74-5 |
| | Joshua Rifkin | LP | Nonesuch 71264 | 1972 |
| | William Neil Roberts | LP | Klavier 510 | 1972 |
| | Eric Rogers | LP | London Phase 4 21105 | 1974 |
| | Wally Rose | LP | Dawn Club 12003 | 47-8 |
| | Wally Rose | LP | Fairmont 102 | 47-8 |
| | Wally Rose | 78 | Good Time Jazz 27 | 50-6 |
| | Wally Rose | 10"LP | GTJ LP-3 | 53-2 |
| | Wally Rose | LP | GTJ M-12034 | 58-12 |
| | Royal Garden Ramblers | LP | (Switzerland) Elite Special 52584 | 79-3 |
| | Tom Shea | LP | (Canada) Ragtime Society 1 | 1963 |
| | Fred Sokolow | LP | Kicking Mule 212 | c. 1982 |
| | South Frisco JB | LP | Stomp Off 1143 | 84-11 |
| | Southland Stingers | LP | Angel S-36074 | 1974 |
| | St. Louis Ragtimers | LP | Ragophile | 1961 |
| | Ton Van Bergeyk | LP | Kicking Mule 114 | r. 1976 |
| | Lu Watters YBJB | 78 | West Coast 110 | 46-6 |
| | Dick Wellstood | LP | Pickwick SPC-3376 | 1974 |
| | Mary Lou Williams | LP | NYPL SJ | 71-10 |
| | Dick Zimmerman | LP | Murray Hill 931079 | 1974 |
| PINK POODLE | | | | |
| Johnson, Charles L. | Dick Zimmerman | LP | Stomp Off 1017 | 1981 |
| PINYWOODS RAG | | | | |
| Cocroft, N. Weldon | Trebor Tichenor | LP | Folkways FS-3164 | 1979 |
| PIPPIN RAG | | | | |
| Marshall, Arthur | Milton Kaye | LP | Golden Crest 31032 | 1974 |
| | Max Morath | LP | Vanguard SRV-310 | r. 1974 |
| PLAY THE RAG | | | | |
| | Sid Philips & Band | 78 | (England) HMV BD-6132 | 50- |
| POISON IVY RAG | | | | |
| Ingraham, Herbert | Dave Jasen | LP | Blue Goose 3001 | 1972 |
| | Knocky Parker | LP | Audiophile AP-91 | |
| | San Francisco Harry | LP | Fantasy 3270 | 1958 |

| Composition | Performer | Record Speed | Record Company/No. | Year-Month |
|---|---|---|---|---|
| **POKER RAG** | | | | |
| Blake, Charlotte | Chrysanthemum Ragtime Band | LP | Stomp Off 1047 | 1983 |
| | Max Morath | LP | Vanguard VSD-79402 | 1977 |
| **POLLY** | | | | |
| Zamecnik, John S. | H. Robinson Cleaver | 78 | (England) Parlophone F-892 | |
| | Zez Confrey Orchestra | 78 | Victor 21010 | 27-8 |
| | Raie Da Costa | 78 | (England) Parlophone R-3534 | 28-3 |
| | Reginald Dixon | 78 | (England) Columbia FB-3624 | |
| | Bert Firman & Orchestra | 78 | (England) Zonophone 5046 | 27-11 |
| | Gerald Marks & Orchestra | 78 | Columbia 1121-D | 27-6 |
| | Constance Mering & Muriel Pollock | 78 | Columbia 1211-D | 27-11 |
| | Ivor Moreton & Dave Kaye (m) | 78 | (England) Parlophone R-1797 | 34-3 |
| | Phil Ohman–Victor Arden & Orchestra | 78 | Brunswick 3305 | r. 26-9 |
| | Pattman | 78 | (England) Columbia 4847 | |
| | Fred Rich & Orchestra | 78 | (England) Columbia 4721 | 28-1 |
| | Sid Roy & Orchestra | 78 | (England) Imperial 1904 | |
| | Wally Rose | LP | Stomp Off 1057 | 1982 |
| | Al Siegel | 78 | (England) Zonophone 5056 | 27-2 |
| | Rudy Starr Three | 78 | (England) Parlophone R-132 | |
| **POLYRAGMIC** | | | | |
| Morath, Max | Max Morath | LP | Vanguard VSD-39/40 | 1967 |
| | Queen City Ragtime Ensemble | LP | Zeno 99 | 1976 |
| | James Tyler Orchestra | LP | Desto 7181 | 1979 |
| **POODLE RAG** | | | | |
| Krenz, Bill | Bill Krenz | 78 | MGM 30706 | 1952 |
| **POOR BUTTERMILK** | | | | |
| Confrey, Zez | Zez Confrey | 78 | Brunswick 2112 | 21-5 |
| | Zez Confrey | 78 | Emerson 10486 | 21-9 |
| | Stanley C. Holt | 78 | (England) Homochord H-448 | 23-9 |
| | John Jensen | LP | Genesis 1051 | 1974 |
| | Milton Kaye | LP | Golden Crest 31040 | 1974 |
| | Arthur Kleiner | LP | Golden Crest 2004 | c. 1967 |
| | Russ Morgan & Eddie Wilser | LP | Decca DL-8746 | 1958 |
| | Vi Palmer (Zez Confrey) | 78 | Banner 2049 | 21-9 |
| | Wayne and Geraldi | LP | Reader's Digest RDA-70-01-05 | 1968 |
| | Dick Wellstood | LP | Jazzology 73 | 1971 |
| **POOR JIMMY GREEN** | | | | |
| Blake, Eubie | Eubie Blake | LP | Columbia C2S-847 | 69-3 |
| | Morton Gunnar Larsen | LP | Stomp Off 1009 | 81-1 |
| **POOR KATIE REDD** | | | | |
| Blake, Eubie | Amherst Saxophone Quartet | LP | Musical Heritage Society 4368 | 80-12 |
| | Eubie Blake | LP | Columbia C2S-847 | 69-3 |
| | Max Morath | LP | Vanguard 79418 | 1979 |

| Composition | Performer | Record Speed | Record Company/No. | Year-Month |
|---|---|---|---|---|
| **POPULAR RAG** | | | | |
| Long, Webb | Victor Military Band | 12"78 | Victor 35515 | 15-12 |
| **POPULARITY** | | | | |
| Cohan, George M. | Harry Breuer Orchestra | LP | Audio Fidelity 3001 | 1960 |
| | Chrysanthemum Ragtime Band | LP | Stomp Off 1123 | 1985 |
| | Vess L. Ossman w/ Orchestra | 78 | Columbia 3529, A-892 | 06-10 |
| | Vess L. Ossman w/ Orchestra | 78 | Zonophone 637 | r. 07-1 |
| | Vess L. Ossman w/ pno | 78 | Sun 45477 | |
| | Pavilion Royale Orchestra | 78 | (France) Grammophon 30735 | |
| | Van Eps–Banta Dance Orchestra | 78 | Pathe 20328 | r. 18-5 |
| | Richard Zimmerman | LP | Murray Hill 60556/5 | 1981 |
| **PORCUPINE RAG** | | | | |
| Johnson, Charles L. | Ballyhooligans (m) | 78 | (England) HMV BD-5131 | 36-10 |
| | Etcetera String Band | LP | Moon 200 | 1975 |
| | New York Military Band | 78 | Edison 50287 | 15-10 |
| | Knocky Parker | LP | Audiophile AP-91 | |
| | Prince's Band | 78 | Columbia A-901 | 09-11 |
| | Red Wing Blackbirds | LP | Stomp Off 1018 | 1981 |
| | Harry Roy Orchestra | 78 | (England) Parlophone F-388 | 36-1 |
| **PORK AND BEANS** | | | | |
| Bennett, Theron | Knocky Parker | LP | Audiophile AP-91 | |
| **PORK AND BEANS** | | | | |
| Roberts, Luckey | All Star JB | 78 | (Belgium) Sphinx 6026 | 50-6 |
| | David Bee Gang | LP | (Belgium) Bally 12005 | 56-5 |
| | Eubie Blake | LP | Eubie Blake Music 2 | 1971 |
| | William Bolcom | LP | Nonesuch 71257 | 1971 |
| | Henri Chaix | LP | (Switzerland) Philips 843813 | 1969 |
| | Bernard Ette Orchestra | 78 | (Germany) Kristall 3009 | 29-12 |
| | Earl Fuller's Orchestra | 78 | Columbia A-2370 | 17-7 |
| | James P. Johnson | LP | Library of Congress 14 | 38-12 |
| | Donald Lambert | LP | IAJRC 23 | c. 1962 |
| | Morton Gunnar Larsen | LP | Stomp Off 1009 | 81-1 |
| | Luckey Roberts | 78 | Circle 1027 | 46-6 |
| | Wally Rose | LP | Fantasy 5016 | 1964 |
| | Roger Shields | LP | Turnabout 34579 | 1974 |
| | Willie the Lion Smith | 10"LP | Dial 305 | 50-1 |
| | Willie the Lion Smith | LP | (England) Black Lion BLP-30123 | 66-11 |
| | Elite Syncopators | LP | Jazzology JC-102 | r. 1989 |
| | Dick Wellstood | LP | Chiaroscuro 109 | 70-11 |
| | Richard Zimmerman | LP | Murray Hill 60556/5 | 1981 |
| | Paul Zukofsky & Robert Dennis | LP | Vanguard SRV-350 | 1975 |
| **PORTO RICO RAG** | | | | |
| Dabney, Ford | John Arpin & Catherine Wilson | LP | (Canada) Fanfare 9023 | r. 1986 |
| | Chrysanthemum Ragtime Band | LP | Stomp Off 1047 | 1983 |
| | George Foley | LP | Stomp Off 1187 | 1988 |

| Composition | Performer | Record Speed | Record Company/No. | Year-Month |
|---|---|---|---|---|
| POSSUM AND TATERS | | | | |
| Hunter, Charles | Knocky Parker | LP | Audiophile AP-89 | |
| | Piano Roll | 10"LP | Riverside RLP-1025 | |
| | Piano Roll | LP | Sounds 1201 | |
| | Alan Rogers | LP | (England) VJM LC-4 | 1965 |
| | Roger Shields | LP | Turnabout 34579 | 1974 |
| | Trebor Tichenor | LP | (Canada) Scroll 102 | 1966 |
| POSSUM RAG | | | | |
| Dobyns, Geraldine | Charlie Rasch | LP | (Canada) Ragtime Society 4 | 1966 |
| POVERTY RAG | | | | |
| Lincoln, Harry J. | Billy Hamilton's Rag Pickers | 78 | Vega 114 | |
| POWDER RAG | | | | |
| Birch, Raymond | Black Diamonds Band (Peerless Orchestra) | 78 | (England) Zonophone 1016 | 12-11 |
| | Fried Potatoes | LP | (Holland) Cat LP-56 | 86-4 |
| | New Orleans Ragtime Orchestra | LP | GHB 210 | 87-1 |
| | Piano Roll | LP | Sounds 1201 | |
| | Royal Military Band | 78 | (England) Edison Bell Winner 2259 | 13-9 |
| | Ton Van Bergeyk | LP | Kicking Mule 114 | r. 1976 |
| | Fred Van Eps w/ Orchestra | Cylinder | U.S. Phonograph Co. 1398 | r. 12-4 |
| | Fred Van Eps w/ Orchestra | 78 | Zonophone 5876 | r. 12-4 |
| PRIDE OF BUCKTOWN | | | | |
| Roberts, Robert S. | Wally Rose | LP | Stomp Off 1057 | 1982 |
| PRIDE OF THE SMOKY ROW | | | | |
| Wilcockson, J. M. | Dawn of the Century Ragtime Orchestra | LP | Arcane 603 | 1973 |
| | Gale Foehner | LP | Stomp Off 1023 | 81-7 |
| | Bill Mitchell | LP | Ethelyn 1750 | 1972 |
| | Piano Roll | LP | Indiana Historical Society 1001 | |
| | David Thomas Roberts | LP | Stomp Off 1021 | 1981 |
| | Richard Zimmerman | LP | Murray Hill 60556/5 | 1981 |
| PRINCESS RAG | | | | |
| Scott, James | Knocky Parker | LP | Audiophile AP-76/77 | 1962 |
| PROCRASTINATION RAG | | | | |
| Cobb, George L. | Chrysanthemum Ragtime Band | LP | Stomp Off 1123 | 1985 |
| | George Foley | LP | Stomp Off 1088 | 1984 |
| PROFICIENCY | | | | |
| Hession, Jim | Jim Hession | LP | Eubie Blake Music 6 | 1973 |
| PROSPERITY RAG | | | | |
| Scott, James | John Jensen | LP | Genesis 1044 | 1974 |
| | Knocky Parker | LP | Audiophile AP-76/77 | 1962 |
| | Keith Taylor | LP | Sami 1001 | 1974 |
| PRYOR FOX TROT | | | | |
| Pryor, Arthur | Victor Military Band | 12"78 | Victor 35411 | r. 14-12 |

| Composition | Performer | Record Speed | Record Company/No. | Year-Month |
|---|---|---|---|---|
| PURDUE RAG | | | | |
| Boyer, Opal | Piano Roll | LP | Indiana Historical Society 1001 | |
| PUSSY FOOT | | | | |
| Hoffman, Robert | New Leviathan Orchestra | LP | Camelback 19328 | 1980 |
| PUTTING ON THE DOG | | | | |
| Shapiro, Ted | Willie Eckstein | 78 | Okeh 40121 | 24-4 |
| QUALITY RAG | | | | |
| Scott, James | T. J. Anderson Orchestra | LP | Smithsonian N-001 | 1975 |
| | W. Arlington Piano Roll | LP | Biograph 1006Q | |
| | John Jensen | LP | Genesis 1044 | 1974 |
| | London Ragtime Orchestra | LP | Stomp Off 1081 | 84-8 |
| | Max Morath | LP | Vanguard VSD-39/40 | 1967 |
| | Knocky Parker | LP | Audiophile AP-76/77 | 1962 |
| | Phoenix Ragtime Ensemble | LP | World Jazz 12 | 77-6 |
| | Piano Roll | LP | Biogragh 1016Q | |
| | Piano Roll | 78 | Circle 5005 | |
| QUALITY SHOUT | | | | |
| Hill, Alex | Paul Howard's Quality Serenaders | 78 | Victor V-38122 | 29-4 |
| QUEEN OF LOVE | | | | |
| Hunter, Charles | David Thomas Roberts | LP | Stomp Off 1021 | 1981 |
| QUIVERY QUAVERS | | | | |
| Thomas, Lloyd | Pall Mall Revellers | 78 | (England) Bosworth 1072 | |
| QWINDO'S RAG | | | | |
| Jasen, David A. | Dave Jasen | LP | Blue Goose 3001 | 1972 |
| RACE DAY RAG | | | | |
| Dallwitz, Dave | Southern Jazz Group | 78 | (Australia) Jazzart 40 | 49-12 |
| RACING DOWN THE BLACK AND WHITES | | | | |
| Carroll, Adam | Tony Caramia | LP | Stomp Off 1209 | 1989 |
| RACKETY RAG | | | | |
| Delcamp, J. Milton | J. Milton Delcamp Piano Roll | LP | Herwin 407 | |
| RAG-A-BIT | | | | |
| Straight, Charley | Charley Straight Piano Roll | LP | Folkways RBF-44 | |
| RAG BABY RAG | | | | |
| Losey, F. H. | Sammy Spear Orchestra | LP | Jubilee 1110 | c. 1952 |
| RAG BAG RAG | | | | |
| Lincoln, Harry | Butch Thompson | LP | Stomp Off 1116 | 84-3 |
| RAG BAG RAG | | | | |
| Taylor, H. S. | Zonophone Orchestra | 78 | Zonophone 5561 | r. 09-12 |
| RAG DOLL | | | | |
| Brown, Nacio Herb | Godfrey Andolfi | 78 | (France) Pathe X-8616 | 31-5 |
| | Anton & Orchestra (m) | 78 | (England) HMV BD-570 | |
| | Victor Arden–Phil Ohman & Orchestra | 78 | Victor 21588 | 28-7 |

| Composition | Performer | Record Speed | Record Company/No. | Year-Month |
|---|---|---|---|---|
| RAG DOLL (continued) | Harry Bidgood & Orchestra | 78 | (England) Broadcast 308 | |
| Brown, Nacio Herb | Raie Da Costa & Orchestra | 78 | (England) Parlophone R-238 | 28-10 |
| | Gil Dech | 78 | (Australia) Columbia 01196 | 28-7 |
| | Reginald Dixon (m) | 78 | (England) Regal Zonophone MR-3385 | |
| | Bert Firman & Rhythm Eight | 78 | (England) Zonophone 5217 | 28-9 |
| | Edna Fischer | 78 | Victor 21384 | 28-4 |
| | Russell Jones | EP | (Australia) Century EPC-2 | 56-3 |
| | Sam Lanin & Orchestra | 78 | Domino 4146 | 28-4 |
| | Abe Lyman's California Orchestra | 78 | Brunswick 3943 | 28-5 |
| | Billy Mayerl | 78 | (England) Columbia 5154 | 28-10 |
| | Constance Mering & Muriel Pollack | 78 | Columbia 1447-D | 28-6 |
| | Ivor Moreton & Dave Kaye (m) | 78 | (England) Parlophone F-550 | |
| | New Mayfair Novelty Orchestra (m) | 78 | (England) HMV BD-683 | |
| | Pickard's Chinese Syncopators | 78 | (England) HMV B-5528 | 28-6 |
| | Rawicz & Landauer | 78 | (Austria) HMV AM-1957 | 29-5 |
| | Harry Robbins (m) | 78 | (England) Columbia FB-1355 | |
| | Willard Robison & Orchestra | 78 | Perfect 14972 | 28-4 |
| | B. A. Rolfe Orchestra | 78 | Edison 52268 | 28-4 |
| | Andy Sanella Trio | 78 | Harmony 656-H | |
| | Debroy Somers Band | 78 | (England) Columbia 5038 | |
| | Varsity Four | 78 | Brunswick 3918 | 28-4 |
| | Lawrence Welk & Orchestra | 78 | Coral 61207 | 53-5 |
| | Sid Williams | 78 | Vocalion 15689 | 28-4 |
| RAG OF RAGS | | | | |
| | Mary Lou Williams | 78 | London 1174 | 53-3 |
| RAG PICKER'S RAG | | | | |
| O'Brien, Robert | Richard Zimmerman | LP | Murray Hill 60556/5 | 1981 |
| RAG SENTIMENTAL | | | | |
| Scott, James | Ann Charters | LP | Folkways FG-3563 | 1961 |
| | Knocky Parker | LP | Audiophile AP-76/77 | 1962 |
| | Piano Roll | LP | Biograph 1016Q | |
| RAG TRADE RAG | | | | |
| Franks, Gordon | Gordon Franks Orchestra | 45 | (England) Parlophone R-4910 | 1962 |
| RAGAMUFFIN | | | | |
| Greer, Jesse | Victor Arden & Phil Ohman | 78 | Victor 21929 | 29-3 |
| | New Mayfair Dance Orchestra | 78 | (England) HMV B-5632 | 29-3 |
| | Rudy Starita | 78 | (England) Columbia 5646 | |
| RAGAMUFFIN RAG | | | | |
| Lange, Arthur | Pacific Coast Ragtimers | LP | Circle CLP-137 | r. 1988 |
| RAG-A-MUFFIN RAG | | | | |
| Pierson, Will T. | Victor Military Band | 78 | Victor 17619 | 14-4 |
| RAGGED RAPIDS RAG | | | | |
| Lamb, Joseph | Milton Kaye | LP | Golden Crest 31035 | 1974 |

| Composition | Performer | Record Speed | Record Company/No. | Year-Month |
|---|---|---|---|---|
| **RAGGED THOUGHTS** | | | | |
| Von Der Mehden, Jr., J. Louis | Pathe Dance Orchestra | 78 | Pathe 29192, 35100 | r. 17-3 |
| | Zonophone Orchestra | 78 | Zonophone 1010 | r. 08-4 |
| **RAGGEDY ANN RAG** | | | | |
| Busch, Louis F. | Joe "Fingers" Carr's Ragtime Band | LP | Capitol T-443 | |
| | Brooke Pemberton | 45 | Warners Bros. 5010 | |
| **RAGGEDY ANNE** | | | | |
| Wellstood, Dick | Dick Wellstood | 78 | Century 4002 | 47-4 |
| **RAGGING THE CHIMES** | | | | |
| Grant, Mel | Professor Ragtime | 78 | Joco 109 | 50-4 |
| **RAGGING THE SCALE** | | | | |
| Claypoole, Edward B. | Anglo-Persians | 78 | Brunswick 4021 | r. 28-9 |
| | Paul Ash Orchestra | 78 | Varsity 649 | 37-3 |
| | Jan August | 45 | Mercury 1367 | 1951 |
| | Ballyhooligans | 78 | (England) HMV BD-5094 | 36-7 |
| | Harry Breuer Orchestra | LP | Audio Fidelity AFSC-5912 | 1960 |
| | Broadway Dance Orchestra | 78 | Edison 51223 | 23-9 |
| | Fud Candrix JB | 78 | (Belgium) Telefunken A-2660 | 38-6 |
| | Fud Candrix & Orchestra | 78 | (Germany) Telefunken A-2660 | 38-6 |
| | Joe "Fingers" Carr | 78 | Capitol 15727 | 51-9 |
| | Joe "Fingers" Carr | LP | Cap. T-280 | c. 1951 |
| | Eddie Condon Orchestra | 78 | Decca 27408 | 50-10 |
| | Conway's Band | 78 | Victor 17850 | 15-8 |
| | Frank Denke | LP | Doric 1408 | 1976 |
| | The Duchess | 78 | London 1338 | |
| | Emerson Military Band | 78 | Emerson 7118 | r. 16-12 |
| | Don Harper | LP | (England) EMI One-Up-2202 | 77-6 |
| | Dick Hyman | LP | Cadence CR-2001 | 1974 |
| | Vernon Geyer | 78 | Montgomery Ward M-7388 | |
| | Grammophon Tanz Orchester | 78 | (Germany) Grammophon 15822 | |
| | Jaudas Society Orchestra | 78 | Edison 50305 | 15-11 |
| | Ben Light | 78 | Tempo 568 | |
| | Vincent Lopez & Orchestra | 78 | Okeh 4921 | r. 23-11 |
| | Jimmy Lunceford & Orchestra | 78 | Decca 1364 | 37-6 |
| | Metropolitan Military Band | 78 | (England) Diamond 0236 | |
| | Russ Morgan & Orchestra | 78 | Brunswick 7925 | 37-7 |
| | Original Excentric Band | 78 | (Germany) Homocord 15986 | 19-12 |
| | Operaphone Band | 78 | Operaphone 1035 | r. 16-1 |
| | Knuckles O'Toole | LP | Grand Award 33-373 | |
| | Pathe Dance Orchestra | 78 | Pathe 30410 | r. 16-4 |
| | Peruna Jazzmen | LP | (Denmark) Storyville SLP-407 | 77-6 |
| | Jack Pleis Orchestra | 78 | London 611 | |
| | Prince's Band | 12"78 | Columbia A-5702 | r. 15-8 |
| | Ragtime Banjo Commission | LP | GHB 154 | 80-8 |
| | Red Roseland Cornpickers | LP | (Sweden) Auviton 2021 | 84-2 |
| | Alvino Rey | 78 | Capitol 15272 | |

| Composition | Performer | Record Speed | Record Company/No. | Year-Month |
|---|---|---|---|---|
| RAGGING THE SCALE (continued) Claypoole, Edward B. | Adrian Rollini Trio | LP | Mercury MG-20011 | 1950 |
| | Sammy Spear Orchestra | LP | Jubilee JLP-1110 | c. 1952 |
| | Three Suns | 78 | Victor 20-3700 | 49-6 |
| | Fred Van Eps | 78 | Victor 18085 | 16-6 |
| | Van Eps Trio | 78 | Paramount 2050 | |
| | Joe Venuti's Blue Four | 78 | Okeh 41432 | 30-5 |
| | Joe Venuti's Blue Four | 78 | Columbia 2765-D | 33-2 |
| | Wayne & Geraldi | LP | Reader's Digest RDA-70-01-05 | 1968 |
| | Paul Whiteman Orchestra | 78 | Decca 2268 | 38-11 |
| | Victor Young Orchestra | 78 | Decca 23952 | 44-10 |
| RAGGY FOX TROT Goffin, Laurence E. | Johnny Gibbs Band | LP | Reader's Digest RDA-70-01-05 | 1968 |
| RAGMAN'S EXERCISE Squires, Harold | Stanley C. Holt | 78 | (England) Homocord 434 | 1923 |
| RAGS TO BURN McFadden, Frank X. | Wally Rose | LP | Blackbird 12010 | 71-6 |
| | Richard Zimmerman | LP | Murray Hill 60556/5 | 1981 |
| RAGTIME BETTY Scott, James | T. J. Anderson Orchestra | LP | Smithsonian N-001 | 1975 |
| | Knocky Parker | LP | Audiophile AP-76/77 | 1962 |
| | Jack Rummel | LP | Stomp Off 1118 | 1985 |
| RAGTIME BOBOLINK Lamb, Joseph | George Foley | LP | Stomp Off 1187 | 1988 |
| | Patrick Gogerty | LP | Sounds Current | 1976 |
| | Dennis James | LP | Concert M-109 | r. 1973 |
| | Jazzou Jones | LP | High Water 101 | 1983 |
| | Milton Kaye | LP | Golden Crest 4127 | 1974 |
| RAGTIME CHIMES Wenrich, Percy | Daryl Ott | LP | Uplift R-0180 | 1980 |
| | Trebor Tichenor | LP | Dirty Shame 2001 | 1973 |
| RAGTIME DANCE Mills, Kerry | Dawn of the Century Orchestra | LP | Arcane 603 | 1973 |
| | Turk Murphy Jazz Band | LP | (Australia) Jazz & Jazz 6357.903 | 1978 |
| | Turk Murphy Jazz Band | LP | Good Time Jazz L-12026 | 50-1 |
| | New Sunshine Jazz Band | LP | Biograph 12058 | 1978 |
| | St. Louis Ragtimers | LP | Paseo 102 | 1968 |
| | Wally Rose | LP | Blackbird 12010 | 71-6 |
| | South Frisco Jazz Band | LP | Stomp Off 1027 | 1981 |
| | Watergate Seven Plus One | LP | Stomp Off 1165 | 87-7 |
| RAGTIME DANCE Joplin, Scott | Marden Abadi | LP | Sine Qua Non 2020 | c. 1979 |
| | Concert Arban | LP | (France) Arion 33786 | 1985 |
| | Graeme Bell | LP | (Australia) Festival L-45545/6 | 74-8 |
| | William Bolcom | LP | NYPL SJ | 71-10 |
| | Budapest Ragtime Orchestra | LP | (Czechoslovakia) Krem SLPX-17794 | 1984 |

| Composition | Performer | Record Speed | Record Company/No. | Year-Month |
|---|---|---|---|---|
| RAGTIME DANCE (continued) | Neville Dickie | LP | (England) Contour 2870-190 | 1972 |
| Joplin, Scott | Neville Dickie | LP | (England) Saydisc SDL-118 | 1966 |
| | Eden Electronic Ensemble | LP | (England) Pye 12101 | 1975 |
| | Myron Floren | LP | Ranwood 8127 | 1974 |
| | Raymond Fonseque Band | LP | (France) Promophone 4 | 73-10 |
| | David Andrew Frost | LP | MHS 3201 | 1975 |
| | Steve Hancoff | LP | Dirty Shame 4553 | 1977 |
| | Dick Hyman | LP | RCA CRL5-1106 | 1975 |
| | Bill Knopf | LP | First Inversion 001 | r. 1983 |
| | Dick Kroeckel | LP | Ragtime GRU-1930 | 1977 |
| | Paul Lolax | LP | Titanic 13 | 1981 |
| | London Ragtime Orchestra | LP | Stomp Off 1081 | 84-8 |
| | Mimi & Russell | LP | Mumpus 791 | r. 1979 |
| | Bill Mitchell | LP | Euphonic 1203 | 1962 |
| | Max Morath | LP | Vanguard VSD-39/40 | 1967 |
| | New England Conservatory | LP | Angel 36060 | 1973 |
| | New Orleans Ragtime Orchestra | LP | ABC AA-1076 | 1977 |
| | New Orleans Ragtime Orchestra | LP | Arhoolie 1058 | 71-5 |
| | Knocky Parker | LP | Audiophile AP-71/72 | 1960 |
| | Knocky Parker & Bill Coffman | LP | Jazzology JCE-82 | c. 1979 |
| | Itzhak Perlman & Andre Previn | LP | Angel S-37113 | 1975 |
| | Piano Roll | LP | Biograph 1013Q | |
| | Ronnie Price | LP | (England) Embassy 31043 | c. 1973 |
| | Queen City Ragtime Ensemble | LP | Zeno 99 | 1976 |
| | Ragtime Orchestra (m) | LP | (Czechoslovakia) Supraphon 1115.1965 | 1976 |
| | Ragtime Society of Frankfurt | LP | (Germany) Joke JLP-205 | 78-2 |
| | The Ragtimers | LP | RCA Camden ACL1-0599 | 1974 |
| | Jean-Pierre Rampal | LP | CBS 37818 | 1982 |
| | Joshua Rifkin | LP | Nonesuch 71248 | 1970 |
| | William Neil Roberts | LP | Klavier 516 | 1973 |
| | Janice Scroggins | LP | Flying Hearts 334 | 87-9 |
| | St. Louis Ragtimers | LP | Ragophile TSLR-007 | 1986 |
| | Bob Tryforous | LP | Puritan 5002 | r. 1976 |
| | Dick Wellstood | LP | Pickwick SPC-3376 | 1974 |
| | Dick Zimmerman | LP | Murray Hill 931079 | 1974 |
| RAGTIME DRUMMER | | | | |
| Lent, James I. | James I. Lent | 78 | (England) HMV GC | 04-5 |
| | James I. Lent w/ Orchestra | 78 | Emerson 779 | |
| | James I. Lent w/ Pryor's Band | 78 | Victor 17042 | 12-4 |
| RAGTIME IN THE HOLLOW | | | | |
| Tichenor, Trebor | Trebor Tichenor | LP | Dirty Shame 2001 | 1973 |
| RAGTIME MELODY | | | | |
| Beasley, William, Stratton, Richard & Hazelwood, Adelaide | Rex Allen & Dixielanders | 78 | Decca 27876 | 51-10 |
| | Lola Ameche | 78 | Mercury 5750 | 51- |
| | Joe "Fingers" Carr | 78 | Capitol 1876 | 51-9 |
| | Eddie Hawks | 78 | Mercury 6364 | |
| | Eddie Smith | 78 | King 1018 | 51- |
| | Del Wood | 78 | Tennessee 800 | 51-11 |

| Composition | Performer | Record Speed | Record Company/No. | Year-Month |
|---|---|---|---|---|
| RAGTIME NIGHTINGALE | | | | |
| Lamb, Joseph | William Albright | LP | Music Masters 20033 | 80-12 |
| | John Arpin | LP | (Canada) Scroll 101 | 1965 |
| | John Arpin & Catherine Wilson | LP | (Canada) Fanfare 9023 | r. 1986 |
| | Dave Dallwitz Ragtime Ensemble | LP | Stomp Off 1098 | 84-8 |
| | Down Home JB | LP | Stomp Off 1190 | 88-8 |
| | Brian Dykstra | LP | Century Advent 5075 | 1974 |
| | Chuck Folds | LP | Jazzways 106/4 | 1974 |
| | Marco Fumo | LP | (Italy) Fonit Cetra 0004 | 83-2 |
| | Patrick Gogerty | LP | Sounds Current | 1976 |
| | Marvin Hamlisch | LP | MCA 2115 | 1974 |
| | Dennis James | LP | Concert M-109 | r. 1973 |
| | Glenn Jenks | LP | Bonnie Banks 103 | 1983 |
| | John Jensen | LP | Genesis GS-1045 | 1974 |
| | Hank Jones | LP | ABC-Paramount 496 | 64-4 |
| | Milton Kaye | LP | Golden Crest 4127 | r. 1974 |
| | David Laibman | LP | Rounder 3040 | r. 1981 |
| | Joseph Lamb | LP | Folkways FG-3562 | 59-8 |
| | Bill Mitchell | LP | Euphonic 1203 | 1962 |
| | Max Morath | LP | Epic LN-24066 | 1963 |
| | Max Morath | LP | Vanguard VSD-39/40 | 1967 |
| | New England Conservatory Ensemble | LP | Golden Crest 31042 | 1975 |
| | Knocky Parker | LP | Audiophile AP-28 | c. 1956 |
| | Knocky Parker & Bill Coffman | LP | Jazzology JCE-81 | r. 1979 |
| | Knocky Parker & Bob Long | LP | Euphonic 1215 | 77-4 |
| | Bob Pilsbury Band | LP | Dirty Shame 1243 | c. 1981 |
| | Royal Ballet Orchestra | LP | CRD 1029 | 1976 |
| | Uptown Lowdown JB | LP | GHB 149 | c. 1980 |
| | Johnny Wittwer | 78 | Jazz Man 20 | 45-12 |
| RAGTIME NIGHTMARE | | | | |
| Turpin, Tom | William Bolcom | LP | Nonesuch 71257 | 1971 |
| | Steve Hancoff | LP | Dirty Shame 4553 | 1977 |
| | Milton Kaye | LP | Golden Crest 31032 | 1974 |
| | Bill Mitchell | LP | Euphonic 1203 | 1962 |
| | New Orleans Ragtime Orchestra | LP | Pearl 8 | 1970 |
| | Steve Pistorious | LP | Jazzology 78 | 1975 |
| | Jim Smart Entertainers | EP | (Australia) East 007 | 65-6 |
| | Ton Van Bergeyk | LP | Kicking Mule 114 | r. 1976 |
| RAGTIME ORIOLE | | | | |
| Scott, James | William Arlington Piano Roll | LP | Biograph 1006Q | |
| | Ken Colyer's Jazzmen | LP | (England) Joy S-194 | 1974 |
| | Glenn Jenks | LP | Bonnie Banks 103 | 1983 |
| | John Jensen | LP | Genesis 1044 | 1974 |
| | Max Morath | LP | Vanguard SRV-310 | r. 1974 |
| | Knocky Parker | LP | Audiophile AP-76/77 | 1962 |
| | Piano Roll | LP | Biograph 1016Q | |

| Composition | Performer | Record Speed | Record Company/No. | Year-Month |
|---|---|---|---|---|
| RAGTIME ORIOLE (continued) | Piano Roll | 78 | Century 4022 | |
| Scott, James | Piano Roll | LP | (England) Saydisc SDL-132 | |
| | Piano Roll | 10"LP | Riverside RLP-1006 | |
| | Wally Rose | LP | Blackbird 12010 | 71-6 |
| | Roger Shields | LP | Turnabout 34579 | 1974 |
| | Ray Smith | LP | (England) Joy S-194 | 1971 |
| | Ray Smith | LP | (England) Stomp ROBB-005 | 68-5 |
| | Butch Thompson | LP | Prairie Home Companion 34817 | 1979 |
| | Fred Van Eps w/ Banta | 78 | Pathe 021088 | 23-9 |
| | Fred Van Eps w/ Burkhart | 78 | Edison 51324 | 24-2 |
| | Fred Van Eps w/ Bobby Van Eps | 78 | V-5 | r. 52-3 |
| RAGTIME RAG | | | | |
| Blake Eubie | Eubie Blake | LP | 20th Century Fox 3003 | 1958 |
| RAGTIME RAZZMATAZZ | | | | |
| Hyman, Dick | Knuckles O'Toole | LP | Grand Award 33-373 | c. 1958 |
| RAGTIME REVELATIONS | | | | |
| Hyman, Dick | Knuckles O'Toole | LP | Grand Award 33-373 | c. 1958 |
| RAGTIME ROBIN | | | | |
| Green, George Hamilton | George Hamilton Green | 78 | Columbia 265-D | 24-12 |
| | Nexus | LP | (Canada) Umbrella 2 | 1976 |
| RAGTIME SKEDADDLE | | | | |
| Rosey, George | Vess L. Ossman | 78 | (England) Berliner 6307 | 00-5 |
| | Pacific Coast Ragtimers | LP | Circle CLP-137 | r. 1988 |
| | Piano Roll | LP | (England) Saydisc 132 | |
| | George Schweinfest | 78 | Columbia 498 | 02-1 |
| | George Schweinfest | 78 | Berliner 238 | 00-9 |
| | George Schweinfest | 78 | Victor 225 | 00-9 |
| RAGTIME TUBA | | | | |
| Dallwitz, Dave | Southern Jazz Group | 78 | (Australia) Memphis 5 | 48-9 |
| | Southern Jazz Group | 78 | (Australia) Wilco 0-115 | 50-5 |
| RAINBOW RIPPLES | | | | |
| Green, George Hamilton | Jack Daniels Original Band | LP | Spring Branch 29403 | 81-6 |
| | George Hamilton Green | 78 | Victor 19944 | 26-1 |
| | Nexus | LP | (Canada) Umbrella 2 | 1976 |
| RAMBLIN' RAG | | | | |
| Krenz, Bill | Bill Krenz | 78 | Coral 61248 | 54-8 |
| RAMBLING IN RHYTHM | | | | |
| Schutt, Arthur | Arthur Schutt | 78 | Harmony 860-H | 28-1 |
| RAMSHACKLE RAG | | | | |
| Snyder, Ted | Dawn of the Century Orchestra | LP | Arcane 602 | 1972 |
| | Prince's Band | 78 | Columbia A-1107 | 11-11 |
| | Arthur Pryor's Band | 78 | Victor 17021 | 11-11 |
| RANDALL'S RAG | | | | |
| | Jelly Roll Morton | 12"78 | Circle JM-21 | 38-5 |

| Composition | Performer | Record Speed | Record Company/No. | Year-Month |
|---|---|---|---|---|
| RANDI'S RAG | | | | |
| Blake, Eubie | Morton Gunnar Larsen | LP | (Sweden) Sonet 1450 | 1978 |
| RAPSCALLION RAG | | | | |
| Busch, Louis | Joe "Fingers" Carr | LP | Capitol T-280 | |
| RATTLESNAKE RAG | | | | |
| Hanson, Eddie & Carr, Joe Fingers | Joe "Fingers" Carr | 78 | Capitol 2257 | 52-7 |
| RAVIOLI RAG | | | | |
| Putnam–Milton–Biondi | Bill Snyder | 78 | Decca 28086 | 52-3 |
| RAYMOND'S RAG | | | | |
| Jasen, David A. | Dave Jasen | LP | Blue Goose 3001 | 1972 |
| RAZZLE DAZZLE | | | | |
| Stokes, Nellie | Bert Bassett | 78 | (England) Jumbo A-349 | 11-1 |
| RED LIGHT RAG | | | | |
| Daily, Pete & Laguna, Eddie | Pete Daily & Chicagoans | 78 | Sunset 7559 | 45-11 |
| RED ONION RAG | | | | |
| Olman, Abe | Indiana University Orchestra | LP | Indiana Historical Society 1001 | 1981 |
| | Knocky Parker | LP | Audiophile AP-92 | |
| | Roy Spangler | 78 | Rex 5026, 5342 | 13-3 |
| RED PEPPER RAG | | | | |
| Lodge, Henry | Danny Alvin's Band | 78 | Rondo 235 | 50-5 |
| | Ballyhooligans (m) | 78 | (England) HMV BD-5130 | 36-10 |
| | Dawn of the Century Orchestra | LP | Arcane 603 | 1973 |
| | Neville Dickie | LP | Stomp Off 1096 | 83-4 |
| | El Cota | 78 | Columbia A-1149 | 12-1 |
| | Empire Military Band | 78 | (England) Beka 41597 | 11- |
| | Famous Band | 78 | (England) Famous 201 | 13-4 |
| | Vic Filmer | LP | Jazzology JCE-58 | 1970 |
| | Adrian Ford | LP | (Australia) Festival L-25119 | 73-12 |
| | Gottlieb's Orchestra | 12"78 | (England) HMV | 12-12 |
| | Grammophon Military Band | 78 | (England) Grammovox A-114 | 12-9 |
| | Grammophon Orchestra | 78 | (Germany) Grammophon 12807 | |
| | Homophone Band | 78 | (England) Homophone 1105 | 12- |
| | Irish Guard's Band | 78 | (England) Guardsman 261 | 13-1 |
| | Jumbo Military Band | 78 | (England) Jumbo 789 | 12-3 |
| | Mayfair Dance Orchestra | 12"78 | (England) HMV C-214 | 12-10 |
| | National Guards Band | 78 | (England) Marathon 120 | 12-7 |
| | New Orleans Ragtime Orchestra | LP | Stomp Off 1213 | 1989 |
| | Odeon Tanz Orchestra | 78 | (Germany) Odeon UAA-57584 | |
| | Palais De Danse | 78 | (Germany) Grammophon 12872 | |
| | Tony Parenti's Ragtime Gang | LP | Jazzology J-21 | 66-4 |
| | Peerless Orchestra | 78 | (England) Zonophone 905 | 12-7 |
| | Piano Roll | LP | Sounds 1201 | |
| | Mike Polad | LP | Jazzology JCE-77 | r. 1975 |
| | Prince's Band | 78 | Columbia 1910, A-1031 | 11-6 |
| | Wally Rose | 78 | Good Time Jazz 26 | 50-6 |

| Composition | Performer | Record Speed | Record Company/No. | Year-Month |
|---|---|---|---|---|
| RED PEPPER RAG (continued) | Wally Rose | 10"LP | GTJ L-3 | 53-2 |
| Lodge, Henry | Wally Rose | LP | GTJ M-12034 | 58-12 |
| | Harry Roy Orchestra | 78 | (England) Parlophone F-302 | 35-7 |
| | Royal Court Orchestra | 78 | (England) Edison Bell Winner 2136 | 12- |
| | Royal Military Band | 78 | (England) Victory A-16 | 12-8 |
| | St. James Meister Orchestra | 78 | (England) Butterfly B-293 | 11-7 |
| | Tanzpalast Orchester | 78 | (Germany) Grammophon 62196 | |
| | Fred Van Eps | 78 | Victor 17033 | 11-12 |
| | Fred Van Eps w/ Orchestra | 78 | Zonophone 5783 | r. 11-9 |
| RED RAMBLER RAG | | | | |
| Niebergall, Julia Lee | Max Morath Band | LP | Vanguard VSD-79402 | 1977 |
| | Knocky Parker | LP | Audiophile AP-92 | |
| | Piano Roll | LP | Indiana Historical Society 1001 | |
| RED RAVEN RAG | | | | |
| Straight, Charley | Pathe Dance Orchestra | 78 | Pathe 30383 | r. 16-3 |
| | Prince's Band | 12"78 | Columbia A-5826 | 16-7 |
| RED ROBIN RAG | | | | |
| | Joe Daniels & Hot Shots | 78 | (England) Parlophone F-1882 | 41-9 |
| RED ROOSTER RAG | | | | |
| Ronfort, G. W. | Pathe Dance Orchestra | 78 | Pathe 30428 | r. 16-6 |
| REFLECTION RAG | | | | |
| Joplin, Scott | Ann Charters | LP | GNP Crescendo 9032 | 1974 |
| | Ann Charters | LP | Portents 3 | |
| | Steen Christensen | LP | (Holland) Jazz Crooner 155.771 | 1977 |
| | Dick Hyman | LP | RCA CRL5-1106 | 1975 |
| | Max Morath | LP | Vanguard SRV-310 | r. 1974 |
| | Knocky Parker | LP | Audiophile AP-71/72 | 1960 |
| | Piano Roll | LP | Biograph 1014Q | |
| | Roger Shields | LP | Turnabout 34579 | 1974 |
| | Dick Zimmerman | LP | Murray Hill 931079 | 1974 |
| REINDEER RAG | | | | |
| Lamb, Joseph | Chris Barber JB | LP | (England) Col. 33SX-1245 | 1960 |
| | John Jensen | LP | Genesis 1045 | 1974 |
| | Milton Kaye | LP | Golden Crest 4127 | 1974 |
| | London Ragtime Orchestra | LP | GHB 199 | 87-2 |
| | New Orleans Ragtime Orchestra | LP | Pearl 7 | 67-9 |
| | New Orleans Ragtime Orchestra | LP | Vanguard VSD-69/70 | 1971 |
| | Keith Nichols | LP | (England) EMI One-Up-2035 | 1974 |
| | Knocky Parker & Robbie Rhodes | LP | Circle CLP-10001 | 1984 |
| | Steamboat Stompers | LP | (Germany) WAM 69076 | 77-6 |
| | Sumpen's Swingsters | LP | (Sweden) Swamp 791 | 79-5 |
| REISENWEBER RAG | | | | |
| LaRocca, Dominic James | Eddie Condon Orchestra | LP | World Pacific 1292 | 1958 |
| | Original Dixieland Jass Band | 78 | Aeolian 1242 | 17-9 |
| RENDESVOUS RAG | | | | |
| Campbell, Brun | Brun Campbell | LP | Euphonic 1202 | 1947 |

| Composition | Performer | Record Speed | Record Company/No. | Year-Month |
|---|---|---|---|---|
| RHAPSODY IN RAGTIME | | | | |
| Blake, Eubie | Eubie Blake | LP | Eubie Blake Music 5 | 1973 |
| | Eubie Blake | LP | (France) RCA FXM1-7157 | 1974 |
| RHAPSODY RAG | | | | |
| Cross, Bud | Winifred Atwell | 78 | (England) Philips PS-182 | |
| RHAPSODY RAG | | | | |
| Jentes, Harry | J. J. Ashton | 78 | (England) Edison Bell Winner 3082 | 16-9 |
| | Victor Cornelius & Jacob Schmidt | 78 | (Germany) Grammophon 49059 | 24-9 |
| | Max Tak | 78 | (Germany) Odeon 313109 | c. 1921 |
| A RHEINWINE RAG | | | | |
| Henneberg, Paul | Arthur Pryor's Band | 78 | Victor 16834 | 11-1 |
| RHYTHM STEP | | | | |
| Elizalde, Fred | Fred Elizalde | 78 | (England) Brunswick 115 | 27-7 |
| | Fred Elizalde & Orchestra | 78 | (England) Brunswick 114 | 27-7 |
| RIALTO RIPPLES RAG | | | | |
| Donaldson, Will & Gershwin, George | John Arpin & Catherine Wilson | LP | (Canada) Fanfare 9023 | r. 1986 |
| | Winifred Atwell | 45 | London 45-1912 | |
| | William Bolcom | LP | Nonesuch H-71284 | c. 1973 |
| | Marvin Hamlisch | LP | MCA 2115 | 1974 |
| | Dick Hyman | LP | Cadence CR-2001 | 1974 |
| | Katia & Marielle Labeque | LP | Angel S-37980 | 1982 |
| | New York Banjo Ensemble | LP | Kicking Mule 224 | |
| | Platte River JB | LP | PRJB Vol. 3 | 1981 |
| | Roger Shields | LP | Turnabout 34579 | 1974 |
| | Soprano Summit II | LP | World Jazz S-13 | 77-12 |
| | Ken Werner | LP | Finnedar SR-9019 | 1978 |
| RICHMOND RAG | | | | |
| Aufderheide, May | Chrysanthemum Ragtime Band | LP | Stomp Off 1123 | 1985 |
| | Indiana University Orchestra | LP | Indiana Historical Society 1001 | 1981 |
| RIGAMAROLE RAG | | | | |
| Kendall, Edwin F. | Joe "Fingers" Carr | LP | Capitol T-280 | |
| RIPPLES OF THE NILE | | | | |
| Roberts, Luckey | Luckey Roberts | 78 | Circle 1028 | 46-5 |
| RIVERSIDE RAG | | | | |
| Cohen, Charles | Neville Dickie | LP | Euphonic ESR-1206 | 1966 |
| | Alain Lesire | LP | (Belgium) Jazz Cats 6983003 | 1982 |
| | Jack Rummel | LP | Stomp Off 1118 | 1985 |
| | Uptown Lowdown Jazz Band | LP | Stomp Off 1030 | 81-10 |
| RIVIERA RAG (aka FRED HELTMAN'S RAG) | | | | |
| Heltman, Fred | Joe "Fingers" Carr | 78 | Capitol 2834 | 53-8 |
| ROCK ISLAND RAG (see BLACK & WHITE RAG) | | | | |
| | Ray Turner | 78 | Capitol 1046 | |

| Composition | Performer | Record Speed | Record Company/No. | Year-Month |
|---|---|---|---|---|
| ROCK ISLAND ROCK | | | | |
| Grant, Mel | Professor Ragtime | 78 | Joco 110 | 50-4 |
| ROCKING HORSE RAG | | | | |
| Bell, Graeme | Graeme Bell's Ragtime Four | 78 | (Australia) Parlophone A-7786 | 52-4 |
| ROCKING MOUNTAIN RAG | | | | |
| | Hometown Boys | 78 | Madison 201 | |
| ROCKY FORD MELON PICKERS | | | | |
| Wilson, Garfield | Queen City Ragtime Ensemble | LP | Stomp Off 1136 | 1986 |
| ROCKY'S RAG (see RUSSIAN RAG) | | | | |
| | Joe "Fingers" Carr | 78 | Capitol 1311 | 50-8 |
| ROMANTIC RAG | | | | |
| Craig, Kathy | Max Morath | LP | Vanguard VSD-79402 | 1977 |
| ROMPING BESSIE | | | | |
| Rossiter | Thomas Malin w/ Orchestra | 78 | Pathe 20376 | r. 18-7 |
| ROOSTER RAG | | | | |
| Pollock, Muriel | Emerson Symphony Orchestra | 78 | Emerson 7162 | r. 17-5 |
| | Max Morath | LP | Vanguard VSD-79402 | 1977 |
| | Wally Rose | 10″LP | Columbia CL-6260 | 53-5 |
| | Starr Military Band | 78 | Starr 10010 | r. 17-6 |
| ROSE LEAF RAG | | | | |
| Joplin, Scott | Ann Charters | LP | Portents 1 | 1958 |
| | Dick Hyman | LP | RCA CRL5-1106 | 1975 |
| | New Orleans Ragtime Orchestra | LP | Vanguard VSD-69/70 | 1971 |
| | Knocky Parker | LP | Audiophile AP-71/72 | 1960 |
| | Piano Roll | LP | Biograph 1008Q | |
| | Joshua Rifkin | LP | Nonesuch 71264 | 1972 |
| | Dick Zimmerman | LP | Murray Hill 931079 | 1974 |
| ROSEBUD RAG | | | | |
| Shea, Tom | Grant Klink | LP | Biogaph 12058 | r. 1979 |
| ROSEWOOD RAG | | | | |
| Heaton, Peter | Knocky Parker | LP | Audiophile AP-91 | |
| ROSS' DOG TROT | | | | |
| Eddie Ross | "Black Face" Eddie Ross | 78 | Vicor 18815 | 21-8 |
| ROUNDHOUSE RAG | | | | |
| Daily, Pete | Pete Daily & Chicagoans | 78 | Sunset 7566 | 45-11 |
| ROXYETTE | | | | |
| | Harry Breuer | 78 | Melotone 12072 | |
| THE ROY RAG | | | | |
| Roy, Harry | Harry Roy Orchestra | 78 | (England) Parlophone R-1896 | 34-7 |
| ROYAL TERMIMUS RAG | | | | |
| Dyer, Warwick | Frank Johnson's Fabulous Dixielanders | 78 | (Australia) Parlophone A-7733 | 49-12 |
| | Southern Jazz Group | 78 | (Australia) Swaggie 1010 | 51-6 |

| Composition | Performer | Record Speed | Record Company/No. | Year-Month |
|---|---|---|---|---|
| **RUBBER PLANT RAG** | | | | |
| Cobb, George L. | George Foley | LP | Stomp Off 1088 | 1984 |
| | Hot Antic Jazz Band | LP | Stomp Off 1155 | 1987 |
| | New Orleans Ragtime Orchestra | LP | Stomp Off 1213 | 1989 |
| | Uptown Lowdown Jazz Band | LP | Yerba Buena Jazz 101 | c. 1985 |
| **RUDY'S RAMBLES** | | | | |
| Starita, Rudy | Rudy Starita | 78 | (England) Decca F-3051 | |
| **RUFENREDDY** | | | | |
| Bargy, Roy & | Roy Bargy | 78 | Victor 19320 | 24-3 |
| Straight, Charley | Henry Lange | 78 | Brunswick 2344 | 22-9 |
| | Fritz Stahmer | 78 | (Germany) Acme 2061 | 24-11 |
| | Ray Turner | 78 | Capitol 2096 | 52-3 |
| **RUMPUS RAG** | | | | |
| Ewell, Don | Don Ewell | EP | Good Time Jazz 1004 | 1946 |
| | Ray Smith | LP | Stomp Off 1162 | 1987 |
| **RUSSIAN RAG** | | | | |
| Cobb, George L. | Dave Apollon & String Orchestra | 78 | Brunswick 6339 | 32-6 |
| | Wilda Baughn | LP | Sacramento Jazz 16 | 1981 |
| | Graeme Bell | LP | (Australia) Par. PMD-07501 | 53-4 |
| | Russ Conway | EP | (England) Col. SEG-7886 | 1959 |
| | Bob Darch | LP | United Artists UAL-3120 | 1960 |
| | Eddy Davis | LP | Pa Da 7401 | 1974 |
| | Dawn of the Century Orchestra | LP | Arcane 603 | 1973 |
| | The Duchess | 78 | (England) Decca F-10140 | 53- |
| | Emerson Military Band | 78 | Emerson 7427, 9107 | r. 18-11 |
| | Jim Europe's Hell Fighters | 78 | Pathe 22087 | 19-3 |
| | Joseph Fiers | 78 | (Belgium) HMV F-256 | 1931 |
| | Chuck Folds | LP | Jazzways 106/4 | 1974 |
| | Earl Fuller's Rector Novelty Orchestra | 78 | Columbia A-2649 | 18-9 |
| | Curly Hicks & Taproom Boys | 78 | Bluebird 10757 | 40-2 |
| | Lou Hooper | LP | (Canada) Radio Canada Int. 380 | 1973 |
| | Max Kortlander Piano Roll | LP | Folkways RBF-43 | |
| | Dick Kroeckel | LP | Ragtime GRU-1930 | 1977 |
| | Donald Lambert | LP | IAJRC 23 | c. 1962 |
| | LeRoy Larsen | LP | Banjar 1784 | 1977 |
| | Joe Loss Orchestra | 78 | (England) HMV BD-6045 | 49-7 |
| | Geoff Love Ragtime Band | LP | (Canada) Quality 753 | 1974 |
| | Mando Boys | LP | Red House 10 | 86-6 |
| | Mayfair Dance Orchestra | 12"78 | (England) HMV C-924 | 19-10 |
| | Monde | 78 | Columbia 272-D | 24-8 |
| | Max Morath | LP | Vanguard VSD-39/40 | 1967 |
| | Ivor Moreton & Dave Kaye | 78 | (England) Parlophone F-2485 | |
| | Ivor Moreton & Dave Kaye (m) | 78 | (England) Parlophone R-1797 | 34-3 |
| | Okeh Dance Orchestra | 78 | Okeh 4002 | r. 19-11 |
| | Pathe Dance Orchestra | 78 | (England) Pathe 5402 | 19-11 |
| | Sid Phillips & Band | 78 | (England) HMV BD-6187 | 54-12 |
| | Pietro | 78 | Victor 18743 | 18-11 |

| Composition | Performer | Record Speed | Record Company/No. | Year-Month |
|---|---|---|---|---|
| RUSSIAN RAG (continued) | Alex Read | LP | (Canada) RCA CTLS-1097 | 67-12 |
| Cobb, George L. | Alex Read Band | LP | (Canada) CBC LM-8 | 66-4 |
| | Regal Dance Orchestra | 78 | (England) Regal G-7570 | 20-7 |
| | Rex Schepp | 78 | Autograph 630 | 24-12 |
| | Duncan Swift | LP | (England) Big Bear 34 | 90-7 |
| | Frank Traynor JB | LP | (Australia) W & G B-1546 | 62-12 |
| | Dick Wellstood | LP | (Germany) MRC 006-32-859 | 77-1 |
| | Dick Wellstood | LP | Jazzology JCE-73 | 1971 |
| | Arthur Young & Youngsters (m) | 78 | (England) Decca F-5645 | 35-8 |
| RUSSIANOVA | | | | |
| Grant, Burt & Arnold, Cecil | Stanley C. Holt | 78 | (England) Homochord H-448 | 23- |
| RUTH'S RAG | | | | |
| Tinnon, Ben | Grinnell Giggers | 78 | Victor 40276 | 30-5 |
| S'MORE | | | | |
| Straight, Charley | Charley Straight Piano Roll | LP | Folkways RBF-44 | |
| SAILIN' ALONG | | | | |
| Andrews, Jimmy | Jimmy Andrews (Frank Banta) | 78 | Banner 6066 | 27-8 |
| SALLY TROMBONE | | | | |
| Fillmore, Henry | Ford Dabney Band | 78 | Aeolian 1243 | 17-11 |
| | Waldo's Ragtime Orchestra | LP | Stomp Off 1007 | 80-10 |
| SALOME'S SLOW DRAG | | | | |
| Campbell, Brun | Brun Campbell | LP | Euphonic 1201 | c. 1947 |
| SALTY DOG RAG | | | | |
| Crowe–Gordy | "Poppa" John Gordy | 78 | Bullet 1097 | |
| | "Poppa" John Gordy | 78 | Victor 20-6656 | 56-9 |
| | "Poppa" John Gordy Band | LP | RCA Victor LPM-1060 | 1955 |
| | Eddie Hill | 78 | Mercury 6383 | 51- |
| SAPHO RAG | | | | |
| Robinson, J. Russell | Tony Parenti's Ragtime Gang | LP | Jazzology J-21 | 66-4 |
| | Knocky Parker | LP | Audiophile AP-91 | |
| | Knocky Parker | LP | Indiana Historical Society 1001 | 1969 |
| | Ron Weatherburn | LP | (England) Alpha LPX-32 | 62-1 |
| SAVOY RAG | | | | |
| Mandell, Pete | Phil Russell (Pete Mandell) | 78 | (England) Edison Bell Winner 4647 | 26-9 |
| SAXANOLA | | | | |
| Doerr, Clyde | Clyde Doerr | 78 | Victor 19028 | 22-9 |
| SAXAPHOBIA | | | | |
| Wiedoeft, Rudy | Rene Dumont | 78 | (England) Parlophone R-371 | 28-12 |
| | Skeets Hurfurt | 78 | Capitol 1154 | 50-7 |
| | Sammy Spear Orchestra | LP | Jubilee 1110 | c. 1952 |
| | Tom Stuip Band | LP | Stomp Off 1177 | 87-12 |
| | Rudy Wiedoeft | 78 | Brunswick 2015 | |
| | Rudy Wiedoeft | 78 | Emerson 1043 | |
| | Rudy Wiedoeft w/ Orchestra | 78 | Triangle | |
| | Rudy Wiedoeft w/ Orchestra | 78 | Victor 18728 | 20-4 |
| | Yerkes Sax Sextette | 78 | Edison 50553 | 19-12 |

| Composition | Performer | Record Speed | Record Company/No. | Year-Month |
|---|---|---|---|---|
| SAXARELLA | | | | |
| Wiedoeft, Rudy | Rudy Wiedoeft | 78 | Edison 51339 | 24-4 |
| | Rudy Wiedoeft | 78 | (England) Zonophone 2675 | |
| | Rudy Wiedoeft w/ Orchestra | 78 | (England) Brunswick 2825 | |
| | Rudy Wiedoeft w/ pno | 78 | Victor 19167 | 23-9 |
| SAXEMA | | | | |
| Wiedoeft, Rudy | Albert White Orchestra | LP | Barbary Coast 33008 | 1958 |
| | Rudy Wiedoeft | 78 | Victor 21152 | 27-12 |
| | Rudy Wiedoeft | 78 | Edison 50862 | 21-9 |
| | Rudy Wiedoeft & Frank Banta | 78 | Columbia 84-D | 24-2 |
| | Rudy Wiedoeft w/ Orchestra | 78 | Vocalion 14088 | |
| SAX-O-PHUN | | | | |
| Wiedoeft, Rudy | Skeets Hurfurt | 78 | Capitol 1154 | 50-7 |
| | George Olsen Orchestra | 78 | Victor 19509 | 24-8 |
| | Rudy Wiedoeft & Frank Banta | 78 | Brunswick 3103 | 26-1 |
| | Rudy Wiedoeft & Oscar Levant | 78 | (England) Columbia 4037 | 26-6 |
| SAX-O-TRIX | | | | |
| Wiedoeft, Rudy & Savino, Domenic | Rudy Wiedoeft & Frank Banta | 78 | Brunswick 3395 | |
| SCALE IT DOWN | | | | |
| O'Neill, Walker | Walker O'Neill | 78 | (England) Homochord H-675 | 24-2 |
| | Walker O'Neill | 78 | (England) HMV B-1806 | 24-3 |
| SCANDALOUS THOMPSON | | | | |
| Johnson, Charles L. | Knocky Parker | LP | Audiophile AP-89 | |
| SCARLET RAG | | | | |
| Cook, Forest L. | Lowell Schreyer | LP | Indiana Historical Society 1001 | 1981 |
| SCOTT JOPLIN'S DREAM | | | | |
| Lamb, Joseph & Joplin, Scott | Milton Kaye | LP | Golden Crest 31035 | 1974 |
| SCOTT JOPLIN'S NEW RAG | | | | |
| Joplin, Scott | Marc Bercovic | LP | (France) Promophone ROM-1 | 1973 |
| | E. Power Biggs | LP | Columbia M-33205 | 1974 |
| | Claude Bolling | LP | (France) CY 733.607 | c. 1980 |
| | Budapest Ragtime Orchestra | LP | (Czechoslovakia) Krem SLPX-17794 | 1984 |
| | Dick Hyman | LP | RCA CRL5-1106 | 1975 |
| | Dave Jasen | LP | Euphonic ESR-1206 | 1966 |
| | Morton Gunnar Larsen | LP | (Norway) Hot Club 6 | 1983 |
| | James Levine | LP | RCA ARL1-2243 | 1976 |
| | Max Morath | LP | Vanguard VSD-39/40 | 1967 |
| | New England Conservatory Ensemble | LP | Golden Crest 31031 | 1973 |
| | New Orleans Ragtime Orchestra | LP | Pearl 8 | 1970 |
| | New Sunshine JB | LP | Flying Dutchman 1-0549 | 1972 |
| | Knocky Parker | LP | Audiophile AP-71/72 | 1960 |
| | Piano Roll | LP | Biograph 1014Q | |
| | Piano Roll | 78 | Jazz Classics 533 | |

| Composition | Performer | Record Speed | Record Company/No. | Year-Month |
|---|---|---|---|---|
| SCOTT JOPLIN'S NEW RAG (continued) | Piano Roll | 10"LP | Riverside RLP-1006 | |
| | Ronnie Price | LP | (England) Embassy 31043 | c. 1973 |
| Joplin, Scott | Queen City Ragtime Ensemble | LP | Stomp Off 1138 | 1986 |
| | Ragtime Society of Frankfurt | LP | (Germany) Joke JLP-217 | 81-10 |
| | Joshua Rifkin | LP | Nonesuch 71248 | 1970 |
| | William Neil Roberts | LP | Klavier 516 | 1973 |
| | Eric Rogers | LP | London Phase 4 21105 | 1974 |
| | Wally Rose | LP | Blackbird 12010 | 71-6 |
| | Wally Rose | 10"LP | Col. CL-6260 | 53-5 |
| | Fred Sokolow | LP | Kicking Mule 212 | c. 1982 |
| | Uptown Lowdown JB | LP | GHB 159 | c. 1980 |
| | Dick Wellstood | LP | Chiaroscuro 109 | 70-11 |
| | Dick Wellstood | LP | Pickwick SPC-3376 | 1974 |
| | Dick Zimmerman | LP | Murray Hill 931079 | 1974 |
| | Zinn's Ragtime String Quartet | LP | Music Minus One 13 | 1974 |
| SCOUTING AROUND | | | | |
| Johnson, James P. | James P. Johnson | 78 | Okeh 4937 | 23-8 |
| SEARCHLIGHT RAG | | | | |
| Joplin, Scott | Marvin Ash | LP | Decca DL-8346 | 56-3 |
| | Marvin Ash | 10"LP | Jazz Man 335 | 1954 |
| | Ann Charters | LP | Sierra Wave 101 | 1974 |
| | Chrysanthemum Ragtime Band | LP | Stomp Off 1196 | 1988 |
| | Brian Dykstra | LP | Orion 83449 | 82-7 |
| | Dick Hyman | LP | RCA CRL5-1106 | 1975 |
| | Glenn Jenks | LP | Bonnie Banks 104 | 1985 |
| | Max Morath | LP | Vanguard SRV-310 | r. 1974 |
| | Knocky Parker | LP | Audiophile AP-71/72 | 1960 |
| | Piano Roll | LP | Biograph 1008Q | |
| | Yannick Singery | LP | (France) Swing SLD-928 | c. 1975 |
| | Tex Wyndham | LP | Fat Cat's Jazz 168 | 1973 |
| | Dick Zimmerman | LP | Murray Hill 931079 | 1974 |
| SENSATION RAG | | | | |
| Lamb, Joseph F. | Black Bottom Stompers | 78 | (Sweden) Gazell 1006 | 50-12 |
| | Mutt Carey's New Yorkers | 78 | Century 4007 | 47-11 |
| | Ann Charters | LP | Sierra Wave 101 | 1974 |
| | Steen Christensen | LP | (Denmark) LB 1 | 1972 |
| | Ken Colyer's Jazzmen | EP | (England) Decca DFE-6466 | 1958 |
| | Ken Colyer's Jazzmen | LP | (England) Joy S-194 | 1974 |
| | Patrick Gogerty | LP | Sounds Current | 1976 |
| | Steve Hancoff | LP | Dirty Shame 4553 | 1977 |
| | John Jensen | LP | Genesis 1045 | 1974 |
| | Hank Jones | LP | ABC-Paramount 496 | 64-4 |
| | Milton Kaye | LP | Golden Crest 4127 | r. 1974 |
| | Joseph Lamb | LP | Folkways FG-3562 | 59-8 |
| | Lawson–Haggart JB | LP | Decca DL-8199 | 1954 |
| | Jack Lidstrom's Hep Cats | EP | (Sweden) Metropolis MEP-224 | 56-10 |

| Composition | Performer | Record Speed | Record Company/No. | Year-Month |
|---|---|---|---|---|
| SENSATION RAG (continued) | David Montgomery & Cecil Lytle | LP | Klavier 533 | 1974 |
| Lamb, Joseph F. | New Black Eagle JB | LP | Dirty Shame 2002 | 73-6 |
| | New Emily Jazz Orchestra | LP | (Italy) EMBI Studio 00J | 81-6 |
| | New England Conservatory Ensemble | LP | Golden Crest 31042 | 1975 |
| | New Iberia Stompers | LP | (England) 77SEU 12/40 | 70-1 |
| | New Orleans Ragtime Orchestra | LP | Pearl 8 | 1970 |
| | Steve Pistorious | LP | Jazzology JCE-78 | 1975 |
| | Richard Wayne's Bearcats | LP | Reader's Digest RDA-70-01-05 | 1968 |
| | Dick Zimmerman | LP | Murray Hill 931079 | 1974 |
| SHIM SHAM DRAG | | | | |
| Wilson, Garland | Garland Wilson | 78 | (England) Brunswick 02283 | 36-9 |
| SHIVERY STOMP | | | | |
| Ellis, Seger | Seger Ellis | 78 | Okeh 41447 | 30-3 |
| | Seger Ellis & Orchestra | 78 | Decca 1275 | 37-3 |
| SHOE STRING RAG | | | | |
| Jasen, David A. | Dave Jasen | LP | Blue Goose 3002 | 1974 |
| SHOW ME RAG | | | | |
| Tichenor, Trebor | Trebor Tichenor | LP | (Canada) Scroll 102 | 1966 |
| SHY AND SLY | | | | |
| Roberts, Luckey | Luckey Roberts | 78 | Circle 1028 | 46-5 |
| SILENCE AND FUN | | | | |
| Mullen, Charles | Regimental Band of the Republic | 78 | A. R. C. 031334 | 06-5 |
| | Sousa's Band | 78 | Victor 4538 | 05-10 |
| SILHOUETTE | | | | |
| Bloom, Rube | Rube Bloom | 78 | Columbia 1195-D | 27-7 |
| | Rube Bloom | 78 | Okeh 40901 | 27-9 |
| SILVER FOX RAG | | | | |
| Lodge, Henry | Turk Murphy Jazz Band | LP | GHB 92 | 72-4 |
| | Turk Murphy Jazz Band | LP | Sonic Arts 14 | 1979 |
| | Prince's Band | 12"78 | Columbia A-5705 | r. 15-10 |
| SILVER ROCKET | | | | |
| Marshall, Arthur | John Arpin | LP | Jazzology 52 | c. 1967 |
| | Milton Kaye | LP | Golden Crest 31032 | 1974 |
| SILVER SWAN RAG | | | | |
| Joplin, Scott | Dawn of the Century Orchestra | LP | Arcane 603 | 1973 |
| | Dick Hyman | LP | RCA CRL5-1106 | 1975 |
| | David Laibman | LP | Rounder 3040 | r. 1981 |
| | Max Morath | LP | Vanguard VSD-39/40 | r. 1981 |
| | Knocky Parker & Bill Coffman | LP | Jazzology 81 | r. 1979 |
| | Piano Roll | LP | Biograph 1010Q | |
| | Myron Romanul | LP | Golden Crest 31042 | 1975 |
| | Ton Van Bergeyk | LP | Kicking Mule 114 | r. 1976 |
| | Terry Waldo | LP | Fat Cat's Jazz 151 | 74-1 |
| | Dick Zimmerman | LP | Murray Hill 931079 | 1974 |

| Composition | Performer | Record Speed | Record Company/No. | Year-Month |
|---|---|---|---|---|
| SIZZLING FINGERS | | | | |
| Lehrer, Ivan | Bill Krenz | 78 | Decca 90499 | 35-12 |
| SLEEPY HOLLOW RAG | | | | |
| Woods, Clarence | John Arpin | LP | (Canada) Scroll 101 | 1965 |
| | John Arpin & Catherine Wilson | LP | (Canada) Fanfare 9023 | r. 1986 |
| | Max Morath | LP | Vanguard 79440 | 1981 |
| | Tex Wyndham | LP | Yerba Buena Jazz 201 | r. 1989 |
| | Richard Zimmerman | LP | Murray Hill 60556/5 | 1981 |
| | Paul Zukofsky & Robert Dennis | LP | Vanguard SRV-350 | 1975 |
| SLEEPY PIANO | | | | |
| Mayerl, Billy | Billy Mayerl | 78 | (England) Columbia 4115 | 26-8 |
| SLEEPY SIDNEY | | | | |
| Scheu, Archie | Johnny Maddox | 45 | Dot 45-15028 | c. 1952 |
| | Johnny Maddox | LP | Redstone 101 | r. 1978 |
| | Sousa's Band | 78 | Victor 16278 | 08-10 |
| SLEW FOOT NELSON | | | | |
| Blake, Eubie | Eubie Blake | LP | Eubie Blake Music 6 | 1973 |
| SLIM TROMBONE | | | | |
| Fillmore, Henry | Canadian Brass | LP | (Canada) Boot 3004 | 1974 |
| SLIPOVA | | | | |
| Bargy, Roy | Frank Banta–Cliff Hess | 78 | Okeh 4825 | r. 23-6 |
| | Roy Bargy Piano Roll | LP | Folkways RF-35 | |
| | Patricia Rossborough | 78 | (England) Parlophone R-1599 | 33- |
| SLIPPERY ELM RAG | | | | |
| Woods, Clarence | William Albright | LP | Music Masters 20033 | 80-12 |
| | Max Morath | LP | Vanguard VSD-39/40 | 1967 |
| | Knocky Parker | LP | Audiophile AP-92 | |
| | Charlie Rasch | LP | (Canada) Ragtime Society 4 | 1966 |
| | Rick Schoenberg | LP | Kicking Mule 107 | r. 1976 |
| | Fred Sokolow | LP | Kicking Mule 212 | c. 1982 |
| | Paul Zukofsky & Robert Dennis | LP | Vanguard SRV-350 | 1975 |
| SLIPPERY FINGERS | | | | |
| Steele, Henry | Percival Mackey's Band | 78 | (England) Columbia 4044 | 26-8 |
| | Snappy Dan (Henry Steele) | 78 | (England) Piccadilly 340 | 29-7 |
| A SLIPPERY PLACE | | | | |
| Hacker, P. M. | First Life Guards Band | 78 | (England) Edison Bell Winner 3052 | 16-9 |
| | Naval Reserve Band | 78 | Columbia A-2627 | 18-7 |
| | Victor Military Band | 78 | Victor 17006 | 11-9 |
| SMART ALEC | | | | |
| Confrey, Zez | John Jensen | LP | Genesis 1051 | 1974 |
| | Milton Kaye | LP | Golden Crest 31040 | 1974 |
| SMASHING THIRDS | | | | |
| Waller, Thomas | Joe Turner | EP | (Switzerland) Columbia SEG-2035 | 1959 |
| | Joe Turner | LP | Pablo 2310-763 | 75-11 |
| | Fats Waller | 78 | Victor V-38613 | 29-9 |

| Composition | Performer | Record Speed | Record Company/No. | Year-Month |
|---|---|---|---|---|
| SMASH-UP RAG | | | | |
| Stevenson, Gwendolyn | Neville Dickie | LP | Euphonic ESR-1206 | 1966 |
| SMILER RAG | | | | |
| Wenrich, Percy | J. J. Ashton | 78 | (England) Imperial 954 | 19-6 |
| | Beka London Orchestra | 78 | (England) Beka 436 | 11-5 |
| | Harry Breuer Orchestra | LP | Audio Fidelity 3001 | 1960 |
| | Dave Dallwitz Ensemble | LP | Stomp Off 1098 | 84-8 |
| | New Sunshine Jazz Band | LP | Flying Dutchman 1-0549 | 1972 |
| | New York Military Band | Cylinder | Edison 10424 | |
| | Vess L. Ossman | 78 | Imperial 45484 | 07- |
| | Vess L. Ossman w/ Orchestra | 78 | Columbia A-972 | 10-12 |
| | Knocky Parker | LP | Audiophile AP-90 | |
| | Piano Roll | 10"LP | (England) London AL-3542 | |
| | Uptown Lowdown Jazz Band | LP | Stomp Off 1030 | 81-10 |
| | Fred Van Eps w/ pno | 78 | Pathe 29081 | |
| | Fred Van Eps w/ pno | 78 | Pathe 30261 | r. 15-9 |
| | Fred Van Eps w/ pno | 78 | Princess 1064 | |
| | Fred Van Eps w/ pno | 78 | Majestic 124 | r. 16-11 |
| | Fred Van Eps w/ pno | 78 | Edison 51514 | 25-2 |
| | Fred Van Eps w/ pno | 78 | V-2 | r. 52-3 |
| | Van Eps Banjo Band | 78 | Paroquette 42 | r. 17-1 |
| | Van Eps Trio | 78 | Victor 17575 | 14-3 |
| | Victor Orchestra | 78 | Victor 16497 | 10-3 |
| | Zonophone Concert Band | 78 | Zonophone 980 | r. 08-3 |
| SMILES AND CHUCKLES | | | | |
| Klickman, F. Henri | Max Morath | LP | Vanguard 79440 | 1981 |
| | Six Brown Brothers | 78 | Victor 18385 | 17-5 |
| | Waldo's Ragtime Orchestra | LP | Stomp Off 1007 | 80-10 |
| SMILING SADIE | | | | |
| Scheu, Archie | Victor Orchestra | 78 | Victor 4745 | 06-3 |
| SMITHSONIAN RAG | | | | |
| Jensen, Jonathan | Piano Roll | LP | Herwin 407 | |
| SMOKY MOKES | | | | |
| Holzmann, Abe | Down Home Jazz Band | LP | Stomp Off 1199 | 88-8 |
| | South Frisco Jazz Band | LP | Stomp Off 1143 | 84-11 |
| SMORGASBORD RAG | | | | |
| Burman, Andrew | Ralph & Bert Bergh | 78 | (Sweden) Metronome J-135 | 50-5 |
| | Reinhold Svensson | 78 | (Sweden) Metronome J-223 | 52-3 |
| SNAPPIN' TURTLE RAG | | | | |
| Cooke, Charles | Chrysanthemum Ragtime Band | LP | Stomp Off 1196 | 1988 |
| SNATCHES | | | | |
| Wellstood, Dick | Dick Wellstood | LP | Chiaroscuro 139 | 1975 |
| | Dick Wellstood | LP | (Switzerland) 88 Up Right 005 | 76-1 |

| Composition | Performer | Record Speed | Record Company/No. | Year-Month |
|---|---|---|---|---|
| **SNEAKAWAY** | | | | |
| Smith, Willie the Lion | Neville Dickie | LP | Stomp Off 1176 | 1988 |
| | Willie the Lion Smith | 78 | Commodore 524 | 39-1 |
| | Willie the Lion Smith | LP | Commodore FL-30.003 | 50-12 |
| | Willie the Lion Smith | LP | RCA Victor LSP-6016 | 67-4 |
| | Willie the Lion Smith | LP | Chiaroscuro 113 | 44-7 |
| | Ralph Sutton | EP | Decca ED-2111 | 53-6 |
| **SNEAKY SHUFFLES** | | | | |
| Lodge, Henry | Mike Polad | LP | Jazzology 77 | r. 1975 |
| **SNEEKY PEET** | | | | |
| Johnson, Charles L. | Elliott Adams | LP | Stomp Off 1198 | 1988 |
| **SNOOKUMS RAG** | | | | |
| Johnson, Charles L. | Terry Waldo | LP | Dirty Shame 1237 | 1974 |
| | Terry Waldo | LP | Fat Cat's Jazz 151 | 74-1 |
| **SNOW FLAKES** | | | | |
| Wirges, Bill | Varsity Four | 78 | Brunswick 3918 | 28-4 |
| **SNOWFLAKES** | | | | |
| Rawicz | Rawicz & Landauer | 78 | (England) Columbia DB-2160 | 42-12 |
| **SOLID IVORY** | | | | |
| Sutton, Jess | Jess Sutton | 78 | New Flexo | 1925 |
| | Jess Sutton | 45 | Tiffany 45-1315 | c. 1955 |
| **SOLILOQUY** | | | | |
| Bloom, Rube | Rube Bloom | 78 | Harmony 164-H | 26-3 |
| | Rube Bloom | 78 | Cameo 1153 | 27-4 |
| | Rube Bloom | 78 | Okeh 40867 | 27-7 |
| | Continental Dance Orchestra | 78 | Banner | 27-8 |
| | Will Donaldson | 78 | Edison 52340 | r. 28-8 |
| | Duke Ellington & Orchestra | 78 | Brunswick 3526 | 27-4 |
| | Eliot Everett & Orchestra | 78 | Victor 22921 | 31-12 |
| | Harry Fields & Marlene Fingerle | 78 | Decca 18241 | 41-7 |
| | Dick Hyman | LP | Cadence CR-2001 | 1974 |
| | Ozzie Nelson Orchestra | 78 | Brunswick 7414 | 35-3 |
| | Don Voorhees Orchestra | 78 | Columbia 1129-D | 27-9 |
| | Paul Whiteman Orchestra | 12"78 | Victor 35828 | 27-6 |
| **SOME BABY** | | | | |
| Lenzberg, Julius | American Republic Band | 78 | Pathe 29014 | |
| | Band | 78 | Little Wonder 34 | |
| | Van Eps Banjo Orchestra | 78 | Columbia A-1594 | 14-7 |
| **SOME PUMPKINS** | | | | |
| Kuhn, Ed | Etcetera String Band | LP | Moon 200 | 1975 |
| **SOMEBODY'S RAG** | | | | |
| Jasen, David A. | Dave Jasen | LP | Folkways FG-3561 | 77-6 |
| **SOMETHIN' DOIN'** | | | | |
| | Nap Hayes & Matthew Prater | 78 | Okeh 45231 | 28-2 |

| Composition | Performer | Record Speed | Record Company/No. | Year-Month |
|---|---|---|---|---|
| SOMETHING DOING | | | | |
| Hayden, Scott & Joplin, Scott | E. Power Biggs | LP | Col. M-33205 | 1974 |
| | William Bolcom | LP | Music Master 0149 | 1981 |
| | Ann Charters | LP | GNP Crescendo 9032 | 1974 |
| | Ann Charters | LP | Portents 3 | |
| | Bill Coffman & Kathy Craig | LP | OTMH 101 | r. 1980 |
| | Neville Dickie | LP | Euphonic ESR-1206 | 1966 |
| | Dick Hyman | LP | RCA CRL5-1106 | 1975 |
| | Scott Joplin Piano Roll | LP | Biograph 1006Q | |
| | Milton Kaye | LP | Golden Crest 31032 | 1974 |
| | Alian Lesire | LP | (Belgium) Jazz Cats 6983003 | 1982 |
| | Knocky Parker | LP | Audiophile AP-71/72 | 1960 |
| | Knocky Parker & Bill Coffman | LP | Jazzology JCE-81 | r. 1979 |
| | Piano Roll | LP | Biograph 1008Q | |
| | Piano Roll | LP | Folkways RBF-7 | |
| | Piano Roll | LP | Sounds 1201 | |
| | Steve Pistorious | LP | Jazzology JCE-78 | 1975 |
| | William Neil Roberts | LP | Klavier 516 | 1973 |
| | Alan Rogers | LP | (England) VJM LC-4 | 1965 |
| | Sigi Schwab | LP | (Germany) Jupiter 6.24831 | c. 1985 |
| | Tom Shea | LP | (Canada) Ragtime Society 1 | 1963 |
| | Southland Stingers | LP | Angel S-36078 | 1974 |
| | Dick Zimmerman | LP | Murray Hill 931079 | 1974 |
| SOUNDS OF AFRICA (aka CHARLESTON RAG) | | | | |
| Blake, Eubie | Eubie Blake (tk. 6) | 78 | Emerson 10434 | 21-7 |
| | Eubie Blake (tk. 4) | LP | Eubie Blake Music 2 | 21-7 |
| SOUTH BOUND RAG | | | | |
| Blake, Blind | Blind Blake | 78 | Paramount 12681 | 28-4 |
| SOUTHERN BEAUTIES RAG | | | | |
| Johnson, Charles L. | Etcetera String Band | LP | Moon 200 | 1975 |
| | Arthur Pryor's Band | 78 | Victor 16073 | 08-9 |
| | Red Wing Blackbirds | LP | Stomp Off 1018 | 1981 |
| SOUTHERN SYMPHONY, A | | | | |
| Wenrich, Percy | Dick Zimmerman | LP | Stomp Off 1049 | 82-8 |
| SPACE SHUFFLE | | | | |
| Frost, Robin | Robbie Rhodes Piano Roll | LP | Herwin 407 | |
| SPAGHETTI RAG | | | | |
| Lyons, George & Yosco, Bob | Ray Anthony & Orchestra | 78 | Capitol 923 | 50-2 |
| | Jan August | 45 | Mercury 9000 | 1950 |
| | Louis Bashell | 78 | Victor 20-5793 | 53-1 |
| | Harry Breuer Orchestra | LP | Audio Fidelity AFSC-5912 | 1960 |
| | Frankie Carle | 78 | Victor 20-3719 | 50-2 |
| | Joe "Fingers" Carr | LP | Capitol T-760 | |

| Composition | Performer | Record Speed | Record Company/No. | Year-Month |
|---|---|---|---|---|
| SPAGHETTI RAG (continued) | Joe "Fingers" Carr & Orchestra | LP | Dot DLP-25705 | |
| Lyons, George & Yosco, Bob | Freeman Clark (m) | 78 | Linden 09 | c. 47- |
| | Jack Fina & Orchestra | 78 | MGM 10610, 30674 | 49-12 |
| | Armand Hug | LP | Golden Crest CR-3064 | 1959 |
| | Beatrice Kay & Kay Jammers | 78 | Columbia 38772 | |
| | Herb Kern | 78 | Decca 24913 | 50-1 |
| | Tiny Little | LP | Brunswick 54030 | |
| | Johnny Maddox (m) | 45 | Dot 45-15365 | |
| | Robert Maxwell | 78 | MGM 12254 | 56- |
| | Robert Maxwell | 78 | Tempo 634 | |
| | Max Morath | LP | Talking Machine 4 | |
| | Russ Morgan Orchestra | 78 | Decca 27930 | 50-4 |
| | Brooke Pemberton | LP | Warner Bros. W-1235 | 1958 |
| | Sammy Spear Orchestra | LP | Mercury MG-20116 | 1954 |
| | Claude Thronhill Orchestra | LP | Decca 8878 | 59-2 |
| SPIRIT OF '49 RAG | | | | |
| Tremer, George H. | George H. Tremer | 78 | Gennett 6242 | 27-8 |
| SPONGE RAG | | | | |
| Simon, W. C. | David Thomas Roberts | LP | Stomp Off 1021 | 1981 |
| SPORTING HOUSE RAG | | | | |
| Morton, Jelly Roll | Jelly Roll Morton | LP | Commodore XFL-14942 | 39-12 |
| SPRING FEELIN' | | | | |
| Thorne, Donald | Donald Thorne | 78 | (England) Columbia 5155 | 28-6 |
| SPRING FEVER | | | | |
| Bloom, Rube | Rube Bloom | 78 | Harmony 164-H | 26-3 |
| | Rube Bloom | 78 | Cameo 1153 | 27-4 |
| | Rube Bloom | 78 | Okeh 40867 | 27-7 |
| | Hans Bund & Herbert Jager | 78 | (Germany) Telefunken A-1375 | 33-2 |
| | Ken Edwards | 78 | (England) Vocalion X-9999 | 27-2 |
| | Lou Hooper | LP | (Canada) Radio Canada Int. 380 | 1973 |
| | Dave Jasen | LP | Blue Goose 3002 | 1974 |
| | Constance Mering & Muriel Pollack | 78 | Columbia 1004-D | 27-5 |
| SPRINGTIME RAG | | | | |
| Pratt, Paul | London Ragtime Orchestra | LP | Stomp Off 1081 | 84-8 |
| | Vic Meyers Orchestra | 78 | Brunswick 2630 | 24-3 |
| | Keith Nichols Orchestra | LP | (England) EMI One-Up 2135 | 1976 |
| | Wally Rose | 78 | Good Time Jazz 44 | 51-7 |
| | Wally Rose | LP | Good Time Jazz M-12034 | 58-12 |
| ST. LOUIS RAG | | | | |
| Turpin, Tom | Band | 78 | Leeds 4320 | |
| | Marc Bercovic | LP | (France) Promophone ROM-1 | 1973 |
| | Claude Bolling | EP | (France) Phililps 424292 | 1962 |
| | Chris Chapman w/ Orchestra | 78 | Victor 4916 | 06-10 |
| | Steen Christensen | LP | (Denmark) LB 1 | 1972 |
| | Chrysanthemum Ragtime Band | LP | Stomp Off 1079 | 1984 |
| | Burt Earle w/ Orchestra | 78 | (England) Favorite 1-64001 | 06-11 |

| Composition | Performer | Record Speed | Record Company/No. | Year-Month |
|---|---|---|---|---|
| ST. LOUIS RAG (continued) | Burt Earle w/ pno | 78 | (England) Odeon 0177 | 06-11 |
| Turpin, Tom | Ron Hanscom | LP | Audiophile AP-88 | 1966 |
| | Hank Jones | LP | ABC-Paramount 496 | 64-4 |
| | Dick Kroeckel | LP | Ragtime GRU-1930 | 1977 |
| | Alain Lesire | LP | (Belgium) Jazz Cats 6983003 | 1982 |
| | Johnny Maddox | LP | Paragon 102 | r. 1978 |
| | Max Morath | LP | Vanguard VSD-39/40 | 1967 |
| | Vess L. Ossman | 78 | I. R. C. 3129 | r. 06-8 |
| | Vess L. Ossman | 78 | Odeon 030810 | c. 07- |
| | Knocky Parker | LP | Audiophile AP-90 | |
| | Piano Roll | 78 | Century 4024 | |
| | Piano Roll | 10″LP | Riverside RLP-1006 | |
| | Arthur Pryor's Band | 78 | Victor 2783 | 04-3 |
| | Queen City JB | LP | Audiophile AP-88 | 1966 |
| | Queen City Ragtime Ensemble | LP | Zeno 99 | 1976 |
| | Wally Rose | LP | Blackbird 12007 | 1968 |
| | Tom Shea | LP | (Canada) Ragtime Society 1 | 1963 |
| | Tom Shea | LP | Stomp Off 1022 | 1981 |
| | Fred Sokolow | LP | Kicking Mule 212 | c. 1982 |
| | St. Louis Ragtimers | LP | Audiophile AP-122 | 1977 |
| | Leo Wijnkamp | LP | Kicking Mule 108 | 1974 |
| ST. LOUIS TICKLE | | | | |
| Barney & Seymore | Scott Anthony | LP | Dawson & Chambers 001 | 1981 |
| | Cinch Military Band | 78 | (England) Cinch 5117 | 13-6 |
| | Jim Couch | 78 | Okeh 40467 | |
| | Kathy Craig | LP | ITMH 101 | r. 1980 |
| | Humphries Brothers | 78 | Okeh 45464 | 30-6 |
| | Morton Gunnar Larsen | LP | (Norway) Philips 9114010 | 76-4 |
| | Morton Gunnar Larsen (m) | LP | Stomp Off 1009 | 81-1 |
| | Humphrey Lyttelton Band | LP | (England) Calligraph 013 | 86-7 |
| | Johnny Maddox | 78 | Dot 1005 | 50-5 |
| | New Orleans Ragtime Orchestra | LP | Pearl 8 | 1970 |
| | New Orleans Ragtime Orchestra | LP | Stomp Off 1213 | 1989 |
| | New York Jazz Repertory Company | LP | Atlantic 1671 | 74-11 |
| | Ossman–Dudley Trio | 78 | Victor 4624, 16092 | 06-1 |
| | Vess L. Ossman w/ Orchestra | 78 | Columbia A-937 | 09-9 |
| | Knocky Parker | LP | Audiophile AP-90 | |
| | Piano Roll | 10″LP | Riverside RLP-1025 | |
| | Steve Pistorious | LP | Jazzology JCE-78 | 1975 |
| | Prince's Band | 78 | Columbia 3249, A-139 | 05-8 |
| | Queen City Ragtime Ensemble | LP | Stomp Off 1138 | 1986 |
| | Charlie Rasch | LP | (Canada) Ragtime Society 4 | 1966 |
| | Gene Rodemich & Orchestra | 78 | Brunswick 2480 | r. 23-10 |
| | Wally Rose | LP | Blackbird 12007 | 1968 |
| | St. Louis Ragtimers | LP | Audiophile AP-122 | 1977 |
| | St. Louis Ragtimers | LP | Ragophile | 1961 |
| | Van Eps Trio (Plantation Trio) | 78 | Victor 16092 | 20-9 |
| | Tex Wyndham | LP | Fat Cat's Jazz 168 | 1973 |

| Composition | Performer | Record Speed | Record Company/No. | Year-Month |
|---|---|---|---|---|
| STATE AND MADISON | | | | |
| Morton, Jelly Roll | Jelly Roll Morton | 12"78 | Circle JM-70 | 38-5 |
| STATE STREET RAG | | | | |
| Bogan & Armstrong | Louie Bluie & Ted Bogan | 78 | Bluebird 5593 | 34-3 |
| STATES RAG MEDLEY #8 | | | | |
| | Piano Roll | 10"LP | Riverside RLP-1025 | |
| STEAMBOAT RAG | | | | |
| Burnett, Ernie | Phil Green & Band | 78 | (England) Decca MW-99 | 43-9 |
| | Ethel Smith | 78 | Decca 27051 | 50-5 |
| | Richard Zimmerman | LP | Murray Hill 60556/5 | 1981 |
| STEEPLECHASE RAG (aka OVER THE BARS) | Dick Hyman Band | LP | Columbia M-33706 | 75-5 |
| Johnson, James P. | James P. Johnson Piano Roll | LP | Biograph 1009 | |
| | Dick Wellstood | LP | Audiophile AP-120 | 75-10 |
| | Richard Zimmerman | LP | Murray Hill 60556/5 | 1981 |
| STEPPING ON THE IVORIES | | | | |
| McLaughlin, John | Duke Yellman | 78 | Edison 52033 | r. 27-7 |
| STOMPIN' 'EM DOWN | | | | |
| Hill, Alex | Alex Hill | 78 | Vocalion 1270 | 29-3 |
| | Ray Skjelbred | LP | Stomp Off 1124 | 1985 |
| STOP IT | | | | |
| Cobb, George | Waldo's Ragtime Orchestra | LP | Stomp Off 1007 | 80-10 |
| STOPTIME RAG | | | | |
| Joplin, Scott | Len Barnard JB | LP | (Australia) Swaggie S-1302 | 1968 |
| | Graeme Bell | LP | (Australia) Festival L-45545/6 | 74-8 |
| | Marc Bercovic | LP | (France) Promophone ROM-1 | 1973 |
| | Black Bottom Stompers | LP | (England) Sunshine SM-5 | 1977 |
| | Ann Charters | LP | GNP Crescendo 9032 | 1974 |
| | Eddy Davis | LP | Pa Da 7401 | 1974 |
| | Lee Erwin | LP | Angel S-36075 | 1974 |
| | Marvin Hamlisch | LP | MCA 2115 | 1974 |
| | Dick Hyman | LP | Project 3 PR-5080 | 1973 |
| | Dick Hyman | LP | RCA CRL5-1106 | 1975 |
| | Katia & Marielle Labeque | LP | Angel S-37980 | 1982 |
| | Knocky Parker | LP | Audiophile AP-71/72 | 1960 |
| | Piano Roll | LP | Biograph 1008Q | |
| | Piano Roll | LP | Sound 1201 | |
| | Cesare Poggi | LP | (Italy) Dire FO-344 | 1979 |
| | Joshua Rifkin | LP | Nonesuch 71305 | 1974 |
| | William Neil Roberts | LP | Klavier 510 | 1972 |
| | Royal Ballet Orchestra | LP | CRD 1029 | 1976 |
| | Tom Shea | LP | (Canada) Ragtime Society 1 | 1963 |
| | Southland Stingers | LP | Angel 36074 | 1974 |
| | Dick Zimmerman | LP | Murray Hill 931079 | 1974 |
| | Zinn's Ragtime String Quartet | LP | Music Minus One 13 | 1974 |
| | Paul Zukofsky & Robert Dennis | LP | Vanguard SRV-350 | 1975 |

| Composition | Performer | Record Speed | Record Company/No. | Year-Month |
|---|---|---|---|---|
| STRENUOUS LIFE | | | | |
| Joplin, Scott | E. Power Biggs | LP | Columbia M-32495 | 1973 |
| | Eden Electronic Ensemble | LP | (England) Pye 12101 | 1975 |
| | Dick Hyman | LP | RCA CRL5-1106 | 1975 |
| | Katia & Marielle Labeque | LP | Angel S-37980 | 1982 |
| | Max Morath | LP | Vanguard 79440 | 1981 |
| | Knocky Parker | LP | Audiophile AP-71/72 | 1960 |
| | Itzhak Perlman & Andre Previn | LP | Angel S-37113 | 1975 |
| | Piano Roll | LP | Biograph 1008Q | |
| | Southland Stingers | LP | Angel S-36078 | 1974 |
| | Dick Zimmerman | LP | Murray Hill 931079 | 1974 |
| SUGAR CANE RAG | | | | |
| Joplin, Scott | E. Power Biggs | LP | Col. M-33205 | 1974 |
| | Boston Pops | LP | Polydor PD-6033 | 1974 |
| | William Cerny | LP | University of Notre Dame | 1975 |
| | Ann Charters | LP | Sierra Wave 101 | 1974 |
| | Brian Dykstra | LP | Century Advent 5075 | 1974 |
| | Dick Hyman | LP | RCA CRL5-1106 | 1975 |
| | James Levine | LP | RCA ARL1-2243 | 1976 |
| | London Ragtime Orchestra | LP | GHB 199 | 87-2 |
| | New England Conservatory Ensemble | LP | Angel S-36060 | 1973 |
| | New Orleans Ragtime Orchestra | LP | GHB 210 | 87-1 |
| | Knocky Parker | LP | Audiophile AP-71/72 | 1960 |
| | Knocky Parker & Bill Coffman | LP | Euphonic 1216 | 77-4 |
| | Itzhak Perlman & Andre Previn | LP | Angel S-37113 | 1975 |
| | Piano Roll | LP | Biograph 1013Q | |
| | The Ragtimers | LP | RCA Camden ACL1-0599 | 74-5 |
| | Joshua Rifkin | LP | Nonesuch 71305 | 1974 |
| | Dick Zimmerman | LP | Murray Hill 931079 | 1974 |
| SUGAR LUMP | | | | |
| Bryan, Fred M. | Pathe Dance Orchestra | 78 | Pathe 70128 | r. 15-9 |
| | Prince's Band | 12"78 | Columbia A-5643 | 15-2 |
| | Victor Military Band | 78 | Victor 17692 | 14-12 |
| A SUMMER BREEZE | | | | |
| Scott, James | Knocky Parker | LP | Audiophile AP-76/77 | 1962 |
| SUNBURST RAG | | | | |
| Scott, James | John Arpin | LP | (Canada) Scroll 103 | 1966 |
| | Dixieland All Stars | LP | Somerset 6700 | 62-7 |
| | John Jensen | LP | Genesis 1044 | 1974 |
| | Left Bank Bearcats | LP | Somerset P-1400 | 1956 |
| | New Orleans Ragtime Orchestra | LP | Pearl 7 | 67-9 |
| | New Orleans Ragtime Orchestra | LP | Vanguard VSD-69/70 | 1971 |
| | Knocky Parker | LP | Audiophile AP-76/77 | 1962 |
| | Piano Roll | LP | Biograph 1016Q | |
| | Piano Roll | LP | Folkways RBF-7 | |
| | Lu Watters & YBJB | 78 | West Coast 103 | 46-6 |

| Composition | Performer | Record Speed | Record Company/No. | Year-Month |
|---|---|---|---|---|
| **SUNFLOWER RAG** | | | | |
| Wenrich, Percy | Joe "Fingers" Carr | LP | Capitol T-760 | |
| **SUNFLOWER SLOW DRAG** | | | | |
| Hayden, Scott & Joplin, Scott | E. Power Biggs | LP | Col. M-32495 | 1973 |
| | Eubie Blake | LP | 20th Century Fox 3003 | 1958 |
| | William Bolcom | LP | Musicmaster 0149 | 1981 |
| | Sune Borg | EP | (Sweden) Efel EP-7201 | 1971 |
| | Budapest Ragtime Orchestra | LP | (Czechoslovakia) Krem SLPX-17794 | 1984 |
| | William Cerny | LP | University of Notre Dame | 1975 |
| | Ann Charters | LP | Portents 1 | 1958 |
| | Dave Dallwitz Ensemble | LP | (Austalia) Swaggie S-1393 | |
| | Eden Electronic Ensemble | LP | (England) Pye 12101 | 1975 |
| | Chuck Folds | LP | Jazzways 106/4 | 1974 |
| | Dick Hyman | LP | RCA CRL5-1106 | 1975 |
| | Hank Jones | LP | ABC-Paramount 496 | 64-4 |
| | Johnny Maddox | LP | Redstone 101 | r. 1978 |
| | Moonlight Ragtime Band | LP | National Geographic 07817 | 1979 |
| | New England Conservatory Ensemble | LP | Angel S-36060 | 1973 |
| | Parenti's Ragtimers | 78 | Circle 1029 | 47-11 |
| | Knocky Parker | LP | Audiophile AP-71/72 | 1960 |
| | Knocky Parker & Bill Coffman | LP | Jazzology JCE-81 | r. 1979 |
| | Phoenix Ragtime Ensemble | LP | World Jazz 12 | 77-6 |
| | Piano Roll | LP | Biograph 1010Q | |
| | Piano Roll | 78 | Circle 5004 | |
| | Ronnie Price | LP | (England) Embassy 31043 | c. 1973 |
| | William Neil Roberts | LP | Klavier 510 | 1972 |
| | Myron Romanul | LP | Angel S-36060 | 1973 |
| | Royal Ballet Orchestra | LP | CRD 1029 | 1976 |
| | Sigi Schwab | LP | (Germany) Jupiter 6.24831 | c. 1985 |
| | Soprano Summit II | LP | World Jazz S-13 | 1974 |
| | Chris Stone | LP | ABC 823 | 1974 |
| | Bob Tryforous | LP | Puritan 5002 | r. 1976 |
| | Dick Wellstood | LP | Pickwick SPC-3376 | 1974 |
| | Dick Zimmerman | LP | Murray Hill 931079 | 1974 |
| **SUNFLOWER TICKLE** | | | | |
| Wenrich, Percy | Trebor Tichenor | LP | Dirty Shame 2001 | 1973 |
| **SUNSHINE CAPERS** | | | | |
| Bargy, Roy | Roy Bargy | 78 | Victor 19320 | 24-3 |
| | Roy Bargy Piano Roll | LP | Folkways RF-35 | |
| **SUPERIOR RAG** | | | | |
| Morton, Jelly Roll | Ophelia Ragtime Orchestra | LP | Stomp Off 1108 | 85-2 |
| | Knocky Parker | LP | Audiophile AP-102 | |
| **SUSAN'S RAG** | | | | |
| Jasen, David A. | Dave Jasen | LP | Blue Goose 3001 | 1972 |
| | Dave Jasen | LP | Euphonic ESR-1206 | 1966 |

| Composition | Performer | Record Speed | Record Company/No. | Year-Month |
|---|---|---|---|---|
| SWANEE RIPPLES RAG | | | | |
|   Blaufuss, Walter E. | Band | 78 | Little Wonder 292 | |
| | Victor Dance Orchestra | 78 | Victor 17585 | 14-2 |
| SWEET AND TENDER | | | | |
|   Bargy, Roy | Roy Bargy Piano Roll | LP | Folkways RF-35 | |
| | George Hicks | LP | Folkways FS-3165 | 1983 |
| | Dave Jasen | LP | Folkways FG-3561 | 77-6 |
| SWEET NOTHINGS | | | | |
|   Rettenberg, Milton | Billy Mayerl | 78 | (England) Columbia 5671 | 29-9 |
| | Shilkret's Rhyth-Melodists | 78 | Victor 21902 | 28-9 |
| | Jack Wilson (m) | 78 | (England) Regal-Zonophone MR-1694 | |
| SWEET PETER | | | | |
|   Morton, Jelly Roll | Jelly Roll Morton | 12"78 | Circle JM-69 | 38-5 |
| | Jelly Roll Morton & Red Hot Peppers | 78 | Victor 23402 | 29-11 |
| SWEET PICKLES | | | | |
|   Bennett, Theron | David Thomas Roberts | LP | Stomp Off 1021 | 1981 |
| | St. Louis Ragtimers | LP | Ragophile | 1961 |
| SWEETIE DEAR | | | | |
|   Jordan, Joe | Sidney Bechet New Orleans Feetwarmers | 78 | Victor 23360 | 32-9 |
| | Claude Bolling & Orchestra | 78 | (France) Pacific HC-90017 | 48-5 |
| | Conway's Band | 78 | Victor 17628 | 14-8 |
| | National Military Band | 78 | Melodisc 702 | |
| SWEETMEATS | | | | |
|   Wenrich, Percy | Chrysanthemum Ragtime Band | LP | Stomp Off 1079 | 1984 |
| | Dawn of the Century Orchestra | LP | Arcane 601 | 1971 |
| | Arthur Pryor's Band | 78 | Victor 5733, 16818 | 09-5 |
| | Zonophone Orchestra | 78 | Zonophone 5287 | |
| SWEETNESS RAG | | | | |
|   Woods, Fannie | London Orchestra | 78 | (England) Cinch 5068 | 13-5 |
| SWIPESY CAKEWALK | | | | |
|   Joplin, Scott & Marshall, Arthur | Chris Barber JB | LP | (England) Col. 33SX-1245 | 1960 |
| | William Bolcom | LP | Music Master 0149 | 1981 |
| | Eric Brooks | 78 | (England) Poydras 17 | 50- |
| | Ann Charters | LP | Sierra Wave 101 | 1974 |
| | Steen Christensen | LP | (Denmark) LBS-1 | 1972 |
| | Ken Colyer's Jazzmen | LP | (England) 77LEU 12/10 | 1964 |
| | Kathy Craig | LP | OTMH 101 | r. 1980 |
| | Bob Darch | LP | United Artists UAL-3120 | 1960 |
| | Brian Dykstra | LP | Orion 83449 | 82-7 |
| | Ray Foxley | LP | (Germany) Jeton 100.3301 | 79-3 |
| | Freetime Jassband | LP | (Holland) Cat LP-25 | 77-12 |
| | David Andrew Frost | LP | MHS 3201 | 1975 |

| Composition | Performer | Record Speed | Record Company/No. | Year-Month |
|---|---|---|---|---|
| SWIPESY CAKEWALK (continued) Joplin, Scott & Marshall, Arthur | Paul Hersh & David Montgomery | LP | RCA Victor ARL1-0364 | 1974 |
| | Dick Hyman | LP | RCA CRL5-1106 | 1975 |
| | Jazzin' Babies | LP | Mabel 6927 | 1983 |
| | Morton Gunnar Larsen | LP | (Norway) Flower ABM-439 | 75-11 |
| | Merseysippi JB | EP | (England) Esquire EP-118 | 55-2 |
| | Merseysippi Jazz Band | 78 | (England) Esquire 10-438 | 55-2 |
| | Mimi & Russell | LP | Mumpus 791 | r. 1979 |
| | Max Morath | LP | Vanguard VSD-39/40 | 1967 |
| | Turk Murphy JB | LP | (Australia) Jazz & Jazz 6357.903 | 78-12 |
| | Turk Murphy JB | LP | Merry Makers 105 | 1970 |
| | New England Conservatory Ensemble | LP | Golden Crest 31042 | 1975 |
| | New Orleans Ragtime Orchestra | LP | ABC AA-1076 | 1977 |
| | Parenti's Ragtimers | 78 | Circle 1031 | 47-11 |
| | Knocky Parker | LP | Audiophile AP-71/72 | 1960 |
| | Knocky Parker & Bill Coffman | LP | Jazzology JCE-81 | r. 1979 |
| | Piano Roll | LP | Biograph 1008Q | |
| | Queen City JB | LP | Zeno 100 | 1976 |
| | William Neil Roberts | LP | Klavier 510 | 1972 |
| | Eric Rogers | LP | London Phase 4 21105 | 1974 |
| | Tom Schmutzler & Harry Malfas | LP | Fleet Street 80-01 | 1980 |
| | Tom Shea | LP | (Canada) Ragtime Society 2 | 64-8 |
| | Stevedore JB | LP | (Holland) Pink Poid 0102 | 80-2 |
| | Steve Waddell Band | LP | Stomp Off 1173 | 87-12 |
| | Dick Zimmerman | LP | Murray Hill 931079 | 1974 |
| THE SYCAMORE Joplin, Scott | Canadian Brass | LP | (Canada) Boot 3004 | 1974 |
| | Ann Charters | LP | Portents 1 | 1958 |
| | Dick Hyman | LP | RCA CRL5-1106 | 1975 |
| | Knocky Parker | LP | Audiophile AP-71/72 | 1960 |
| | Piano Roll | LP | Biograph 1008Q | |
| | Southland Stingers | LP | Angel S-36078 | 1974 |
| | Leo Wijnkamp | LP | Kicking Mule 115 | 1975 |
| | Dick Zimmerman | LP | Murray Hill 931079 | 1974 |
| SYMPHONOLA Lange, Henry | Andrews Instrumental Trio (Henry Lange Trio) | 78 | Perfect 14005 | 22- |
| | Garcia Badenes | 78 | (France) Discolux DF-519 | 32-3 |
| | Stanley C. Holt | 78 | (England) Homochord H-492 | 23-9 |
| | Harry Reser w/ pno | 78 | (England) Columbia 3334 | 23-7 |
| TAKE YOUR PICK Mandell, Pete | Joe Brannelly | 78 | (England) Zonophone 5552 | 30-3 |
| | Michael Danzi | 78 | (Germany) Homokord 4-1988 | 26-10 |
| | Pete Mandell w/ pno | 78 | (England) Duo D-523 | 28-9 |
| | Pete Mandell & Savoy Orpheans | 78 | (England) HMV B-5035 | 26-3 |
| | Phil Russell (Pete Mandell) | 78 | (England) Edison Bell Winner 4647 | 26-9 |

| Composition | Performer | Record Speed | Record Company/No. | Year-Month |
|---|---|---|---|---|
| TAMING THE TENOR | | | | |
| Fillis, Len & Bright, Sid | Len Fillis & Sid Bright | 78 | (England) Columbia 4161 | |
| TANGO RAG | | | | |
| Jordan, Joe | Lois Delano | LP | (Canada) Arpeggio 1205 | 1968 |
| TANTALIZING TINGLES | | | | |
| Bernard, Mike & Violinsky, Sol | Mike Bernard | 78 | Columbia A-1386 | 13-6 |
| TAR BABIES RAG | | | | |
| Johnson, Charles L. | Knocky Parker | LP | Audiophile AP-92 | |
| | Roger's Band | 78 | Paroquette 72 | r. 17-3 |
| TATTERS | | | | |
| Dickie, Neville | Neville Dickie | LP | (England) Contour 2870-190 | 1972 |
| TEASIN' THE IVORIES | | | | |
| Schutt, Arthur | Arthur Schutt | 78 | (England) Regal G-8046 | 23-7 |
| TEASING RAG | | | | |
| Pratt, Paul | Elliott Adams | LP | Stomp Off 1198 | 1988 |
| TEASING RAG | | | | |
| | Ex-Dixieland Bobcats | 78 | Crystalette 649 | 45- |
| TEASING THE CAT | | | | |
| Johnson, Charles L. | Rishell Dance Band | 78 | Rishell 5430 | |
| | Roger's Military Band | 78 | Paroquette 38 | r. 17-1 |
| | Van Eps–Banta Dance Orchestra | 78 | Pathe 20087 | 16-12 |
| | Van Eps Trio | 78 | Victor 18226 | 16-12 |
| | Richard Zimmerman | LP | Murray Hill 60556/5 | 1981 |
| TEASING THE FRETS | | | | |
| Colicchio, Ralph | Michele Ortuso | 78 | (England) HMV B-3651 | 29-11 |
| TEASING THE FRETS | | | | |
| Lucas, Nick | Nick Lucas | 78 | Brunswick 2536 | 23-11 |
| | Nick Lucas | 78 | Brunswick 6508 | 32-12 |
| | Nick Lucas | 78 | Pathe 020794 | 22-6 |
| TEASING THE KLASSICS | | | | |
| Christensen, Axel W. | Axel Christensen | 78 | Okeh 4973 | 23-10 |
| | Axel Christensen | 78 | Paramount 20173 | |
| TEASING THE PIANO | | | | |
| | Coco Colignon Rhythm | 78 | (Germany) Telefunken A-2642 | 38-6 |
| TEDDY IN THE JUNGLE | | | | |
| Freeberg, Edward J. | David Thomas Roberts | LP | Stomp Off 1021 | 1981 |
| | Richard Zimmerman | LP | Murray Hill 60556/5 | 1981 |
| TEDDY TROMBONE | | | | |
| Fillmore, Henry | Trombone Trio | 78 | Tempo 576 | |
| | West End Jazz Band | LP | Stomp Off 1085 | 84-8 |
| | Albert White Orchestra | LP | Barbary Coast 33008 | 1958 |
| TEDDY'S RAG | | | | |
| | Walter Dobschinski & Orchestra | 78 | (Germany) Odeon 0-28590 | 53-6 |

| Composition | Performer | Record Speed | Record Company/No. | Year-Month |
|---|---|---|---|---|
| TEK-NIK-ALITY RAG | | | | |
| Johnson, Arnold | Arnold Johnson Piano Roll | LP | Herwin 407 | |
| TEMPERAMENTAL RAG | | | | |
| Deiro, Guido | Guido Deiro | 78 | Columbia A-2834 | 18-9 |
| TEMPTATION RAG | | | | |
| Lodge, Henry | Marvin Ash | LP | Jump J12-9 | 1947 |
| | Burt Bales | 10″LP | GTJ 19 | 49-10 |
| | Kenny Ball JB | LP | Kapp KL-1314 | 1963 |
| | Ballhaus Orchester | 78 | (Germany) Odeon 308274 | 14- |
| | Ballyhooligans | 78 | (England) HMV BD-5065 | 36-4 |
| | Ballyhooligans (m) | 78 | (England) HMV BD-5130 | 36-10 |
| | Sidney Bechet w/ Claude Luter's Orchestra | 78 | (France) Vogue 5020 | 49-11 |
| | David Bee & Busy Bees | 78 | (France) Columbia FP-1023 | |
| | David Bee Orchestra | LP | (France) Col. FP-1023 | |
| | Beka London Orchestra | 78 | (England) Beka 436 | 11-5 |
| | Graeme Bell & Ragtime Four | 78 | (Australia) Parlophone A-7824 | 53-4 |
| | Ralph & Bert Bergh | 78 | (Sweden) Metronome J-135 | 50-5 |
| | Black Diamonds Band | 78 | (England) Zonophone 771 | 11-11 |
| | Claude Bolling | LP | (France) Philips 70341 | 1966 |
| | Sharkey Bonano & Band | 78 | Capitol 15703 | 50-7 |
| | Bugle Call Raggers | 78 | (England) Decca F-5479 | 35-3 |
| | Joe "Fingers" Carr | LP | Cap. T-760 | |
| | Cattani's Orchestra | 78 | (England) Ariel 2077 | 12- |
| | Arthur Collins | 78 | Columbia A-826 | r. 10-6 |
| | Arthur Collins | 78 | Sonora 5052 | |
| | Russ Conway | EP | (England) Col. SEG-7886 | 1959 |
| | Victor Cornelius & Jacob Schmidt | 78 | (Germany) Grammophon 49059 | 24-9 |
| | Billy Cotton Orchestra | 78 | (England) Regal Zonophone MR-1688 | |
| | Crooks | LP | (Sweden) Opus 3 Nr. 7916 | 1979 |
| | Mario De Pietro | 78 | (England) Parlophone F-1078 | |
| | Neville Dickie | LP | (England) Contour 2870-190 | 1972 |
| | Otto Dobrindt | 78 | (Germany) Odeon 0-31372 | 38-8 |
| | Empire Guards Band | 78 | (England) Olympic 37 | 12-4 |
| | Pee Wee Erwin Dixieland Band | LP | United Artists UAL-4010 | 58-10 |
| | Doc Evans Band | 10″LP | Audiophile AP-34 | 1956 |
| | Famous Band | 78 | (England) Famous 137 | 13-4 |
| | Joseph Fiers | 78 | (Belgium) HMV F-219 | c. 1930 |
| | Larry Fotine Band | LP | Bel Canto SR-1009 | |
| | Erik Frank Trio | 78 | (Sweden) Sonora 566 | 42-8 |
| | Georgie's Varsity Five | LP | HiFi R-805 | 1959 |
| | Joe Glover's Cotton Pickers | LP | Epic LN-3581 | |
| | Benny Goodman Sextet | 78 | Columbia 39121 | 50-11 |
| | Grammophon Orchestra | 78 | (Germany) Grammophon 12805 | |
| | Grammovox Military Band | 78 | (England) Grammovox A-114 | 12-9 |
| | Chris Hamilton | 78 | London 1210 | |
| | Imperial Regimental Band | 78 | (England) Pathe 8549 | 12-1 |

| Composition | Performer | Record Speed | Record Company/No. | Year-Month |
|---|---|---|---|---|
| TEMPTATION RAG (continued) | Irish Guards' Band | 78 | (England) Bell Disc 305 | 11-6 |
| Lodge, Henry | Irish Guards' Band | 78 | (England) Best Tone 177 | |
| | Irish Guards' Band | 78 | (England) Dacapo 419 | 12-7 |
| | Lawson–Haggart JB | LP | Decca DL-8199 | 1954 |
| | Nisse Lind | 78 | (Sweden) Toni 627 | 37-12 |
| | Louisiana Symphony Orchestra | 78 | (England) Edison Bell Winner 2030 | 11-12 |
| | Geoff Love Ragtime Band | LP | (Canada) Quality 753 | 1974 |
| | Memphis Nighthawks | LP | Delmark 216 | 1977 |
| | New Orleans Ragtime Orchestra | LP | GHB 210 | 87-1 |
| | New York Military Band | Cylinder | Edison 10406 | |
| | Odeon Dance Orchestra | 78 | (Germany) Odeon 311586 | |
| | Orchestra Tzigane du Pavillion Royale | 78 | (France) Grammophon 30736 | |
| | Palais de Danse | 78 | (Germany) Grammophon 12872 | 12-11 |
| | Palais de Danse | 78 | (Germany) Pathe 416 | |
| | Palm Court Orchestra | LP | (Australia) K-Tel NA-628 | r. 1986 |
| | Papa Bue's JB | 10"LP | (Denmark) Storyville SLP-156 | 62-6 |
| | Knocky Parker & Patrick Gogerty | LP | Euphonic 1215 | 77-4 |
| | Pasadena Roof Orchestra | LP | (England) Transatlantic 314 | 75-12 |
| | Piano Roll | LP | (England) Saydisc SDL-132 | |
| | Cesare Poggi | LP | (Italy) Dire FO-344 | 1979 |
| | Prince's Band | 78 | Columbia A-854 | 09-11 |
| | Arthur Pryor's Band | 78 | Victor 16511 | 10-6 |
| | Arthur Pryor's Band (m) | 78 | Victor 16542 | 10-6 |
| | Rainy City JB | 78 | Exner 6 | 47-12 |
| | Razzberrie Ragtimers | LP | Razzberrie 32888 | 1979 |
| | Rhythm Rascals | 78 | (England) Crown 7 | 35-6 |
| | George Robb | EP | (Canada) Periwinkle PER-7311 | 1973 |
| | Wally Rose | LP | Fairmont 102 | 47-8 |
| | Wally Rose & Rhythm | 78 | Jazz Man 7 | 42-3 |
| | Harry Roy Orchestra | 78 | (England) Parlophone F-102 | 35-1 |
| | Harry Roy Orchestra (m) | 78 | (England) Parlophone F-338 | 35-11 |
| | Harry Roy Orchestra (m) | 78 | (England) Parlophone F-1568 | 39-2 |
| | Royal Military Band | 78 | (England) Victory A-55 | 12-8 |
| | Yannick Singery | LP | (France) Swing SLD-928 | c. 1975 |
| | St. James Meister Orchestra | LP | (England) Butterfly B-293 | 11-7 |
| | Monty Sunshine JB | LP | (England) DJM 26088 | 1965 |
| | Rolf Syversen | 78 | (Norway) Telefunken T-8224 | 39-1 |
| | Tanzpalast Orchestra | 78 | (Germany) Grammophon 62196 | |
| | Donald Thorne | 78 | (England) Decca F-6807 | 38- |
| | Sidney Torch | 78 | (England) Columbia FB-1133 | 35- |
| | Fred Van Eps & Albert Benzler | Cylinder | U.S. Everlasting 1260 | |
| | Barrie Vye | 78 | Exner 6 | 47-12 |
| | Dick Wellstood | 10"LP | GHB 1 | c. 1951 |
| | Jay Wilbur Band | 78 | (England) Rex 8485 | 35-5 |
| | Arthur Young & Youngsters (m) | 78 | (England) Decca F-5645 | 35-8 |
| | Richard Zimmerman | LP | Murray Hill 60556/5 | 1981 |
| | Zonophone Orchestra | 78 | Zonophone 5679 | r. 11-1 |

| Composition | Performer | Record Speed | Record Company/No. | Year-Month |
|---|---|---|---|---|
| TENNESSEE JUBILEE | | | | |
| Broady, Thomas | Trebor Tichenor | LP | Dirty Shame 2001 | 1973 |
| A TENNESSEE MAPLE LEAF | | | | |
| Rummel, Jack, Joplin, Scott & Hunter, Charles | Jack Rummel | LP | Stomp Off 1118 | 1985 |
| A TENNESSEE TANTALIZER | | | | |
| Hunter, Charles | Morton Gunnar Larsen (m) | LP | Stomp Off 1009 | 81-1 |
| | Bill Mitchell | LP | Euphonic 1203 | 1962 |
| | Knocky Parker | LP | Audiophile AP-90 | |
| TENT SHOW RAG | | | | |
| Campbell, Brun | Brun Campbell | LP | Euphonic 1202 | 1947 |
| TENTH INTERVAL RAG | | | | |
| Ruby, Harry | Gene Rodemich & Orchestra | 78 | Brunswick 2599 | 24-2 |
| TEXAS FOX TROT | | | | |
| Guion, David | Chrysanthemum Ragtime Band | LP | Stomp Off 1079 | 1984 |
| | Jaudas Society Orchestra | 78 | Edison 50625 | 20-3 |
| | Richard Zimmerman | LP | Murray Hill 60556/5 | 1981 |
| TEXAS RAG | | | | |
| Jackson, C. W. | David Thomas Roberts | LP | Stomp Off 1021 | 1981 |
| | Richard Zimmerman | LP | Murray Hill 60556/5 | 1981 |
| TEXAS SHOUT (see TRILBY RAG) | | | | |
| | Cow Cow Davenport | 78 | Vocalion 1291 | 29-5 |
| THAT AMERICAN RAGTIME DANCE | | | | |
| Jasen, David A. | Dave Jasen | LP | Blue Goose 3001 | 1972 |
| THAT BANJO RAG | | | | |
| Roberts, Dick | The Banjo Kings | 78 | Good Time Jazz 47 | |
| THAT CAPTIVATING RAG | | | | |
| Wellinger, Charles | John Arpin | LP | (Canada) Harmony 6026 | 1970 |
| THAT CERTAIN PARTY | | | | |
| Kelley, Tom | Brooke Pemberton | LP | Warner Bros. W-1235 | 1958 |
| THAT DEMON RAG | | | | |
| Smith, Russell | John Hasse | LP | Sunflower 501 | 1980 |
| | Piano Roll | LP | Indiana Historical Society 1001 | |
| THAT ECCENTRIC RAG | | | | |
| Robinson, J. Russell | Buster Bailey Sextet | 78 | Varsity 8356 | 40-6 |
| | Eddy Bayard JB | LP | Stomp Off 1145 | 1986 |
| | Sharkey Bonano JB | 78 | Cap. 15705 | 50-1 |
| | Dave Brennan JB | LP | (England) VJM LC-12 | 1971 |
| | Raymond Burke JB | 10"LP | Southland SLP-227 | 1960 |
| | Castle JB | 78 | Castle 14 | 50-9 |
| | Ken Colyer's Jazzmen | LP | (England) K.C. Records GNO-101 | 1965 |
| | Cotton Town JB | LP | (Holland) CTE SLP-7905 | 78-12 |
| | Bob Crosby Orchestra | 78 | Odeon 286027 | 42-1 |

| Composition | Performer | Record Speed | Record Company/No. | Year-Month |
|---|---|---|---|---|
| THAT ECCENTRIC RAG (continued) | Kenny Davern Trio | LP | Fat Cat's Jazz FCJ-207 | 79-12 |
| | Wild Bill Davison Band | LP | (Switzerland) Jaylin P-19811 | 81-1 |
| Robinson, J. Russell | Wild Bill Davison JB | 78 | Circle 1023 | 47-7 |
| | Johnny DeDroit Orchestra | 78 | Okeh 40240 | 24-10 |
| | Dorsey Brothers Orchestra | 78 | Decca 1304 | 35-2 |
| | Dukes of Dixieland | LP | Audio Fidelity AF-1860 | 1957 |
| | Dutch Swing College Band | LP | (Holland) Philips BL-7579 | 62-8 |
| | Pee Wee Erwin JB | 78 | King 15073 | 50-8 |
| | Bernard Ette Orchestra | 78 | (Germany) Vox 1713 | 24-12 |
| | Doc Evans JB | 78 | Art Floral 102 | 49-2 |
| | Doc Evans JB | LP | Audiophile XL-329 | 1955 |
| | Doc Evans JB | LP | Soma MG-1209 | 57-6 |
| | Evergreen Classic JB | LP | Triangle Jazz 110 | 1987 |
| | Flatfoot Stompers | LP | (Holland) Timeless SJP-529 | 84-10 |
| | Friars Society Orchestra | 78 | Gennett 5009 | 22-8 |
| | Henry Hall Orchestra | 78 | (England) Col. FB-1818 | 37-10 |
| | Happy JB | LP | Happy Jazz 201 | c. 1970 |
| | Harbour JB | LP | (Holland) Dankers 113118 | 67-12 |
| | Hazy-Gate Bellhops | LP | (Holland) Kimball 58027534 | 71-5 |
| | Art Hodes | 78 | Jazz Record 1004 | 40-3 |
| | Hot Shots | LP | (Germany) Happy Bird 90123 | 83-4 |
| | Indiana U. Ragtime Orchestra | LP | Indiana Historical Society 1001 | 1981 |
| | Max Kaminsky JB | 78 | Commodore 560 | 44-6 |
| | Lawson–Haggart JB | LP | Decca 8199 | 1954 |
| | London Ragtime Orchestra | LP | Stomp Off 1081 | 84-4 |
| | Rod Mason's JB | LP | (Germany) Happy Bird 5008 | 74-2 |
| | Merseysippi JB | 10″LP | (England) Esquire 20-093 | 58-5 |
| | New Orleans Ragtime Orchestra | LP | (Sweden) Sonet 709 | 76-3 |
| | Keith Nichols Ragtime Orchestra | LP | (England) EMI One-Up-2135 | 76-2 |
| | Red Nichols Five Pennies | 78 | Brunswick 3627 | 27-8 |
| | Red Nichols Five Pennies | LP | Cap. T-1228 | 59-3 |
| | Original Memphis Five | 78 | Perfect 14105 | 23-2 |
| | Oriole Orchestra | 78 | Br. 2616 | 24-2 |
| | Papa Bue's Viking JB | LP | (Denmark) Storyville SLP-150 | 61-6 |
| | Tony Parenti's Downtown Boys | LP | Jazzology J-11 | 1961 |
| | Pasadena Roof Orchestra | LP | (England) Transatlantic 15918 | 1974 |
| | Pearl Street JB | LP | Proud Mother 3 | 79-7 |
| | Mike Pembroke Hot Seven | LP | Jazzology J-24 | 76-10 |
| | Peruna Jazzmen | LP | Stomp Off 1003 | 80-4 |
| | Platte River JB | LP | PRJB Vol. 3 | 1981 |
| | Red Roseland Cornpickers | LP | Stomp Off 1153 | 87-1 |
| | J. Russell Robinson | 78 | Eagle 901 | r. 47-9 |
| | Maxim Saury Band | LP | (France) Decca 99058 | 71-5 |
| | Savoy Orpheans | 78 | (England) Col. 3432 | 24-4 |
| | Muggsy Spanier's Ragtime Band | 78 | Bluebird B-10417 | 39-7 |
| | Jack Teagarden Orchestra | LP | Bethlehem BCP-32 | 54-11 |
| | This Is Jazz All Stars | 10″LP | Circle L-423 | 47-4 |

| Composition | Performer | Record Speed | Record Company/No. | Year-Month |
|---|---|---|---|---|
| THAT ECCENTRIC RAG | Gosta Torner Orchestra | 78 | (Germany) Telefunken A-5396 | 49-10 |
| (continued) | Alex Welch Dixielanders | 78 | (England) Decca F-10538 | 55-4 |
| Robinson, J. Russell | Dick Wellstood Jazz Band | LP | Fat Cat's Jazz 207 | 79-12 |
| | Alex Welsh Dixielanders | 78 | (England) Decca F-10538 | 55-4 |
| | Brian White JB | LP | Jazzology J-116 | 86-4 |
| THAT ERRATIC RAG | | | | |
| Robinson, J. Russel | Tony Parenti's Ragtime Gang | LP | Jazzology J-21 | 66-4 |
| THAT EVER-LOVIN' RAG | | | | |
| Byron, Walter | Joe "Fingers" Carr | 78 | Capitol 2081 | |
| | Billy Cotton | 78 | (England) Decca F-9814 | |
| | Guy Lombardo Orchestra | 78 | Decca 28536 | 51-11 |
| | Ivor Moreton & Dave Kaye | 78 | (England) Parlophone F-2484 | |
| | Buddy Morrow Orchestra | 78 | Victor 20-4543 | 52-1 |
| | Sid Phillips Band | 78 | (England) HMV BD-6111 | 51-9 |
| THAT FLYING RAG | | | | |
| Pryor, Arthur | National Military Band | 78 | Phono Cut 5024 | |
| | Arthur Pryor's Band | 78 | Victor 17021 | r. 12-2 |
| THAT FUTURISTIC RAG | | | | |
| Bloom, Rube | Rube Bloom | 78 | Okeh 41073 | 28-2 |
| | George Hicks | LP | Folkways FS-3165 | 1983 |
| THAT MOANING TROMBONE | | | | |
| Bethel | Jim Europe's Band | 78 | Pathe 22085 | 19-3 |
| | Murray Pilcer's Jazz Band | 78 | (England) Edison Bell Winner 3292 | 19-1 |
| | Sammy Spear Orchestra | LP | Mercury MG-20116 | 1954 |
| THAT PECULIAR RAG | | | | |
| Fagan, Fred M. | Mike Bernard | 78 | Columbia A-1313 | 12-12 |
| | Sharkey Bonano Jazz Band | 78 | Capitol 1078 | 50-1 |
| | Ed Morton | 78 | Columbia A-1058 | 11-7 |
| THAT RAG | | | | |
| Browne, Ted | Arthur Pryor's Band | 78 | Victor 16043 | 08-9 |
| THAT RIPPING RAG | | | | |
| Wildman, F. Collis | Casino Orchestra | 78 | (England) Regal G-6141 | 14-1 |
| | Empire Military Band | 78 | (England) Beka 696 | 13-3 |
| | National Symphony Orchestra | 78 | (England) Marathon 195 | 12-12 |
| | Peerless Orchestra | 78 | (England) Zonophone | 13-3 |
| | Ragtime Orchestra | 78 | (England) HMV C-268 | |
| | Royal Court Orchestra | 78 | (England) Edison Bell Winner 2319 | 13- |
| THAT SENTIMENTAL RAG | | | | |
| Tilton, Mabel | Max Morath Band | LP | Vanguard VSD-79402 | 1977 |
| THAT TEASIN' RAG | | | | |
| Jordan, Joe | Ken Colyer's Jazzmen | LP | (England) VJM 35 | 1969 |
| | Lois Delano | LP | (Canada) Arpeggio 1205 | 1968 |
| | Down Home Jazz Band (m) | | Stomp Off 1217 | 89-10 |
| | Bunk Johnson Jazz Band | LP | Columbia ML-4802 | 47-12 |
| | Joe Jordan | LP | Stereoddities C-1990 | 1962 |

| Composition | Performer | Record Speed | Record Company/No. | Year-Month |
|---|---|---|---|---|
| THAT TEASIN' RAG (continued) | Louisiana Repertory Jazz Ensemble (m) | LP | Stomp Off 1140 | 86-6 |
| Jordan, Joe | New Orleans Ragtime Orchestra | LP | Vanguard VSD-69/70 | 1971 |
| | Original Dixieland Five (m) | 78 | Victor 25502 | 36-11 |
| | Original Dixieland Jass Band | 78 | Victor 18255 | 17-2 |
| | Waldo's Ragtime Orchestra | LP | Stomp Off 1007 | 80-10 |
| THAT'S A PLENTY | | | | |
| Pollack, Lew | Alexander's JB | 78 | Ragtime 1052 | 50-9 |
| | Henry "Red" Allen Band | LP | Roulette R-25015 | 57-5 |
| | Pete Allen | LP | (England) Black Lion 12174 | 78-10 |
| | Jimmy Archey JB | LP | (France) Barclay BLP-84001 | 1955 |
| | Kenny Ball JB | EP | (England) Par. GEP-8733 | 58-10 |
| | Barrelhouse JB | LP | (Austria) L & R 40020 | 1982 |
| | Sweet Emma Barrett JB | LP | Southland SLP-241 | 1963 |
| | Basin Street Six | LP | Mercury MG-25111 | 1951 |
| | Eddy Bayard JB | LP | Stomp Off 1145 | 1986 |
| | Sidney Bechet JB | LP | Riverside RLP-149 | 47-3 |
| | Sidney Bechet Hot Six | 10"LP | Blue Note BLP-7020 | 51-11 |
| | Bechet–Spanier Quartet | 12"78 | HRS 2002 | 40-4 |
| | Graeme Bell JB | LP | (Australia) Festival FL-30908 | 62-8 |
| | Adrian Bentzon | LP | (Denmark) Tono 2-18266 | 53-11 |
| | Ralph & Bert Berg | 78 | (Sweden) Metronome J-165 | 50-4 |
| | Acker Bilk JB | LP | (Czechoslovakia) Supraphon 026499 | 1964 |
| | Harry Blons JB | LP | Mercury MG-20222 | 1956 |
| | Bluebird Military Band | 78 | Bluebird B-3303 | 38-8 |
| | Boll Weevil JB | LP | GHB 33 | 1963 |
| | Sharkey Bonano JB | 78 | Kappa 120 | 49-6 |
| | Borgy Borgerson JB | EP | (Canada) Periwinkle PER-7311 | 1973 |
| | Bridge Town JB | LP | (Holland) Jazz Crooner JC-2910743 | 1974 |
| | Brunies Brothers | 10"LP | American Music 651 | 1957 |
| | Jan Burgers JB | LP | (Holland) Artone POS-242 | 1966 |
| | Dick Carey JB | LP | Golden Crest CR-3024 | 1957 |
| | Joe "Fingers" Carr | LP | Warner Bros. W-1389 | 1960 |
| | Casa Loma Orchestra | LP | Capitol ST-1400 | 1960 |
| | Castle JB | LP | GTJ L-12037 | 1959 |
| | Papa Celestin JB | LP | Imperial 9199 | 1956 |
| | Ceres Band | LP | (Germany) Munich BM-15042 | 1979 |
| | Colgate Hi-Five | LP | Golden Crest CR-3099 | 1959 |
| | Max Collie's Rhythm Aces | LP | (Holland) Beerendonk 9996 | 80-1 |
| | Eddie Condon Gang | LP | Columbia CL-1089 | 57-8 |
| | Eddie Condon Gang | LP | Jazzology J-50 | 68-12 |
| | Eddie Condon's Barrelhouse Gang | 78 | Signature 28130 | 43-11 |
| | Russ Conway | EP | (England) Col. SEG-7886 | 1959 |
| | Pete Daily's Chicagoans | LP | Eclectic E-71 | 1945 |
| | Jack Daniels' Original Band | LP | Spring Branch SB-29403 | 81-6 |
| | Darktown Strutters | 78 | (Switzerland) Chant du Monde 29138 | 50-2 |

| Composition | Performer | Record Speed | Record Company/No. | Year-Month |
|---|---|---|---|---|
| THAT'S A PLENTY (continued) | Wallace Davenport JB | LP | (France) Black & Blue 33172 | 80-7 |
| Pollack, Lew | Kenny Davern Trio | LP | Fat Cat's Jazz FCJ-207 | 79-12 |
| | Trump Davidson Band | LP | (Canada) Sound Canada SC-7702 | 1969 |
| | Wild Bill Davison Band | 78 | Commodore 1511 | 43-11 |
| | Wilbur DeParis JB | LP | Atlantic 1318 | 59-4 |
| | Neville Dickie | LP | (England) Contour 2870-190 | 1972 |
| | Dixie Five | 78 | United 1000 | 50-8 |
| | Dixie Rebels | LP | Command 33-801 | 1959 |
| | Dixiecats | LP | Roulette R-25015 | 57-5 |
| | Dixieland Pipers | EP | (Holland) Col. SEGH-28 | 57-5 |
| | Dixieland Rhythm Kings | LP | Fat Cat's Jazz 177 | 76-12 |
| | Dixieland Wanderers | 45 | (Holland) Pan 2004 | 69-3 |
| | Walter Dobschinsky Band | EP | (Germany) Electrola 1C134-32428/29 | 52-1 |
| | Jimmy Dorsey Band | 78 | Col. 38710 | 50-1 |
| | Tommy Dorsey Orchestra | 78 | Vic. 25363 | 36-6 |
| | Down Home JB | LP | Stomp Off 1190 | 88-8 |
| | Dukes of Dixieland | LP | Victor LPM-2982 | 1955 |
| | Dukes of Dixieland | LP | Vik LVA-1025 | 55-5 |
| | Dutch Swing College Band | 78 | (Holland) Decca M-32772 | 50-1 |
| | East End Jazz Men | EP | (Sweden) Gazell GEP-26 | 59-1 |
| | Eli's Chosen Six | LP | Col. CL-736 | 55-6 |
| | Empire City Six | 10"LP | Stardust SD-101 | |
| | Doc Evans JB | 78 | Disc 6074 | 47-4 |
| | Doc Evans Band | 10"LP | Audiophile XL-329 | c.1955 |
| | Doc Evans Band | 10"LP | Soma MG-1208 | 1957 |
| | Fatty George Band | 10"LP | Mastertone JML-010 | 55-9 |
| | Lennie Felix | LP | (England) Col. 33SX-1144 | 59-6 |
| | Firehouse Five Plus Two | LP | GTJ L-12040 | 60-3 |
| | Pete Fountain Band | LP | Coral CRL-57334 | 1960 |
| | Erik Frank Ensemble | 78 | (England) Decca F-44068 | 47-5 |
| | French Market JB | LP | Flying Dutchman BDL1-1239 | 1975 |
| | Georgians JB | LP | (Argentina) Vic AVS-4438 | 76-9 |
| | Walt Gifford's New Yorkers | LP | Delmark DL-206 | 52-4 |
| | Harry Gold Pieces of Eight | LP | (England) Lake 5003 | 84-9 |
| | Nat Gonella's Georgians | 78 | (England) Par. F-832 | 37-7 |
| | Benny Goodman's Boys | 78 | Voc. 15705 | 28-6 |
| | Benny Goodman Sextet | 78 | Cap. 15766 | 47-12 |
| | Guardia Vieja JB | 78 | (Argentina) TK S-5234 | 1953 |
| | Bobby Hackett JB | LP | Capitol T-962 | 55-10 |
| | Bobby Hackett JB | LP | Flying Dutchman FD-10159 | 1973 |
| | Happy Wanderers | EP | (England) Esquire EP-177 | 57-3 |
| | Harbour JB | LP | (Holland) Imperial 50052-24302 | 70-4 |
| | Lance Harrison Band | LP | (Canada) RCA Victor PC-1043 | 65-4 |
| | Earl Hines Band | LP | GNP 9043 | 56-3 |
| | Earl Hines Orchestra | 78 | Decca 182 | 34-9 |
| | Al Hirt Band | LP | Vic LPM-2497 | 62-1 |

| Composition | Performer | Record Speed | Record Company/No. | Year-Month |
|---|---|---|---|---|
| THAT'S A PLENTY (continued) | Art Hodes Band | 78 | Jazz Record 1009 | 46-3 |
| Pollack, Lew | Pee Wee Hunt Band | LP | Capitol T-573 | 1957 |
| | Dick Hyman | LP | (England) Sonet 734 | 77-4 |
| | Port Jackson JB | EP | (Australia) Carinia 45-EPJ-3083 | 58-11 |
| | Conrad Janis JB | 10"LP | London LTZ-U15095 | 51-1 |
| | Frank Johnson Band | 78 | (Australia) Swaggie S-1001 | 50-10 |
| | Jonah Jones Quartet | EP | Cap. EAP1-1039 | 58-4 |
| | Jumping Jacks | EP | (Sweden) Karisell KSEP-3033 | 56-10 |
| | Jungle Cats | LP | (Switzerland) Elite Special SJLP-6320 | 76-9 |
| | Kid Ory JB | LP | GTJ L-12004 | 54-8 |
| | Kid Ory JB | 10"LP | Jazz Pan LP-8 | 44-4 |
| | KXYZ Novelty Band | 78 | Bluebird B-5832 | 35-1 |
| | Yank Lawson's JB | 78 | Signature 28108 | 44-12 |
| | Nisse Lind Trio | 78 | (Sweden) Sonet 3519 | 39-2 |
| | Paul Lingle | LP | Euphonic 1220 | 1951 |
| | Jack London's JB | LP | Sound of New Orleans 1004 | 1976 |
| | Mike LoScalzo JB | 78 | Black & White 1215 | 45-5 |
| | Louisiana Rhythm Kings | 78 | Voc. 15784 | 29-2 |
| | Rick Lundy's Saints | LP | Westminster WP-6113 | 1958 |
| | Claude Luter Orchestra | EP | (France) Vogue EPL-7644 | 59-5 |
| | Fess Manetta | LP | Jazzology JCE-6 | 57-5 |
| | Lew Marcus | 10"LP | Savoy XP-8052 | 47-3 |
| | Matty Matlock Band | LP | Warner Bros. B-1262 | 58-11 |
| | Clyde McCoy Orchestra | LP | Circle CLP-82 | 51-3 |
| | Jimmy McPartland Band | LP | RCA Camden CAL-549 | 59-5 |
| | Metronome Quintet | 10"LP | (England) Philips B-10105 | 53-9 |
| | Midnight Jazzmen | EP | (England) Embassy WEP-1033 | c. 1960 |
| | Milan College Jazz | 78 | (Italy) Col. CQ-2705 | 53-5 |
| | Ray Miller Orchestra | 78 | Br. 4224 | 29-1 |
| | Miff Mole Band | 78 | Okeh 41232 | 29-4 |
| | Turk Murphy JB | LP | Fairmont 111 | 50-6 |
| | Fumio Nanri Orchestra | LP | (Japan) Col. SW-7036 | |
| | Phil Napoleon Orchestra | 78 | Variety 669 | 37-9 |
| | Louis Nelson Band | LP | Nola LP-7 | 70-5 |
| | Rick Nelson Band | LP | Jazzology J-123 | c. 1970 |
| | New Harlem Ramblers | LP | (Switzerland) Elite Special SJLP-6333 | 82-5 |
| | New Hot Players | 78 | (Switzerland) Elite Special 4200 | 43-6 |
| | New Orleans Joymakers | LP | (England) Paragon PLE-S104 | 73-10 |
| | New Orleans Rhythm Kings | 78 | Gennett 5105 | 23-3 |
| | New Ragtime Band | LP | (France) Mode 9857 | 70-10 |
| | Albert Nicholas Band | 10"LP | (Poland) Muza L-0161 | 57-6 |
| | Red Nichols Five Pennies | LP | Broadway Intermission 130 | 59-8 |
| | Red Nichols Five Pennies | 78 | Jump 20 | 49-3 |
| | North Country JB | LP | Adirondack 1007 | 81-8 |
| | Orange Peels | LP | Inter-Varsity 1201 | c. 1960 |

| Composition | Performer | Record Speed | Record Company/No. | Year-Month |
|---|---|---|---|---|
| THAT'S A PLENTY (continued) | Original Atlanta Footwarmers | 78 | Bell 585 | 28-1 |
| Pollack, Lew | Original Salty Dogs | LP | (Australia) Jazz & Jazz 6437158 | 79-6 |
| | Matty Matlock Paducah Patrol | LP | Warner Bros. W-1262 | 1959 |
| | Panigal JB | LP | (Italy) RCA A72V0134 | 57-5 |
| | Tony Parenti's Melody Boys | 78 | Okeh 40308 | 25-1 |
| | Harry Parry Sextet | 78 | (England) Par. R-3187 | 49-2 |
| | Lina Patruno Band | LP | (Italy) Carosello CLE-21015 | 75-5 |
| | Bert Peck Band | LP | Paula 2225 | c. 1973 |
| | Eddie Pequenino Rockers | EP | (Argentina) Orfeo 10012 | 58-11 |
| | Sid Phillips Band | 10"LP | (England) HMV DLP-1164 | |
| | Phoenix JB | LP | (France) Black & Blue 33418 | 84-5 |
| | Danny Polo Swing Stars | 78 | (England) Decca F-6550 | 37-10 |
| | Nannie Porres Band | 45 | (Sweden) HMV X-8603 | 57-5 |
| | Preacher Rollo's Saints | 10"LP | MGM E-220 | 53-3 |
| | Ray Price JB | LP | (Australia) Ata SATAL-165/6 | 1971 |
| | Sammy Price Blusicians | 10"LP | (France) Guilde du Jazz 1236 | 56-2 |
| | Leon Prima JB | LP | Southland 210 | 54-10 |
| | Prince's Band | 12"78 | Col. A-5582 | 14-7 |
| | Prowizorka JB | LP | (Holland) Timeless TTD-526 | 85-12 |
| | Rainy City Stompers | LP | (Germany) Ocean 44.017 | 87-1 |
| | Freddie Randall Band | 78 | (England) Par. R-3382 | 51-1 |
| | Rhythm Maniacs | 78 | (England) Decca F-1573 | 29-10 |
| | Trevor Richards Trio | LP | Crescent 4 | 75-3 |
| | John Rindfleisch Orchestra | LP | (Germany) Fontana 9294078 | 75-11 |
| | River Boat Five | 10"LP | Mercury MG-20379 | 1958 |
| | Riverboat Stompers | LP | (Italy) R.S. 1001 | 82-7 |
| | Riverside JB | EP | (Italy) Pro Musica PMB-7081 | 58-7 |
| | Rivertown JB | EP | (Germany) Metronome MEP-1731 | 58-10 |
| | Roman JB | 78 | (Italy) HMV HN-2947 | 51-11 |
| | Billy Rowland | LP | RCA Victor LPM-1872 | 1958 |
| | Harry Roy Tiger Ragamuffins | 78 | (England) Par. F-484 | 36-6 |
| | Stan Rubin Tigertown Five | LP | Coral CRL-57238 | 1957 |
| | Stan Rubin Tigertown Five | 10"LP | Jubilee LP-5 | 53-5 |
| | Salt City Five | 10"LP | Jubilee JLP-13 | 1955 |
| | Santa Anita Band | 78 | (Argentina) Vic. 60-2017 | 1950 |
| | Maxim Saury Band | 10"LP | (France) Pathe ST-1141 | 1961 |
| | Pete Savory Band | LP | (Canada) Pelican 101 | 77-9 |
| | Bob Scobey JB | 78 | Ragtime 1052 | 50-9 |
| | Sextette From Hunger | 78 | MacGregor 1011 | 49- |
| | Shakey City Seven | LP | Esquire 32-194 | 62-3 |
| | Frank Signorelli | LP | Kapp 1005 | 1955 |
| | Six Sounds Jazzband | EP | (Germany) Philips 42345 | 62-12 |
| | Chuck Slate Band | LP | Trutone 520.337 | 1972 |
| | Society Jazzmen | LP | (New Zealand) TJF PRA-2375 | 70-3 |
| | Muggsy Spanier Band | LP | Jazum LP-34 | 53-10 |
| | Muggsy Spanier JB | LP | (England) Rarities 33 | 47-3 |
| | Muggsy Spanier JB | 78 | Manhattan A-20-3 | 45-3 |

| Composition | Performer | Record Speed | Record Company/No. | Year-Month |
|---|---|---|---|---|
| THAT'S A PLENTY (continued) | Sammy Spear Band | LP | London LA-38001 | 1963 |
| Pollack, Lew | Spokane Falls Brass Band | LP | Folkways FTS-32325 | 83-12 |
| | Spring Street Stompers | LP | Williams LP-1 | 54-3 |
| | Squadronaires | 78 | (England) Decca F-8127 | 41-6 |
| | Lou Stein Band | LP | Jubilee LP-1019 | 1954 |
| | Rex Stewart Dixielanders | LP | Concert Hall 1202 | 53-6 |
| | Lew Stone Band | 78 | (England) Decca F-5271 | 34-4 |
| | Storyville Stompers | LP | Olympia 61186 | c. 1986 |
| | Joe Sullivan Trio | LP | Riverside RLP-12-202 | 1951 |
| | Ralph Sutton Trio | LP | Chazjazz 105 | 79-12 |
| | Reinhold Svensson | 78 | (Sweden) Sonora 623 | 44-2 |
| | Swiss Dixie Stompers | LP | (Switzerland) Newland 701 | 69-11 |
| | Tailgate Ramblers | LP | Jazzology J-43 | c. 1960 |
| | Jack Teagarden JB | LP | New World 5009 | 52-2 |
| | Kid Thomas Band | LP | Riverside RLP-365 | 61-1 |
| | Butch Thompson | LP | Triangle Jazz 105 | 84-2 |
| | Tin Town Tooters | LP | (Holland) Sweet Audio 84102 | 84-10 |
| | Johnnie Tozer Band | 78 | (Australia) Process 293 | 41-1 |
| | Joe Venuti & Marion McPartland | LP | Halcyon 112 | 73-7 |
| | Vestre Jazzvaerk | LP | (Denmark) Kong Paere 10 | 79-5 |
| | Pinky Vidacovich Band | 10"LP | Southland SLP-228 | 1960 |
| | Lu Watters YBJB | 78 | West Coast 108 | 46-5 |
| | Richard Wayne's Bearcats | LP | Reader's Digest RDA-70-01-05 | 1968 |
| | Chick Webb Orchestra | LP | (England) Jazz Panorama 2 | 37-2 |
| | George Wein Sextet | 10"LP | Bethlehem BCP-6050 | 60-6 |
| | Dick Wellstood | LP | Fat Cat's Jazz 207 | 79-12 |
| | West Music Club Orchestra | LP | (Belgium) Swing 1002 | 85-1 |
| | George Wettling Trio | 78 | Black & White 27 | 44-7 |
| | White Eagle JB | LP | (Germany) Biton 2117 | 79-11 |
| | Mark White's Dixielanders | EP | (England) Decca DFE-6553 | 58-10 |
| | Johnny Wiggs Band | 78 | Commodore 642 | 50-11 |
| | Windjammers | LP | Monomoy LP-6004 | 1962 |
| THOROUGHBRED RAG | | | | |
| Lamb, Joseph | John Jensen | LP | Genesis 1045 | 1974 |
| | Milton Kaye | LP | Golden Crest 4127 | 1974 |
| THREE IN ONE | | | | |
| | East Texas Serenaders | 78 | Brunswick 379 | 29-11 |
| THRILLER RAG | | | | |
| Aufderheide, May | Albion JB | LP | Stomp Off 1206 | 90-3 |
| | Chris Barber JB | LP | (England) Nixa 505 | 1956 |
| | Bunk Johnson's Jazz Band | 78 | Jazz Information 11 | 42-10 |
| | Chrysanthemum Ragtime Band | LP | Stomp Off 1123 | 1985 |
| | Climax JB | LP | (Canada) Baby Grand SE-1030 | 1977 |
| | Max Collie's Rhythm Aces | LP | (Holland) Beerendonk 9997 | 80-1 |
| | Ken Colyer's Jazzmen | LP | (England) Decca LK-4176 | 1956 |
| | Ken Colyer's Jazzmen | LP | (England) Joy S-194 | 1974 |

| Composition | Performer | Record Speed | Record Company/No. | Year-Month |
|---|---|---|---|---|
| THRILLER RAG (continued) | Neville Dickie | LP | (England) Saydisc SDL-118 | 1966 |
| Aufderheide, May | John Hasse | LP | Sunflower 501 | 1980 |
| | Indiana U. Orchestra | LP | Indiana Historical Society 1001 | 1981 |
| | Max Morath Band | LP | Vanguard VSD-79402 | 1977 |
| | Papa Benny Band | LP | (Denmark) Storyville SLP-156 | 62-12 |
| | Papa Bue's JB | 10″LP | (Denmark) Storyville SLP-101 | 58-11 |
| | Knocky Parker | LP | Audiophile AP-91 | |
| | Westend Stompers | LP | (England) Sweet Folk & Country 083 | 78-8 |
| | Richard Zimmerman | LP | Murray Hill 60556/5 | 1981 |
| TICKLE RAG | | | | |
| Monsbourgh, Ade | Lazy Ade & Band | 78 | (Australia) Ampersand 10 | 45-5 |
| | Len Barnard Jazz Band | 45 | (Australia) Swaggie 4514 | 58-12 |
| | Graham Coyle | 45 | (Australia) Swaggie 4514 | 55-12 |
| TICKLE THE IVORIES | | | | |
| Herzer, Wallie | Casino Orchestra | 78 | (England) Columbia 2778 | 17-1 |
| | Chrysanthemum Ragtime Band | LP | Stomp Off 1123 | 1985 |
| | Edgar Fairchild & Ralph Rainger(m) | 12″78 | Victor 35845 | 27-9 |
| | First Life Guards | 78 | (England) Edison Bell Winner 3104 | 16-9 |
| | Frantic Freddy | 45 | London 45-1775 | |
| | Brooke Pemberton | LP | Warner Bros. W-1235 | 1958 |
| | Sammy Spear Orchestra | LP | Mercury MG-20116 | 1953 |
| | Albert White Orchestra | LP | Barbary Coast SLP-33002 | |
| TICKLED PINK | | | | |
| Rowland, William S. | George Hicks | LP | Folkways FS-3165 | 1983 |
| TICKLED TO DEATH | | | | |
| Hunter, Charles | William Arlington Piano Roll | LP | Biograph 1006Q | |
| | John Arpin | LP | (Canada) Scroll 101 | 1965 |
| | Grammophon Orchestra | 78 | (Germany) Grammophon 12799 | |
| | High Society JB | LP | Stomp Off 1010 | 81-3 |
| | Percy Honri | 78 | (England) Edison Bell Winner 2501 | 13- |
| | LeRoy Larson | LP | Banjar 1784 | 1977 |
| | New Orleans Ragtime Orchestra | LP | Stomp Off 1213 | 1989 |
| | Knocky Parker | LP | Audiophile AP-89 | |
| | Peerless Orchestra | 78 | (England) Zonophone 997 | 12-12 |
| | Piano Roll | LP | (England) Saydisc 132 | |
| | Prince's Band | 78 | Columbia A-972 | 10-12 |
| | Regal Military Band | 78 | (England) Regal G-6687 | 14-2 |
| | Richard Zimmerman | LP | Murray Hill 60556/5 | 1981 |
| TIDDLE-DE-WINKS | | | | |
| Morris, Melville | Charley Straight Piano Roll | LP | Folkways RBF-44 | |
| TIN PAN RAG | | | | |
| Busch, Louis | Joe "Fingers" Carr | 45 | (Holland) Warner Bros. 5149 | |
| TOAD STOOL RAG | | | | |
| Lamb, Joseph | John Jensen | LP | Genesis 1045 | 1974 |
| | Milton Kaye | LP | Golden Crest 31035 | 1974 |

| Composition | Performer | Record Speed | Record Company/No. | Year-Month |
|---|---|---|---|---|
| TODDLIN' | | | | |
| Johnson, James P. | James P. Johnson | 78 | Okeh 4937 | 23-8 |
| TOMATO SAUCE | | | | |
| Longshaw, Fred | Fred Longshaw | 78 | Columbia 14080-D | 25-6 |
| TOO MUCH MUSTARD | | | | |
| Macklin, Cecil | Joe "Fingers" Carr | LP | Cap. T-280 | c. 1952 |
| | Joe "Fingers" Carr | LP | Warner Bros. W-1389 | 1960 |
| | Joe "Fingers" Carr's Brass Band | LP | Warner Bros. W-1456 | 1962 |
| | Chrysanthemum Ragtime Band | LP | Stomp Off 1123 | 1985 |
| | Clyde Valley Stompers | LP | (England) Pye NJL-23 | 1959 |
| | Max Collie's Rhythmn Aces | LP | (England) Black Lion 12181 | 1978 |
| | Wilbur DeParis JB | LP | Atlantic 1233 | 52-9 |
| | Armand Hug (m) | LP | Land O'Jazz 3475 | 75-4 |
| | Mandell Novelty Concert Band | LP | Reader's Digest RDA-70-01-05 | 1968 |
| | Merseysippi JB | 10"LP | (England) Esquire 20-063 | 56-4 |
| | National Promenade Band | 78 | Edison 50135 | 1914 |
| | New Orleans Ragtime Orchestra | LP | Pearl 8 | 1970 |
| | New Sunshine JB | LP | Biograph 12058 | 1978 |
| | Steve Pistorious | LP | Jazzology JCE-78 | c. 1975 |
| | Red Onion JB | 10"LP | Empirical 106 | 54-9 |
| | Sammy Spear Orchestra | LP | Jubilee JLP-1110 | c. 1952 |
| TOO MUCH MUSTARD (see TRES MOUTARDE) | | | | |
| TOO MUCH RASPBERRY | | | | |
| Russell, Sidney K. | Dave Jasen | LP | Folkways FG-3561 | 77-6 |
| TOOTS | | | | |
| Arndt, Felix | Dr. Clarence Penney w/ Felix Arndt | 78 | Victor 17694 | 14-8 |
| TOP LINER RAG | | | | |
| Lamb, Joseph | Brian Dykstra | LP | Advent 5021 | 1976 |
| | Patrick Gogerty | LP | Sounds Current | 1976 |
| | Dave Jasen | LP | Blue Goose 3002 | 1974 |
| | John Jensen | LP | Genesis 1045 | 1974 |
| | Milton Kaye | LP | Golden Crest 4127 | 1974 |
| | Joseph Lamb | LP | Folkways FG-3562 | 59-8 |
| | Morton Gunnar Larsen | LP | (Sweden) Sonet SLP-1450 | 1978 |
| | Max Morath | LP | Vanguard SRV-310 | r. 1974 |
| | Roland Nadeau | LP | VQR 2625 | 1979 |
| | Piano Roll | LP | Dot DLP-25321 | |
| | Wally Rose | LP | GTJ M-12034 | 58-12 |
| | Wally Rose | 78 | Good Time Jazz 44 | 51-7 |
| | Richard Zimmerman | LP | Murray Hill 60556/5 | 1981 |
| TORRID DORA | | | | |
| Cobb, George L. | George Foley | LP | Stomp Off 1187 | 1988 |
| TOWN TALK | | | | |
| Olson, Elmer | Elliott Adams | LP | Stomp Off 1198 | 1988 |
| | George Hicks | LP | Folkways FS-3165 | 1983 |

| Composition | Performer | Record Speed | Record Company/No. | Year-Month |
|---|---|---|---|---|
| TOWN TOPIC RAG | | | | |
| Lada, Anton & Williams, Spencer | Louisiana Five | 78 | Emerson 10241 | 19-12 |
| TRAININ' THE FINGERS | | | | |
| Reser, Harry F. | Harry Reser | 78 | Edison 52647 | r. 29-10 |
| TRAMP RAG | | | | |
| Batten, Joseph | Joseph Batten | 78 | (England) Popular P-656 | 12- |
| TRES MOUTARDE | | | | |
| Macklin, Cecil | J. Lawrence Cook | 78 | Abbey 15060 | |
| | Empire Military Band | 78 | (England) Beka 1079 | 15-12 |
| | Jim Europe's Band | 12"78 | Victor 35359 | 13-12 |
| | Gottlieb's Orchestra | 78 | (England) HMV B-132 | 11-10 |
| | Hager's Band | 78 | Rex 5082 | |
| | Imperial Symphony Orchestra | 78 | (England) Pathe 197 | 11-9 |
| | Mayfair Dance Orchestra | 12"78 | (England) HMV C-319 | 13-10 |
| | Prince's Band | 78 | Columbia A-1307 | 13-2 |
| | Victor Military Band | 78 | Victor 17292 | 13-2 |
| | Marek Weber & Orchestra | 78 | (Germany) Pathe P-1106 | |
| TRIANGLE JAZZ BLUES | | | | |
| LeClere, Irwin | Dave Jasen | LP | Blue Goose 3002 | 1974 |
| | Max Kortlander Piano Roll | LP | Folkways RBF-43 | |
| | New Leviathan Orchestra | LP | Camelback 19328 | 1980 |
| | Wally Rose | 10"LP | Columbia CL-6260 | 53-5 |
| | Wally Rose | LP | Stomp Off 1057 | 1982 |
| | Wally Rose & YBJB Rhythm | 78 | West Coast 120 | 46-6 |
| TRICKY FINGERS | | | | |
| Blake, Eubie | Amherst Saxophone Quartet | LP | Musical Heritage Society 4368 | 80-12 |
| | Eubie Blake | LP | Chiaroscuro 170 | 1972 |
| | Eubie Blake | LP | Columbia C2S-847 | 68-12 |
| | Eubie Blake | LP | Eubie Blake Music 5 | 1973 |
| | Morton Gunnar Larsen | LP | (Norway) Flower 439 | 75-12 |
| | Keith Nichols | LP | (England) EMI One-Up-2085 | 1975 |
| TRICKY SAM | | | | |
| Morris, George E. | George Clinton w/pno (George Morris) | 78 | (England) Victory 270 | 30-4 |
| TRICKY TRIX | | | | |
| Jentes, Harry | George Foley | LP | Stomp Off 1187 | 1988 |
| | Cecil Norman | 78 | (England) Homochord D0-020 | 26- |
| TRILBY RAG | | | | |
| Morgan, Carey | Conway's Band | 12"78 | Victor 35487 | 15-8 |
| | George Foley | LP | Century Advent 778 | 1977 |
| | Pathe Dance Orchestra | 78 | Pathe 70131 | r. 15-9 |
| | Wally Rose | 10"LP | Columbia CL-6260 | 53-5 |

| Composition | Performer | Record Speed | Record Company/No. | Year-Month |
|---|---|---|---|---|
| TRIPLETS | | | | |
| Green, George Hamilton | George Hamilton Green | 78 | Edison 50625 | 19-12 |
| | George Hamilton Green | 78 | Victor 19944 | 26-1 |
| | George Hamilton Green's Novelty Orchestra | 78 | Emerson 10169 | |
| | Nexus | LP | (Canada) Umbrella 2 | 1976 |
| TROUBADOUR RAG | | | | |
| Scott, James | John Arpin | LP | (Canada) Scroll 103 | 1966 |
| | William Bolcom | LP | Nonesuch 71299 | 1974 |
| | Glenn Jenks | LP | Bonnie Banks 104 | 1985 |
| | John Jensen | LP | Genesis 1044 | 1974 |
| | Knocky Parker | LP | Audiophile AP-76/77 | 1962 |
| TROUBLESOME IVORIES | | | | |
| Blake, Eubie | Amherst Saxophone Quartet | LP | Musical Heritage Society 4368 | 80-12 |
| | Eubie Blake | LP | 20th Century Fox 3003 | 1958 |
| | Eubie Blake | LP | Columbia C2S-847 | 68-12 |
| | Eubie Blake | LP | Eubie Blake Music 6 | 1973 |
| | Eubie Blake | LP | (France) RCA FXM1-7157 | 1974 |
| | Paul Kosmala | LP | Mark 5660 | 1979 |
| | Keith Nichols | LP | (England) EMI One-Up-2035 | 1974 |
| | Roger Shields | LP | Turnabout 34579 | 1974 |
| | Terry Waldo | LP | Fat Cat's Jazz 151 | 74-1 |
| TROUBLESOME RAG | | | | |
| Morton, Jelly Roll | Knocky Parker | LP | Audiophile AP-102 | |
| TRY AND PLAY IT | | | | |
| Ohman, Philmore | Mike Loscalzo | 78 | Olympic 1426 | r. 23-2 |
| | Arthur Schutt | 78 | (England) Regal G-8032 | 23-7 |
| | Tom Waltham | 78 | (France) Pathe 9608 | 23-10 |
| | Willie White | 78 | Pathe 021102 | 23-4 |
| TRY ME | | | | |
| Straight, Charley | Charley Straight Piano Roll | LP | Folkways RBF-44 | |
| TURKEY TROT RAG | | | | |
| Danmark, Ribe | Red Wing Blackbirds | LP | Stomp Off 1018 | 1981 |
| TURKISH TOWEL RAG | | | | |
| Allen, Thomas S. | Chrysanthemum Ragtime Band | LP | Stomp Off 1047 | 1983 |
| | Georgie's Varsity Five | LP | HiFi R-805 | 1959 |
| | Albert White's Orchestra | LP | Fantasy 3292 | |
| TURKISH TROPHIES | | | | |
| Egan, Sara | Harry Breuer Orchestra | LP | Audio Fidelity AFSC-5912 | 1960 |
| TWELFTH STREET HA CHA CHA | | | | |
| Bowman, Euday | Joe "Fingers" Carr & Band | 45 | Capitol F-4163 | |

| Composition | Performer | Record Speed | Record Company/No. | Year-Month |
|---|---|---|---|---|
| TWELFTH STREET RAG | | | | |
| Bowman, Euday Louis | Oscar Aleman | 78 | (Argentina) Odeon 22310 | 46-4 |
| | Tony Almerico JB | LP | Vik LX-1057 | 1956 |
| | All Star Trio | 78 | Victor 18713 | 20-10 |
| | Albert Ammons | 78 | Mercury 8040 | 46-11 |
| | William Arlington (pr) | LP | Biograph 1006Q | |
| | Louis Armstrong & Hot Seven | 78 | Columbia 35663 | 27-5 |
| | Jan August (m) | 78 | Mercury 70541 | 1955 |
| | Burt Bales | 78 | Good Time Jazz 9 | 49-12 |
| | Count Basie Orchestra | 78 | Vocalion 4886 | 39-4 |
| | Sidney Bechet & Claude Luter Orchestra | 78 | (France) Vogue 5139 | 52-11 |
| | Sidney Bechet & New Orleans Feetwarmers | 78 | Victor 20-3120 | 41-10 |
| | David Bee & Busy Bees | 78 | (France) Columbia DF-1023 | |
| | David Bee Gang | LP | (France) Col. FP-1023 | 1955 |
| | Belmonte Orchestra | 78 | Columbia 40423 | |
| | Jimmy Blade | 78 | Rondo 111 | |
| | Eric Borchard's Jazz Band | 78 | (Germany) Grammophon 20160 | 24-11 |
| | Borgy Borgerson JB | LP | (Canada) Reunion 1000 | 1980 |
| | Boston Pops | LP | Polydor PD-6033 | 1974 |
| | Euday L. Bowman | 78 | Bowman 11748 | 48-11 |
| | Jimmy Bracken's Toe Ticklers | 78 | Banner 6441 | 29-6 |
| | Harry Breuer Orchestra | LP | Audio Fidelity AFSC-5912 | 1960 |
| | Teddy Buckner JB | LP | Vogue LA-257-30 | 1956 |
| | Joe Bushkin | 10"LP | Allegro-Royale 1590 | 1946 |
| | Brun Campbell | 78 | Echoes 1, Brun | 47- |
| | Johnny Campbell JB | 45 | (Denmark) RCA 45-1041 | 60-4 |
| | Fud Candrix JB | LP | (Belgium) Fiesta LPIS-1002 | 1954 |
| | Frankie Carle | 78 | Columbia 35572 | 48- |
| | Joop Carlquist & Orchestra | 78 | (Germany) Telefunken A-10347 | 41-6 |
| | Joe "Fingers" Carr | 78 | Capitol 15894 | 52-6 |
| | Joe "Fingers" Carr | LP | Cap. T-345 (maybe on 78) | |
| | Joe "Fingers" Carr | LP | Cap. T-760 | |
| | JoAnn Castle | LP | Ranwood R-8011 | |
| | Roland Cedermark | LP | (Sweden) Round Up LPR-054 | 1979 |
| | Freeman Clark | 78 | Linden 09 | |
| | Clyde Valley Stompers | LP | (England) Pye NJL-26 | 1960 |
| | Connie's Inn Orchestra | 78 | Crown 3212 | 31-10 |
| | Russ Conway | EP | (England) Col. SEG-7886 | 1959 |
| | Billy Cotton's Band | 78 | (England) Regal Zonophone MR-2185 | 36-5 |
| | Crazy Otto | 78 | Decca 29503 | 55-3 |
| | Joe Daniels & Orchestra | 78 | (England) Parlophone F-844 | 37-7 |
| | Trump Davidson Band | LP | (Canada) CTL S-5021 | 63-4 |
| | Deep River Orchestra | 78 | Perfect 14816 | 27-4 |
| | Werner Deinert & Orchestra | 78 | (Germany) Metrophon 7052 | 52- |

| Composition | Performer | Record Speed | Record Company/No. | Year-Month |
|---|---|---|---|---|
| TWELFTH STREET RAG (continued) | Wilbur DeParis JB | LP | Atlantic 1336 | 60-5 |
| | Vic Dickenson JB | LP | Jazzways 106/3 | 74-2 |
| Bowman, Euday Louis | Walter Dobschinski & Orchestra | 78 | (Germany) Amiga 1216 | 49-3 |
| | Red Dougherty Band | LP | Audiophile AP-29 | c. 1954 |
| | Dry Throat Five | LP | Stomp Off 1114 | 85-6 |
| | Dukes of Dixieland | LP | Audio Fidelity AF-1928, AF-5928 | 1959 |
| | Duke Ellington Orchestra | 78 | Capitol 2980 | |
| | Duke Ellington's Juggle Band | 78 | Brunswick 6038 | 31-1 |
| | Elliot Brothers | 78 | MGM 11501 | 53-4 |
| | Alan Elsdon JB | LP | (England) Ace of Clubs ACL-1099 | 61-11 |
| | Excelsior Marimba Band | 78 | (England) Columbia 3042 | 20-10 |
| | Farsans Band | LP | (Sweden) Coop 793 | 1979 |
| | Shep Fields | 78 | Bluebird 6817 | 37-2 |
| | Jack Fina & Orchestra | 78 | MGM 10251, 30674 | 47-12 |
| | Firehouse Five Plus Two | 78 | Good Time Jazz 29 | 50-10 |
| | Freddie Fisher & Orchestra | 78 | Decca 3359 | 40-6 |
| | Freddie Fisher & Orchestra | 78 | Regent 125 | |
| | Myron Floren | LP | Ranwood 8127 | 1974 |
| | Gabriel Formiggini | 78 | (Germany) Vox 01307 | 1925 |
| | Pete Fountain Dixielanders | LP | RCA Camden CAL-727 | 56-6 |
| | Rene Franc Quartet | LP | (Germany) Amiga 855696 | 79-5 |
| | Erik Frank Sextet | 78 | (England) Decca F-44147 | 51-1 |
| | Frank Froeba | 78 | Hit 8005 | 42-7 |
| | Earl Fuller's Orchestra | 78 | Columbia A-2298 | 17-6 |
| | Georgia Cotton Pickers | 78 | Harmony 1090-H | 30-1 |
| | Jeff Gledhill | 78 | Tempo 754 | |
| | Morton Gould Orchestra | 78 | Columbia 4541-M | |
| | Bill Grah | 78 | (Austria) Mastertone 7020 | 56-2 |
| | Ken Griffin | EP | (England) Esquire EG-9 | |
| | Guardia Vieja JB | 78 | (Arg) TK S-5234 | 1953 |
| | Erwin Halletz & Orchestra | 78 | (Austria) Austroton 8357 | 50-3 |
| | Lionel Hampton & Orchestra | 78 | Victor 26362 | 39-6 |
| | Hauulea Entertainers | 78 | Okeh 45461 | 30-6 |
| | Sherman Hayes & Orchestra | 78 | Aristocrat 103 | |
| | Bobby Henderson | LP | Vanguard VRS-8511 | 56-11 |
| | Fletcher Henderson Orchestra | 78 | Crown 3212 | 31-10 |
| | Milt Herth | 78 | Decca 1344 | 36-12 |
| | Milt Herth | 78 | Decca 24450 | 47-9 |
| | Milt Herth | 78 | (England) Brunswick 02294 | 36-6 |
| | Art Hodes Band | LP | (England) Rarities 35 | 47-3 |
| | Honey Duke (Johnny Marvin) | 78 | Harmony 115-H | 26-1 |
| | Sol Hoopi's Novelty Trio | 78 | Columbia 1189-D | 27-10 |
| | Sol Hoopi's Orchestra | 78 | Decca 2280 | 38-12 |
| | Georgie Hormel | 78 | MacGregor 1028 | |
| | Hotcha Mundharmonika-Trio | 78 | (Dutch) Phillips P-34463 | 52-8 |
| | Armand Hug | LP | Golden Crest CR-3064 | 1959 |
| | Percy Humphry Band | 10"LP | Center CEN-13 | 1953 |

| Composition | Performer | Record Speed | Record Company/No. | Year-Month |
|---|---|---|---|---|
| TWELFTH STREET RAG (continued) | Pee Wee Hunt & Orchestra | 78 | Capitol 15105 | 48-5 |
| | Imperial Marimba Band | 78 | Edison 50743 | 21-8 |
| Bowman, Euday Louis | Jazz O'Maniacs | LP | Stomp Off 1071 | 84-2 |
| | Jazz Studio Three | 10"LP | Decca DL-8014 | 55-1 |
| | Dink Johnson | LP | Euphonic 1201 | c. 1948 |
| | Jonah Jones Sextet | LP | Circle CLP-83 | 44-10 |
| | Richard M. Jones | 78 | Gennett 5174 | 23-6 |
| | Jubilee Dixielanders | 78 | (Italy) Fonola 6722-3 | 52-2 |
| | Kern–Sloop–Arey | 78 | Tempo 978 | |
| | Andy Kirk & 12 Clouds of Joy | 78 | Decca 18123 | 40-11 |
| | Willie the Rock Knox | 10"LP | Waldorf 33-151 | 1955 |
| | Max Kortlander & Victor Arden | 78 | Pathe 20467 | 20-7 |
| | Bob Laine Quartet | 78 | (Sweden) Cupol 9031 | 53-10 |
| | LeRoy Larson | LP | Banjar 1781 | 1973 |
| | Cy Laurie's Band | EP | (England) Esquire EP-210 | 56-5 |
| | Lawson–Haggart JB | 10"LP | Decca DL-5456 | 53-1 |
| | Jimmy Leach & Harry Farmer | 78 | (England) Columbia FB-2850 | |
| | Jimmy Leach & Organolians | 78 | (England) Columbia FB-40288 | |
| | Marc Leferriere Band | EP | (France) Pacific 90426 | 1960 |
| | Bernie Leighton | LP | Cameo 1005 | 1958 |
| | Leningrad Dixieland | LP | (Russia) Melodija D-21485-6 | 67-12 |
| | Ted Lewis & Band | 78 | Columbia A-3972 | 23-4 |
| | Liberace | 78 | Columbia 40217, 50061 | 54- |
| | Liberace | 78 | Daytone 101 | |
| | Ben Light | 78 | Capitol 2530 | |
| | Tiny Little | LP | GNP-Crescendo 2120 | 1978 |
| | Pink Lindsey & Bluebirds | 78 | Bluebird 6221 | 35-8 |
| | Geoff Love Ragtime Band | LP | (Canada) Quality 753 | 1974 |
| | Loyal Central Jazz Ensemble | LP | (Canada) Madness AVR-7933 | 79-9 |
| | Claude Luter JB | LP | (Argentina) Odeon LDM-91009 | 1957 |
| | Abe Lyman's California Orchestra | 78 | Brunswick 3316 | 26-9 |
| | Abe Lyman's California Orchestra | 78 | Brunswick 6314 | 32-5 |
| | Gloves McGinty | LP | (England) London 38002 | c. 1963 |
| | Johnny Maddox | LP | Blythwood 103 | c. 1986 |
| | Johnny Maddox | 78 | Dot 15057 | |
| | Fess Manetta | LP | Jazzology JCE-6 | 57-5 |
| | Johnny Marvin | 78 | Edison 51709 | r. 26-5 |
| | Johnny Marvin & William Carola | 78 | Victor 20386 | 26-12 |
| | Fabio Mataloni | 78 | (Italy) Parlophone TT-9580 | 52-6 |
| | Eddie "Piano" Miller | 78 | Rainbow 70033 | |
| | Susan Miller | 78 | Columbia 40423 | |
| | Missouri Jazz Band (Willard Robison) | 78 | Banner 6031 | r. 27-8 |
| | Marvin Montgomery | LP | Audiophile AP-83 | c. 1969 |
| | Art Mooney JB | LP | MGM E-3616 | 1957 |
| | Bennie Moten's Orchestra | 78 | Victor 20946 | 27-6 |
| | Mulcays | 78 | Essex 407 | |

| Composition | Performer | Record Speed | Record Company/No. | Year-Month |
|---|---|---|---|---|
| TWELFTH STREET RAG (continued) | Don Neely Orchestra | LP | Merry Makers 111 | c. 1982 |
| | Louis Nelson Band | LP | Nola LP-7 | 70-5 |
| Bowman, Euday Louis | New Orleans JB | LP | (Argentina) Elite ELE-77004 | 73-3 |
| | New Sunshine JB | LP | Flying Dutchman 1-0549 | 1972 |
| | Roy Newman's Boys | 78 | Vocalion 03240 | 35-10 |
| | Ray Nolan Band | 78 | (Argentina) Music Hall 5035 | 52-5 |
| | Red Norvo & Orchestra | 78 | Capitol 10187 | |
| | Phil Ohman Orchestra | LP | Camay CA-3006 | |
| | Old Apple Trio | 78 | Victor 24311 | 33-4 |
| | Old Timers | LP | (Poland) Muza XLO-842 | 72-1 |
| | Kid Ory JB | LP | (Denmark) Storyville SLP-6016 | 55-2 |
| | Kid Ory JB | LP | Verve MGV-1022 | 1959 |
| | Kid Ory's JB | LP | Dixieland Jubilee 213 | 49-10 |
| | Kid Ory Band | 78 | D. J. 213 | 49-10 |
| | Will Osborne Orchestra | 78 | Decca 1534 | 37-8 |
| | Papa Bue's JB | 10"LP | (Denmark) Storyville SLP-156 | 62-6 |
| | Papa French JB | LP | Nobility LP-702 | 1965 |
| | Joe Paradise & Band | 78 | (England) Parlophone F-356 | 35-11 |
| | Santo Pecora Band | 78 | Clef 8925 | 50-3 |
| | Knocky Parker Bearkats | LP | Circle CLP-10001 | 1984 |
| | Jad Paul | LP | Liberty 3107 | c. 1959 |
| | Donald Peers | 78 | (England) HMV B-9763 | 49- |
| | Brooke Pemberton | LP | Warner Bros. W-1235 | 1958 |
| | Sid Phillips Orchestra | LP | (England) Rediffusion ZS-15 | 62-6 |
| | Piano Roll | LP | Dot DLP-25321 | |
| | Ray Price JB | 45 | (Australia) CBS BA-221049 | 63-8 |
| | Harold Ramsay | 78 | (England) Parlophone F-606 | 36-8 |
| | Charlie Rasch | LP | C. K. 39987/39988 | 78-3 |
| | Red Garters | LP | (Australia) Camden 156 | 70-3 |
| | Rega Dance Orchestra | 78 | Okeh 4196 | 20-9 |
| | Alan Rhodes Jazzmen | 10"LP | (Australia) Planet PZ-010 | 56-6 |
| | Rhythm Wreckers | 78 | Vocalion 3523 | 37-3 |
| | John Rindfleisch Orchestra | LP | (Germany) Fontana 9294078 | 75-11 |
| | River Boat Five | 10"LP | Mercury MG-20378 | 1958 |
| | Harry Robbins | 78 | (England) Columbia FB-1160 | 35-10 |
| | Harry Roy Orchestra | 78 | (England) Parlophone R-1568 | 33-6 |
| | Harry Roy Orchestra (m) | 78 | (England) Parlophone F-338 | 35-11 |
| | Maxin Saury Band | 10"LP | (France) Pathe ST-1133 | 60-6 |
| | Joe Schirmer & Orchestra | 78 | Magnolia 500 | |
| | Tom Schmutzler & Harry Malfas | LP | Fleet Street 80-01 | 1980 |
| | Yuzuru Sera Band | LP | (Japan) Canyon C20R-0014 | 79-5 |
| | Six Brown Brothers | 78 | Emerson 10205 | r. 20-7 |
| | Six Lemons | 78 | (Japan) Vic. A-5130 | 1953 |
| | Slew Foot Five w/ Grady Martin | 78 | Decca 29146 | 54-4 |
| | Slugger Ryan | LP | Judson 3015 | 1958 |
| | Roy Smeck & Art Kahn | 78 | Challenge 576 | 28-2 |
| | Roy Smeck & Art Kahn | 78 | Regal 8528 | 28-2 |

| Composition | Performer | Record Speed | Record Company/No. | Year-Month |
|---|---|---|---|---|
| TWELFTH STREET RAG (continued) Bowman, Euday Louis | Roy Smeck | 78 | Edison 52287 | r. 28-6 |
| | Arthur Smith | 78 | MGM 10294 | 48- |
| | Jerry Smith | LP | Ranwood R-8126 | 1974 |
| | Willie the Lion Smith | 78 | (France) Royal Jazz 735 | 49-12 |
| | Willie the Lion Smith | LP | (Germany) Saba SB-15101 | 66-11 |
| | Willie the Lion Smith | LP | MPS/BASF BAP-5055 | 1966 |
| | Elmer Snowden Band | LP | Riverside RLP-348 | 60-12 |
| | Southern Jazz Group | 78 | (Australia) Wilco 0-117 | 50-5 |
| | Southern-Aires | 78 | B. M. 1007 | |
| | Lou Stein Band | LP | Mercury MG-20271 | 1960 |
| | Leath Stevens & Orchestra | 78 | Vocalion 4350 | 38-6 |
| | Reinhold Svensson | 78 | (Sweden) Tono 3022 | 49-3 |
| | Sveriges Jazzband | LP | (Sweden) RCA PL-40087 | 77-12 |
| | Victor Sylvester Orchestra | 78 | (England) Columbia FB-3488 | |
| | Eva Taylor & Clarence Williams | 78 | Okeh 4805 | 23-2 |
| | Jack Teter Trio | 78 | Brunswick 80222 | 53-5 |
| | Charles Thompson | LP | Euphonic 1221 | c. 1960 |
| | Three Jacks | 78 | Okeh 41102 | 28-6 |
| | Tin Pan Stompers | LP | (Canada) Mercury 135.502 | 67-10 |
| | Art & Dotty Todd | 78 | Diamond 3002 | |
| | Sidney Torch | 78 | (England) Columbia FB-1132 | 34-12 |
| | Gosta Torner Orchestra | 78 | (Sweden) Artist B-3009 | 49-2 |
| | Frank Trapani Band | LP | Maison Bourbon 6 | c. 1970 |
| | Triola Pick Up Jazz Group | 78 | (Finland) Triola 8019 | 50-3 |
| | Joe Turner | 78 | (Swiss) Columbia 1305 | 50- |
| | Arpad Varosz Orchestra | 78 | (Germany) Homokord B-372 | 23-12 |
| | Varsity Ragtime Band | 78 | Varsity 106, 270 | |
| | Benny Vasseur Orchestra | LP | (France) Festival FLP-128 | 58-5 |
| | Vasseur–Paquinet Orchestra | LP | (France) Festival FLP-123 | 1958 |
| | Mike Vax Band | LP | Sacramento Jazz 28 | 85-7 |
| | Vestre Jazzvaerk | LP | (Denmark) Kong Paere 10 | 79-5 |
| | Village Stompers | LP | Epic LN-24235 | c. 1966 |
| | Vox American Jazz Band | 78 | (Germany) Vox 01307 | 23- |
| | Fats Waller & Rhythm | 78 | Victor 25087 | 35-6 |
| | Cy Watts & Jazzmen | 78 | (Australia) Jazzart 19 | 49-6 |
| | Moe Wechsler | LP | Roulette R-25002 | 1958 |
| | Lou Weertz | 78 | MGM 30684 | 52-6 |
| | Randy Weston Trio | LP | Riverside RLP-12-203 | 55-8 |
| | Ted White's Collegians | 78 | Oriole 960 | 27-4 |
| | Kurt Widmann & Orchestra | 78 | (Germany) Odeon 0-28264 | 51-11 |
| | Del Wood | LP | RCA Camden ADL2-0778 | 55-5 |
| | Del Wood | 78 | Republic 7036 | |
| | Alonzo Yancey | 78 | Session 10-015 | 43-12 |
| | Arthur Young & Youngsters (m) | 78 | (England) Decca F-5645 | 35-8 |
| | Richard Zimmerman | LP | Murray Hill M-60556/5 | 1981 |

| Composition | Performer | Record Speed | Record Company/No. | Year-Month |
|---|---|---|---|---|
| TWILIGHT RAG | | | | |
| Johnson, James P. | James P. Johnson | LP | Folkways FJ-2850 | 45-5 |
| | James P. Johnson Piano Roll | LP | Biograph 1009Q | |
| TWO DOLLAR RAG | | | | |
| Busch, Louis F. | Professor Lou Busch | 78 | Capitol 15436 | 51-3 |
| | Joe "Fingers" Carr (m) | 78 | Capitol 3883 | |
| TWO-MELODY RAG (see THE ENTERTAINER'S RAG) | | | | |
| | Ben Light & Rhythm | 78 | Tempo 1206 | |
| UNCANNY BANJO | | | | |
| Fillis, Len & Bright, Sid | Len Fillis | 78 | (England) Decca F-2379 | 31-1 |
| | Len Fillis & Sid Bright | 78 | (England) Columbia 4643 | 27-2 |
| | Jack Hylton's Hyltonians | 78 | (England) HMVB-5279 | 27-5 |
| UNIVERSAL RAG | | | | |
| Botsford, George | Piano Roll | LP | Herwin 407 | |
| UNKNOWN BLUES | | | | |
| Henderson, Fletcher | Fletcher Henderson | 78 | Black Swan 2026 | 21-9 |
| UP AND DOWN IN CHINA | | | | |
| Robison, Willard | Willard Robison | 78 | Autograph 601 | 24-9 |
| UP AND DOWN THE KEYS | | | | |
| Ohman, Philmore | Mike Loscalzo | 78 | Olympic 1426 | r. 23-2 |
| UPRIGHT AND GRAND | | | | |
| Banta, Frank & DeRose, Peter | George Foley | LP | Century Advent 778 | 1977 |
| | Frank Banta & The Ambassadors | 78 | Vocalion 14671 | 23-8 |
| | Frank Banta & Dave Grupp | 78 | Pathe 02113 | r. 24-5 |
| VALENTINE STOMP | | | | |
| Waller, Thomas | Eddie Bernard | 78 | (France) Blue Starr 56 | 47-10 |
| | Henry "Thins" Francis | LP | Mephistopheles 103 | 89-1 |
| | Dick Hyman | LP | Project 3 PR-5080 | 1973 |
| | Fats Waller | 78 | Victor V-38554 | 29-8 |
| VANITY RAG | | | | |
| Pratt, Paul | Knocky Parker | LP | Audiophile AP-91 | |
| VARIETY RAG | | | | |
| Tierney, Harry Austin | Richard Zimmerman | LP | Murray Hill 60556/5 | 1981 |
| VICTORY RAG | | | | |
| Scott, James | Ann Charters | LP | Folkways FG-3563 | 1961 |
| | John Jensen | LP | Genesis 1044 | 1974 |
| | Knocky Parker | LP | Audiophile AP-76/77 | 1962 |
| VIRGINIA CREEPER | | | | |
| Mayerl, Billy | George Hicks | LP | Folkways FS-3165 | 1983 |
| | Billy Mayerl | 78 | (England) HMV B-2203 | 25-11 |
| VIRGINIA RAG | | | | |
| Harris, Sydney P. | Knocky Parker | LP | Audiophile AP-90 | |

| Composition | Performer | Record Speed | Record Company/No. | Year-Month |
|---|---|---|---|---|
| WAILANA | | | | |
| Pratt, Paul | Richard Zimmerman | LP | Murray Hill 60556/5 | 1981 |
| WALHALLA RAG | | | | |
| Pratt, Paul | Chrysanthemum Ragtime Band | LP | Stomp Off 1123 | 1985 |
| | Indiana University Orchestra | LP | Indiana Historical Society 1001 | 1981 |
| | Piano Roll | LP | (England) Saydisc 132 | |
| WALL STREET RAG | | | | |
| Joplin, Scott | William Bolcom | LP | Nonesuch 71257 | 1971 |
| | Ann Charters | LP | Folkways FG-3563 | 1961 |
| | Brian Dykstra | LP | Orion 83449 | 82-7 |
| | Paul Hersh & David Montgomery | LP | RCA Victor ARL1-0364 | 1974 |
| | Dick Hyman | LP | RCA CRL5-1106 | 1975 |
| | Mimi & Russell | LP | Mumpus 791 | r. 1979 |
| | Max Morath | LP | Vanguard SRV-351 | r. 1976 |
| | New England Conservatory Ensemble | LP | Golden Crest 31031 | 1973 |
| | New Orleans Ragtime Orchestra | LP | Stomp Off 1213 | 1989 |
| | Darryl Ott | LP | Uplift R-0180 | 1980 |
| | Knocky Parker | LP | Audiophile AP-71/72 | 1960 |
| | Piano Roll | LP | Biograph 1010Q | |
| | Southland Stingers | LP | Angel S-36074 | 1974 |
| | Dick Zimmerman | LP | Murray Hill 931079 | 1974 |
| | Zonophone Orchestra | 78 | Zonophone 5603 | r. 10-3 |
| WALPER HOUSE RAG | | | | |
| Lamb, Joseph | Milton Kaye | LP | Golden Crest 31035 | 1974 |
| WALTZ IN RAGTIME | | | | |
| Busch, Louis F. | Joe "Fingers" Carr | 78 | Capitol 15727 | 51-9 |
| WATERLOO RAG | | | | |
| Ashwander, Donald | Donald Ashwander | LP | Upstairs 1 | 1973 |
| WATERMELON TRUST | | | | |
| Thompson, Harry C. | David Thomas Roberts | LP | Stomp Off 1132 | 1981 |
| | Terry Waldo (m) | LP | Stomp Off 1002 | 80-7 |
| | Waldo's Ragtime Orchestra | LP | Stomp Off 1007 | 80-10 |
| WATERMELON WHISPERS | | | | |
| Green, George Hamilton | American Republic Band | 78 | Pathe 29218 | |
| | George Hamilton Green w/Orchestra | 78 | Emerson 991 | |
| WEEPING WILLOW | | | | |
| Joplin, Scott | Ann Charters | LP | Portents 1 | 1958 |
| | Bill Coffman & Kathy Craig | LP | OTMH 101 | r. 1980 |
| | Neville Dickie | LP | (England) Saydisc SDL-118 | 1966 |
| | Brian Dykstra | LP | Orion 83449 | 82-7 |
| | John Hasse | LP | Sunflower 501 | 1980 |
| | Dick Hyman | LP | RCA CRL5-1106 | 1975 |
| | Scott Joplin Piano Roll | LP | Biograph 1006Q | |

| Composition | Performer | Record Speed | Record Company/No. | Year-Month |
|---|---|---|---|---|
| WEEPING WILLOW (continued) | Milton Kaye | LP | Golden Crest 31032 | 1974 |
| Joplin, Scott | Alain Lesire | LP | (Belgium) Jazz Cats 6983003 | 1982 |
| | James Levine | LP | RCA ARL1-2243 | 1976 |
| | Paul Lolax | LP | Titanic 13 | r. 1981 |
| | Moonlight Ragtime Band | LP | National Geographic 07817 | 1979 |
| | Keith Nichols | LP | (England) EMI One-Up-2035 | 1974 |
| | Knocky Parker | LP | Audiophile AP-71/72 | 1960 |
| | Knocky Parker & Bill Coffman | LP | Euphonic 1216 | 77-4 |
| | Piano Roll | 78 | Circle 5005 | |
| | Queen City Ragtime Ensemble | LP | Zeno 99 | 1976 |
| | Ragtime Banjo Commission | LP | GHB 154 | 80-8 |
| | Joshua Rifkin | LP | Nonesuch 71305 | 1974 |
| | Sigi Schwab | LP | (Germany) Jupiter 6.24831 | c. 1985 |
| | Yannick Singery | LP | (France) Swing SLD-928 | c. 1975 |
| | Swingle II | LP | Col. PC-34194 | 1975 |
| | Trebor Tichenor | LP | Dirty Shame 2001 | 1973 |
| | Bob Tryforous | LP | Puritan 5002 | r. 1976 |
| | Dick Zimmerman | LP | Murray Hill 931079 | 1974 |
| | Richard Zimmerman | LP | Murray Hill 60556/5 | 1981 |
| WEEPING WILLOW RAG | | | | |
| Fischler, H. A. | Piano Roll | 10"LP | (England) London AL-3542 | |
| WELLER'S HOSPITALITY | | | | |
| Parrish, Terry | Elite Syncopators | LP | Jazzology 102 | r. 1989 |
| WEST COAST RAG | | | | |
| Ezell, Will | Will Ezell | 78 | Paramount 12549 | 27-9 |
| WEST DALLAS DRAG | | | | |
| Hearn, L. | Rob Cooper | 78 | Bluebird 5459 | 34-4 |
| WEST DALLAS DRAG #2 | | | | |
| Cooper, Rob | Rob Cooper | 78 | Bluebird 5947 | 35-1 |
| WHIPPED CREAM | | | | |
| Wenrich, Percy | Fred Van Eps w/ Orchestra | 78 | Columbia A-1294 | 13-2 |
| WHIPPIN' THE IVORIES | | | | |
| Siegel, Al | Al Siegel | 78 | (England) Zonophone 2945 | 27-2 |
| WHIPPING THE KEYS | | | | |
| Goold, Sam | Tony Caramia | LP | Stomp Off 1209 | 1989 |
| | Sam Goold | 78 | Okeh 4850 | 23-6 |
| | Wally Rose | LP | Blackbird 12010 | 71-6 |
| WHIPPOORWILL RAG | | | | |
| Jordan, Joe | Lois Delano | LP | (Canada) Arpeggio 1205 | 1968 |
| WHIRLWIND RAG | | | | |
| Robinson, J. Russell | Tony Parenti Ragtime Gang | LP | Jazzology J-21 | 66-4 |
| WHISTLE RAG | | | | |
| Andrews, David | Harry Gold's Pieces of Eight | LP | London LL-1338 | 50-7 |

| Composition | Performer | Record Speed | Record Company/No. | Year-Month |
|---|---|---|---|---|
| WHISTLING PIANO MAN | | | | |
| Smith–Wood–Vaughan | Johnny Maddox | 78 | Dot 15365 | |
| WHITEWASH MAN | | | | |
| Schwartz, Jean | J. J. Ashton | 78 | (England) Edison Bell Winner 3082 | 16-10 |
| | Arthur Collins | 78 | Zonophone 5475 | |
| | Clancy Hayes Band | LP | ABC-Paramount 591 | 1966 |
| | Merseysippi Jazz Band | LP | (England) Decca DFE-6251 | 55-1 |
| | Merseysippi Jazz Band | 78 | (England) Esquire 10-438 | 55-2 |
| | Turk Murphy Jazz Band | LP | Atlantic 1613 | 71-9 |
| | Vess L. Ossman w/ pno | 78 | Victor 16302 | 09-3 |
| | Palais de Danse Orchestra | 78 | (Germany) Pathe 420 | |
| | Arthur Pryor's Band | 78 | Victor 16306 | 09-3 |
| | Fred Sokolow | LP | Kicking Mule 212 | c. 1982 |
| | Ralph Sutton | 78 | Circle 1052 | 49-1 |
| | Fred Van Eps w/ Orchestra | 78 | Columbia A-1118 | 11-11 |
| | Fred Van Eps | 78 | Pathe 29082 | c. 12- |
| | Fred Van Eps w/ pno | 78 | Pathe 30262 | r. 15-9 |
| | Fred Van Eps w/ Orchestra | 78 | Pathe 20094 | r. 16-11 |
| | Tex Wyndham | LP | Fat Cat's Jazz 168 | 1974 |
| WHITTLING REMUS | | | | |
| Broady, Thomas | Knocky Parker | LP | Audiophile AP-89 | |
| | Richard Zimmerman | LP | Murray Hill 60556/5 | 1981 |
| WHOA, NELLIE! | | | | |
| Gould, George | Chrysanthemum Ragtime Band | LP | Stomp Off 1168 | 1987 |
| | Paul Lingle | LP | Euphonic 1227 | 1951 |
| | Paul Whiteman Orchestra | 78 | Victor 19641 | 24-9 |
| | Richard Zimmerman | LP | Murray Hill 60556/5 | 1981 |
| WHOA, YOU HEIFER! | | | | |
| Verges, Al | Columbia Orchestra | 78 | Columbia A-165 | |
| | Humphrey Lyttelton Band | LP | (England) Calligraph 013 | 86-7 |
| WHY WE SMILE | | | | |
| Hunter, Charles | John Hancock | LP | Stomp Off 1025 | 1982 |
| WIGGLE RAG | | | | |
| Botsford, George | Elite Syncopators | LP | Jazzology 102 | r. 1989 |
| | Knocky Parker | LP | Audiophile AP-91 | |
| WILD CAT BLUES | | | | |
| Waller, Thomas & Williams, Clarence | Sidney Bechet JB | LP | Riverside RLP-149 | 47-4 |
| | Sidney Bechet W. C. Luter Orchestra | 45 | (France) Vogue 45-704 | 55-10 |
| | Pierre Braslavsky & Orchestra | 78 | (France) Selmer 2976 | 49-4 |
| | Henri Chaix | EP | (Switzerland) Philips 422869 | 1965 |
| | Mike Daniels JB | LP | (England) Col. 33SX-1256 | 60-3 |
| | Neville Dickie | LP | (England) Pizza Express 5507 | 81-3 |
| | Henry "Thins" Francis | LP | Mephistopheles 103 | 89-1 |
| | Dick Hyman | LP | Stomp Off 1141 | 86-6 |
| | Steve Lane's Southern Stompers | LP | Stomp Off 1040 | 1982 |
| | Claude Luter & Band | 78 | (France) Harmo J-3001 | 48-2 |

| Composition | Performer | Record Speed | Record Company/No. | Year-Month |
|---|---|---|---|---|
| WILD CAT BLUES (continued) | Midnight Stompers | EP | (Sweden) Col. SEG-30 | 57-2 |
| Waller, Thomas & Williams, Clarence | Mimosa's New Orleans Band | 78 | (France) Vogue V-5090 | 51-4 |
| | Keith Nichols | LP | (England) EMI One-Up-2135 | 1976 |
| | Monte Sunshine JB | LP | Stomp Off 1110 | 85-4 |
| | Monte Sunshine Trio | 78 | (Denmark) Storyville KB-206 | 53-4 |
| | Fats Waller Piano Roll | LP | Biograph 1005Q | |
| | Dick Wellstood | LP | Chiaroscuro 183 | 78-1 |
| | Westend Stompers | LP | (England) Sweet Folk & Country 083 | 78-8 |
| | Bob Wilbur & Dick Wellstood | LP | Parkwood 103 | 84-5 |
| | Bob Wilbur's Wildcats | 78 | Commodore 584 | 47-2 |
| | Clarence Williams' Blue Five | 78 | Okeh 4925 | 23-7 |
| WILD CHERRIES RAG | | | | |
| Snyder, Ted | John Arpin | LP | (Canada) Scroll 103 | 1966 |
| | Frank Banta | 78 | Gennett 4735 | 21-5 |
| | Black Diamonds Band | 78 | (England) Zonophone 771 | 11-11 |
| | Harry Breuer Orchestra | LP | Audio Fidelity 3001 | 1960 |
| | Grammophon Orchestra | 78 | (Germany) Grammophon 12805 | r. 10-1 |
| | Dick Kroeckel | LP | Ragtime GRU-1930 | 1977 |
| | Dave Laibman | LP | Kicking Mule 107 | r. 1976 |
| | LeRoy Larson | LP | Banjar 1781 | 1973 |
| | Edward Meeker | 78 | Edison 10291 | |
| | Eddie Morton | 78 | Columbia A-737 | 09-10 |
| | Eddie Morton | 78 | Victor 16792 | 10-7 |
| | Knuckles O'Toole | LP | Grand Award 33-373 | |
| | Knocky Parker | LP | Audiophile AP-90 | |
| | Ragtime Banjo Commission | LP | GHB 154 | 80-8 |
| | Ray Templin | LP | Euphonic 1219 | 1980 |
| | Victor Orchestra | 78 | Victor 16472 | 10-1 |
| | Terry Waldo Orchestra | LP | Stomp Off 1069 | 83-6 |
| | Albert White Orchestra | LP | Barbary Coast 33008 | 1958 |
| | Zonophone Orchestra | 78 | Zonophone 5496 | r. 09-6 |
| WILD FLOWER RAG | | | | |
| Williams, Clarence | Armand Hug | LP | (Austrialia) Swaggie 1281 | 1972 |
| | Armand Hug | 78 | Capitol 987 | 49-10 |
| | Keith Nichols Syncopators | LP | Stomp Off 1135 | 86-1 |
| | Knocky Parker | LP | Audiophile AP-49 | 1958 |
| | Knocky Parker | 78 | Paradox 8 | 49-4 |
| | Clarence Williams | 78 | Okeh 8604 | 28-7 |
| | Clarence Williams & Orchestra | 78 | QRS 7033 | 28-11 |
| WINDY CITY | | | | |
| Wiley, Arnold | Arnold Wiley | 78 | Brunswick 7113 | 29-7 |
| WINE ROOM RAG | | | | |
| Tichenor, Trebor | Trebor Tichenor | LP | Folkways FS-3164 | 1979 |
| WINTER GARDEN RAG | | | | |
| Olman, Abe | Indiana University Orchestra | LP | Indiana Historical Society 1001 | 1981 |
| | Knocky Parker | LP | Audiophile AP-92 | |
| | Keith Smith Jazz Band | LP | (England) 77LEU 12/9 | |
| | Lee Stafford | 78 | Castle 10 | 50-1 |

| Composition | Performer | Record Speed | Record Company/No. | Year-Month |
|---|---|---|---|---|
| WIZZLE DOZZLE | | | | |
| Bell, Harry & Johnson, Lloyd | Jared Carter | LP | Indiana Historical Society 1001 | 1981 |
| WORLD'S FAIR RAG | | | | |
| Babcock, Harvey M. | Chrysanthemum Ragtime Band | LP | Stomp Off 1168 | 1987 |
| | Richard Zimmerman | LP | Murray Hill 60556/5 | 1981 |
| X. L. RAG | | | | |
| Settle, L. Edgar | David Thomas Roberts | LP | Stomp Off 1021 | 1981 |
| | Trebor Tichenor | LP | (Canada) Scroll 102 | 1966 |
| | Richard Zimmerman | LP | Murray Hill 60556/5 | 1981 |
| YANKEE LAND | | | | |
| Hoffman, Max | Vess L. Ossman w/ Orchestra | 78 | Columbia 3155, A-230 | r. 05-6 |
| | Vess L. Ossman w/ pno | 78 | Victor 4461, 16781 | r. 05-10 |
| YELLOW ROSE RAG | Ragtime Banjo Commission | LP | GHB 154 | 1980 |
| Waldo, Terry | Terry Waldo | LP | Dirty Shame 1237 | 1974 |
| YOU TELL 'EM IVORIES | | | | |
| Confrey, Zez | Tony Caramia | LP | Stomp Off 1209 | 1989 |
| | Zez Confrey | 78 | Brunswick 2112 | 21-6 |
| | Zez Confrey | 78 | Emerson 10523 | 22-2 |
| | Max Darewski | 78 | (England) Zonophone 2336 | 23-3 |
| | Ernest Harrison | 78 | (England) Meloto S-1318 | 22- |
| | Stanley C. Holt | 78 | (England) Homochord H-383 | 23-2 |
| | Dick Hyman | LP | RCA XRL1-4746 | 1983 |
| | John Jensen | LP | Genesis 1051 | 1974 |
| | Milton Kaye | LP | Golden Crest 31040 | 1974 |
| | Arthur Kleiner | LP | Golden Crest 2004 | c. 1967 |
| | Isidore Maurice | 78 | (England) Aco G-15131 | 23-1 |
| | Russ Morgan & Eddie Wilser | LP | Decca DL-8746 | 1958 |
| | Dick Palmer (Zez Confrey) | 78 | Arto 9082 | r. 21-10 |
| | Vi Palmer (Zez Confrey) | 78 | Banner 2059 | 22-2 |
| | Philip Porter | 78 | (England) Guardsman 1245 | |
| | Frank Westphal | 78 | Columbia A-3800 | 22-12 |
| | Harold Willoughby | 78 | (England) Columbia 3219 | 22-12 |
| YOU'VE GOT TO BE MODERNISTIC | Great Day New Orleans Singers | 78 | Okeh 8755 | |
| Johnson, James P. | James P. Johnson | 78 | Brunswick 2762 | 30-1 |
| | James P. Johnson & Orchestra | 78 | Victor V-38099 | 29-11 |
| ZAM-A-ZAM RAG (see ZAMP-A-ZAMP RAG) | | | | |
| ZAMP-A-ZAMP RAG | | | | |
| Wagner, Ernest F. | Emerson Military Band | 78 | Emerson 7225 | r. 17-9 |
| | Rishell Dance Band | 78 | Rishell 5430 | |
| ZAMPA RAG | | | | |
| Deiro, Guido | Guido Deiro | 78 | Columbia A-2969 | 20-6 |

# APPENDIX 2

## Ragtime Piano Rollography

The piano roll came into being at the start of the ragtime era, thus documenting early local and regional rags from its beginning. The first rolls only used sixty-five notes of the piano and were called, oddly enough, 65 note rolls. Perforations in rolls were cut by machine, precisely following the pencil lines drawn by an arranger on a paper master. Arranging consisted of planning the placement of holes to conform to the notes of published sheet music, then adding extra holes to enlarge the sound.

The most prolific of all piano roll arrangers, J. Lawrence Cook arranging a roll.

As capabilities expanded, so too did the range of the roll, utilizing all eighty-eight notes and from 1901 on, rolls were automatically made using the entire keyboard. Arrangers added a third and fourth hand to magnify and augment the sound thus obtained.

This rollography lists the rag compositions alphabetically and by roll label, noting if the rag is part of a medley by the use of (m) next to the roll number. If the medley has a name of its own instead of a generic "rag medley," it is noted alongside the label and its number. If the roll is handplayed, the artist is listed next to the roll number. IF the roll is an early one, the designation of (65 note) is given immediately after the roll number. Sixty-five note rolls are always machine cut without any artist playing the arrangement. This listing is for rolls manufactured and sold in the United States.

AEROPLANE RAG (Jack Glogau)
US Music 65859
US Music 6300 (m), *States Rag Medley #13*

AFRICAN HUNTER (Edwin Kendall)
Artistyle 90194
Universal 93075

AFRICAN PAS' (Maurice Kirwin)
Connorized 6045 (65 note)

AGGRAVATION RAG (George L. Cobb)
US Music 63869

AGITATION RAG (Robert Hampton)
Artempo 3027, Dave Kaplan
Classics of Ragtime 0102
Connorized 10312, W. Arlington
US Music 7051

ALABAMA JIGGER (Edward Claypoole)
US Music 65934

ALABAMA RAG (Joseph Lamb)
Classics of Ragtime 0103

ALABAMA SLIDE (Charles L. Johnson)
Universal 6315
US Music 7367

ALASKAN RAG (Joseph Lamb)
Classics of Ragtime 0054

ALKALI IKE RAG (Albert Perfect)
QRS 32444
QRS 32466 (m), Hillcrest
QRS 32501 (m), *Artola Medley*

ALL THE MONEY (Charles L. Johnson)
Connorized 4439

ALLIGATOR BAIT (Hal G. Nichols)
US Music 65369

AMAZON RAG (Teddy Hahn)
Chase and Baker 1904-J (65 note)
Lyric 4074

AMERICAN BEAUTY RAG (Joseph Lamb)
Aeolian 104054 (65 note)
Aeolian 300874
Angelus 91255
Artempo 1878, Ernest Stevens

Classics of Ragtime 0154
Connorized 3083
Dominant 10511
Kimball B-7007
Master Record 1077
Metrostyle 104054
Metrostyle 300874
QRS 100299, Max Kortlander
Royal 4418
Supertone 870765 (m), *Popular Rag Medley*
Supertone 863312
Universal 100595 (65 Note)
Universal 300875
US Music 7065 (m), *States Rag Medley #19*
US Music 66312

AMERICAN DANCERS (Bob Alden)
Royal 3065

AMERICAN JUBILEE RAG (Edward Claypoole)
Artempo 10046, Steve Williams
Arto 88129, Valentine
Autokrat 60302
Connorized 3361
Metro Art 202964, Ted Eastwood
Metrostyle-Themodist 302836
Perfection 86852, Valentine and Gardner
Universal 302837
US Music 8104

AMERICAN RAG (Harry L. Newman and Roy Barton)
Kimball C-5472
Rolla Artis 50100, Phil Goldberg
Supertone 820347
US Music 1052 (m)
US Music 62047

ANGEL FOOD RAG (Al F. Marzian)
Supertone 862338
US Music 66238

ANOMA RAG (Ford Dabney)
Connorized 10289, William Axtmann
Supertone 847314
US Music 64714

APEDA RAG (Dave Harris)
Connorized 2444
Full scale 17547 (m), *Latest Ragtime Hits #2*

QRS 31387 (m), *Rag Medley*
Rhythmodik B-6223, Fred Schmitz

APPLE JACK RAG (Charles L. Johnson)
QRS 03373 (65 note)
QRS 30924
QRS 32329

APPLE SASS (Harry Belding)
Connorized 2852
Connorized 20377, W. Arlington
Dominant 10321
Pianostyle 35218
QRS 32104
Supertone 867335
US Music 66735

APRIL FOOL RAG (Jean Schwartz)
QRS 31047

ARABIAN RAG (George Gould)
Royal 4664

ARKANSAS TUSSLE (M. G. Wittman)
Virtuoso 1202 (65 note)

ARCTIC SUNSET (Joseph Lamb)
Classics of Ragtime 0104

ASHY AFRICA (Percy Wenrich)
Classics of Ragtime 0052
QRS X-3123

AT A RAGTIME RECEPTION (Ben Jerome)
Connorized 6029 (65 note)
QRS 3375
Universal 4241 (65 note)
Universal 86765
Virtuoso 1217 (65 note)

AVIATION RAG (Mark Janza)
US Music 65518

AVIATOR RAG (Irene Giblin)
Angelus A-90467 (m), *Rag Medley #18*
QRS 30999
QRS 03443 (65 note)
Universal 78717 (m), *Rag Medley #18*
Universal 95965 (m), *Rag Medley #18*
US Music 64730

A BAG OF RAGS (W. R. McKanlass)
Angelus 90886 (65 note)
Connorized 4617 (65 note)
Connorized 2060
88 Note 99675
Electra 80196
QRS 31171
US Music 65247

BANANA PEEL RAG (Gus Winkler)
Kimball B-5499, 6499
Pianostyle 35584
QRS 31408 (m), *Rag Medley for Dancing*
US Music 65890

BANANA SPLIT RAG (A. M. Gifford)
US Music 7622

BANJO RAG (E. K. Bennett)
Aeolian 77445 (65 note)
Electra 77445
Melographic X-560
QRS 31408 (m), *Rag Medley for Dancing*
Supertone 830385
Universal 90905
US Music 3085 (65 note)
US Music 63085

BANTAM STEP (Harry Jentes)
Artempo 9055, May Fisher
Ideal 3310
Perfection 86632, George Gershwin
QRS 100340, Harry Jentes
Rolla Artis 50253, Helen Thall
Uni-Record 202685, George Gershwin
Universal 101269 (m), *An O.K. Medley* (65 note)
Universal 302599 (m), *An O.K. Medley*
Universal 302553
US Music 7852

BARBED WIRE RAG (Herbert Spencer)
Kimball C-6528
QRS 30838
QRS 03296 (65 note)
Universal 77829 (65 note)
Universal 92425
US Music 63874

BARBER POLE RAG (Charles L. Johnson)
Classics of Ragtime 0006

BARREL HOUSE RAG (Fate Marable and Clarence Williams)
Kimball 7142

BEE HIVE RAG (Joseph Lamb)
Classics of Ragtime 0079

BEEDLE-UM-BO (Raymond Birch)
Connorized 4444 (65 note)

BEES AND HONEY RAG (Les Copeland)
Universal 202759, Les Copeland

BEES WAX RAG (Harry J. Lincoln)
QRS 31082
US Music 65161

BEHAVE YOURSELF (Roy Bargy)
Melodee 204043, Roy Bargy
Recordo 66070, Roy Bargy

BELL HOP RAG (Fred Bryan)
Artempo 2878, Steve Williams
Metro-Art 202066, Paul Paris
QRS 31943
Starr 1145
Uni-Record 202067, Paul Paris

BING BING (Mel B. Kaufman)
Ampico 66991, Vincent Lopez
Ideal 4002

BINGO RAG (F. R. Losey)
QRS 03376 (65 note)
QRS 30927

BIRD-BRAIN RAG (Joseph Lamb)
Classics of Ragtime 0094

BITTERSWEETS RAG (Lora M. Hudson)
Royal 3582
US Music 6858

BLACK AND BLUE RAG (Hal Nichols)
Kimball B-6600
Master Record 1075
Royal 3467
US Music 66370

BLACK AND WHITE RAG (George Botsford)
Aeolian 1159, Clyde Ridge
Artona 502
Capitol 95125
Connorized 4405 (65 note)
Connorized 130
Cremona "A" 978 (m)
Diamond 1993
Dominant 10121
Excello 1242
Electra 76714
Kimball B-5257
Lakeside 3531
Melographic 01034
Melographic 98715
Metrostyle-Themodist 78521 (65 note)
Metrostyle-Themodist 98712
QRS X-3953
QRS 8825, Rudy Erlebach
QRS 30720
Selected 89
Supertone 10005
Supertone 813353
Universal 75569 (65 note)
Universal 98715
US Music 1353 (65 note)
US Music 65399 (m), *Rag Potpourri*
US Music 61353

BLACK BAWL (Harry Thompson)
QRS X-3426

BLACK BEAUTY RAG (Jean Schwartz)
Kimball B-5317
Metrostyle 94711 (m), *Rag Medley*
QRS 03399 (65 note)
QRS 30952
Universal 94715 (m), *Rag Medley #13*
US Music 4670 (65 note)

BLACK CAT RAG (Frank Wooster and Ethyl Smith)
Connorized 4333 (65 note)
Diamond 11003
Kimball C-5131
Kimball J-2666
Metrostyle 862510
QRS X-3328

Universal 71855 (65 note)
Universal 86255

BLACK DIAMOND RAG (Harry J. Lincoln)
US Music 66795

BLACK DIAMOND RAG (Henry Lodge)
Connorized 4609 (65 note)
Connorized 2016
Fall Scale 10423
Kimball C-6441
QRS 31227
US Music 65287

A BLACK HAND (Robert Hoffman)
QRS X-3911

BLACK JACK RAG (Charley Straight)
QRS 100705, Charley Straight

BLACK SATIN (Clarence Woods)
QRS 30590
US Music 9235

BLACK SMOKE (Charles L. Johnson)
Chase and Baker 1036-J (65 note)
QRS 30284
QRS 3783
Virtuoso 1408 (65 note)

BLACK WASP RAG (H. A. Fischler)
Artistone 31686
QRS 03424 (65 note)
QRS 30978
US Music 64878

BLACK SMITH RAG (Rednip)
Ideal 2939
Pianostyle 47654

BLAME IT ON THE BLUES (Charles Cooke)
Artempo 4614, Howard Lutter
Ideal 01418
Imperial 55310, Zema Randale
Kimball B-6941
Perfection 86437, Arthur Prescott
Pianostyle 35142
QRS 31816
QRS 41850 (m), *Bon-Bon Medley*
Rolla Artis 50166, H. Connor
Rolla Artis 50165 (m), *One Step Medley #3,* Phil Goldberg and
    J. E. Anderlik
Uni-Record 202383, Felix Arndt
US Music 66403
US Music 7109 (m), *States Blue Medley #21*
Winner 1416

BLOOIE BLOOIE (Edythe Baker)
Universal 203545, Edythe Baker

BLUE BLAZES RAG (Arthur Sizemore)
US Music 3927 (65 note)

BLUE CLOVER (Max Kortlander)
QRS 100879, Max Kortlander
Rhythmodik Z-106583, Harry Shipman

BLUE GOOSE RAG (Raymond Birch)
Kimball B-7009
Metrostyle-Themodist 6316
Pianostyle 35922
Universal 6317
US Music 7662
US Music 8007 (m), *States Rag Medley #66*

BLUE GRASS RAG (Joseph Lamb)
Classics of Ragtime 0008

BLUE JAY RAG (Frank B. Wooster)
QRS X-3737
US Music 1340

BLUE NOTE RAG (Phillips)
Metrostyle-Themodist 303226

BLUE RIBBON RAG (May Aufderheide)
QRS 03379 (65 note)
QRS 30930

BLUE STREAK (Roy Bargy)
Imperial 513600, Roy Bargy
Recordo 64770, Roy Bargy

BOHEMIA RAG (Joseph Lamb)
Classics of Ragtime 0083
QRS 100015

BOLO RAG (Albert Gumble)
Connorized 4431 (65 note)
Full Scale 13003
Metrostyle-Themodist 91442
QRS 03075 (65 note)
QRS 30659
Universal 76839 (65 note)
Universal 91445

BOMBS AND BULLETS (E.G. Ruth)
QRS 33023

BON TON (Luckey Roberts)
Artempo 4624, Howard Lutter
Metrostyle-Themodist 302036
Universal 302037

BOOGIE RAG (Wilbur Sweatman)
Artempo 12805, Howard Lutter
Perfection 87153, Frank C. Weston
Pianostyle 46488
US Music 8578, Constance Winters and Ray Earle

BOOMERANG RAG (George Botsford)
Metrostyle-Themodist 302636
Universal 302637
US Music 68047

BOOSTER (Mayhew Lake)
Artempo 11406, Howard Lutter

BORNEO RAG (Neil Moret)
Connorized 4554 (65 note)
Connorized 1781
QRS 03452 (65 note)
QRS 31008
US Music 64891

BOWERY BUCK (Tom Turpin)
American 676
Baldwin 186-D
Chase and Baker 76 (65 note)
Connorized 4044 (65 note)
Kimball J-1168
QRS 3532
Simplex 1332 (65 note)
Universal 8355 (65 note)
US Music 65635
Virtuoso 1478 (65 note)

BRAZILIAN NUT (Sol Wolerstein)
QRS 32165

BREAD AND BUTTER (Ted Eastwood)
Metro Art 203016, Ted Eastwood
Uni-Record 203017, Ted Eastwood

BREEZE FROM ALABAMA (Scott Joplin)
Classics of Ragtime 0018

BROADWAY RAG (James Scott)
Classics of Ragtime 0130

BROWNIE RAG (Frank Wooster and Max Wilkins)
QRS X-3358

BUBBLES RAG (W. C. Powell)
Lyric 4097

BUCK-EYE RAG (George Botsford)
Royal 5212
Uni-Record 300559

BUD RAG (Budd L. Cross)
US Music 62351

BUDDY CARTER'S RAG (Jelly Roll Morton)
Classics of Ragtime (m) 0124

BUFFALO RAG (Tom Turpin)
Classics of Ragtime 0070

BUGLE CALL RAG (Eubie Blake and Carey Morgan)
Artrio-Voltem 7580
Connorized 3222
DeLuxe 15340
Harmonic 14840
Imperial 19403
Imperial 56540, Zema Randale
Marvel 2138
Perfection 86643, Gertrude Baum
Pianostyle 35740
QRS 32547
Rolla Artis 50248, H. Connor
Supertone 78323
Universal 101269 (m), *An O.K. Medley* (65 note)
Universal 302599 (m), *An O.K. Medley* (65 note)
Universal 302559
US Music 7823

BUGS RAG (Nina Kohler)
US Music 66099

BULL DOG RAG (Douglas Henderson)
Glockenspiel 1011, Douglas Henderson

BULLY RAG (James E. C. Kelly)
Connorized 1697
Connorized 4543 (65 note)
Cremona A978 (m)
Electra 76496
QRS 03433 (65 note)
QRS 31559 (m), Tout-Bowe
QRS 30988
Universal 95455 (m), *Rag Medley #15*
US Music 64842

BUMBLE BEE (Harry A. Tierney)
Connorized 4480 (65 note)
Connorized 1347

BUNCH OF NOISE RAG (Louis Mentel)
QRS 03279 (65 note)
QRS 30821

BUNNY-BOY (Eric Gatty)
Full Scale 17547 (m), *Latest Ragtime Hits #2*

BUNNY HUG RAG (Harry De Costa)
88 Note 99505
US Music 65379

BUZZER RAG (May Aufderheide)
Melographic 4618 (65 note)
QRS 03359 (65 note)
QRS 30910
US Music 3373 (65 note)

CACTUS RAG (Lucian P. Gibson)
US Music 8000

CALICO RAG (Lee B. Grabbe)
QRS X-3564
QRS 30476

CALICO RAG (Nat Johnson)
Duo Art 1523, Frank Banta
Musicnote 1100
QRS 100193, Nat Johnson
Rolla Artis 50042, George Evans
US Music 6911

CALIFORNIA SUNSHINE (Harry Jentes)
Ampico 20934
Artistone 31987
Pianostyle 35491
QRS 100277, Max Kortlander
Rhythmodik A-7362, Harry Jentes
Supertone 862361
US Music 66261

CALIOPE RAG (Sylvester and Charles Hartlaub)
US Music 65700

CAMPUS RAG (Ben Richmond)
Full Scale 14853

CANADIAN CAPERS (Henry Cohen)
Duo-Art 1772, Erlebach and Milne
Kimball C-6950
Pianostyle 47974
QRS 32166

QRS 1785, Max Kortlander
QRS 1785, J. Lawrence Cook
Rolla Artis 50090, Henry Cohen
US Music 7722

CANDLE STICK RAG (Abe Olman)
QRS 03365 (65 note)
QRS 30916

CANNON BALL (Joseph Northup)
Chase and Baker 2673-F (65 note)
Connorized 581
Connorized 4303 (65 note)
Connorized 10341, William Axtmann
Kimball B-5396
Kimball F-6154 (m), *King of Ragtime*
QRS 100058, Ed M. Pirsell
QRS 30083
QRS 9821, J. Lawrence Cook
QRS X-3447 (65 note)
Supertone 812333
Universal 74357 (65 note)
US Music 65399 (m), *Rag Potpourri*
US Music 61233

CAPRICE RAG (James P. Johnson)
Artempo 12415, James P. Johnson
Classics of Ragtime 0149
Metro Art 203176, James P. Johnson
Perfection 87023, James P. Johnson
Pianostyle 46415
Universal 203177, James P. Johnson

CAR BAR LICK ACID (Clarence Wiley)
Classics of Ragtime 0153
Connorized 584
Connorized 4181 (65 note)
Kimball B-5654
QRS X-3766 (65 note)
QRS 30550
Universal 77299 (65 note)

CAROLINA FOX TROT (Will Vodery)
Artempo 1845, Will Randolph
Connorized 2794
Dominant 10304
Electra 80671
QRS 31619
Rhythmodik E-9402, Fred Schmitz
Supertone 867375
US Music 6775

CAROLINA SHOUT (James P. Johnson)
Aeolian 1547, J. Lawrence Cook
Artempo 12975, James P. Johnson
QRS 100999, James P. Johnson

CARPET RAGS (Raymond W. Connor)
Connorized 4189 (65 note)
Connorized 583
Kimball B-5293
QRS 3980
Virtuoso 1589 (65 note)

CASCADES (Scott Joplin)
    Classics of Ragtime 0084
    Connorized 4172 (65 note)
    Connorized 430
    Connorized 6047
    Connorized 854 (m), *Rag Portfolio*
    QRS 30088
    QRS X-3465 (65 note)
    QRS 31559 (m), Tout-Bowe
    QRS CEL-153, William Bolcom

CASTLE DOGGY (James Reese Europe)
    Melo-Art 91668
    Metrostyle-Themodist 302038
    Universal 302039

CASTLE HOUSE RAG (James Reese Europe)
    Artempo 836, Steve Williams
    Electra 80614 (m), *Castles' Modern Dances*
    Kimball C-6628
    Pianostyle 35651 (m), *Castle Fox Trot Medley*
    QRS 31544
    QRS 31637 (m), *All Seasons Medley*
    Rhythmodik B-8873, Oscar Lifshey
    US Music 66448

CAT'S PAJAMAS (Harry Jentes)
    Connorized 20873, Bert Reeves
    Melodee 204139, Harry Jentes
    QRS 101023, Harry Jentes

CATARACT RAG (Robert Hampton)
    Artempo 1865, Steve Williams
    Classics of Ragtime 0122
    Connorized 3055
    QRS 32270
    US Music 6668

CAULDRON RAG (Axel Christensen)
    QRS 100005, Axel Christensen

A CERTAIN PARTY (Tom Kelley)
    Electra 76436
    Kimball B-5318
    Universal 93515 (m), *Rag Medley #9*
    US Music 64602

CHAMPAGNE RAG (Joseph Lamb)
    Classics of Ragtime 0119
    US Music 64523

CHANTICLEER RAG (Albert Gumble)
    Connorized 4527 (65 note)
    Connorized 1615
    QRS 03293 (65 note)
    QRS 30835
    QRS 100140, Ferdinand Steindel
    Universal 96465 (m), *Rural Medley*
    US Music 63875
    US Music 65364 (m), *Chanticleer Medley*

CHARLESTON RAG (Eubie Blake)
    Ampico 54174-E, Eubie Blake

CHATTERBOX RAG (George Botsford)
    Connorized 4531 (65 note)
    Connorized 1645
    Full Scale 12123
    QRS 03364 (65 note)
    QRS 30915
    Royal 4192
    Universal 78565
    Universal 95125
    US Music 64618
    US Music 4618

CHECKERBOARD RAG (E. W. Jimerson)
    QRS 32548
    US Music 7371

CHECKERS (Harry J. Lincoln)
    US Music 66217

CHECKERS (Nellie Stokes)
    QRS 30365
    QRS 31443 (m), *Rag Medley*

CHECKS RAG (Reuben Lawson)
    Lyric 4096 (65 note)

CHEESE AND CRACKERS (Homer Denney)
    QRS 30749
    QRS 03207 (65 note)

CHEESE AND CRACKERS (Egbert Van Alstyne)
    QRS 100261, Egbert Van Alstyne

CHEVY CHASE (Eubie Blake)
    Artempo 2227, Steve Williams
    Classics of Ragtime 0029
    88 Note 23964
    Electra 86392
    Rhythmodik B-I0652, Pete Wendling and W. E. D.
    US Music 7669

CHEWIN' THE RAG (Fred Heltman)
    Connorized 2236
    QRS 200292, Fred Heltman
    Solo Style A-5482, Albert Gumble and Fred Arno
    US Music 65630

CHICKEN CHARLIE (Ashley Ballou)
    Kimball B-5121
    QRS X-3314 (65 note)
    QRS 30407

CHICKEN CHOWDER (Irene Giblin)
    Connorized 4319 (65 note)
    Connorized 1385
    Electra 73595
    Kimball B-5092
    QRS X-3407 (65 note)
    QRS 30429
    Universal 73595 (65 note)
    US Music 61365
    Virtuoso 1654 (65 note)

CHICKEN PATTY (Theodore Morse)
    QRS X-398l (65 note)

CHICKEN PRANKS (Max Kortlander and Lee Roberts)
Kimball 7190
QRS 100648, Max Kortlander

CHILI SAUCE RAG (H. A. Fischler)
Electra 76538
Universal 78645
Universal 95455 (m), *Rag Medley #15*
US Music 4597 (65 note)

CHILLY BILLY BEE (Lewis F. Muir)
QRS 03295 (65 note)
QRS 30837
Universal 93515 (m), *Rag Medley #9*

CHIMES (Homer Denney)
Aeolian 102752 (65 note)
Angelus 25821 (65 note)
Angelus 90222
Metrostyle-Themodist 93491
Metrostyle-Themodist 100121
Universal 27133
Universal 93495
Universal 78275 (65 note)
US Music 65304

CHINESE RAG (A. Copeland)
Rolla Artis 50068, A. Copeland

CHOCOLATE CREAMS (Warren Camp)
QRS 03266 (65 note)
QRS 30806
US Music 3240 (65 note)

CHOW-CHOW (Robert Hoffman)
QRS 03184 (65 note)
QRS 30731

CHOW-CHOW RAG (Phil Schwartz)
US Music 3366 (65 note)

CHROMATIC RAG (Will Held)
US Music 67906

CLASSIC RAG (Neil Moret)
Connorized 4488 (65 note)
Connorized 1474
QRS 30695
Royal 4163
Universal 77667 (m), *Rag Medley #2* (65 note)
Universal 94345 (m), *Rag Medley #2*
US Music 61469

CLASSICAL SPASM (Harry Thomas)
Ampico 57533, Harry Thomas
Rhythmodik 19913, Harry Thomas

CLASSY RAG (Lillian Lawler)
Kimball C-6421
QRS 32225

CLEOPATRA RAG (Joseph Lamb)
Classics of Ragtime 0048
Standard A-1273 (m)

CLIMAX RAG (James Scott)
Aeolian 301036
Angelus 01333
Artempo 1857, Steve Williams
Metrostyle 104364 (65 note)
Metrostyle 301036
QRS 100395, Max Kortlander
QRS 9889 (m)
Universal 100797 (65 note)
Universal 301037
US Music 66433

CLOUD KISSER (Raymond Birch)
Cremona "A"-978 (m)
US Music 64818
US Music 470 (m)

CLOVER BLOSSOM RAG (Fred Heltman)
QRS 100062, Fred Heltman
Supertone 854378
US Music 65478

CLOVER CLUB (Felix Arndt)
Metro-Art 201988, Felix Arndt
QRS 100814, Felix Arndt
Uni-Record 201989, Felix Arndt
Universal 301499

COLE SMOAK (Clarence St. John)
Connorized 4335 (65 note)
Connorized 1387
QRS X-3677 (65 note)
QRS 30514

COLONIAL GLIDE (Paul Pratt)
QRS 03351 (65 note)
QRS 30901

COLONIAL RAG (Julius Lenzberg and Ernest Ball)
Artempo 2535, Steve Williams
Electra 80718
Master Record 1317
QRS 31726
Rhythmodik A-11802, Pete Wendling and W. E. D.
US Music 66838

COLORED FINGERS RAG (Clarence Johnson)
Columbia 95130, Clarence Johnson

COLUMBIA RAG (Irene Giblin)
US Music 3676 (65 note)

COMET RAG (Ed C. Mahoney)
US Music 64830

CONTENTMENT RAG (Joseph Lamb)
Artempo 2815, Steve Williams
Classics of Ragtime 0107
QRS CEL-139, Max Morath
US Music 7050

COON BAND PARADE RAG (James Reese Europe)
Kimball B-5123
Universal 69805

CORN ON THE COB (Cliff Hess)
 Melodee 204133, Cliff Hess

COTTON BOLLS (Charles Hunter)
 Chase and Baker 900 (65 note)
 Classics of Ragtime 0127
 Connorized 4154 (65 note)
 Kimball B-5405 (65 note)
 QRS 3641 (65 note)
 Virtuoso 1802 (65 note)

A COTTON PATCH (Charles A. Tyler)
 Aeolian 8491 (65 note)
 American 476
 US Music 1052 (m)
 Virtuoso 1804 (65 note)

COTTON TIME (Charles N. Daniels)
 Connorized 4526 (65 note)
 Connorized 1617
 Full Scale 5823
 QRS 03360 (65 note)
 QRS 30911
 Universal 93555
 US Music 64592

COTTONTAIL RAG (Joseph Lamb)
 Classics of Ragtime 0095

COUNTRY CLUB (Scott Joplin)
 Classics of Ragtime 0043
 QRS CEL-150, William Bolcom

CRAB APPLES RAG (Percy Wenrich)
 Connorized 4422 (65 note)
 Connorized 574
 Electra 77536
 QRS 30684
 US Music 1458 (65 note)

CRACKER JACK RAG (E. W. Francis)
 US Music 3159 (65 note)

CRADLE ROCK (Abe Frankl and Phil Kornheiser)
 Autokrat 60279
 Connorized 3368
 QRS 100503, Charley Straight
 Rolla Artis 50325, Billie King (Charley Straight)

CRAZY BONE RAG (Charles L. Johnson)
 Artempo 976, Ernest Stevens
 Electra 80492
 Full Scale 19323
 Full Scale 19717 (m), *Latest Ragtime Hits #4*
 Herbert 81344
 Kimball C-6621
 US Music 65903
 US Music 6300 (m), *States Rag Medley #13*

CRAZY HORSE RAG (Roscoe Carter)
 QRS 03290 (65 note)
 QRS 30832

CRIMSON RAMBLER RAG (Harry A. Tierney)
 Connorized 2273
 Kimball B-6335

QRS 31045
US Music 64973

CUBAN RAG (Armando Romeu)
 Universal 52624

CUBIST RAG (Tom Griselle)
 Ampico 54924, Tom Griselle w/ Victor Arden
 DeLuxe B-6639, Thomas Griselle
 Melodee 203743, Frank Banta
 Rhythmodik F-19504, Thomas Griselle and Victor Arden

CUM BAC RAG (Charles L. Johnson)
 Connorized 2215
 Diamond 12133
 Kimball C-6120
 QRS 31197
 Royal 4226
 Universal 98565
 US Music 5237 (65 note)
 US Music 65237

CURIOSITY (James E. C. Kelly)
 Connorized 4523 (65 note)
 Connorized 1618
 Electra 76398
 Lyric 2109
 Universal 93545 (m), *Rag Medley #10*
 US Music 64581

CUTTIN' UP (Charles G. Haskell)
 Connorized 4436 (65 note)
 QRS X-3672 (65 note)
 Universal 73745

CYCLONE IN DARKTOWN (George D. Barnard)
 American 6964

CYCLONE RAG (E. G. Rieman)
 Wurlitzer 34-5 (m), *Medley #6*

DAFFODILS (James E. C. Kelly)
 US Music 65180

DAFFYDIL RAG (J. R. Shannon)
 QRS 100013, Stanford Robar

DAHOMEAN RAG
 QRS 100004, R.M.

DAINTINESS RAG (James P. Johnson)
 Metro-Art 203106, James P. Johnson
 Pianostyle 46432, 4 hand arr.
 Universal 203107, James P. Johnson

DAINTY FOOT GLIDE (G. M. Tidd)
 Ideal 7000

DAINTY MISS (Bernard Barnes)
 Duo-Art 68956, Robert Armbruster

DANCING SHADOWS (Ernie Golden)
 QRS 4192, Max Kortlander
 Recordo 616700 (m), *Dinner Mosaic #6*, Max Kortlander

DANCING TAMBOURINE (W. C. Polla)
 Acme 3292
 Ampico 68361, J. Milton Delcamp

Duo-Art 713430, Pauline Alpert
Hit 330, J. Lawrence Cook
Imperial 06669
Jewel 20004, Earl Brooks
Pennant 93811
Playrite 5357, Armand Muth
QRS 4081, Max Kortlander

DANDELION RAG (Ted Barron)
Connorized 4497 (65 note)
Connorized 2966 (m), *Bunch of Rags*
Connorized 1506
QRS 03234 (65 note)
QRS 30771
US Music 3122 (65 note)

DARKEY TODALO (Joe Jordan)
Aeolian 100531
Full Scale 12143
Universal 78529
Universal 94775

DAT LOVIN' RAG (Bernie Adler)
American 4066 (m), *Popular Favorites Series*
Angelus 25672 (65 note)
Chase and Baker 4029 (65 note)
Connorized 4426 (65 note)
Connorized 867
Electra 76929
Full Scale 12633
Melographic 4029 (65 note)
Melographic 0981
Universal 76929 (65 note)
Universal 90865
US Music 61074

DEIRO RAG (Herman Schultz)
National 1071
Royal 3411
Supertone 862348
US Music 66248

DELIRIOUS RAG (Harry Thomas and Willie Eckstein)
Metro Art 203064, Harry Thomas
Universal 203065, Harry Thomas

DELIRIUM TREMENS RAG (F. Henri Klickmann)
US Music 65944

DESECRATION RAG (Felix Arndt)
Aeolian 104474 (65 note)
Angelus 91341
Artempo 2389, Steve Williams
Connorized 3102
Ideal 06504
Imperial 52035, Zema Randale
Metro-Art 201638, Felix Arndt
Metrostyle-Themodist 301094, Felix Arndt
Universal 100869 (65 note)
Universal 201639, Felix Arndt
Universal 301095
US Music 66889

DEUCES WILD (Max Kortlander)
QRS 100836, Max Kortlander

DEUCES WILD RAG (Hubert Bauersachs)
Connorized 20864, Rastus Lee

DILL PICKLES (Charles L. Johnson)
American 11613
Arto 2781, Ethel Clayton
Autokrat 60201
Columbia 95120
Connorized 4393 (65 note)
Connorized 423
Electra 2781
Full Scale 11613
Kimball B-5198
Lakeside 6531
Lyric 2126
Melographic 0364
Melographic 1280
Perfection 813356
Perfection 2781, Ethel Clayton
QRS 30473
QRS 8460, J. Lawrence Cook
Supertone 4393 (65 note)
Supertone 10013
Universal 90615
US Music 61356

DIMPLES (Leroy Colburn)
Aeolian 77619 (65 note)

DINGLE POP HOP (Harry A. Tierney)
US Music 64938

DIPPY DITTY (Charley Straight)
Imperial 511770, Charley Straight

DISCHORD RAG (Annette Stone)
Imperial 51363, A. E. Copeland
US Music 66380

DISH RAG (Floyd D. Godfrey)
QRS 03251 (65 note)
QRS 30789

DISH RAG (Richard Goosman)
Connorized 4407 (65 note)

DITTO (Roy Bargy)
Imperial 513000, Roy Bargy

DIXIE DOODLES (Josef Rubens)
QRS 31374 (m), *Rag Medley*

DIXIE KISSES (Phil Ohman)
QRS 100884, Phil Ohman

DIXIE RAG (Irene Giblin)
Artistone 31889
US Music 65832

DIZZY FINGERS (Zez Confrey)
Ampico 65581, Zez Confrey
QRS 101060, Victor Arden
QRS 614680, Victor Arden
US Music 14229, Lee Sims

DOCKSTADER RAG (Les Copeland)
Aeolian 102114 (65 note)
Aeolian 99992

Universal 79717 (65 note)
Universal 99995
US Music 65595

DOCTOR BROWN (Fred Irvin)
Kimball B-7002
QRS 100214, Charley Straight
US Music 6909
US Music 7067 (m), *States Fox-Trot Medley #20*

DOHERTY RAG (Harry Stephenson)
US Music 65227

DOLL DANCE (Nacio Herb Brown)
Acme 3236
Ampico 67741-F, Adam Carroll
Atlas 3236, Fred Seibert
Challenge 9043, Charlie Garland
Duo-Art 713376, Constance Mering
Hit 260
Imperial 06583
Jewel 4966, Al Burton
Pianostyle 49932
Playrite 5322, Phil Duval
QRS 101067, Max Kortlander
QRS 4014, Ted Baxter
QRS 4014, Max Kortlander
Recordo 615430, Max Kortlander
Recordo 616700 (m), *Dinner Mosaic #6,* Max Kortlander
Supertone 4011, Charlie Garland
US Music 44419

DON'T JAZZ ME, I'M MUSIC (James Scott)
Classics of Ragtime 0159

DOPE (W. C. Powell)
Melographic 01427
QRS 03196 (65 note)
QRS 30739
US Music 64576
Virtuoso 80212

DOROTHY RAG (Nat Johnson)
US Music 7289

DOWN HOME RAG (Wilbur Sweatman)
Aeolian 103262 (65 note)
Artempo 1305, Steve Williams
Connorized 2568
88 Note 300527 (m), *A Bear*
Master Record 743
Metro-Art 200868, Felix Arndt
Metrostyle-Themodist 300386
QRS 31777
QRS 100072 (m), *Tango Medley*
QRS 31912 (m), *Poetique Foxtrot Medley*
QRS 9700, J. Lawrence Cook
Rhythmodik C-8563
Royal 3307
65N 100235 (m), *A Bear Turkey Trot* (65 note)
Supertone 852381
Uni-Record 200869, Felix Arndt
Universal 100075 (65 note)
Universal 300387

US Music 6999 (m), *States Fox-Trot Medley*
US Music 65281
US Music 7202
Vocalstyle 9041

DUSTING THE KEYS (Edward Claypoole)
Columbia 667, Wayne Love
International 92423

DUSTY RAG (May Aufderheide)
Connorized 4392 (65 note)
Connorized 315
Kimball B-5433
QRS 03199 (65 note)
QRS 41654 (m), *Aufderheide Melodic Ideas*
Standard 76152

DYNAMITE RAG (Paul Biese and F. Henri Klickman)
National 1073
Supertone 863340
Supertone 870765 (m), *Popular Rag Medley*
US Music 66340
US Music 7065 (m), *States Rag Medley #19*

DYNAMITE RAG (Joseph Lamb)
Classics of Ragtime 0085

DYNAMITE RAG (J. Russel Robinson)
Full Scale 7233 (m), *Casey Jones*

EASY MONEY (A. H. Tournade)
Connorized 4179 (65 note)

EASY WINNERS (Scott Joplin)
Classics of Ragtime 0021
QRS 3749
QRS CEL-134, Max Morath
Virtuoso 5602 (m), *Scott Joplin's Best Rags*

ECCENTRIC (J. Russel Robinson)
Connorized 3077 (m), *Jubilee One-Step Medley*
Dominant 10472
QRS 31211
QRS 9699, J. Russel Robinson (J. L. Cook)
US Music 8173
US Music 65469

EDWARD J. MELLINGER RAG (E. J. Mellinger)
Connorized 10248, E. Bergeson
Connorized 2800 (m), *Raggy Rags Medley*
Keiselhorst 5001
QRS 31443 (m), *Rag Medley*
Supertone 863323
US Music 66323

EFFICIENCY RAG (James Scott)
Metrostyle 303152
Universal 303153
US Music 8397
Wurlitzer 202243 (m)

EGYPTIAN RAG (Percy Wenrich)
Metrostyle-Themodist 100732 (m), *Timely Tunes Medley #42*
(65 note)
QRS 03427 (65 note)
QRS 30982

Universal 95715 (m), *Timely Tunes Medley #42*
US Music 4656 (65 note)
US Music 64656

EIGHT O'CLOCK RUSH RAG (Bess Rudisill)
US Music 65242

ELEPHANT RAG (Malvin Franklin)
Connorized 2448
Connorized 4723
Pianostyle 35479
Rhythmodik A-6372, Malvin Franklin
US Music 65993

ELITE SYNCOPATIONS (Scott Joplin)
Classics of Ragtime 0015

EMPIRE CITY RAG (Frank Broekoven)
US Music 65061

THE ENTERTAINER (Scott Joplin)
Ampico 40121, Bill Flynt
Cecilian 6046
Classics of Ragtime 0108
Connorized 6046 (65 note)
QRS X-308l (65 note)
QRS 9857 (m), *Scott Joplin's Ragtime Medley,* J. Lawrence Cook
QRS 10-518, Oakes and Williams
QRS 30358
QRS CEL-138, Max Morath

ENTERTAINER'S RAG (Jay Roberts)
Aeolian 18866 (m), *Latest Ragtime Hits #3*
Arto 80375
Connorized 2543
Connorized 20350, W. Arlington
Diamond 15483
Electra 80375
Full Scale 17593
Imperial 54294, Jack Clyde
Kimball C-6569
Mignon 1631, Meta Haight
Perfection 80375
Rhythmodik B-8183, Mabel Wayne
Rolla Artis 50040, J. Gordon
Supertone 860443
QRS 100355, Max Kortlander
US Music 66043
Victory 1276

ESTHER RAG (David Reichstein)
US Music 7111

ETHIOPIA RAG (Joseph Lamb)
Classics of Ragtime 0074
US Music 2254 (65 note)

EUGENIA RAG (Scott Joplin)
Classics of Ragtime 0042
QRS 03183 (65 note)
QRS 30730
US Music 1710 (65 note)

EUPHONIC SOUNDS (Scott Joplin)
Artrio-Angelus 90193 (m)
Classics of Ragtime 0059

Metrostyle 102302 (m)
QRS CEL-151, William Bolcom
Universal 77987 (m)
Universal 92715 (m), *Rag Medley #6*
US Music 3871 (65 note)

EVERGREEN RAG (James Scott)
Classics of Ragtime 0155
QRS 32269
US Music 7278

EVERYBODY TWO STEP (Wallie Herzer)
Angelus 25963 (65 note)
Angelus 90912
Connorized 2173
Connorized 3829
Full Scale 14923
Kimball F-6263 (m), *Popular Song Hits #2*
Kimball C-6l64
QRS 31027
Rhythmodik B-5252, Fred A. Schmitz
Royal 4300
Supertone 695418 (65 note)
Supertone 845418
Universal 99845
Universal 94505 (m), *Rag Medley #11*
US Music 65500 (m), *States Medley # 5*
US Music 64518
Virtuoso 81014
Vocalstyle 1530

EVERYBODY'S RAG (Dan Goldsmith and Robert Sharp)
US Music 65499

EVOLUTION RAG (Thomas Allen)
Perfection 80459
Supertone 860397
US Music 66097

EXCELSIOR RAG (Joseph Lamb)
Classics of Ragtime 0123
Supertone 822355
US Music 62255

FANATIC RAG (Harry Tierney)
QRS 03432 (65 note)
QRS 30987
Universal 78679
Universal 95905 (m), *Rag Medley #16*

FASCINATOR (James Scott)
Classics of Ragtime 0081

FASHION RAG (Chas. Cohen)
Herbert 80916
QRS 31177
US Music 65254
US Music 65679 (m), *States Rag Medley #8*
Virtuoso 80916

FASHIONETTE (Jack Glogau and Robert King)
Ampico 69741, Vincent Lopez

FASTEP (Charley Straight)
Imperial 511560, Charley Straight

FATHER KNICKERBOCKER (Edwin E. Wilson)
QRS X-3852 (65 note)

THE FAVORITE (Scott Joplin)
Chase and Baker 2051 (65 note)
Classics of Ragtime 0040
Connorized 4173 (65 note)
QRS X-3345 (65 note)

FELICITY RAG (Scott Joplin and Scott Hayden)
Classics of Ragtime 0106
Kimball B-6781
US Music 65050

FIDDLER'S RAG (Trovato and A. C. Manning)
Aeolian 79405 (65 note)
QRS 31168
Royal 4195
US Music 65260

FIDDLESTICKS RAG (Al B. Coney)
QRS 31315
US Music 65443

FIDDLESTICKS RAG (Florence Wilson)
QRS 03335 (65 note)
QRS 30880
US Music 64650

FIG LEAF RAG (Scott Joplin)
Classics of Ragtime 0064
Play-Rite 573, Rastus Lee
QRS 03073 (65 note)
QRS 30141
QRS 9497 (m), *Scott Joplin's Ragtime Piano Medley,* J. Lawrence Cook
Virtuoso 5667 (65 note)

FINGER BREAKER (Jelly Roll Morton)
Classics of Ragtime 0053

FIRE CRACKER RAG (Will Held)
QRS 03464 (65 note)
QRS 31021

FIREFLY RAG (Joseph F. Lamb)
Classics of Ragtime 0009

FIREWORKS (Roy Wetzel)
QRS 100240, Roy Wetzel

FIVE LITTLE BROWN JUGS (Lawrence B. O'Connor)
Connorized 4475 (65 note)
Connorized 1321

FIZZ WATER (Eubie Blake)
Electra 86393, Gertrude Baum
QRS 31908 (m), *Cupid*
US Music 67230
US Music 7297 (m), *States Dance Medley #38*

FLAPPERETTE (Jesse Greer)
Ampico 68421-B, Roy Bargy
QRS 101068, Max Kortlander
QRS 4068, Max Kortlander
QRS 9686, J. Lawrence Cook
QRS Recordo 615600, Max Kortlander

QRS Recordo 616700 (m), *Dinner Mosaic #6,* Max Kortlander
Sterling 06650
US Music 44463, Fred Parsons

FLEUR DE LIS RAG (Harry Tierney)
Connorized 4580 (65 note)
QRS 31067
Universal 96985 (m), *Rag Medley #21*
US Music 65011

FLORIDA RAG (George Lowry)
American 662
Chase and Baker 3124 (65 note)
Connorized 4258 (65 note)
QRS X-3367 (65 note)
Universal 72559 (65 note)

FLY PAPER RAG (A. Lorne Lee)
QRS 03202 (65 note)
QRS 30744

FLYER RAG (Frieda Aufderheide)
Connorized 4424 (65 note)

FOOLISHNESS RAG (Mort Weinstein)
Connorized 4588 (65 note)
Connorized 1941
QRS 31097
Supertone 850376
US Music 65076

FOOT WARMER (Harry Puck)
Herbert 81476

FOXIE FEET (Paul Pratt)
US Music 8551, M. E. Brown and Paul Pratt

FRANCO-AMERICAN RAG (Jean Schwartz)
Aeolian 77527 (65 note)
Connorized 4477 (65 note)
Connorized 1323
QRS 02022 (65 note)
QRS 20536
US Music 3345 (65 note)

FRECKLES (Larry Buck)
QRS X-3594 (65 note)
QRS 30484

FRENCH PASTRY RAG (Les Copeland)
Metro-Art 202652, Les Copeland
Rolla Artis 50024, Maud Adams
Uni-Record 202653, Les Copeland
US Music 66695

FRENZIED RAG (Joseph H. Miller)
Connorized 4371 (65 note)
QRS X-3914 (65 note)
US Music 1709 (65 note)

FRISCO RAG (Harry Armstrong)
Connorized 4559 (65 note)
Connorized 1809
QRS 03232 (65 note)
QRS 30769
Starr 1809

Universal 92275 (m), *Rag Medley #3*

FROG-I-MORE RAG (Jelly Roll Morton)
Classics of Ragtime 0038

FROG LEGS RAG (James Scott)
Classics of Ragtime 0145
Connorized 4301 (65 note)
Connorized 582
Electra 76202
Kimball B-5132
Kimball F-6154 (m), *King of Ragtime*
Melographic 0804
QRS X-3570 (65 note)
QRS 9762, J. Lawrence Cook
US Music 1255 (65 note)
US Music 64709
US Music 61255

FROSTY RAG (Webb Long)
US Music 64747

FUN BOB RAG (Percy Wenrich)
Classics of Ragtime 0002

FUNERAL RAG (Max Kortlander)
QRS 100306, Max Kortlander
US Music 66032

FUNNY FOLKS (W. C. Powell)
Chase and Baker 1854 (65 note)
Connorized 4331 (65 note)
QRS X-3344 (65 note)

FUSS AND FEATHERS RAG (F. H. Moreland)
Universal 71139

FUZZY WUZZY RAG (Al Morton)
Kimball B-7001
QRS 32252
US Music 7275

GEE WHIZ (Sam Ewing)
US Music 4508 (65 note)
US Music 64508

GEORGIA GRIND (Ford Dabney)
Connorized 3172
Dominant 10583
Imperial 06229
Metrostyle-Themodist 6082
Metrostyle-Themodist 302214 (m), *Azaza*
Perfection 80754
Pianostyle 35248
QRS 32253
QRS 32298 (m), *Eulalia One-Step Medley*
Uni-Record 202415, Felix Arndt
Universal 101149 (m), *Azaza* (65 note)
Universal 302215 (m), *Azaza*
Universal 6083
US Music 43912

GEORGIA RAG (Albert Gumble)
Aeolian Metrostyle 94261 (m), *Rag Medley #12*
Connorized 4525 (65 note)
Connorized 1622

QRS 03388 (65 note)
QRS 30939
Universal 94265 (m), *Rag Medley #12*
US Music 64679

GINGER SNAP RAG (Horace K. Dugdale)
Angelus 25566
Universal 74989 (65 note)
Virtuoso 5622 (65 note)

GLAD RAG (Ribe Danmark)
US Music 64157

GLADIOLUS (Scott Joplin)
American 12623
Artrio-Angelus 90002
Classics of Ragtime 0058
Electra 76896
Kimball C-6529
Metrostyle-Themodist 79513
Metrostyle-Themodist 92261
Full Scale 12623
QRS X-3928 (65 note)
Standard 76836
QRS 30162
Universal 92265
Universal 77769 (65 note)
Virtuoso 5777 (65 note)

GLORIA (Fred Hager and Justin Ring)
Ampico 63041-E, Vincent Lopez

GOIN' SOME (James Nonnahs)
US Music 63425

GOLD DUST TWINS RAG (Nat Johnson)
Connorized 2569
Royal 3371
Supertone 860344
US Music 66044

GOLDEN SPIDER RAG (Charles L. Johnson)
Electra 80030
QRS 03378 (65 note)
QRS 30929
Royal 6089 (m)
Universal 97275 (m), *Rag Medley #22*
US Music 64666

GOLDEN TROPHIES RAG (Erwin R. Schmidt)
Rolla Artis 50085, Erwin R. Schmidt

GOOD AND PLENTY RAG (Joseph F. Lamb)
Classics of Ragtime 0090

GOOD GRAVY RAG (Harry Belding)
Connorized 2484
Kimball B-6366
US Music 65979
US Music 6300 (m), *States Rag Medley #13*

GRACE AND BEAUTY (James Scott)
Angelus 90969
Connorized 20460, W. Arlington
88 N 80260
Electra 80260

Kimball B-6317
Metrostyle 102604
Metrostyle 300118
QRS S-3026 (m)
QRS 31388 (m), *Dance Medley*
QRS CEL, 137, Max Morath
Supertone 83294
Universal 79839
Universal 300119
US Music 63294
US Music 65399 (m), *Rag Potpourri*
US Music 65162 (m), *Grace and Beauty Medley*

GRAND CONCERT RAG (E. Philip Severin)
Capitol 95128

GRANDPA'S SPELLS (Jelly Roll Morton)
Vocalstyle 50487, Jelly Roll Morton

GRAVEL RAG (Charlotte Blake)
Connorized 4432 (65 note)
QRS 03099 (65 note)
QRS 30668
Universal 78067

GREASED LIGHTNING (Joseph F. Lamb)
Classics of Ragtime 0078

GREAT SCOTT RAG (James Scott)
Classics of Ragtime 0146
QRS 31138

GREENWICH WITCH (Zez Confrey)
QRS 101022, Zez Confrey

GRIZZLY BEAR RAG (George Botsford)
Aeolian 6162 (65 note)
Connorized 3671 (65 note)
Connorized 1533
Connorized 1515 (m), *Our Own Medley*
Full Scale 4723
Kimball B-5288
Melographic X-628
Melographic 01875
Metrostyle 79593 (65 note)
Metrostyle-Themodist 93081
QRS 03299 (65 note)
QRS 30842
Starr 4723
Universal 93085
Universal 77815 (65 note)
US Music 64135
Virtuoso 6234 (m), *A-Double Medley* (65 note)

GROWLS (Alfred E. Cooper)
US Music 65030

GULBRANSEN RAG (Herb Willett)
US Music 66036

HALLEY'S COMET (Harry J. Lincoln)
QRS 03381 (65 note)
QRS 30932
US Music 64148

HAM AND (Arthur Marshall)
Classics of Ragtime 0005

HAM BONES RAG (Homer Denney)
Connorized 2157
Supertone 856378
US Music 65678
US Music 6300 (m), *States Rag Medley #13*

HANKY PANK (Harry G. Robinson andClifford Adams)
Kimball B-6798
US Music 66575
US Music 7022 (m), *States Popular Medley #17*

HAPPY HOPS (Howard Lutter)
Artempo 13215, Howard Lutter

HAPPY LULU RAG (Alfonso Hart)
QRS 31236

HAPPY RAG (R. G. Grady)
Pianostyle 35352

HARD BOILED RAG (Louis Mentel)
US Music 4013 (65 note)

HARLEM RAG (Tom Turpin)
Classics of Ragtime 0067
QRS 3912

HARLEM STRUT (James P. Johnson)
Aeolian 1450, J. Lawrence Cook
QRS 101014, James P. Johnson
Wurlitzer 1557 (m)

HARMONY RAG (Hal Nichols)
Artistone 41717
Royal 6089 (m)
Universal 97275 (m), *Rag Medley #22*

HARRIMAN CAKE WALK (Lee S. Roberts)
Perfection 202424, Felix Arndt
QRS 100211, Lee S. Roberts
QRS 32206
Uni-Record 202425, Felix Arndt
US Music 7446

HARRY FOX TROT (Lew Pollack)
Perfection 87270, Archie Stephens

HAUNTING RAG (Julius Lenzberg)
Full Scale 10103
QRS 31161
QRS 100044, Felix Arndt
Uni-Record 200623
Universal 98275 (m), *Rag Medley #23*
US Music 65179
Virtuoso 80874

HAVANA RAG (Maurice Kirwin)
Connorized 4372 (65 note)
Connorized 1262
QRS X-3922 (65 note)
QRS 30613

HAYTIAN RAG (Ford Dabney)
Connorized 4551 (65 note)
Connorized 1776
US Music 64613

HEARTS AND HANDS (a.k.a. THOSE HARMELODIC
BLUES, Phil Goldberg)
QRS 100244, Phil Goldberg

HEAVY ON THE CATSUP (Lewis Muir)
Master Record 1120
US Music 6391

HELENDORO RAG (Nat Johnson)
Supertone 72369
US Music 7269

HELIOTROPE BOUQUET (Louis Chauvin and Scott Joplin)
Classics of Ragtime 0022
US Music 1076 (65 note)

HIGH STEPPER (Lew Pollack)
Rolla Artis 50446, Billy King

HILARITY RAG (James Scott)
Angelus 91069
Connorized 3056
Connorized 3105 (m), *Autumn Leaves Medley*
Dominant 10492
Kimball C-5248
Kimball F-6154 (m), *King of Ragtime*
Metrostyle 103174 (65 note)
Metrostyle 300278
QRS 31379 (m), *Rag Medley*
Standard 80343
Supertone 845342
Universal 100017 (65 note)
Universal 300279
US Music 4542 (65 note)
US Music 65399 (m), *Rag Potpourri*
US Music 64542

HIPPODROME RAG (Herman E. Schultz)
Rolla Artis 50481, Herman E. Schultz

HOBBLE RAG (Will Morrissey)
QRS 04594 (65 note)
QRS 31050
QRS 41299

HOLY MOSES (C. Seymore)
QRS X-3803
QRS 30570

HOMESPUN RAG (Thos. Allen)
Aeolian 102204 (65 note)
Aeolian 300052
Angelus 90927
Herbert 81091
Universal 79779 (65 note)
Universal 300053

HOMESPUN RAG (Austin S. Benson)
QRS 03317 (65 note)
QRS 30860
US Music 64551

HONEY RAG (Egbert Van Alstyne)
QRS 03190 (65 note)
US Music 3357

HONEYMOON RAG (Abe Olman)
Connorized 4434 (65 note)
QRS 03404 (65 note)
QRS 30957
Universal 96475 (m), *Rag Medley #19*
US Music 64234

HONEY MOON RAG (James Scott)
Artempo 9935, Steve Williams
Classics of Ragtime 0098
Metro-Art 203008, Felix Arndt
Universal 203009, Felix Arndt
US Music 8143

HONEYSUCKLE RAG (George Botsford)
Electra 80229
QRS 31172
US Music 65510

HOOSIER GIRL RAG (Emil Seidel)
Vocalstyle 50161

HOOSIER RAG (Sophus Jergensen)
QRS X-3795 (65 note)

HOOSIER RAG (Julia Lee Niebergall)
QRS X-3880 (65 note)
QRS 30598
US Music 1360 (65 note)

HORSESHOE RAG (Julia Lee Niebergall)
Kimball B-6475
Melographic 02187
QRS 03460 (65 note)
QRS 31017
US Music 65150
US Music 66074
US Music 65679 (m), *States Rag Medley #8*

HOT AIR RAG (F. A. Walker)
Kimball A-5821
QRS X-3986 (65 note)

HOT CABBAGE (Homer Denney)
QRS 03201 (65 note)
QRS 30743

HOT CHOCOLATE RAG (Malvin Franklin and Arthur Lange)
Connorized 4429 (65 note)
QRS 03063 (65 note)

HOT CINDERS (Joseph F. Lamb)
Classics of Ragtime 0088

HOT HANDS (Charley Straight)
Ideal 1437
Kimball B-7013
Melographic 1282
QRB 100266 (m), *Bamberger Autograph Medley*
QRS 100223, Charley Straight
Uni-Record 202733, Felix Arndt

US Music 7739
US Music 8007 (m), *States Rag Medley #66*

HOT HOUSE RAG (Paul Pratt)
Artempo 1887, Steve Williams
Kimball B-6838
Supertone 10029
Supertone 866365
US Music 6665

HOT OFF THE GRIDDLE (James White)
Starr 9291

HOT SCOTCH RAG (H. A. Fischler)
QRS 03411 (65 note)
QRS 30964
Supertone 847380
US Music 64780
US Music 65679 (m), *States Rag Medley #8*

HOT STUFF (Howard Lutter)
Artempo 12925, Howard Lutter

HOT TAMALES (I. M. Lawson)
Connorized 4410 (65 note)
Connorized 960
QRS X-3700 (65 note)

HUDSON RAG (Lora Hudson)
Ampico 21157 (m), *Popular Ragtime Hits #5*
Connorized 2633
Full Scale 21157 (m), *Popular Ragtime Hits #5*
Kimball C-6510
Royal 3428
Supertone 863301
US Music 66301

HUMORESQUE RAG (Charles E. Gall)
Pianostyle 45232
QRS 100317, Max Kortlander
Rhythmodik A-6872, Malvin Franklin

HUMORESTLESS (Zez Confrey)
Ampico 64381-F, Zez Confrey

HUMPTY DUMPTY RAG (Charley Straight)
Ampico 21157 (m), *Popular Ragtime Hits #5*
Artempo 728, Ernest Stevens
Connorized 2707
Full Scale 21157 (m), *Popular Ragtime Hits #5*
Metro-Art 201574, Felix Arndt
Pianostyle 35308
QRS 31888
QRS 100137, Charley Straight
Supertone 870765 (m), *Popular Rag Medley*
Uni-Record 201575, Felix Arndt
US Music 66369
US Music 7065 (m), *States Rag Medley #19*

HUNGARIAN RAG (Julius Lenzberg)
Artistone 31979
Electra 80491
Excello 1376
Connorized 4745 (65 note)
Connorized 2533

Connorized 10340, W. Arlington
Full Scale 19717 (m), *Latest Ragtime Hits #4*
Perfection 80491
QRS 31387 (m), *Rag Medley*
QRS 31374 (m), *Rag Medley*
Rhythmodik B-6842, Edwin F. Kendall
Supertone 861323
Supertone 870765 (m), *Popular Rag Medley*
US Music 66123
US Music 7065 (m), *States Rag Medley #19*

HUNTING THE BALL (Max Kortlander)
QRS 100470, Max Kortlander

HURRICANE RAG (Frederick Johnson)
QRS 31245
US Music 65091

HYACINTH RAG (George Botsford)
Ampico 2203, Botsford and Gumble
Connorized 4611 (65 note)
Connorized 2029
Full Scale 10733
Full Scale 11115 (m), *Rag Bag*
QRS 31167
SoloStyle A-3022, Botsford and Gumble
Supertone 851389
US Music 65189
US Music 65438 (m), *A Winsome Widow*

HYPNOTIC RAG (Ed Mahoney)
Aeolian 102204 (65 note)
Aeolian 300048
Electra 80253
Universal 79777 (65 note)
Universal 300049
US Music 65506

HYSTERICS RAG (Paul Biese and F. Henri Klickman)
US Music 6985

ICYCLES RAG (Jas. E. C. Kelly)
Connorized 4383 (65 note)
Kimball B-6093
QRS 03109 (65 note)
QRS 30673

I'M ALABAMA BOUND (Robert Hoffman)
US Music 65338

IMP RAG (Webb Long)
US Music 4161 (65 note)

IN A MIST (Bix Beiderbecke)
Duo-Art 1928, Constance Mering

INCANDESCENT RAG (George Botsford)
Aeolian 103894 (65 note)
Aeolian 300772
Electra 80516
Kimball B-6495
Metrostyle-Themodist 300773
Metro-Art 201236, Felix Arndt
QRS 31390
QRS 31384 (m), *Rag Medley*

Royal 3417
Uni-Record 201237, Felix Arndt
Universal 300176
Universal 100489 (65 note)
Supertone 861341

INDIA RUBBER (Duke Baier)
QRS 100469, Max Kortlander

INK SPLOTCH RAG (Clifford Adams)
Kimball B-6314
QRS 30687

INNOCENCE RAG (Harry A. Tierney)
QRS 31146
Standard 80243
US Music 65557

INNOVATION (James P. Johnson)
Metro-Art 203254, James P. Johnson
Universal 203255, James P. Johnson

INTERFERENCE (Maurice Wetzel)
QRS 10-084, Hi Babbit

INTERMISSION RAG (Chas. Wellinger)
QRS 32454
US Music 7673

INVITATION RAG (Les Copeland)
Aeolian 79199
Electra 80033
National 1101
QRS 31120
Royal 3198
Supertone 850386
Universal 97685
US Music 65086

IRRESISTIBLE RAG (Lora M. Hudson)
QRS 32533
US Music 7589

IRRESISTIBLE RAG (W. C. Powell)
QRS 03319 (65 note)
QRS 30862

ISHUDWORRY (Robert M. Storer)
A.M.A. 91157
Aeolian 103572 (65 note)
Aeolian 300566
Angelus 91134
Master Record 1106
QRS 31607
QRS 31635 (m), *Frivolity*
Royal 4375
Supertone 858347
Universal 100279 (65 note)
Universal 300567
US Music 65847

ITSIT (Charley Straight)
QRS 100600, Charley Straight

IVORY RAG (Louis F. Busch)
QRS 8854, J. Lawrence Cook

JACK FROST RAG (Archie Scheu)
QRS X-3487 (65 note)
QRS 30453

JACK RABBIT RAG (Donald Garcia)
US Music 3535 (65 note)
Wurlitzer 203782

JACKIE (J. Milton Delcamp)
Welte Y-6116, J. Milton Delcamp

JAG RAG (Arthur C. Morse)
US Music 66064

JAMAICA JINGER RAG (Egbert Van Alstyne)
Aeolian 101864 (65 note)
Aeolian 99462
Connorized 1407
Connorized 2191
Electra 80127
Full Scale 10845 (m), *Latest Hits #15*
QRS 31269
QRS 100036, Egbert Van Alstyne
Royal 3268
Universal 79549 (65 note)
Universal 99465
US Music 65315

JAPANESE RAG (Mose Gumble)
QRS 3877

JASS BAND RAG (Frank S. Butler)
Connorized 20677, H. Claar
Rolla Artis 50598, N. Weyend

JAXON RAG (Lucius Dunn)
Connorized 4395 (65 note)
Connorized 244
QRS X-3960 (65 note)
QRS 30622
US Music 1249 (65 note)

JAY ROBERTS RAG (Jay Roberts)
QRS 31236
QRS 31559 (m), *Tout-Bowe*

JAY WALK (Zez Confrey)
Ampico 66821, Zez Confrey

JAZAMINE (Max Kortlander)
QRS 100812, Max Kortlander

JERSEY RAG (Joseph F. Lamb)
Classics of Ragtime 0035

JERUSHA PEPPER (Jay G. Coffman)
Kimball B-5431

JIM JAMS (Roy Bargy)
Imperial 513140, Roy Bargy
Melodee 204025, Roy Bargy

JINX RAG (Lucian P. Gibson)
Connorized 4598 (65 note)
Universal 98275 (m), *Rag Medley #23*
US Music 7562

JOHNSON RAG (Henry Kleinkauf and Guy Hall)
QRS 8572, J. Lawrence Cook

JOLLY JINGLES RAG (F. H. Losey)
Supertone 861340
US Music 6140

JOY RAG (Jay Roberts)
QRS 31230
US Music 65715
US Music 6300 (m), *States Rag Medley #13*

JUMPING JACK (Rube Bloom, Bernie Seaman and
Marvin Smolev)
Duo-Art, Rube Bloom
Melodee 47695, Rube Bloom

JUNGLE TIME (E.P. Severin)
Connorized 4206 (65 note)
Connorized 1052
Connorized 854 (m), *Rag Portfolio*
Kimball M-2561 (m), *Rag Portfolio*
QRS X-3274 (65 note)

JUNK MAN RAG (Luckey Roberts)
Aeolian 103454 (65 note)
Aeolian 18866 (m), *Latest Ragtime Hits #3*
Connorized 2409
88 Note 300505
Electra 80410
Kimball B-6496
Kimball E-6557 (m), *Tango Medley*
Metro-Art 200984, Felix Arndt
Metrostyle-Themodist 6140
Perfection 80410
Pianostyle 35138
QRS 100063, Stanford Robar
QRS 100074, Sallie Heilbronner and Mabel Cripe
QRS 31559 (m), *Tout-Bowe*
Uni-Record 200985, Felix Arndt
Universal 6141
Universal 100205 (65 note)
Universal 300504
US Music 65919
US Music 6720 (m), *States Medley #15*
Connorized 2447 (m), *Summer Melodies*

JUST A RAG (Lee S. Roberts)
QRS 100008, Lee S. Roberts

JUST ASK ME (Charles Hunter)
QRS X-3093 (65 note)

JUSTIN-TYME (Roy Bargy)
Imperial 513800, Roy Bargy
Melodee 204045, Roy Bargy

KALAMITY KID (Ferd Guttenberger)
Classics of Ragtime 0131
Connorized 1626
QRS 03238 (65 note)
QRS X-3886 (65 note)
QRS 30775

KANGAROO HOP (Melville Morris)
Artempo 8414, Dave Kaplan
Connorized 3224
DeLuxe 15371
Ideal 1427
Imperial 55660, Lewis J. Fuiks
Metrostyle-Themodist 302412
Perfection 66595, George Gershwin
QRS 100319, Charley Straight
Rolla Artis 50273, Billie King
Uni-Record 202583, Ruben
Universal 302413
Universal 302485 (m), *A-Wide-Awake*
Universal 101245 (m)
US Music 7606

KANSAS CITY RAG (James Scott)
Classics of Ragtime 0132
Connorized 4334 (65 note)
Connorized 1560
QRS X-3796 (65 note)
QRS 30566

KEEN KUT-UPS (Armand Muth)
Staffnote 2039, Armand Muth

KENTUCKY BEAUTY (Albert Gumble and
Monroe Rosenfeld)
QRS X-3382 (65 note)
QRS 30424
US Music 1081 (65 note)

KENTUCKY RAG (Floyd Willis)
Connorized 4631 (65 note)

KETCHUP RAG (Irene M. Giblin)
QRS 03311 (65 note)
QRS 30854
US Music 3873 (65 note)

KEWPIE (Gene Rose)
Duo-Art 73558, Pauline Alpert

KIMBERLY RAG (H. H. Hoyt, Jr.)
US Music 3153 (65 note)

KING OF RAGS (Sherman Swisher)
Metrostyle 6274
QRS 03097 (65 note)
Universal 6275

KING OF THEM ALL (William M. Simpson)
QRS 03267 (65 note)
QRS 30807

KING PORTER STOMP (Jelly Roll Morton)
QRS 9595, J. Lawrence Cook
Vocalstyle 50480, Jelly Roll Morton

KINKLETS (Arthur Marshall)
Classics of Ragtime 0080
QRS X-3689 (65 note)
QRS 30519

KISMET RAG (Scott Joplin and Scott Hayden)
    Classics of Ragtime 0039
    Kimball B-6793
    US Music 65819

KITTEN ON THE KEYS (Zez Confrey)
    Aeolian 1213, Bob Sawyer
    Ampico 60621, Herbert Clair
    Columbia 488, Gus Drobegg
    International 2179
    Melodee 204023, Rudy Erlebach
    Metro-Art 203928, Rudy Erlebach
    Pianostyle 48013
    QRS 101003, Zez Confrey
    QRS 10-353, Al Eldridge
    Supertone 5234, Gus Drobegg
    Vocalstyle 12228, Willsey
    Welte DeLuxe Y-6l95, Adam Carroll

KLASSICLE RAG (Cecil Duane Crabb)
    Cremona A-978 (m)
    QRS 03449 (65 note)
    QRS 31005
    US Music 64882

KLU-LUKUM RAG (Claude P. Christopher and Carl T. Williams)
    US Music 3195 (65 note)

KNICE AND KNIFTY (Charley Straight)
    Imperial 512260, Charley Straight
    Melodee 204039, Roy Bargy

KNICK KNOCKS RAG (Phil Schwartz)
    Perfection 80751
    QRS 32135
    US Music 7311

KNIGHT HUBERT (William Bolcom)
    QRS CEL-154, William Bolcom

KNOCKOUT DROPS (F. Henri Klickman)
    Connorized 20776, H. Claar
    Imperial 53533, Zema Randale
    US Music 4690 (65 note)
    US Music 64690
    Virtuoso 80693

LA PETITE BOSTON RAG (Reva Marie Ritch)
    US Music 65081

LAGOON RAG (Louis Mentel)
    QRS 03276 (65 note)
    QRS 30818

LASSES (Lucy Thomas)
    QRS X-3346

LAZY BONES (Charley Straight)
    QRS 100500, Charley Straight

LEAP FROG RAG (Edwin F. Kendall)
    Connorized 4430 (65 note)
    QRS 03039 (65 note)
    QRS 30644

LEMON DROPS (Mike Bernard)
    Connorized 4597 (65 note)
    US Music 65711

LEMONS AND LIMES (Cora Salisbury)
    Farrand 123
    Full Scale 123
    QRS 03270 (65 note)
    QRS 30812
    US Music 3074 (65 note)

LEOLA TWO-STEP (Scott Joplin)
    Classics of Ragtime 0036

LET'S GO (Charley Straight)
    QRS 100204, Charley Straight
    US Music 7641

LET'S TRY IT (Max Kortlander)
    QRS 100660, Max Kortlander

LEVEE RAG (Fred E. Gates)
    Connorized 10269, E. Bergeson

LI'L JOE (Max Kortlander)
    QRS 100706, Max Kortlander

LILY QUEEN (Arthur Marshall)
    Classics of Ragtime 0020

LILY RAG (Charles Thompson)
    US Music 6797
    US Music 7299 (m), *States Popular Medley #40*

LIMBER JACK (Richardson and Joseph)
    Ampico 52804, Victor Arden

LION TAMER'S RAG (Mark Janza)
    Connorized 2674 (m), *Ragpicking*
    Full Scale 15904
    Full Scale 17547 (m), *Latest Ragtime Hits #2*
    US Music 65604

LITTLE BIT OF RAG (Paul Pratt)
    US Music 8005

LITTLE ROCK GETAWAY (Joe Sullivan)
    QRS 8706, as played by Bob Zurke

LITTLE STICKS 0' LICORICE (Ray Ruddy)
    US Music 65265

LIVE WIRES RAG (Adaline Shepard)
    Connorized 4576 (65 note)
    Connorized 1884
    Kimball B-5605
    Melographic 01901
    Metrostyle 959852 (m), *Rag Medley #17*
    QRS 30162 (65 note)
    Universal 78697
    Universal 95985 (m), *Rag Medley #17*

LOG CABIN RAG (Ferd Guttenberger)
    Connorized 1218
    QRS 03237 (65 note)
    QRS 30774

LOG CABIN RAG (James R. Shannon)
US Music 6934

LOPEZ RAG (J. R. Lopez)
International 1055

LOUISIANA RAG (Leon Block)
Artistone 31593
Full Scale 12415
Universal 96535 (m), *Rag Medley #20*

LOUISIANA RAG (Theo Northrup)
Aeolian 102574 (65 note)
Aeolian 95411
Aeolian 8190 (65 note)
Simplex 1188 (65 note)
Universal 78619 (65 note)
Universal 88995
Universal 95415
Virtuoso 2973 (65 note)

LUNDBERG SPECIAL (Peter Lundberg)
Classics of Ragtime 0137

MACADAMIAN SCUFFLE (David A. Jasen)
Blues Tone 137140, David Jasen

MADAGASCAR MANGLE (Vinton Freedley)
US Music 65455

MAGNETIC RAG (Scott Joplin)
Classics of Ragtime 0165
Connorized 10266, Scott Joplin
88 N 26274

MAGPIE RAG (Malvin Franklin)
QRS 03088 (65 note)

MAJESTIC RAG (Ben Rawls and Royal Neel)
Kimball B-7082
QRS 31688
US Music 6673

MANDO RAG (R. G. Ingraham)
US Music 6667

MANDY'S BROADWAY STROLL (Thos. E. Broady)
Chase and Baker 307 (65 note)
Classics of Ragtime 0162

MANHATTAN RAG (Fred Brownold)
QRS 3862

MANHATTAN RAG (Edwin F. Kendall)
Connorized 4312 (65 note)
Connorized 1055

MAPLE LEAF RAG (Scott Joplin)
Aeolian 1040, Clyde Ridge
American 493
American 4066 (m), *Popular Favorites Series*
American 95101
Ampico 40131, Bill Flynt
Angelus 25383 (65 note)
Aristo 4066 (m), *Popular Favorites: Ragtime*

Artempo 9976, Steve Williams
Arto 8440
Artrio-Angelus 90080
Autokrat 60223
Autopiano 1363 (65 note)
Capitol 95101
Chase and Baker 1731 (65 note)
Classics of Ragtime 0065
Connorized 4028 (65 note)
Connorized 148
Connorized 2966 (m), *Bunch of Rags*
Connorized 10265, Scott Joplin
Electra 8440
Full Scale 493
Full Scale 4066 (m), *Popular Favorites Series*
Imperial 510300
Kimball B-5087
Kimball F-6154 (m), *King of Ragtime*
Little Wonder 212
Lyric 2276
Melographic 0369
Melographic 1731 (65 note)
Metro-Art 202704, Scott Joplin
Metrostyle-Themodist 89961
Perfection 8440
Pianostyle 35143
QRS 148
QRS X-3817 (65 note)
QRS 30900
QRS 100419, Max Kortlander
QRS 7308, J. Lawrence Cook
QRS 9725, Scott Joplin (sic) J. Lawrence Cook
Rollo Mexico 1205
Royal 4078
Simplex 1655 (65 note)
Starr 8057
Supertone 10029
Supertone 813368
Uni-Record 202705, Scott Joplin
Universal 8440 (65 note)
Universal 11060
Universal 89965
US Music 61368
US Music 65399 (m), *Rag Potpourri*
Virtuoso 80891
Virtuoso 5602 (m), *Scott Joplin's Best Rags*

MARDI GRAS RAG (George Lyons and Bob Yosco)
US Music 66427

MASHED POTATOES (C. L. Woolsey)
QRS 31118
US Music 64995

MAURICE RAG (William H. Penn)
QRS 31271
US Music 65395

MEADOW LARK RAG (Tom Pitts)
US Music 7998

MEDIC RAG (Calvin Woolsey)
Kimball B-5309
Melographic 02270
QRS 03362 (65 note)
QRS 30913
Standard 77857
Universal 77857
Universal 92525
US Music 63966

MEDITATION (Lee Sims)
Ampico 6876l-E, Lee Sims

MEL-O-DEE RAG (Harry Stover)
Melodee 203557, Harry Stover

MELODY MAN (Charles Gillen)
US Music 64720

MELODY RAG (Charles L. Johnson)
Cremona A-978 (m)
Full Scale 8973
QRS 31229
Supertone 848308
US Music 64808

MELROSE RAG (Hubert Bauersachs)
Connorized 20861, Sybil Court

MEMPHIS RAG (Percy Wenrich)
US Music 2068 (65 note)

MERRY-GO-ROUND RAG (Gus Edwards)
Aeolian 77339 (65 note)
Aristo 3224
Full Scale 3224
QRS 03146 (65 note)
QRS 30703
Universal 90895
US Music 2215 (65 note)
Virtuoso 5883 (65 note)

MERRY WIDOW RAG (Eubie Blake)
QRS CEL-125, Eubie Blake

MERRY WIDOW RAG (E. Clinton Keithley)
Connorized 4391 (65 note)
Connorized 866
QRS 03156 (65 note)
QRS 30709

METEOR RAG (Arthur Morse)
Columbia 95129

MIDNIGHT RAG (Gus Winkler)
Supertone 856386
US Music 65686

MIDNIGHT TROT (George L. Cobb)
QRS 32588
Rolla Artis 50129, Jack Chapman

MIDNIGHT WHIRL RAG (Silvio Hein)
Aeolian 301142
Universal 301143

MINSTREL BAND (Albert Gumble)
Virtuoso 5957 (65 note)

MINSTREL MAN (J. Russel Robinson)
QRS 9001, J. Russel Robinson (J. Lawrence Cook)
US Music 65156

MISERABLE RAG (Malvin M. Franklin)
US Music 7418

MISERY RAG (Carlton Colby)
Connorized 20452, A. Hyland
Kimball C-6763
Klean-Kut 4662
QRS 31642
US Music 6963

MISS CUTEY RAG (Phil Schwartz)
QRS 100018, Phil Schwartz

MISSISSIPPI TEASER (Hugh Canon)
US Music 65299

MISSOURI AUTUMN RAG (Trebor J. Tichenor)
Classics of Ragtime 0147

MISSOURI BREEZE (Trebor J. Tichenor)
Classics of Ragtime 0086

MISSOURI RAG (W. C. Powell)
QRS 03024 (65 note)
QRS 30640

MISSOURI RAG (a.k.a. THAT HAND-PLAYED RAG, David Silverman and Arthur Ward)
Connorized 20758, H. Claar

MISSOURI ROMP (Arthur Marshall)
Classics of Ragtime 0168

MITINICE (Charley Straight)
QRS 100475, Charley Straight
Rolla Artis 50298, Billie King (Charley Straight)

MIZZOURA MAG'S CHROMATIC RAG (H. H. Farris)
Aeolian 70409 (65 note)

MODESTY RAG (James Scott)
Classics of Ragtime 0019

MOON SLIDE RAG (Claude W. Smith)
QRS 32329

MOOSE RAG (Ted Johnson)
Electra 80293
QRS 31386 (m), *Rag Medley*
Supertone 856342
US Music 65642

MORE NOISE RAG (Louis Mentel)
QRS 03160 (65 note)
QRS 30712
US Music 4014 (65 note)

MOTOR BUS RAG (Annie Houston)
US Music 6674

MOVIE RAG (J. S. Zamecnik)
Aeolian 18573
Aeolian 18866 (m), *Latest Ragtime Hits #3*
Electra 80472
QRS 31443 (m), *Rag Medley*
Rhythmodik A-7512, Malvin Franklin

MOW-EM-DOWN (Charley Straight and Rube Bennett)
Imperial 511940, Charley Straight

MUSIC BOX RAG (Luckey Roberts)
Aeolian 301744
Artempo 2236, Will Randolph
Connorized 2890
Electra 86394 (m), *Fox Trot Medley #3*
QRS 32123
Triumph 10336
Universal 301745
US Music 6908

MUSLIN RAG (Mel B. Kaufman)
Metrostyle-Themodist 303402
Universal 303403

MUTILATION RAG (Zema Randale)
Imperial 53154, Zema Randale

MUTT AND JEFF (P. L. Eubank)
Connorized 2600
Connorized 4762
Royal 3442
Supertone 863365
US Music 66365

MY BABY'S RAG (Charley Straight)
Rolla Artis 50297, Billie King (Charley Straight)

MY FAVORITE RAG (James S. White)
QRS 32463
Rolla Artis 50201, James S. White
US Music 7454

MY PET (Zez Confrey)
Ampico 60631, Herbert Clair
QRS 100827, Zez Confrey

NAKED DANCE (Jelly Roll Morton)
Classics of Ragtime 0028

NANETTE (Adam Carroll)
Ampico 68211, Adam Carroll

NAT JOHNSON'S RAG (Nat Johnson)
Herbert
Pianostyle 35566

NERVOUS RAG (Bernard E. Fay and Blackford)
US Music 64704

NEW ERA RAG (James Scott)
Classics of Ragtime 0152

NEW HIPPODROME RAG (Herman E. Schultz)
Rolla Artis 50032, H. M. Norton
US Music 6694

NEW RUSSIAN RAG (George L. Cobb)
Vocalstyle 50409, Buck Johnson

NEW YORK RAG (George C. Durgan)
QRS 31116

NICE AND EASY (Cliff McKay)
US Music 8291

NICE AND EASY (Charley Straight)
Rolla Artis 50338, Billie King (Charley Straight)

NIFTY NONSENSE (Charley Straight)
Imperial 511510, Charley Straight

NIGGER TOE RAG (H. A. Fischler)
Aeolian Metrostyle 94261 (m), *Rag Medley #12*
Electra 76482
QRS 03391 (65 Note)
QRS 30942
Universal 94265 (m), *Rag Medley #12*

NIGHTINGALE RAG (see RAGTIME NIGHTINGALE)

1915 RAG (Harry A. Tierney)
Aeolian 103624 (65 note)
Aeolian 300618
Ampico 20503
Ampico 20777 (m), *Popular Ragtime Hits*
Electra 80362
Full Scale 20503
Full Scale 20177 (m), *Popular Ragtime Hits*
Metrostyle-Themodist 300619
Perfecta S-6464
Universal 100317 (65 note)

NOBODY'S RAG (David A. Jasen)
Blues Tone 137100, David A. Jasen

NOISY NOTES RAG (Ralph Wray)
QRS 32065

NONETTE (Herbert Spencer)
Electra 80219
Metrostyle-Themodist 99915
QRS 31311

NONPAREIL RAG (Scott Joplin)
Classics of Ragtime 0012
Connorized 4401 (65 note)
Virtuoso 5602 (m), *Scott Joplin's Best Rags*

NONSENSE RAG (R. G. Grady)
QRS 03410 (65 note)
QRS 30963
US Music 64823

NOTORIETY RAG (Kathryn Widmer)
Ampico 20344
Artempo 928, Howard Lutter
Electra 80582
Full Scale 20344
QRS 31386 (m), *Rag Medley*
US Music 66188

NOVELTY RAG (May Aufderheide)
Kimball C-5904
QRS 03463 (65 Note)
QRS 31020
US Music 64940

OCTOPUS RAG (John O. Erlan)
Chase and Baker 3285 (65 note)

OCTOROON (Keith Nichols)
Jazzmaster 20

OH YOU ANGEL (Ford Dabney)
Full Scale 12334
US Music 64769

OH YOU DEVIL (Ford Dabney)
Connorized 4496 (65 note)
Connorized 1514
Full Scale 12334
QRS 03179 (65 note)
QRS 30726
Universal 77837 (65 note)
Universal 92465
US Music 62270
Virtuoso 5931 (65 note)

OH YOU DRUMMER (J. Leubrie Hill)
QRS

OH YOU SALLY RAG (Clarence Jones)
QRS 31105

OH YOU TURKEY (Henry Lodge)
Rhythmodik A-9212, Fred Arno and F. A. S.

OLD CROW RAG (George Botsford)
Classics of Ragtime 0160
Electra 76014
QRS 03169 (65 note)
US Music 2991 (65 note)

OLD FOLKS RAG (Wilbur Sweatman)
Aeolian 104472 (65 note)
Aeolian 6138
88 N 301093
Electra 80701 (m), *Fox Trot Medley #1*
Metro-Art 201846, Felix Arndt
Metrostyle-Themodist 301346 (m), *Fox Trot Medley*
QRS 31530
Uni-Record 201847, Felix Arndt
Universal 100867 (65 note)
Universal 6139
Universal 301347 (m), *Fox Trot Medley*
US Music 66547

OLD HOME RAG (Joseph F. Lamb)
Classics of Ragtime 0092

OLD LEVEE DAYS (Trebor J. Tichenor)
Classics of Ragtime 0136

OLD VIRGINIA RAG (Clyde Douglass)
QRS 03010 (65 note)
QRS 30631

OMEOMY (Roy Bargy)
Imperial 513980, Roy Bargy

ON THE PIKE (James Scott)
Classics of Ragtime 0157

ON THE RIVIERA (Alfred J. Doyle)
Connorized 3779 (65 note)
US Music 65022

ON THE RURAL ROUTE (Paul Pratt)
US Music 7952

OPERA HOUSE RAG (Robert Darch)
Classics of Ragtime 0118

OPERATIC NIGHTMARE (Felix Arndt)
Autokrat 60329
Imperial 56710, Zema Randale
Metro-Art 202832, Felix Arndt
QRS 100482, Jeff Waters
Universal 202833, Felix Arndt
US Music 8275

OPERATIC RAG (Julius Lenzberg)
Connorized 2867
Electra 80731
Little Wonder 198
Perfection 80731, O. L. Metz and B. Morgan
QRS 31972
Rolla Artis 50075, Walter Ford
Universal 23393
US Music 6902
Victory 1255
Winner 1405

OPHELIA RAG (James Scott)
Classics of Ragtime 0099
US Music 64138

ORIGINAL BLUES (Ted S. Barron)
US Music 6944
US Music 7109 (m), *States Blue Medley #2*

ORIGINAL CHICAGO BLUES (James White)
Connorized 20511, A. Hyland
Imperial 54510, Zema Randale
QRS 32157

ORIGINAL RAGS (Scott Joplin)
Aeolian Grand 20428 (65 note)
Chase and Baker 147-J (65 note)
Classics of Ragtime 0151
Connorized 4051 (65 note)
Connorized 843
Connorized 2035l, W. Arlington
Kimball J-1185 (65 note)
Kimball C-5063
Melographic 0370
QRS 3268 (58 note)
Universal 2508 (65 note)
Virtuoso 3533 (65 note)
Virtuoso 5602 (m), *Scott Joplin's Best Rags*

ORINOCO (S. L. Clary)
QRS 3798
QRS 30288

ORINOCO (Cecil Duane Crabb)
QRS 31016
US Music 65039

ORPHEUM RAG (Charles Frank)
Supertone 861390
US Music 6190

OUT STEPPIN' (Charley Straight)
Imperial 510000, Charley Straight
QRS 100650, Charley Straight

OYSTER RAG (Tom Lyle)
Connorized 4532 (65 note)
Connorized 1653
QRS 03325 (65 note)
QRS 30870
US Music 64158

PALM BEACH RAG (Luckey Roberts)
Connorized 3183
Kimball B-7008
QRS 31772
US Music 6907

PALM LEAF RAG (Scott Joplin)
Classics of Ragtime 0063
Kimball B-5824
QRS X-3034 (65 note)
QRS 30342
Virtuoso 5602 (m), *Scott Joplin's Best Rags*

PAN-AM RAG (Tom Turpin)
Classics of Ragtime 0141

PANAMA RAG (C. Seymour)
Connorized 4275 (65 note)
Connorized 857
Chase and Baker 2682 (65 note)
Full Scale 12093
QRS X-3448
Universal 68287 (65 note)
Universal 87115
Virtuoso 3567 (65 note)
Royal 4026
US Music 7625

PANSY BLOSSOMS (Charles L. Johnson)
US Music 2324 (65 note)

PARAGON RAG (Scott Joplin)
Classics of Ragtime 0024
QRS CEL-152, William Bolcom
US Music 3865 (65 note)
US Music 75378 (m)

PARAMOUNT RAG (James Scott)
Classics of Ragtime 0037
Music Note 1074

PASTIME RAG (Henry Lodge)
Full Scale 19717 (m), *Latest Ragtime Hits #4*
Pianostyle 35483
Pianostyle 85487

PASTIME RAG #1 (Artie Matthews)
Classics of Ragtime 0030
Supertone 860371
US Music 66071

PASTIME RAG #2 (Artie Matthews)
Classics of Ragtime 0031

PASTIME RAG #3 (Artie Matthews)
Classics of Ragtime 0032
Perfection 86738, Fred Murtha (a.k.a. George Gershwin)

PASTIME RAG #4 (Artie Matthews)
Classics of Ragtime 0033

PASTIME RAG #5 (Artie Matthews)
Classics of Ragtime 0034

PATRICIA RAG (Joseph Lamb)
Classics of Ragtime 0047

PEACE AND PLENTY (James Scott)
Classics of Ragtime 0050

PEACEFUL HENRY (E. Harry Kelly)
Aeolian 20790 (58 note)
Chase and Baker 915-J (65 note)
Connorized 4121 (65 note)
Connorized 4507 (m), *Fascinating Two-Step* (65 note)
Connorized 586
Kimball J-1528 (65 note)
Simplex 1639 (65 note)
Starr 4121
Universal 11362 (65 note)
Universal 63525 (65 note)
Virtuoso 3618 (65 note)

PEACH (Arthur Marshall)
Classics of Ragtime 0071

PEACHERINE RAG (Scott Joplin)
Classics of Ragtime 0041
Connorized 6047 (65 note)

PEACHES AND CREAM (Percy Wenrich)
Angelus 25590 (65 note)
Kimball J-3123 (65 note)
QRS X-3673 (65 note)
Universal 75485 (65 note)

PEARL OF THE HAREM (Harry P. Guy)
Aeolian 60595 (65 note)
American 2653
Chase and Baker 376 (65 note)
Connorized 4108 (65 note)
QRS 3853
QRS 30306

THE PEARLS (Jelly Roll Morton)
Classics of Ragtime 0101

PEEK-A-BOO RAG (Charles L. Johnson)
    Supertone 869364
    US Music 66964

PEGASUS RAG (James Scott)
    Classics of Ragtime 0073

PEKIN RAG (Joe Jordan)
    Virtuoso 3633 (65 note)

PEKIN RAG (Harry W. Martin)
    US Music 65938

PEPPER SAUCE (H. A. Fischler)
    US Music 64645

PERCY (Archie W. Scheu)
    Connorized 4441 (65 note)
    QRS X-3863 (65 note)

PERFECT RAG (Jelly Roll Morton)
    Classics of Ragtime 0055

PEROXIDE RAG (C. L. Woolsey)
    QRS 31100
    US Music 65547

PERPETUAL RAG (Harry Thomas and Willie Eckstein)
    Metro-Art 203062, Harry Thomas
    Universal 203063, Harry Thomas

PERSIAN LAMB RAG (Percy Wenrich)
    Classics of Ragtime 0128
    QRS 03049 (65 note)
    QRS 30647

PETTICOAT LANE (Euday Bowman)
    US Music 7484
    US Music 7656 (m), *States Blue Medley #50*

PHILOPENA RAG (McKinstry)
    Royal 4027

PIANO MANIA (Billy Fazioli)
    Connorized 20872, Bert Reeves

PIANO RAG (Russell Franck)
    US Music 66517

PIANOFLAGE (Roy Bargy)
    Ampico 68751, Roy Bargy
    Imperial 513130, Roy Bargy
    Melodee 204047, Roy Bargy
    Picturoll 884
    Recordo 67630, Roy Bargy

PIANOPHIEND (Reuben J. Haskin)
    US Music 6699

PIANOPHIENDS RAG (George Botsford)
    Metrostyle 94711 (m), *Rag Medley*
    Universal 78475 (m), *Rag Medley #13*
    Universal 94715 (m), *Rag Medley #13*

PICCALILLI RAG (George A. Reeg, Jr.)
    Connorized 4618 (65 note)
    QRS 31180
    US Music 65221

PICKLED BEETS RAG (Ed Kuhn)
    QRS 03441 (65 note)
    QRS 30997

PICKLES AND PEPPERS (Adaline Shepherd)
    Arto 75449, Ben Hurst
    Electra 75449
    Full Scale 4073
    Kimball C-5395
    Metrostyle 77693 (65 note)
    QRS X-3987 (65 note)
    QRS 30719
    Perfection 75449, Ben Hurst
    Universal 75449 (65 note)
    Universal 90845

PIERCE CITY RAG (Trebor J. Tichenor)
    Classics of Ragtime 0087

PIFFLE RAG (Gladys Yelvington)
    QRS 03465 (65 note)
    QRS 31022
    QRS 31539 (m), *Tout-Bowe Rag Medley*
    US Music 64887

PIGEON WING RAG (Charles L. Johnson)
    US Music 2232 (65 note)

PINEAPPLE RAG (Scott Joplin)
    Angelus 90193 (m)
    Classics of Ragtime 0060
    Herbert 80422
    Lyon and Healy 6067
    Metrostyle 102303 (m)
    QRS 10-524, Oakes and Williams
    QRS CEL-156, William Bolcom
    Universal 77987 (m)
    Universal 92715 (m), *Rag Medley #6*

PINEYWOOD RAG (Adam Minsel)
    US Music 3092 (65 note)

PINK POODLE RAG (Charles L. Johnson)
    Classics of Ragtime 0161

PINOCHLE RAG (Seymour Furth)
    Herbert 81419
    Pianostyle 35414

PIPING ROCK (J. Fred Coots)
    Universal 203495, J. Fred Coots

THE PIPPIN (Arthur Marshall)
    Classics of Ragtime 0069

PIRATE RAG (Henneman)
    Artempo 13195, Henneman

PITTER-PATTER RAG (Jos. M. Daly)
    QRS 31374 (m), *Rag Medley*

PLAYER PIANO RAG (Marcella A. Henry)
    Kimball 7582

PLAYMOR (Charley Straight)
    QRS 100571, Charley Straight

PLENTY O' PEPPER RAG (Bien)
QRS 31613

POISON IVY (Herbert Ingraham)
Connorized 4403 (65 note)
Connorized 399
Electra 77316
Kimball J-3245 (65 note)
QRS 30696
Virtuoso 5892 (65 note)

POISON RAG (C. L. Woolsey)
QRS 31101

POKER RAG (Charlotte Blake)
QRS 03174 (65 note)
QRS 30723
Supertone 821392
US Music 62192

POLAR BEAR RAG (George Howard)
Connorized 4301 (65 note)
QRS 31122
Universal 96535 (m), *Rag Medley #20*
US Music 64709

POLLY (J. S. Zamecnik)
Ampico 6724l-E, J. Milton Delcamp

POLYRAGMIC (Max Morath)
QRS CEL-136, Max Morath

POOR JIM (James Chapman)
QRS X-3084 (65 note)

POP CORN MAN (Jean Schwartz)
QRS 30419 (65 note)
QRS 30972
Universal 95145 (m), *Rag Medley #14*
US Music 64694

POPULAR RAG (Webb Long)
Angelus 26058 (m), *A-Startler* (65 note)
QRS 31319
Universal 101217 (m), *A-Startler* (65 note)
Universal 302433 (m), *A-Startler*
US Music 65466

PORCUPINE RAG (Charles L. Johnson)
Connorized 4502 (65 note)
Connorized 1544
Kimball B-5516
QRS 03217 (65 note)
QRS 30756
Universal 92275 (m), *Rag Medley #3*

PORK AND BEANS (Theron Bennett)
QRS 03081 (65 note)
US Music 1321 (65 note)
US Music 61321

PORK AND BEANS (Luckey Roberts)
Artistone 31992
Supertone 861386
US Music 66186

PORTO RICO RAG (Ford Dabney)
Connorized 4585 (65 note)
Full Scale 11603
Metro-Art 200462, Felix Arndt
Uni-Record 200463, Felix Arndt
Universal 78527
Universal 95405
US Music 64726

POSSUM AND 'TATERS (Charles Hunter)
Connorized 4098 (65 note)
Connorized 854 (m), *Rag Portfolio*
Kimball M-256l (m), *Rag Portfolio*
QRS 3465 (65 note)

POSSUM RAG (Geraldine Dobyns)
Melographic 01246 (65 note)
Metrostyle-Themodist 77321
Universal 85619 (65 note)
US Music 1306 (65 note)

POVERTY RAG (Harry J. Lincoln)
QRS 03274 (65 note)
QRS 30816
Wurlitzer 203782

POWDER RAG (Raymond Birch)
Angelus 25655 (65 note)
Connorized 4435 (65 note)
Full Scale 7224
Kimball C-5l85
Kimball F-6154 (m), *King of Ragtime*
Metrostyle 959852 (m), *Rag Medley #17*
QRS 03150 (65 note)
QRS 30686
Supertone 814346
Universal 77975 (65 note)
Universal 78697
Universal 95985 (m), *Rag Medley #17*
US Music 61446

POWDER RAG (a.k.a. HUSTLING RAG, Roy Stevenson)
Connorized 4402 (65 note)
Connorized 1142

PRATTLES (Paul Pratt)
US Music 7916

PRIDE OF THE SMOKY ROW (J. M. Wilcockson)
Kimball C-5887
Supertone 847399
US Music 64799

PRINCESS RAG (James Scott)
Classics of Ragtime 0133
US Music 64846

PROMENADE RAG (Marie White)
Kimball 6056
Melographic 02546
US Music 65113

PROSPERITY RAG (James Scott)
Classics of Ragtime 0075
US Music 7905

PURDUE RAG (Opal Boyer)
US Music 66480

PURDUE SPIRIT (Edward J. Freeberg)
QRS 03252 (65 note)
QRS 30791
US Music 65602

PUSS IN BOOTS (Henry Lange)
US Music 10149, Henry Lange

PUSSY FOOT RAG (Robert Hoffman)
Herbert 81574
QRS 31908 (m), *Cupid*

QUALITY RAG (James Scott)
Connorized 20461, W. Arlington
Kimball C-6778 (m)
QRS 32226
QRS 32346 (m), *A Rich Mixture*
US Music 5270 (65 note)
US Music 65270

QUEEN OF LOVE (Charles Hunter)
QRS 3419 (65 note)

QUEEN RAG (Floyd Willis)
Connorized 4562 (65 note)
Connorized 1831
QRS 31111
US Music 64988
US Music 65679 (m), *States Rag Medley #8*

QUEEN OF RAGS (Walter L. Dunn)
US Music 65658

RACE TRACK BLUES (Les Copeland)
Metro-Art 202752, Les Copeland
Universal 202753, Les Copeland

RACKETY-RAG (J. Milton Delcamp)
Republic 47708, J. Milton Delcamp

RAG A BIT (Charley Straight)
Imperial 511760, Charley Straight

RAG-A-MINOR (Julius Lenzberg)
QRS 33272

RAG-A-MUFFIN RAG (Will T. Pierson)
Supertone 862331
US Music 66231

RAG-A-TAG RAG (Al W. Brown)
Autopiano 92305 (m), *Rag Medley #4*
US Music 63713

RAG BABY MINE (George Botsford)
Aeolian 301394
Universal 301395

RAG BABY RAG (F. R. Losey)
QRS 03363 (65 note)
QRS 30914
US Music 3061 (65 note)

RAG BAG RAG (Harry J. Lincoln)
Kimball
QRS 03374 (65 note)

QRS 30925
US Music 2045 (65 note)
Virtuoso 5934 (65 note)

RAG CARPET (Sol Levy)
Connorized 4622 (65 note)
QRS 31266
US Music 65342

RAG DOLL (Nacio Herb Brown)
Ampico 69351, Victor Arden
Imperial 07005
Playrite 5479, Armand Muth
QRS 101070, Max Kortlander
Supertone 4159, John Hunnert

RAG PICKERS RAG (Robert O'Brien)
Full Scale 12943
Melographic 0365 (65 note)
QRS X-3886 (65 note)
Universal 75327 (65 note)
Universal 91755

RAG SENTIMENTAL (James Scott)
Music Note 1075
US Music 8737

RAG WITH NO NAME (Warren Camp)
Connorized 2674 (m), *Ragpickins*
Full Scale 9733
QRS 31243
Supertone 862465
US Music 66265

RAGGED EDGES (Otto Frey)
QRS 3431 (65 note)
QRS 30986

RAGGED JACK (Jack Bradshaw)
US Music 3009 (65 note)

RAGGED TERRY RAG (Margaret A. White)
US Music 6901

RAGGED THOUGHTS (Louis Von der Mehden)
QRS 31053

RAGGING THE SCALE (Ed Claypoole)
Artrio-Angelus 7550, William Berge
Artempo 5052, Dave Kaplan
Autokrat 60075
Connorized 3117
Connorized 3125 (m), *Raggy Fox Trot Medley*
DeLuxe 15165
Dominant 10538
Dyna-Record 50015, Hilda Wehmeier
Harmony 110923
Herbert 81994 (m), *The Hunter Fox Trot Medley*
Ideal 02410, J. Caldwell Atkinson
Imperial 55530, Zema Randale
Kimball B-6926
Marvel 2143
Metrostyle-Themodist 302196
Orient 2186
Perfection 86400, Joseph Fecher

Pianostyle 35170
QRS 100263, Charley Straight
QRS 41951 (m), *Crown Medley #3*
QRS 6236, Max Kortlander
Rhythmodik A-13172, Pete Wendling
Rollo Artis 50155, Clarence Jones
Universal 101159 (65 note)
Universal 302197
US Music 7590
Winner 2410

RAGGY FOX TROT (Laurence E. Goffin)
US Music 7561

RAGS TO BURN (Frank X. McFadden)
QRS X-3016 (65 note)

RAGTIME BETTY (James Scott)
Classics of Ragtime 0129
Electra 76018
Electra 80021

RAGTIME BOBOLINK (Joseph Lamb)
Classics of Ragtime 0091

RAGTIME CHIMES (Percy Wenrich)
QRS 31046
US Music 65017
US Music 65703 (m), *Percy Wenrich Medley*

RAGTIME DANCE (Scott Joplin)
Classics of Ragtime 0013
QRS X-3626 (65 note)

RAGTIME FOLLIES (May Olive Arnold)
Kimball B-6046

RAGTIME JIM (A. Fred Phillips)
Connorized 2317
Melographic X-548
QRS 31336
QRS 100069, Phil Schwartz
QRS 31366 (m), *Tango Medley*
Supertone 855387
US Music 65587

RAGTIME JINGLES (Al J. Markgraf)
Ampico 50694, Pete Wendling
Artempo 9945, Steve Williams
Autokrat 60215
QRS 32593

RAGTIME MELODY (William Beasley, Dick Stratton, and
Adelaide Hazelwood)
QRS 8807, J. Lawrence Cook

RAGTIME NIGHTINGALE (Joseph Lamb)
Artempo 3855, Steve Williams
Classics of Ragtime 0046
Metrostyle 302002
Standard A-1237 (m)
Universal 302003
US Music 7373

RAGTIME NIGHTMARE (Tom Turpin)
Classics of Ragtime 0125

Connorized 4149 (65 note)
QRS 3789 (65 note)

RAGTIME ORIOLE (James Scott)
Angelus 91182
Artempo 1898, Steve Williams
Connorized 10311, W. Arlington
88 N 80353
Kimball C-6787
Metrostyle 103672 (65 note)
Metrostyle 300642
QRS 100278, Max Kortlander
QRS 32228
Supertone 853411
Triumph 8090 (65 note)
Universal 100345 (65 note)
Universal 300643
US Music 65311

RAGTIME SPECIAL (Joseph F. Lamb)
Classics of Ragtime 0068

RAH RAH BOY (Wallie Herzer)
Universal 94505 (m), *Rag Medley #11*

RAMSHACKLE RAG (Ted Snyder)
Angelus 90510
Full Scale 8633
Kimball B-5560
Melographic 4865 (65 note)
QRS 03438 (65 note)
QRS 30993
QRS 100016, C. C. Jones
Universal 11333 (65 note)
Universal 96575
US Music 65099

RAPID TRANSIT (Joseph Lamb)
Classics of Ragtime 0077

RASTUS RAG (H. A. Fischler)
QRS 03386 (65 note)
QRS 30937
US Music 2864 (65 note)

RATS (M. K. Miller)
Connorized 2853
Kimball A-6856
Selected 179
Starr 9320
Triumph 10322
US Music 6808
US Music 8851

RAVIOLI RAG (Frank Lucanese and Charles Lucotti)
Rolla Artis 50036, J. E. Anderlik

RAZZLE DAZZLE (Nellie Stokes)
QRS 03281 (65 note)
QRS 30823
US Music 3312 (65 note)

THE REAL STUFF (Ed N. Pirsell)
QRS 200262, Ed N. Pirsell

RED CLOVER (Max Kortlander)
QRS 100874, Max Kortlander

RED FOX-TROT (Albert Gumble)
US Music 8547

RED HEAD RAG (Irene Franklin and Burt Green)
US Music 3617 (65 note)
US Music 63617

RED ONION RAG (Abe Olman)
QRS 31216
US Music 65292

RED PEPPER (Henry Lodge)
Connorized 4536 (65 note)
Connorized 1681
Full Scale 5563
Kimball C-5468
Metrostyle 94741
QRS 03398 (65 note)
QRS 30951
Supertone 10034
Supertone 47357
Universal 8507
Universal 94745
US Music 64757

RED RAMBLER RAG (Julia Lee Niebergall)
Melographic 02631
QRS 31314
US Music 65411

RED RAVEN (Carl E. Olson)
US Music 4635 (65 note)

RED RAVEN RAG (Charley Straight)
Kimball B-6955
QRS 100270, Charley Straight
Universal 302547

RED RIBBON RAG (Z. M. Van Tress)
QRS 32067

REFLECTION RAG (Scott Joplin)
Classics of Ragtime 0016

REINDEER RAG (Joseph Lamb)
Barker Roll 009
Classics of Ragtime 0143
US Music 7272
US Music 7345 (m), *States Popular Dance Medley #41*

RHAPSODY IN RAGTIME (Eubie Blake)
QRS CEL-123, Eubie Blake

RHAPSODY RAG (Budd Cross)
QRS 31058
US Music 64814

RHAPSODY RAG (Harry Jentes)
Connorized 4586 (65 note)
Connorized 1927
Connorized 2966 (m), *Bunch of Rags*
Full Scale 12964
Universal 96515
US Music 64765

RHINOCEROUS RAG (Young)
Master Record 652

RHINEWINE RAG (Paul Henneberg)
QRS 31201

RIALTO RIPPLES RAG (George Gershwin and Will Donaldson)
Pianostyle 46479
Metro-Art 202934, George Gershwin
Uni-Record 202935, George Gershwin
US Music 8461

RICHMOND RAG (May Aufderheide)
QRS 30136

RIG-A-JIG RAG (Nat D. Ayer)
Aeolian 102142 (65 note)
Aeolian 300014
Rhythmodik, Nat D. Ayer
Starr 967
Universal 79735 (65 note)
Universal 300015
US Music 65422

RIGAMAROLE RAG (Edwin Kendall)
Perfection 80295
QRS 31099
US Music 4628 (65 note)
US Music 64628

RIGHT OFF THE GRIDDLE RAG (Ed N. Pirsell)
QRS 200282, Ed N. Pirsell

RINALDO RAG (Rinaldo)
US Music 1052 (m)

RIVERSIDE RAG (Charles Cohen)
Kimball
QRS 03473 (65 note)
QRS 31030

RIZZY BOO
US Music 66166

ROCKY MOUNTAIN FOX (Les Copeland)
Uni-Record 202725, Les Copeland

ROLLIN' THE BONES (Harry Jentes)
Metro-Art 203266, Harry Jentes

ROODLE-DI-DOO (Archie L. Hamilton)
US Music 8060

ROOSTER RAG (Muriel Pollock)
Classics of Ragtime 0148
Duo-Art 1549, Frank Banta
US Music 68429

ROSE LEAF RAG (Scott Joplin)
Classics of Ragtime 0025
Connorized 4473 (65 note)
Connorized 1336

ROSEWOOD RAG (Peter Heaton)
QRS 3165 (65 note)
US Music 3841 (65 note)

ROTATION RAG (Al Sweet)
QRS 31098
US Music 65143

ROYAL FLUSH RAG (George Botsford)
Angelus A-90467 (m), *Rag Medley #18*
Artistone 31627
QRS 03437 (65 note)
QRS 30992
Universal 78717 (m), *Rag Medley #18*
Universal 95965 (m), *Rag Medley #18*
US Music 64835

RUBBER HEELS RAG (E. W. Hille)
QRS 100022, E. W. Hille

RUBBER PLANT RAG (George L. Cobb)
QRS 03273 (65 note)
QRS 30815
US Music 63322
US Music 65399 (m), *Rag Potpourri*

RUBIES AND PEARLS (Harry A. Tierney)
QRS 31247
US Music 65336

RUBY RAG (Harry Ruby)
Metro-Art 203256, George Gershwin and Rudy Erlebach

RUFENREDDY (Charley Straight)
Ampico 68641-E, Roy Bargy
Artrio-Angelus 2080, Roy Bargy
Imperial 511360, Charley Straight
Melodee 204027, Roy Bargy

RUSSIAN PONY RAG (Don Ramsay)
Universal 77665 (65 note)
Universal 92035
US Music 63629

RUSSIAN RAG (George L. Cobb)
International 1058
QRS 33297
QRS 100870, Max Kortlander

S 0 S (K. W. Bradshaw and Joe McGrade)
Keynote 1174

S'MORE (Charley Straight)
QRS 100409, Charley Straight
Rolla Artis 50291, Billie King (Charley Straight)

SACRILEGIOUS RAG (Samuel A. Perlstein)
Connorized 20582, Samuel A. Perlstein

SAFETY PIN CATCH (Lewis Fuiks)
US Music 3559 (65 note)

ST. LOUIS RAG (Tom Turpin)
Angelus 25701
Chase and Baker 2150-J (65 note)
Classics of Ragtime 0082
Connorized 4143 (65 note)
Connorized 1460
QRS X-3057 (65 note)
QRS 9978, Hi Babit
Simplex 1772 (65 note)
Starr 1460
Virtuoso 4516 (65 note)

ST. LOUIS TICKLE (Barney and Seymore)
Aeolian 70947 (65 note)
American 519
Aristo 6404
Chase and Baker 3305 (65 note)
Connorized 4232 (65 note)
Connorized 461
Connorized 854 (m), *Rag Portfolio*
Connorized 6404
Electra 76947
Full Scale 6404
Kimball B-5220
Melographic 01062
QRS X-3343 (65 note)
Simplex 8440 (65 note)
Universal 80747
Virtuoso 4517 (65 note)
Vocalstyle 12601, Buck Johnson

SAM FOX TROT (George Howard)
Electra 85132
QRS 100189 (m), Ferdinand Steindel
US Music 7080
Winner 4900

SANDPAPER RAG (H.E. Elman and S. Lew Schwab)
US Music 63533

SANDY RIVER RAG (Thos. Allen)
Herbert 81391
Pianostyle 35478

SAPHO RAG (J. Russel Robinson)
QRS 03243 (65 note)
QRS 30781
QRS 9000, J. Russel Robinson (J. Lawrence Cook)
US Music 63439

SASKATOON RAG (Phil Goldberg)
QRS 32016
Rolla Artis 50069, Phil Goldberg
US Music 7223

SATISFIED (Theron Bennett)
QRS X-3041

SCANDALOUS THOMPSON (Charles L. Johnson)
Aeolian 8169 (65 note)
American 2922
Perforated D-169 (65 note)
Simplex 1167 (65 note)
Virtuoso 4122 (65 note)

SCARECROW RAG (Will Morrison)
US Music 66387

SCOTT JOPLIN'S NEW RAG (Scott Joplin)
American 11263
Angelus 90806
Classics of Ragtime 0121
Connorized 4632 (65 note)
Connorized 2121
Full Scale 11263
Kimball C-6132

Metrostyle-Themodist 99362
Universal 79527
Universal 99365
QRS 31282
QRS 9857 (m), J. Lawrence Cook
QRS CEL-135, Max Morath
US Music 65357

SCRAMBLE RAG (Louis Mentel)
US Music 65045

SCRUB RAG (A. W. Mueller)
US Music

SEARCHLIGHT RAG (Scott Joplin)
Classics of Ragtime 0011
QRS X-3866 (65 note)
QRS 30595

SEDALIA RAG (Fred Hoeptner)
Classics of Ragtime 0097

SENSATION RAG (Joseph Lamb)
Classics of Ragtime 0142
Connorized 4469 (65 note)
Connorized 1303
Electra 77624
QRS 03302 (65 note)
QRS 30845
QRS 9497 (m), J. Lawrence Cook

SEXTETTE RAG (Malvin Franklin)
Rhythmodik B-8273, Malvin Franklin

SHAVE 'EM DRY (Sam Wishnuff)
Musicnote 1080
US Music 8398

SHAY-KA-LEG (Lewis J. Fuiks)
Imperial 58670, Lewis J. Fuiks

THE SHEATH (William E. Weigel)
US Music 2348 (65 note)

SHIMMIE SHOES (Max Kortlander)
QRS 100847, Max Kortlander

SHINE OR POLISH RAG (Fred Heltman)
US Music 7052

SHOE TICKLER RAG (Wilbur Campbell)
Classics of Ragtime 0001

SHOVEL FISH RAG (Harry Cook)
Chase and Baker 3952 (65 note)
Connorized 4364 (65 note)
Connorized 1062
QRS 03043 (65 note)
QRS 30156

SHREVEPORT STOMP (Jelly Roll Morton)
Vocalstyle 50461, Jelly Roll Morton

SILENCE AND FUN (Charles E. Mullen)
US Music 1077 (65 note)

SILVER BUCKLE RAG (Joseph Sikorra)
Full Scale 193
Full Scale 1097

Herbert
QRS 03340 (65 note)
QRS 30887
US Music 64546

SILVER KING (Charles L. Johnson)
Kimball C-5325
Melographic 4568 (65 note)
Melographic 01635
Supertone 823354
US Music 62354

SILVER ROCKET RAG (Arthur Marshall)
Classics of Ragtime 0169

SILVER SWAN (Scott Joplin)
Classics of Ragtime 0167
Master Record 1239
National Music 123
QRS 31533

SILVER TRUMPETS (Viviani)
QRS 12564

SKY ROCKETS RAG (E. Philip Severin)
Connorized 4619 (65 note)
Connorized 2070
Electra 80159
QRS 31309
US Music 65427

SLEEPY LOU (Irene Giblin)
Connorized 4326 (65 note)
Connorized 858
US Music 1088

SLEEPY SIDNEY (Archie Scheu)
Connorized 4440 (65 note)
Electra 75565 (65 note)
QRS X-3741 (65 note)
Universal 75565 (65 note)
Virtuoso 5474

SLIPOVA (Roy Bargy)
Imperial 513070, Roy Bargy
Melodee 203999, Roy Bargy

SLIPPERY ELM RAG (Clarence Woods)
Classics of Ragtime 0100
Supertone 860375
US Music 66075

SMASHUP RAG (Gwendolyn Stevenson)
Kimball D-7053
QRS 31908 (m), *Cupid*
Standard 4346 (65 note)
US Music 6986

THE SMILER (Percy Wenrich)
Chase and Baker 3992 (65 note)
Classics of Ragtime 0003
Connorized 4472 (65 note)
Connorized 1340
Duo-Art 5551, Felix Arndt
Metro-Art 200398, Felix Arndt
QRS 30606

Royal 3129
Uni-Record 200399, Felix Arndt
Universal 3361 (65 note)

SMILES AND CHUCKLES (F. Henri Klickman)
Artempo 13135, Worth
Pianostyle 46701
Supertone 87498
US Music 8798

SMITHSONIAN RAG (Jon Jensen)
QRS

SNAPPIN' TURTLE RAG (Charles Cooke)
QRS 31389
QRS 31384 (m), *Rag Medley*

SNAPPY RAG (Ree Mercelle)
US Music 3840 (65 note)

SNEAKY PETE RAG (Charles L. Johnson)
Virtuoso 5379

SNEAKY SHUFFLES (Henry Lodge)
US Music 64640

SNOWBALL RAG (Nellie Stokes)
QRS X-3892 (65 note)
Universal 74707

SOCIETY RAG (Nat Johnson)
US Music 65460

SOFT PEDAL RAG (Sanford Robar, a.k.a. Lee S. Roberts)
QRS 100017, Sanford Robar (Lee S. Roberts)

SOFT SHOE RAG
Aeolian 102862 (65 note)
Aeolian 300138 (m)
Universal 79865 (65 note) (m)
Universal 300139 (m)

SOLILOQUY (Rube Bloom)
Ampico 68613, J. Milton Delcamp
Duo-Art 71477, Rube Bloom

SOME BLUES, FOR YOU ALL (Theron Bennett)
Diamond 18493
Universal 6303
US Music 7752

SOMETHING DOING (Scott Joplin and Scott Hayden)
Classics of Ragtime 0115
Connorized 4433 (65 note)
Connorized 10278, Scott Joplin
Lyric 2763
QRS 30396
QRS 30786
Royal 3389
Starr 4433
Supertone 860355
QRS X-3284 (65 note)
US Music 6055

SON SET RAG (Ted Browne)
88 N 27864
US Music 7746

SOUP AND FISH RAG (Pete Wendling and Harry Jentes)
Rhythmodik A-8112, Mabel Wayne

SOUR GRAPES (Will B. Morrison)
Connorized 4747 (65 note)
Connorized 2539

SOUTHERN BEAUTIES (Charles L. Johnson)
Chase and Baker 3925 (65 note)
Melographic 0365
QRS 30616

SOUTHERN SYMPHONY (Percy Wenrich)
QRS 03308 (65 note)

SPAGHETTI RAG (George Lyons and Bob Yosco)
Connorized 4495 (65 note)
Connorized 1520
QRS 8641, J. Lawrence Cook
US Music 64042

SPASM RAG (Torn Shea)
Classics of Ragtime 0135

SPECKLED SPIDER RAG (Harry French)
Kimball C-6237
QRS 03421 (65 note)
QRS 30975
US Music 3925 (65 note)

SPONGE (W. C. Simon)
Connorized 4600 (65 note)
Connorized 2219 (m), *Two-Step Special #4*
QRS 31139
US Music 65203
US Music 65679 (m), *States Rag Medley #8*

SPOTS (Edward A. Blake)
Connorized 4474 (65 note)
Connorized 1342

SPRING-TIME RAG (Paul Pratt)
Classics of Ragtime 0072
Metrostyle 302454
Universal 101259 (m), *Blue Fox Medley* (65 note)
Universal 302455
Universal 302573 (m), *Blue Fox Medley*
US Music 7672

SQUIRREL RAG (Paul Biese and F. Henri Klickman)
Connorized 2674 (m), *Ragpickins*
Supertone 863422
US Music 66322

STATES RAG MEDLEY #8
US Music 65679

STATES RAG MEDLEY #13
US Music 6300

STATES RAG MEDLEY #19
US Music 7065

STATES BLUE MEDLEY #21
US Music 7109

STATES RAG MEDLEY #66
US Music 8007

STEAMBOAT RAG (Ernie Burnett)
    QRS 32411
    QRS 32466 (m), Hillcrest
    US Music 66794

STEEPLECHASE RAG (James P. Johnson)
    Metro-Art 203178, James P. Johnson
    Universal 203179, James P. Johnson

STEWED CHICKEN RAG (Glenn C. Leap)
    US Music 8303

STEWED PRUNES (Oscar Lorraine)
    US Music 64623

STOPTIME RAG (Scott Joplin)
    Classics of Ragtime 0044
    QRS 03248 (65 note)
    QRS 30786
    US Music 3466 (65 note)

STRAIGHT GOODS (Charley Straight)
    Rolla Artis 50328, Billie King (Charley Straight)

STRATFORD HUNCH (Jelly Roll Morton)
    Vocalstyle 50485, Jelly Roll Morton

STRENUOUS LIFE (Scott Joplin)
    Classics of Ragtime 0010
    Connorized 4090 (65 note)
    QRS X-3625 (65 note)

SUCH IS LIFE (Charles Cooke)
    QRS 32452
    Universal 101249 (65 note)
    Universal 302493
    US Music 7816
    US Music 8007 (m), *States Rag Medley #66*

SUGAR CANE RAG (Scott Joplin)
    Classics of Ragtime 0017
    Connorized 4421 (65 note)

SUGAR LUMP RAG (Fred Bryan)
    Artempo 2206, Steve Williams
    Electra 85105 (m), *Fox Trot Medley #2*
    Pianostyle 35146
    US Music 7024
    Victory 1289

SUMMER BREEZE (James Scott)
    Classics of Ragtime 0156

SUNBURST RAG (James Scott)
    Classics of Ragtime 0158
    Kimball B-6794
    Supertone 822361
    US Music 2261 (65 note)
    US Music 62261
    US Music 1052 (m)

SUNFLOWER BABE (Fred Heltman)
    QRS 30745

SUNFLOWER RAG (Percy Wenrich)
    QRS 31063
    Universal 96985 (m), *Rag Medley #21*

US Music 64979
US Music 65679 (m), *States Rag Medley #8*

SUNFLOWER SLOW DRAG (Scott Joplin and Scott Hayden)
    American 1072
    Angelus 25330 (65 note)
    Chase and Baker 637 (65 note)
    Classics of Ragtime 0109
    Connorized 4082 (65 note)
    Connorized 844
    Sterling 271 (65 note)
    Universal 8479 (65 note)
    Virtuoso 4555 (65 note)
    Virtuoso 5602 (m), *Scott Joplin's Best Rags*

SUNFLOWER TICKLE (Dolly Richmond)
    US Music 2063 (65 note)

SUNSET RAG (Fred M. Bryan)
    Electra 85105 (m), *Fox Trot Medley #2*
    QRS 31760

SUNSHINE CAPERS (Roy Bargy)
    Imperial 513080, Roy Bargy
    Melodee 204003, Roy Bargy

SUNSHINE FROM THE FINGERS (Zez Confrey)
    QRS 9167, Zez Confrey

SUPERIOR RAG (Jelly Roll Morton)
    Classics of Ragtime 0124

SURE FIRE RAG (Henry Lodge)
    Master Record 703

SWAMPTOWN SHUFFLE (H. W. Jones)
    Connorized 4068

SWANEE RAG (Charles L. Johnson)
    88 N 99105 (m), *Rag Medley #25*
    Kimball B-7075
    US Music 65321

SWANEE RIPPLES RAG (Walter Blaufuss)
    Aeolian 301268
    Artempo 1477, Steve Williams
    Connorized 2604
    Electra 80685
    Kimball C-6553
    Metro-Art 201804, Paul Paris
    QRS 31335
    QRS 100048, Pierre LaFontaine
    Rose Valley 1020
    Supertone 857416
    Uni-Record 201805, Paul Paris
    Universal 301269
    US Music 65716

SWEET AND TENDER (Roy Bargy)
    Imperial 512980, Roy Bargy

SWEET PICKENS (Charley Straight)
    Imperial 510740, Charley Straight
    Metrostyle-Themodist 303374
    Music Note 1078
    Universal 303375

SWEET PICKLES (Theron Bennett)
Chase and Baker 3867 (65 note)

SWEET POTATOES RAG (Justin Ringleben)
QRS X-3742 (65 note)
QRS 30540

SWEETMEATS (Percy Wenrich)
QRS 30833

SWEETNESS (Fannie B. Woods, a.k.a. Charles L. Johnson)
Barkeroll 003
Connorized 2319
Connorized 2348 (m), *Broadway Melodies*
QRS 31301
Rhythmodik B-5302, Gumble and Arno
Supertone 854349
US Music 65449

SWINGY RAG (Joseph Fecher)
Perfection 86518, Joseph Fecher

SWIPESY CAKEWALK (Scott Joplin and Arthur Marshall)
Classics of Ragtime 0045
Connorized 4087 (65 note)
QRS 3988 (65 note)
QRS 30328

SYCAMORE RAG (Scott Joplin)
Classics of Ragtime 0014
Connorized 4320 (65 note)
QRS X-3283 (65 note)
QRS 30395

SYNCOPATED FOX TROT (E. S. Teal)
Kimball A-7076

SYNCOPATED SYMPHONY (Duke Baier)
Keynote 30112, Pete Batesti

SYNCOPER (William E. Macquin)
Artempo 3296, Steve Williams
QRS 32255
Uni-Record 202049, William E. Macquin
US Music 7138

TANGLE FOOT RAG (Fleta Jan Brown)
QRS X-3607

TANGLEFOOT RAG (F. H. Losey)
Universal 95145 (m), *Rag Medley #14*
US Music 64513

TANTALIZER RAG (Frank S. Butler)
Connorized 20500, W. Arlington

TANTALIZING TINGLES (Mike Bernard and Sol Violinsky)
Supertone 860398
US Music 66098

TAR BABIES (Charles L. Johnson)
Connorized 9173
88 N 99105 (m), *Rag Medley #25*
Full Scale 9173
QRS 31233
US Music 64804

TAR BABY RAG (Gertrude Cady)
Aeolian 66125 (65 note)
Perforated D-1233
QRS X-3162 (65 note)
Virtuoso 4711 (65 note)

TATTERED MELODY RAG (Hilda Ossusky)
US Music 64686
US Music 65679 (m), *States Rag Medley #8*

TEASING THE CAT (Charles L. Johnson)
Artempo 10255, Howard Lutter
Kimball B-7099
Metro-Art 203018, Felix Arndt
Uni-Record 203019, Felix Arndt
US Music 8149

TEASING THE KLASSICS (Axel Christensen)
Recordo M-615270, Axel Christensen
US Music 11398, Axel Christensen

TEDDY IN THE JUNGLE (Edward J. Freeberg)
QRS 03242 (65 note)
QRS 30780

TEK-NIK-ALITY RAG (Arnold Johnson)
Imperial 512220, Arnold Johnson

TEMPTATION RAG (Henry Lodge)
Connorized 4482 (65 note)
Connorized 1407
Diamond 1913
Full Scale 4853
Imperial 04414
Kimball B-5120
Kimball F-6154 (m), *King of Ragtime*
Melographic 01874
Metrostyle 79031 (65 note)
Metrostyle-Themodist 91532
Perfection 77550
QRS 03208 (65 note)
QRS 30750
QRS 9967, Dick Watson
Supertone 830347
Triumph 7799 (m), *Ragtime Grace*
Universal 76615 (65 note)
Universal 91535
US Music 63047
Virtuoso 80279

TEN PENNY RAG (Clarence Brandon and Billy Smythe)
QRS 41672 (m), *Popular Medley #3*

TENNESSEE JUBILEE (Thomas Broady)
Classics of Ragtime 0163
Connorized 4095 (65 note)
QRS 3483 (65 note)

TENNESSEE TANTALIZER (Charles Hunter)
Connorized 4091 (65 note)

TENTH INTERVAL RAG (Ted Eastwood and Harry Ruby)
Aeolian 301234
Metro-Art 202992, Ted Eastwood
Rolla Artis 50060, Phil Goldberg
Universal 301235

TEXAS FOX TROT (Dave Guion)
    Ampico 54853, Muriel Pollock
    Artempo 13145, Howard Lutter
    Connorized 20625, A. Hyland
    Metro-Art 203406, Rudy Erlebach and Herzog
    Rhythmodik E-19383, Lew Pollack
    Universal 203407, Erlebach and Herzog

TEXAS RAG (C. W. Jackson)
    Angelus 25314
    Universal 69055 (65 note)
    Universal 87135

TEXAS STEER RAG (George Botsford)
    Connorized 4515 (65 note)
    Connorized 1609
    Virtuoso 5989

THAT BLISSFUL RAG (George H. Bliss)
    QRS 100110, George H. Bliss

THAT BULL FROG RAG (George Thomas)
    Kimball 7203
    Rolla Artis 50667, Norman Weyand

THAT CONTAGIOUS RAG (Edward J. Mellinger)
    Connorized 2800 (m), *Raggy Rags Medley*
    QRS 31386 (m), *Rag Medley*

THAT CORRUGATED RAG (Edward Mellinger)
    US Music 5138 (65 note)
    US Music 65138

THAT DAWGGONE RAG (Maurice Smith)
    Supertone 863350
    Supertone 870765 (m), *Popular Rag Medley*
    US Music 66350
    US Music 7065 (m), *States Rag Medley #19*

THAT DEMON RAG (Russell Smith)
    Connorized 3158 (65 note)
    Connorized 3189 (m), *One-Step Medley #8*
    QRS 31145
    US Music 65515

THAT DEVILISH GLIDE (R. G. Grady)
    QRS 31342
    Starr 924

THAT DREAMY RAG (Bernie Adler)
    QRS 30702
    Universal 77309 (65 note)

THAT EASY RAG (Edward J. Mellinger)
    QRS 32064

THAT ECCENTRIC RAG (see ECCENTRIC)

THAT ENTERTAINING RAG (Arthur Wellesley)
    QRS 31218
    US Music 5552

THAT GIGGLIN' RAG (Howard Githens)
    Connorized 2700
    US Music 65569
    Virtuoso 81106

THAT GOSH-DARNED TWO STEP RAG (M. K. Miller)
    Aeolian 1390, Clyde Ridge (actually recut of Supertone 10036)
    Connorized 2799
    Kimball B-6855
    QRS 31702
    Supertone 10036
    Supertone 859398
    Triumph 10307
    US Music 65998

THAT HAND PLAYED RAG (David Silverman and Arthur Ward; see MISSOURI RAG)
    QRS 100107, David H. Silverman

THAT IRRESISTIBLE RAG (Fay Parker)
    QRS 31637 (m), *All Seasons One-Step Medley*
    US Music 66383

THAT LEFT-HAND RAG (Charles Humfeld)
    Connorized 2232
    Electra 6712
    Full Scale 16073
    Full Scale 17547 (m), *Latest Ragtime Hits #2*

THAT NATURAL RAG (Ettore Fisichelli)
    Connorized 4620 (65 note)
    QRS 31232
    US Music 65332

THAT PECULIAR RAG (F. M. Fagan)
    Connorized 1731 (m), *Honeysuckle Medley*
    Diamond 12023
    Full Scale 11913
    Melographic 4904
    QRS 41369
    Selected 32
    Universal 96435
    US Music 64773
    US Music 65293 (m), *States Medley #2*

THAT PLEASING RAG (J. Fred O'Connor)
    Electra 80106
    US Music 65232
    QRS 31169

THAT RAG (Ted Browne)
    Autopiano 10369 (65 note)
    Connorized 4384 (65 note)
    Electra 75709
    QRS X-3920 (65 note)
    QRS 30612
    Universal 75709 (65 note)

THAT SCANDALOUS RAG (Edwin Kendall)
    Electra 80318
    QRS 31379 (m), *Rag Medley*
    US Music 65794

THAT SNEAKY CREEPY TUNE (Egbert Van Alstyne)
    QRS 200282, Egbert Van Alstyne

THAT SPANISH RAG (Seymour Furth)
    Ampico 2641, Seymour Furth
    Connorized 4490 (65 note)
    Connorized 1495

Full Scale 6893
Metrostyle-Themodist 92391
Rhythmodik B-1462, Seymour Furth
Royal 3128
Universal 77809 (65 note)
Universal 92395

THAT TANGO RAG (C. Roy Larson)
US Music 66459

THAT TEASIN' RAG (Joe Jordan)
Connorized 4478 (65 note)
Connorized 1370
Metrostyle 77667 (m), *Rag Medley #2*
QRS 04102 (65 note)
QRS 40795
Universal 94345 (m), *Rag Medley #2*
US Music 2188 (65 note)
Virtuoso 5953 (65 note)
Virtuoso 6050 (m), *Airy Airs* (65 note)

THAT TICKLIN' RAG (Mike Bernard)
Melographic 4683
Metrostyle-Themodist 93451
QRS 30891
QRS 9889 (m)
QRS 03344 (65 note)
Universal 78215 (65 note)
Universal 93455
US Music 64660

THAT TIRED RAG (Charlotte Blake)
QRS 03428 (65 note)
QRS 30983

THAT TUNEFUL RAG (Buel Risinger)
US Music 65006
US Music 65679 (m), *States Rag Medley #8*

THAT'S A PLENTY (Lew Pollack)
88 N 24923
Electra 80674
Connorized 20768, H. Claar with Billy Munson
Marvel 1012
Metrostyle-Themodist 301228
Pianostyle 35614
QRS 9584, J. Lawrence Cook
Rhythmodik E-11892, Pete Wendling and W. E. D.
Rhythmodik J-12295 (m), *Medley #16,* Pete Wendling
Universal 301229
US Music 6649

38th STREET RAG (a.k.a. LES COPELAND'S RAG, Les Copeland)
Metro-Art 200296, Les Copeland
Metrostyle 102132 (65 note)
Metrostyle 300006
Rolla Artis 50067, Phil Goldberg)
Universal 79727 (65 note)
Universal 300007

THOROUGHBRED RAG (Joseph Lamb)
Classics of Ragtime 0093

THOSE HARMELODIC BLUES (a.k.a. HEARTS AND HANDS, Phil Goldberg)
US Music 28939, Phil Goldberg

THE THRILLER (May Aufderheide)
Angelus 25770 (65 note)
Angelus 90172
Metrostyle 79453
QRS 03288 (65 note)
QRS 30830
Universal 77727 (65 note)
Universal 92775
US Music 2992 (65 note)

TICKLE THE IVORIES (Wallie Herzer)
Ampico 20777 (m), *Popular Ragtime Hits*
Ampico 68433 (m), *Ziegfeld Follies,* Fairchild and Rainger
Autokrat 60240
Connorized 2587
Diamond l953
Full Scale 19882
Full Scale 20777 (m), *Popular Ragtime Hits*
Metrostyle 104504 (65 note)
Metrostyle-Themodist 301154
Monarch 1044
Pianostyle 35147
Popular Roll 10917
QRS 31339
QRS 31366 (m), *Tango Medley*
QRS 100066, Joe Collins
Supertone 857342
Universal 100889 (65 note)
Universal 301155
US Music 65742

TICKLED TO DEATH (Charles Hunter)
Aeolian 8189 (65 note)
American 745
Chase and Baker 1363 (65 note)
Connorized 20349, W. Arlington
Full Scale 14343
Kimball C-5688
Otto Higel 010606 (m), *Rag Medley #1*
Simplex 1187 (65 note)
Universal 88625
Virtuoso 4746 (65 note)

TIDDLE DE WINKS (Melville Morris)
Autokrat 60304
Autokrat 29765 (m), *Fox Trot Medley #12*
DeLuxe 15431, Margaret Schlesselman
Ideal 1446
Metro-Art 203052, George Gershwin
Metrostyle-Themodist 303004
Metrostyle-Themodist 105244 (m), *A High Roller*
Rolla Artis 50337, Billie King (Charley Straight)
Universal 303005
Universal 303032 (m), *A High Roller*
US Music 8187

TOAD STOOL RAG (Joseph Lamb)
Classics of Ragtime 0089

TOBOGGAN RAG (John F. Barth)
US Music 65608

TOKIO RAG (Henry Lodge)
American 12032
Connorized 4633 (65 note)
Metrostyle 101892 (65 note)
Metrostyle 00512
QRS 31286
Universal 79567 (65 note)
Universal 99515
US Music 65405

TOM AND JERRY RAG (Jerry Cammack)
Classics of Ragtime 0004

TOM CAT RAG
Vocalstyle 13268, Dick Osgood

TOOTS (Felix Arndt)
Angelus 91554
Artempo 12915, Lester Albertson
Connorized 20370, C. Herman Kornbau with
    Gladys Aldrich
Metro-Art 201842, Felix Arndt
Metrostyle-Themodist 301474
Uni-Record 201843, Felix Arndt
Universal 301475

TOP LINER RAG (Joseph Lamb)
Artempo 8834, Howard Lutter
Classics of Ragtime 0027
Metro-Art 202626, Felix Arndt
Uni-Record 202627, Felix Arndt
US Music 7671
US Music 8007 (m), *States Rag Medley #66*

A TOTALLY DIFFERENT RAG (May Aufderheide)
QRS X-3380 (65 note)
QRS 30931
QRS 41654 (m), *Aufderheide Melodic Ideas*
US Music 64230

TOWN TALK (Elmer Olson)
US Music 9100

TREBOR'S STOMP (Pete Diller)
Classics of Ragtime 0140

TRIANGLE JAZZ BLUES (Irwin Leclere)
Kimball 7135
QRS 100631, Max Kortlander

TRICKY TRIX (Harry Jentes)
Melodee 204149, Harry Jentes

TRILBY RAG (Carey Morgan)
Connorized 3070
Metrostyle-Themodist 6236
Perfection 86508, Gertrude Baum
Pianostyle 35205
QRS 100461, Lee S. Roberts
QRS 32257
QRS 32298 (m), *Eulalia One-Step Medley*
Universal 6237

TROUBADOUR RAG (James Scott)
Classics of Ragtime 0166
Music Note 1175

TROUBLE MAKER RAG (Claude Messinger)
Kimball B-6790
QRS 03332 (65 note)
QRS 30877
US Music 66582 (Kieselhorst K-5002 is same)

TROUBLE RAG (Will Morrison and C. Duane Crabb)
QRS 03028 (65 note)
QRS 30140
US Music 1069 (65 note)

TROUBLESOME IVORIES (Eubie Blake)
QRS CEL-124, Eubie Blake

TRY ME (Charley Straight)
QRS 100406, Charley Straight
Rolla Artis 50281, Billie King (Charley Straight)

TURKISH TOWEL RAG (Thomas S. Allen)
QRS 31202
US Music 65210

TURKISH TROPHIES (Sara B. Egan)
Kimball C-5256

12th STREET RAG (Euday Bowman)
Aeolian 1022, Bob Sawyer
Ampico 205161 (m), *Biminy,* J. Milton Delcamp
Artempo 74130
Connorized 20374, W. Arlington
DeLuxe 15486, Frank Black
Kimball B-6958
Kimball 10027
Majestic 1371
Melodee 3893, Edythe Baker
Metrostyle-Themodist 303342
Pianostyle 10903
Pianostyle 47631
Pop 1234, Bud Sawyer
QRS 1188, Max Kortlander
QRS 1188, J. Lawrence Cook
QRS CEL-119, Liberace
Universal 303343
US Music 7198
US Music 8733
Vocalstyle 11758, Hunt and Davidson

TWILIGHT RAG (James P. Johnson)
Metro-Art 203274, James P. Johnson and Edwin E. Wilson

TWIST AND TWIRL (Les Copeland)
Metro-Art 202754, Les Copeland
Universal 202755, Les Copeland

TWO-KEY RAG (Joe Hollander)
Artempo 9355, Howard Lutter
Connorized 3354
DeLuxe 15402, Ed Sheppard and Charles Shisler
Kimball B-7067
Metrostyle-Themodist 302848
QRS 32665

Rolla Artis 50288, Billie King (Charley Straight)
Universal 302849

U-TE-ZER RAG (E. Mutchler)
US Music 6820

UNCLE TOM'S CABIN (Harry A. Tierney)
Electra 76600
QRS 03445 (65 note)
QRS 31001
Universal 95905 (m), *Rag Medley #16*
US Music 64871
US Music 65679 (m), *States Rag Medley #8*

UNIVERSAL RAG (George Botsford)
Angelus 25987 (65 note)
Metrostyle-Themodist 10382 (65 note)
Metrostyle-Themodist 300282
Universal 100019 (65 note)
Universal 300283

UNIVERSAL RAG (Charley Straight)
QRS 100801, Charley Straight

UNIVERSAL RAG (Frank Wooster)
QRS X-3457 (65 note)
QRS 30441

UNIVERSITY RAG (Marie A. White)
Kimball 6055
QRS 31110
US Music 65063

VANITY RAG (Paul Pratt)
QRS 03152 (65 note)
QRS 30708
US Music 62299

VARIETY RAG (Harry A. Tierney)
Perfection 80277
US Music 65625

VENTURA RAG (Louis Mentel)
QRS 03055 (65 note)
QRS 30649

VESTAL PRESS RAG (Jon Jensen)
QRS CU-172, Jon Jensen

VIVACITY RAG (Frank C. Keithley)
US Music 64785

WAILANA RAG (Paul Pratt)
US Music 7917

WAIMAN RAG (J. R. Shannon)
Connorized 4521 (65 note)
Connorized 1639
Universal 78069 (m), *Rag Medley #17* (65 note)
Universal 93015 (m), *Rag Medley #17*
US Music 64160

WALHALLA (Paul Pratt)
Melographic 4601 (65 note)
QRS 30918
US Music 3555 (65 note)

WALL STREET RAG (Scott Joplin)
Classics of Ragtime 0057
Master Record 653
Virtuoso 5952 (65 note)

WASH DAY RAG (Charles Goeddel)
US Music 66618

WASHIN' BLUES (Frank Black)
DeLuxe 15482, Frank Black

WATERMELON TRUST (Harry C. Thompson)
Virtuoso 5121 (65 note)

WEDDING BELLS RAG (Al B. Coney)
Supertone 850300
Universal 96475 (m), *Rag Medley #19*
US Music 65000

WEEPING WILLOW RAG (H. A. Fischler)
QRS 03417 (65 note)
QRS 30970
US Music 65400

WEEPING WILLOW (Scott Joplin)
Classics of Ragtime 0117
Connorized 10277, Scott Joplin
Connorized 4411 (65 note)
Connorized 400
Connorized 2016
QRS X-3303 (65 note)
QRS 30404
US Music 65482

WEIRD RAG (Phil Schwartz)
QRS 31219
US Music 65353

WHIPPED CREAM RAG (Percy Wenrich)
Connorized 4748 (65 note)
Connorized 2541
Herbert 81283
Metrostyle 103154 (65 note)
Metrostyle 300244
Pianostyle 35531
Rhythmodik A-8512, Pete Wendling
Royal 4294
Supertone 856315
Universal 100005 (65 note)
Universal 300245
US Music 65615

WHIRLWIND (J. Russel Robinson)
US Music 65194

WHISTLES RAG (Trevor Sauks)
US Music 3224 (65 note)

WHITEWASH MAN (Jean Schwartz)
Connorized 4451 (65 note)
Connorized 1166
QRS 03180 (65 note)
QRS 30727
Royal 4034
Supertone 811351

US Music 61151
Virtuoso 5927 (65 note)

WHITTLING REMUS (Thomas Broady)
Chase and Baker 201 (65 note)
Classics of Ragtime 0164
Perforated D-522
Virtuoso 5179 (65 note)

WHO LET THE COWS OUT? (Charles Humfeld)
Connorized 4509 (65 note)
Connorized 1550
Connorized 1515 (m), *Our Own Medley*
Universal 78069 (m), *Rag Medley #17* (65 note)
Universal 93015 (m), *Medley #17*

WHO'S WHO (Melville Morris)
US Music 8545

WHOA NELLIE (George Gould)
QRS 32214
US Music 7352
US Music 7426 (m), *States Popular Medley #43*

WHOA! YOU HEIFFER (Al Verges)
Connorized 4194 (65 note)
Connorized 1438
Connorized 3081 (m), *Sterling One-Step Medley*

WIG WAG RAG (Harry Thompson)
QRS 31166
US Music 65374

WIGGLE RAG (George Botsford)
QRS 03303 (65 note)
QRS 30847
US Music 3360 (65 note)

WILD CAT BLUES (Thomas Waller and Clarence Williams)
Automatic A-1418

WILD CHERRIES (Ted Snyder)
Aeolian 77479 (65 note)
American 4066 (m), *Popular Favorites Series*
Aristo 4066 (m), *Popular Favorites Ragtime*
Connorized 4453 (65 note)
Connorized 1154
Electra 76924
Full Scale 3513
Herbert 80262
Melographic 01577
Metrostyle-Themodist 78611 (65 note)

QRS 03074 (65 note)
QRS 100030, Sanford Robar (Lee S. Roberts)
QRS 30658
Rhythmodik B-343, Hans Hanke
Universal 90355
US Music 1137 (65 note)
US Music 61137
US Music 65399 (m), *Rag Potpourri*
Virtuoso 80282
Vocalstyle 1164

WILD FLOWER RAG (Clarence Williams)
Kimball 7143

WILD MAN RAG (Edward J. Mellinger)
Connorized 2800 (m), *Raggy Rags*

WILL O' THE WISP RAG (Richard Haasz)
Melographic 02639
QRS 03458 (65 note)
QRS 31015

WILLETT RAG (Herb Willett)
Universal S-2517

WILLIAM'S WEDDING (Harry A. Tierney)
QRS 31114

WINTER GARDEN RAG (Abe Olman)
Imperial 185
Supertone 856389
US Music 65689

YANKEE DOODLE RAG (Garfield Wilson)
Kimball B-5694

YANKEE LAND (Max Hoffman)
Connorized 4210 (65 note)
QRS 30086
Universal 65835 (65 note)

YELLOW ROSE RAG (Terry Waldo)
Echoes 210

ZIG ZAG RAG (H. Anderson)
QRS 20659

ZU ZU RAG (Max Fischler)
Ampico 52603, Victor Arden
Kimball A-7080
Rhythmodik E-17663, Victor Arden
Welte B-3880, Ted Oliver

# APPENDIX 3

## Published Rags in America

Back of an 1899 music store. Sheet music is stocked in racks on wall behind bookkeeper.

| Title | Composer | Date | Publisher | City |
|---|---|---|---|---|
| "A" NATURAL | Joe Mauro | December 28, 1908 | H. A. Triggs | Denver, CO |
| AERO RAG | Bert F. Grant | April 30, 1910 | O'Neil and Story | Boston, MA |
| AEROPLANE RAG | Jack Glogau | January 25, 1913 | Will Rossiter | Chicago, IL |
| AFFINITY RAG | Irene Cozad | September 19, 1910 | J. W. Jenkins | Kansas City, MO |
| AFRICAN 400 | Charles J. Roberts | April 26, 1909 | Carl Fischer | New York, NY |
| AFRICAN HUNTER | Edwin Kendall | April 8, 1909 | Seminary Music | New York, NY |
| AFRICAN PAS' | Maurice Kirwin | December 29, 1902 | John Stark and Son | St. Louis, MO |
| AFRICAN REVERIE | H. B. Newton | September 8, 1900 | F. A. Mills | New York, NY |
| AFRICAN RIPPLES | Thomas "Fats" Waller | April 20, 1931 | Joe Davis | New York, NY |
| AFRICAN SMILE | Paul Eno | May 5, 1906 | Walter Jacobs | Boston, MA |
| AGGRAVATION RAG | George L. Cobb | March 1, 1910 | Walter Jacobs | Boston, MA |
| AGITATION RAG | Robert Hampton | January 10, 1915 | Stark Music Company | St. Louis, MO |
| AIN'T I LUCKY | Bess Rudisell | April 18, 1905 | Jerome H. Remick | Detroit, MI |
| AKRON RAG | Melvin Champion | December 16, 1911 | M. D. Swisher | Philadelphia, PA |
| ALABAMA HOP | Phil H. Kaufman | September 8, 1908 | Self | Los Angeles, CA |
| ALABAMA JIGGER | Ed Claypoole | January 28, 1913 | Joseph W. Stern | New York, NY |
| ALABAMA RAG | Joseph F. Lamb | 1964 | Mills Music | New York, NY |
| ALABAMA RAG | Wynona Smith | 1918 | James S. White | Boston, MA |
| ALABAMA SHUFFLE | Roy Barton | February 4, 1910 | Sunlight Music | Chicago, IL |
| ALABAMA SLIDE | Charles L. Johnson | July 21, 1915 | Forster Music | Chicago, IL |
| ALASKA RAG | Alec M. Malin | August 4, 1915 | Echo Music Publishing Co | Seattle, WA |
| ALASKAN RAG | Joseph F. Lamb | June 27, 1966 | Oak Publishing | New York, NY |
| ALFALFA RAG | Frank W. Ryan | July 25, 1910 | Self | Troy, KS |
| ALHAMBRA | George Nageleisen | May 25, 1912 | Self | Arion, OH |
| ALHAMBRA RAG | Roy Steventon and C. Morris Haigh | March 14, 1910 | Steventon and Haigh | Covington, KY |
| ALISON RAG | Karl Edgar Johnson | April 14, 1916 | Nomad Publishing | St. Joseph, MO |
| ALL OF A TWIST | Billy Mayerl | August 21, 1925 | Sam Fox | Cleveland, OH |
| ALL OF A TWIST RAG | Frank E. Hersom | 1920 | Walter Jacobs | Boston, MA |
| ALL THE GRAPES | James Fahy | July 1, 1908 | Self | Springfield, MO |
| ALL THE MONEY | Raymond Birch | March 13, 1908 | Charles L. Johnson | Kansas City, MO |

Charles L. Johnson

| Title | Composer | Date | Publisher | City |
|---|---|---|---|---|
| ALLEN GLIDE | Louise Allen | 1915 | Syndicate Music | St. Louis, MO |
| ALLIGATOR BAIT | Hal G. Nichols | January 27, 1912 | F. A. Mills | New York, NY |
| AMAZON RAG | Teddy Hahn | February 11, 1904 | Miller–Arnold | Cincinnati, OH |
| AMERICAN BEAUTY | Joseph F. Lamb | December 27, 1913 | Stark Music Company | St. Louis, MO |
| AMERICAN DANCERS | Bob Alden | July 2, 1908 | Jerome H. Remick | New York, NY |
| AMERICAN JUBILEE | Ed Claypoole | June 24, 1916 | Broadway Music | New York, NY |
| AMERICAN RAG | John N. Lang | September 6, 1917 | Self | Indianapolis, IN |
| AMERICAN SUNSHINE RAG | Louis Altman | March 27, 1917 | Altman and Fuss | Patchogue, NY |
| ANGEL FOOD | Al F. Marzian | December 16, 1911 | Forster Music | Chicago, IL |
| ANNIVERSARY RAG | Glyn Williams | December 7, 1915 | Self | Columbus, OH |
| ANOMA | Ford Dabney | December 14, 1910 | Jerome H. Remick | New York, NY |
| ANTIQUARY | Billy Mayerl | March 9, 1926 | Sam Fox | Cleveland, OH |
| ANY OLD RAG | Bert Beyerstedt | 1915 | Self | Jacksonville, FL |
| ANY OLD RAG | Richard Goosman | June 2, 1909 | Self | Cincinnati, OH |
| APEDA RAG | Dave Harris | March 12, 1913 | Waterson, Berlin, and Snyder | New York, NY |
| APPETITE PETE | H. H. Kratz | December 13, 1909 | F. B. Haviland | New York, NY |
| APPLE BLOSSOM RAG | Hattie Turner | 1914 | Dugdale | Washington, DC |
| APPLE JACK | Charles L. Johnson | April 7, 1909 | Vandersloot Music | Williamsport, PA |
| APPLE SASS RAG | Harry Belding | 1914 | Buck and Lowney | St. Louis, MO |
| APRIL FOOL RAG | Jean Schwartz | May 1, 1911 | Jerome H. Remick | Detroit, MI |
| APRON RAG | George D. Lewis | July 15, 1911 | Maurice Shapiro | New York, NY |
| ARABIAN RAG | George Gould | November 2, 1917 | Sherman, Clay | San Francisco, CA |
| ARCADIA RAG | Albert L. Klein | March 14, 1914 | Self | St. Louis, MO |
| ARCTIC SUNSET | Joseph F. Lamb | 1964 | Mills Music | New York, NY |
| ARLENE'S DOILIES | Thomas P. Quinn | November 6, 1980 | Self | Los Angeles, CA |
| ARM BREAKER | Fred Rose | April 7, 1923 | Jack Mills | New York, NY |
| ARMADILLO | Clarence F. Brown | May 29, 1911 | Thomas Goggan and Brothers | Galveston, TX |
| ASHY AFRICA | Percy Wenrich | October 29, 1903 | Buck and Carney | Chicago, IL |
| AT A COFFEE COLORED PARTY | O. S. Wald | February 6, 1899 | Canton MPC | Canton, OH |
| AT A RAGTIME RECEPTION | Ben M. Jerome | March 21, 1900 | Howley, Haviland | New York, NY |
| AUDACITY | Zez Confrey | October 17, 1936 | Robbins Music | New York, NY |
| AUNT DINAH'S HEAD RAG | W. R. Sawyer | February 27, 1912 | Self | Russell, WY |
| AUNT JEMIMA'S BIRTHDAY | Rube Bloom | May 15, 1931 | Robbins Music | New York, NY |
| AUTO RAG | T. H. Trenholm | June 2, 1905 | Self | Cambridge, MA |
| AVIATION RAG | Mark Janza | 1910 | Keithley–Marzian Company | Louisville, KY |
| AVIATOR RAG | Irene M. Giblin | December 15, 1910 | Jerome H. Remick | Detroit, MI |
| AXEL GREASE | Axel Christensen | January 26, 1924 | Jack Mills | New York, NY |
| B and O RAG | John L. Armsey | February 19, 1917 | Self | Akron, OH |
| BACHELOR'S BUTTON | W. C. Powell | May 3, 1909 | J. W. Jenkins | Kansas City, MO |
| BACK TO LIFE | Charles Hunter | November 18, 1905 | Charles K. Harris | New York, NY |
| BAG OF RAGS | W. R. McKanlass | January 22, 1912 | Joseph M. Daly | Boston, MA |
| BALE O' COTTON | Mark Janza | December 18, 1914 | A. F. Manian | New Albany, IN |
| BALTIMORE BLUES | Henry Lodge | June 20, 1917 | Jerome H. Remick | New York, NY |

| Title | Composer | Date | Publisher | City |
|---|---|---|---|---|
| BALTIMORE BUCK | Harry Brown | October 13, 1905 | Vinton Music | Boston, MA |
| BALTIMORE CONVENTION RAG | Stephen Corbin | October 1, 1912 | H. Kirkus Dugdale | Washington, DC |
| BALTIMORE TODALO | Eubie Blake | 1975 | Eubie Blake Music | New York, NY |
| BANANA PEEL RAG | Gus Winkler | January 24, 1913 | Forster Music | Chicago, IL |
| BANDIT KING RAG | G. W. Haskins and J. A. Poston | November 20, 1914 | Mellinger Music | St. Louis, MO |
| BANJO RAG | E. K. Bennett | April 13, 1912 | Joseph Krolage Music | Cincinnati, OH |
| BANTAM STEP | Harry Jentes | February 21, 1916 | Shapiro, Bernstein | New York, NY |
| BARBEQUE RAG | Mamie Thornton | 1909 | Emerson Music | Cincinnati, OH |
| BARBED WIRE RAG | Herbert Spencer | March 14, 1910 | Jerome H. Remick | NewYork, NY |
| BARBER POLE RAG | Charles L. Johnson | April 3, 1911 | Hal G. Nichols Company | Denver, CO |
| BARBER SHOP RAG | Bill Krenz | January 19, 1953 | Mills Music | New York, NY |
| BARNYARD RAG | Timothy Jones | December 15, 1913 | John T. Hall | New York, NY |
| BARREL HOUSE RAG | Fate Marable and Clarence William | November 9, 1916 | Williams and Piron | New Orleans, LA |
| BASEBALL RAG | Mata Wulff | 1910 | Self | Indianapolis, IN |
| BEAN SOUP BLUES | Jess H. Valentine | April 19, 1918 | Pace and Handy | Memphis, TN |
| BEAR CLUB RAG | Joseph Hensberg | January 8, 1912 | Empire Music | Seattle, WA |
| BEAR TRACKS | Edward C. Barroll | April 10, 1930 | Rubank | Chicago, IL |
| BEAUTIFUL SENSATION RAG | Lew J. Novy | October 9, 1916 | National Music | Chicago, IL |
| BEEDLE-UM-BO | Raymond Birch | December 17, 1908 | Charles L. Johnson | Kansas City, MO |
| BEES WAX | Harry J. Lincoln | August 19, 1911 | Vandersloot Music | Williamsport, PA |
| BEHAVE YOURSELF | Roy Bargy | June 27, 1922 | Sam Fox | Cleveland, OH |
| BELL HOP RAG | Frederick Bryan | December 30, 1914 | Joseph W. Stern | New York, NY |
| BENZINE RAG | Edward A. Denish | October 10, 1910 | Harrison MPC | Providence, RI |
| BIG BEN | Thomas S. Allen | 1916 | Walter Jacobs | Boston, MA |
| BIG SANDY RAG | Verne Bestor | | | |
| BILLIE RITCHIE RAG | Margaret E. Crump | 1915 | Self | |
| BILLIKEN RAG | E. J. Stark | February 21, 1913 | Stark Music Company | St. Louis, MO |
| BILLY POSSUM | Walter H. Wayland | April 8, 1909 | Self | Girard, KS |
| BILLY POSSUM RAG | B. Claude Davis | August 27, 1909 | Self | Valdosta, GA |
| BING! BING! | Mel B. Kaufman | January 20, 1915 | Plaza Music | New York, NY |
| BINGO RAG | F. H. Losey | March 28, 1910 | Vandersloot Music | Williamsport, PA |
| BIRD-BRAIN RAG | Joseph F. Lamb | 1964 | Mills Music | New York, NY |
| BIRDS' CARNIVAL | Zez Confrey | October 7, 1935 | Robbins Music | New York, NY |
| BLACK AND BLUE RAG | Hal G. Nichols | January 2, 1914 | Sam Fox | Cleveland, OH |
| BLACK AND WHITE RAG | George Botsford | 1908 | Jerome H. Remick | New York, NY |
| BLACK BAWL | Harry C. Thompson | June 16, 1905 | W. C. Polla | Chicago, IL |
| BLACK BEAUTY | Jean Schwartz | November 9, 1910 | Jerome H. Remick | Detroit, MI |
| BLACK CANARY | Harry A. Tierney | May 5, 1911 | Ted Snyder Company | New York, NY |
| BLACK CAT RAG | Lina Mumford | July 5, 1901 | Self | Grand Rapids, MI |
| BLACK CAT RAG | Frank Wooster and Ethyl B. Smith | September 7, 1905 | Frank Wooster Company | St. Louis, MO |
| BLACK CROW | Max Schuldt, Jr. | 1912 | Self | Chippewa Falls, WI |

| Title | Composer | Date | Publisher | City |
|---|---|---|---|---|
| BLACK CROW RAG | Tommy Moreland | April 24, 1914 | Self | Idaho Falls, ID |
| BLACK DEVIL RAG | C. C. Muth | March 27, 1919 | Self | Chicago, IL |
| BLACK DIAMOND RAG | Emmett E. Fawcett | December 26, 1908 | Groene Music | Cincinnati, OH |
| BLACK DIAMOND RAG | Harry J. Lincoln | September 23, 1914 | Vandersloot Music | Williamsport, PA |
| BLACK DIAMOND RAG | Henry Lodge | February 5, 1912 | M. Witmark and Sons | New York, NY |
| BLACK FEATHER | Irene M. Giblin O'Brien | November 13, 1908 | Vinton Music | Chicago, IL |
| BLACK HAND | Robert Hoffman | February 24, 1908 | John H. Keyser | New Orleans, LA |
| BLACK HAND RAG | George A. Norton | December 31, 1910 | Self | Denver, CO |
| BLACK HILLS RAG | Joseph Liljenberg | January 22, 1914 | Self | Lead, SD |
| BLACK KEY KAPERS | Silvio DeRienzo | January 7, 1929 | Alfred and Company | New York, NY |
| BLACK SMOKE | Charles L. Johnson | 1902 | Carl Hoffman Music | Kansas City, MO |
| BLACK WASP RAG | H. A. Fischler | February 21, 1911 | Vandersloot Music | Williamsport, PA |
| BLACKSMITH RAG | Rednip | April 14, 1920 | Ted Garton Music | Boston, MA |
| BLAME IT ON THE BLUES | Charles L. Cooke | March 3, 1914 | Jerome H. Remick | New York, NY |
| BLARNEY KISSES | Holmes Travis | June 10, 1911 | M. L. Carlson | Chicago, IL |
| BLIND BOONE'S SOUTHERN RAG MEDLEY #1 | Blind Boone | October 22, 1908 | Allen Music | Columbia, MO |
| BLIND BOONE'S SOUTHERN RAG MEDLEY #2 | Blind Boone | November 1, 1909 | Allen Music | Columbia, MO |
| BLUE BLAZES | Arthur L. Sizemore | July 8, 1909 | Victor Kremer | Chicago, IL |
| BLUE GOOSE | Raymond Birch | January 3, 1916 | Forster Music | Chicago, IL |
| BLUE GRASS RAG | Joseph F. Lamb | 1964 | Mills Music | New York, NY |
| BLUE GRASS RAG | Charley Straight | November 11, 1918 | Joe Morris | New York, NY |
| BLUE GRASS RAG | Ernest S. Williams | October 23, 1909 | Self | Boston, MA |
| BLUE JAY RAG | Frank Wooster | June 22, 1907 | Self | St. Louis, MO |
| BLUE MOON | Max Kortlander and Lee S. Roberts | May 9, 1918 | Lee S. Roberts | Chicago, IL |
| BLUE MOON TWO STEP | E. M. Cook | 1906 | H. A. Sturm | Cincinnati, OH |
| BLUE NOTE BLUES | Billy James | September 7, 1922 | F. B. Haviland | New York, NY |
| BLUE RIBBON RAG | May Aufderheide | October 3, 1910 | J. H. Aufderheide | Indianapolis, IN |
| BLUE RIBBON RAG | Irwin Dash | 1911 | Longbrake and Edwards | Philadelphia, PA |
| BLUE STREAK | Roy Bargy | 1921 | Forster Music | Chicago, IL |
| BLUE STREAK RAG | Richard Wegenhardt | November 5, 1912 | Self | Cincinnati, OH |
| BLUFFTON CARNIVAL RAG | Verdi Karns | August 14, 1899 | Self | Bluffton, IN |
| BLUIN' THE BLACK KEYS | Arthur Schutt | February 24, 1926 | Robbins–Engel | New York, NY |
| BOB'S CHILI RAG | Robert E. Cleary | November 11, 1921 | Self | Spokane, WA |
| BOBETTE | Bernard Barnes | August 4, 1926 | Weeks and Winge | San Francisco, CA |
| BOHEMIA RAG | Joseph F. Lamb | February 17, 1919 | Stark Music Company | St. Louis, MO |
| BOHEMIAN RAG | Gus Edwards and Louis Silvers | June 2, 1914 | Jerome H. Remick | New York, NY |
| BOILED OWL | Margaret Wooden | April 28, 1911 | Self | Flint, MI |
| BOLO RAG | Albert Gumble | November 11, 1908 | Jerome H. Remick | New York, NY |
| BOMBSHELL | Thomas R. Confare and Morris S. Silver | 1909 | Charles I. Davis | Cleveland, OH |
| BON TON | C. Luckeyth Roberts | May 7, 1915 | G. Ricordi | New York, NY |

| Title | Composer | Date | Publisher | City |
|---|---|---|---|---|
| BONE DRY | Sidney Landfield | November 15, 1918 | Jerome H. Remick | New York, NY |
| BONE HEAD BLUES | Leo Gordon | 1917 | Walter Jacobs | Boston, MA |
| BOOGIE RAG | Wilbur Sweatman | September 21, 1917 | Shapiro, Bernstein | New York, NY |
| BOOMERANG RAG | George Botsford | June 21, 1916 | Jerome H. Remick | New York, NY |
| BOOSTER | Mayhew L. Lake | December 12, 1913 | Carl Fischer | New York, NY |
| BORDER BLUES RAG | Guy A. Surber | October 6, 1916 | Self | Mercedes, TX |
| BORNEO RAG | Neil Moret | April 8, 1911 | Jerome H. Remick | Detroit, MI |
| BOUNCING ON THE KEYS | Ed Claypoole | December 31, 1924 | Jack Mills | New York, NY |
| BOWERY BUCK | Tom Turpin | March 6, 1899 | Robert DeYong | St. Louis, MO |
| BRAIN-STORM RAG | Bud Manchester | June 3, 1907 | Stark Music Company | New York, NY |
| BRAZILIAN NUT | Sol Wolerstein | May 5, 1915 | Jerome H. Remick | New York, NY |
| BREAK THE PIANO | Billy James | March 27, 1918 | Self | Philadelphia, PA |
| BREAKIN' THE PIANO | Billy James | May 20, 1922 | Jack Mills | New York, NY |
| BREEZE FROM ALABAMA | Scott Joplin | December 29, 1902 | John Stark and Son | St. Louis, MO |
| BRIC-A-BRAC RAG | Maurice Porcelain | 1906 | Vinton Music | Boston, MA |
| BRITTWOOD RAG | Eubie Blake | 1975 | Eubie Blake Music | New York, NY |
| BROADWAY RAG | Marcella A. Henry | October 1, 1917 | Christensen School | Chicago, IL |
| BROADWAY RAG | Eva Nieman | June 28, 1910 | Self | Cincinnati, OH |
| BROADWAY RAG | W. C. Powell | April2, 1909 | T. B. Harms | New York, NY |
| BROADWAY RAG | James Scott | January 3, 1922 | Stark Music Company | St. Louis, MO |
| BROKEN BUTTONS | Harrison E. Baumbaugh | September 24, 1925 | Jack Mills | New York, NY |
| BRONCO BILLY | Nell Wright Slaughter | October 7, 1914 | Bush and Gerts | Dallas, TX |
| BRONCHO BUCK | Edward C. Barroll | March 2, 1914 | Mid-West Music | St. Louis, MO |
| BROWNIE RAG | Frank Wooster and Max Wilkens | November 15, 1905 | Frank Wooster | St. Louis, MO |
| BRUN CAMPBELL EXPRESS | Tom Shea | June 27, 1966 | Oak Publishing | New York, NY |
| BRUSH CREEK RAG | Eleanora Beauchamp | July 25, 1913 | Geo. Jennings | Cincinnati, OH |
| BUBBLES | M. M. Nash | September 27, 1911 | Standard Music | Chicago, IL |
| BUCCANEER | Phil Kussel | March 15, 1911 | United Music Publishing | Cincinnati, OH |
| BUD RAG | Budd L. Cross | July 22, 1909 | Sam Fox | Cleveland, OH |
| BUDWEISER RAG | Grace Kuykendall | June 13, 1908 | Self | Morgantown, KY |
| BUFFALO DISH RAG | Bernisne G. Clements | September 23, 1910 | F. B. Haviland | New York, NY |
| BUFFALO MEANS BUSINESS | George L. Cobb | June 14, 1909 | Louis C. Snyder | Buffalo, NY |
| BUFFALO RAG | Tom Turpin | November 2, 1904 | Will Rossiter | Chicago, IL |
| BUG-HOUSE RAG | Randolph C. Newton and Will E. Skidmore | 1916 | Skidmore Music Company | Kansas City, MO |
| BUGAVUE RAG | George W. Fairman | 1902 | William Dowler | Marion, OH |
| BUGLE CALL RAG | Eubie Blake and Carey Morgan | January 27, 1916 | Joseph W. Stern | New York, NY |
| BUGS RAG | Nina B. Kohler | January 22, 1913 | Self | Sherman, TX |
| BULL DOG RAG | Geraldine Dobyns | November 19, 1908 | Anderson–Rienhardt Company | Memphis, TN |
| BULL MOOSE RAG | K. M. Gilham | November 12, 1912 | Self | Alameda, CA |
| BULLY RAG | James E. C. Kelly | February 10, 1911 | Kelly, Geiger, and Becker | Cincinnati, OH |
| BULLY RAG | J. Fred O'Connor | January 3, 1910 | F. A. Mills | New York, NY |

| Title | Composer | Date | Publisher | City |
|---|---|---|---|---|
| BUM RAG | J. Schiller | July 1, 1904 | Pioneer Music | Chicago, IL |
| BUMBLE BEE RAG | E. Clinton Keithley | 1909 | Keith Music | Louisville, KY |
| BUMBLE BEE RAG | Harry A. Tierney | November 24, 1909 | Ted Snyder Company | New York, NY |
| BUNCH OF BURR HEADS | Percy Fullinwider | 1903 | W. H. Willis | Cincinnati, OH |
| BUNCH OF NOISE | Louis Mentel | June 17, 1908 | Mentel Brothers | Cincinnati, OH |
| BUNDLE OF RAGS | Robert S. Roberts | December 17, 1897 | Phillip Kussel | Cincinnati, OH |
| BUNNY HUG RAG | Kenneth V. Abendana | January 20,1913 | Globe Music | New York, NY |
| BUNNY HUG RAG | George L. Cobb | August 4,1913 | Charles E. Roat Music | Battle Creek, MI |
| BUNNY HUG RAG | Harry DeCosta | May 1, 1912 | Waterson, Berlin, and Snyder | New York, NY |
| BUNNY-BOY | Eric C. Garry | November 22, 1912 | Joseph W. Stern | New York, NY |
| BURNING RAGS | Bess Rudisell | July 1, 1904 | Samuel Simon | St. Louis, MO |
| BURNING THE KEYS | Robert Marine | 1928 | Self | New York, NY |
| BUSINESS IN TOWN | Donald Ashwander | June 27, 1966 | Oak Publishing | New York, NY |
| BUSTER RAG | Bessie M. Powell | 1915 | Whitmore Publishing | Scranton, PA |
| BUTCHER RAG | Louis Mentel | November 22, 1912 | Mentel Brothers | Cincinnati, OH |
| BUZZER RAG | May Aufderheide | September 4, 1909 | J. H. Aufderheide | Indianapolis, IN |
| CABBAGE LEAF RAG | Les Copeland | November 2, 1909 | Marsh and Needles | Wichita, KS |
| CABBAGE RAG | Bertha Stanfield | November 24, 1911 | Spiker and McMillen | Joplin, MO |
| CABERAVINGS | Richard A. Whiting | March 31, 1914 | Jerome H. Remick | New York, NY |
| CACTUS RAG | Lucian P. Gibson | May 10, 1916 | Stark Music Company | St. Louis, MO |
| CALICO RAG | Richard G. Behan | February 1, 1909 | Self | Newark, NJ |
| CALICO RAG | Lee B. Grabbe | November 16, 1905 | Emmett and Johns | Chicago, IL |
| CALICO RAG | Nat Johnson | October 19, 1914 | Forster Music | Chicago, IL |
| CALICO RAG | Les Jones | August 9, 1953 | Self | LaHabra, CA |
| CALIFORNIA SUNSHINE | Harry Jentes | November 29, 1913 | Theron C. Bennett | New York, NY |
| CALIOPE RAG | Sylvester L. Hartlaub and Charles L. Hartlaub | June 30, 1911 | Joseph Krolage Music | Cincinnati, OH |
| CALL 'EM TOODLES | Corrie Huddleston | April 19, 1921 | Jack Mills | New York, NY |
| CALLA LILLY RAG | Logan Thane | 1907 | Stark Music Company | New York, NY |
| CALLIOPE RAG | James Scott | June 27, 1966 | Oak Publishing | New York, NY |
| CAMPUS RAG | Benjamin Richmond | April 27, 1911 | Charles D. Gallagher | New York, NY |
| CAN YOU BEAT IT RAG | Frederick Christeen | 1911 | Henry B. Kronlage | New Orleans, LA |
| CAN YOU DO THAT? | G. E. Fuller | 1900 | Self | Hallstead, PA |
| CAN'T THINK OF THE NAME | Bernard B. Brin and Al Newman | 1922 | Melody Shop | Seattle, WA |
| CANADIAN CAPERS | Gus Chandler, Henry Cohen, and Bert White | March 26, 1915 | Roger Graham | Chicago, IL |
| CANDIED CHERRIES | Lucien Denni | October 26, 1911 | J. W. Jenkins | Kansas City, MO |
| CANDLE-STICK RAG | Abe Olman | February 12, 1910 | J. H. Aufdierheide | Indianapolis, IN |
| CANDY | Clarence Jones | 1909 | John Arnold | Cincinnati, OH |
| CANDY KID | Floyd Bartlett | March 22, 1911 | H. Kirkus Dugdale | Washington, DC |
| CANDY RAG | Robert Bircher | October 4, 1909 | Self | St. Louis, MO |
| CANHANIBALMO RAG | Arthur Pryor | August 8, 1911 | Carl Fischer | New York, NY |
| CANNED CORN RAG | George L. Cobb | March 1, 1910 | Bell Music | Buffalo, NY |

| Title | Composer | Date | Publisher | City |
|---|---|---|---|---|
| CANNIBAL RAG | Ed Dangel | 1911 | Evans–Dangel Music | Boston, MA |
| CANNON BALL | Jos. C. Northup | April 17, 1905 | Victor Kremer | Chicago, IL |
| CAPITOL CITY RAG | Catherine W. O'Connor | June 17, 1905 | Self | New Haven, CT |
| CAPTIVATIN' RAG | Harry Ellman and S. Lew Schwab | March 16, 1910 | Wellworth Music | St. Louis, MO |
| CAR-BARLICK ACID RAG | Clarence C. Wiley | August 9, 1901 | Self | Oskaloosa, IA |
| CARMEN RAG | Serverino Giovannoli | November 13, 1912 | Self | McMunnville, TN |
| CARNATION | Clyde D. Douglas | 1903 | John Stark and Son | St. Louis, MO |
| CAROLINA FOX TROT | Will H. Vodery | July 7, 1914 | Joseph W. Stern | New York, NY |
| CAROLINA ROMP | Will H.Vodery | July 14, 1913 | Joseph W. Stern | New York, NY |
| CAROLINA SHOUT | James P. Johnson | October 16, 1925 | Clarence Williams Music | New York, NY |
| CARPET RAGS | Ray W. Conner | December 10, 1902 | Joe Morris | Philadelphia, PA |
| CARR'S HOP | Lou Busch | March 5, 1952 | Chatsworth Music | New York, NY |
| CASCADES | Scott Joplin | August 22, 1904 | John Stark and Son | St. Louis, MO |
| CASTLE DOGGY | Ford Dabney and James Reese Europe | 1915 | G. Ricordi | New York, NY |
| CASTLE HOUSE RAG | James R. Europe | March 9, 1914 | Joseph W. Stern | New York, NY |
| CAT GRIN RAG | Flora Bergman | November 8, 1910 | Ted Snyder Company | New York, NY |
| CAT'S PAJAMAS | Harry Jentes | January 10, 1923 | Jack Milia | New York, NY |
| CATARACT | Robert Hampton | July 27,1914 | Stark Music Company | St. Louis, MO |
| CAULDRON RAG | Axel Christensen | April 26, 1909 | Christensen School | Chicago, IL |
| CAZADOR | H. L. Berger | 1906 | Graul Publishing | Detroit, MI |
| CEDAR CREST RAG | Meade Graham | March 14, 1924 | Song Shop | Dallas, TX |
| CELESTIAL RAG | Joe Glover | April 14, 1959 | Melrose Music | New York, NY |
| CENTENNIAL RAG | John Arpin | April 1, 1966 | BMI Canada Ltd. | Toronto, CN |
| CENTENNIAL RAG | Charles Roy Cox | 1912 | Buckeye Music | Columbus, OH |
| CENTURY PRIZE | Arthur Marshall | June 27, 1966 | Oak Publishing | New York, NY |
| CERISE | Jesse L. Williams | August 1, 1914 | Self | Lincoln, NE |
| CERTAIN PARTY | Tom Kelly | October 3, 1910 | Maurice Shapiro | New York, NY |
| CHAMPAGNE RAG | Joseph F. Lamb | September 15, 1910 | Stark Music Company | St. Louis, MO |
| CHANGES | Ed Claypoole | November 23, 1922 | Jack Mills | New York, NY |
| CHANTICLEER RAG | Albert Gumble | March 22, 1910 | Jerome H. Remick | New York, NY |
| CHARLESTON RAG | Eubie Blake | 1975 | Eubie Blake Music | New York, NY |
| CHARMING RAG | Alamanzer Leon Dupuis | May 1, 1913 | Self | Lowell, MA |
| CHASING THE CHICKENS | Abe Olman and Raymond Walker | June 29, 1917 | Forster Music | Chicago, IL |
| CHASING THE FOX | J. Louis Merkur | August 4, 1928 | Jack Mills | New York, NY |
| CHASING THE FOX | Percy Wenrich | June 5, 1922 | Forster Music | Chicago, IL |
| CHATTERBOX RAG | George Bohford | October 4, 1910 | Jerome H. Remick | Detroit, MI |
| CHECKER | Bulah Arens | 1908 | Carlin and Lennox | Indianapolis, IN |
| CHECKER RAG | Dan Goldsmith | November 18, 1911 | Self | Winnepeg, CN |
| CHECKERBOARD RAG | Elijah Jimerson | 1914 | Syndicate Music | St. Louis, MO |
| CHECKERBOARD RAG | Harry A. Tierney | May 13, 1911 | Ted Snyder Company | New York, NY |
| CHECKERS | Harry J. Lincoln | November 1, 1913 | Vandersloot Music | Williamsport, PA |
| CHEESE AND CRACKERS | Homer Denney | September 15, 1909 | Self | Cincinnati, OH |

| Title | Composer | Date | Publisher | City |
|---|---|---|---|---|
| CHERRY LEAF RAG | El Cota | September 20, 1909 | Victor Kremer | Chicago, IL |
| CHESTNUT VALLEY RAG | Trebor J. Tichenor | June 27, 1966 | Oak Publishing | New York, NY |
| CHESTNUTS | Percy Wenrich | November 7, 1906 | Arnett–Delonais | Chicago, IL |
| CHEVY CHASE | Eubie Blake | October 28, 1914 | Joseph W. Stern | New York, NY |
| CHEWIN' THE RAG | E. C. Kammermayer | 1900 | Self | Los Angeles, CA |
| CHEWIN' THE RAG | Fred Heltman | September 6, 1912 | Popular Music Publishers | Cleveland, OH |
| CHIC | A. C. Brockmeyer | September 15, 1918 | Crescent Publishing Company | St. Louis, MO |
| CHICAGO BREAKDOWN | Jelly Roll Morton | January 12, 1926 | Melrose Brother | Chicago, IL |
| CHICAGO TICKLE | Harry A. Tierney | August 8, 1913 | Charles T. French | New York, NY |
| CHICKEN CHARLIE | Ashley Ballou | February 9, 1905 | W. C. Polla | Chicago, IL |
| CHICKEN CHOWDER | Irene M. Giblin | April 12, 1905 | Jerome H. Remick | Detroit, MI |
| CHICKEN DANCE | Herbert Cortess | July 17, 1913 | Chauncey Van Demark | Kyserike, NY |
| CHICKEN PATTY | Theodore Morse | April 24, 1908 | F. B. Haviland | New York, NY |
| CHICKEN PRANKS | Max Kortlander and Lee S. Roberts | 1917 | Self | Chicago, IL |
| CHICKEN'S RAG | Rafael Balseiro | September 23, 1915 | J. Fischer and Bro. | New York, NY |
| CHILI CON CARNE | Elmer B. Griffith | March 6, 1911 | Rinker Music | Lafayette, IN |
| CHILI PEPPER | Fred W. Longshaw | September 18, 1925 | Perry Bradford Music | New York, NY |
| CHILI SAUCE | H. A. Fischler | September 24, 1910 | Vandersloot Music | Williamsport, PA |
| CHILLS AND FEVER | Theron C. Bennett | August 27, 1912 | Sam Fox | Cleveland, OH |
| CHILLY BILLY BEE RAG | Lewis F. Muir | January 5, 1910 | J. Fred Helf | New York, NY |
| CHIMES | Homer Denney | July 20, 1910 | Joseph Krolage Music | Cincinnati, OH |
| CHIPPEWA RAG | Myrtle Hoy | March 22, 1911 | Windsor Music | Chicago, IL |
| CHOCOLATE CREAMS RAG | Warren Camp | September 20, 1909 | Victor Kremer | Chicago, IL |
| CHOCOLATE SWEETS | Walter G. Wilmarth | 1902 | E. F. Droop and Sons | Washington, DC |
| CHOP SUEY RAG | Edward Hayne | September 20, 1915 | Self | Chicago, IL |
| CHOPIANO | Henry Lange | March 6, 1922 | Jack Mills | New York, NY |
| CHOW CHOW | Robert Hoffman | 1909 | Crescent Music | New Orleans, LA |
| CHOW-CHOW RAG | Phil Schwartz | August 12, 1909 | Jerome H. Remick | Detroit, MI |
| CHROMATIC CAPERS | George L. Cobb | June 12, 1925 | Walter Jacobs | Boston, MA |
| CHROMATIC RAG | Will Held | March 10, 1916 | Stark Music Company | St. Louis, MO |
| CHROMATIC RAG | Pete Wendling and Ed Gerhart | May 17, 1916 | Waterson, Berlin, and Snyder | New York, NY |
| CINCINNATI RAG | W. C. Powell | June 21, 1909 | Arnett–Delonais | Chicago, IL |
| CINDER-ELLA RAG | Mabel L. Asher | May 24, 1910 | Self | San Diego, CA |
| CLASSIC RAG | Neil Moret | April 3, 1909 | Jerome H. Remick | New York, NY |
| CLASSICANNA | Henry Lange | May 4, 1923 | Waterson, Berlin, and Snyder | New York, NY |
| CLASSY RAG | Lillian M. Lawier | August 15, 1917 | Self | New Orleans, LA |
| CLASSY RAG | Ethel S. Phillips | February 27, 1915 | Self | Fort Worth, TX |
| CLAUDIA RAG | Grace Shaw | 1910 | Gottfried and McMillan | Joplin, MO |
| CLEOPATRA RAG | Joseph F. Lamb | June 16, 1915 | Stark Music Company | St. Louis, MO |
| CLIMAX RAG | James Scott | March 5, 1914 | Stark Music Company | St. Louis, MO |
| CLIMBERS | Arthur L. Sizemore | July 27, 1911 | Stark Music Company | St. Louis, MO |

| Title | Composer | Date | Publisher | City |
|---|---|---|---|---|
| CLOUD KISSER | Raymond Birch | January 3, 1911 | Charles L. Johnson | Kansas City, MO |
| CLOVER BLOSSOM RAG | Fred Heltman | July 30, 1910 | Self | Cleveland, OH |
| CLOVER BLOSSOM RAG | Bud Manchester | August 17, 1912 | Stark Music Company | St. Louis, MO |
| CLOVER CLUB | Felix Arndt | May 9, 1918 | Sam Fox | Cleveland, OH |
| CLOVER LEAF | John Lind | October 16, 1905 | Self | Cincinnati, OH |
| CLOVER LEAF RAG | Edith Haynes-Wall | 1909 | Self | Groom, TX |
| CLOVER LEAF RAG | Cy Seymour | March 1, 1909 | Albright Music | Chicago, IL |
| CLUB CABIN | S. Em. Duguay | 1903 | Le Passe-Temps | Montreal, CN |
| COAXING THE IVORIES | Robert Marine | June 1, 1928 | Self | New York, NY |
| COAXING THE PIANO | Zez Confrty | March 6, 1922 | Jack Mills | New York, NY |
| COFFEE RAG | Lily Coffee | July 21, 1915 | W. C. Munn Company | Houston, TX |
| COLD FEET RAG | Mamie Williams | 1907 | J. W. Jenkins | Kansas City, MO |
| COLDWATER RAG | Mollie F. Cloud | August 7, 1913 | G. L. Dearing | Lincoln, NE |
| COLE SMOAK | Clarence H. St. John | December 28, 1906 | John Stark and Son | St. Louis, MO |
| COLLARS AND CUFFS | Clarence H. St. John | December 23, 1907 | Stark Music Company | New York, NY |
| COLLEGE RAG | William Hunter | December 17, 1910 | Herald Square Music | New York, NY |
| COLLEGE RAG | Ruth Knipperberg | July 22, 1910 | Self | Milwaukee, WI |
| COLONIAL GLIDE | Paul Pratt | January 13, 1910 | J. H. Aufderheide | Indianapolis, IN |
| COLONIAL RAG | Ernest R. Ball and Julius Lenzberg | October 3, 1914 | M. Witmark and Sons | New York, NY |
| COLUMBIA RAG | Armorell Cochran | November 8, 1913 | Luckhardt and Belder | New York, NY |
| COLUMBIA RAG | Irene M. Giblin | March 5, 1910 | Jerome H. Remick | New York, NY |
| COMET RAG | Leslie C. Groff | 1910 | Self | Chicago, IL |
| COMET RAG | Jean J. Haas | 1910 | Bixby and Castle | Buffalo, NY |
| COMET RAG | Ed C. Mahoney | November 10, 1910 | Joseph M. Daly | Boston, MA |
| COMET RAG | Alfred V. Peterson | April 22, 1910 | Self | Salt Lake City, UT |
| CONEY ISLAND DIP | Addison J. Ressegue | July 10, 1901 | Union Music | Cincinnati, OH |
| CONEY ISLAND GIRL | Homer Denney | February 26, 1906 | Self | Cincinnati, OH |
| CONEY ISLAND TICKLE | Alfred Gasdorf | 1906 | Self | Newport, KY |
| CONTENTMENT RAG | Joseph F. Lamb | January 10, 1915 | Stark Music Company | St. Louis, MO |
| COON BAND PARADE | James R. Europe | October 14, 1905 | Sol Bloom | New York, NY |
| COON CAN | Edward Derville | 1901 | Sol Bloom | Chicago, IL |
| COPPER KING RAG | Marguerite Ray | October 12, 1912 | Hatch and Loveland | Los Angeles, CA |
| CORN CRACKER RAG | Eugene S. Pyle | June 19, 1911 | Self | Campbell, MO |
| CORN ON THE COB | Cliff Hess | October 17, 1923 | Jack Mills | New York, NY |
| CORN PALACE | Ray Stewart Soladay | September 22, 1915 | Advocate Printers | Fulton, SD |
| CORN SHUCKS RAG | Ed Kuhn | 1908 | J. W. Jenkins | Kansas City, MO |
| CORN TASSLE RAG | E. Earle Marx | June 11, 1912 | Self | Lincoln, NE |
| CORONATION RAG | Winifred Atwell | April 22, 1953 | Jefferson Music | New York, NY |
| COTTON | Albert Von Tilzer | 1907 | York Music | New York, NY |
| COTTON BELT RAG | Irma V. Dawson | April 29, 1916 | Thomas Goggan and Brothers | Galveston, TX |
| COTTON BELT RAG | J. H. O'Bryan | August 5, 1908 | Self | Mooleyville, KY |
| COTTON BOLLS | Charles Hunter | June 7, 1901 | Frank G. Fite | Nashville, TN |
| COTTON LEAF RAG | Len Larimer | February 13, 1911 | H. Kirkus Dugdale | Washington, DC |

| Title | Composer | Date | Publisher | City |
|---|---|---|---|---|
| COTTON PATCH | Charles A. Tyler | July 31, 1902 | J. W. Jenkins | Kansas City, MO |
| COTTON PICKERS CARNIVAL | Maurice Taube | January 2, 1904 | William R. Haskins Company | Brooklyn, NY |
| COTTON STATES RAG | Annie Ford McKnight | February 19, 1910 | Cocroft Music | Thomasville, GA |
| COTTON TIME | Charles N. Daniels | September 26, 1910 | Jerome H. Remick | Detroit, MI |
| COTTONTAIL RAG | Joseph F. Lamb | 1964 | Mills Music | New York, NY |
| COUNTRY CLUB | Scott Joplin | October 30, 1909 | Seminary Music | New York, NY |
| COZY CORNER RAG | Carroll Stephens | April 28, 1911 | F. B. Haviland | New York, NY |
| CRAB APPLES | Percy Wenrich | January 27, 1908 | Brehm Brothers | Erie, PA |
| CRACKED ICE | George L. Cobb | 1918 | Walter Jacobs | Boston, MA |
| CRACKER JACK RAG | E. W. Francis | November 5, 1909 | Victor Kremer | Chicago, IL |
| CRADLE ROCK | Abe Frankl and Phil Komheiser | August 11, 1916 | Leo Feist | New York, NY |
| CRAPS | L. Z. Phillips | 1908 | J. Goldsmith and Sons | Memphis, TN |
| CRAPS | Will E. Skidmore | May 21, 1910 | Cosmopolitan Music | Little Rock, AR |
| CRASH!!! | Gus Van and Joe Schenck | April 14, 1914 | Will Rossiter | Chicago, IL |
| CRAZY BONE RAG | Charles L. Johnson | March 29, 1913 | Forster Music | Chicago, IL |
| CRAZY HORSE RAG | Roscoe Carter | August 18, 1909 | Victor Kremer | Chicago, IL |
| CRAZY QUILT | Lawrence L. Willey | March 8, 1910 | Self | Manchester, NH |
| CRIMSON RAMBLER RAG | Harry A. Tierney | May 19, 1911 | Ted Snyder Company | New York, NY |
| CROSS WORD PUZZLE | Charles Olson | March 23, 1925 | Jack Mills | New York, NY |
| CROSSED HANDS | Saul Sieff | November 24, 1925 | Villa Moret | San Francisco, CA |
| CUBIST | Tom Griselle | June 1, 1918 | Artmusic | New York, NY |
| CUBISTIC RAG | George L. Cobb | October 14, 1927 | Walter Jacobs | Boston, MA |
| CUCUMBER RAG | W. C. Powell | December 9, 1910 | Joe Morris | New York, NY |
| CUM-BAC RAG | Charles L. Johnson | December 22, 1911 | Jerome H. Remick | Detroit, MI |
| CURIOSITY | James E. C. Kelly | May 17, 1910 | Ballard and Kelly | Cincinnati, OH |
| CURL-I-CUES | Walter E. Miles | August 10, 1945 | Sam Fox | New York, NY |
| CUTE AND PRETTY | Melville Morris | September 26, 1917 | Jerome H. Remick | New York, NY |
| CUTTER | Elma Ney McClure | July 18, 1909 | O. K. Houck | Memphis, TN |
| CUTTIN' UP | Charles G. Haskell | December 31, 1906 | Jerome H. Remick | New York, NY |
| CYCLONE | Ferde Grofe | April 7, 1923 | Jack Mills | New York, NY |
| CYCLONE | Edward G. Rieman | July 21,1908 | Self | Cincinnati, OH |
| CYCLONE IN DARKTOWN | George D. Barnard | December 30, 1910 | Carl Fischer | New York, NY |
| CYCLONE RAG | F. Brown | April 12, 1909 | Fritz and Floyd | Cleveland, OH |
| DAFFODILS | James E. C. Kelly | January 5,1912 | Joseph Krolage Music | Cincinnati, OH |
| DAFFY DINGIES | Harry Raymond | January 16,1901 | Raymond and Wood | Buffalo, NY |
| DAFFYDILL RAG | Waiman | December 29,1911 | Grinnell Bros. | Detroit, MI |
| DAINTY DOLL | Bernard Barnes | 1934 | Sherman, Clay | San Francisco, CA |
| DAINTY FOOT GLIDE | G. M. Tidd | February 16, 1915 | Self | Marion, OH |
| DAINTY MISS | Bernard Barnes | November 24, 1924 | Sherman, Clay | San Francisco, CA |
| DAISY RAG | Fred Heltman | December 5, 1908 | Sam Fox | Cleveland, OH |
| A DAISY RAG | C. Kenneth Yoder | 1916 | Self | Bellfontaine, OH |
| DAKOTA RAG | O. H. Andersen | June 7, 1899 | S. Brainard's Sons | Chicago, IL |
| DANCE OF THE CROCODILES RAG | H. H. Whiting | October1, 1912 | Self | Sanford,ME |

| Title | Composer | Date | Publisher | City |
|---|---|---|---|---|
| DANCE OF THE NOTES | Phil Saltman | November 30, 1935 | Robbins Music | New York, NY |
| DANCING ANIMAL CRACKERS | Harry DeCosta and Herbert Steiner | April 22, 1929 | Mills Music | New York, NY |
| THE DANCING DEACON | Frederick M. Bryan | 1918 | Pace and Handy | New York, NY |
| DANCING FINGERS | Earl Hines | November 16, 1935 | Modern Standard | Chicago, IL |
| DANCING SHADOWS | Ernie Golden | September 29, 1927 | Al Piantadosi | New York, NY |
| DANCING TAMBOURINE | W. C. Polla | August 4, 1927 | Harms, Inc. | New York, NY |
| DANDELION | Ted S. Barron | October 23, 1909 | M. Witmark and Sons | New York, NY |
| DANGER RAG | Vivian A. Tillotson | May 23, 1912 | Self | Hope, ND |
| DANSOPATION | Martin K. Mortensen | November 26, 1923 | Hearst Music | Winnipeg, CN |
| DARKIES' SPRING SONG | Egbert Van Alstyne | 1901 | Will Rossiter | Chicago, IL |
| DARKEY TODALO | Joe Jordan | November 15, 1910 | Harry Von Tilzer Music | New York, NY |
| DARKTOWN CAPERS | Walter Starck | December 15, 1897 | Shattinger Music | St. Louis, MO |
| DAT CACKLIN' RAG | Kenneth W. Bradshaw | September 26, 1911 | H. Kirkus Dugdale | Washington, DC |
| DAT JOHNSON RAG | N. Clark Smith and C. E. Matchett | 1910 | Marsh and Needles | Wichita, KS |
| DAT LOVIN' RAG | Bernard Adler | 1908 | F. B. Haviland | New York, NY |
| DAT'S IT | Sebastian Lutz | November 10, 1903 | Hakenjos | New Orleans, LA |
| DAVE'S RAG | David A. Jasen | June 28, 1979 | The Big Three | New York, NY |
| DEIRO RAG | Guido Deiro | December 18, 1913 | Jerome H. Remick | New York, NY |
| DEL MAR RAG | Joe Sullivan | 1945 | Robbins Music | New York, NY |
| DELIGHIFUL RAG | Lester Sill | January 19, 1914 | Warner C. Williams | Indianapolis, IN |
| DELIRIUM TREMENS RAG | F. Henri Klickmann | January 20, 1913 | Harold Rossiter | Chicago, IL |
| DELTA RAG | Virginia A. Birdsong | December 20, 1913 | L. Grunewald Company | New Orleans, LA |
| DEMON RAG | John E. Broderick | June 20, 1918 | W. C. DeForest | Sharon, PA |
| DERBY DAY RAG | Leafy Colvin | May 26, 1909 | Self | Kansas City, MO |
| DESECRATION | Felix Arndt | September 29, 1914 | G. Ricordi | New York, NY |
| DESERT KING RAG | B. Leroy Massie | 1911 | Redewill | Phoenix, AZ |
| DESIRE RAG | Charles DeGeorge | 1918 | Buffalo Music | Buffalo, NY |
| DEUCES WILD | Max Kortlander | November 17, 1923 | Jack Mills | New York, NY |
| DEUCES WILD RAG | Hubert Bauersachs | October 19, 1922 | Self | St. Louis, MO |
| DEVIL RAG | Frank R. Powell | 1907 | Self | Kansas City, MO |
| DEVILISH RAG | Lew Roberts | April 27, 1908 | Lew Roberts Music | Nashville, TN |
| DEX | Armond C. Rhodehamel | June 5, 1909 | Self | Indianapolis, IN |
| DIABOLO RAG | Dorothy I. Wahl | March 11, 1908 | Victor Kremer | Chicago, IL |
| DIAMOND RAG | H. A. Cholmondeley | 1908 | Self | Cincinnati, OH |
| DICTY'S ON SEVENTH AVENUE | Eubie Blake | 1971 | Edward B. Marks Music | New York, NY |
| DILL PICKLES RAG | Charles L. Johnson | 1906 | Carl Hoffman Music | Kansas City, MO |
| DIMPLES AND SMILES | Alfred H. Cooper | 1913 | Joseph Krolage Music | Cincinnati, OH |
| DIMPLEY SMILES | Harry C. Thompson | 1915 | Crest Music | Chicago, IL |
| DINGLE POP HOP | Harry A. Tierney | April 12, 1911 | Ted Snyder Company | New York, NY |
| DINGY'S SERENADE | Roy Mullendore | December 10, 1898 | Carlin and Lennox | Indianapolis, IN |
| DIPLOMAT RAG | William H. Hickman | January 25, 1910 | Self | Covington, KY |
| DISCHORD RAG | Annette Stone | February 1, 1915 | Popular Music Publishers | New York, NY |
| DISH RAG | Saul Bluestein | 1909 | Self | Memphis, TN |

| Title | Composer | Date | Publisher | City |
|---|---|---|---|---|
| DISH RAG | Floyd D. Godfrey | 1909 | Charles C. Adams and Company | Peoria, IL |
| DISH RAG | Richard Goosman | August 14, 1908 | Charles I. Davis | Cleveland, OH |
| DISH RAG | John Nelson | 1915 | J. R. Hall | |
| DIXIE BLOSSOMS | Percy Wenrich | July 16, 1906 | Jerome H. Remick | Detroit, MI |
| DIXIE DIMPLES | Frank Loewenstein | August 5, 1911 | Will Rossiter | Chicago, IL |
| DIXIE DIMPLES | James Scott | 1918 | Will L. Livernash Music | Kansas City, MO |
| DIXIE DOODLES | Josef Ruben | September 9, 1913 | Jerome H. Remick | New York, NY |
| DIXIE KICKS | Percy Wenrich | September 14, 1908 | McKinley Music | Chicago, IL |
| DIXIE KISSES | E. Clinton Keithley | 1909 | Keith Music | Louisville, KY |
| DIXIE LIFE RAG | Frank E. Brown | September 21, 1920 | Self | Walton, NY |
| DIXIE QUEEN | Robert Hoffman | 1906 | Cable Company | New Orleans, LA |
| DIXIE RAG | Irene M. Giblin | February 8, 1913 | Joseph M. Daly | Boston, MA |
| DIXIE RAG | Al Lewis | July 21, 1908 | Koninsky Music | Troy, NY |
| DIXIE RAG | Gustav Roberti | October 14, 1922 | Self | New Haven, CT |
| DIXIE SLOW DRAG | Robert Hoffman | 1903 | Cable Company | New Orleans, LA |
| DIZZY FINGERS | Zez Confrey | November 17, 1923 | Jack Mills | New York, NY |
| DOCKSTADER RAG | Les Copeland | November 29, 1912 | Jerome H. Remick | New York, NY |
| DOCTOR BROWN | Fred Irvin | October 27, 1914 | Jerome H. Remick | New York, NY |
| DOG ON THE PIANO | Ted Shapiro | September 5, 1924 | Jack Mills | New York, NY |
| DOGZIGITY RAG | Billie Taylor | June 1, 1910 | Ted Snyder Company | New York, NY |
| DOLL DANCE | Nacio Herb Brown | July 6, 1927 | Sherman, Clay | San Francisco, CA |
| DOLL RAGS | Homer A. Hall | May 4, 1906 | Victor Kremer | Chicago, IL |
| DOLL RAGS | Bernard Ungar | 1909 | Hits Publishing Company | Cincinnati, OH |
| DOMINO RAG | Clarence E. Brandon | July 30, 1913 | Syndicate Music | St. Louis, MO |
| DOMINO RAG | Richard Glade | September 12, 1908 | Self | Chicago, IL |
| DOMINO RAG | Reba Powers | March 28, 1908 | Lew Roberts Music | Nashville, TN |
| DOMINO RAG | Harry L. Sack | May 10, 1907 | Self | Milwaukee, WI |
| DON'T JAZZ ME-RAG | James Scott | September 18, 1921 | Stark Music Company | St. Louis, MO |
| DOODLE BUG | Cliff Hess | August 30, 1915 | Waterson, Berlin, and Snyder | New York, NY |
| DOPE | W. C. Powell | April 28, 1909 | Joseph Flanner | Milwaukee, WI |
| DOROTHY | Frank Banta and Jimmy McHugh | May 7, 1929 | Jack Mills | New York, NY |
| DOUBLE FUDGE | Joe Jordan | December 20, 1902 | Hunleth Music | St. Louis, MO |
| DOUBLE M RAG | Joe Morris and William Morris | March 25, 1914 | William Morris Publishing Company | Detroit, MI |
| DOWN HOME RAG | Wilbur Sweatman | September 18, 1911 | Will Rossiter | Chicago, IL |
| DOWN SOUTH | C. A. Grimm | February 23, 1907 | Jerome H. Remick | Detroit, MI |
| DOWN TOWN RAG | Frank Signorelli and George Carrozza | April 7, 1923 | Jack Mills | New York |
| DRAGGY RAGS | D. P. Argo | August 29, 1908 | Sterling Publishing Company | Aberdeen, OH |
| DREAMY RAG | Ethel M. McKray | August 16, 1912 | Globe Music | New York, NY |
| DUSKY DAMSELS RAG | F. W. Sanger | July 17, 1905 | Pioneer Music | Chicago, IL |
| DUST' EM OFF | George L. Cobb | 1920 | Walter Jacobs | Boston, MA |

| Title | Composer | Date | Publisher | City |
|---|---|---|---|---|
| DUSTY RAG | May Aufderheide | February 6, 1908 | Duane Crabb Publishing Company | Indianapolis, IN |
| DUTCH MILL RAG | A. J. Babich | January 3, 1916 | Dutch Mill Company | Omaha, NE |
| DYNAMITE | Paul Biese and F. Henri Klickmann | September 18, 1913 | Will Rossiter | Chicago, IL |
| DYNAMITE RAG | J. Russel Robinson | October 1, 1910 | Southern California Music | Los Angeles, CA |
| DYNAMITE RAG | Samuel J. Stokes | August 14, 1908 | Self | New Orleans, LA |
| EASY MONEY | Will D. Moyer | October 11, 1915 | William C. Stahl | Milwaukee, WI |
| EASY MONEY | A. H. Tournade | January 27, 1905 | Hakenjos | New Orleans, LA |
| EASY WINNERS | Scott Joplin | October 10, 1901 | Self | St. Louis, MO |
| EATIN' TIME RAG | Irene Cozad | April 27, 1913 | J. W. Jenkins | Kansas City, MO |
| ECCENTRIC | J. Russel Robinson | October 17, 1923 | Jack Mills | New York, NY |
| ECHO OF SPRING | Willie the Lion Smith | April 4, 1935 | Clarence Williams Music | New York, NY |
| EDUCATIONAL RAG | William L. Needham | February 26, 1914 | Self | Chicago, IL |
| EDWARD MELLINGER RAG | Edward J. Mellinger | 1913 | Stark Music Company | St. Louis, MO |
| EFFICIENCY RAG | James Scott | January 10, 1917 | Stark Music Company | St. Louis, MO |
| EGYPTIAN RAG | Percy Wenrich | November 16, 1910 | Jerome H. Remick | New York, NY |
| EIGHT O'CLOCK RUSH RAG | Bess Rudisell | September 29, 1911 | Sear–Wilson Music | Chicago, IL |
| ELECTRIC PARK RAG | Jean Ledies | | Lenge and Venuto | Kansas City, MO |
| ELECTRIC RAG! | Glennie C. Batson | April 11, 1914 | L. Grunewald Company | New Orleans, LA |
| ELECTRIC RAG! | Mary Gilmore | February 23, 1914 | W. M. Bodine | Kansas City, KS |
| ELEPHANT RAG | Malvin M. Franklin | June 3, 1913 | Jerome H. Remick | New York, NY |
| ELEVENTH STREET RAG | Euday Bowman | July 15, 1918 | Bowman and Ward | Gary, IN |
| ELITE SYNCOPATIONS | Scott Joplin | December 29, 1902 | John Stark and Son | St. Louis, MO |
| EMPIRE CITY RAG | Frank Broekhoven | January 14, 1911 | Sunlight Music | Chicago, IL |
| ENCORE RAG | Tad Fischer | February 3, 1912 | O. K. Houck | Memphis, TN |
| ENTERTAINER | Scott Joplin | December 29, 1902 | John Stark and Son | St. Louis, MO |
| ENTERTAINER'S RAG | Jay Roberts | September 30, 1910 | Pacific Coast Music | Oakland, CA |
| ERRATIC | J. Russel Robinson | October 17, 1923 | Jack Mills | New York, NY |
| ESKIMO SHIVERS | Billy Mayerl | August 21, 1925 | Sam Fox | Cleveland, OH |
| ESTELLE | Frankie Carle | November 15, 1930 | Mills Music | New York, NY |
| ESTHER | David Reichstein | January 9, 1915 | Mellinger Music | St. Louis, MO |
| ETHIOPIA RAG | Joseph F. Lamb | 1909 | Stark Music Company | New York, NY |
| EUGENIA | Scott Joplin | February 26,1906 | Will Rossiter | Chicago, IL |
| EUPHONIC SOUNDS | Scott Joplin | October 30, 1909 | Seminary Music | New York, NY |
| EVERGREEN RAG | James Scott | 1915 | Stark Music Company | St. Louis, MO |
| EVERYBODY TWO STEP | Wallie Herzer | June 30, 1910 | Self | San Francisco, CA |
| EVERYBODY'S RAG | Dan Goldsmith and Robert D. Sharp | November 9, 1909 | Darrow and Sharp | Denver, CO |
| EVERYBODY'S RAG | Mayme B. Zechmann | 1909 | Self | Sioux City, IA |
| EVOLUTION RAG | Thomas S. Allen | 1979 | The Big Three | New York, NY |
| EXCELSIOR RAG | Joseph F. Lamb | 1909 | Stark Music Company | New York, NY |
| EXTR'ORDINARY RAG | Otto Motzan | March 22, 1915 | T. B. Harms | New York, NY |
| EYE OPENER | Bob Zurke and Julian Matlock | April 10, 1939 | Leo Feist | New York, NY |
| FADETTES CALL | Grace Gooding | April 28, 1914 | Jerome H. Remick | New York, NY |

| Title | Composer | Date | Publisher | City |
|---|---|---|---|---|
| FAMOUS PLAYERS RAG | Harry Baisden | September 27, 1915 | Baisden and Poole | Ft. Dodge, IA |
| FANATIC RAG | Harry A. Tierney | February 15, 1911 | Ted Snyder Company | New York, NY |
| FANCY FINGERS | Burn Knowles | July 14, 1936 | ABC Standard | New York, NY |
| FASCINATOR | James Scott | September 23, 1903 | Dumars Music | Carthage, MO |
| FASHION RAG | Charles Cohen | January 17, 1912 | Vandersloot Music | Williamsport, PA |
| FASHIONETTE | Jack Glogau and Robert A. King | June 28, 1928 | Shapiro, Bernstein | New York, NY |
| FATHER KNICKERBOCKER | Edwin E. Wilson | August 19, 1907 | Joseph W. Stern | New York, NY |
| FAVORITE | Scott Joplin | June 23, 1904 | A. W. Perry and Sons | Sedalia, MO |
| FAVORITE RAG | Willard Bailey | 1900 | Puntenney and Eutsler | Columbus, OH |
| FEATHER FINGERS | Claude Lapham | May 14, 1928 | Alfred and Company | New York, NY |
| FEEDIN' THE KITTY | George L. Cobb | 1919 | Walter Jacobs | Boston, MA |
| FELICITY RAG | Scott Joplin and Scott Hayden | July 27, 1911 | Stark Music Company | St. Louis, MO |
| FELIX RAG | H. H. McSkimming | March 19, 1910 | Self | Kiowa, KS |
| FERN LEAF RAG | Hobart E. Swan | April 5, 1906 | Self | Kearney, NE |
| FESTIVAL RAG | David A. Jasen | June 28, 1979 | The Big Three | New York, NY |
| FIDDLE STICKS | Florence Wilson | April 12, 1910 | Joseph Flanner | Milwaukee, WI |
| FIDDLER'S RAG | Trovato and A. C. Manning | November 6, 1911 | Leo Feist | New York, NY |
| FIDDLESTICKS | Al B. Coney | June 17, 1912 | Will Rossiter | Chicago, IL |
| FIDDLING GEORGE | J. P. Doss | 1905 | Thomas Goggan and Brothers | Galveston, TX |
| FIDGETY FINGERS | Norman J. Elholm | February 27, 1923 | Jack Mills | New York, NY |
| FIG LEAF RAG | Scott Joplin | February 24, 1908 | Stark Music Company | New York, NY |
| FIG LEAF RAG | William Lawrence | June 7, 1909 | Self | Philadelphia, PA |
| FINE FEATHERS | Larry Briers | 1923 | Jack Mills | New York, NY |
| FINESSE | Bernard Maltin and Ray Doll | April 11, 1929 | Santley Bros. | New York, NY |
| FINGER BREAKER | Jelly Roll Morton | 1975 | Edwin H. Morris | New York, NY |
| FINGER BUSTER | Willie the Lion Smith | October 15, 1934 | Clarence Williams Music | New York, NY |
| FINICKY FINGERS | Lou Busch | March 5, 1952 | Chatsworth Music | New York, NY |
| FIRE CRACKER RAG | Will Held | May 5, 1911 | Charles H. Henderson | Corry, PA |
| FIREFLY RAG | Joseph F. Lamb | 1964 | Mills Music | New York, NY |
| FISHIN' FOR FLATS | Billy James | August 22, 1922 | Jack Mills | New York, NY |
| FIVE LITTLE BROWN JUGS RAG | Lawrence B. O'Connor | April 30, 1909 | Joseph M. Daly | Boston, MA |
| FIZZ WATER | Eubie Blake | October 28, 1914 | Joseph W. Stern | New York, NY |
| FLAP JACKS RAG | J. Bowie Gouger | December 20, 1916 | Self | Dallas, TX |
| FLAPPERETTE | Jesse Greer | February 22, 1926 | Jack Mills | New York, NY |
| FLEUR DE LIS | Harry A. Tierney | August 16, 1911 | Joseph W. Stern | New York, NY |
| FLICKER RED RAG | Robert R. Darch | December 30, 1953 | Red-Dog Saloon | Juneau, AK |
| FLOATING ALONG | Henry Fredericks | August 8, 1914 | McKinley Music | Chicago, IL |
| FLORIDA CRACKER | Ellis Brooks | February 22, 1898 | S. Brainard's Sons | Chicago, IL |
| FLORIDA RAG | George L. Lowry | September 25, 1905 | Joseph W. Stern | New York, NY |
| FLUFFY RUFFLES | Jack Glogau | November 27, 1928 | Bibo, Bloedon, and Lang | New York, NY |
| FLUFFY RUFFLES | Frank C. Keithley | February 1, 1908 | Monroe | Chicago, IL |

| Title | Composer | Date | Publisher | City |
|---|---|---|---|---|
| FLUFFY RUFFLES | Joe Zimmerman | November 27, 1928 | Bibo, Bloedon, and Lang | New York, NY |
| FLUFFY RUFFLES GIRLS RAG | Marion I. Davis | February 19, 1908 | Charles I. Davis | Cleveland, OH |
| FLUFFY RUFFLES RAG | Harry Cook | December 9, 1907 | Self | Louisville, KY |
| FLY PAPER RAG | A. Lorne Lee | April 15, 1909 | A. H. Goetting | Toronto, CN |
| FONTELLA RAG | Ethyl B. Smith | August 5, 1907 | Thiebes–Stierlin Music | St. Louis, MO |
| FOOL 'EM FINGERS | Odgard C. Stemland | 1929 | Self | Minneapolis, MN |
| FOOLIN' AROUND | Henry W. Ross | November 3, 1922 | Jack Mills | New York, NY |
| FOOLISHEAD | Russell Griffen and Edith Miller | May 27, 1911 | Griffen Music Publishing | Rochester, NY |
| FOOLISHNESS RAG | Mort Weinstein | August 21, 1911 | Harold Rossiter | Chicago, IL |
| FOOT WARMER | Harry Puck | February 20, 1914 | Kalmar and Puck | New York, NY |
| FORTY-SECOND STREET RAG | Les Copeland and Jack Smith | December 2, 1913 | Waterson, Berlin, and Snyder | New York, NY |
| FOX-TERRIER RAG | John N. Lang | May 1, 1915 | Self | Indianapolis, IN |
| FRANCO-AMERICAN RAG | Jean Schwartz | October 13, 1909 | Jerome H. Remick | New York, NY |
| FRANKFORT RAG | Maude M. Thurston | January 14, 1909 | Self | Chicago, IL |
| FRECKLES | Larry Buck | November 25, 1905 | W. C. Polla | Chicago, IL |
| FRECKLES | Fleta B. Davis | November 30, 1908 | Self | Indianapolis, IN |
| FRED HELTMAN'S RAG | Fred Heltman | February 16, 1918 | Self | Cleveland, OH |
| FRENCH PASTRY RAG | Les Copeland | September 1, 1914 | Jerome H. Remick | New York, NY |
| FRENZIED RAG | Joseph H. Miller | November 6, 1905 | C. Melbourne | Chicago, IL |
| FRIAR TUCK RAG | Jop Lincott | 1898 | Self | Chicago, IL |
| FRIDAY NIGHT | Donald Ashwander | December 30, 1976 | Edward B. Marks Music | New York, NY |
| FRIED CHICKEN RAG | Ella Hudson Day | February 27, 1912 | Thomas Goggan and Brothers | Galveston, TX |
| FRIGID FROLICS | A. L. Marx | June 5, 1905 | Self | Superior, WI |
| FRISCO FRAZZLE | Nat Johnson | June 27, 1912 | M. Witmark and Sons | New York, NY |
| FRISCO RAG | Harry Armstrong | November 6, 1909 | M. Witmark and Sons | New York, NY |
| FRIVOLOUS RAGS | Flora L. Noll | March 12, 1918 | A. W. Perry's Sons | Sedalia, MO |
| FROG LEGS RAG | James Scott | December 10, 1906 | John Stark and Sons | New York, NY |
| FROG-I-MORE RAG | Jelly Roll Morton | 1946 | R. J. Carew | Washington, DC |
| FROGGIE MOORE | Jelly Roll Morton, Benjamin F. Spikes, and John C. Spikes | April 16, 1923 | Spikes Brothers | Los Angeles, CA |
| FULL MOON | Roy G. Carew | January 13, 1909 | Puderer Publishing Company | New Orleans, LA |
| FULL OF TRICKS | Robert Marine | 1928 | Self | New York, NY |
| FUN BOB | Percy Wenrich | March 30, 1907 | Arnett–Delonais | Chicago, IL |
| FUNNY BONES | Calvin Lee Woolsey | July 17, 1909 | Jerome H. Remick | New York, NY |
| FUNNY FOLKS | W. C. Powell | February 25, 1904 | W. C. Polla Company | Chicago, IL |
| FUSS AND FEATHERS | J. C. Halls | September 7, 1909 | United States Music | Williamsport, PA |
| FUSS AND FEATHERS | F. L. Moreland | August 22, 1904 | John Stark and Son | St. Louis, MO |
| FUSSIN' AROUND | William C. Isel | 1915 | Walter Jacobs | Boston, MA |
| FUSSY FLOSSIE | Charles H. Hagedon | March 25, 1908 | Wiegel | Minneapolis, MN |
| FUZZY IDEAS | C. E. Hoxworth | July 12, 1913 | Self | Sumner, IA |
| FUZZY WUZZY | Frank C. Keithley | August 24, 1908 | Keithley–Joy Music | Des Moines, IA |
| FUZZY WUZZY RAG | Al Morton | May 4, 1915 | Pace and Handy | Memphis, TN |

| Title | Composer | Date | Publisher | City |
|---|---|---|---|---|
| GALLERY GODS DELIGHT | Joseph H. Denck | 1905 | O. K. Houck | Memphis, TN |
| GARDEN OF EDEN | William Bolcom | May 24, 1971 | Edward B. Marks Music | New York, NY |
| GASOLINE RAG | Louis Mentel | July 23, 1906 | Mentel Brothers | Cincinnati, OH |
| GATLING GUN RAG | Oreste Migliaccio | April 17, 1908 | George Mitchell | New York, NY |
| GAY BIRDS | Ed Claypoole | December 1, 1924 | Jack Mills | New York, NY |
| GAYETY | Harry Sosnik | February 4, 1935 | Robbins Music | New York, NY |
| GEE WHIZ | Sam H. Ewing | September 23, 1908 | Self | Princeton, IN |
| GEORGIA BALL | Burt H. Flanders | June 30, 1910 | Sapp | Eastman, GA |
| GEORGIA GIGGLE RAG | Will L. Livernash | 1918 | Self | Kansas City, MO |
| GEORGIA GRIND | Ford Dabney | March 12, 1915 | Joseph W. Stern | New York, NY |
| GEORGIA RAG | Albert Gumble | December 15, 1910 | Jerome H. Remick | Detroit, MI |
| GEORGIA RAINBOW | Leo Gordon | 1916 | Walter Jacobs | Boston, MA |
| GHOST OF THE PIANO | Arthur Schutt | March 5, 1923 | Jack Mills | New York, NY |
| GIDDY DITTY | Zez Confrey | October 24, 1935 | Exclusive Publications | New York, NY |
| GIGGLER | Chauncey Haines | April 5, 1905 | Jerome H. Remick | Detroit, MI |
| GINGER | Mrs. Wm. Neal McCoy | 1908 | Globe Music | New York, NY |
| GINGER SNAP RAG | Horace K. Dugdale | August 3, 1907 | H. Kirkus Dugdale and Corbitt | Washington, DC |
| GINGER SNAPS | Rosario Bourdon | December 27, 1928 | Harms, Inc. | New York, NY |
| GINGER SNAPS | Egbert Van Alstyne | 1904 | Will Rossiter | Chicago, IL |
| GIT BIZZY | Hardaway Frazer | October 31, 1905 | Pioneer Music | Chicago, IL |
| GLAD CAT RAG | Will Nash | 1905 | Pioneer Music | Chicago, IL |
| GLAD RAG | Glen W. Caldwell | June 1, 1909 | Self | Los Angeles, CA |
| GLAD RAG | Ribe Danmark | May 18, 1910 | Jerome H. Remick | Detroit, MI |
| GLAD RAG | R. G. Grady | September 22, 1910 | Gamble Hinged Music | Chicago, IL |
| GLAD RAG | Lew Roberts | December 3, 1907 | Lew Roberts Music | Nashville, TN |
| GLAD RAGS | Anna Hughes Carpenter | September 18, 1907 | George Jaberg | Cincinnati, OH |
| GLAD RAGS | George Gould | October 27, 1911 | H. W. Williams | San Francisco, CA |
| GLAD RAGS | W. E. Nuss | 1911 | Windsor Music | Chicago, IL |
| GLAD RAGS | Harry Williams | October 27, 1911 | H. W. Williams | San Francisco, CA |
| GLADIOLUS RAG | Scott Joplin | September 24, 1907 | Joseph W. Stern | New York, NY |
| GLEN OAKS RAG | Axel Christensen | November 26, 1912 | Christensen School | Chicago, IL |
| GLIDE AWAY RAG | Frank C. Keithley | July 5, 1910 | Keithley–Joy Music | Des Moines, IA |
| GLORIA | Fred Hager and Justin Ring | August 30, 1923 | Robbins–Engel | New York, NY |
| GOBLER RAG | Libbie Allen | August 30, 1913 | Shattinger Music | St. Louis, MO |
| GOIN' SOME | James Nonnahs | January 5, 1910 | Grinnell Bros. | Detroit, MI |
| GOIN' SUM | J. Dechant | 1908 | Gearhart and Tilton | Fresno |
| GOING SOME | Marcel Francis Dumas | April 2, 1909 | Philip Werlein | New Orleans, LA |
| GOING SOME | Mabel Harrison | | Carl Hoffman Music | Kansas City, MO |
| GOING SOUTH | Palmer Jones and Will Riley | November 24, 1914 | Jerome H. Remick | New York, NY |
| GOING TO PIECES | Karl Kaffer | October 20, 1915 | Jerome H. Remick | New York, NY |
| GOLD BAR RAG | Max Morath | October 20, 1964 | Hollis Music | New York, NY |
| GOLD DUST RAG | D. M. Headricks | 1911 | Charles I. Davis | Cleveland, OH |

| Title | Composer | Date | Publisher | City |
|---|---|---|---|---|
| GOLD DUST TWINS RAG | Nat Johnson | June 20, 1913 | Forster Music | Chicago, IL |

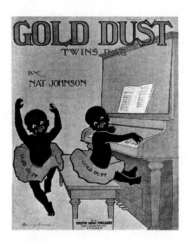

| Title | Composer | Date | Publisher | City |
|---|---|---|---|---|
| GOLDEN GATE RAG | F. B. Mueller and A. H. Zeller | October 2, 1913 | Emitgar Company | Los Angeles, CA |
| GOLDEN SMILE | Garfield Wilson | May 22, 1912 | Will Rossiter | Chicago, IL |
| GOLDEN SPIDER | Charles L. Johnson | November 30, 1910 | Vandersloot Music | Williamsport, PA |
| GOOD AND PLENTY RAG | Joseph F. Lamb | 1964 | Mills Music | New York, NY |
| GOOD BYE BLUES | George L. Cobb | May 27, 1916 | Charles E. Roat Music | Battle Creek, MI |
| GOOD BYE RAG | Carleton L. Colby | May 17, 1920 | Harold Rossiter | Chicago, IL |
| GOOD GRAVY RAG | Harry Belding | January 18, 1913 | Buck and Lowney | St. Louis, MO |
| GOOD YEARS | Teddie Beth Hardy | October 20, 1964 | Hollis Music | New York, NY |
| GOSSIPERS RAG | Norwood M. Grant | May 16, 1905 | Self | Middleport, OH |
| GRACE AND BEAUTY | James Scott | November 12, 1909 | Stark Music Company | St. Louis, MO |
| GRAND CONCERT RAG | E. Philip Severin | February 11, 1918 | Self | Moline, IL |

| Title | Composer | Date | Publisher | City |
|---|---|---|---|---|
| GRANDPA'S SPELLS | Jelly Roll Morton | August 20, 1023 | Melrose Brothers | Chicago, IL |
| GRASSHOPPER RAG | Leon Eleizer | April 28, 1909 | Victor Kremer | Chicago, IL |
| GRAVEL RAG | Charlotte Blake | December 22, 1908 | Jerome H. Remick | New York, NY |
| GREAT MORRIS RAG | Marjorie Burgess | 1974 | Emerson Music Company | Melrose, MA |
| GREAT SCOTT RAG | James Scott | August 18, 1909 | Allen Music | Columbia, MO |
| GREEN MILL RAG | Marcella A. Henry | 1918 | Christensen School | Chicago, IL |
| GREEN RAG | Evangeline Green | July 8, 1913 | Shapiro Music | New York, NY |
| GREEN RAG | Jack Murfree | February 10, 1911 | Murfree Music | Boston, MA |
| GREENWICH WITCH | Zez Confrey | August 4, 1921 | Jack Mills | New York, NY |
| GRIDIRON RAG | Dave Johnson | 1910 | Emerson Music | Cincinnati, OH |
| GRIZZLY BEAR RAG | George Botsford | April 18, 1910 | Ted Snyder Company | New York, NY |
| GROWLS | Alfred H. Cooper | July 21, 1911 | Joseph Krolage Music | Cincinnati, OH |
| GUM SHOE | E. J. Stark | January 10, 1917 | Stark Music Company | St. Louis, MO |
| GUN-COTTON RAG | Merle Von Hagen | June 7, 1916 | Jerome H. Remick | New York, NY |
| GUNPOWDER RAG | Roy W. Spangler | February 10, 1910 | Joe Morris | Philadelphia, PA |
| GYPSY RAG | Gypsy Countess Verona | November 24, 1916 | T. B. Harms | New York, NY |
| HALIFAX RAG | H. D. Carter | March 15, 1910 | Cocroft Music | Thomasville, GA |
| HALLEY'S COMET | Harry J. Lincoln | June 11, 1910 | Vandersloot Music | Williamsport, PA |
| HALLOWE'EN RAG | Arthur Manlowe | March 6, 1911 | Will Rossiter | Chicago, IL |
| HAM AND! | Arthur Marshall | February 24, 1908 | Stark Music Company | New York, NY |
| HAM BONES | Homer Denney | January 30, 1912 | Joseph Kroiage Music | Cincinnati, OH |
| HANDFUL OF KEYS | Thomas "Fats" Waller | December 29, 1930 | Southern Music Publishing Company | New York, NY |
| HANKY PANK | Clifford Adams and Harry G. Robinson | May 4, 1914 | M. Witmark and Sons | New York, NY |
| HAPPY DIXIE RAG | Joe Scott | October 10, 1913 | Self | Tuscaloosa, AL |
| HAPPY FEELINGS RAG | Dan Desdumes | May 10, 1912 | Self | Omaha, NE |
| HAPPY GO LUCKY RAG | John M. Fait | July 3, 1918 | Pace and Handy | Chicago, IL |
| HAPPY JACK | Jack Lampe | 1903 | Lampe Music Company | Buffalo, NY |
| HAPPY LULU RAG | Alfonso Hart | July 25, 1912 | Self | Milwaukee, WI |
| HAPPY RAG | R. G. Grady | September 4, 1913 | Ajax Music | Chicago, IL |
| HAPPY SAMMY | Fred C. Schmidt | October 15, 1906 | Cable Company | New Orleans, LA |
| HARD BOILED RAG | Louis Mentel | March 10, 1910 | Mentel Brothers | Cincinnati, OH |
| HARD KNOTS | Vicory Barker Tunstall | April 23, 1906 | Self | Crockett, TX |
| HARDWOOD RAG | Jack Sight | May 3, 1909 | J. W. Jenkins | Kansas City, MO |
| HAREM SCAREM RAG | Lem Trombley | | Self | Kalamazoo, MI |
| HAREM SKIRT RAG | Harold H. Hampson | 1913 | Marsh and Needles | Wichita, KS |
| HARLEM RAG | Tom Turpin | December 17, 1897 | Robert DeYong | St. Louis, MO |
| HARLEM RAG (ARR. #2) | Tom Turpin | March 6, 1899 | Robert DeYong | St. Louis, MO |
| HARLEM RAG (ARR. #3) | Tom Turpin | 1899 | Joseph W. Stern | New York, NY |
| HARLEQUINS' GRAND MARCH | Harold Dixon | October 7, 1927 | Self | New York, NY |
| HARMONY RAG | Hal G. Nichols | September 25, 1911 | Sam Fox | Cleveland, OH |
| HARPSICHORD RAG | Buddy Weed | April 13, 1955 | Tee Kaye Music | New York, NY |
| HARRIMAN CAKE WALK | Lee S. Roberts | September 17, 1915 | Self | Chicago, IL |
| HARRY FOX TROT | Lew Pollack | June 12, 1918 | Maurice Richmond | New York, NY |

| Title | Composer | Date | Publisher | City |
|---|---|---|---|---|
| HAUNTING RAG | Julius Lenzberg | December 4, 1911 | M. Witmark and Sons | New York, NY |
| HAVANA RAG | Maurice Kirwin | August 22, 1904 | John Stark and Son | St. Louis, MO |
| HAYTIAN RAG | Ford Dabney | October 4, 1910 | Jerome H. Remick | Detroit, MI |
| HAZLESPLITTER | Charles Pigg | August 11, 1906 | Pioneer Music | Chicago, IL |
| HEAVY ON THE CATSUP | Lewis F. Muir | December 26, 1913 | F. A. Mills | New York, NY |
| HELIOTROPE BOUQUET | Louis Chauvin and Scott Joplin | December 23, 1907 | Stark Music Company | New York, NY |
| HELIOTROPE RAG | Edmund Braham | 1906 | A. H. Goetting | Springfield, MA |
| HELTER-SKELTER RAG | Emma Bila | November 18, 1914 | Marks–Goldsmith Company | Washington, DC |
| HEN CACKLE RAG | Charles L. Johnson | January 31, 1912 | J. W. Jenkins | Kansas City, MO |
| HESITATIN' HEZ' | Willmont U. Webb | October 27, 1904 | Self | Buffalo, NY |
| HI-JINX | Harold Berg and Fred A. Libby | April 8, 1929 | Sam Fox | Cleveland, OH |
| HI-YELLER | Sal Rugoff and Bernard Schmidt | 1918 | Richmond Music | New York, NY |
| HICKORY NUTS RAG | Abe Losch | June 4, 1928 | Vandersloot Music | Williamsport, PA |
| HIFALUTIN RAG | Henry Lodge | March 28, 1918 | M. Witmark and Sons | New York, NY |
| HIGH HATTIN' | Zez Confrey | July 16, 1924 | Jack Mills | New York, NY |
| HIGH JINKS | Whidden and Conrad | 1910 | Leo Feist | New York, NY |
| HIGH LIFE RAG | Harry Levinsohn and Robert D. Sharp | 1913 | Robert D. Sharp Music Company | Denver, CO |
| HIGH STEPPER RAG | Lew Pollack | January 25, 1917 | Joe Morris | New York, NY |
| HIGHTOWER RAG | Winnifred Hightower | August 31, 1914 | Self | Fort Worth, TX |
| HILARITY RAG | James Scott | September 15, 1910 | Stark Music Company | St. Louis, MO |
| HINGES | Teddy Hahn | September 16, 1909 | Symplex | Cincinnati, OH |
| HIPPOCAMPUS TWO-STEP | Peter Lundberg | October 20, 1964 | Hollis Music | New York, NY |
| HIT OR MISS | Buck Wilson | November 17, 1923 | Jack Mills | New York, NY |
| HOBBLE RAG | Luther B. Hayes | April 22, 1911 | Hayes and Mardis | Covington, KY |
| HOBBLE RAG | Will Morrissey | April 7, 1911 | F. B. Haviland | New York, NY |
| HOBBLE SKIRT DRAG | Sylvester E. George | December 21, 1910 | Maurice Shapiro | New York, NY |
| HOBBLE SKIRT RAG | R. Rembert Goldsby | December 22, 1910 | E. Witzmann | Memphis, TN |
| HOLLY AND MISTLETOE RAG | Geraldine Dobyns | 1909 | Philip Werlein | New Orleans, LA |
| HOLLY RAG | Raymond Litzenberger | November 25, 1911 | Self | Wilkes-Barre, PA |
| HOLLYHOCK | Billy Mayerl | December 21, 1927 | Sam Fox | Cleveland, OH |
| HOLY MOSES RAG | Cy Seymour | April 26, 1906 | Arnett–Delonais | Chicago, IL |
| HOLY SMOKES | Franz Von Loew | 1916 | Universal Music | Duluth, MN |
| HOME SPUN RAG | Thomas S. Allen | February 14, 1913 | Joseph M. Daly | Boston, MA |
| HOMESPUN RAG | Austin S. Benson | June 2, 1910 | Charles K. Harris | New York, NY |
| HONEY LOU-LU RAG | Charles Johnston | 1915 | P. J. Howley | New York, NY |
| HONEY MOON RAG | James Scott | August 15, 1916 | Stark Music Company | St. Louis, MO |
| HONEY RAG | Egbert Van Alsyne | July 7, 1909 | Jerome H. Remick | Detroit, MI |
| HONEYMOON RAG | Lawrence B. O'Connor | July 5, 1910 | Ernest S. Williams | Boston, MA |
| HONEYMOON RAG | Abe Olman | November 23, 1908 | W. B. Morrison | Indianapolis, IN |
| HONEYSUCKLE | J. Louis Merkur | December 22, 1927 | Jack Mills | New York, NY |
| HONEYSUCKLE RAG | George Botsford | December 19, 1911 | Jerome H. Remick | New York, NY |

| Title | Composer | Date | Publisher | City |
|---|---|---|---|---|
| HOOSIER RAG | Sophus Jergensen | October 21, 1905 | Abby Music | Indianapolis, IN |
| HOOSIER RAG | Julia Lee Niebergall | November 1, 1907 | Jerome H. Remick | New York, NY |
| HOP SCOTCH | George L. Cobb | 1921 | Walter Jacobs | Boston, MA |
| HORSE LAUGH | Sam H. Ewing | 1909 | Self | Cleveland, OH |
| HORSESHOE RAG | Julia Lee Niebergall | April 1, 1911 | J. H. Aufderheide | Indianapolis, IN |
| HOT AIR RAG | F. A. Walker | April 27, 1907 | Self | Mount Healthy, OH |
| HOT AIR RAG | Thomas V. White | December 24, 1900 | M. D. Swisher | Philadelphia, PA |
| HOT ASHES | Earl K. Smith | October 28, 1909 | Levan Music | Chicago, IL |
| HOT CABBAGE | Homer Denney | July 31, 1908 | Self | Cincinnati, OH |
| HOT CHESTNUTS | George J. Trinkhaus | December 16, 1910 | Herald Square Music | New York, NY |
| HOT CHOCOLATE RAG | Malvin M. Franklin and Arthur Lange | April 6, 1909 | Joseph W. Stern | New York, NY |
| HOT CINDERS | Joseph F. Lamb | 1964 | Mills Music | New York, NY |
| HOT FINGERS | Joe Gold | October 15, 1925 | Jack Mills | New York, NY |
| HOT FINGERS | Robert Marine | June 1, 1928 | Self | New York, NY |
| HOT HANDS | Charley Straight | February 16, 1916 | Jerome H. Remick | New York, NY |
| HOT HOUSE RAG | Paul Pratt | July 27, 1914 | Stark Music Company | St. Louis, MO |
| HOT IVORIES | Ray Sinatra | April 11, 1927 | Bibo, Bloedon, and Lang | New York, NY |
| HOT OFF THE GRIDDLE | James White | December 31, 1915 | Frank K. Root | Chicago, IL |
| HOT RAG | S. R. Lewis | March 19, 1900 | S. Brainard's Sons | Chicago, IL |
| HOT SCOTCH RAG | H. A. Fischler | January 7, 1911 | Vandersloot Music | Williamsport, PA |
| HOT STUFF | D. E. Maharb | August 7, 1911 | Backman and Backman | New York, NY |
| HOT TAMALE MAN! | Herbert Ingraham | March 5, 1909 | Shapiro Music | New York, NY |
| HUMMER RAG | J. Rollie Bibb | July 25, 1917 | Warner C. Williams | Indianapolis, IN |
| HUMORESTLESS | Zez Confrey | March 12, 1925 | Jack Mills | New York, NY |
| HUMPTY DUMPTY | Charley Straight | January 13, 1914 | M. Witmark and Sons | New York, NY |
| HUMPY'S BUCK | Charles Humfeld | January 30, 1914 | Self | St. Louis, MO |
| HUNGARIAN RAG | Julius Lenzberg | June 26, 1913 | Jerome H. Remick | New York, NY |
| HURON GLIDE | W. R. McKanlass | March 25, 1913 | McKanlass and Marone | Port Huron, MI |
| HURRICANE RAG | Joe Glover | April 14, 1959 | Melrose Music | New York, NY |
| HURRICANE RAG | Frederick G. Johnson | 1910 | Self | Wilkes-Barre, PA |
| HURRY A LITTLE | Charles Cooper | 1904 | H. H. Sparks | Toronto, CN |
| HUSTLING RAG | Roy Steventon and Lloyd Kidwell | 1914 | Great Eastern | Cincinnati, OH |
| HUTCHINSON BRO'S RAG | William H. Stockwell | August 7, 1911 | Hutchinson Bros. | Shreveport, LA |
| HYACINTH RAG | George Botsford | December 11, 1911 | Jerome H. Remick | New York, NY |
| HYPNOTIC RAG | Ed C. Mahoney | October 4, 1912 | Joseph M. Daly | Boston, MA |
| HYPNOTIZER RAG | Clarence H. Graham | September 24, 1910 | Maurice Shapiro | New York, NY |
| HYSTERICS RAG | Paul Biese and F. Henri Klickmann | December 23, 1914 | Jerome H. Remick | New York, NY |
| I'M ALABAMA BOUND | Robert Hoffman | September 28, 1909 | Robert Ebberman | New Orleans, LA |
| ICYCLES | James E. Kelly | November 11, 1907 | Jerome H. Remick | New York, NY |
| IDAWANNA | Newell Chase | May 2, 1929 | Sherman, Clay | San Francisco, CA |
| IGLOO STOMP | Bill Wirges | January 26, 1927 | Alfred and Company | New York, NY |
| IMAGINATION | Fud Livingston | October 6, 1927 | Robbins Music | New York, NY |

| Title | Composer | Date | Publisher | City |
|---|---|---|---|---|
| IMP RAG | Webb Long | June 21, 1910 | Self | Wichita, KS |
| IMPERIAL RAG | Walter M. Davis | March 15, 1910 | Self | Chicago, IL |
| IMPERIAL RAG | Joseph M. Eshelman | July 29, 1908 | Self | Reading, PA |
| IMPERIAL RAG | Billie Talbot | November 28, 1914 | Bush and Gerts | Dallas, TX |
| IN A MIST | Bix Beiderbecke | November 18, 1927 | Robbins Music | New York, NY |
| IN COLORED CIRCLES | Fred L. Neddermeyer | October 7, 1898 | Self | Columbus, OH |
| IN THE GROOVE | Willie the Lion Smith | August 18, 1936 | Mills Music | New York, NY |
| IN THE SPOTLIGHT | Jerry Jarnagin | September 5, 1924 | Jack Mills | New York, NY |
| INCANDESCENT RAG | George Botsford | October 21, 1913 | Jerome H. Remick | New York, NY |
| INCLINATION FOX-TROT | Frank A. Anderson | 1916 | Louis H. Ross | Boston, MA |
| INDIA RUBBER | Duke Baier | December 12, 1913 | Baier and Slagle | Fort Wayne, IN |
| INK SPLOTCH RAG | Clifford Adams | 1909 | A. Hospe Company | Omaha, NE |
| INNOCENCE | Harry A. Tierney | June 24, 1911 | Ted Snyder Company | New York, NY |
| INTERMISSION RAG | Charles Wellinger | January 6, 1916 | Roger Graham | Chicago, IL |
| INVITATION RAG | Les Copeland | December 20, 1911 | Jerome H. Remick | Detroit, MI |
| IRIDESCENCE | Phil Saltman | July 12, 1938 | Robbins Music | New York, NY |
| IRISH CONFETTI | George L. Cobb | 1918 | Walter Jacobs | Boston, MA |
| IRMENA RAG | Axel Christensen | March 9, 1908 | Christensen School | Chicago, IL |
| IRRESISTIBLE RAG | W. C. Powell | March 14, 1910 | Church, Paxson | New York, NY |
| ISHUDWORRY | Robert Milton Storer | April 22, 1914 | Charles Edward Storer | St. Louis, MO |
| IT'S A BIRD! | Cliff Hess | December 28, 1905 | Groene Music | Cincinnati, OH |
| IVORY CHIPS | Phil Ohman | October 8, 1929 | Robbins Music | New York, NY |
| IVORY KAPERS | Giff Fahrmeyer | November 19, 1929 | Vandersloot Music | Williamsport, PA |
| J. J. J. RAG | Joe Jordan | April 17, 1905 | Pekin Publishing | Chicago, IL |
| JACK FROST | Archie W. Scheu | March 26, 1906 | Self | Cincinnati, OH |
| JACK FROST RAG | William Haskins | November 14, 1928 | Denton and Haskins | New York, NY |
| JACK IN THE BOX | Zez Confrey | December 30, 1927 | Jack Mills | New York, NY |
| JACK RABBIT RAG | H. J. Beckerman | 1914 | American Music | Chicago, IL |
| JACK RABBIT RAG | Donald Garcia | January 24, 1910 | Vandersloot Music | Williamsport, PA |
| JAGTIME JOHNSON'S RAGTIME MARCH | Fred L. Ryder | June 14, 1901 | McKinley Music | Chicago, IL |
| JAMAICA JINGER | Egbert Van Alstyne | March 19, 1912 | Jerome H. Remick | Detroit, MI |
| JAPANESE RAG | Mose Gumble | March 25, 1901 | W. H. Willis | Cincinnati, OH |
| JAPANIMO | Arthur D. Porter | January 15, 1906 | John Arnold | Cincinnati, OH |
| JASS BAND RAG | Frank S. Butler | August 1, 1917 | Self | New York, NY |
| JAXON RAG | Edward G. Byers and Lucius C. Dunn | February 24, 1908 | Victor Kremer | Chicago, IL |
| JAY ROBERTS RAG | Jay Roberts | December 16, 1911 | Forster Music | Chicago, IL |
| JAY WALK | Zez Confrey | February 12, 1927 | Jack Mills | New York, NY |
| JAZZ MASTER | Billy Mayerl | August 4, 1925 | Sam Fox | Cleveland, OH |
| JAZZ MISTRESS | Billy Mayerl | September 25, 1925 | Sam Fox | Cleveland, OH |
| JAZZARISTRIX | Billy Mayerl | November 4, 1925 | Sam Fox | Cleveland, OH |
| JERUSHA PEPPER | Jay G. Coffman | March 26, 1908 | Victor Kremer | Chicago, IL |
| JES' DANDY | Joe Solman | March 5, 1923 | Jack Mills | New York, NY |
| JESTER RAG | W. R. McKanlass | 1917 | Buck & Lowney | St. Louis, MO |

| Title | Composer | Date | Publisher | City |
|---|---|---|---|---|
| JIM CROW RAG | Lizzie Mowen | January 3, 1910 | C. C. Powell | Fort Wayne, IN |
| JIM JAMS | Roy Bargy | June 27, 1922 | Sam Fox | Cleveland, OH |
| JINGLES | James P. Johnson | July 1, 1926 | Clarence Williams Music | New York, NY |
| JINGO | Edwin Gale | 1907 | W. H. Croner | Columbus, OH |
| JINX RAG | Lucian P. Gibson and Jesse Dukes | December 7, 1911 | Lucian P. Gibson | St. Louis, MO |
| JITNEY BUS RAG | Grover Thompson | September 1, 1915 | Marks–Goldsmith Company | Washington, DC |
| JOHNNY-JUMP-UPS | Syndey S. Barker | February 20, 1905 | Sherman, Clay | San Francisco, CA |
| JOHNSON RAG | Guy Hall and Henry Kleinkauf | February 28, 1917 | Self | Wilkes-Barre, PA |
| JOLLY JINGLES RAG | F. H. Losey | September 24, 1913 | Vandersloot Music | Williamsport, PA |
| JOY BOY | A. J. Weidt | 1916 | Walter Jacobs | Boston, MA |
| JOY RAG | Jay Roberts | December 15, 1911 | Forster Music | Chicago, IL |
| JUGGLING THE PIANO | Sam A. Perry | December 1, 1924 | Jack Mills | New York, NY |
| JUMPING JACK | Rube Bloom and Bernie Seaman | July 3, 1928 | ABC Standard | New York, NY |
| JUMPING JACK | Chet Ferguson | 1917 | Daniels and Wilson | San Francisco, CA |
| JUNGLE TIME | E. Philip Severin | February 23, 1905 | Self | Moline, IL |
| JUNK MAN RAG | C. Luckeyth Roberts | May 26, 1913 | Joseph W. Stern | New York, NY |
| JUST A LI'L RAG | Urban A. Schick | November 20, 1915 | Shattinger Music | St. Louis, MO |
| JUST ASK ME | Charles Hunter | April 5, 1902 | Frank G. Fite | Nashville, TN |
| JUST MISSED | Clarence W. Murphey | September 4, 1912 | Self | St. Louis, MO |
| JUST NOISE | C. I. Stewart | June 4, 1906 | Southwestern Music | Tulsa, OK |
| JUSTIN-TIME | Roy Bargy | June 27, 1922 | Sam Fox | Cleveland, OH |
| KAISER'S RAG | Clare Mast | 1915 | Self | Edgerton, OH |
| KALAMITY KID | Ferd Guttenberger | 1909 | Self | Macon, GA |
| KANGAROO HOP | Melville Morris | November 24, 1915 | Jerome H. Remick | New York, NY |
| KANSAS APPLEKNOCKER | Frank Frank | August 16, 1909 | F. B. Haviland | New York, NY |
| KANSAS CITY RAG | James Scott | January 2, 1907 | Stark Music Company | St. Louis, MO |
| KANSAS CITY STOMP | Jelly Roll Morton | August 20, 1923 | Melrose Brothers | Chicago, IL |
| KAUTIOUS KITTENS | Silvio DeRienzo | May 26, 1930 | Alfred and Company | New York, NY |
| KEE TO KEE | Ted Eastwood and Eugene Platzmann | September 28, 1917 | Artmusic | New York, NY |
| KEEK-ES-MAN-DAH! | C. Bellstedt | 1906 | Ilsen and Company | Cincinnati, OH |
| KEEP-A-MOVIN' | Al Sweet | May 2, 1910 | Ted Snyder Company | New York, NY |
| KEEP BUSY | Hardaway Fraser | July 2, 1912 | Globe Music | New York, NY |
| KEEP FINGERING | Willie the Lion Smith | March 11, 1938 | Mills Music | New York, NY |
| KEEP OFF THE GRASS | James P. Johnson | July 1, 1926 | Clarence Williams Music | New York, NY |
| KEEP YOUR TEMPER | Willie the Lion Smith | September 19, 1925 | Clarence Williams Music | New York, NY |
| KEHAMA RAG | Emma A. Bouska | March 12, 1909 | Victor Kremer | Chicago, IL |
| KENTUCKY BEAUTY | Albert Gumble and Monroe H. Resenfeld | February 20, 1904 | Joseph W. Stern | New York, NY |
| KENTUCKY RAG | Marcella A. Henry | July 1, 1917 | Christensen School | Chicago, IL |
| KENTUCKY RAG | John H. Tenney | May 8, 1905 | Joseph Placht and Son | St. Louis, MO |
| KENTUCKY RAG | Floyd Willis | September 30, 1908 | Self | Covington, KY |

| Title | Composer | Date | Publisher | City |
|---|---|---|---|---|
| KERRY MILLS' RAGTIME DANCE | Kerry Mills | February 8, 1909 | F. A. Mills | New York, NY |
| KETCHUP RAG | Irene M. Giblin | March 5, 1910 | Jerome H. Remick | New York, NY |
| KEWPIE | Gene Rose | April 4, 1929 | Sherman, Clay | San Francisco, CA |
| KEY STONE RAG | Willie Anderson | 1921 | Stark Music Company | St. Louis, MO |
| KEYBOARD KAPERS | Hunter L. Kahler | July 2, 1934 | M. M. Cole | Chicago, IL |
| KEYBOARD KLASSIC | Robert Marine | June 1, 1928 | Self | New York, NY |
| KEYBOARD KONVERSATION | Vee Lawnhurst | April 9, 1923 | Jack Mills | New York, NY |
| KIMBERLY RAG | H. H. Hoyt, Jr. | November 5, 1909 | Victor Kremer | Chicago, IL |
| KINDA CARELESS | Zez Confrey | July 16, 1924 | Jack Mills | New York, NY |
| KING BAGGOT'S RAG | G. W. Lowe | February 19, 1914 | Self | Columbia, KY |
| KING OF RAGS | Bob Haney | 1900 | Self | Keokuk, IA |
| KING OF RAGS | Sherman Swisher | 1908 | Self | Philadelphia, PA |
| KING OF THEM ALL | William Murray Simpson | November 20, 1909 | McKinley Music | Chicago, IL |
| KING PORTER STOMP | Jelly Roll Morton | December 6, 1924 | Melrose Brothers | Chicago, IL |
| KINKLETS | Arthur Marshall | December 10, 1906 | Stark Music Company | New York, NY |
| KINKY | Carrie E. Zeman | November 5, 1906 | Andreas Music | Davenport, IA |
| KINKY HEAD | George E. Rausch | 1910 | Self | Omaha, NE |
| KINKY KINKS | Louis K. Carroll | 1907 | Self | Manchester, OH |
| KISMET RAG | Scott Joplin and Scott Hayden | February 21, 1913 | Stark Music Company | St. Louis, MO |
| KISSING BUG RAG | Charles L. Johnson | 1909 | Keith Music | Louisville, KY |
| KITCHEN TOM | Eubie Blake | 1975 | Eubie Blake Music | New York, NY |
| KITTEN ON THE KEYS | Zez Confrey | July 8, 1921 | Jack Mills | New York, NY |
| KITTY WOBBLE | Waylande Gregory | 1920 | Self | Pittsburg, KS |
| KLASSICLE RAG | Cecil Duane Crabb | April 10, 1911 | J. H. Aufderheide | Indianapolis, IN |
| KLINKERS | Albert Stedman | 1906 | Empire Music | Boston, MA |
| KLONDIKE RAG | George Botsford | January 23, 1908 | William R. Haskins Company | New York, NY |
| KLU-LUKUM RAG | Claude P. Christopher and Carl T. Williams | 1909 | Lew Roberts Music | Nashville, TN |
| KNICE AND KNIFTY | Roy Bargy and Charley Straight | February 7, 1922 | Sam Fox | Cleveland, OH |
| KNICK KNOCKS | Phil Schwartz | March 29, 1915 | Sam Fox | Cleveland, OH |
| KNOCKOUT DROPS | F. Henri Klickmann | December 8, 1910 | Victor Kremer | Chicago, IL |
| KRAZY KAT | Ben Ritchie | November 6, 1911 | Self | New York, NY |
| LACE EMBROIDERY | Bob Zurke | April 10, 1939 | Leo Feist | New York, NY |
| LADY SLIPPERS RAG | Raymond Birch | May 26, 1910 | Charles L. Johnson | Kansas City, MO |
| LAGOON BREEZE | Louis Mentel | September 28, 1903 | Mentel Brothers | Cincinnati, OH |
| LAGOON RAG | Louis Mentel | August 5, 1907 | Mentel Brothers | Covington, KY |
| LAKESIDE WHISTLE RAG | Carl H. Copenhaver | June 4, 1912 | Frank Harding | New York, NY |
| LASSES | Lucy Thomas | December 28, 1905 | Groene Music | Cincinnati, OH |
| LAST RAG | William Bolcom | December 30, 1976 | Edward B. Marks Music | New York, NY |
| LATONIA RAG | Leon Donaldson | July 23, 1903 | American Music | St. Louis, MO |
| LAUGHING AT THE IVORIES | Theo Uden Masman | February 15, 1926 | Jack Mills | New York, NY |
| LAUGHING DICK RAG | Riffe H. Smith | 1908 | Louis Grunewald | New Orleans, LA |

| Title | Composer | Date | Publisher | City |
|---|---|---|---|---|
| LAURETTE | Frank Banta | March 4, 1929 | Robbins Music | New York, NY |
| LAUTERBACH | Ernest A. Ittner | November 24, 1906 | Victor Kremer | Chicago, IL |
| LAWN EYRIE RAG | Jesse Rehkopf | 1905 | Pioneer Music | Chicago, IL |
| LAZY LUKE | George J. Philpot | December 10, 1904 | Walter Jacobs | Boston, MA |
| LEAP FROG | Edwin F. Kendall | July 2, 1908 | Jerome H. Remick | New York, NY |
| LEMON DROPS | Mike Bernard | December 31, 1910 | Joe Morris | New York, NY |
| LEMONS | Ollie McHugh | October 28, 1907 | H. A. Sturm Music | Cincinnati, OH |
| LEMONS AND LIMES | Cora Salisbury | November 1, 1909 | Will Rossiter | Chicago, IL |
| LEOLA | Scott Joplin | 1905 | American Music | St. Louis, MO |
| LEONA RAG | Leona Coker | April 19, 1906 | Self | St. Joseph, MO |
| LET'S GO | Charley Straight | December 30, 1915 | Jerome H. Remick | New York, NY |
| LEVEE RAG | Fred E. Gates | December 7, 1914 | Gates and Jacobson | Cincinnati, OH |
| LEVEE RAG | Charles E. Mullen | September 29, 1902 | Will Rossiter | Chicago, IL |
| LIGHTNING | Clarence Jones | December 26, 1908 | Groene Music | Cincinnati, OH |
| LILY QUEEN | Arthur Marshall and Scott Joplin | November 8, 1907 | Willis Woodward | New York, NY |
| LILY RAG | Charles Thompson | 1914 | Syndicate Music | St. Louis, MO |
| LION TAMER RAG | Mark Janza | January 2, 1913 | A. F. Marzian | Louisville, KY |
| LIP-STICK | Ted Murray and Charles Rosoff | February 4, 1928 | Harms, Inc. | New York, NY |
| LITTLE BIT O' HONEY | E. Clinton Keithley | March 15, 1909 | Keith Music | Louisville, KY |
| LITTLE JACK'S RAG | Arthur Marshall | October 29, 1976 | Hawthorne Books | New York, NY |
| LITTLE ROCK GETAWAY | Joe Sullivan | April 1, 1938 | Leo Feist | New York, NY |
| LITTLE STICKS O'LICORICE | Ray Ruddy | December 29, 1911 | Jerome H. Remick | New York, NY |
| LIVE WIRES RAG | Adaline Shepherd | November 16, 1910 | Harold Rossiter | Chicago, IL |
| LOG CABIN RAG | Ferd Guttenberger | 1908 | Self | Macon, GA |
| LOG CABIN RAG | James R. Shannon | November 9, 1914 | Forster Music | Chicago, IL |
| LONDON RAG | David A. Jasen | June 28, 1979 | The Big Three | New York, NY |
| LONG ISLAND RAG | Ida B. Robinson | February 13, 1912 | Self | Bellport, NY |
| LOOSE ELBOWS | Billy Mayerl | March 9, 1926 | Sam Fox | Cleveland, OH |
| LOOSE FINGERS | Maurice E. Swerdlow | May 31, 1923 | Sam Fox | Cleveland, OH |
| LOPEZ RAG | J. R. Lopez | August 31, 1918 | Self | Memphis, MO |
| LOPEZ SPEAKING | Harry Jentes | August 27, 1926 | Robbins–Engel | New York, NY |
| LOPEZIANA | Louis Alter | August 9, 1926 | Robbins–Engel | New York, NY |
| LOST RAG | Herbert Ingraham | March 5, 1909 | Shapiro Music | New York, NY |
| LOTTA TRIX | Robert Marine | June 1, 1928 | Self | New York, NY |
| LOTUS CLUB RAG | Ernie Burnett | September 24, 1919 | Keystone Music | St. Joseph, MO |
| LOUISIANA RAG | Leon Block | February 6, 1911 | Will Rossiter | Chicago, IL |
| LOUISIANA RAG | Theo. H. Northrup | October 20, 1897 | Thompson Music | Chicago, IL |
| LOUISIANA RAG | Harry A. Tierney | May 3, 1913 | Joseph Krolage Music | Cincinnati, OH |
| LOUISIANA RAG | Edward R. Wagner | May 5, 1908 | Treece and Bowen | Herrin, IL |
| LOVER'S LANE GLIDE | Calvin Lee Woolsey | October 5, 1914 | Self | St. Joseph, MO |
| LOVEY-DOVEY | George Botsford | May 19, 1910 | Ted Snyder Company | New York, NY |
| LOVEY-DOVEY | Charles L. Johnson | 1907 | Charles L. Johnson | Kansas City, MO |
| LUCKY DOG | Herbert Bryan Marple | January 15, 1917 | Sherman, Clay | San Francisco, CA |

| Title | Composer | Date | Publisher | City |
|---|---|---|---|---|
| LUCKY LOU | Frank C. Keithley | 1906 | Keithley–Joy Music | Des Moines, IA |
| LUSITANIA RAG | Edward R. Wagner | May 5, 1908 | Treece and Bowen | Herrin, IL |
| MAD FINGERS | Billy James | April 24, 1930 | Mills Music | New York, NY |
| MADAGASCAR MANGLE | Vinton Freedley | February 3, 1912 | Jerome H. Remick | New York, NY |
| MADE IN GERMANY | Karl Schmidt | 1906 | Frank K. Root | Chicago, IL |
| MAGNETIC RAG | Scott Joplin | July 21, 1914 | Self | New York, NY |
| MAGPIE RAG | Malvin M. Franklin | December 15, 1908 | Joseph W. Stern | New York, NY |
| MAH JONG | Sid Reinherz | March 5, 1924 | Jack Mills | New York, NY |
| MAJESTIC RAG | Ben Rawls and Royal Neel | May 14, 1914 | Bush and Gerts | Dallas, TX |
| MAKE BELIEVE RAG | David A. Jasen | June 28, 1979 | The Big Three | New York, NY |
| MANDO RAG | Robert George Ingraham | July 10, 1914 | Stark Music Company | St. Louis, MO |
| MANDY'S BROADWAY STROLL | Thomas E. Broady | 1898 | Henry A. French | Nashville, TN |
| MANHATTAN RAG | Fred Brownold | December 28, 1901 | John Stark and Son | St. Louis, MO |
| MANHATTAN RAG | Edwin F. Kendall | August 23, 1906 | Joseph W. Stern | New York, NY |
| MANHATTAN RAG | Frank Signorelli and Deane Kincaide | July 3, 1963 | Bregman, Vocco, and Conn | New York, NY |
| MANILLA RAG | Gregorio Domingo | March 14, 1916 | Self | Liberal, KS |
| MANILLA RAG | Zellah Edith Sanden | 1898 | Lyon and Healy | Chicago, IL |
| MAPLE LEAF RAG | Scott Joplin | September 18, 1899 | John Stark and Son | Sedalia, MO |
| MARATHON RAG | Whitney Combes | February 26, 1909 | Nightingale Music | New York, NY |
| MARDI GRAS RAG | George Lyons and Bob Yosco | February 24, 1914 | George W. Meyer Music | New York, NY |
| MARIGOLD | Billy Mayerl | June 18, 1928 | Sam Fox | Cleveland, OH |
| MARILYNN | Wheeler Wadsworth and Victor Arden | July 7, 1919 | Forster Music | Chicago, IL |
| MARINE SYNCOPATIONS | Robert Marine | June 1, 1928 | Self | New York, NY |
| MARITA | Bill Krenz | December 14, 1934 | M. M. Cole | Chicago, IL |
| MARY JANE RAG | Robert Klock | 1909 | Philip Werlein | New Orleans, LA |
| MASHED POTATOES | Calvin Lee Woolsey | August 12, 1911 | Self | Braymer, MO |
| MATTIE'S RAGS | Mattie C. Thompson | April 22, 1916 | Self | Little Rock, AR |
| MAURICE RAG | William H. Penn | April 16, 1912 | Self | New York, NY |
| MAY BLOOM RAG | Ramond Henry Willis | March 4, 1904 | Self | Boulder, CO |
| MEADOW LARK RAG | Tom Pitts | 1916 | Charles N. Daniels Music | San Francisco, CA |
| MEADOW LARK RAG | Jean Rameau | May 10, 1910 | Self | Butte, MT |
| MEASLES RAG | Arthur H. Nokes | November 4, 1913 | H. Kirkus Dugdale | Winnipeg, CN |
| MEDDLESOME | Clarence H. St. John | October 8, 1908 | Stark Music Company | New York, NY |
| MEDIC RAG | Calvin Lee Woolsey | April 13, 1910 | Jerome H. Remick | New York, NY |
| MEDICAL RAG | Lucas and Phelps | 1912 | Broadway Music | New York, NY |
| MEDITATION | Lee Sims | 1927 | Robbins | New York, NY |
| MEER-SHAM RAG | Cliff Irvin | January 30, 1914 | H. Kirkus Dugdale | Washington, DC |
| MELANCHOLY CHARLIE | Frank Crum | March 9, 1927 | Robbins Music | New York, NY |
| MELODY MAN | Charles Gillen | December 28, 1910 | Theodore Morse Music | New York, NY |
| MELODY RAG | Raymond Birch | January 3, 1911 | Charles L. Johnson | Kansas City, MO |
| MELROSE RAG | Hubert Bauersachs | December 29, 1921 | Self | St. Louis, MO |
| MEMPHIS RAG | Percy Wenrich | September 14, 1908 | McKinley Music | Chicago, IL |
| MEPHISTO RAG | S. C. Baumann | January 13, 1909 | L. Grunewald | New Orleans, LA |

| Title | Composer | Date | Publisher | City |
|---|---|---|---|---|
| MEPHISTO RAG | Anthony J. Stasny | August 20, 1908 | Self | Cleveland, OH |
| MERRY MINNOW | Pauline Alpert | November 29, 1935 | Mills Music | New York, NY |
| MERRY WIDOW GLAD RAG | Victor Maurice | 1908 | Metropolitan Music | New York, NY |
| MERRY WIDOW RAG | E. Clinton Keithley | March 5, 1908 | Keith Music | Louisville, KY |
| MERRY-GO-ROUND RAG | Gus Edwards | November 11, 1908 | Self | New York, NY |
| MERRY-GO-ROUND RAG | Ralph Larsh | January 8, 1918 | Self | Chicago, IL |
| METEOR RAG | Arthur C. Morse | 1920 | Walter Jacobs | Boston, MA |
| METROPOLITAN RAG | Anna Case | March 21, 1917 | T. W. Allen | Newark, NJ |
| METROPOLITAN RAG | A. R. Langermann and F. C. Humsinger | July 30, 1912 | Langermann and Humsinger | New Orleans, LA |
| MEW MEW RAG | H. Taylor Weeks | December 17, 1910 | Ted Snyder Company | New York, NY |
| MICHIGAN RAG | Adrian Carter | May 28, 1910 | Self | Battle Creek, MI |
| MICROBE | Webb Long | April 22, 1909 | Marsh and Needles | Wichita, KS |
| MIDNIGHT RAG | Gus Winkler | June 17, 1912 | Forster Music | Chicago, IL |
| MIDNIGHT TROT | George L. Cobb | April 5, 1916 | Will Rossiter | Chicago, IL |
| MIDNIGHT WHIRL RAG | Silvio Hein | January 26, 1914 | T. B. Harms | New York, NY |
| MIKE'S WASHBOARD RAG | David A. Jasen | June 2, 2002 | Katherine Reynolds | Minneapolis, MN |
| MILKMAN'S RAG | Shep Camp | April 28, 1913 | F. B. Haviland | New York, NY |
| MINNESOTA RAG | Axel Christensen | July 10, 1913 | Christensen School | Chicago, IL |
| MINNESOTA STREET RAG | Fred Swanson | November 5, 1903 | Self | St. Paul, MN |
| MINSTREL BAND RAG | Albert Gumble | April 30, 1909 | Jerome H. Remick | New York, NY |
| MINSTREL MAN | J. Russel Robinson | July 27, 1911 | Stark Music Company | St. Louis, MO |
| MISERABLE RAG | Malvin M. Franklin | June 19, 1915 | Waterson, Berlin, and Snyder | New York, NY |
| MISERY BLUES | Henry Lodge | May 1, 1918 | M. Witmark and Sons | New York, NY |
| MISS MOLLY | Hirshfield and Levy | 1903 | Fred J. Hamill | Chicago, IL |
| MISSISSAUGA RAG | Austin E. Kitchen | December 6, 1974 | Eldorado Music | Mississauga, CN |
| MISSISSIPPI RAG | Alfred Gasdorf | 1914 | Great Eastern | Cincinnati, OH |
| MISSISSIPPI SHIVERS | Zez Confrey | July 16, 1924 | Jack Mills | New York, NY |
| MISSISSIPPI SMILAX | H. Harry Landrum | 1907 | J. W. Jenkins | Kansas City, MO |
| MISSISSIPPI TEASER | Hugh Canon | February 27, 1911 | O. K. Houck | Memphis, TN |
| MISSOURI MAZE | Ulysses E. Cross | March 21, 1913 | E. W. Berry Music | Kansas City, MO |
| MISSOURI RAG | Maie Fitzgerald | December 20, 1900 | A. W. Perry and Sons | Sedalia, MO |
| MISSOURI RAG | W. C. Powell | November 8, 1907 | Joe Morris | Philadelphia, PA |
| MISSOURI RAG | David Silverman and Arthur Ward | March 10, 1919 | Weile Publishing | St. Louis, MO |
| MISSOURI ROMP | Arthur Marshall | June 27, 1966 | Oak Publishing | New York, NY |
| MISTER BUZZ SAW | Jean Kastowsky | March 17, 1916 | C. L. Barnhouse | Oskaloosa, IA |
| MODERNESQUE | Charles E. Wilkinson | April 10, 1930 | Rubank | Chicago, IL |
| MODERNISTIC | James P. Johnson | November 3, 1933 | Clarence Williams Music | New York, NY |
| MODESTY | James Scott | September 15, 1920 | Stark Music Company | St. Louis, MO |
| MODULATIONS | Clarence Jones | April 17, 1923 | Will Rossiter | Chicago, IL |
| MOLLY CODDLE RAG | Julius De Van | 1907 | George H. Remington | Cincinnati, OH |
| MONKEY MOTION RAG | O. E. Keenan | July 17, 1911 | W. H. Willis | Cincinnati, OH |
| MONKEY RAG | Wheatley Davis | April 17, 1911 | O. K. Houck | Memphis, TN |
| MONOGRAMS | Homer Denney | 1911 | Self | Cincinnati, OH |

| Title | Composer | Date | Publisher | City |
|---|---|---|---|---|
| MONUMENTAL ECHOES | F. G. Howland | 1900 | Self | Schuyleville, NY |
| MOONLIGHT RAG | Henry Lodge | May 5, 1913 | M. Witmark and Sons | New York, NY |
| MOONSHINE RAG | Edward Hudson | May 10, 1916 | Stark Music Company | St. Louis, MO |
| MOOSE RAG | Ted Johnson | March 7, 1910 | Brehm Brothers | Erie, PA |
| MOP RAG | Merton T. Buckley | January 25, 1912 | Self | Wichita, KS |
| MOP RAG | Helen S. Eaton | October 20, 1909 | Jerome H. Remick | Detroit, MI |
| MORE NOISE RAG | Louis Mentel | May 12, 1909 | Mentel Brothers | Cincinnati, OH |
| MOSQUITO BITES | Edwin F. Kendall | July 13, 1907 | Seminary Music | New York, NY |
| MOTOR BOAT RAG | Henry W. Gaul | November 9, 1911 | Tropwen Music | Newport, KY |
| MOTOR BUS | Annie Houston | July 25, 1914 | Bush and Gerts | Dallas, TX |
| MOUSE'S HOOFS | Zez Confrey | December 9, 1935 | Exclusive Publications | New York, NY |
| MOUSIE IN THE PIANO | Joe Keden | October 29, 1928 | Al Piantadosi | New York, NY |
| MOUSTACHE JOHNSON | Dora Loucks Hillman | March 24, 1909 | Webb Rockefeller Miller | Chicago, IL |
| MOVIE RAG | John S. Zamecnik | August 6, 1913 | Sam Fox | Cleveland, OH |
| MOVING RAG | Earl E. Edmonds | February 13, 1912 | Joseph Krolage Music | Cincinnati, OH |
| MUD CAT RAG | Bill Krenz | November 24, 1953 | Mills Music | New York, NY |
| MUNKI DOODLE DUM | Chester A. Freeman | April 10, 1903 | B. J. Tiemann | New York, NY |
| MUSETTE | Ferde Grofe | July 25, 1928 | Robbins Music | New York, NY |
| MUSIC BOX RAG | C. Luckeyth Roberts | October 23, 1914 | Joseph W. Stern | New York, NY |
| MUSIC SHOP RAG | J. F. Cohen | 1915 | Morrison Music Shop | Indianapolis, IN |
| MUSICAL ZIG ZAGS | O. J. Goehmer | July 24, 1905 | Thiebes–Stierlin Music Company | St. Louis, MO |
| MUSLIN RAG | Mel B. Kaufman | December 16, 1918 | Forster Music | Chicago, IL |
| MUTILATION RAG | Zema Randale | July 31, 1915 | Cable Company | Chicago, IL |
| MUTT AND JEFF RAG | Phillip E. Eubank | January 12, 1912 | Self | Tahlequah, OK |
| MUTT AND JEFF RAG | M. C. Rowe and William Arthurs | 1911 | Gotham–Attucks Music | New York, NY |
| MY AEROPLANE JANE | G. L. Trombley | February 25, 1911 | Self | Kalamazoo, MI |
| MY FAVORITE RAG | James White | September 20, 1915 | Roger Graham | Chicago, IL |
| MY PET | Zez Confrey | March 11, 1921 | Jack Mills | New York, NY |
| MY RAG | Amerigo V. Bafunno | June 28, 1907 | Bafunno Bros. Music | St. Louis, MO |
| NAKED DANCE | Jelly Roll Morton | 1950 | Tempo Music | Washington, DC |
| NANETTE | Adam Carroll | July 14, 1927 | Robbins Music | New York, NY |
| NAPPY LEE | Joe Jordan | December 15, 1903 | James E. Agnew | Des Moines, IA |
| NAT JOHNSON'S RAG | Nat Johnson | December 16, 1911 | Forster Music | Chicago, IL |
| NATIONAL COLORS RAG | Marcella A. Henry | June 1, 1917 | Christensen School | Chicago, IL |
| NATURAL GAS RAG | Oscar F. Hanna | June 14, 1910 | Self | Lexington, KY |
| NAUGHTY NAURETTE | Lew Pollack | September 15, 1927 | Jack Mills | New York, NY |
| NAUTICAL NONSENSE | George L. Cobb | 1917 | Walter Jacobs | Boston, MA |
| NAVY BLUE RAG | Leo Piersanti | 1919 | National Music | Chicago, IL |
| NERVOUS NUCKLES | Norman J. Elholm | December 7, 1923 | Jack Mills | New York, NY |
| NERVOUS RAG | Bernard E. Fay and Blackford | June 20, 1910 | Jerome H. Remick | Detroit, MI |
| NERVY GEORGE | Viola Dominique | May 13, 1903 | Self | New Orleans, LA |
| NEUTRALITY RAG | W. F. Lewinski | 1915 | | |
| NEW BLACK EAGLE BUCK | Max Morath | December 30, 1976 | Edward B. Marks Music | New York, NY |

| Title | Composer | Date | Publisher | City |
|---|---|---|---|---|
| NEW DIXIE RAG | Thomas M. Byrne | December 24, 1910 | Self | Fort Worth, TX |
| NEW ERA RAG | James Scott | June 1, 1919 | Stark Music Company | St. Louis, MO |
| NEW HIPPODROME | Herman E. Schultz | September 1, 1914 | Jerome H. Remick | New York, NY |
| NEW ORLEANS BUCK | A. C. Bernard | 1904 | Hakenjos | New Orleans, LA |
| NEW ORLEANS RAG | Castro Carazo | 1960 | Mills | New York, NY |
| NEW RUSSIAN RAG | George L. Cobb | May 16, 1923 | Will Rossiter | Chicago, IL |
| NEW STANDARD RAG | Elliot L. Adams | 1974 | Paragon Sheet Music | Lodi, CA |
| NEW YORK RAG | George C. Durgan | August 1, 1910 | Union Music Company | Boston, MA |
| NEWS RAG | Glenn C. Leap | 1910 | Swibar Publishing | Indianapolis, IN |
| NIAGARA RAG | Laverne Hanshaw | October 3, 1914 | Bush and Gerts | Dallas, TX |
| NICE AND EASY | Cliff McKay | October 17, 1916 | Jerome H. Remick | New York, NY |
| NICEST, SWEETEST, CUTEST RAG | Herbert Ingraham | March 5, 1909 | Shapiro Music | New York, NY |
| NICKEL IN THE SLOT | Zez Confrey | April 6, 1923 | Leo Feist | New York, NY |
| NICKELODEON RAG | Ada M. Burnett | April 3, 1909 | Alf E. Burnett and Company | Cincinnati, OH |
| NIGGER-TOE RAG | H. A. Fischler | April 20, 1910 | Vandersloot Music | Williamsport, PA |
| NIGHTINGALE RAG | Lester Sill | January 19, 1914 | Warner C. Williams | Indianapolis, IN |
| NITRIC-ACID RAG | Edward Hudson | January 3, 1922 | Stark Music Company | St. Louis, MO |
| NO-ZE | Homer Denney | February 7, 1905 | Self | Cincinnati, OH |
| NOBODY'S BUSINESS | Axel Christensen | July 11, 1923 | Forster Music | Chicago, IL |
| NOBODY'S RAG | David A. Jasen | June 28, 1979 | The Big Three | New York, NY |
| NOISY NOTES RAG | Ralph Wray | March 1, 1915 | Mellinger Music | St. Louis, MO |
| NONETTE RAG | Herbert Spencer | August 16, 1912 | Will Rossiter | Chicago, IL |
| NONPAREIL | Scott Joplin | 1907 | Stark Music Company | St. Louis, MO |
| NONSENSE RAG | R. G. Grady | January 14, 1911 | Joseph W. Stern | New York, NY |
| NOODLES | Percy Wenrich | August 21, 1906 | Arnett–Delonais | Chicago, IL |
| NOODLIN' | Tom Griselle | May 30, 1923 | Richmond–Robbins | New York, NY |
| NORTH POLE RAG | John Lind | October 14, 1909 | Self | Cincinnati, OH |
| NORTH POLE RAG | Samuel J. Stokes | November 1, 1909 | Louis Grunewald | New Orleans, LA |
| NOTHING DOIN' RAG | Frances Willard Neal | November 4, 1914 | Bush and Gerts | Dallas, TX |
| NOTORIETY | Kathryn L. Widmer | July 31, 1913 | Jerome H. Remick | New York, NY |
| NOVELTY RAG | May Aufderheide | April 11, 1911 | J. H. Aufderheide | Indianapolis, IN |
| NUCKLES O'TOOL WOULDS'T RIDE AGAIN | Claude Bolling | 1970 | Famous Music | New York, NY |
| O YOU SWEET RAG | James Palao | December 11, 1911 | Dugdale | New Orleans, LA |
| OAK LEAF RAG | Arthur L. Sizemore | May 10, 1911 | Self | Mankato, MN |
| OCTAGON RAG | Horace Dowell | January 5, 1903 | Alcorn and Hutsell | Nashville, TN |
| OCTAVE RAG | Frank Weeks | March 20, 1917 | Self | Osborne, KS |
| OCTOPUS RAG | John Oliver Erlan | January 14, 1907 | Darrow and Quadland | Chicago, IL |
| OFF THE ELBOW | Joe Keden | September 5, 1929 | Al Piantadosi | New York, NY |
| OH YOU ANGEL | Ford Dabney | January 4, 1911 | Maurice Shapiro | New York, NY |
| OH YOU RAG | Josephine Becker | 1909 | Emerson Music | Cincinnati, OH |
| OH YOU SALLY RAG | Clarence Jones | April 29, 1911 | John Arnold | Cincinnati, OH |
| OH YOU TIGERS | Anna de Varennes | 1909 | Self | Bay City, MI |

| Title | Composer | Date | Publisher | City |
|---|---|---|---|---|
| OH YOU TURKEY | Henry Lodge | January 20, 1914 | Waterson, Berlin, and Snyder | New York, NY |
| OH! WILLIE, PLAY THAT THING | Bill Krenz | May 23, 1952 | Mills Music | New York, NY |
| OH! YOU DARKEYS | Henry Lange | May 4, 1923 | Waterson, Berlin, and Snyder | New York, NY |
| OH! YOU DEVIL | Ford Dabney | July 2, 1909 | Maurice Shapiro | New York, NY |
| OH! YOU RAG | Sydney Chapman | April 16, 1910 | Koninsky Music | Troy, NY |
| OKISKO RAG | Harry S. G. Stoudt | September 18, 1915 | Self | Medina, OH |
| OLD CARPET RAG | Jennie Aaron | February 2, 1911 | Tolben R. Ingram Music | Denver, CO |
| OLD CROW RAG | George Botsford | April 13, 1909 | Jerome H. Remick | New York, NY |
| OLD FOLKS RAG | Wilbur Sweatman | April 14, 1914 | Joseph W. Stern | New York, NY |
| OLD HOME RAG | Joseph F. Lamb | 1964 | Mills Music | New York, NY |
| OLD KENTUCK | Frank Schmuhl | October 3, 1898 | W. J. Dyer and Bro. | St. Paul, MN |
| OLD PROFESSOR | Dick Hyman | April 18, 1955 | Hollis Music | New York, NY |
| OLD TOM-CAT ON THE KEYS | Bob Zurke | November 4, 1940 | Leo Feist | New York, NY |
| OLD VIRGINIA RAG | Clyde Douglass | December 19, 1907 | W. C. Parker | New York, NY |
| OLGA | Chas. F. Gall | July 14, 1913 | Joseph W. Stern | New York, NY |
| ON THE BAYOU | Theo. H. Northrup | September 2, 1898 | American Musical Association | Chicago, IL |
| ON THE PIKE | James Scott | April 13, 1904 | Dumars Music | Carthage, MO |
| ON THE RIVIERA | Alfred J. Doyle | June 24, 1911 | Ted Snyder Company | New York, NY |
| ON THE RURAL ROUTE | Paul Pratt | May 10, 1917 | Stark Music Company | St. Louis, MO |
| ONE FINGER JOE | Rube Bloom | May 15, 1931 | Robbins Music | New York, NY |
| ONE FOR AMELIA | Max Morath | October 20, 1964 | Hollis Music | New York, NY |
| ONE MORE RAG | Minnie Berger | 1909 | Stark Music Company | St. Louis, MO |
| ONE O'THEM THINGS! | James Chapman and Leroy Smith | 1904 | Joseph Placht and Son | St. Louis, MO |
| OPALESCENT RAG | Opal A. Allyn | | Self | Modesto, IL |
| OPERA HOUSE RAG | Robert R. Darch | August 19, 1960 | The Ragtime Music | Virginia City, NV |
| OPERA RAGS | E. Chouteau Legg | May 13, 1903 | J. W. Jenkins | Kansas City, MO |
| OPERATIC NIGHTMARE | Felix Arndt | August 2, 1916 | Sam Fox | Cleveland, OH |
| OPERATIC RAG | Julius Lenzberg | October 27, 1914 | Jerome H. Remick | New York, NY |
| OPHELIA RAG | James Scott | June 6, 1910 | Stark Music Company | St. Louis, MO |
| ORANGE LEAF RAG | Strauss L. Lloyd | February 5, 1908 | Self | Inverness, FL |
| ORIENTAL BLUES | Jack Newlon | May 25, 1933 | Self | Glenside, PA |
| ORIGINAL BLUES | Ted S. Barron | May 11, 1914 | Metropolitan Music | New York, NY |
| ORIGINAL CHICAGO BLUES | James White | March 8, 1915 | Frank K. Root | Chicago, IL |
| ORIGINAL RAGS | Scott Joplin | March 15, 1899 | Carl Hoffman Music | Kansas City, MO |
| ORIGINOLA | Hunter L. Kahler | July 2, 1934 | M. M. Cole | Chicago, IL |
| ORINOCO | Cecil Duane Crabb | March 5, 1909 | J. H. Aufderheide | Indianapolis, IN |
| OTTAWA RAG | George E. Lynn | 1913 | Northern Music | |
| OUT OF THE SOUTH | Willard Robison | April 21, 1926 | Robbins–Engel | New York, NY |
| OVER AND UNDER | Arnold Johnson | April 7, 1923 | Jack Mills | New York, NY |
| OVER THE BARS | James P. Johnson | February 15, 1939 | Clarence Williams Music | New York, NY |
| OVER THE ICE | Bill Wirges | January 26, 1927 | Alfred and Company | New York, NY |
| OYSTER RAG | Tom Lyle | May 9, 1910 | Jerome H. Remick | New York, NY |

| Title | Composer | Date | Publisher | City |
|---|---|---|---|---|
| PACIFIC RAG | James Watson | June 2, 1913 | Self | Vancouver, CN |
| PAGE MR. PIANIST | Henry Lange | April 7, 1923 | Jack Mills | New York, NY |
| PALM BEACH | C. Luckeyth Roberts | October 23, 1914 | Joseph W. Stern | New York, NY |
| PALM LEAF RAG | Scott Joplin | November 14, 1903 | Victor Kremer | Chicago, IL |
| PAN-AM RAG | Tom Turpin Arr. Arthur Marshall | June 8, 1966 | Oak Publishing | St. Louis, MO |
| PANAMA RAG | Cy Seymour | August 15, 1904 | Albright Music | Chicago, IL |
| PANSY BLOSSOMS | Charles L. Johnson | June 28, 1909 | American Music | Chicago, IL |
| PARAGON RAG | Scott Joplin | October 30, 1909 | Seminary Music | New York, NY |
| PARAMOUNT RAG | Harry Baisden | June 26, 1915 | Self | Fort Dodge, IA |
| PARAMOUNT RAG | James Scott | November 24, 1917 | Stark Music Company | St. Louis, MO |
| PASTIME RAG | Henry Lodge | April 28, 1913 | M. Witmark and Sons | New York, NY |
| PASTIME RAG NO. 1 | Artie Matthews | August 15, 1913 | Stark Music Company | St. Louis, MO |
| PASTIME RAG NO. 2 | Artie Matthews | 1913 | Stark Music Company | St. Louis, MO |
| PASTIME RAG NO. 3 | Artie Matthews | 1916 | Stark Music Company | St. Louis, MO |
| PASTIME RAG NO. 4 | Artie Matthews | September 15, 1920 | Stark Music Company | St. Louis, MO |
| PASTIME RAG NO. 5 | Artie Matthews | 1918 | Stark Music Company | St. Louis, MO |
| PATHETIC RAG | Axel Christensen | 1913 | Christensen School | Chicago, IL |
| PATRICIA RAG | Joseph F. Lamb | November 19, 1916 | Stark Music Company | St. Louis, MO |
| PATSY | Sam A. Perry | November 12, 1925 | Robbins Music | New York, NY |
| PATSY LOU | Muriel Pollock | August 19, 1935 | Joe Davis | New York, NY |
| PEACE AND PLENTY | James Scott | December 1, 1919 | Stark Music Company | St. Louis, MO |
| PEACEFUL HENRY | E. Harry Kelly | 1901 | Carl Hoffman Music | Kansas City, MO |
| PEACH | Arthur Marshall | December 7, 1908 | Stark Music Company | New York, NY |
| PEACH BLOSSOMS | Maude Gilmore | 1910 | Charles L. Johnson | Kansas City, MO |
| PEACHERINE RAG | Scott Joplin | March 18, 1901 | John Stark and Son | St. Louis, MO |
| PEACHES AND CREAM | Percy Wenrich | November 27, 1905 | Jerome H. Remick | New York, NY |
| PEACHTREE STREET RAG | John Chagy | 1977 | Kjos West | San Diego, CA |
| PEANUTS | Ethel Earnist | July 20, 1911 | Charles L. Johnson | Kansas City, MO |
| PEAR BLOSSOMS | Scott Hayden | 1966 | Oak Publishing | New York, NY |
| PEARL OF THE HAREM | Harry P. Guy | April 19, 1901 | Willard Bryant | Detroit, MI |
| PEARL'S RAG | William E. Pearl and W. H. Bell | January 10, 1914 | H. Kirkus Dugdale | Washington, DC |
| PEARLS | Jelly Roll Morton | August 20, 1923 | Melrose Brothers | Chicago, IL |
| PEEK-A-BOO RAG | Charles L. Johnson | September 28, 1914 | Forster Music | Chicago, IL |
| PEEK-A-BOO RAG | Warren and Edwards | 1905 | Newton | Chicago, IL |
| PEEKABOO PEEK | Gussie Goodfried | 1911 | F. A. Mills | New York, NY |
| PEGASUS | James Scott | September 15, 1920 | Stark Music Company | St. Louis, MO |
| PEKIN RAG | Joe Jordan | September 24, 1904 | Jordan and Motts Pekin Publishing | Chicago, IL |
| PEKIN RAG | Harry W. Martin | 1910 | Emerson Music | Cincinnati, OH |
| PENNANT RAG | Percy Wenrich | September 12, 1913 | Charles I. Davis | Cleveland, OH |
| PEPPER SAUCE | H. A. Fischler | September 24, 1910 | Vandersloot Music | Williamsport, PA |
| PERCY | Archie W. Scheu | 1909 | Self | Chicago, IL |
| PERILS OF PAULINE | Pauline Alpert | June 22, 1927 | Jack Mills | New York, NY |
| PEROXIDE | Calvin Lee Woolsey | May 3, 1910 | Self | Braymer, MO |

| Title | Composer | Date | Publisher | City |
|---|---|---|---|---|
| PERPETUAL RAG | B. W. Castle | May 15, 1908 | Bixby and Castle | Buffalo, NY |
| PERSIAN LAMB RAG | Percy Wenrich | June 15, 1908 | Walter Jacobs | Boston, MA |
| PETER PAN RAG | Leonie Ecuyer | 1906 | Self | New Orleans, LA |
| PETTICOAT LANE | Euday Bowman | August 14, 1915 | J. W. Jenkins | Kansas City, MO |
| PETTIN' THE KEYS | Allister Wylie | January 31, 1924 | Richmond–Robbins | New York, NY |
| PHANTOM RAG | Sol Violinsky and Al W. Brown | June 9, 1911 | J. Fred Helf | New York, NY |
| PIANIST RAG | Frank Schwarz | 1917 | Winn School of Popular Music | New York, NY |
| PIANO CAPERS | Allister Wylie | January 31, 1924 | Richmond–Robbins | New York, NY |
| PIANO MANIA | William Fazioli | May 26, 1922 | Jack Mills | New York, NY |
| PIANO MARMALADE | Willie the Lion Smith | June 8, 1937 | Mills Music | New York, NY |
| PIANO PAN | Phil Ohman | October 10, 1922 | Richmond–Robbins | New York, NY |
| PIANO PHUN | Louis Alter | November 14, 1925 | Robbins–Engel | New York, NY |
| PIANO PRANKS | Silvio DeRienzo | April 3, 1929 | Alfred and Company | New York, NY |
| PIANO PUZZLE | Ralph Reichenthal | February 26, 1923 | Jack Mills | New York, NY |
| PIANO RAG | Russell J. Frank | May 5, 1913 | Forster Music | Chicago, IL |
| PIANO SALAD | George L. Cobb | January 19, 1923 | Walter Jacobs | Boston, MA |
| PIANO SAUCE | George L. Cobb | August 13, 1927 | Hub Music | Boston, MA |
| PIANO TUNER'S WALKAWAY RAG | Orion Wilson and Rabe | 1915 | Wilson and Rabe | Indianapolis, IN |
| PIANOFLAGE | Roy Bargy | June 27, 1922 | Sam Fox | Cleveland, OH |
| PIANOGRAM | Ralph Rainger | October 8, 1929 | Robbins Music | New York, NY |
| PIANOLA | Frank Westphal | August 2, 1923 | Jack Mills | New York, NY |
| PIANOLA CONCERT RAG | Otto Welcome | September 1, 1922 | American Standard | Chicago, IL |
| PIANOLA RAG | Bill Krenz | December 29, 1953 | Mills Music | New York, NY |
| PIANOPHIEND | Reuben J. Haskin | August 26, 1914 | Buckeye Music | Columbus, OH |
| PIANOPHIENDS RAG | George Botsford | May 17, 1909 | William R. Haskins Company | New York, NY |
| PICCALILI RAG | Herbert Ingraham | March 5, 1909 | Shapiro Music | New York, NY |
| PICCALILI RAG | George A. Reeg, Jr. | 1912 | Daly Music | Boston, MA |
| PICKANNINY RAG | Irene M. Giblin | January 2, 1909 | Sam Fox | Cleveland, OH |
| PICKLED BEETS RAG | Ed Kuhn | January 1, 1910 | J. W. Jenkins | Kansas City, MO |
| PICKLES AND PEPPERS | Adaline Shepherd | November 7, 1906 | Joseph Flanner | Milwaukee, WI |
| PIFFLE RAG | Gladys Yelvington | April 8, 1911 | J. H. Aufderheide | Indianapolis, IN |
| PIGEON WING RAG | Charles L. Johnson | July 26, 1909 | Will Rossiter | Chicago, IL |
| PIKE PIKERS RAG | Ida G. Bierman | August 4, 1904 | W. C. Polla | Chicago, IL |
| PIN CUSHION RAG | R. G. Grady | October 28, 1909 | Levan Music | Chicago, IL |
| PINE APPLE RAG | Scott Joplin | October 12, 1908 | Seminary Music | New York, NY |
| PINEYWOOD RAG | Adam Minsel | August 18, 1909 | Victor Kremer | Chicago, IL |
| PINK POODLE | Charles L. Johnson | May 6, 1914 | Forster Music | Chicago, IL |
| PINOCHOLE RAG | Seymour Furth | February 11, 1911 | Joe Morris | New York, NY |
| PINYWOODS RAG | Nellie Weldon Cocroft | October 16, 1909 | Cocroft Music | Thomasville, GA |
| PIPE DREAM | Mose Gumble | March 3, 1902 | Shapiro, Bernstein | New York, NY |
| PIPE THE PIPER | Joe Keden | July 12, 1937 | ABC Standard | New York, NY |
| PIPPIN | Arthur Marshall | December 7, 1908 | Stark Music Company | New York, NY |

| Title | Composer | Date | Publisher | City |
|---|---|---|---|---|
| PIPPINS | Ed C. Mahoney | October 16, 1909 | Colonial Music | Boston, MA |
| PIRATE RAG | E. A. Windell | January 14, 1905 | Self | Enid, OK |
| PITTER-PATTER RAG | Jos. M. Daly | April 1, 1910 | Joseph M. Daly | Boston, MA |
| PLAYIN' POSSUM | J. Mahlon Duganne | January 18, 1909 | Joseph W. Stern | New York, NY |
| POISON IVORIES | Harry Akst and Walter Haenschen | July 23, 1923 | Richmond–Robbins | New York, NY |
| POISON IVY | Arthur John Drees | March 27, 1919 | Self | St. Louis, MO |
| POISON IVY | Herbert Ingraham | March 9, 1908 | Maurice Shapiro | New York, NY |
| POISON RAG | Calvin Lee Woolsey | May 3, 1910 | Self | Braymer, MO |
| POKER RAG | Charlotte Blake | June 3, 1909 | Jerome H. Remick | New York, NY |
| POLAR BEAR RAG | George P. Howard | December 1, 1910 | Wilson Music | San Francisco, CA |
| POLKA DOTS RAG | Reuben Lawson | 1907 | Self | Cincinnati, OH |
| POLLY | John S. Zamecnik | February 25, 1929 | Sam Fox | Cleveland, OH |
| POLYRAGMIC | Max Morath | October 20, 1964 | Hollis Music | New York, NY |
| POODLE RAG | Bill Krenz | August 12, 1954 | Mills Music | New York, NY |
| POOR BUTTERMILK | Zez Confrey | August 5, 1921 | Jack Mills | New York, NY |
| POOR JIM | James Chapman | August 17, 1903 | Joseph Placht and Son | St. Louis, MO |
| POOR JIMMY GREEN | Eubie Blake | 1975 | Eubie Blake Music | New York, NY |
| POOR KATIE REDD | Eubie Blake | 1975 | Eubie Blake Music | New York, NY |
| POP CORN MAN | Jean Schwartz | December 15, 1910 | Jerome H. Remick | Detroit, MI |
| POPULAR RAG | Webb Long | July 30, 1912 | Martin and Adams Music | Wichita, KS |
| POPULARITY | George M. Cohan | August 27, 1906 | F. A. Mills | New York, NY |
| PORCUPINE RAG | Charles L. Johnson | September 15, 1909 | M. Witmark and Sons | New York, NY |
| PORK AND BEANS | Theron C. Bennett | January 26, 1909 | Victor Kremer | Chicago, IL |
| PORK AND BEANS | C. Luckeyth Roberts | June 24, 1913 | Joseph W. Stern | New York, NY |
| PORTO RICO RAG | Ford Dabney | December 14, 1910 | Maurice Shapiro | New York, NY |
| PORTUGUESE RAG | Mike L. Baird | May 28, 1972 | Dottie Bee Music | Pasadena, CA |
| POSSUM RAG | Geraldine Dobyns | June 11, 1907 | O. K. Houck | Memphis, TN |
| POSSUM AND TATERS | Charles Hunter | April 20, 1900 | Henry A. French | Nashville, TN |
| POTLATCH TICKLE | Donald A. Robertson | July 17, 1911 | Empire Music | Seattle, WA |
| POVERTY RAG | Harry J. Lincoln | October 27, 1909 | Vandersloot Music | Williamsport, PA |
| POWDER RAG | Raymond Birch | August 20, 1908 | Charles L. Johnson | Kansas City, MO |
| POWDER RAG | Roy Steventon and Lloyd Kidwell | 1906 | Steventon and Kidwell | Covington, KY |
| POWDER RAG | Jones Yow | April 13, 1906 | Will Rossiter | Chicago, IL |
| POWER HOUSE | Raymond Scott | August 4, 1937 | Circle Music | New York, NY |
| POZZO | Vincent Rose | November 8, 1916 | Jerome H. Remick | New York, NY |
| PRAIRIE QUEEN | Tom Shea | June 28, 1963 | Ragtime Society | Toronto, CN |
| PRESS CLUB RAG | Axel Christensen | November 22, 1912 | Christensen School | Chicago, IL |
| PRETTY PEGGY | John Queen Slye | May 17, 1905 | Self | Washington, DC |
| PRETTY POL' | Little Jack Little | October 3, 1927 | ABC Standard | New York, NY |
| PRIDE OF BUCKTOWN | Robert S. Roberts | 1897 | Phillip Kussel | Cincinnati, OH |
| PRIDE OF THE SMOKY ROW | J. M. Wilcockson | February 5, 1911 | Self | Hammond, IN |
| PRINCESS RAG | James Scott | 1911 | Stark Music Company | St. Louis, MO |
| PRINCESS RAG | Gayle Von Kamacke Wood | 1915 | Self | Cedar Rapids, IA |

| Title | Composer | Date | Publisher | City |
|---|---|---|---|---|
| PROCRASTINATION RAG | George L. Cobb | June 29, 1927 | Walter Jacobs | Boston, MA |
| PROGRESSIVE RAG | Tobe Brown | July 3, 1913 | Christensen School | Chicago, IL |
| PROSPERITY RAG | James Scott | March 10, 1916 | Stark Music Company | St. Louis, MO |
| PUBLICITY RAG | Henry P. Menges | December 18, 1911 | Charles H. Loomis | New Haven, CT |
| PUDNIN TAME | Theron C. Bennett | March 25, 1909 | Jerome H. Remick | New York, NY |
| PUNCH AND JUDY | Paul Vincent | July 9, 1928 | Triangle Music | New York, NY |
| PUPPETS SUITE | Billy Mayerl | June 1, 1927 | Sam Fox | Cleveland, OH |
| PURDUE RAG | Opal Boyer | February 9, 1914 | Self | Lafayette, IN |
| PURDUE SPIRIT | Edward J. Freeberg | May 14, 1909 | Rinker Music | Lafayette, IN |
| PUSSY FOOT | Robert Hoffman | 1914 | Walter Jacobs | Boston, MA |
| PUT 'EN ON THE BRAKES | Charles Olson | October 3, 1927 | Self | Minneapolis, MN |
| PUTTING ON THE DOG | Ted Shapiro | October 17, 1923 | Jack Mills | New York, NY |
| PYRAMYTHS | Jess Sutton | March 5, 1923 | Jack Mills | New York, NY |
| QUALITY | James Scott | July 27, 1911 | Stark Music Company | St. Louis, MO |
| QUALITY RAG | Ella Hudson Day | March 2, 1909 | J. P. Nuckolls | Dallas, TX |
| QUEEN OF CONEY ISLAND | Alfred Gasdorf | 1904 | Self | Cincinnati, OH |
| QUEEN OF LOVE | Charles Hunter | June 21, 1901 | Henry A. French | Nashville, TN |
| QUEEN OF RAGS | Walter Dunn | June 21, 1909 | Self | Atlanta, GA |
| QUEEN RAG | Floyd Willis | June 16, 1911 | Joseph Krolage Music | Cincinnati, OH |
| QUEEN RAGLAN | A. E. Henrich | June 13, 1902 | Henry A. French | Nashville, TN |
| QUEEN SUGAR BEET RAG | M. M. Moore | 1912 | Self | San Jose, CA |
| QWINDO'S RAG | David A. Jasen | June 28, 1979 | The Big Three | New York, NY |
| RA! RA! RA! | Floyd Reuter | December 5, 1910 | Kauffman Music | Sedalia, MO |
| RABBIT FOOT RAG | Al Harriman | November 30, 1910 | Self | Boston, MA |
| RACE HORSE RAG | Mike Bernard | September 11, 1911 | Joe Morris | Philadelphia, PA |
| RACING DOWN THE BLACK AND WHITES | Adam Carroll | April 3, 1926 | Harms, Inc. | New York, NY |
| RADIO RAG | Lillian W. Shackford | October 10, 1927 | C. I. Hicks Music | Boston, MA |
| RAG A MUFFIN RAG | Arthur Lange | 1909 | Mignon Ziegfeld | New York, NY |
| RAG ALLEY DREAM | Mattie Harl Burgess | 1902 | Will Rossiter | Chicago, IL |
| RAG BABY MINE | George Botsford | March 28, 1913 | Jerome H. Remick | New York, NY |
| RAG BABY RAG | F. H. Losey | October 27, 1909 | Vandersloot Music | Williamsport, PA |
| RAG BAG RAG | Harry J. Lincoln | May 17, 1909 | Vandersloot Music | Williamsport, PA |
| RAG BAG RAG | H. S. Taylor | September 4, 1909 | Self | Elizabeth, NJ |
| RAG CARPET | Sol Levy | February 5, 1912 | M. Witmark and Sons | New York, NY |
| RAG DE LUXE | Elmer Olson and Scott Cowles | November 20, 1913 | Van Publishing | Minneapolis, MN |
| RAG DOLL | Nacio Herb Brown | March 20, 1928 | Sherman, Clay | San Francisco, CA |
| RAG DOLL CARNIVAL | Zez Confrey | August 10, 1945 | Mills Music | New York, NY |
| RAG LA JOIE | Jerry Cammack | 1918 | Stark Music Company | St. Louis, MO |
| RAG OF RAGS | William E. Macquinn | January 25, 1915 | Chappell and Company | New York, NY |
| RAG PICKER'S RAG | Robert J. O'Brien | October 19, 1901 | Union Music Company | Cincinnati, OH |
| RAG SENTIMENTAL | James Scott | 1918 | Stark Music Company | St. Louis, MO |
| RAG TAGS RAG | Harry Thomas | May 10, 1909 | Delmar Music | Montreal, CN |
| RAG TIME CHIMES | Egbert Van Alstyne | October 16, 1900 | Will Rossiter | Chicago, IL |

| Title | Composer | Date | Publisher | City |
|---|---|---|---|---|
| RAG TIME CHIMES | Percy Wenrich | July 26, 1911 | Jerome H. Remick | New York, NY |
| RAG TIME FIEND | Scotty McClure | December 30, 1914 | Self | Des Moines, IA |
| RAG TIME JOKE | Andy L. Burke | December 7, 1905 | Self | Galesburg, IL |
| RAG TIME NIGHTMARE | Tom Turpin | April 13, 1900 | Robert DeYong | St. Louis, MO |
| RAG WITH NO NAME | Warren Camp | May 23, 1911 | Self | Seattle, WA |
| RAG-A-MINOR | Julius Lenzberg | October 8, 1917 | T. B. Harms | New York, NY |
| RAG-A-MORE | George Nolton | May 19, 1924 | Master Music | Chicago, IL |
| RAG-A-MUFFIN | William F. Peters | May 26, 1913 | M. Witmark and Sons | New York, NY |
| RAG-A-MUFFIN RAG | Will T. Pierson | October 3, 1913 | Sam Fox | Cleveland, OH |
| RAG-A-TAG RAG | Al W. Brown | February 16, 1910 | Leo Feist | New York, NY |
| RAG-GED | Joe Perry | April 23, 1930 | Self | New York, NY |
| RAG-O-RHYTHM | Harry Jentes | May 17, 1924 | Self | New York, NY |
| RAG-TIME DAUD | Dawn Renfro | January 2, 1906 | Self | St. Elmo, IL |
| RAGAMUFFIN | Jesse Greer | January 18, 1929 | Spier & Coslow | New York, NY |
| RAGGED EDGES | Otto Frey | February 28, 1911 | Victor Kremer | Chicago, IL |
| RAGGED JACK | Jack Bradshaw | September 15, 1909 | Victor Kremer | Chicago, IL |
| RAGGED TERRY | Margaret Agnew White | 1913 | Bush and Gerts | Dallas, TX |
| RAGGED THOUGHTS | J. Louis von der Mehden | August 10, 1906 | Carl Fischer | New York, NY |
| RAGGEDY-ANN RAG | Lou Busch | March 5, 1952 | Chatsworth Music | New York, NY |
| RAGGETY RAG | Meryle Payne | October 19, 1910 | Fordi Music | Los Angeles, CA |
| RAGGIN' RUDI | William Bolcom | August 22, 1974 | Edward B. Marks Music | New York, NY |
| RAGGIN' THE BLUES | Bill Krenz and Allan Clark | April 24, 1953 | Mills Music | New York, NY |
| RAGGING THE SCALE | Ed Claypoole | April 2, 1915 | Broadway Music | New York, NY |
| RAGGITY-RAG | J. B. Lafreniere | 1907 | Delmar Music | Montreal, CN |
| RAGGY FOX TROT | Laurence E. Goffin | October 20, 1915 | Jerome H. Remick | New York, NY |
| RAGGY RAG | Floyd Willis | 1909 | W. H. Willis | Cincinnati, OH |
| RAGMAN'S EXERCISE | Harold D. Squires | April 3, 1922 | Jack Mills | New York, NY |
| RAGOLOGY | Forest L. Traylor | March 25, 1912 | Self | Petersburg, IN |
| RAGOVITCH RAG | Walter Lipman | July 22, 1910 | Self | Chicago, IL |
| RAGS TO BURN | Frank X. McFadden | November 28, 1899 | J. W. Jenkins | Kansas City, MO |
| RAGTIME BETTY | James Scott | October 5, 1909 | Stark Music Company | New York, NY |
| RAGTIME BOBOLINK | Joseph F. Lamb | 1964 | Mills Music | New York, NY |
| RAGTIME DANCE | Scott Joplin | December 21, 1906 | Stark Music Company | New York, NY |
| RAGTIME EYES | W. C. Powell | 1907 | P. J. Howley | New York, NY |
| RAGTIME FOLLIES | May Olive Arnold | October 31, 1910 | Self | Mobile, AL |
| RAGTIME JIM | A. Fred Phillips | November 21, 1912 | Jerome H. Remick | New York, NY |
| RAGTIME JINGLES | Al J. Markgraf | March 15, 1916 | Self | San Francisco, CA |
| RAGTIME NIGHTINGALE | Joseph F. Lamb | June 10, 1915 | Stark Music Company | St. Louis, MO |
| RAGTIME ORIOLE | James Scott | December 10, 1911 | Stark Music Company | St. Louis, MO |
| RAGTIME PARADE IN DARKTOWN | William A. Calhoun | 1899 | Groene Music | Cincinnati, OH |
| RAGTIME PATSY | O. Wellington Snell | September 12, 1903 | Self | Boston, MA |
| RAGTIME RAZZMATAZZ | J. Gaines | September 2, 1958 | Record Songs | New York, NY |
| RAGTIME REFRESHMENTS | William L. Needham | 1903 | Golden Rule Music | Chicago, IL |

| Title | Composer | Date | Publisher | City |
|---|---|---|---|---|
| RAGTIME AND REVELATIONS | J. Gaines | September 2, 1958 | Record Songs | New York, NY |
| RAGTIME RIGGLES | Isidor Heidenreich | 1902 | Hunleth Music | St. Louis, MO |
| RAGTIME RIPPLES | Percy Wenrich | September 14, 1908 | McKinley Music | Chicago, IL |
| RAGTIME SHOWERS | Kathryn Athol Morton | May 3, 1902 | Richard A. Saalfield | New York, NY |
| RAGWEED RAG | Harry Bussler | June 26, 1911 | H. Kiskus Dugdale | Washington, DC |
| RAH RAH BOY!!! | Wallie Herzer | November 18, 1908 | Herzer and Brown | San Francisco, CA |
| RAINDROPS | Bill Wirges | June 12, 1928 | Self | New York, NY |
| RAMBLER | Walter G. Haenschen and Arthur F. Beyer | 1906 | Stark Music Company | New York, NY |
| RAMBLIN' RAG | Bill Krenz | July 11, 1952 | Mills Music | New York, NY |
| RAMBLING IN RHYTHM | Arthur Schutt | November 5, 1927 | Jack Mills | New York, NY |
| RAMBLING RAGS | L. J. Meyerholtz | 1908 | C. C. Powell | Fort Wayne, IN |
| RAMSHACKLE RAG | Ted Snyder | March 10, 1911 | Ted Snyder Company | New York, NY |
| RAPID FIRING RAG | C. Kenneth Yoder | November 13, 1915 | Self | Bellefontaine, OH |
| RAPSCALLION RAG | Lou Busch | March 5, 1952 | Chatsworth Music | New York, NY |
| RASTUS RAG | H. A. Fischler | September 21, 1909 | Vandersloot Music | Williamsport, PA |
| RATHSKELLER DRAG | Walter L. Dunn | December 31, 1910 | Self | Atlanta, GA |
| RATS!!! | M. Kendree Miller | October 1, 1914 | Bush and Gerts | Dallas, TX |
| RATTLE SNAKE RAG | Clyde W. Headley | December 19, 1910 | H. Kirkus Dugdale | Washington, DC |
| RATTLER RAG | Susie Wells | December 7, 1912 | Self | Henrietta, TX |
| RATTLESNAKE RAG | Lou Busch and Eddie Hansen | December 29, 1952 | Chatsworth Music | New York, NY |
| RATTLESNAKE RAG | Ethwell Hanson | April 9, 1917 | Self | Neenah, WI |
| RAVIOLI RAG | Frank Lucanese and Charles Lucotti | July 21, 1914 | Jerome H. Remick | New York, NY |
| RAVLINS | Floyd Willis | May 20, 1910 | W. H. Willis | Cincinnati, OH |
| RAYMOND'S RAG | David A. Jasen | June 28, 1979 | The Big Three | New York, NY |
| RAZZLE DAZZLE | Lilburn Kingsbury and Alma Smith | July 6, 1905 | | Detroit, MI |
| RAZZLE DAZZLE | Nellie M. Stokes | October 20, 1909 | Jerome H. Remick | Detroit, MI |
| REAL RAG | Lawrence W. Blair | November 22, 1912 | Lew Roberts Music | Nashville, TN |
| REAL SWING RAG | Oswald Thumser | 1908 | Bafunno Bros. Music | St. Louis, MO |
| RED AND BLACK RAG | Robert Reynolds | 1909 | Emerson Music | New York, NY |
| RED CLOVER | Max Kortlander | October 17, 1923 | Jack Mills | New York, NY |
| RED DEVIL RAG | Lucien Denni | September 19, 1910 | J. W. Jenkins | Kansas City, MO |
| RED FOX TROT | Albert Gumble | August 23, 1917 | Jerome H. Remick | New York, NY |
| RED MOUSE RAG | Wilbur Piper | August 15, 1910 | H. R. McClure Company | Sidney, OH |
| RED ONION RAG | Abe Olman | January 17, 1912 | George W. Meyer Music | New York, NY |
| RED ONION RAG | Roy Steventon and Lloyd Kidwell | November 11, 1911 | Associated Music | Cincinnati, OH |
| RED PEPPER | Henry Lodge | December 19, 1910 | M. Witmark and Sons | New York, NY |
| RED PEPPERS | F. P. Aukens | April 10, 1910 | F. B. Haviland | Cleveland, OH |
| RED RAG | Jack Murfree | December 1, 1910 | Murfree Music | Boston, MA |
| RED RAMBLER RAG | Julia Lee Niebergall | July 16, 1912 | J. H. Aufderheide | Indianapolis, IN |
| RED RAVEN | Carl E. Olson | August 30, 1910 | Olson–Edwards Music | Wichita, KS |
| RED RAVEN RAG | Harry Kimpton | March 16, 1908 | Self | Baudette, MN |

| Title | Composer | Date | Publisher | City |
|---|---|---|---|---|
| RED RAVEN RAG | Charley Straight | December 30, 1915 | Jerome H. Remick | New York, NY |
| RED RIBBON RAG | Z. M. Van Tress | February 1, 1915 | Self | Houston, TX |
| RED SLIPPER RAG | Glenn Rowell | January 6, 1965 | Bregman, Vocco, and Conn | New York, NY |
| REFLECTION RAG | Scott Joplin | December 4, 1917 | Stark Music Company | St. Louis, MO |
| REGAL RAG | Lily Coffee | January 24, 1916 | Self | Houston, TX |
| REINDEER | Joseph F. Lamb | 1915 | Stark Music Company | St. Louis, MO |
| REINETTE RAG | David Reichstein | June 14, 1913 | Christensen School | Chicago, IL |
| REISENWEBER RAG | Dominic J. LaRocca | June 4, 1918 | Leo Feist | New York, NY |
| REMINGTON RAG | Martie Stoltz | 1909 | Groene Music | Cincinnati, OH |
| REMORSE BLUES | Henry Lodge | July 30, 1917 | Jerome H. Remick | New York, NY |
| RESTLESS RAG | Sarah E. Cook | August 5, 1908 | Victor Kremer | Chicago, IL |
| REXALL RAG | J. Meredith Daniel | November 24, 1914 | Self | Manson, IA |
| RHAPSODY IN RAGTIME | Eubie Blake | 1975 | Eubie Blake Music | New York, NY |
| RHAPSODY RAG | Budd L. Cross | January 28, 1911 | Sam Fox | Cleveland, OH |
| RHAPSODY RAG | Harry Jentes | January 17, 1911 | Maurice Shapiro | New York, NY |
| RHINEWINE RAG | Paul Henneberg | June 12, 1912 | Carl Fischer | New York, NY |
| RHYTHMIC FANTASY | Phil Saltman | February 9, 1929 | Denton and Haskins | New York, NY |
| RIALTO RIPPLES | George Gershwin and Will Donaldson | June 6, 1917 | Jerome H. Remick | New York, NY |
| RICHMOND RAG | May Aufderheide | December 12, 1908 | J. H. Aufderheide | Indianapolis, IN |
| RIFFIN' | Willie the Lion Smith | March 21, 1938 | Mills Music | New York, NY |
| RIG-A-JIG | Nat D. Ayer | August 2, 1912 | Jerome H. Remick | New York, NY |
| RIG-A-JIG RAG | William Schroeder | February 20, 1917 | M. Witmark and Sons | New York, NY |
| RIGAMAROLE | Harold Mooney | January 30, 1935 | Luz Brothers | New York, NY |
| RIGAMAROLE RAG | Edwin F. Kendall | 1910 | Jerome H. Remick | New York, NY |
| RINALDO RAG | Rinaldo | June 17, 1909 | Ted Snyder Company | New York, NY |
| RING-TUM-DIDDIE | Fred Heltman | January 13, 1912 | Popular Music Publishers | Cleveland, OH |
| RIO DE JANEIRO | Willard Robison | September 14, 1926 | Robbins–Engel | New York, NY |
| RIP RAG | Miriam Todd | 1911 | P. F. Sarver | Piqua, OH |
| RIPPLES RAG | Camilla Thiele | June 24, 1912 | Peerless Music | Janesville, WI |
| RISING MOON | M. Mae Serviss | January 15, 1912 | H. Kirkus Dugdale | Washington, DC |
| RITA | J. Russel Robinson and Bemie Cummins | May 20, 1929 | Vincent Youmans Music | New York, NY |
| RIVAL RAG | Ada LaVerne Rogers | September 1, 1910 | Eaton Music | New York, NY |
| RIVER | Edwin A. Burkart | February 18, 1911 | Amo Music | Cincinnati, OH |
| RIVERSIDE RAG | Charles Cohen | August 8, 1910 | Self | Binghamton, NY |
| ROBARDINA RAG | E. Warren Furry | September 6, 1902 | Balmer and Weber Music | St. Louis, MO |
| ROCHELLE | Bill Krenz | December 15, 1934 | M. M. Cole | Chicago, IL |
| ROCHESTER FAIR | Lawrence Leon Wiley | July 17, 1914 | Self | Rochester, NY |
| ROCHESTER RAG | J. C. Mills | December 1, 1912 | H. Kirkus Dugdale | Washington, DC |
| ROCKY FORD MELON PICKERS | A. Garfield Wilson | November 6, 1902 | Pepin and Triggs | Denver, CO |
| ROCKY RAGS | Isidore Seidel | April 26, 1911 | Self | Indianapolis, IN |
| ROLLER-SKATERS RAG | Sam Gompers | 1906 | Self | New Orleans, LA |
| ROMANTIC RAG | Kathy Craig | December 30, 1976 | Edward B. Marks Music | New York, NY |
| ROOSTER RAG | Muriel Pollock | February 26, 1917 | Joseph W. Stern | New York, NY |

| Title | Composer | Date | Publisher | City |
|---|---|---|---|---|
| ROSE LEAF RAG | Scott Joplin | November 15, 1907 | Joseph M. Daly | Boston, MA. |
| ROSEWOOD RAG | Peter M. Heaton | March 22, 1909 | Victor Kremer | Chicago, IL |
| ROTATION RAG | Al Sweet | September 19, 1911 | Shapiro Music | New York, NY |
| ROUGH HOUSE RAG | W. E. Smith | 1905 | | |
| ROUND UP RAG | Con Conrad and Weedon | October 17, 1911 | F. A. Mills | New York, NY |
| ROUND UP RAG | Jerome Shay | August 4, 1909 | Fred Fischer Music | New York, NY |
| ROUSTABOUT RAG | Paul Sarebresole | 1897 | Louis Grunewald | New Orleans, LA |
| ROYAL FLUSH RAG | George Botsford | March 27, 1911 | Jerome H. Remick | Detroit, MI |
| ROYAL PURPLE | Errol Croom | November 20, 1913 | P. J. Howley | New York, NY |
| RUBBER PLANT RAG | George L. Cobb | June 14, 1909 | Walter Jacobs | Boston, MA |
| RUBE BENNETT'S RAGGEDY RAG | Rube Bennett | February 27, 1914 | Waterson, Berlin, and Snyder | New York, NY |
| RUBIES AND PEARLS | Harry A. Tierney | June 24, 1911 | Ted Snyder Company | New York, NY |
| RUFENREDDY | Roy Bargy and Charley Straight | November 14, 1921 | Sam Fox | Cleveland, OH |
| RUNNING UP AND DOWN | Henry Cohen | March 5, 1928 | Bibo, Bloedon, and Lang | New York, NY |
| RUSSIAN PONY RAG | Don Ramsay | August 27, 1909 | Walter Jacobs | Boston, MA |
| RUSSIAN RAG | George L. Cobb | April 27, 1918 | Will Rossiter | Chicago, IL |
| S. O. S. | Kenneth W. Bradshaw and Joe McGrade | 1919 | Stark Music Company | St. Louis, MO |
| SAFETY PIN CATCH | Lewis Fuiks | December 8, 1909 | Thompson Music | Chicago, IL |
| SAILING ALONG OVER THE KEYS | Silvio DeRienzo | March 5, 1928 | Bibo, Bloedon, and Lang | New York, NY |
| SAINT LOUIS RIPPLE RAG | Paul Burmeister | July 1, 1912 | Self | St. Louis, MO |
| SAKES ALIVE | Stephen Howard | May 2, 1903 | M. Witmark and Sons | New York, NY |
| SALOME RAG | Samuel J. Stokes | March 22, 1909 | Self | New Orleans, LA |
| SALT AND PEPPER RAG | Herbert Ingraham | March 5, 1909 | Shapiro Music | New York, NY |
| SALTED PEANUTS | Sydney Chapman | September 27, 1911 | Koninsky Music | Troy, NY |
| SAN FRANCISCO PRETTY GIRL RAG | Walter Shannon | November 17, 1910 | San Francisco Music | San Francisco, CA |
| SAND PAPER RAG | Harry Ellman and Lew Schwab | January 12, 1910 | Stark Music Company | St. Louis, MO |
| SANDELLA RAG | Edward Hudson | September 18, 1921 | Stark Music Company | St. Louis, MO |
| SANDY RIVER RAG | Thomas S. Allen | 1915 | Walter Jacobs | Boston, MA |
| SAPHO RAG | J. Russel Robinson | October 5, 1909 | Stark Music Company | St. Louis, MO |
| SARATOGA GLIDE | Harry L. Newman | 1909 | Sunlight Music | Chicago, IL |
| SARONOFF RAG | Silvio Hein | May 15, 1913 | T. B. Harms | New York, NY |
| SASKATOON RAG | Phil Goldberg | March 15, 1915 | Roger Graham | Chicago, IL |
| SASSAFRAS RAG | J. Levy | May 22, 1905 | Arnett–Delonais | Chicago, IL |
| SASSAFRAS SAM | George Grace | September 14, 1908 | McKinley Music | Chicago, IL |
| SATISFACTION | Percy B. Keenan | 1908 | Charles B. Loomis Music | New Haven, CT |
| SAY WHEN | George L. Cobb | 1919 | Walter Jacobs | Boston, MA |
| SCALE IT DOWN | Walker O'Neil | September 5, 1924 | Jack Mills | New York, NY |
| SCANDALOUS THOMPSON | Charles L. Johnson | May 27, 1899 | J. W. Jenkins | Kansas City, MO |
| SCARECROW RAG | Frank Baer | 1911 | Evans–Dangel Music | Boston, MA |
| SCARECROW RAG | Will B. Morrison | April 15, 1911 | J. H. Aufderheide | Indianapolis, IN |
| SCARLETT RAG | Forest L. Cook | April 3, 1911 | Self | Huntington, IN |

| Title | Composer | Date | Publisher | City |
|---|---|---|---|---|
| SCHULTZMEIER RAG | B. R. Whitlow | March 5, 1914 | Stark Music Company | St. Louis, MO |
| SCIZZOR BILL | Logan Sizemore | June 5, 1909 | Victor Kremer | Chicago, IL |
| SCOTCH RYE | E. W. Anderson | 1909 | Tolbert R. Ingram Music | Denver, CO |
| SCOTT JOPLIN'S NEW RAG | Scott Joplin | May 1, 1912 | Joseph W. Stern | New York, NY |
| SCOUTIN' AROUND | James P. Johnson | September 18, 1925 | Perry Bradford Music | New York, NY |
| SCRAMBLE RAG | Louis Mentel | June 30, 1911 | Mentel Brothers | Cincinnati, OH |
| SCRAMBLED EGGS | James A. Brennan | February 16, 1914 | O. E. Story | Boston, MA |
| SCRAMBLES | Sid Reinherz | April 30, 1928 | Robbins Music | New York, NY |
| SCRAPS FROM THE RAG BAG | Hubert Tanner | 1906 | Self | Plymouth, IN |
| SCREEN DOOR RAG | Marjorie Burgess | 1973 | Self | Boston, MA |
| SCROOCHIN' UP RAG | Lena Martin | August 11, 1911 | Self | East Redford, VA |
| SCRUB RAG | Alfred W. Brinkmeyer | April 30, 1910 | Self | St. Louis, MO |
| SCRUB RAGS | Arthur W. Mueller | 1904 | Arnold Publishing Company | Cincinnati, OH |
| SEA WEEDS RAG | Abe Olman | December 9, 1910 | Joe Morris | New York, NY |
| SEABISCUITS RAG | William Bolcom | May 24, 1971 | Edward B. Marks Music | New York, NY |
| SEARCH LIGHT RAG | Scott Joplin | August 12, 1907 | Joseph W. Stern | New York, NY |
| SEN-SEN RAG | Russell B. Harker | May 5, 1910 | Jerome H. Remick | New York, NY |
| SENSATION RAG | Joseph F. Lamb | October 8, 1908 | Stark Music Company | New York, NY |
| SENSIBLE RAG | Ed Avey | 1914 | Self | Cherry Vale, KS |
| SERVICE RAG | Adolph Hansen | June 12, 1919 | Self | Omaha, NE |
| SHADOW RAG | William Brunsvold | December 16, 1910 | F. B. Haviland | New York, NY |
| SHAKA FOOT | Ferd Guttenberger | September 12, 1933 | Self | Macon, GA |
| SHAMROCK RAG | Euday Bowman | March 14, 1916 | J. W. Jenkins | Kansas City, MO |
| SHAVE 'EM DRY | Sam Wishnuff | May 10, 1917 | Stark Music Company | St. Louis, MO |
| SHEATH | William E. Weigel | December 8, 1908 | John Arnold | Cincinnati, OH |
| SHIMMIE SHOES | Max Kortlander | October 17, 1923 | Jack Mills | New York, NY |
| SHINE OR POLISH RAG | Fred Heltman | April 24, 1914 | Fred Heltman Company | Cleveland, OH |
| SHOCK RAG | Elmer Olson | 1911 | A. W. Pinger | Minneapolis, MN |
| SHOE STRING RAG | David A. Jasen | June 28, 1979 | The Big Three | New York, NY |
| SHOE TICKLER RAG | Wilbur Campbell | April 11, 1911 | Southern California Music | Los Angeles, CA |
| SHOOTIN' THE AGATE | Thomas A. Schmutzler | December 30, 1976 | Edward B. Marks Music | New York, NY |
| SHOOTIN' THE CHUTES | Larry Briers | March 5, 1924 | Jack Mills | New York, NY |
| SHOVEL FISH | Harry Cook | October 4, 1907 | Herman Straus and Sons | Louisville, KY |
| SHOW ME RAG | Trebor J. Tichenor | December 30, 1976 | Edward B. Marks Music | New York, NY |
| SHOWBOAT RAG | Bill Krenz and Thomas J. Filas | November 24, 1953 | Mills Music | New York, NY |
| SHREVEPORT STOMPS | Jelly Roll Morton | April 1, 1925 | Melrose Brothers | Chicago, IL |
| SHY AND SLY | C. Luckeyth Roberts | May 7, 1915 | G. Ricordi | New York, NY |
| SIC 'EM PRINZ | Alfred Gasdorf | 1905 | Self | Newport, KY |
| SILENCE AND FUN | Charles E. Mullen | December 22, 1904 | Will Rossiter | Chicago, IL |
| SILHOUETTE | Rube Bloom | May 9, 1927 | Triangle Music | New York, NY |
| SILK HOSE RAG | Omar L. Sims | December 15, 1916 | Buckeye Music | Columbus, OH |
| SILVER BUCKLE RAG | Joseph Sikorra | February 24, 1910 | Joseph Flanner | Milwaukee, WI |
| SILVER KING RAG | Charles L. Johnson | April 5, 1909 | Thompson Music | Chicago, IL |

| Title | Composer | Date | Publisher | City |
|---|---|---|---|---|
| SILVER LEAF RAG | Dan Goldsmith | October 17, 1911 | Imperial Music | Winnepeg, CN |
| SILVER ROCKET | Arthur Marshall | June 27, 1966 | Oak Publishing | New York, NY |
| SILVER SWAN RAG | Scott Joplin | 1971 | Maple Leaf Club | Los Angeles, CA |
| SILVER TIP | Frederick Owens Hanks | May 12, 1914 | Jerome H. Remick | New York, NY |
| SIMPLICITY RAG | Eugene Ellsworth | April 15, 1912 | Standard Music | Chicago, IL |
| SKI DO RAG | Alfred Gasdorf | March 19, 1906 | Ilsen and Company | Cincinnati, OH |
| SKIDDING | Ed Claypoole | April 7, 1923 | Jack Mills | New York, NY |
| SKIPINOVA | Glen Barton | May 20, 1926 | Jack Mills | New York, NY |
| SKY ROCKETS | E. Philip Severin | June 10, 1911 | Self | Moline, IL |
| SLAM BANG RAG | Joseph A. Helmers | January 27, 1910 | Self | Cincinnati, OH |
| SLEEPY HOLLOW RAG | Clarence Woods | 1918 | Will L. Livernash Music | Kansas City, MO |
| SLEEPY LOU | Irene M. Giblin | November 15, 1906 | Jerome H. Remick | New York, NY |
| SLEEPY PIANO | Billy Mayerl | July 15, 1926 | Sam Fox | Cleveland, OH |
| SLEEPY SIDNEY | Archie W. Scheu | August 22, 1907 | Self | Cincinnati, OH |
| SLIPOVA | Roy Bargy | November 14, 1921 | Sam Fox | Cleveland, OH |
| SLIPPERY ELM RAG | Herbert Ingraham | March 5, 1909 | Shapiro Music | New York, NY |
| SLIPPERY ELM RAG | Clarence Woods | 1912 | Self | Fort Worth, TX |
| SLIPPERY FINGERS | Henry Steele | January 8, 1927 | Jack Mills | New York, NY |
| SLIPPERY PLACE | P. M. Hacker | July 26, 1911 | Jerome H. Remick | New York, NY |
| SLIPPERY STEPS | Bert Leach | April 15, 1915 | Traler–Elliot Company | Atlantic City, NJ |
| SLIVERS | Harry Cook | March 18, 1909 | Central Music | St. Louis, MO |
| SLIVERS | Maude Gilmore | 1909 | Charles L. Johnson | Kansas City, MO |
| SMART ALEC | Zez Confrey | December 27, 1933 | Mills Music | New York, NY |
| SMASH UP RAG | Gwendolyn Stevenson | December 2, 1914 | Jerome H. Remick | New York, NY |
| SMILER RAG | Percy Wenrich | January 2, 1907 | Arnett–Delonais | Chicago, IL |
| SMILES AND CHUCKLES | F. Henri Klickmann | October 8, 1917 | Frank K. Root | Chicago, IL |
| SMILING BILL | Jack Schuesler | May 13, 1911 | Self | Covington, KY |
| SMILING SADIE | Archie W. Scheu | April 20, 1905 | Self | Cincinnati, OH |
| SNAPPIN' TURTLE | Charles L. Cooke | October 27, 1913 | Jerome H. Remick | New York, NY |
| SNAPPY RAG | Harry J. Palmer | 1914 | Self | Mankato, MN |
| SNAPPY RAG | Edwin H. See | October 28, 1913 | Regent Music | Lake Charles, LA |
| SNEAKAWAY | Willie the Lion Smith | August 21, 1937 | Mills Music | New York, NY |

Willie the Lion.

| Title | Composer | Date | Publisher | City |
|---|---|---|---|---|
| SNEAKY SHUFFLES RAG | Henry Lodge | October 4, 1910 | Jerome H. Remick | Detroit, MI |
| SNEEKY PEET | Charles L. Johnson | January 10, 1907 | J. W. Jenkins | Kansas City, MO |
| SNIPES | Mamie Williams | November 1, 1909 | Carl Hoffman Music | Kansas City, MO |
| SNOOKUMS RAG | Charles L. Johnson | February 9, 1918 | Forster Music | Chicago, IL |
| SNOW SHOES | Bill Wirges | January 26, 1927 | Alfred and Company | New York, NY |
| SNOWBALL | Nellie M. Stokes | February 23, 1907 | Jerome H. Remick | Detroit, MI |
| SNOWBALL BABE | C. Roland Flick | 1900 | Frank G. Fite | Nashville, TN |
| SNUFFUNS | Harold Dixon | October 31, 1927 | Self | New York, NY |
| SNUGGLE PUP | George L. Cobb | March 4, 1929 | Walter Jacobs | Boston, MA |
| SOAP BUBBLES RAG | Charles F. Myers | 1907 | Vinton Music | Boston, MA |
| SOAP SUDS | Irene M. Giblin | March 1, 1906 | Jerome H. Remick | New York, NY |
| SOCIETY RAG | Nat Johnson | June 27, 1912 | Forster Music | Chicago, IL |
| SOFT SHOE DANCER | Dent Mowrey | 1933 | Carl Fischer | New York, NY |
| SOLILOQUY | Rube Bloom | June 21, 1926 | Triangle Music | New York, NY |
| SOLITAIRE RAG | Clara Campbell Igelman | December 26, 1909 | Wilson Music | Richmond, IN |
| SOME BABY | Julius Lenzberg | December 29, 1913 | Jerome H. Remick | New York, NY |
| SOME BLUES, FOR YOU ALL | Theron C. Bennett | January 8, 1916 | Joe Morris | New York, NY |
| SOME CLASS RAG | S. E. Roberts | May 9, 1912 | Shapiro Music | New York, NY |
| SOME JAZZ | S. J. Stocco | 1919 | Jerome H. Remick | New York, NY |
| SOME PUMPKINS | Ed Kuhn | 1908 | W. B. Allen Music | Columbia, MO |
| SOME RAG | Willie Eckstein | January 10, 1911 | Delmar Music | Montreal, CN |
| SOME STUFF | Lindsay McPhail | February 24, 1923 | Self | Chicago, IL |
| SOME WAMPUS CAT RAG | James Wickiser | November 14, 1913 | H. Kirkus Dugdale | Washington, DC |
| SOMETHING DOING | Scott Joplin and Scott Hayden | February 24, 1903 | Val A. Reis Music | St. Louis, MO |
| SOMETHING DOING SOON | Regina Morphy Voitier | February 23, 1905 | Philip Werlein | New Orleans, LA |
| SON SET RAG | Ted Browne | December 7, 1915 | Buck and Lowney | St. Louis, MO |
| SOPHISTICATED RHYTHM | Bill Krenz | January 22, 1935 | M. M. Cole | Chicago, IL |
| SORORITY RAG | Margaret Bartlett | March 22, 1909 | Thompson Music | Chicago, IL |
| SOUP AND FISH RAG | Harry Jentes and Pete Wendling | December 11, 1913 | George W. Meyer Music | New York, NY |
| SOUR GRAPES RAG | Will B. Morrison | November 11, 1912 | Self | Indianapolis, IN |
| SOUTH DAKOTA RAG | Dee Cort Keith Hammitt | January 22, 1913 | H. Kirkus Dugdale | Washington, DC |
| SOUTH DAKOTA RAG | Joseph Liljenberg | February 2, 1902 | Self | Canova, SD |
| SOUTHERN BEAUTIES | Charles L. Johnson | October 12, 1907 | Jerome H. Remick | New York, NY |
| SOUTHERN BLOSSOMS | Harold G. Mitchell | January 20, 1905 | Self | Los Angeles, CA |
| SOUTHERN CHARMS | Rube Bloom | May 15, 1931 | Robbins Music | New York, NY |
| SOUTHERN ROSES | Joe Bren | August 22, 1904 | Shapiro, Remick | Detroit, MI |
| SOUTHERN SHUFFLE | T. Palmer Stephens | February 19, 1912 | H. Kirkus Dugdale | Washington, DC |
| SOUTHERN SNEEZE | Harry A. Slee | March 26, 1906 | Joseph Placht and Brother | St. Louis, MO |
| SOUTHERN SNOWBALLS | LaRue E. Black | December 30, 1907 | Vinton Music | Chicago, IL |
| SOUTHERN SYMPHONY | Percy Wenrich | April 13, 1910 | Jerome H. Remick | New York, NY |
| SPAGHETTI RAG | George Lyons and Bob Yosco | April 11, 1910 | Maurice Shapiro | New York, NY |
| SPARKLER RAG | Horace Smith Wilson | November 12, 1908 | Victor Kremer | Chicago, IL |

| Title | Composer | Date | Publisher | City |
|---|---|---|---|---|
| SPARKLES | Charles B. Ennis | 1909 | W. B. Morrison | Indianapolis, IN |
| SPARKLES | Phil Ohman | June 12, 1935 | Robbins Music | New York, NY |
| SPARKS | Theo Uden Masman | 1928 | Marks Music | New York, NY |
| SPASM RAG | Tom Shea | March 21, 1963 | Ragtime Society | Toronto, CN |
| SPATTER RAG | Elmer Olson | 1912 | A. W. Pinger | Minneapolis, MN |
| SPECKLED SPIDER RAG | Harry French | April 6, 1910 | Victor Kremer | Chicago, IL |
| SPEEDOMETER RAG | William B. Dale | November 7, 1912 | H. Kirkus Dugdale | Washington, DC |
| SPINAL CHORDS | Silvio DeRienzo | March 5, 1928 | Bibo, Bloedon, and Lang | New York, NY |
| SPITFIRE | Roy Allen | 1910 | F. B. Haviland | New York, NY |
| SPITFIRE RAG | E. Grazia Nardini | January 19, 1914 | Self | San Francisco, CA |
| SPITFIRE RAG | Elsie Grace Rafael | May 20, 1909 | Weller–Hartman Music | New York, NY |
| SPLINTERS | Maude Gilmore | May 21, 1909 | Charles L. Johnson | Kansas City, MO |
| SPONGE RAG | Walter C. Simon | 1911 | Self | New Orleans, LA |
| SPOTS | Edward A. Blake | October 8, 1909 | W. H. Willis | Cincinnati, OH |
| SPRING FEVER | Rube Bloom | June 21, 1926 | Triangle Music | New York, NY |
| SPRING HOLIDAY | Rube Bloom | May 15, 1931 | Robbins Music | New York, NY |
| SPRING TIME RAG | Paul Pratt | January 4, 1916 | Stark Music Company | St. Louis, MO |
| SPRINT SPLINTER RAG | Dena Merle Lantz | June 4, 1908 | Victor Kremer | Chicago, IL |
| SQUIGGILUM DRAG | Harry Gasdorf | 1911 | Gasdorf Music | Newport, KY |
| SQUIRREL FOOD RAG | R. G. Grady | 1916 | Olympic Music | Cincinnati, OH |
| SQUIRREL RAG | Paul Biese and F. Henri Klickmann | October 9, 1913 | Will Rossiter | Chicago, IL |
| ST. LOUIS MULE | Jean Ledies | 1914 | Wolf–Camp | St. Louis, MO |
| ST. LOUIS RAG | Tom Turpin | November 2, 1903 | Sol Bloom | New York, NY |
| ST. LOUIS TICKLE | Barney and Seymore | August 20, 1904 | Victor Kremer | Chicago, IL |
| ST. VITUS DANCE | Herbert Ingraham | March 5, 1909 | Shapiro Music | New York, NY |
| STACK 'EM UP | H. Leo Levy and Luis C. Russell | August 25, 1927 | Joe Davis | New York, NY |
| STATE FAIR CADONIAN | Horace C. Rudisell | August 5, 1910 | Kauffman Music Company | Sedalia, MO |
| STEAM ROLLER RAG | Mary E. B. Redus | October 12, 1912 | Shapiro Music | New York, NY |
| STEAMBOAT RAG | Ernie Burnett | 1914 | Syndicate Music | St. Louis, MO |
| STENOTYPIC RAG | Ben Kilmer, Jr. | May 15, 1915 | A. W. Perry and Sons | Sedalia, MO |
| STEP ON IT | Silvio DeRienzo | July 2, 1927 | Alfred and Company | New York, NY |
| STEPPIN' ON THE IVORIES | Wallace A. Johnson | October 15, 1924 | T. Presser | Philadelphia, PA |
| STEPPING ON THE IVORIES | John McLaughlin | August 4, 1927 | M. Witmark and Sons | New York, NY |
| STEWED CHICKEN RAG | Glenn C. Leap | April 22, 1912 | Self | New York, NY |
| STEWED PRUNES RAG | Oscar Lorraine | November 16, 1910 | Jerome H. Remick | New York, NY |
| STOP IT | George L. Cobb | 1919 | Walter Jacobs | Boston, MA |
| STOP RAG | C. A. Reccius | April 14, 1913 | A. F. Marzian | Louisville, KY |
| STOP YOUR KIDDIN' | Ferde Grofe and Jimmy McHugh | November 24, 1922 | Jack Mills | New York, NY |
| STOP-TROT RAG | Cass. Freeborn | March 3, 1914 | M. Witmark and Sons | New York, NY |
| STOPTIME RAG | Scott Joplin | June 4, 1910 | Joseph W. Stern | New York, NY |
| STORYVILLE SPORT | Tom Shea | 1966 | Ragtime Society | Toronto, CN |
| STREAMERS RAG | E. Earle Marx | August 18, 1909 | Victor Kremer | Chicago, IL |
| STRENOUS LIFE | Scott Joplin | 1902 | John Stark and Son | St. Louis, MO |

| Title | Composer | Date | Publisher | City |
|---|---|---|---|---|
| STUMBLING (Paraphrase) | Zez Confrey | July 1, 1922 | Leo Feist | New York, NY |
| STUNG RAG | Albert A. Stoll | June 26, 1909 | J. Placht and Brother | St. Louis, MO |
| SUCH A RAG | Carl H. Copenhaver | February 27, 1913 | Frank Harding | New York, NY |
| SUCH IS LIFE | Charles L. Cooke | December 30, 1915 | Jerome H. Remick | New York, NY |
| SUGAR CANE RAG | Scott Joplin | April 21, 1908 | Seminary Music | New York, NY |
| SUMMER BREEZE | James Scott | March 14, 1903 | Dumars Music | Carthage, MO |
| SUMTHIN DOIN | Florence M. Wood | April 1, 1904 | Automatic Perforating Company | New York, NY |
| SUNBEAMS | Bill Wirges | May 31, 1929 | Self | New York, NY |
| SUNBURST RAG | James Scott | 1909 | Stark Music Company | New York, NY |
| SUNFLOWER BABE | Fred Heltman | February 20, 1909 | Self | Cleveland, OH |
| SUNFLOWER RAG | Percy Wenrich | July 26, 1911 | Jerome H. Remick | New York, NY |
| SUNFLOWER SLOW DRAG | Scott Joplin and Scott Hayden | March 18, 1901 | John Stark and Son | St. Louis, MO |
| SUNFLOWER TICKLE | Dolly Richmond | September 14, 1908 | McKinley Music | Chicago, IL |
| SUNNY SOUTH RAG | Clyde Spence | October 16, 1907 | Globe Music | New York, NY |
| SUNSET | Allen P. Dougherty and Max Mayer | February 9, 1907 | North–Western Music | Seattle, WA |
| SUNSET RAG | Frederick Bryan | October 21, 1914 | Joseph W. Stern | New York, NY |
| SUNSHINE CAPERS | Roy Bargy | February 7, 1922 | Sam Fox | Cleveland, OH |
| SUNSTROKE RAG | M. W. Myers | October 2, 1911 | Joe Morris | Philadelphia, PA |
| SUPPER CLUB | Harry Carroll | March 14, 1917 | Jerome H. Remick | New York, NY |
| SURE FIRE RAG | Henry Lodge | March 15, 1910 | Victor Kremer | Chicago, IL |
| SUSAN'S RAG | David A. Jasen | June 28, 1979 | The Big Three | New York, NY |
| SWAMPTOWN SHUFFLE | Harry W. Jones | 1902 | Medbery Music | Chicago, IL |
| SWANEE RAG | Charles L. Johnson | March 18, 1912 | Sam Fox | Cleveland, OH |
| SWANEE RIPPLES | Walter E. Blaufuss | December 27, 1912 | Frank Clark Music | Chicago, IL |
| SWEET AND TENDER | Roy Bargy | April 17, 1923 | Will Rossiter | Chicago, IL |
| SWEET BUNCH | Morley Caldwell | September 15, 1904 | Pioneer Music | Chicago, IL |
| SWEET NOTHINGS | Milton J. Rettenberg | September 28, 1928 | Ager, Yellen, and Bornstein | New York, NY |
| SWEET PICKIN'S RAG | Charley Straight | April 30, 1918 | Forster Music | Chicago, IL |
| SWEET PICKLES | George E. Florence | October 23, 1907 | Victor Kremer | Chicago, IL |
| SWEET POTATOES | Justin Ringleben | November 20, 1906 | Seminary Music | New York, NY |
| SWEET SIXTEENTHS | William Albright | December 30, 1976 | Edward B. Marks | New York, NY |
| SWEETIE DEAR | Joe Jordan | November 26, 1906 | Jordan and Cook | Chicago, IL |
| SWEETMEATS | Percy Wenrich | February 18, 1907 | Arnett–Delonais | Chicago, IL |
| SWEETNESS | Fannie B. Woods | June 14, 1912 | Forster Music | Chicago, IL |
| SWEETY, WON'T YOU BE KIND TO ME | D. W. Batsell | August 14, 1913 | Self | Florence, AL |
| SWELL AFFAIR | Bert Potter | August 27, 1904 | George M. Krey | Boston, MA |
| SWIPESY CAKE WALK | Scott Joplin and Arthur Marshall | July 21, 1900 | John Stark and Son | St. Louis, MO |
| SWISS CHEESE RAG | A. E. Bohrer | December 1, 1913 | Self | New York, NY |
| SYCAMORE | Scott Joplin | July 18, 1904 | Will Rossiter | Chicago, IL |
| SYCAMORE SAPLIN | Theron C. Bennett | April 9, 1910 | Jerome H. Remick | Detroit, MI |
| SYMPATHETIC JASPER | E. L. Catlin | 1905 | John Stark and Son | St. Louis, MO |

| Title | Composer | Date | Publisher | City |
|---|---|---|---|---|
| SYMPATHETIC RAG | Arthur M. Siebrecht | June 2, 1911 | Self | Lexington, KY |
| SYMPHONOLA | Henry Lange | March 6, 1922 | Jack Mills | New York, NY |
| SYMPHONY RAG | J. A. Cotter | May 3, 1913 | Cotter's Theatrical and Musical | Peoria, IL |
| SYNCOPATED ECHOES | Elmer Olson | December 8, 1920 | W. A. Quincke | Los Angeles, CA |
| SYNCOPATED FOX TROT | E. S. Teall | December 15, 1915 | Joseph W. Sturtevant | New York, NY |
| SYNCOPATING THE SCALES | Arthur Schutt | November 3, 1922 | Jack Mills | New York, NY |
| TAKE IT EASY | Axel Christensen | February 9, 1924 | Jack Mills | New York, NY |
| TALK OF THE TOWN | Elijah Jimerson and M. Cranston | 1919 | Syndicate Music | St. Louis, MO |
| TANGLE FOOT RAG | Fleta Jan Brown | December 14, 1906 | Joseph W. Stern | New York, NY |
| TANGLEFOOT | E. A. Storman | 1899 | Self | St. Louis, MO |
| TANGLEFOOT RAG | John F. James | May 5, 1910 | Jerome H. Remick | New York, NY |
| TANGLEFOOT RAG | F. H. Losey | May 21, 1910 | Vandersloot Music | Williamsport, PA |
| TANGO | Joe Jordan | January 16, 1913 | Will Rossiter | Chicago, IL |
| TANGO RAG | L. T. Dunlap | August 21, 1913 | Owl Music | Wilkes-Barre, PA |
| TANGO RAG | Abe Olman | January 6, 1914 | Joe Morris | New York, NY |
| TANGOLIZING RAG | Ray Collins | October 15, 1914 | H. Kirkus Dugdale | Washington, DC |
| TANTALIZER RAG | Frank S. Butler | April 10, 1916 | Mellinger Music | St. Louis, MO |
| TANTALIZING TINGLES | Mike Bernard and Solly Ginsberg | February 18, 1913 | Waterson, Berlin, and Snyder | New York, NY |
| TAR BABIES | Charles L. Johnson | January 3, 1911 | Charles L. Johnson | Kansas City, MO |
| TAR BABY | Gertrude Cady | May 19, 1904 | H. L. Walker | New York, NY |
| TATTERED MELODY RAG | Hilda Ossusky | December 15, 1910 | Jerome H. Remick | Detroit, MI |
| TATTERS | Charles Cohen | October 2, 1906 | Sam Fox | Cleveland, OH |
| TEASING RAG | Paul Pratt | 1912 | Charles A. Meyers | Chicago, IL |
| TEASING THE CAT | Charles L. Johnson | August 19, 1916 | Forster Music | Chicago, IL |
| TEASING THE KLASSICS | Axel Christensen | June 25, 1923 | Forster Music | Chicago, IL |
| TECHNIC TOUCH RAG | Harold B. Knox | November 4, 1913 | H. Kirkus Dugdale | Washington, DC |
| TEDDY BEAR RAG | Hattie Goben | October 18, 1907 | Self | Dallas, TX |
| TEDDY IN THE JUNGLE | Edward J. Freeberg | February 8, 1910 | Rinker Music | Lafayette, IN |
| TEDDY'S PARDNERS | Horace Dowell | 1903 | Frank G. Fite | Nashville, TN |
| TEE NA NAH | Harry Weston | May 30, 1910 | L. Grunewald Company | New Orleans, LA |
| TEMPTATION RAG | Henry Lodge | September 9, 1909 | M. Witmark and Sons | New York, NY |
| TEMPUS RAGORUM | Marshall M. Bartholomew | February 21, 1906 | Self | New York, NY |
| TEN PENNY RAG | Clarence E. Brandon and Billy Smythe | December 6, 1911 | Brandon and Smythe | St. Louis, MO |
| TENNESSEE JUBILEE | Thomas E. Broady | 1899 | Henry A. French | Nashville, TN |
| TENNESSEE RAG | Severino Giovannoli | July 26, 1912 | Self | Cookeville, TN |
| TENNESSEE RAG | George McDade and Henry Watterson | October 26, 1908 | Victor Kremer | Chicago, IL |
| TENNESSEE TANTALIZER | Charles Hunter | November 19, 1900 | H. A. French | Nashville, TN |
| TENTH INTERVAL RAG | Harry Ruby | January 2, 1924 | Stark and Cowan | New York, NY |
| TEX TANGLE FOOT RAG | F. J. Boyer | October 1, 1912 | H. Kirkus Dugdale | Washington, DC |
| TEXAS FOX TROT | David Guion | August 16, 1915 | M. Witmark and Sons | New York, NY |

| Title | Composer | Date | Publisher | City |
|---|---|---|---|---|
| TEXAS RAG | Callis W. Jackson | June 5, 1905 | Self | Dallas, TX |
| TEXAS RAG | Frank Orth | November 6, 1909 | Mack and Orth | Philadelphia, PA |
| TEXAS STEER | George Botsford | October 15, 1909 | Jerome H. Remick | Detroit, MI |
| TEXAS WIGGLE RAG | Ermon Smith | April 8, 1914 | H. Kirkus Dugdale | Washington, DC |
| THAT AMERICAN RAG | L. Vertugno and W. H. Kuney | November 26, 1912 | Oelwein Music | Oelwein, IA |
| THAT AMERICAN RAGTIME DANCE | David A. Jasen | June 28, 1979 | The Big Three | New York, NY |
| THAT ANGELL RAG | Henry P. Schaefer | November 21, 1914 | Regent Music | Lake Charles, LA |
| THAT BOMBSHELL RAG | Jean Rameau | February 21, 1912 | Self | Ely, NV |
| THAT BULL FROG RAG | George W. Thomas | July 27, 1917 | Williams and Piron | New Orleans, LA |
| THAT CAPTIVATING RAG | Ruth Orndorff | February 23, 1912 | Self | Kendallville, IN |
| THAT CAPTIVATING RAG | Charles Wellinger | September 8, 1914 | Self | Hamilton, CN |
| THAT CHERRY RAG | Edna Chappell Tiff | January 30, 1914 | H. Kirkus Dugdale | Washington, DC |
| THAT CHINESE RAG | Albert Stedman | 1910 | G. W. Setchell | Boston, MA |
| THAT CONTAGIOUS RAG | Edward J. Mellinger | February 21, 1913 | Stark Music Company | St. Louis, MO |
| THAT CONTAGIOUS RAG | Wilbur Piper | 1911 | Self | Sidney, OH |
| THAT CORRUGATED RAG | Edward J. Mellinger | July 27, 1911 | Stark Music Company | St. Louis, MO |
| THAT CRAZY RAG | Frank Broekhoven | December 1, 1911 | Self | New Orleans, LA |
| THAT DAHM RAG | Phil J. Dahm | April 13, 1912 | Self | Chicago, IL |
| THAT DANDY RAG | W. L. Rand | October 3, 1912 | Jerome H. Remick | Detroit, MI |
| THAT DAWGGONE RAG | Maurice K. Smith | March 18, 1914 | W. A. Quincke | Los Angeles, CA |
| THAT DEMON RAG | Russell Smith | January 27, 1911 | I. Seidel Music | Indianapolis, IN |
| THAT DIXIE DIP | Dippy Dip | October 14, 1912 | Frank K. Root | Chicago, IL |
| THAT DIXIE RAG | Victor Moulton | August 27, 1912 | McKinley Music | Chicago, IL |
| THAT DIZZY RAG | Earl S. Rogers | May 15, 1916 | Harmony Music | Lafayette, IN |
| THAT DOG GONE RAG | W. H. Petway | 1911 | Self | Nashville, TN |
| THAT DYNAMITE RAG | Guy Arter | June 14, 1915 | Self | Prairie City, IL |
| THAT EASY RAG | Edward J. Mellinger | October 9, 1914 | Mellinger Music | St. Louis, MO |
| THAT ECCENTRIC RAG | J. Russel Robinson | January 22, 1912 | I. Seidel Music | Indianapolis, IN |
| THAT ENTERTAINING RAG MUSIC | Arthur Wellesley | January 3, 1912 | George W. Meyer | New York, NY |
| THAT ENTICING TWO STEP | Blanch M. Tice | March 1, 1913 | Self | Sioux City, IA |
| THAT ERRATIC RAG | J. Russel Robinson | 1940 | Self | New York, NY |
| THAT EVER LOVIN' RAG | Walter Byron | March 28, 1952 | Johnstone–Montei | New York, NY |
| THAT EVERLASTING RAG | Will Held | April 25, 1911 | Charles E. Roat Music | Battle Creek, MI |
| THAT FASCINATING RAG | Walter Rolfe | September 27, 1911 | J. W. Jenkins | Kansas City, MO |
| THAT FASCINATING TEMPLE RAG | C. S. and H. H. Byron | 1910 | House of Laemmle | Chicago, IL |
| THAT FLYING RAG | Arthur Pryor | August 8, 1911 | Carl Fischer | New York, NY |
| THAT FUTURISTIC RAG | Rube Bloom | April 9, 1923 | Jack Mills | New York, NY |
| THAT GIGGLIN' RAG | Howard M. Githens | August 1, 1912 | Clarice Manning Company | New York, NY |
| THAT GOSH-DARNED TWO STEP RAG | M. Kendree Miller | March 7, 1913 | Bush and Gerts | Dallas, TX |
| THAT GRAVITATING RAG | Carl Eckerle | February 10, 1914 | Self | Cincinnati, OH |

| Title | Composer | Date | Publisher | City |
|---|---|---|---|---|
| THAT HAND PLAYED RAG | David Silverman and Arthur Ward | 1914 | Silverman and Ward | St. Louis, MO |
| THAT HARMONIZING RAG | James J. DeZego | January 28, 1914 | Harmony Music | New York, NY |
| THAT HATEFUL RAG | Bertha Allen | July 21, 1925 | Self | Des Moines, IA |
| THAT HESITATING RAG | Roy Hatfield | April 19, 1910 | Self | West Milton, OH |
| THAT HINDU RAG | George L. Cobb | October 15, 1910 | Walter Jacobs | Boston, MA |
| THAT HUNGARIAN RAG | Arthur H. Gutman | October 29, 1910 | Joe Morris | New York, NY |
| THAT HYPNOTIC RAG | Leon M. Block | February 24, 1913 | Cahn and Block | Shreveport, LA |
| THAT IRRESISTIBLE RAG | S. Charles Lavin | August 6, 1910 | Ted Snyder Company | New York, NY |
| THAT IRRESISTIBLE RAG | Fay Parker | 1913 | Syndicate Music | St. Louis, MO |
| THAT IRRESISTIBLE RAG | Lucy B. Phillips | 1912 | Charles L. Johnson | Kansas City, MO |
| THAT JUMPING RAG | Irma Hult | April 8, 1914 | H. Kirkus Dugdale | Washington, DC |
| THAT MADRID RAG | Julius Lenzberg | May 31, 1911 | Ted Snyder Company | New York, NY |
| THAT MOANING SAXOPHONE RAG | Harry Cook and Tom Brown | September 18, 1913 | Will Rossiter | Chicago, IL |
| THAT MOVING PICTURE RAG | Willard A. Thomas | June 12, 1913 | Thomas Goggan and Brothers | Galveston, TX |
| THAT NATURAL RAG | Ettore Bernardo Fisichelli | November 2, 1911 | Ted Snyder Company | New York, NY |
| THAT NEKOMA RAG | Floyd V. Swanson | March 9, 1914 | Self | Moline, IL |
| THAT NEW REGENERATION RAG | Lester Stewart Holland | October 11, 1915 | Self | San Pedro, CA |
| THAT NIFTY RAG | S. E. Roberts | 1911 | George F. Briegel | New York, NY |
| THAT NOBBY RAG | Louis Fontaine | April 1, 1913 | Self | Colville, WA |
| THAT PECULIAR RAG | F. M. Fagan | September 12, 1910 | Aubrey Stauffer | Chicago, IL |
| THAT PICTURE SHOW RAG | Horace Rosamond | October 31, 1913 | Self | Stanford, TX |
| THAT PLEASING RAG | J. Fred O'Connor | November 29, 1911 | Harold Rossiter | Chicago, IL |
| THAT POSTAL RAG | E. L. McKenzie | September 22, 1910 | Self | Portland, OR |
| THAT POTATOE BUG RAG | Axel Christensen | December 1, 1916 | Christensen School | Chicago, IL |
| THAT PUZZLIN' RAG | Chris Smith | 1912 | F. B. Haviland | New York, NY |
| THAT QUEEN CITY RAG | O. B. Kramer | 1916 | Connett Sheet Music | Newport, KY |
| THAT RAG | Ted Browne | April 6, 1907 | Thiebes–Stierlin Music | St. Louis, MO |
| THAT REAL RAG | J. W. Mooney | 1914 | Mooney and Spears | New York, NY |
| THAT RUNAWAY RAG | Vincent Baluta | April 23, 1914 | Samuel H. Speck | New York, NY |
| THAT SCANDALOUS RAG | Edwin F. Kendall | November 22, 1912 | John Franklin Music | New York, NY |
| THAT SENTIMENTAL RAG | Mabel Tilton | May 6, 1913 | Leo Feist | New York, NY |
| THAT SPARKLING RAG | Frank A. Goulart | September 25, 1911 | Self | Dorchester, MA |
| THAT SPOOKY RAG | Will J. Elener | April 20, 1912 | H. Kirkus Dugdale | Washington, DC |
| THAT SPOONEY DANCE | Jean Schwartz | July 6, 1910 | Jerome H. Remick | Detroit, MI |
| THAT STOP TIME RAG | Ernie Erdman | October 1, 1912 | Tell Taylor | Chicago, IL |
| THAT TANGO RAG | C. Roy Larson | March 16, 1914 | Charles H. Henderson | New York, NY |
| THAT TANTALIZING RAG | Thelma Kay | January 22, 1913 | H. Kirkus Dugdale | Washington, DC |
| THAT TEASING RAG | Joe Jordan | December 24, 1909 | Joseph W. Stern | New York, NY |
| THAT TEXAS RAG | Nell Wright Watson | 1914 | Bush and Gerts | Dallas, TX |
| THAT TICKLING RAG | Mike Bernard | July 27, 1910 | Charles K. Harris | New York, NY |
| THAT TIGER RAG | W. J. Rawson, Jr. | October 6, 1911 | Self | Aberdeen, SD |
| THAT TIRED FEELIN' | Joe Arzonia | 1906 | Joe Morris | Philadelphia, PA |

| Title | Composer | Date | Publisher | City |
|---|---|---|---|---|
| THAT TIRED RAG | Charlotte Blake | February 11, 1911 | Jerome H. Remick | Detroit, MI |
| THAT TOUCHY KID RAG | Bertha Stanfield | 1912 | Self | Baxter Springs, KS |
| THAT TUNEFUL RAG | Buel B. Risinger | January 14, 1911 | Sunlight Music | Chicago, IL |
| THAT WHISTLING RAG | Joseph M. Foley | May 18, 1912 | Self | Tharold, CN |
| THAT'S A PLENTY | Lew Pollack | February 25, 1914 | Joe Morris | New York, NY |
| THAT'S IT | Charles C. Miller | December 23, 1912 | Self | Billings, MT |
| THEATORIUM RAG | Leon M. Block | March 5, 1909 | Self | Pine Bluff, AR |
| THELMA RAG | W. M. Reiff | 1905 | C. C. Powell | Fort Wayne, IN |
| THIRTY-EIGHTH STREET RAG | Les Copeland | January 17, 1913 | Waterson, Berlin, and Snyder | New York, NY |
| THOMAS BROTHERS' RAG | Maurice B. Thomas | June 20, 1906 | Sanders and Stayman | Washington, DC |
| THOROUGHBRED RAG | Joseph F. Lamb | 1964 | Mills Music | New York, NY |
| THREE HUNDRED GREEN | A. E. Jeffers | June 16, 1913 | Self | Springfield, MO |
| THREE WEEKS RAG | Harold G. Mitchell | May 22, 1908 | Southern California Music | Los Angeles, CA |
| THRILLER | May Aufderheide | September 4, 1909 | J. H. Aufderheide | Indianapolis, IN |
| THUNDERBOLT RAG | Frank S. Butler | 1913 | Gotham–Attucks Music | New York, NY |
| THUNDERBOLT RAG | Samuel J. Stokes | August 19, 1910 | Self | New Orleans, LA |
| THUNDERBOLT RAG | Fred T. Whitehouse | August 23, 1909 | Self | Barberton, OH |
| TICKLE IT | Thomas Buster Page | August 10, 1912 | Self | Lima, OH |
| TICKLE THE IVORIES | Wallie Herzer | January 25, 1913 | Jerome H. Remick | New York, NY |
| TICKLED PINK | William S. Rowland | December 30, 1976 | Edward B. Marks Music | New York, NY |
| TICKLED TO DEATH | Charles Hunter | May 11, 1901 | Frank G. Fite | Nashville, TN |
| TICKLED TO DEATH | Ralph Larsh | 1936 | Ralph Larsh | Chicago, IL |
| TICKLER | Frances Cox | 1908 | Charles L. Johnson | Kansas City, MO |
| TICKLISH RAG | J. P. Traxler | January 6, 1905 | Self | Lorain, OH |
| TIDDLE-DE-WINKS | Melville Morris | September 16, 1916 | Jerome H. Remick | New York, NY |
| TIERNEY RAG | Harry A. Tierney | August 8, 1913 | Charles T. French | New York, NY |
| TIN PAN RAG | Lou Busch | March 5, 1952 | Chatsworth Music | New York, NY |
| TIN WHISTLE BLUES | Frank Capie | September 4, 1918 | Jerome H. Remick and Company | New York, NY |
| TIPSY TOPSY | Joe Keden | January 18, 1927 | Jack Mills | New York, NY |
| TOAD STOOL RAG | Joseph F. Lamb | 1964 | Mills Music | New York, NY |
| TOBOGGAN RAG | John F. Barth | August 27, 1912 | Sam Fox | Cleveland, OH |
| TODDLIN' | James P. Johnson | September 18, 1925 | Perry Bradford Music | New York, NY |
| TODDLING | William Axst and Erno Rapee | April 30, 1923 | Richmond–Robbins | New York, NY |
| TOKIO RAG | Henry Lodge | May 27, 1912 | M. Witmark and Sons | New York, NY |
| TOLD AT TWILIGHT | Ed Kneisel | September 24, 1925 | Jack Mills | New York, NY |
| TOM AND JERRY RAG | Jerry Cammack | 1913 | St. Louis Publishing Company | St. Louis, MO |
| TOM BROWN'S TRILLING TUNE | Charles L. Cooke | December 20, 1916 | Buck and Lowney | St. Louis, MO |
| TOM CAT RAG | Harry Weston | 1912 | Music Shop | New Orleans, LA |
| TOM-BOY | W. F. Bradford | February 18, 1907 | Arnett–Delonais | Chicago, IL |
| TOMATO SAUCE | Fred W. Longshaw | September 18, 1925 | Perry Bradford Music | New York, NY |
| TOMFOOLERY | Tom Griselle | August 30, 1923 | Robbins Music | New York, NY |
| TOO MUCH RASPBERRY | Sydney King Russell | September 6, 1916 | Self | Berkeley, CA |

| Title | Composer | Date | Publisher | City |
|---|---|---|---|---|
| TOODLES | Clarence C. Jones | June 2, 1916 | Joseph Krolage Music | Cincinnati, OH |
| TOOTH PICK RAG | Gladys Andrews | August 25, 1912 | Bixby Bros. | Buffalo, NY |
| TOOTS | Felix Arndt | November 27, 1915 | G. Ricordi | New York, NY |
| TOP LINER RAG | Joseph F. Lamb | January 4, 1916 | Stark Music Company | St. Louis, MO |
| TOPSEY'S DREAM | Henry Williams | May 11, 1903 | Shattinger Music | St. Louis, MO |
| TORPEDO | George Oscar Young | June 5, 1917 | Daniels and Wilson | San Francisco, CA |
| TORRID DORA | George L. Cobb | December 28, 1921 | Will Rossiter | Chicago, IL |
| TOTALLY DIFFERENT RAG | May Aufderheide | July 16, 1910 | J. H. Aufderheide | Indianapolis, IN |
| TOWN TALK | Elmer Olson | November 27, 1917 | E. F. Bickhart's Song Shop | Minneapolis, MN |
| TOWN TALK | Rube Richardson and James S. White | 1910 | James S. White | Boston, MA |
| TOY PIANO RAG | Bill Krenz and Eddie Ballantine | December 23, 1954 | Mills Music | New York, NY |
| TOY TOWN TOPICS | Harold Dixon | October 7, 1927 | Self | New York, NY |
| TRANSFORMATION RAG | Babe Taylor | February 15, 1915 | Howard L. Dodge | Long Beach, CA |
| TREY O' HEARTS RAG | A. E. Holch | December 22, 1915 | Self | Cripple Creek, CO |
| TRIANGLE JAZZ BLUES | Irwin P. Leclere | February 21, 1917 | Triangle Music | New Orleans, LA |
| TRICKY FINGERS | Eubie Blake | 1971 | Edward B. Marks Music | New York, NY |
| TRICKY TRIX | Harry Jentes | June 13, 1923 | Jack Mills | New York, NY |
| TRILBY RAG | Carey Morgan | May 11, 1915 | Joseph W. Stern | New York, NY |
| TRILLIUM RAG | Tom Shea | October 20, 1964 | Hollis Music | New York, NY |
| TROUBADOUR RAG | James Scott | February 7, 1919 | Stark Music Company | St. Louis, MO |
| TROUBLE | C. Duane Crabb and Will B. Morrison | November 23, 1908 | Morrison and Crabb | Indianapolis, IN |
| TROUBLE MAKER RAG | Claude Messenger | August 2, 1910 | Charles H. Henderson | Corry, PA |
| TROUBLESOME IVORIES | Eubie Blake | 1971 | Edward B. Marks Music | New York, NY |
| TRY AND PLAY IT | Phil Ohman | August 5, 1922 | Richmond–Robbins | New York, NY |
| TUCKER TROT | Jules Buffano | January 4, 1921 | Will Rossiter | Chicago, IL |
| TURKEY TROT | Ribe Danmark | July 2, 1912 | Jerome H. Remick | New York, NY |
| TURKISH TOWEL RAG | Thomas S. Allen | January 16, 1912 | Walter Jacobs | Boston, MA |
| TURKISH TROPHIES | Sara B. Egan | May 31, 1907 | Will Rossiter | Chicago, IL |
| TURPENTINE RAG | Jessie Murphy | November 10, 1905 | Self | Greenville, TX |
| TWELFTH STREET RAG | Euday Bowman | August 31, 1914 | Euday Bowman | Fort Worth, TX |
| TWILIGHT WHISPERS | King W. Baker | June 16, 1919 | Self | Rumsey, KY |
| TWINKLE DIMPLES RAG | Edward C. Barroll and Hattie Leonara Smith | March 2, 1914 | Mid-West Music | St. Louis, MO |
| TWINKLE TOES | Harold Potter | 1927 | Jack Mills | New York, NY |
| TWINKLES | Harry Jentes | June 1, 1925 | Robbins–Engel | New York, NY |
| TWO-KEY RAG | Joe Hollander | April 19, 1916 | H. Lesser and Brother | New York, NY |
| U. OF M. HARMONY RAG | Frank Stori | May 26, 1914 | Samuel H. Speck | Menomonie, WI |
| UNCLE SAMMY AT THE PIANO | Clarence Gaskill | February 26, 1923 | Jack Mills | New York, NY |
| UNCLE TOM'S CABIN RAG | Harry A. Tierney | March 14, 1911 | Joseph W. Stern | New York, NY |
| UNCLE ZEKE'S MEDLEY RAG | Bertha Stanfield | 1912 | Self | Baxter Springs, KS |
| UNEEDA RAG TIME | Bayard W. Craig | May 25, 1900 | Self | Elizabeth, NJ |
| UNIVERSAL RAG | Frank Wooster | 1905 | John Stark and Son | St. Louis, MO |
| UNIVERSITY RAG | Claude V. Frisinger | August 28, 1911 | Self | Urbana, IL |

| Title | Composer | Date | Publisher | City |
|---|---|---|---|---|
| UNIVERSITY RAG | Frayser Hinton and Donald Stonebraker | 1914 | Hinton | Memphis, TN |
| UNIVERSITY RAG | Ruth Knippenburg | June 1, 1912 | Pollworth Music Publishing Company | Milwaukee, WI |
| UNNAMED RAG | Frank Pallma | 1917 | Self | Minneapolis, MN |
| UP AND DOWN IN CHINA | Willard Robison | September 14, 1926 | Robbins–Engel | New York, NY |
| UP AND DOWN THE KEYS | Phil Ohman | September 30, 1922 | Richmond–Robbins | New York, NY |
| UPRIGHT AND GRAND | Frank Banta and Peter DeRose | September 1, 1923 | Richmond–Robbins | New York, NY |
| VARSITY RAG | Paul Pratt | April 17, 1909 | J. H. Aufderheide | Indianapolis, IN |
| VARIETY RAG | Harry A. Tierney | July 1, 1912 | George W. Meyer Music | New York, NY |
| VARSITY DAYS | Frank W. Ryan | September 30, 1907 | Self | Topeka, KS |
| VELMA CHOCOLATES | Ernst Otto | August 7, 1909 | Self | Davenport, IA |
| VENTURA RAG | Louis Mentel | March 12, 1907 | Mentel Brothers | Cincinnati, OH |
| VERY RAGGY | Mrs. Merrill Morgan | June 10, 1907 | Self | Rotan, TX |
| VICTORY RAG | James Scott | 1921 | Stark Music Company | St. Louis, MO |
| VIRGINIA CREEPER | Mae Davis | December 21, 1907 | Walter Jacobs | Boston, MA |
| VIRGINIA CREEPER | Billy Mayerl | October 12, 1925 | Sam Fox | Cleveland, OH |
| VIRGINIA CREEPER RAG | Chas. H. Roth | 1909 | Roth and Redding | Washington, DC |
| VIRGINIA RAG | Bryant Gallagher | December 7, 1916 | Mentel Brothers | Cincinnati, OH |
| VIRGINIA RAG | Sydney P. Harris | July 22, 1907 | Self | New York, NY |
| VIRGINIA RAG | Isham E. Jones | November 11, 1913 | Jones Brothers | Saginaw, MI |
| VIRGINIA RAG | Harriet Reynolds Marchant | February 19, 1912 | H. Kirkus Dugdale | Washington, DC |
| VIVACITY RAG | Frank C. Keithley | February 5, 1910 | New York and Chicago Music | Chicago, IL |
| VOLCANIC RAG | Leah Monks Robb | 1911 | Gotham–Attucks Music | New York, NY |
| WAIMAN RAG | James R. Shannon | June 27, 1910 | Grinnell Bros. | Detroit, MI |
| WALHALLA | Paul Pratt | January 13, 1910 | J. H. Aufderheide | Indianapolis, MN |
| WALL STREET RAG | Scott Joplin | February 23, 1909 | Seminary Music | New York, NY |
| WASH DAY RAG | Charles Goeddel | October 14, 1911 | Panella and Murray Music | Pittsburgh, PA |
| WASH RAG | F. H. Losey | November 16, 1910 | Carl Fischer | New York, NY |
| WATER BUG | Walter E. Miles | November 9, 1925 | Sam Fox | Cleveland, OH |
| WATER QUEEN | Homer Denney | June 8, 1906 | Denney and Flanigan | Cincinnati, OH |
| WATER WAGON BLUES | George L. Cobb | 1919 | Walter Jacobs | Boston, MA |
| WATERMELON | Harry S. Krossin | 1909 | Self | Minneapolis, MN |
| WATERMELON MOSE | Floyd Willis | November 9, 1907 | Self | Covington, KY |
| WATERMELON TRUST | Harry C. Thompson | May 25, 1906 | Barron and Thompson | New York, NY |
| WEAVING AROUND RAG | Lawrence A. Mirchel | January 20, 1913 | Sam Fox | Cleveland, OH |
| WEBSTER GROVE RAG | Axel Christensen | March 31, 1915 | Christensen School | Chicago, IL |
| WEDDING BELLS RAG | Al B. Coney | December 10, 1910 | Will Rossiter | Chicago, IL |
| WEEPING WILLOW | H. A. Fischler | January 16, 1911 | Vandersloot Music | Williamsport, PA |
| WEEPING WILLOW | Scott Joplin | June 6, 1903 | Val A. Reis Music | St. Louis, MO |
| WEIRD RAG | Phil Schwartz | September 18, 1911 | Will Rossiter | Chicago, IL |
| WELSH RAREBIT | Maude E. Palmiter | 1907 | R. V. Gould | Rockford, IL |
| WHAT IS IT? | Oswald E. Planchard | 1906 | Cable Company | New Orleans, LA |

| Title | Composer | Date | Publisher | City |
|---|---|---|---|---|
| WHAT'S YOUR HURRY? | Effie Kamman | January 19, 1923 | Jerome H. Remick | New York, NY |
| WHIPPED CREAM | Percy Wenrich | January 18, 1913 | Wenrich–Howard | New York, NY |
| WHIPPIN' THE KEYS | Sam Goold | 1923 | Stark and Cowan | New York, NY |
| WHIRL WIND | J. Russel Robinson | December 11, 1911 | Stark Music Company | St. Louis, MO |
| WHITE RAG | Ella White | February 9, 1911 | W. A. Cantrell | Charleston, WV |
| WHITE SEAL RAG | Kittie M. Hamel | October 21, 1907 | Jerome H. Remick | New York, NY |
| WHITEWASH MAN | Jean Schwartz | September 8, 1908 | Cohan and Harris | New York, NY |
| WHITTLING REMUS | Thomas E. Broady | April 20, 1900 | Henry A. French | Nashville, TN |
| WHO GOT THE LEMON? | Marcella A. Henry | June 26, 1909 | Self | Peru, IL |
| WHO LET THE COWS OUT | Charles Humfeld | March 10, 1910 | Howard and Browne Music | St. Louis, MO |
| WHO'S WHO | Melville Morris | June 6, 1917 | Jerome H. Remick | New York, NY |
| WHOA! MAUDE | Will H. Etter | July 29, 1905 | Thomas Goggan and Brothers | Galveston, TX |
| WHOA! NELLIE | George Gould | 1915 | Charles N. Daniels Music | San Francisco, CA |
| WHOA! YOU HEIFER | Al Verges | October 13, 1904 | Hakenjos | New Orleans, LA |
| WHY WE SMILE | Charles Hunter | September 28, 1903 | Frank G. Fite | Nashville, TN |
| WIDE AWAKE RAG | Jessie Spaenhower | November 3, 1915 | Marks–Goldsmith Company | Washington, DC |
| WIG-WAG RAG | Harry C. Thompson | November 9, 1911 | Leo Feist | New York, NY |
| WIGGLE RAG | George Botsford | October 15, 1909 | Jerome H. Remick | Detroit, MI |
| WILD CAT BLUES | Thomas "Fats" Waller and Clarence Williams | September 24, 1923 | Clarence Williams Music | New York, NY |

Fats Waller.

| | | | | |
|---|---|---|---|---|
| WILD CHERRIES | Ted Snyder | September 23, 1908 | Ted Snyder Company | New York, NY |
| WILD FLOWER RAG | Clarence Williams | August 21, 1916 | Williams and Piron Music | New Orleans, LA |
| WILD FLOWER RAG | Carlotta Williamson | August 27, 1910 | Colonial Music | Boston, MA |
| WILD GRAPES RAG | Clarence Jones | 1910 | Emerson Music | Cincinnati, OH |
| WILD-FIRE RAG | Holmes Travis | April 5, 1911 | M. L. Carlson | Chicago, IL |
| WILL O' THE WISP RAG | Richard Haasz | April 3, 1911 | Charles H. Henderson | Corry, PA |
| WILLIAM'S WEDDING | Harry A. Tierney | June 23, 1911 | Ted Snyder Company | New York, NY |
| WILSON'S FAVORITE RAG | Otto L. Stock, Jr. | July 11, 1913 | Self | Pine Island, MN |
| WINNIE'S ARRIVAL | Edna Ralya | 1905 | W. H. Willis | Cincinnati, OH |
| WINTER GARDEN RAG | Abe Olman | December 5, 1912 | Will Rossiter | Chicago, IL |

| Title | Composer | Date | Publisher | City |
|---|---|---|---|---|
| WIPPIN' THE IVORIES | Henry Lange | May 4, 1923 | Waterson, Berlin, and Snyder | New York, NY |
| WIRELESS RAG | Adaline Shepherd | August 21, 1909 | Standard Music | Chicago, IL |
| WISE GAZABO | Frank C. Keithley | 1905 | Keithley-Carl Publishing | Newton, IA |
| WISH BONE | Charlotte Blake | March 6, 1909 | Jerome H. Remick | New York, NY |
| WIZZLE DOZZLE | Harry Bell and Lloyd L. Johnson | April 25, 1910 | Bell and Johnson | Princeton, IN |
| WOOLWORTH RAG | F. Henri Klickmann | May 7, 1913 | Ajax Music | Chicago, IL |
| WOOZY | A. E. Groves | December 14, 1903 | Arnett–Delonais | Chicago, IL |
| WORLD'S FAIR RAG | Harvey M. Babcock | May 13, 1912 | Self | San Francisco, CA |
| WOUNDED LION | Karl C. Robertson | June 19, 1911 | Self | Kansas City, MO |
| WYOMING PRANCE | Kerry Mills | November 14, 1910 | F. A. Mills | New York, NY |
| X-RAY RAG | O. Lee Shoemaker | May 18, 1914 | Self | Denver, CO |
| X.L. RAG | L. Edgar Settle | December 21, 1903 | A. W. Perry and Sons | Sedalia, MO |
| YANKEE DOODLE RAG | Garfield Wilson | June 15, 1911 | Will Rossiter | Chicago, IL |
| YANKEE GIRL | Harry L. Stone | December 24, 1919 | Self | Spokane, WA |
| YANKEE LAND | Max Hoffman | August 31, 1904 | Rogers Bros. Music | New York, NY |

To Jerry from his pal Max
Aug 2 - 38

Max Hoffman.

| | | | | |
|---|---|---|---|---|
| YELLOW BRIDGE | Frankie Gooch McCool | December 29, 1899 | Self | Indianapolis, IN |
| YELLOW ROSE RAG | Will H. Etter | September 1, 1904 | L. Grunewald Company | New Orleans, LA |
| YELLOW ROSE RAG | Terry Waldo | December 30, 1976 | Edward B. Marks Music | New York, NY |
| YIDDISH RAG | A. Traxler | August 15, 1902 | Self | Sharon, PA |
| YOESTIC TWO STEP | Harry N. Koverman | 1904 | W. H. Willis | Cincinnati, OH |
| YOU TELL 'EM, IVORIES | Zez Confrey | August 5, 1921 | Jack Mills | New York, NY |
| YUMURI | Jos. LaCalle | April 25, 1903 | Joseph W. Stern | New York, NY |
| YVONETTE | Bill Krenz | February 1, 1935 | M. M. Cole | Chicago, IL |

| Title | Composer | Date | Publisher | City |
|---|---|---|---|---|
| ZEPHYR | Bill Krenz | February 12, 1935 | M. M. Cole | Chicago, IL |
| ZIG ZAG RAG | H. Anderson | November 21, 1910 | Charles K. Harris | New York, NY |
| ZIG ZAG RAG | Bob Emmerich | 1926 | Triangle Music | New York, NY |
| ZINZINNATI | Nancy Bierbaum | 1907 | Self | Cincinnati, OH |
| ZU-ZU RAG | Max E. Fischler | August 30, 1916 | John Franklin Music | New York, NY |

# Index

Note: Page numbers in **boldface** indicate a subject with its own entry.

# C

"Cactus Rag," **1**
Cakewalk, **31–32**, 197–198
"California Sunshine," 1, **32**
"Calliope Rag," **32**
"Campbell Cakewalk," **34**
Campbell, Sanford Brunson, 10, 22, **33–34**, 42, 50–51, 65, 69, 79, 81, 192, 251
Cammack, Jerry, 259
Can Ragtime Be Surpressed?, **34–36**
"Canadian Capers," **36**, 297–299
"Cannon Ball," **37**
"Caprice Rag," **37**
"Car-Barlick-Acid Rag-Time," **37**, 300, 456
"Carolina FoxTrot," **37**
"Carolina Shout," xvii, **38**, 107, 300–301, 456
Carr, Joe "Fingers," xvii, 28–29, 88, 209–213, 224
"Cascades, The," **38–39**
"Castle House Rag," **39**
"Cat's Pajamas, The," **39**
"Cataract Rag," 1, **39**
"Champagne Rag," **39**
Chapman, James and Leroy Smith, **163**
"Charleston Rag," **40**, 304
"Chatterbox Rag," 38, **39**
Chauvin, Louis, **40–42**, 85
"Chestnut Street in the 90s," **42**
"Chevy Chase, The," **42**
"Chicago Breakdown," **42**
"Chicago Tickle," **42**
"Chicken Chowder," **43**
"Chills and Fever," **43**
Christensen, Axel, 34–36, **43–44**, 192–193
"Chromatic Rag," **44**
Claypoole, Edward, 2, 188–189
"Cleopatra Rag," **45**
"Climax Rag," **45**
"Clover Club," **45**
"Coaxing the Piano," **45**
Cobb, George L., 2, 23, **45–47**, 90, 145, 156, 175, 224, 236, 275
Cohan, George Michael, 181
Cohen, Henry, 36
"Cole Smoak," **47**
"Colonial Glide," **47**
Confare, Thomas, 23, 37
Confrey, Edward Elzear (Zez), 2, 45, **47–50**, 79, 82, 88, 92, 99, 102, 123, 154, 156–157, 177, 232, 268, 282
"Contentment Rag," **50**, 308–309, 458
Cook, Harry, 231
Cooke, Charles L., 19, 302
Copeland, Leslie C., 12, 50–52, 59, 77, 97, 187, 222, 265
"Coronation Rag," **52**
"Cotton Bolls," **52**
"Cotton Patch, A," **52**
"Cotton Time," **53**
"Cottontail Rag," **53**

"Country Club," **53**
"Crab Apples," **53**
"Cradle Rock," **53**
"Crazy Bone Rag," 54, 181
"Crazy Otto, The," **54**
"Creole Belles," 32, 87
"Cum-Bac," **54**, 311, 459

# D

Dabney, Ford T., 79, 159, 181
Daily, Pete & Chicagoans, 88, 207
"Daintiness Rag," 37
Daniels, Charles Neil, 53, 64, 66, 105, 165, 178–180, 193, 215–216
Darch, Bob, 32, **55–56**, 88, 128, 173, 210, 255
"Darkey Todalo, A," **56**
Dawn of the Century Ragtime Orchestra, 210
Day, Ella Hudson, 77
"Delmar Rag" (Thompson), 1, **57**
"Deuces Wild," **57**
"Dew Drop Alley Stomp" 57
"Dickie, Neville," 88, 213
"Dill Pickles Rag," **57**, 105, 178, 180, 192, 216, 314–316, 460
"Dixie Dimples," **58**
"Dixie Kisses," **58**
"Dixie Queen," **59**
"Dockstader Rag, The," **59**
"Doctor Brown," **59**
"Dog on the Piano," **59**
"Doll Dance," xvii, **60**, 318–319, 461
"Don't Jazz Me-Rag," **60**
"Double Fudge," **60**
Douglass, Clyde, 162
"Down Home Rag," **60**
"Dusty Rag," **61**

# E

Early Ragtime, 1897–1905, 63–66
"Easy Winners, The," **66**
"Eccentric," **66–67**
Eckstein, Willie, **67**, 88, 156
"Efficiency Rag," **67**
"Eleventh Street Rag," **67**
"Elite Syncopations," **68**, 324
"Entertainer, The," (Joplin), **68–69**, 110, 212, 324–327. 462
"Entertainer's Rag, The," (Roberts), **69**
"Erratic," **69**
"Essay in Ragtime," **69**
"Ethiopia Rag," **69**
"Eugenia," **70**
"Euphonic Sounds," **70**
Europe, James Reese, 38
"Evergreen Rag," **70**

"Everybody Two Step," 180
"Evolution Rag," **70**
"Excelsior Rag," **71**
Ezell, Will, 65, 277

# F

"Fascinator, The," **73**
"Favorite, The," **73**
"Felicity Rag," **73**
"Fig Leaf Rag," **74**, 111, 331, 463
"Finger Breaker, The," **74**
"Firefly Rag," **74**
Fischler, H.A., 16
"Fizz Water," **74**
"Floating Along," **75**
Florence, George E., *See* Bennett, Theron
"Florida Rag," **75**
"Fourth Man Rag," **75**
"Frances," **75**
Frankl, Abe and Phil Kornheiser, 53
Franklin, Malvin M., 91
"Freakish," **75**
"Freckles," **76**
"Fred Heltman's Rag," 1, **76**
"Fredericks, Henry," **75**
Freeberg, Edward J., 249
"French Pastry Rag," **77**
"Fried Chicken Rag," **77**
"Frog-I-More Rag," 74, **77**
"Frog Legs Rag," **77–78**, 227
"Funeral Rag," **78**
"Funny Bones," **78**
"Funny Folks," **78**

# G

Garnett, Blind Leroy, 65, 134
"Georgia Grind," **79**
Giblin, Irene, 43
Gibson, Lucien P., 1, 104
"Giddy Ditty," **79**
"Ginger Snap Rag," **79**
"Glad Rag," **80**
"Gladiolus Rag," **80**
Goffin, Laurence E., 189
"Good and Plenty Rag," **80**
Gordon, Leo *See* Cobb, George L.
Gould, George, 277
"Grace and Beauty," **80**, 339–340, 464–465
"Grandpa Stomps," **81**
"Grandpa's Spells," **81**, 340–342
"Greased Lightning," **81**
"Great Scott Rag," **81**
"Greenwich Witch," **82**

"Gulbransen Rag," **82**
Gumble, Albert, 23, 181
Gumble, Mose, 193, 215
Guttenberger, Ferdinand A., 121, 221

# H

Hahn, Teddy, 3–4
"Ham And!," **83**
Hamlisch, Marvin, 207, 212
Hampton, Robert, 1, 2, 39, 142
"Handful of Keys," xvii, **83**
Harding, W.N.H., 117
"Harlem Rag," **83–84**, 199, 344–345
Hayden, Scott, 73, **84–85**, 122, 173, 236, 246
"Heavy on the Catsup," **85**
Held, Will, 44
"Heliotrope Bouquet," **85**
"Hilarity Rag," **86**
History of Ragtime Recordings, **86–89**
Hoffman, Max, 66, 194, 281
Hoffman, Robert, 59, 97
"Honey Moon Rag," **89**
"Honey Rag," **89**
"Honeysuckle Rag," **90**
Honky-Tonk Piano, 208, 209
"Hoosier Rag," **90**
"Hop Scotch," **90**
"Horseshoe Rag," **90**
"Hot Chocolate Rag," 1, **91**
"Hot Cinders," **92**
"Hot Hands," **92**
"Hot House Rag," **92**
House of Lords, 175, 255, 275
Humfeld, Charles, 277
"Humorestless," **92**
"Hungarian Rag," 2, **92**, 180
Hunt, Pee Wee & Orchestra, 89, 207
Hunter, Charles, 9, 52, 63, **93–94**, 119, 182, 185, 251, 257, 278
"Hyacinth," **94**
Hyman, Richard Roven. 88, **95**, 161, 200, 209, 211, 212, 213

# I

"I'm Alabama Bound," **97**, 195
"Incandescent Rag, The," **97**
"Invitation Rag," **97**, 196
Irvin, Fred, 59

# J

"J. J. J. Rag," **99**
"Jack in the Box," **99**

# S

St. Louis Ragtimers, 88, 210, 213, 255–256
"St. Louis Tickle," 166, 196, **238,** 252
Stark, E.J., 15
Stark, John, 116–117, 127, 142, 191, 216, 227, **239–241**
"Steeplechase Rag," **241**
Sting, The, xvii, 110, 207, 212
"Stompin' 'Em Down," **241**
"Stop It," **242**
"Stoptime Rag," **242**
"Strenuous Life, The," **244**
Straight, Charley, 2, 92, 123, 187, 224, 235, **242–243,** 267
Stride Ragtime, **244–245**
"Sugar Cane," **245**
"Summer Breeze, A," **245**
"Sunburst Rag," **245**
"Sunflower Slow Drag," **246**
"Swanee Ripples," **246**
Sweatman, Wilbur, C.S., 60
"Sweet and Tender," **246,** 423
"Sweet Pickles," **246–247**
"Swipesy Cakewalk," **247**
"Sycamore, The," **247**
"Sycamore Saplin'," **247**

# T

"Talk of the Town," **249**
"Tantalizing Tingles," 14
"Teasing the Cat," **249**
"Teddy in the Jungle," **249**
"Temptation Rag," 131, **249–250**
"Ten Penny Rag," **250**
"Tennessee Jubilee, A," **250**
"Tennessee Tantalizer, A," **251**
"Tent Show Rag," **251**
"Texas Rag," **251**
"That Demon Rag," **251**
"That Eccentric Rag," 221
"That Futuristic Rag," **251**
"That Rag," **252**
"That Teasin' Rag," **252**
"That's a Plenty," **252**
"They All Played the Maple Leaf Rag," 88, 151, 212
Thomas, Harry, 2, 174
Thompson, Charles Hubbard, 1, 25, 39, 40, 55, 57, 122, 130, 142, 208, **252–253**
Thompson, Harry C., 15, 275
"Thoroughbred Rag," **253**
Three over Four, 15, 57, 90, 123, 130, 173, 180, 199, 229, 232, **253,** 264
"Thriller, The," **254**
Tichenor, Trebor Jay, xxiii, 66, 88, 101, 192, 202, 203, 210, 211, 212, **254–256**
"Tickled to Death," **257**
"Tiddle-De-Winks," **257**

Tierney, Harry Austin, 42, 135, 181, 257–258, 267, 271
Tin Pan Alley Steals from Ragtime Composers, **259**
"Tin Pan Rag," **259**
"Toad Stool Rag," **259**
"Tom and Jerry Rag," **259**
"Too Much Raspberry," 1, **260**
"Top Liner Rag," **260,** 437, 488
"Torpedo Rag," **260**
"Totally Different Rag, A," **260**
"Town Talk," **260**
"Triangle Jazz Blues," 1, **260–261,** 438
"Trilby Rag," 65, **261**
"Troubadour Rag," **261**
"Troublesome Ivories," **262**
Turpin, Thomas M. J., 25–26, 27, 63, 83–84, 142, 169, 201, **262–263**
"Twelfth Street Rag," 89, 209, **264–265,** 439, 440–444, 488
"Twist and Twirl," **265**

# U

"Uncle Tom's Cabin," **267**
Underwood, Sugar, 57, 65
"Universal Rag," (Botsford), **267**
"Universal Rag," (Straight-McKay), **267**
"Up and Down in China," **268**

# V

"Valentine Stomp," **269**
Van Alstyne, Egbert, 89, 99, 181, 200
Van Eps, Fred, 10, 87, 165, 215, **269–271**
"Variety Rag," **271**
"Victory Rag," **271**
"Vivacity Rag," **271**
Vodery, Will, 37, 114

# W

Waldo, Terry, 88, 131, 212–213, 236
"Wall Street Rag," **273**
Waller, Thomas Wright, 83, 88, 269, **273–274**
"Walper House Rag," **274**
"Water Wagon Blues," **275**
"Watermelon Trust, The," **275**
Watters, Ly & Yerba Buena Jazz Band, xvii, 88, 206, 224
"Weeping Willow," **275**
Wendling, Pete, 237
Wenrich, Percy, 53, 173, 175, 181, 200, 232, 259, **275–276**